CURRENT LEGAL PROBLEMS 2006

Volume 59

CURRENT LEGAL PROBLEMS 2006

VOLUME 59

Edited by
JANE HOLDER
and
COLM O'CINNEIDE

Assistant Editor
CHRISTOPHER CAMPBELL-HOLT

On behalf of the Faculty of Laws
University College London

OXFORD
UNIVERSITY PRESS

OXFORD
UNIVERSITY PRESS

Great Clarendon Street, Oxford OX2 6DP

Oxford University Press is a department of the University of Oxford.
It furthers the University's objective of excellence in research, scholarship,
and education by publishing worldwide in

Oxford New York

Auckland Cape Town Dar es Salaam Hong Kong Karachi
Kuala Lumpur Madrid Melbourne Mexico City Nairobi
New Delhi Shanghai Taipei Toronto

With offices in

Argentina Austria Brazil Chile Czech Republic France Greece
Guatemala Hungary Italy Japan Poland Portugal Singapore
South Korea Switzerland Thailand Turkey Ukraine Vietnam

Oxford is a registered trade mark of Oxford University Press
in the UK and in certain other countries

Published in the United States
by Oxford University Press Inc., New York

First published 2007

British Library Cataloguing in Publication Data
Data available

Library of Congress Cataloging in Publication Data
Data available

Typeset by Newgen Imaging Systems (P) Ltd., Chennai, India
Printed in Great Britain
on acid-free paper by
Biddles Ltd., King's Lynn

ISBN 978–0–19–921211–8

1 3 5 7 9 10 8 6 4 2

Editors' Preface

As editors we pursue the best legal scholarship, from both established academics and relative newcomers, regardless of subject matter or theme. This policy produces widely diverse chapters, born from different schools of thought, and parts of the world, and engaging varying methodological approaches, all given in the context of the series of public lectures which forms the backbone of annual volumes of published papers, such as this. Nonetheless, from an editorial point of view, it is satisfying when several chapters coalesce around a particular idea or ideas, thereby reinforcing the strength of a particular contribution and the volume as a whole. This is certainly our experience with this volume, the first part of which is concerned with the basic foundations of law: rights, rules, and constitutions.

Nigel Simmonds opens the volume with an analysis of the foundations of core legal concepts—judgment and legality—with which he examines the status and nature of legal systems as a whole. Departing from Hart, he concludes that the quality of being 'law' is derived from more than just adherence to the relevant rules of recognition: the status of rules as 'law' is dependent upon the approximation of this system to an abstract idea of law. This argument, Simmonds accepts, is not without its difficulties, though he goes on to explain skilfully the justificatory force of legality, equating law with freedom in the sense of independence, and relating governance and the rule of law. In summary, Simmonds elucidates, and challenges, the arguments of certain grandees of legal philosophy—Hart, Fuller, Raz, and even Nietszche—and brings these arguments to bear on the most basic of questions—what is law? Such a question, he concludes, cannot be separated from the idea of justice.

Continuing the ideas of legality and justice, Trevor Allan examines the Human Rights Act from a constitutional perspective, by focusing upon the meaning of the requirement that legislation should be construed compatibly with European Convention rights, at least in so far as it is 'possible to do so'.[1] Allan identifies a substantial overlap between the Convention rights and the constitutional rights that the courts have identified as basic common law commitments. He extends this discussion of the boundaries of legitimate interpretation into an analysis of the intricate and complex relationship between statute and the common law.

[1] s 3 Human Rights Act 1998.

Neil Walker considers the relationship between the European constitution and the tradition, or 'shadow', of state constitutions. In so doing he carries out a thoughtful and close examination of the constitutional credibility of the EU, particularly when viewed from this tradition. This is an important work for 'EU watchers', but also those working in other fields, because of the significance of constitutional change for methods of regulation and 'governance'. Walker instils a sense of the dynamic quality of constitution making and constitutional change and succeeds in supporting the case that the EU constitutional order is unique, particularly given its formal integrity and generative power to develop rules.

For Cheryl Saunders, the role of foreign law in the course of constitutional adjudication in the United States opens up the question of interpretation of law and, as with the previous chapters, also raises questions about legitimacy, justice, and judicial method. Saunders employs a broad comparative analysis, and gleans insights from private international law, reaching the conclusion that greater adherence to standards of accuracy, relevance, and justifiability are needed, and sometimes reference to the *legal context* of a particular foreign law. But, she also recognises that in this area the principal catalysts for change—supranational and international law and the forces of globalisation—are manifest and further encourage convergence of the broad conceptual foundations on which constitutions are based.

Moving on to the practical consequences of upholding or denying constitutional rights, Robert Reiner primarily examines the rise of 'law and order' politics, including the new punitiveness in crime control policies. Reiner traces the impact of the human rights agenda on this area, most notably in terms of due process requirements. However, in this context he also highlights the development of hybrid offences whereby criminal sanctions attach to breach of orders that are initially determined by civil processes, ASBOs (Anti-Social Behaviour Orders) being a prime example. A key observation is that there are a variety of alternative, often conflicting, conceptions of crime apart from, and often in conflict with, the legal. In general, Reiner's (admittedly dystopian) chapter, providing a vision of 2020 based on current trends, acts as an important successor to Michael Freeman's state-of-the-art representation of liberal and left thinking about law and order in the 1980s.[2] Fittingly, Reiner concludes that 'unless there is some mitigation of neo-liberalism, and the inequality and egoism it carries with it, there is no real hope of reversing the deep pressures that have driven crime up, and assured the ascendancy of law and order politics. Law and order in 2020 would realize the worst visions of 1984.'

[2] Michael Freeman, 'Law and Order in 1984' (1984) *Current Legal Problems* 175.

Jörg Fedtke examines a specific manifestation of the 'law and order' debate, the contentious project to issue identity cards to United Kingdom citizens which forms the subject of the Identity Cards Act 2006. Fedtke considers in particular the controversial powers linking the future access to certain public services to the production of an identity card, which raises so many constitutional and rights-based concerns. But he also looks to Germany's experience in using modern information technology to counter terrorism and crime, and broadens this into a comparative analysis of the German and United Kingdom systems, their motivations and logics.

A second set of chapters explores the intriguing and important interface between academic and legal practice, with several academics trying to clear a path through the (often legislative) mess of very real legal problems. Of all the obtuse, confusing, and overly complex areas of the law currently taxing lawyers, judges, and teachers of law, the role of *mens rea* in cases of statutory conspiracy stands out as particularly problematic. In his chapter on this subject, David Ormerod seeks (successfully—this paper was cited by the House of Lords[3]) to influence judicial opinion in favour of workable solutions for resolving this most 'perfect current legal problem'.

A radical reappraisal of the law relating to undue influence is equally vigorously pursued by Mindy Chen-Wishart. She argues that the normative basis of this doctrine is mired in a debate as to whether it stems from a claimant's defective consent or a defendant's reprehensible procurement of that consent. Drawing on Hart and Raz, Chen-Wishart then suggests that a better conceptual underpinning for the doctrine can be found in the legitimacy of the 'perfectionist action of the state', when directed towards protecting and enhancing the personal autonomy of the individual. Chen-Wishart's arguments are compelling, and she develops this 'relational' theory of undue influence by drawing both on black letter doctrine and legal theory to present a new and convincing 'multi-dimensional' perspective on this often abstruse common law doctrine.

Similarly clearing a way through an undergrowth of confusing and contradictory conceptual growths is Charles Mitchell, with his analysis of primary and secondary equitable obligations. He calls for clarity in distinguishing secondary 'substantial' rights to damages from remedies, and in determining when the primary rights of beneficiaries to have their trust property appropriately maintained or disbursed by a trustee may and should be analytically distinct from secondary rights to compensation. Mitchell's chapter is invaluable as an exercise in rigour and common law reasoning, bringing as it does close analysis to bear on a messy and opaque area.

3 See *R v Saik* [2006] UKHL 18, para 99, *per* Lady Hale.

A final set of chapters illuminates areas of the discipline of law which are frequently overlooked. We are particularly pleased to include Peter Alldridge's chapter on 'locating disability law', which is a first in this series on this subject. This examines the development of a relatively new and important area of legal analysis, 'disability law', drawing upon the work done within the discipline of disability studies to illuminate a wide range of legal issues which touch upon the lives, status, and dignity of persons with disabilities. Alldridge emphasises that the discourse of 'disability rights' and equality norms, while important, is not sufficient to capture and frame the multiple ways in which law and disability interface.

Alison Clarke examines the emergence of new forms of commons—she sharply points out that law fails to provide adequate mechanisms by which new commons might come into existence and evolve in response to changing social and economic pressures and preferences. As she argues, '[l]egal rules have the potential both to facilitate and to discourage the development of successful commons. We need to look more closely at our legal institutions to ensure that they are doing the former and not the latter.'

Judith Freedman examines the academically neglected issue of tax avoidance. She argues powerfully that if there is a distinct problem of tax avoidance, then it is at least in part the consequence of governmental attitudes to taxation and defects in the tax system at large. She suggests that reliance upon appeals to 'corporate social responsibility' will not be sufficient to address well-established patterns of behaviour, and that a range of solutions must be deployed which take account of the task and role of the government to define what kind of behaviour is 'acceptable' or 'fair'.

Richard Fentiman also brings conceptual clarity and rigour to bear on the problem of the extent to which 'foreign' law should be viewed through the lens of English legal norms and practice, or, to reverse the question, to what degree English courts should 'mimic' a foreign court's treatment of their foreign law. He concludes that, while compromise to reflect the realities of complex litigation is inevitable, there is no need to adhere unthinkingly to the 'old shibboleth' that foreign laws are evidential facts, and not laws capable of recognition and application by English courts. Again, Fentiman's analysis reflects a common theme that runs throughout much of this volume: resistance to the unquestioning assumption that doctrines resting on shaky normative and conceptual foundations will 'do' when dealing with real and complex current legal conundrums.

The final two contributions to this year's volume come from eminent US contributors, indicating not just the persistence of strong and valued academic links across the Atlantic, but also the existence of shared legal problems. John Jackson surveys the progress of the World Trade Organisation (WTO) after ten years of its existence, examining its evolving jurisprudence and organisational functioning against the backdrop of the shifting economic and policy landscape of globalisation. From his unique viewpoint as an academic who has been closely involved with the development of the WTO, Jackson provides a comprehensive overview of the WTO's initial decade and outlines where its adolescence might bring new legal and policy challenges to the forefront.

Jonathan Wiener's chapter on 'Better Regulation' is an excellent example of the influence of ideas from the United States upon methods of governance in the European Union. Initially a product of the Nixon government, 'better regulation' initiatives, including forms of impact assessment, are now 'sweeping Europe', and are in particular reshaping the European Commission's work programme. Wiener addresses the key question—will such initiatives make a difference, or 'is better regulation better'? In responding, he examines the arguments that better regulation operates as a form of (disguised) deregulation, and concludes that the initiative could indeed yield better results in the form of improved regulatory policies and outcomes. In broader terms, like Saunders and Jackson (in this volume), Wiener is concerned with the products of globalisation, in terms of the mutual borrowing of legal ideas across many countries and the creation of new hybrid legal concepts. Similar themes resonate throughout all of this year's set of chapters, which taken together survey some interesting terrain and indicate possible resolutions to persisting legal problems.

Finally, we would like to thank (in no particular order) all those who chaired the series of public lectures in this series over 2005–6: Lord Steyn, Shainila Pradhan, Lord Justice Sedley, Lord Justice Hooper, Lady Hale, Lord Brown, Lord Hope, Lord Phillips, Lord Hoffmann, Lord Justice Brooke, Professor Jeffrey Jowell, Lady Justice Arden, Lord Mance, Lord Justice Laws, Lord Rodger, Sir Gavin Lightman, Sir James Mumby, Lord Justice Ward, and Lord Justice Neuberger. Their willingness to give up their time and energy to chair the lectures, and to participate in the discussions that follow, are greatly appreciated by us and add a unique dimension to the *Current Legal Problems* series.

Jane Holder and Colm O'Cinneide
UCL
2006

Contents

Table of Cases xiii

Judgment and Legality 1

NE Simmonds, *Reader in Jurisprudence in the University of Cambridge; Fellow of Corpus Christi College, Cambridge*

Parliament's Will and the Justice of the Common Law: The Human Rights Act in Constitutional Perspective 27

TRS Allan, *Professor of Public Law and Jurisprudence, University of Cambridge; Fellow of Pembroke College, Cambridge*

European Constitutionalism in the State Constitutional Tradition 51

Neil Walker, *Professor of European Law, European University Institute*

Comparative Constitutional Law in the Courts: Is There a Problem? 91

Cheryl Saunders, *Professor of Law, University of Melbourne*

Law and Order—A 20:20 Vision 129

Robert Reiner, *Professor of Law, School of Law, London School of Economics and Political Science*

Identity Cards and Data Protection: Public Security Interests and Individual Freedom in Times of Crisis 161

Jörg Fedtke, *Reader, Faculty of Laws, University College London*

Making Sense of *Mens Rea* in Statutory Conspiracies 185

David Ormerod, *Professor of Law, University of Leeds*

Undue Influence: Vindicating Relationships of Influence 231

MINDY CHEN-WISHART, *Fellow and Tutor in Law, Merton College, University of Oxford*

Equitable Rights and Wrongs 267

CHARLES MITCHELL, *Professor of Law, King's College London*

Locating Disability Law 289

PETER ALLDRIDGE, *Drapers' Professor of Law, Queen Mary, University of London*

Creating New Commons: Recognition of Communal Land Rights within a Private Property Framework 319

ALISON CLARKE, *Senior Lecturer in Laws, Faculty of Laws, UCL*

The Tax Avoidance Culture: Who is Responsible? Governmental Influences and Corporate Social Responsibility 359

JUDITH FREEDMAN, *Professor of Law, Worcester College, University of Oxford*

Laws, Foreign Laws, and Facts 391

RICHARD FENTIMAN, *Reader in Private International Law, Queens' College, University of Cambridge*

The World Trade Organization After Ten Years: The Role of the WTO in a Globalized World 427

JOHN JACKSON, *Professor of Law, Georgetown University, Washington, DC*

Better Regulation in Europe 447

JONATHAN B WIENER, *William R and Thomas L Perkins Professor of Law, Environmental Policy and Public Policy, Duke University, Durham, NC*

Index 519

Table of Cases

UNITED KINGDOM

A and Others v Secretary of State for the Home Department [2004] UKHL 56, [2005] 2 AC 68 . . . . . 41, 44, 49–50
Adams v Cape Industries Plc [1990] 2 WLR 657 403
Agip (Africa) v Jackson [1990] Ch 265 212
Ahmed Angullia bin Hadjee Mohamed Salleh Angullia v Estate and Trust Agencies (1927) Limited [1938] AC 624 280
Alfred McAlpine Construction Limited v Panatown Limited [2000] UKHL 43, [2001] 1 AC 518 270
Allcard v Skinner (1887) LR 36 Ch D 145 . . . . . 234, 237–239, 249, 254–255, 258–260, 266
Allied Irish Bank v Byrne [1995] 2 FLR 325 258
Archibald v Fife Council [2004] UKHL 32, [2004] 4 All ER 303 304
Armitage v Nurse [1998] Ch 241 . . . . . 274, 284
Arthur JS Hall & Co (a firm) v Simons [2002] 1 AC 615 272
Ashby v Blackwell (1765) 2 Eden 299 282
Attorney-General for New Zealand v Ortiz [1984] AC 1 403
Attorney-General's Reference (No. 3 of 1992) [1994] 1 WLR 409 217
Attorney-General's Reference (No. 4 of 2003) [2004] EWCA Crim 1944 226
Attorney-General v Blake [2000] UKHL 45, [2001] 1 AC 268 270
Attorney-General v R [2003] UKPC 22 . . . . . 236, 257
Attorney-General v Times Newspapers Limited [1974] AC 273 99
Atwal v Massey (1971) 56 Cr App R 6 211
Bacon v Clark (1837) 2 My & Cr 294 280
Bairstow v Queen's Moat Houses Plc [2001] EWCA Civ 712, [2001] 2 BCLC 531 283
Banco Exterior v Thomas [1997] 1 WLR 221 258
Bank of Credit & Commercial International (Overseas) Limited v Gokal and others (Commercial Court 21 December 1999) 258
Bank of Credit & Commerce International SA v Aboody [1990] 1 QB 923 . . . . . 234, 256, 259
Bank of Montreal v Stuart [1911] AC 120 260
Bank of Scotland v Bennett [1997] 1 FLR 801 263
Barclays Bank v Coleman [2002] 2 AC 773 259
Barclays Bank v O'Brien [1995] 1 All ER 438 258
Barclays Mercantile Business Finance Limited v Mawson [2004] UKHL 51, [2005] STC 1 . . . . . 363–364, 367, 380, 384
Bartlett v Barclays Bank Trust Co Limited (No. 2) [1980] Ch 515 . . . . . 280, 283–284
BCCI v Hussain [2000] EWCA Civ 395 233
Beauane Properties Limited v Palmer [2005] EWHC 817, [2006] Ch 79 345
Bettison v Langton [2001] UKHL 24, [2002] 1 AC 27 336
Black-Clawson International Ltd. v Papierwerke Waldhof-Aschaffenburg AG [1975] AC 591 36

Bostock v Flyer (1865) LR 1 Eq 26 . . . 282
Box Parish Council v Lacey [1979] 1 All ER 113 . . . 341
Brando v Barnett (1846) 12 Cl & F 787 . . . 405
Bren v Williams (1996) 186 CLR 71 . . . 274
Bristol & West Building Society v Mothew [1998] Ch 1 . . . 283
British American Elevator Co v Bank of North America [1919] AC 658 . . . 281
Buerger v New York Life Assurance Co (1927) 96 LJKB 930 . . . 398
Bumper Development Corporation v Commissioner of Police of the Metropolis [1991] 1 WLR 1362 . . . 392, 407
Butigan v Nugus-Fancey [2000] EGCS 67 . . . 258
Buttle v Saunders [1950] 2 All ER 193 . . . 277
Caffrey v Derby (1801) 6 Ves 488 . . . 281, 287
Campbell v Campbell (Ch 21 February 1996) . . . 258
Chaplin v Young (1864) 33 Beav 330 . . . 279
Cheese v Thomas [1994] 1 WLR 129 . . . 234, 237, 254, 257
Churchill v Walton [1967] 2 AC 224 . . . 188, 190–192, 197, 220, 229
CIR v Challenge Corporation Limited [1986] STC 548 . . . 363
Clark v Prus [1995] NPC 41 . . . 233, 255
Clark v Novacold Limited [1999] EWCA Civ 1091, [1999] ICR 951 . . . 310
Clingham v Royal Borough of Kensington and Chelsea; R v Crown Court at Manchester, ex parte McCann and others [2002] UKHL 39, [2003] 1 AC 787 . . . 135
Clough v Bond (1838) 3 My & Cr 490 . . . 281
Cocker v Quayle (1830) 1 Russ & M 353 . . . 280, 285
Collins v Brebner [2000] Lloyds Rep PN 587 . . . 283
Cooper v Wandsworth Board of Works (1863) 14 CB (NS) 180 . . . 45
Coppard v Allen (1864) 4 Giff 497 . . . 273
Corporacion del Cobre de Chile v Sogemin Metals Limited [1997] 1 WLR 1396 . . . 284
Corporation of Ludlow v Greenhouse (1827) 1 Bligh (NS) 18 . . . 276
Cowan v Scargill [1985] 2 Ch 270 . . . 277
Crédit Lyonnaise Bank Nederland NV v Burch [1997] 1 All ER 144 . . . 234, 256, 260
Dailey v Dailey [2003] UKPC 65, [2003] 3 FCR 369 . . . 257
Dalmia Dairy Industries Limited v National Bank of Pakistan [1978] 2 Lloyd's Rep 233 . . . 399
Dance v Goldingham (1873) LR 8 Ch App 902 . . . 277
Davies v Norwich Union Life Insurance Society (1999) 78 P & CR 119 . . . 255
Debenhams Retails Plc v Customs and Excise Commissioners [2004] EWHC 1540, [2004] STC 1132 . . . 389
Di Sora v Phillips (1863) 33 LJ Ch 129 . . . 403, 412
Dowse v Gorton [1891] AC 190 . . . 283
Drew v Daniel [2005] EWCA Civ 507, [2005] 2 FCR 365 . . . 236, 263
Dynamit AG v Rio Tinto Co [1918] AC 260 . . . 411
Eaves v Hickson (1861) 30 Beav 136 . . . 282
Eglington v Lamb (1867) 15 LT 657 . . . 412
Eid v Al-Kazemt (No. 1) [2004] EWHC 2129 . . . 236
El Ajou v Dollar Land Holdings Plc [1993] 3 All ER 717 . . . 403
El Amria [1981] 2 Lloyd's Rep 119 . . . 397
Eleftheria, The [1970] P 94 . . . 397

Evan v Dell [1937] 1 All ER 349 213
Ex parte Anderson (1878) 8 Ch App 807 280
Ex parte Belchier (1754) Amb 218 282
Ex parte Kelly & Co (1879) 11 Ch D 306 280
F & K Jabbour v Custodian of Israeli Absentee Property [1954] 1 WLR 139 418
Fitzpatrick v Sterling Housing Association [2001] 1 AC 27 38
Fitzwood Pty Limited v Unique Goal Pty Limited (in liquidation) [2002] FCAFC 285 277
Fourie v Allan le Roux [2005] EWCA Civ 204 . . . . . 412, 419
Fox v Fox (1870) LR 11 277
Furniss v Dawson [1984] STC 15 362
General & Finance Facilities Limited v Cooks Cars (Romford) Limited [1963] 1 WLR 644 279
Ghaidan v Godin-Mendoza [2004] UKHL 30, [2004] 2 AC 557 . . . . . 28, 36, 38–40
Glanville v Glanville [2002] EWHC 1587 258
Goldsworthy v Brickell [1987] Ch 378 235
Gray v Binny (1879) 7 R 332 249
Green v Weatherill [1929] 2 Ch 213 280
Greene King Plc v Stanley and others [2001] EWCA Civ 1966, [2002] BPIR 491 234–235
Guepratte v Young (1851) 4 De G & Sim 217 409
Gwembe Valley Development Co Limited v Koshy (No. 3) [2003] EWCA Civ 1048, [2004] 1 BCLC 131 283
Hall v Hall (1868) L R 1 P & D 257
Hammond v Osborn [2002] EWCA Civ 885, [2002] WTLR 1125 . . . . . 234–237, 255–256, 262
Hampshire County Council v Milburn [1990] 2 All ER 257 341
Harding v Wealands [2006] UKHL 32 391
Hasham v Zenab [1960] AC 316 278
Head v Gould [1898] 2 Ch 250 . . . . . 274, 279
Heaton v Bell [1970] AC 728 376–377
Hilton v Barker Booth & Eastwood (a firm) [2005] UKHL 8, [2005] 1 WLR 567 283
Hudson v Cobetts [2005] All ER (D) 258 258
Hughes v Hughes [2005] EWHC 469, [2005] 1 FCR 679 . . . . . 236, 257
Hulbert v Avens [2003] EWHC 76, [2003] WTLR 387 283
Humphreys v Humphreys [2004] EWHC 2201, [2005] FCR 712 . . . . . 234, 255, 257
Hussein v Chong Fook Kam [1970] AC 942 208
Iliffe v Trafford [2001] EWHC 469 284
Inland Revenue Commissioners v Duke of Westminster [1936] AC 1 . . . . . 362, 377
Inland Revenue Commissioners v Scottish Provident Institution [2004] UKHL 52, [2005] STC 15 364
Inland Revenue Commissioners v Willoughby [1997] STC 995 363
Irvani v Irvani [2000] 1 Lloyd's Rep 412 257
Jabbour v Custodian of Israel Absence Property [1954] 1 WLR 139 398
Jackson v Attorney-General [2005] 3 WLR 733 . . . . . 99, 101, 106–107, 115, 118, 124
Jennings v Cairns [2003] EWCA Civ 1935, [2004] WTLR 361 . . . . . 234, 236–237
Jepson v Chief Constable of West Mercia [2003] EWHC 3318 292

Jervis v Harris [1996] Ch 195 281
Job v Job (1875) 6 Ch D 562 282
Jobson v Palmer [1893] 1 Ch 71 282
Johnson v Agnew [1980] AC 367 279
Johnson v EBS Pensioner Trustees Limited and another [2002]
EWCA Civ 164, [2002] Lloyd's Rep PN 309 258
Johnson v Youden [1950] 1 KB 544 210
Jones v Lewis (1750) 2 Ves Sen 240 282
Kan Ping Bang [1979] AC 609 211
Kemp v Burn (1863) 4 Giff 348 274
Knight v Haynes Duffell, Kentish & Co (a firm) [2003] EWCA Civ 223 279
Krajina v Tass Agency [1949] 2 All ER 274 398
Langton v Langton [1995] 2 FLR 890 .... 233, 237
Law Debenture Trust Corp v Ural Caspian Oil Corp Limited [1995] Ch 152 270
Lazard Brothers v Midland Bank [1933] AC 289 398
Leader v Stevens [2005] EWCA Civ 50 236
Learoyd v Whitely (1887) 12 AC 727 274
Leeds Industrial Co-operative Soc v Slack [1924] AC 851 276
LEP Air Services Limited v Rolloswin Investments Limited [1973] AC 331 270
Lipkin Gorman v Karpnale Limited [1992] 4 All ER 331 284
Lloyd v Attwood (1859) 3 De G & J 614 274
Low v Bouverie [1891] 3 Ch 82 274
Macklin v Dousett [2004] EWCA Civ 904, [2005] WTLR 1561 .... 236, 255, 257
MacNiven v Westmoreland Investments Limited [2001]
UKHL 6, [2001] STC 237 364
Magnus v Queensland National Bank (1888) Ch D 406 280–281
Mahoney v Purnell [1996] 3 All ER 61 251
Maitland v Bateman (1843) 13 LJ Ch 273 271
Male v Roberts (1800) 3 Esq 163 409
Malhotra v Choudury [1980] Ch 52 279
Masbreq Bank Plc v Tulsiani and another (Ch 2 May 2001) 258
Matthews v Ministry of Defence [2003] UKHL 4, [2003] 1 AC 1163 270
McGregor v Michael Taylor [2002] 2 Lloyd's Rep 468 .... 259, 265
MCC Proceeds Inc v Bishopsgate Investment Trust Plc [1999]
CLC 417 .... 399–402, 404–406, 423
M'Donnel v White (1865) 9 HLC 570 273
Mercer v Denne [1904] 2 Ch 534 342
Meredith v Lackschewitz-Martin and another [2002] EWHC 1462, [2002]
WTLR 1451 .... 234, 255
Metall and Rohstoff AG v Donaldson Lufkin & Jenrette Inc [1990] 1 QB 391 276
Morgan Grenfell & Co Limited v SACE [2001]
EWCA Civ 1932 .... 400–402, 404–406, 423
Morley v Loughan [1893] 1 Ch 736 259
Morley v Morley (1678) 2 Ch Cas 2 282
Mortgage Agency Services Number Two Limited v Chater [2003]
EWCA Civ 490, [2004] 1 P & CR 4 .... 234, 236
Mostyn v Fabrigas (1774) 1 Cowp 161 396
Mother Bertha Music Limited v Bourne Music Limited (unreported)
31 July 1997 411

Mounsey v Ismay 1 H & C 729 342
Moyna v Secretary of State for Work and Pensions [2003] UKHL 44, [2003] 1 WLR 1929 311
MPC v Caldwell [1982] AC 341 . . . . 195–197, 199–200
Murad v Al-Saraj [2005] WTLR 1573 287
Mutual Finance Limited v John Wetton & Sons Limited [1937] 2 KB 389 262
Naidoo v Naidu (Ch 1 November 2000) 257
National Commercial Bank (Jamaica) Limited v Hew [2003] UKPC 51 . . . . . . 236, 257
National Shipping Corp v Arab [1971] 2 Lloyd's Rep 363 410
National Westminster Bank v Morgan (1985) AC 686 258
National Westminster Bank v Spectrum Plus Limited [2005] UKHL 41 98
Nationwide Building Society v Bulmer Radmore (a firm) [1999] PNLR 606 281
Nelson v Bridport (1845) 8 Beav 527 398
Nestle v National Westminster Bank Plc [1993] 1 WLR 1260 283
New Windsor Corporation v Mellor [1975] Ch 380 . . . . 337, 342
OBG Limited v Allan [2005] EWCA Civ 106, [2005] QB 762 270
Olszanecki v Hillocks [2002] EWHC 197, [2004] WTLR 975 283
Ord v Noel (1820) 5 Madd 438 277
Österreichische Landerbank v S'Elite Limited [1981] 1 QB 565 . . . . 410, 414
O'Sullivan v Management Agency and Music Limited [1985] QB 428 234
Oxfordshire County Council v Oxford City Council [2006] UKHL 15, [2006] 2 WLR 719 . . . . 336–337, 341–343, 345
Oxley v Hiscock [2004] EWCA Civ 546, [2004] 3 WLR 715 277
Padden v Arbuthnot Pensions and Investments Limited [2004] EWCA Civ 582, [2004] CP Rep 36 277
Padgham and another v Rochell and another (Ch 1 November 2002) 255, 257
Papouis v Gibson-West [2004] EWHC 396, [2004] WTLR 485 . . . . 236, 257, 261
Papouski v Papouski [2004] EWHC 668, [2004] 2 P & CR DG10 257
Parkasho v Singh [1967] 1 All ER 737 399
Partington v Reynolds (1858) 4 Drew 253 282
Pesticcio v Huet [2004] EWCA Civ 372, [2004] WTLR 699 . . . . 234, 236–237, 255
Photo Productions Limited v Securicor Transport Limited [1980] AC 827 270
Polessk, The [1996] 2 Lloyd's Rep 40 410
Portman Building Society v Dusangh [2000] 80 P & CRD 20 . . . . 256, 258
Powell v Wilshire [2004] EWCA Civ 534, [2005] 1 QB 117 277
Prudential Assurance Co Limited v Newman Industries Limited (No. 2) [1982] Ch 204 419
Quinton v Proctor [1998] 4 VR 469 277
R v A (No 2) [2001] UKHL 25, [2002] 1 AC 45 . . . . 29, 41
R v Ali [2005] EWCA Crim 87, [2006] QB 332 . . . . 187, 204–206, 226
R v Anderson [1986] AC 27 . . . . 188, 218
R v Baden [1993] 1 WLR 509 212
R v Bolton (Toger John) (1992) 94 Cr App R 74 217
R v Clayton (1943) 33 Cr App R 113 190–191
R v DPP, ex parte Pretty [2001] UKHL 61, [2002] 1 AC 800 292
R v Drew [2003] UKHL 25, [2003] 2 Cr App R 371 47
R v Easom [1971] 2 QB 315 222
R v El Kurd [2001] Crim LR 234 . . . . 198, 203
R v Forsyth [1997] 2 Cr App R 299 214

R v G [2004] AC 1034 .... 197, 216
R v Griffiths (1974) 60 Cr App R 14 .... 208, 412
R v Hall (1985) 81 Cr App R 260 .... 207–208, 215
R v Harmer [2005] EWCA Crim 1 202–205
R v Harris (1987) 84 Cr App R 75 214
R v Hinks [2001] 2 AC 241 .... 232, 237, 255
R v Hussain [2002] 2 Cr App R 26 .... 203, 215, 226, 237, 259, 262
R v Jacobs [1944] KB 417 190
R v John M Jones (1974) 59 Cr App R 120 216
R v Khan (1990) 91 Cr App R 29 217
R v Lambert [2001] UKHL 37, [2002] 2 AC 545 .... 29, 36, 39
R v Matthews [2003] 2 Cr App R 30 218
R v Mills (1963) 47 Cr App R 49 223
R v Mir 22 April 1994, The Times 194–196
R v Montila [2005] 1 Cr App R 425 .... 198–199, 201–203, 205, 226
R v Morgan [1976] AC 203 225
R v Mulcahy (1868) LR 3 HL 306 188
R v Naguib [1917] 1 KB 359 408
R v Offen [2001] 1 WLR 253 47–48
R v O'Hadhmaill [1996] Crim LR 509 223
R v Oxfordshire County Council, ex parte Sunningwell Parish Council [2000] 1 AC 335 336
R v Pollman (1809) 2 Camp 20 230
R v Quayle [2005] EWCA Crim 1415, [2005] 1 WLR 3642 292
R v Rizvi [2003] EWCA Crim 3575 .... 197–201, 205, 211, 214–215
R v Ryan, The Times, 13 October 1999 .... 194, 196
R v Saik [2006] UKHL 18, [2006] 2 WLR 993 .... 185, 197–198, 200–201, 230
R v Sakavickas [2004] EWCA Crim 2686, [2005] 1 WLR 857 .... 193–194, 200–201
R v Sangha (1988) 87 Cr App R 88 195
R v Secretary of State for the Home Department, ex parte Pierson [1998] AC 539 .... 30, 43
R v Secretary of State for the Home Department, ex parte Rehman [2001] UKHL 47, [2003] 1 AC 153 50
R v Secretary of State for the Home Department, ex parte Simms [2000] 2 AC 115 .... 30, 45
R v Secretary of State for the Home Department, ex parte Venables [1998] AC 407 43
R v Singh [2003] EWCA Crim 3712 226
R v Sorsky (1944) 30 Cr App R 84 190–191
R v Souter [1971] 2 All ER 1151 199
R v Williams [2004] 2 LRC 499 216
R v Winson [1969] 1 QB 371 212
R v Woollin [1999] 1 Cr App R 8 218
R (Anderson) v Secretary of State for the Home Department [2002] UKHL 46, [2003] 1 AC 837 .... 28, 42–43, 49
R (Beresford) v Sunderland City Council [2003] UKHL 60, [2004] 1 AC 889 .... 336, 342–343
R (Daly) v Secretary of State for the Home Department [2001] 2 AC 532 32

R (Laing Homes Limited) v Buckinghamshire County Council [2003] EWHC 1578, [2004] 1 P & CR 36 345
R (on the application of Burke) v General Medical Council [2005] EWCA Civ 1003, [2005] 3 WLR 1132 292
R (on the application of Pro Life Alliance) v BBC [2002] EWCA Civ 297, [2003] UKHL 23, [2004] 1 AC 185 32–34
Randall v Randall [2004] EWHC 2258, [2005] WTLR 119 . . . . 234, 236–237, 255–256
Re Anglo-French Co-operative Soc (1882) 21 Ch D 492 279
Re Banque des Marchands de Moscou [1958] Ch 182 398
Re Brocklehurst's Estate [1978] 1 Ch 14 . . . . 237, 257, 259–261
Re Brogden (1888) LR 38 Ch D 546 273
Re Chapman [1896] 2 Ch 763 284
Re Cohn [1945] Ch 5 398
Re Craig [1971] Ch 95 . . . . 234, 255, 263
Re Duckwari Plc (No. 2) [1999] Ch 268 281
Re Ellenborough Park [1956] Ch 131 349
Re Fish [1893] 2 Ch 413 277
Re Helbert Wagg & Co [1956] Ch 323 403
Re Jenkins [1903] 2 Ch 362 282
Re Killick (deceased), Killick v Poutney and another [2000] WTLR 41 262–263
Re Knox's Trusts [1895] 2 Ch 483 277
Re Lake [1903] 1 KB 439 282
Re Locker's ST [1977] 1 WLR 1323 277
Re Morris (deceased), Special Trustees for Great Ormond Street Hospital for Children v Rushin and others (Ch 19 April 2000) 234–235, 255
Re Patten (1883) 52 LJ Ch 787 282
Re S (Minors) (Care Order: Implementation of Care Plan) [2002] UKHL 10, [2002] 2 AC 291 28
Re Sandeman's WT [1937] 1 All ER 368 277
Re Stevens [1898] 1 Ch 162 . . . . 280, 283
Re Tebbs [1976] 1 WLR 924 284
Re Tillott [1892] 1 Ch 86 277
Re Wells [1962] 1 WLR 874 277
Re Whitely (1886) 33 Ch D 347 274
Re Windsor Steam Coal Co (1901) Limited [1929] 1 Ch 151 279
Rhone v Stephens [1994] 2 WLR 429 349
Roads v Central Trains [2004] EWCA Civ 1541 . . . . 306, 309
Roper v Taylor's Garage [1951] 2 TLR 284 . . . . 211–212, 214
Rosenfeld v Ransley [2004] EWHC 2962 . . . . 236, 257
Ross v Ryanair & Stansted Airport [2004] EWCA Civ 1751, [2005] 1 WLR 2447 306–307
Rossano v Manufacturers Life Insurance Co [1996] 2 QB 352 398
Royal Bank of Scotland v Etridge [2001] 4 All ER 449 . . . . 233–236, 238, 240, 245, 249, 255, 258–260, 262, 264, 266
Royal Brunei Airlines v Tan [1995] 2 AC 378 212
Saif Ali v Sydney Mitchell & Co (a firm) [1980] AC 198 274
Salway v Salway (1831) 2 Russ & M 215 280
Sanders v Parry [1967 1 WLR 753 283

Saunders v Vautier (1841) 4 Beav 115 356
Saxby v Fulton [1909] 2 KB 208 . . . . 403, 412
Schmidt v Rosewood Trust Limited [2003] UKPC 26, [2003] 2 AC 709 274
Sennar (No. 2), The [1985] 1 WLR 490 397
Shaker v Al-Bedrawi [2002] 4 All ER 835 . . . . 409, 419–423
Shepherd v Mouls (1845) 4 Hare 400 282
Simpson v Simpson [1992] 1 FLR 601 . . . . 237, 255
Smith v Acton (1858) 26 Beav 210 277
Speight v Gaunt (1883) 9 App Cas 1 274
Spirit of Independence, The [1999] 1 Lloyd's Rep 43 411
Stafford Allen & Sons Limited v Pacific Steam Navigation Co [1956] 1 Lloyd's Rep 629 . . . . 398, 412
Steeples v Lee [1998] 1 FLR 138 234
Sutton v Wilders (1871) LR 12 Eq 373 282
Swindle v Harrison [1997] 4 All ER 705 283
Target Holdings Limited v Redferns [1996] AC 421 . . . . 274, 280–281, 283–286
Telephone Rentals Plc v Burges Salmon & Co (CA 9 April 1987) 271
Templeton Insurance Limited v Pennington Solicitors LLP [2005] EWHC 2885 277
Thoburn v Sunderland City Council [2002] EWHC 195 98
Thornton v Stokill (1855) 1 Jur 751 282
Tolten, The [1946] 2 All ER 372, [1946] P 135 403
Tufton v Sperni (1952) 2 T L R 516 257
Turkey v Awadh [2005] EWCA Civ 382, [2005] 2 FCR 7 . . . . 236, 257
Ultraframe (UK) Limited v Fielding [2005] EWHC 1638 281
United Australia v Barclays Bank Limited [1941] AC 1 271
Universe Tankships Inc of Monrovia v International Transport Workers Federation (the Universe Sentinel) [1983] AC 366 . . . . 238, 246
Vale v Armstrong and another [2004] EWHC 1160, [2004] WTLR 1471 . . . . 234, 255, 257
W T Ramsay Limited v IRC [1981] STC 174 . . . . 362, 364
Walker v Symonds (1818) 3 Swans 1 284
Walters v Babergh DC (1983) 82 LGR 235 270
Warner v Metropolitan Police Commissioner [1969] 2 AC 256 211–213
Watson v Huber (Ch 9 March 2005) 234, 255
Watts v Girdlestone (1843) 6 Beav 188 282
Western National Bank of New York v Perez, Triana & Co (1860) 6 TLR 366 410
Westminster City Council v Croyalgrange Limited (1986) 83 Cr App R 155 211
White and Carter (Councils) Limited v McGregor [1962] AC 413 275
Wight v Olswang (No. 2) (2000) 2 ITELR 689 274
Wiglesworth v Wiglesworth (1852) 16 Beav 269 279
Wilcock v Muckle [1952] 1 KB 367 . . . . 162, 182
Williams v Bailey (1866) LR 1 LH 200 262
Williams v Roffey Brothers & Nicholls (Contractors) Limited [1991] 1 QB 1 245
Williams v Williams [2003] EWHC 742, [2003] WTLR 1371 . . . . 234, 237
Woolwich Plc v Gomm [2000] 79 P & CR 61 . . . . 237, 262
Wright v Cherrytree Finance Limited and others [2001] EWCA Civ 449, (2001) 82 P & CR DG 10 . . . . 234, 236
Wright v Hodgkinson [2004] EWHC 3091, [2005] WTLR 435 234

Wright v Morgan [1926] AC 788 282
Wroth v Tyler [1974] Ch 30 279
Zamet v Hyman [1961] 1 WLR 1442 234

EUROPE

European Union

Alpharma Inc v Council 2002 WL 31338, Case T-70/99 480
Amministrazione delle Finanze Dellostato v Essevi [1981] ECR 1413 73
Commission of the European Communities v French Republic, Case 1/00 2001 E.C.R. I- 09989 480
Costa v ENEL [1964] ECR 585 72
European Parliament v Council and Commission, Joined Cases C-317/04 and C-318/04 [2006] All ER (D) 05 (Jun) 162
Francovich and Bonifaci v Italy [1991] ECR I-5357 74
Germany v Commission [1987] ECR 3203 74
Germany v European Parliament and Council [2000] ECR I-8419 74
Halifax Plc, Leeds Permanent Development Services Limited, County Wide Property Investments Limited v Commissioners of Customs and Excise Case C-255/02 21 February 2006 . . . . 363, 389
Marks and Spencer Plc v Halsey Case C-446/03, [2006] STC 237 383
Opinion 1/91 [1991] ECR I-6079 72
Pfizer Animal Health SA v Council, Case T-13/99 2002 WL 31337 . . . . 467, 480–481, 511
Re Draft Agreement on a European Economic Area [1991] ECR 6102 72
Rewe-Handelgesellschaft Nord mnH v Hauptzollant Kiel Saarland [1976] ECR 1805 74
Rewe-Zentralfinanz eG and Rewe-Zentral AG v Landwirtschaftskammer für das Saarland [1976] ECR 1989 74
Simmenthal SpA v Commission [1979] ECR 777 73
Van Gend en Loos v Nederlandse Administratie der Belastingen [1963] ECR 1 72

European Court of Human Rights

Engel v Netherlands (1979–80) 1 EHHR 647 135
J A Pye (Oxford) Limited v United Kingdom (2006) 43 EHRR 3 345
Pretty v United Kingdom (2002) 35 EHRR 1 292
Stafford v United Kingdom 35 EHRR 1121 43

Germany

Case 1 BvR 518/02 (2006) 171
Volkzählungs (1983) BVerfGE 65 172

COMMONWEALTH

Australia

Al Kateb v Godwin (2004) 219 CLR 562 96
Alexander v Perpetual Trustees (WA) Limited (2004) 216 CLR 109 280
Armstrong v East West Airlines (Operations) Limited NSW Sup Ct (Eq) (3 February 1994) 280

Attorney-General for New South Wales v Trethowan (1931) 44 CLR 394 107
Attorney-General (WA) v Marquet (2003) 217 CLR 545 107
Austin v Austin (1906) 3 CLR 516 274
Australian Capital Television v Commonwealth (1992) 171 CLR 106 99–100
BP Exploration Limited v Hunt [1980] 1 NSWLR 496 411
Clayton v Heffron (1960) 105 CLR 214 107
Colour Control Centre Pty Limited v Ty NSW Sup Ct (Eq) (24 July 1995) 283
Commercial Bank of Australia Limited v Amadio (1983) 46 ALR 402 236
Damberg v Damberg [2001] NSWCA 87 .... 408, 410, 412, 415–418, 420, 422–423
Davies v Williams [2003] NSWCA 371 277
Elder's Trustee and Executor Co Limited v Higgins (1963) 113 CLR 426 282
Fouche v The Superannuation Fund Board (1952) 88 CLR 609 .... 274, 277
George v Macdonald NSW Sup Ct (Eq Div) (6 February 1992) 277
Glazier Holdings Pty Ltd v Australian Men's Health Pty Ltd NSW Sup Ct (Eq) (22 January 2001) 281, 284
Island Realty Investments Limited v Douglas (1985) 19 ETR 56 281
Lang v Australian Broadcasting Commission (1997) 189 CLR 520 .... 97, 99
Mabo v State of Queensland (No. 2) (1992) 175 CLR 1 319
McCann v Switzerland Insurance Australia Limited (2000) 203 CLR 579 281
McGinty v Western Australia (1995) 186 CLR 140 .... 99, 102, 117–118, 123
Meehan v Glazier Holdings Pty Limited (2002) 54 NSWLR 146 .... 281, 284
Milirrpum v Nabalco Pty Limited (1971) 17 FLR 141 319
Neilson v Overseas Projects Corporation of Victoria Limited [2005] HCA 54 .... 416–418, 423–424
New Cap Reinsurance Corp Limited v General Cologne Re Australia Limited (2004) 7 ITELR 295 279
Permanent Building Society v Wheeler (1994) 11 WAR 187 282
Randall v Lubrana NSW Sup Ct (Eq Div) (31 October 1975) 274
Re Dawson [1966] 2 NSWR 211 280–281
Re French Caledonia Travel Service Pty Limited (in liquidation) (2003) 59 NSWLR 361 280
Regie Nationale des Usines Renault SA v Zhang (2002) 210 CLR 491 416
Spellson v George (1987) 11 NSWLR 300 274
Taylor v Attorney-General of Queensland (1917) 23 CLR 457 107
Turner v TR Nominees Pty Limited NSW Sup Ct (Eq) (3 November 1995) 280
Waxman v Waxman (2004) 7 ITELR 162 .... 280, 283
Wickstead v Browne (1992) 30 NSWLR 1 280
Wik Peoples v Queensland (1996) 187 CLR 1 319
Yorta Yorta Aboriginal Community v Victoria [2002] HCA 58 319

Canada

Amosin v The Mercury Bell (1986) 66 NR 361 .... 409, 413–414, 419, 422
Canson Enterprises Limited v Boughton & Co [1991] 3 SCR 534 284–285
Dixon v Attorney-General (British Columbia) (1989) 59 DLR (4th) 247 103
Fales v Canada Permanent Trust Co [1977] 2 SCR 302 283
Glebe Sugar Refining Company Limited v The Trustees of the Port and Harbour of Greenoch [1921] SCR 72 116
Gray v Kerslake [1958] SCR 3 413

Hellens v Densmore [1957] SCR 768 413
Hill v Church of Scientology of Toronto [1995] 2 SCR 1130, (1995) 126 DLR (4th) 129 .... 97, 99–100, 103, 115, 117–118, 122, 124
Hodgkinson v Simms [1994] 3 SCR 377 283
Inmet Mining Corp v Homestake Canada Inc (2003) 24 BCLR (4th) 1 279
Reference re Electoral Boundaries Commission Act (1991) 81 DLR (4th) 161 .... 99, 103
Sansregret v R [1985] 1 SCR 570 216
Semelhago v Paramadevan [1996] 2 SCR 415 279
The Queen v Canada Trustco Mortgage Co [2005] SCC 54 388
United States of America v Dynar [1997] 2 SCR 462 210
Youyang Pty Limited v Miner Ellison Morris Fletcher (2003) 212 CLR 484 .... 281, 285

Hong Kong

Mok Chi Keung v Mok Chi Hoi (2003) 215 HKCU 1 277

New Zealand

Bank of New Zealand v New Zealand Guardian Trust Co Limited [1999] 1 NZLR 664 283
Chirnside v Fay (No. 2) [2005] 3 NZLR 689 283
Foreman v Kingston [2004] 1 NZLR 841 274
Re Mulligan [1998] 1 NZLR 481 283

South Africa

Du Plessis v De Klerk 1996 (3) SA 850 97
Executive Council of Western Cape Legislature v President of the Republic of South Africa 1995 (4) SA 877 .... 99, 105, 112, 115, 117–118, 125
Harris v Minister of the Interior 1952 (2) 428 107
Minister of the Interior v Harris 1952 (4) 769 107
N K v Minister of Safety & Security 2005 (6) SA 419 125
State v T Makwanyane (1995) (3) SALR 391 101

ISRAEL

Rubinstein v Minister of Defence 52 (5) PD 481 (1997) 99, 104, 115, 118, 123
United Mizrahi Bank / United Bank Hamiezrachi Limited v Migdal Co-operative Village (1995) 49 (4) PD 221 .... 98, 105

UNITED STATES OF AMERICA

Andrus v Sierra Club 442 US 347 (1979) 465
Atkins v Virginia 536 US 304 (2002) 91–93, 110
Bowers v Hardwick 478 US 558 (2003) 117
Calvert Cliffs Coordinating Committee v AEC, 449 F 2d (DC Cir 1971) 465, 471
Chlorine Chemistry Council v EPA 206 F 3d 1286 (DC Cir 2000) 479
Doe v Mutual of Omaha Insurance Co 179 F 3d 557 (1999) 301

Drury v McGarvie (1993) SC 95, (1993) SLT 987 300
Hyde v United States 225 US 747 (1912) 188
Industrial Union Department, AFL-CIO v American Petroleum Institute
448 US 607 (1980) 480
Lawrence v Texas 539 US 558 (2003) 91–93, 117
Leather Industries v EPA 40 F 3d 392 (DC Cir 1994) 479
McElroy v McAllister 1949 SC 100 411
New York Times v Sullivan 376 US 254 (1964) 99, 104, 122, 124
Pinkerton v United States 328 US 640 (1946) 228
Printz v United States 521 US 898 (1997) 91–93, 99, 123
Public Citizen v United States Trade Representative 5 F 3d 549
(DC Cir 1993) 465
Roper v Simmons 16 L Ed 2d 1 (2005) 92–93, 100, 110, 117
Stryker's Bay Neighborhood Council Inc v Karden 444 US 223 (1980) 465, 506
Thomson v Oklahoma 487 US 815 (1988) 91
Trop v Dulles 356 US 86 (1958) 91
United States v Rabinovich 238 US 78 (1915) 228
Washington v Glucksberg 521 US 702 (1997) 91

Judgment and Legality

NE Simmonds[1]

Legal Theory and its Object

Unlike a theory of light or a theory of electricity, a theory of law is never wholly independent of its object. For law exists only in the form of a very complex structure of shared understandings and expectations. The problem of law's nature springs from the fact that these settled understandings do not fit together in easy and obvious ways. We then find ourselves asking what law must be, if these various settled understandings are true.

Why would we feel the need to answer that question? After all, the very fact that the question seems hard to answer[2] suggests that legal systems can get along pretty adequately without any fully satisfactory grasp of law's nature. Our settled understandings could contain tensions or even downright contradictions, and yet they might still sustain a perfectly workable body of thought and practice. As Wittgenstein observed, a contradiction need not be seen as 'the local symptom of a sickness of the whole body' because, once we understand where and how such contradictions arise, they need 'not make our language less usable'.[3]

Our need to gain a coherent understanding of law's nature is grounded in two related considerations. In the first place, the idea of law occupies a prominent place within the moral and political values of our civilization. We need clearly to grasp that idea if we are to adopt an intelligent and

[1] This essay is an expanded version of the lecture delivered at University College London on 9 February 2006.

[2] People have wrestled with it for two millennia at least. See for example the passage from Xenophon quoted in S Paulson, 'Introduction' in H Kelsen, *Introduction to the Problems of Legal Theory*, trans B L and S L Paulson (Oxford: Clarendon Press, 1992), pp xxii–xxiii. See also J Ober, 'Law and Political Theory' in M Gagarin and D Cohen (eds) *The Cambridge Companion to Ancient Greek Law* (Cambridge: Cambridge University Press, 2005): 'By the late classical period, jurisprudence, in the extended sense of "philosophical writing about law" was a feature of Athenian political theorizing and litigants in Athenian courts made jurisprudential arguments to mass juries', 394); 'By the mid fourth century . . . jurisprudence had become an integral part of the public discourse of law', 408.

[3] L Wittgenstein, *Remarks on the Foundations of Mathematics* (Oxford: Blackwell, 1964), 51, 104.

critical reflective stance in relation to those values. Secondly, law is not simply a body of practices aimed at muddling through. Legal decisions must be justified, not as pragmatic exercises of power, but as applications of principle. The need for principled justification creates a dynamic that ultimately gives rise to legal theory. Particularly when, in an adjudicative context, the most fundamental questions of lawmaking authority and legality are reached, the search for some principled basis to guide the decision will inevitably generate an inquiry into the nature of law. Legal thought is always partly reflexive, in so far as it is guided by reflection upon its own nature.[4] Combining these two points, we may say that legal thought is reflexive because and in so far as it constantly seeks to relate its normative and justificatory force to some of our most basic moral and political values. The perennial character of the debate concerning law's nature may show us that sophisticated legal systems can function without having found a satisfactory resolution, but it also shows us that they cannot function without constantly reopening the debate. The idea of law is not a simple descriptive term for extant legal systems so much as the organizing focus for juristic reflections within those systems.[5]

Contemporary legal theorists have devoted a good deal of energy to the question of how the theory of law is related to its object. Many of them take the view that legal theory should not adopt the perspective of those who seek to guide their practical reasoning by law. The inquiry into the nature of law is, on this account, not only reflective but also disengaged. It seeks to describe the character of a pervasive social phenomenon from the viewpoint of an observer who notes and takes account of, but does not adopt, the outlook of participants. Those who reject this conception of legal theory are seen as guilty of a simple error: they confuse questions about 'law', that is to say, questions about the nature of law as such, with questions about 'the law', that is, questions about the content or validity of the laws of this or that jurisdiction.

The 'detached observer' view of legal theory, if I may so style it, runs into quite a few problems. In the first place, while the position is presented

[4] I have suggested elsewhere that legal thought can take a 'reflexive' or a 'non-reflexive' form. The non-reflexive form of legal thought would be instantiated by systems possessing a basic rule of recognition. The present essay is intended to suggest that no legal order can ever be wholly non-reflexive. See N E Simmonds, 'Jurisprudence as a Moral and Historical Inquiry' (2005) 18 *Canadian Journal of Law and Jurisprudence* 249, 274.

[5] It is, I think, in this way that we might best understand the observations of lawyers such as Philip Allott: '[L]egislative texts and reported cases are not themselves the law. They do not even contain the law. The law is somewhere else and something else.' P Allott, *The Health of Nations: Society and Law beyond the State* (Cambridge: Cambridge University Press, 2002), 43.

as a methodological thesis about the nature of philosophical inquiry into law, it seems to rest upon a substantive claim about law's nature. For it assumes that legal thought is guided by something like a basic rule of recognition, rather than being guided by thought about the nature of law itself. If legal thought is guided, at least in part, by reflection upon the nature of law as such, then the question 'what is the law, within this jurisdiction?' cannot be disconnected from the question 'what is law?'

Once we have admitted the possibility that legal thought may itself be guided by reflection upon the nature of law, some further questions arise. How, for example, are claims about the nature of law, made from within the practice of law,[6] to be related to the view of law's nature presented by the detached observer? Let us suppose that the detached observer's conclusions are at odds with some at least of the claims concerning law's nature made within the practices of law. How then must the detached observer regard those latter claims? To view them as false might seem a tempting option, but it is not clear that the option is available: for one can scarcely purport to be offering a detached theory that is disengaged from the practice if one is simultaneously to invoke that theory as revealing the falsity of claims made within the practice. Most probably, the detached observer will be seduced by an equally tempting and permanently available option: claims made within the practice can be reconstrued as not being what they seem. Not really claims about the nature of law, but complex forms of legal argument warranted by the system's inclusive 'rule of recognition'; or, not really claims about the nature of law so much as open-ended political debates that for some undisclosed reason are conducted under a convention requiring them to be formulated as debates about the nature of law.[7]

Finally, of course, the advocate of the detached observer view will need to explain the point or value of his inquiry. The point, of course, need not be a practical or moral point: to feel worried about the value of the detached approach, we need not be committed to the view that philosophical understanding must have a payoff in terms of moral prescriptions. Rather our worries may be exclusively concerned with the intellectual value of the proposed inquiry. For it is by no means obvious that law must possess a unitary nature of the kind that the detached legal theorist seems to be looking for.

[6] Remember that the possibility of such claims cannot be denied without assuming the truth of a substantive thesis about law's nature, in violation of the idea that the detached observer view represents a purely methodological thesis.

[7] For this view, see T Honoré, *Making Law Bind* (Oxford: Oxford University Press, 1987), 32.

Nietzsche famously observed that only that which has no history is definable.[8] His point is that long-standing human practices come to be composed of multiple layers of historically accrued meaning, so that they are repositories of an irreducible semiotic complexity. In the case of the practices of law, Nietzsche's view offers a plausible explanation for how there comes to be a long-standing dispute concerning law's nature. A detached observer of legal systems might seek to discover whether this is indeed so: does the dispute concerning law's nature spring from some widespread confusion that is capable of being dispelled? Or does it reflect the irreducible semiotic complexity of the practices of law? In the latter event, what part does the dispute play within the workings of a legal order? Can the main strands in that complexity be delineated with the help of historical inquiry? These, it seems to me, are the questions that a detached observer might sensibly ask once the Nietzschean possibility has been broached. But these are not the questions typically asked by philosophers of law.[9]

From the viewpoint of the participant, as opposed to the detached observer, genealogy may not be enough. Genealogical inquiry may, of course, have subversive implications, but these are not intrinsic to its nature. Genealogy will be subversive only when it reveals, at the heart of the institution, motivations or beliefs that cannot be acknowledged and endorsed while one continues to support the institution in question. Setting that subversive possibility on one side, the revelation of multiple competing layers of meaning in our practice may simply accentuate the need to strive for a degree of univocality. Our ascription of univocal meaning to the practice will not form part of a detached inquiry, but part of our reflective and critical engagement with our shared moral life.[10] From this perspective, the attempt to arrive at a coherent account of law's nature is closely analogous to the attempt to arrive at a coherent morality in the face of our knowledge that our shared moral life and inherited moral views may be the product of many diverse and potentially conflicting traditions of thought.

From the viewpoint of the detached observer, however, all that is to be recorded is the semiotic complexity itself, and the part that it plays in the

[8] F Nietzsche, *The Genealogy of Morals*, second essay, section 13 (various edns and trans).

[9] This is to be lamented, even from the viewpoint of a morally engaged inquiry into law's nature.

[10] 'For we speak of the essence of a thing when we think of value as the principle of its being.' G Radbruch, *The Legal Philosophies of Lask, Radbruch and Dabin*, trans by Kurt Wilk (Cambridge, Mass: Harvard University Press, 1950), 51.

workings of the practice. Advocates of the detached observer view need to tell us why they assume that a univocal 'nature' of law can be discovered, or appropriately sought after, once our moral understandings and engagements are set on one side.

The Problem

Allow me to begin by reminding you of some settled understandings that we have about law, for they will play a part in the argument which is to follow:

1. Judicial opinions are addressed amongst others to the litigants and to other citizens, and are intended to explain the justification for the decision.
2. In that justification, the status of certain rules as laws plays a key part. Defendants are ordered to pay damages, for example, because they have violated laws, and not just because they have violated rules accepted for whatever reason by the judge.

Surely, an adequate legal theory ought to be able to explain these facts, or ought at least to be consistent with them.

But how are these facts to be explained? What must law be that it can coherently be regarded as offering a justification for the state's use of force? What exactly does 'justification' mean in the context of the judgment? Are we speaking of a moral justification? Or are we speaking of some purely 'technical' justification, that consists solely in the subsumability of an action under established rules without any assumption that the application of the rules is morally required or permissible?

Most of the great classical philosophies of law took the justification involved here to be a form of moral justification. In offering an account of the nature of law they were, in effect, answering the question of what law must be, if it is to be capable of justifying the use of force. It is for this reason that so much of the history of the philosophy of law involves rival accounts of the relationship between those two most fertile concepts of the western legal tradition, *ius* and *lex*.

Kant's philosophy of law is in the first place a theory about *ius* or Recht, which Kant takes to be the ordered set of principles that are consistent with our freedom: 'the sum of conditions under which the choice of one can be united with the choice of another in accordance with a universal law of freedom'.[11] Although a system of wholly posited laws is possible, 'a natural law would still have to precede it, which would establish the authority of the lawgiver'.[12] Consequently, the principles of Recht represent 'the immutable principles for any giving of positive law'.[13]

Hobbes, by contrast, wishes to reduce the idea of law to *lex* alone, rejecting the thought that enactments can be law only by virtue of their groundedness in *ius*. To this end, he cunningly exploits the association of *ius* with individual rights, rather than the idea of *ius* as a matrix of juridical values and principles. At the same time, he seizes upon the fact that the then most influential theory of *ius*, that of Grotius, centred upon the idea of a basic right to self-preservation. Whereas for Grotius, such a right gave rise to non-overlapping domains of entitlement constituting an ordered body of principles, Hobbes argues that the structure of human interaction is such that a basic right to self-preservation will generate endemic conflict, requiring the enactment of positive law to create boundaries between jointly possible, non-overlapping domains of entitlement. Rather than *lex* being grounded in *ius* therefore, *lex* and *ius* are for Hobbes fundamentally antithetical concepts.[14] The coercive force of law is justified, not by reference to the principles of *ius*, but by the inability of men to overcome the deadly conflict inherent in the idea of *ius*, without the intervention of lawmaking authority.

More recently, philosophers have adopted a variety of perspectives from which it is hard to see how inquiry into the nature of something can also be a normative inquiry into justifications.[15] Consequently, many legal theorists have sought to detach inquiry into the nature of law from the broader domain of political philosophy.[16] They take it for granted

[11] I Kant, *The Metaphysics of Morals*, 6: 230 in *The Cambridge Edition of the Works of Immanuel Kant: Practical Philosophy*, trans by M J Gregor, (Cambridge: Cambridge University Press, 1996), 387.

[12] ibid 379.

[13] ibid 386.

[14] T Hobbes, *Leviathan*, ch 24 (various edns).

[15] See on this, Simmonds, n 4 above, 254–60.

[16] John Gardner adopts a somewhat different line in his essay 'Legal Positivism: 5½ Myths' (2001) 46 *American Journal of Jurisprudence* 199. Rather than detaching inquiry into law's nature from political philosophy, he claims that legal positivism 'is not a whole theory of law's nature, after all', 210. '(L)egal positivism explains what it is for a law to be legally valid in the thin *lex* sense, such that the question arises of whether it is also legally valid in the thicker *ius* sense, i.e. morally binding qua law', 227. It seems to follow that a 'whole theory of law's nature' would address the issue of law's moral bindingness. Gardner presents his account of legal positivism not as a revision of legal positivism, but as a myth-dispelling correction of popular misunderstandings of the positivist position. Yet the distinction between 'thick' and 'thin' senses of 'legal validity', combined with the idea that a 'whole theory of law's nature' must explain law's moral bindingness, amounts to a position that Hart clearly and explicitly rejects. See, for example, Hart's comments on the very similar theory offered by Finnis, in H L A Hart, *Essays in Jurisprudence and Philosophy*

that a knowledge of law's content, of the kind imparted by university law schools, is a form of social scientific knowledge, not a matter of moral wisdom or moral understanding. At the same time, they are aware that propositions of law are action-guiding prescriptions, not descriptions of social facts. This sets the agenda, for it is not immediately obvious how a knowledge of action-guiding prescriptions, as opposed to a knowledge of the fact that certain prescriptions have been issued, or are likely to be acted upon, can be a form of social-scientific knowledge. The most familiar response to this agenda is Hart's theory of law.

Hart's Middle Way

Hart saw himself as confronting a field structured by two main positions: one asserting a clear separation between law and morality, but offering a reductivist analysis of propositions of law as descriptive or predictive statements, while the other position points out the inadequacy of such analyses, but concludes on that basis that the normative character of law can be captured only by a theory that grounds law in morality.

Between these two positions, Hart seeks to trace a middle way. He tries to demonstrate that the prescriptive action-guiding character of propositions of law can be preserved without grounding law in morality. The central core of his theory consists in a demonstration that it is possible to have a partially[17] autonomous body of normative reasoning that is not reducible to some more familiar domain of normative reasoning such as morality or prudence.

This solution depends upon the idea of a basic rule of recognition accepted by officials. When such a rule is accepted, it creates a field of normative reasoning bounded by the basic rule. Propositions of law have to be understood as moves within that field of reasoning. Propositions concerning legal validity, legal rights, and so forth express action-guiding conclusions about the applicability of the rule of recognition or the rules stemming from it.

Of course, such a body of normative reasoning could not be sustained if people had no reason to engage in it. In this sense, the social existence of such practices of reasoning depends upon the agents' reasons for

(Oxford: Oxford University Press, 1983), 12. There is equally little doubt that this type of theory would have been rejected by Kelsen.

[17] 'Partially' autonomous because of the unavoidable occurrence of penumbral cases, where the rules will not yield a determinate answer.

participation. But Hart thinks that reasons for engaging in the practice need not be moral reasons. Officials must regard the rule of recognition as a common public standard for judicial decision, but they may take this view for non-moral reasons.[18] Reasons for accepting the rule of recognition may be diverse, and it is precisely this diversity that entitles us to treat the domain of legal reason as partially autonomous from the general body of practical reasoning.

An analogy might be a game, where one's reasons for playing the game may be quite diverse, and this is what leads us to distinguish between reasons within the game and reasons for playing the game. For example, I may play a game with a child because I want to please the child, and not because I want to win a game; but if I am genuinely to play the game, the moves that I make within the game must be aimed at winning. If the child perceives that I am not trying to win but to lose, they may object that I am not really playing the game.

This is quite different from, say, the practice of prayer. Here, if I am genuinely to engage in the practice, my reasons for so engaging must be of an appropriate kind: however meticulously I comply with the necessary rituals, I am not really praying if my reason for engaging in the practice is of an inappropriate kind. The conventional rituals that make up a particular form of prayer offer a mode of expression, rather than an autonomous body of reasons. The convention of kneeling in order to pray, for example, is intended to express some of the attitudes and beliefs that are intrinsic to sincere prayer. These attitudes and beliefs might be expressed in other ways, in the context of other practices of prayer. Hence my reasons for kneeling might be specific to my engagement in this particular form of prayer. But they are not detachable from the background of beliefs making up my reasons for praying: they are intended to express those background beliefs. Within a game, by contrast, my reasons for trying to strike the ball accurately and on target may be internal to the game and quite distinct from my reasons for playing the game in the first place.

Hart's idea of legal reasons as detachable from our reasons for engaging in the practices of law overlooks, or perhaps denies, the possibility of legal reasons being fully intelligible only in so far as the practices embody a commitment to certain guiding values. For, as I have suggested elsewhere, it is possible that the most significant 'step from the pre-legal into the legal world'[19] is to be found, not in the 'invention' of a rule of recognition, but

[18] H L A Hart, *Essays on Bentham* (Oxford: Oxford University Press, 1982), 159.
[19] H L A Hart, *The Concept of Law* (2nd edn) (Oxford: Clarendon Press, 1994), 94.

in the growing understanding that practices of reliable rule-enforcement can realize forms of freedom and independence that would not otherwise be conceivable.[20] Rather than thinking of the institutions of law as invented for this or that purpose, we might better think of them as coalescing from earlier practices of governance and dispute resolution, before coming to be perceived as expressing certain values, the nature and possibility of which had not previously been appreciated. Some entrenched philosophical assumptions encourage us to think of moral reflection as invariably the evaluation of persons and acts by reference to general standards, or as the critical inquiry into the basis of such general standards. In fact, a good deal of moral reflection is concerned to understand values by considering some concrete practice that partly or wholly realizes the value. The realization stands to the value realized in an expressive relation, so that our intellectual access to the value is through its realization: here we do not apply a pre-existing abstract knowledge of value to particulars; nor is it appropriate to think of the features of the particular as constraining an interpretation grounded in an independent knowledge of value.

Legality and the Rule of Recognition

Hart's idea of a partially autonomous domain of reasons depends upon a denial of the possibility of meaningfully asking certain questions about the rule of recognition itself. We can ask factual questions about it—is it in fact accepted?—or moral questions—is it a good rule?—but we cannot ask juridical questions about it. We cannot meaningfully inquire into the rule's legal validity, as it is the ultimate criterion of legal validity.[21]

It is in this way that Hart seeks to block the regress of questions about legality that generates, by way of response, Kelsen's theory of the basic norm, a theory that Kelsen himself described as the minimum of natural law without which a cognition of law is impossible.[22] Hart's thesis is linked in turn to certain other aspects of his theory, such as his characterization of adjudicative decisions on the penumbra of the rule of recognition, or in contexts where that rule is breaking down, as political rather than juridical.[23]

[20] Simmonds, n 4 above, 261–2.

[21] Hart, n 19 above, 107–10.

[22] H Kelsen, *General Theory of Law and State* (Cambridge, Mass: Harvard University Press, 1945), 437.

[23] Hart, n 19 above, 147–54. See also J M Eekelaar, 'Principles of Revolutionary Legality' in *Oxford Essays in Jurisprudence: second series*, A W B Simpson (ed) (Oxford: Clarendon Press, 1973).

These are very important claims, from any point of view. Yet the thesis on which they are grounded looks very much like a tautology. For Hart has in effect defined legal validity in terms of derivability from the rule of recognition, so that it of course follows that the concept cannot be applied to the rule itself. Can such important substantive conclusions be justified by reference to a tautology?

To address the substantive issues involved here, we need to ask whether claims about validity in Hart's sense really exhaust the domain of the juridical. And, to ask this question, we must shift from Hart's concept of 'legal validity' to the broader notion of 'legality', understood as the property of being law.[24]

Pursuing this strategy, we must ask whether one can meaningfully ask questions about the legality of the rule of recognition. Well, it seems to me that one can. Nor do I have in mind the theoretician's question of whether the rule of recognition of a system of law should be thought of as itself a law, or as the non-legal practice on which the law is founded. I am thinking of a much more obvious question, which concerns the status of the system of rules as a whole.

Not all systems of rules derived from a basic rule of recognition are systems of laws. There could be a basic rule of recognition in certain games, for example, where the game is complex and regulated by some official body. But a system of rules might fail to constitute a system of law even though the system provided the basis for governance within a community. A system of governance might possess a rule of recognition, with an associated body of partially autonomous normative reasoning, and yet we might hesitate to describe it as a body of law. Suppose, for example, that the rules stemming from the basic rule of recognition do not purport to guide the conduct of citizens, but simply confer discretionary coercive powers upon various officials, and direct the officials to employ their powers with a view to advancing various objectives. Or suppose that the rules stemming from the rule of recognition set out sufficient conditions for the use of sanctions against citizens, but not necessary conditions, with the result that officials feel free to deploy the state's coercive apparatus against individual citizens whenever they consider that desirable as a way of advancing governmental objectives. Or, if you do not like my examples, take some examples from Fuller: imagine a system where all the

[24] Why not simply ask about the adequacy of Hart's account of 'legal validity'? The answer is, I think, that the term 'validity' is used in a variety of ways by legal theorists but, in its ordinary usage, it tends to be connected with the deliberate exercise of legal powers. Consequently, a focus on the concept of 'legal validity' can create an in-built theoretical bias towards conceptions of law as deliberately enacted in the exercise of legal powers.

rules are kept secret, or all are retrospective, or where the officials never act in accordance with the rules.[25] In systems of this sort, citizens would not guide their conduct by reference to rules but by the prediction of official sanctions.[26] We would I think hesitate to describe these systems as systems of law.[27]

In expressing a doubt about the status of such systems as law, are we expressing a doubt about the legality, the quality of being law, of the relevant rules of recognition? After all, the deviation from legality seems, in at least some of these examples, more likely to have sprung from the way in which lawmakers and other officials have exercised their powers than from some deficiency in the rule of recognition itself. No matter: we have identified a question concerning the legality of the system of rules as a whole, however we describe the question, and this seems to suggest that questions of legality can arise outside of the limited domain that is bounded by the rule of recognition.

At this point, Hart's supporters will doubtless say that I have confused different questions. For when Hart excludes the possibility of questions about the validity of the rule of recognition, he means to sustain the autonomy of the domain of legal reasons by demonstrating that those reasons cannot exist beyond the bounding outer limit of that domain. His concern is with the action-guiding rules and normative considerations that make up the field of legal reason. But my question about the legality of the rule of recognition forms no part of the normative reasoning guiding action or decision within the legal order: it is a conceptual or classificatory question about the status of the system as a whole, including its rule of recognition. The conflation is concealed by the word 'legality', which is ambiguous as between on the one hand, 'the derivability of one rule from another, or the subsumability of an action under a rule' and on the other, 'the property of being law'. In the first sense, 'legality' refers to a property that is relevant within the field of legal reason, while in the second broader sense it may not do so; and, in the case of my 'classificatory' question, it does not do so.

At first this seems a sound reply to a very misguided challenge. But in fact it reveals a problem in Hart's theory. For it invites us to regard the normative or justificatory force of the rules as entirely a function of

[25] L Fuller, *The Morality of Law* (rev edn) (New Haven: Yale University Press, 1969), ch 2.

[26] N E Simmonds, 'Rights at the Cutting Edge' in M Kramer, N E Simmonds, and H Steiner, *A Debate Over Rights* (Oxford: Clarendon Press, 1998), 166.

[27] For the present we can take this to be a claim about our semantic intuitions. In due course we will discover that such understandings are inchoate moral insights rather than mere reflections of settled linguistic usage.

their derivability from the rule of recognition, regardless of their status as law. This conflicts with one of the settled understandings from which our argument began: the idea that, in the judicial justification for the ordering of sanctions, the status of the relevant rules as law plays a key part.

To see the point, imagine a judge who informs the defendant that he is to be punished because he has violated a rule stemming from the basic rule of recognition that the judge and his colleagues accept. Why should the defendant care about that? Why should anyone regard this, without more, as a justification for the decision? How then can the judge regard it, without more, as a justification for the decision? The intelligibility of the purported justification is thrown still further into doubt if we remember that, according to Hart, the judge may accept the basic rule for purely non-moral reasons.

What the judge needs to add is the claim that the rule violated was a law. This still provides us with a source of puzzlement, but it is now the philosophical puzzlement that seeks for a deeper elucidation of our settled moral understandings, rather than the straightforward puzzlement of finding someone's remarks wholly at odds with those understandings. The claim that the rule violated was law, moreover, is not a classificatory or conceptual afterthought forming no part of the justificatory reasoning: it is a central, indeed, the central, element in that reasoning.

If I am sentenced by a judge for breaking some rule, and I suggest that the system to which the rule belongs is not a system of law, the judge may well refuse to consider my argument. For it is that very system that forms the basis of the judge's authority, so that he or she may well feel that the judicial role and oath of office exclude consideration of the argument. But to say this is not to say that the argument is irrelevant in principle.

For related reasons, a consideration of the nature of the system as a whole may not form part of the justificatory reasoning that is expressly set out in the judgment: but this is not to say that certain assumptions about the system as a whole (specifically, the assumption that it is a system of law) are not presupposed by the justification offered in the judgment.

If we are to have a theory of law that is compatible with the settled understandings from which my argument began, it cannot present legal justificatory argument as bounded by the rule of recognition. For the status of rules as law plays a key part in the justification, and that status always depends upon more than derivability from a basic rule of recognition. It depends upon the approximation of the system of rules to an abstract idea of law.

Justification

Hart's supporters will of course say that they have no need to show that judicial decisions are justified. But my response is that they do need to explain how adjudicative legal reasoning could intelligibly be offered as a justification, and they need to explain that in a way that is compatible, so far as possible, with our settled understandings. This they have failed to do, and the failure has two aspects that it is important to distinguish, because the second failure is ultimately of greater significance than the first:

1. It is impossible to understand how any official could think that the acceptance of a rule of recognition by himself and his colleagues, for what might be entirely non-moral reasons, could without more be offered as a justification for the ordering of force against a defendant.
2. On Hart's account, as reconstructed above, it seems that the justificatory force of the rules is entirely a matter of derivability from the rule of recognition. Consequently, the status of the rules as law plays no part in the justificatory reasoning, while our settled understandings tell us that such status is critical to the justification.

The first point challenges Hart's account of the partial autonomy of legal reasons, by suggesting that derivability from an accepted rule of recognition could never, on its own, provide a basis for justifying the use of force in the form of sanctions. Consequently, it could not, without more, intelligibly be offered by the judge as a justification for the use of force. Derivability from a rule of recognition will provide a justification for sanctions only if it forms a part of a broader body of reasoning which draws on considerations lying outside the domain of reasoning that is bounded by the rule of recognition.

Now it might be suggested, in response to the first point, that the justification offered by Hartian officials is not at all unintelligible: they are saying, in effect, 'That's just how we do things around here'. They do not appeal to any deeper reasons, but simply to the fact of a shared practice. We might not find this a convincing or attractive justification for the use of force, but it could be argued that it is perfectly intelligible.[28]

There are indeed contexts where people can quite intelligibly seek to justify their action by saying 'That's just how we do things around here'.

[28] This argument was pressed upon me when I delivered this essay as a lecture at University College London. It is for this reason that I consider it here.

But the contexts are such that they reveal a range of moral or prudential considerations tacitly underpinning the appeal to shared practice. For example, in some situations we need to coordinate action in pursuit of a goal and, for that reason, a familiar pattern of coordination may be invoked on the grounds of its settled and familiar nature. Here, the appeal to shared practice is intelligible as a justification in so far as we take the context of the need for coordination in pursuit of a goal for granted. A full explanation of the justification, however, would have to go beyond the simple appeal to shared practice in order to set out the relevant justificatory circumstances.

In other contexts, the justification 'Its just how we do things around here' might be addressed to someone who has recently joined the community in question, and the tacit background suggestion would be that such a newcomer should submit to the established ways of the long-standing members of the community. A full explanation of the justification would have to do much more than point to the shared practice: it would have to appeal to the right of the community to govern its own way of life, the need for newcomers to submit to that way of life if it is not to be eroded, and perhaps the idea that the newcomer has consented to a duty of compliance by joining the community in the first place.

In other words, 'That's just how we do things around here' is not intelligible as a justification for the use of force if it is truly no more than an appeal to shared practice. In those contexts where it does seem to be intelligible, its intelligibility is always derived from a range of further values forming part of the tacit assumptions structuring our understanding of the situation.

A different response to my first objection is to be found in Neil MacCormick's familiar argument about the 'underpinning reasons' for official acceptance of the rule of recognition. MacCormick observes that legal rules and principles are treated as conclusive reasons for decisions, but 'what gives these reasons conclusiveness as justifications is the tacit presupposition of the obligatory character of respect for criteria of recognition'. MacCormick goes on to argue that an essential element of the officials' attitude towards the rule of recognition must be 'some conscious commitment to pursuing the political values which are perceived as underpinning it, and to sustaining in concrete form the political principles deemed inherent in the constituted order of the society in question'. He says that this 'is not inconsistent with Hart's thesis'.[29]

[29] N MacCormick, *Legal Reasoning and Legal Theory* (rev edn) (Oxford: Clarendon Press, 1994), 139–40.

Some confusion is introduced into the argument by MacCormick's description of the 'underpinning reasons' as giving 'conclusiveness' to the justifications that are offered by invoking legal rules. In the absence of such underpinning reasons, the purported 'justifications' would be unintelligible, not simply inconclusive; and, even given the existence of such underpinning reasons, the justification is not 'conclusive', for there may always be competing considerations of an extra-legal sort. But let us ignore this complicating factor, which probably represents no more than a slip on MacCormick's part.

It is of course perfectly true that, if we assume that the officials have moral reasons of the type adverted to by MacCormick for accepting the rule of recognition, and we treat the judgment as tacitly relying upon those moral reasons, the judgment's invocation of the rule of recognition becomes intelligible as a justification. But it is surely a mistake to say that this 'is not inconsistent with Hart's thesis', for it acknowledges the presence of a necessary connection between law and morality in a way that is very much at odds with Hart's positivism.[30] In fact, MacCormick's view undercuts our warrant for separating the reasons obtaining within the practice of law from the reasons we may have for engaging in that practice in the first place. On MacCormick's account, a full and proper engagement in the practice requires that one has reasons of an appropriate sort for one's engagement: for, without such reasons, one's legal reasoning cannot sincerely and intelligibly be offered as a justification for judicial decision.

It is, no doubt, for reasons such as these that Hart tries to make clear his rejection of the idea that if the judgment is to be intelligible as a justification the judge must accept the rule of recognition for moral reasons:

> [T]hough the judge is ... committed to following the rules his view of the moral merits of doing so ... is irrelevant. His view of the merits may be favourable or unfavourable, or simply absent, or, without dereliction of his duty as a judge, he may have formed no view of the moral merits.[31]

It might be thought that Hart's unwillingness to concede ground on this point may also have been sustained by two further considerations. On closer examination, however, we find that neither of these considerations serves adequately to explain Hart's steadfast refusal to admit a necessary moral element into the officials' 'internal point of view'.

[30] Needless to say, I reject John Gardner's suggestion that Hart did not intend to deny the existence of such necessary connections. See Gardner, n 16 above.

[31] Hart, n 18 above, 159.

In the first place, we might note that his later remarks, such as those just quoted, concerning the nature of judicial acceptance of the rule of recognition were made in response to Raz's theory that legal duties are a species of moral duty and that judges must regard the law as morally binding, or pretend to do so. In fact Hart could have rejected Raz's argument, without rejecting the need for moral 'underpinning reasons'. For the relevant underpinning reasons might serve to render the use of force morally permissible, without themselves entailing a duty, incumbent on the citizen, to comply with the law. Raz's arguments against the view that laws make force permissible without purporting morally to obligate the citizen are really question-begging, for they ignore the possibility that claims concerning legal duties could be construed as reporting the moral propriety of demanding certain actions as due under the rules, together with the moral permissibility of employing force as a response to breach of such rules.[32]

Hart may also have been influenced by the belief that it is just factually false to say that all judges take a moral attitude towards the law. Certainly he expressed such a view in correspondence with Michael Moore.[33] But if this was Hart's motivation, it rested upon a simple error. For, as I have argued elsewhere, the status of law as embodying a moral ideal is fully compatible with the possibility of officials fulfilling the requirements of their role while being motivated by entirely non-moral reasons.[34] It is far more likely, therefore, that Hart resisted the idea of a necessary moral element within the internal point of view because he took legal positivism to require the denial of any such necessary connections.[35]

Quite apart from the question of whether MacCormick's view is consistent with Hart's theory, and whether Hart could or should have accepted amendments along the lines of MacCormick's suggestion, my second problem still remains. For officials might accept a rule of recognition for moral reasons of the sort that MacCormick describes, and yet their acceptance of that rule might nevertheless be unrelated to the status of the rule of recognition, and the system to which it gives rise, as a system of law. Their invocation of an individual rule as a justification for the ordering of sanctions would itself be unrelated to the status of that rule as law. Consequently, a Hartian theory amended along the lines MacCormick

32 See J Raz, *The Morality of Freedom* (Oxford: Clarendon Press, 1986), 27.

33 M S Moore, *Educating Oneself in Public: Critical Essays in Jurisprudence* (Oxford: Oxford University Press, 2000), 3.

34 N E Simmonds, 'Law as a Moral Idea' (2005) 55 *University of Toronto Law Journal* 61, 73–4.

35 See n 30 above, and Gardner, n 16 above.

proposes would still fail to capture the second of the two settled understandings from which my argument began.

Rejecting as he did proposed amendments to his theory, such as those offered by Raz and MacCormick, Hart insisted that the judgment does not offer a moral justification for the decision. Judges, when they speak of the subject's legal duty, 'may mean to speak in a technically confined way' that is concerned only with what 'may legally be demanded or exacted'.[36] 'Justification' is here understood as entirely a matter of the relationship between the individual decision and the rules being applied, without any presupposition that the application of the rules is itself morally permissible. The possibility of such a technically confined form of reasoning is itself, of course, exhibited by Hart's demonstration that it is possible to have an autonomous form of normative reasoning, the autonomy of which is qualified only by the occurrence of penumbral cases. But is the law such a body of reasoning?

One way to approach this question is to imagine in concrete detail a practice that could appropriately be thought of as involving a technically confined form of reasoning, without any intention of offering a moral justification. After all, in deciding what import is to be attached to a form of discourse, we must pay close attention to the context in which it is offered.

Imagine then a practice whereby officials must report to higher authority after making a decision, carefully demonstrating that, in their decision, they applied the relevant body of rules correctly. This would indeed be a 'technically confined' form of reasoning, for it might set on one side all issues about the moral propriety of applying these rules. But we only have to imagine such a practice to see that judicial judgment is not a practice of this sort. A judgment is not a report to higher authority. Nor is it a report to higher authority combined with some clarificatory remarks, for the benefit of the public, about how the law will be applied in future cases. It is a setting forth of the justification of the decision, and is addressed to the litigants amongst others. This was one of the settled understandings from which we began, and we have seen no reason to abandon it.

A better concept of law

The upshot of the argument so far is that, in the judicial judgment, the status of a rule as law plays a key part in the justification offered. And the status of a rule as law can never depend solely upon its derivability from a

[36] Hart, n 18 above, 266.

rule of recognition, but always depends also upon the legality of the system as a whole. Our task now is to construct a concept of law that incorporates these ideas and explains how legality can be given a justificatory role within the judgment.

It is important to see the difficulties that are intrinsic to any serious attempt to accommodate the second of our two initial settled understandings: the idea that, in the judicial justification for the sanction, the status of certain rules as law plays a key part. If the role of legality, understood as the property of being law, within the judgment is to be understood, we must find some property that law necessarily possesses, which could be regarded as bearing upon the justification of the use of force.[37] For our settled understanding is that the justificatory relevance of a rule springs at least in part from its status as law. Justificatory force is not a matter of derivability from a rule of recognition alone, nor is it simply a function of the rule's just and reasonable content. The most fruitful starting point in our search for an appropriate theory is provided by the work of Lon Fuller.

Fuller's argument should be understood as proceeding in two steps. In the first step, he invites us to consider various fairy-tale situations where there is a system of governance that we would not regard as law: situations where there are no rules; where all of the rules are kept secret; where all of the rules are retrospective; where officials never act in accordance with the rules; and so forth. We are then invited to see that reflection upon these situations yields eight 'desiderata' for law. When taken together, these eight desiderata amount to an archetype of law. Instances of law count as such, not by satisfying some set of defining criteria that are satisfied equally by all other non-marginal instances of law, but by approximation to the archetype.

In the second step of Fuller's argument, he claims that the archetype of law is recognizable as a moral ideal. Fuller never succeeded in explaining the moral nature of the archetype. My explanation is that, to the extent that law, understood in terms of the archetype, is realized, citizens governed by law will enjoy domains of permissible conduct that are independent of the will of anyone, but dependent solely on the rules. This makes the citizen free, in precisely the sense in which freedom is the antithesis of slavery. For

[37] For present purposes it is not necessary to address the question of how precisely legality bears upon the justification for the use of force. Within the judgment, the law seems to be taken as a conclusive justification: but this may rest upon background assumptions relating to the degree of justice attained in the system as a whole. In principle, our settled understandings might be explained by the idea that legality is a necessary condition for the justified use of force; a necessary and sufficient condition; or even a non-conclusive reason supporting but not requiring the use of force.

the slave may possibly enjoy more options than the free man: but the options are always dependent upon the will of his master. To equate freedom with the number of options that one has available is to say that the connection between slavery and unfreedom is purely contingent.[38]

This explains the justificatory force of legality, understood as the quality of being law. To show that a rule is law is to show that it forms part of a system of universality, necessity, and independence: that is to say, a system of general rules and principles—universality—that are given peremptory force and are reliably enforced—necessity—as the only way in which political expression can be given to the idea of peremptory force, given the circumstances of the real world. Such a system of reliably enforced rules represents the only conditions within which one can live in political community and nevertheless enjoy a degree of freedom—independence. The existence of such a domain requires that the law be enforced, an analytic proposition, and therefore the value of such a domain justifies the law's enforcement.

Governance and the Rule of Law

It may at first seem paradoxical to equate law with freedom in any sense. For is not law a constraint on freedom and a source of subjection to the power of others? The answer is that it is governance that subjects us to power. Law is a specific form of governance that renders that subjection compatible with a degree of freedom as independence.

Legal theorists have sometimes fostered confusion here by collapsing the distinction between a non-legal but organized form of governance and the idea of governance by law.[39] The work of Raz provides an illustration of this. In his essay 'The Rule of Law and its Virtue', Raz makes two moves. First, he argues that the concept of 'law' is quite distinct from the notion of 'the rule of law'. Secondly, he argues that the rule of law is only a negative virtue, in two senses: 'conformity to it does not cause good except through avoiding evil and the evil which is avoided is evil which could only have been caused by the law itself'.[40] The first move must be sound before the second move can be justified: for how can the rule of law protect us from evils that only the law can cause, if 'the rule of law' is not a distinct concept from the concept of 'law'?

[38] Simmonds, n 34 above.

[39] In collapsing this distinction, they render unintelligible the thought that law may be the basis of the state's authority.

[40] J Raz, *The Authority of Law* (Oxford: Oxford University Press, 1979), 224.

According to Raz, the term 'law' can be used in both a lay sense and a technical lawyers' sense: 'For the lawyer anything is law if it meets the conditions of validity laid down in the system's rule of recognition or in other rules of the system.... To the layman . . . the law is essentially a set of open, general, and relatively stable laws'.[41] The value of the rule of law therefore requires that the making of particular laws, or legal orders, should be guided by open and relatively stable general rules.[42]

One should not postulate such a dualism in our thinking about law too casually. We should not, without some compelling reason, treat the word 'law' as bearing different senses when it is used generally, and when it is employed in the phrase 'the rule of law'. This follows from general principles of intellectual hygiene; but resistance to such a dualism should be particularly strong in this case. For, as Raz concedes elsewhere, one of our most 'common images' of the rule of law holds that 'the rule of law is an ideal rooted in the very essence of law', so that '(i)n conforming to it the law does nothing more than be faithful to its own nature'.[43]

Raz, however, believes that he has such compelling reasons. For, without the dualism of senses, he argues, the idea of government by law would be a tautology rather than a substantive ideal: 'Actions not authorised by law cannot be the actions of the government as a government'.[44] Since all governmental actions are authorized by law, or they would not be governmental actions, it is impossible, without introducing a duality of senses of 'law', to account for the idea that the 'rule of law' is a constraint on government.[45]

At first glance, Raz's argument seems to rest upon a remarkably legalistic understanding of the notion of government. It is in many contexts perfectly reasonable to speak of legally unauthorized acts of government: as when, for example, the members of the government have acted in a carefully coordinated way to achieve a certain goal, and have presented themselves as acting in their capacity as the government. When we speak of the rule of law as a constraint on government, one might say, it is this sense of government that we generally have in mind. Raz anticipates this response, however. He suggests that, if this is what 'the rule of law' means, then it amounts to no more than the requirement that people, including governments, should obey the law. The 'rule of law' in this sense is simply law and order applied to government. But, he tells us 'There is more to the rule of law than the law and order interpretation allows'.[46]

[41] ibid 213. [42] ibid.

[43] J Raz, 'Formalism and the Rule of Law' in R George (ed), *Natural Law Theory* (Oxford: Clarendon Press, 1992) 309. [44] Raz, n 40 above, 212.

[45] ibid. [46] ibid.

There is a good deal of confusion in Raz's argument. His argument might be put as follows. The rule of law is taken to be a constraint upon government. Either 'government' is construed legalistically or it is construed sociologically. If it is construed sociologically, the idea of the rule of law is simply the idea that the government, like everyone else, should obey the law; and this 'law and order' view fails to capture much of what we mean by 'the rule of law'. If, on the other hand, the notion of government is construed legalistically, the rule of law, the idea of a government of laws, becomes a tautology rather than a substantive value. It becomes a tautology, that is, if we fail to acknowledge a dualism in the notion of 'law'.

The fallacy in this argument is surely clear. Suppose that we construe the notion of government sociologically, as the coordinated actions of certain individuals or role-occupants who present themselves as acting in their role as members of the government. The idea of the rule of law is not simply the idea that these individuals should obey the law. For it encompasses also the idea that force should not be used against citizens except in response to the breach of some published, prospective rule by that citizen. This is a different idea from the bare notion of obedience to the extant legal provisions. For those provisions may permit the use of discretionary violence by governmental officials. In deploying such violence against citizens, the officials would not then be disobeying the law; but the regime of which they are a part would be guilty of a serious departure from the rule of law.

I conclude that it is possible for us to avoid the danger of tautology without adopting Raz's dualism, because it is possible, in our explication of the notion of the rule of law, to define government sociologically without reducing the idea of the rule of law to the bare idea of obedience to law.

Raz's mistake here is closely related to another claim he makes: one which is not mistaken so much as misleading. It will be recalled that, in proposing a contrast between the lawyerly and lay senses of 'law', Raz tells us that 'For the lawyer anything is law if it meets the conditions of validity laid down in the system's rule of recognition or in other rules of the system'.[47] If, for the moment, we accept the positivist account of the rule of recognition, Raz's claim is basically correct. But it is correct only when the system of which we are speaking is a system of law. And, as we have seen, it is possible to imagine systems characterized by the existence of a rule of recognition, which nevertheless fail to constitute legal systems.

[47] ibid 213.

Consequently, the lawyerly and lay senses of 'law' seem to be related after all. The lawyer is applying a rule of recognition. But derivability from such a rule confers legal status only if the rule of recognition is part of a system of law; and it will not be a system of law unless it to some extent approximates to the ideal of the rule of law.

All of this reflects our ordinary understandings. For, do we not think of the rule of law as the situation where law rules? And the situation where law rules is not, as Raz seems to think, simply the situation where the law is obeyed, for it involves a certain content for the law, a content that excludes the conferment of extensive discretionary power upon officers of the state. If the conferment of discretion were to be very extensive, citizens would guide their conduct by prediction of official behaviour rather than by reference to the legal rules: we might well conclude that such a system of governance is not an instance of law at all. Hence, law is realized to the extent that the rule of law obtains.[48]

Refining the Archetype

Once we have seen that the archetype of legality is a moral ideal, we have no reason to accept Fuller's eight precepts as final. Fuller shows us that complete failure in any one of the eight desiderata will result in something which is not a body of law at all. In this way, Fuller is able to draw upon our settled understandings of what will and will not count as a legal system. But it does not really follow from this that the best account of the archetype is to be found in the eight desiderata without more. Once we have perceived that the eight desiderata are recognizable as a moral ideal, we see that the initial settled understandings from which we began were in fact inchoate moral insights. We are then in a position to try to refine those moral insights, and to deepen our understanding of the ideal by reflecting upon the conditions that would be involved in its realization.

Our revisions will reflect a deepening moral understanding, informed by experience, of what is required to realize the domain of universality, necessity, and independence. Within the Aristotelian tradition, the distinction between moral knowledge and technical knowledge is precisely the absence, within moral knowledge, of a clear priority for our conception of

[48] Raz seems unable even to envisage this as a possibility. Thus, he contemptuously dismisses Weinrib's suggestion that the form of law is also an ideal to which all law should conform, on the basis that the relevant form cannot be a guiding ideal for law in so far as law must already conform to it, or it would not be law: See Raz, n 43 above, 320.

the end over our understanding of the means: our understanding of the end is in part a product of the experience of pursuing it, and is for that reason never fully complete. Moral philosophy after Kant has developed in ways that obstruct our philosophical comprehension of such forms of moral knowledge, and this has made it hard for us to understand the older tradition of philosophical thought about law's nature.[49]

The experience that should inform our moral reflections is experience of attempts to realize the moral ideal. One aspect of our historical experience of law that invites such reflection is the existence, within developed legal systems, of doctrinal legal scholarship. The practice of doctrinal legal scholarship is central to the rule of law as we know it, but it is also problematic: for the propositions of law offered by the doctrinal scholar often go beyond anything that could be justified directly by reference to authority.[50]

The present argument offers us a basis on which we can understand how the propositions of doctrinal legal scholarship can be put forward as propositions of law.[51] For, if legality is not simply a matter of derivability from a rule of recognition but of approximation to an ideal archetype, the doctrinal scholar's propositions might count as law in virtue of moving the system of doctrine as a whole closer to the archetype. We need to see what features of the archetype, when duly refined beyond the bare eight Fullerian desiderata, cast light upon the practices of doctrinal legal scholarship.

In my work so far I have sought to explain the practices of doctrinal legal scholarship by pointing out that the notion of 'followability', one of Fuller's eight desiderata, has richer implications than Fuller allows. A system of rules may consist of rules that are individually performable but not jointly performable; or the rules may be jointly performable, but not compatible with a tolerable way of life that satisfies basic human needs so that they will not in fact be complied with. Furthermore, people can follow rules only if they have some grasp of what those rules require

[49] Simmonds, n 4 above, 254–60.

[50] See N E Simmonds, 'Protestant Jurisprudence and Modern Doctrinal Scholarship' (2001) 60 *Cambridge Law Journal* 271.

[51] Inclusive legal positivists could, if they wished, explain the status of propositions in doctrinal legal scholarship, but their explanation would be empty. For any such explanation would omit a most important feature of the situation. Within those systems where there is a strong tradition of doctrinal legal scholarship, lawyers would be unlikely to say that the practices of that scholarship simply reflect the criteria of legality contained in the rule of recognition: they would more probably claim that those practices, whether or not they reflected the requirements of a rule of recognition, embodied a soundly based appreciation of the nature of law and of its relationship to other values, such as justice.

in all the multifarious circumstances of human life. They can only have such a grasp if the rules resonate to some extent with their background moral ideas. The doctrinal scholar can be understood as offering propositions of law in so far as his propositions bring the system of rules as a whole closer to the archetype when that is understood as including this enriched notion of 'followability' in the rules.

Some Brief Remarks about Legality and Justice

In the end, however, the practices of doctrinal reasoning, whether in the judgment or the treatise, can never really be separated from the idea of justice. Why is this?

There will always be penumbral cases.[52] The judge's duty is a duty of fidelity to law, and that is not simply a duty to follow the rule of recognition, but a duty to be guided by the idea of law which that rule must itself embody if it is to enjoy justificatory force. But what does this duty imply in the context of the penumbral case?

In the first place we should notice that no default strategy will work: in other words, the judge's duty in the penumbral case cannot be anything like a duty always to decide in favour of the defendant, on the grounds that the law is unclear.[53] The reason is very simple: there is no discernible boundary between the core case and the penumbral case, the distinction between the two being a continuous one. A default strategy involves a discontinuous strategy of adjudication: the judge is required to decide core cases one way by applying the rules and penumbral cases a different way by giving judgment for the defendant. But a discontinuous strategy of adjudication cannot be mapped onto a continuous distinction.

It would not help to say that the default strategy of deciding cases in favour of the defendant should be adopted only in situations where it is perfectly clear that the case is a penumbral case. For the principle on

[52] The notion of a 'penumbral case' is, of course, a theory-dependent idea. The theory upon which it depends views law as a finite system of rules, and holds that some cases are not resolvable on the basis of the rules alone: these are the 'penumbral' cases. My object is to show that, once one has properly understood the idea of law, the judge's duty of fidelity to law leads to a viewpoint from which the distinction between the 'core' and the 'penumbra' can be transcended as lacking any deep theoretical significance.

[53] For the suggestion that such a strategy is the appropriate way to implement a concern for 'fair warning' and the protection of expectations, see R Dworkin, *Laws Empire* (Oxford: Hart Publishing, 1998), ch 4. For further criticism of Dworkin's argument, see N E Simmonds, 'Why Conventionalism Does Not Collapse into Pragmatism' (1990) *Cambridge Law Journal* 63.

which the judge was then acting would require him or her to distinguish between cases where the situation is clearly penumbral and cases where the situation is not-so-clearly, or only possibly, penumbral. And this distinction is no clearer than the one between core cases and penumbral cases. In an individual case, it might indeed be crystal clear that the case is a penumbral situation about which reasonable people may disagree. What must be remembered, however, is that if judges are to observe fidelity to law they must act on the basis of articulable principles, and the principle which would need to be invoked in order to justify a default decision in the defendant's favour, even in the context of a clearly penumbral case, would be too uncertain to be workable.

Judges often have to make do with vaguely formulated principles, of course. But the adoption of a general default rule for penumbral cases, or for 'clearly penumbral' cases, would place an irreducibly vague concept at the heart of adjudication in such a way that it would potentially affect the whole of the law. Fidelity to law requires an effort to reduce such uncertainties whenever reasonably possible, and it precludes adoption of a default strategy.

In the penumbral case, the best the judge can do, from the viewpoint of legality, is to decide the case justly. For justice consists of objective principles that apply to all cases with equality and impartiality—to doubt this is to say that there is no justice, only beliefs about justice. In the absence of a clearly applicable legal rule, the closest that the judge can come to respecting the value of independence from the will of another is to be guided by his understanding of the value of justice.

To say that judges should decide cases justly may seem to be a yawn-inducing platitude. But it must be remembered that my claim is that such a decision is required by the value of fidelity to law, and not simply by the general duty incumbent upon everyone to act justly.

The real importance of this duty to decide penumbral cases justly, however, lies in its pervasive implications. For we have already seen that a discontinuous strategy of adjudication in relation to penumbral cases is impossible: one cannot map a discontinuous strategy onto a continuous distinction, so the judge should not adopt a principle requiring core cases to be decided in one way, and penumbral cases to be decided differently. Consequently, the judicial concern for justice, a concern that is rooted in the duty of fidelity to law, cannot be limited to penumbral cases. Justice must be relevant to every case. The judges must, so to speak, read the law as a body of texts concerning justice.

When we read Plato's *Republic*, we read it on the understanding that it is a book about justice. Understanding Plato is not a technical exercise in the application of semantic rules, or hermeneutical guidelines. We interpret what Plato is saying partly by drawing upon our own understanding of the object to which he is referring. We are, as it were, alongside Plato thinking about justice in dialogue with him. Moreover, to read the text properly, we must read it with a certain degree of submissiveness: we must read on the assumption that it is possible for us to learn from the text. It is misleading to speak of the text as a 'constraint' upon possible interpretations.

Now clearly, this interpretative posture will be easier to adopt in some contexts than in others. Very bad books, based on little real understanding, can be very hard to understand: indeed, we may conclude that there is not much about them to be understood. Deliberation about how the gaps and uncertainties in such books are to be filled will not, in all probability, prove to be profitable. Similarly, legal systems offer us less interpretative guidance the further they depart from the requirements of justice. Legality and justice are distinct concepts and values, and are capable of competing with each other. But each of the two values can be fully realized only in conjunction with the other.

Parliament's Will and the Justice of the Common Law: The Human Rights Act in Constitutional Perspective

TRS Allan

Introduction

Does the requirement of section 3 of the Human Rights Act (HRA) that legislation should be construed compatibly with European Convention rights, in so far as it is 'possible to do so', really alter British constitutional law? The Act apparently reaffirms the common law presumption that Parliament does not intend to legislate contrary to the United Kingdom's international law obligations—a presumption readily displaced (according to orthodoxy) by clear contrary enactment. It is, perhaps, no longer necessary to search for 'ambiguity' as an excuse to displace the 'ordinary' meaning of a provision with one that better complies with the European Convention on Human Rights. There is an analogy with the principle of legality that narrows the scope of broadly framed powers in order to safeguard common law constitutional rights. The meaning that prima facie the words would most readily convey gives way to a different meaning—a sense that they would not bear if the Convention rights were not accorded the high respect that, by official acknowledgement and legal tradition, they now enjoy.

It is widely supposed, however, that section 3 authorizes—even demands—an interpretative approach that would otherwise be unprecedented and illegitimate. But it is hard to see how that view could be consistent with the preservation (by section 3(2)(b) of the HRA) of the validity of legislation incompatible with the Convention. For if the Act overrides or displaces ordinary principles of interpretation, otherwise applicable, it would appear to authorize a process of interpretation-cum-revision in order to *render* a statute compatible with the Convention, subject only to some (highly uncertain) constraints of judicial modesty, in recognition of Parliament's superior credentials as primary lawmaker. An ability to alter or revise a statute's meaning, in exercise of a strong 'interpretative obligation',[1] reduces its supposedly unchallengeable validity (along with parliamentary sovereignty) from substance to mere form. How can we both affirm Parliament's freedom to legislate inconsistently with the Convention and assert the right to give its enactments a special meaning to ensure compatibility?[2]

If, as Lord Nicholls of Birkenhead suggests, section 3 authorizes the attribution of a sense that 'departs from the unambiguous meaning the legislation would otherwise bear',[3] the highly elastic nature of interpretation in the face of a threat to constitutional rights has been conceded. When the moral importance of the matter in issue is sufficiently pressing, it is now acknowledged, the court's interpretative function cannot 'depend critically upon the particular form of words' enacted. Questions of great constitutional principle should not depend on the outcome of a 'semantic lottery'.[4] The notional limits of the interpretative function may be preserved by the reflection that Parliament could not have intended the courts to 'adopt a meaning inconsistent with a fundamental feature of legislation';[5] but the significance of the decision in *Ghaidan* should not be missed. The court, in effect, amended the Rent Act 1977 by adding homosexual partners to the categories of relationship which qualified the survivor to become the statutory tenant on the death of the original tenant. Lord Millett objected that the court's 'reading' clashed with the statute's implicit requirement that partners must be 'of the opposite sex'; it contradicted the ordinary meaning of the language. The revision made by the majority was surely justified, nonetheless, because the provisions would otherwise have violated rights of survivors of homosexual partnerships under Articles 8 and 14 of the Convention; and no convincing reasons had been suggested that could excuse or justify such discrimination.

In *Anderson*, Lord Steyn asserted that section 3 was 'not available where the suggested interpretation is contrary to express statutory words or is by implication necessarily contradicted by the statute'.[6] And in *Lambert*,

[1] See eg *Ghaidan v Godin-Mendoza* [2004] UKHL 30, [2004] 2 AC 557 [30] (Lord Nicholls of Birkenhead).

[2] Cf C Gearty, *Principles of Human Rights Adjudication* (Oxford: Oxford University Press, 2004), 25. Gearty seeks to show how the judges can 'pull off the trick of being positive law servants and natural law masters at one and the same time'; but the compromise he defends often looks precarious.

[3] *Ghaidan* [31].

[4] ibid. Cf. Lord Rodger of Earlsferry at [123].

[5] ibid [33] (Lord Nicolls). Cf. *In re S (Minors) (Care Order: Implementation of Care Plan)* [2002] UKHL 10, [2002] 2 AC 291 [40].

[6] *R (Anderson) v Secretary of State for the Home Department* [2002] UKHL 46, [2003] 1 AC 837 [59].

Lord Hope stated that resort to section 3 will not be possible if 'the legislation contains provisions . . . which expressly contradict the meaning which the enactment would have to be given to make it compatible' with the Convention.[7] The same was true if the statute contains provisions that have this effect by necessary implication.[8] We are supposing, however, that the statutory language, if given its ordinary meaning, does entail an infringement of Convention rights; that is why resort to section 3 is necessary. If, then, we adopt a Convention-compatible meaning, nonetheless, are we not contradicting what the statute would otherwise provide?

Lord Hope considered that the ordinary meaning of the Misuse of Drugs Act 1971 was that the defendant bore the persuasive burden of proof on the issue of his knowledge that the substance in his possession was a controlled drug; yet he was willing to treat the relevant provisions as imposing only an evidential burden. There is no difference here between explicit and implicit instructions. What is implied depends on what is expressed; but the true meaning of what is expressed reflects the appropriate style of interpretation. If, then, section 3 is to do its job, the supposed semantic fetters must yield. If, on its face, a statute appears to cast the burden of establishing a defence on the accused, it is implied that he must be convicted if the jury is not persuaded of its truth. If, however, the statute may properly be read to mean that the accused need only adduce credible evidence in support of that defence, the implication is quite different: he cannot be convicted unless the jury is persuaded that the defence is false.

Our perplexities over the operation of the Human Rights Act should awaken us to deeper problems far below the surface of its beguiling phraseology; and we cannot resolve these perplexities until we confront those underlying questions. Conceptual analysis, in particular, must play second fiddle to our normative judgments: references to 'legislative intent' or the 'separation of powers' or a 'fundamental feature' of the statute can amount to little more than summary restatements of such judgments in specific instances calling for decision. When is a statutory feature to be identified as 'fundamental'? We need, in each case, a theory of the statute in question that explains its application to (what we take to be) its central or primary instances and in the light of which we can assess its relevance to more doubtful cases. Parliamentary 'sovereignty' itself can be invoked as a constitutional absolute only by averting one's gaze from

[7] *R v Lambert* [2001] UKHL 37, [2002] 2 AC 545 [79].
[8] See also *R v A (No 2)* [2001] UKHL 25, [2002] 1 AC 45 [108].

the creative, evaluative nature of judicial interpretation, faithful to the requirements of the rule of law. It is a *formal* doctrine only, providing no guidance as to the true meaning, in any particular case, of Parliament's sovereign commands.[9]

Lord Hoffmann invoked the formal doctrine when he asserted, in *Simms*,[10] that Parliament could 'legislate contrary to fundamental principles of human rights' provided that, through the use of explicit language, it was willing 'to accept the political cost'. The case concerned the extent to which statutory powers of prison management were confined by common law principles of freedom of speech and recourse to legal process to correct a mistaken conviction. Since there is likely to be very little 'political cost' to curtailing prisoners' rights, the surrender of judicial responsibility suggested here endangers the rule of law. In practice, however, the 'principle of legality', which commends an interpretation of general words that respects the basic rights of the individual, can usually provide an acceptable outcome in particular cases. In substance, then, the courts can apply 'principles of constitutionality' akin to those existing in countries 'where the power of the legislature is expressly limited by a constitutional document'.[11] In Britain, the common law itself provides the requisite constitutional foundation.

Any adequate appraisal of the new British bill of rights must locate its role within the wider common law constitution, which in substance it both reflects and strengthens. There is naturally a substantial overlap between the Convention rights and the constitutional rights that the courts have identified as basic common law commitments. Fundamental liberties of speech, conscience, and association, for example, enjoy a protected constitutional status as intrinsic elements of the rule of law.[12] Together with such fundamental principles as the presumption of innocence in criminal proceedings, they play a critical role in the interpretation of statutes. It is rightly assumed that 'Parliament legislates for a European liberal democracy founded on the principles and traditions of the common law'.[13] The 'presumptions of general application', which are 'not easily displaced by a statutory text',[14] possess an enduring constitutional status, independent of any current legislative will.

[9] See T Allan, 'Legislative Supremacy and Legislative Intention: Interpretation, Meaning, and Authority' [2004] 63 *CLJ* 685.

[10] *R v Secretary of State for the Home Department, ex p Simms* [2000] 2 AC 115, 131.

[11] ibid.

[12] See generally T Allan, *Constitutional Justice: A Liberal Theory of the Rule of Law* (Oxford: Oxford University Press, 2001).

[13] *R v Secretary of State for the Home Department, ex p Pierson* [1998] AC 539 (Lord Steyn).

[14] Sir Rupert Cross, *Statutory Interpretation*, 3rd edn by John Bell and Sir George Engel (London: Butterworths, 1995), 165–6.

Constitutional thought in Britain suffers from a deep-rooted ambivalence that constantly threatens to confuse our legal analysis in specific instances. Two rival conceptions of the legal order compete for our allegiance; and we cannot hope to attain a coherent view of the Human Rights Act, or any other significant feature of our partly 'unwritten' constitution, until we resolve our dilemma clearly and decisively. The *Constitution of Will* confronts the *Constitution of Reason*. Absolute parliamentary sovereignty is the prime ingredient of the former; and, formally at least, the Act preserves it: not only may any of the fundamental rights it enshrines be overridden by explicit statutory command, but the entire edifice of legal protection may, on this view, be swept away by the simple device of legislative repeal. If this is the brilliant reconciliation of the public interest and human rights, democracy and the rule of law, allegedly forged by the Human Rights Act, the foundations of our freedom are precarious indeed.

The interpretative requirement of section 3, however, acknowledges a first principle of the Constitution of Reason: the citizen should be treated by government in accordance with the standards of justice or fairness widely recognized as fundamental to political morality, without arbitrary exception or unjustified discrimination. From this perspective, the presumption in favour of a Convention-compatible interpretation will be very strong indeed. We should not lightly conclude that Parliament has violated its own professed commitments by denying to some the freedom or dignity it preserves for others; and where the suggested invasions of freedom or dignity would be very severe, it is doubtful whether such conclusions could ever be justifiably drawn. We should, therefore, question the idea that the boundary between legitimate 'interpretation' of statutes, on the one hand, and impermissible 'legislation' or 'amendment', on the other, is marked by textual constraints that operate independently of the judge's normative conclusions. For this is a feature of the Constitution of Will that the Constitution of Reason denies.

If, then, the Human Rights Act has truly changed the British constitution, it is largely because it was planted in fertile soil. And if it represents a true reconciliation between ideals of legality and democracy, it is surely one that the common law had, to a substantial degree, already provided for. At the level of specific application, moreover, fundamental rights are intrinsically matters of the general law, in the sense that they depend on a legal judgment attuned to all relevant circumstances, within the broadest range of 'relevance'. It makes little sense, therefore, to treat the Act as a self-contained code, governing the relationship between courts and Parliament. Nor should we try to find some standard formula, or generally applicable test, to enable us to distinguish between 'reading' legislative instructions and 'revising' or 'amending' them. Abstracted from specific context, a general test or formula is empty. As Lord Steyn has said, in law 'context is everything';[15] and what is 'possible', or impossible, in matters of statutory interpretation depends, therefore, on the strength and urgency (in the circumstances) of the rule of law's demands.

Interpretation, Meaning, and Authority

The rival claims of the two constitutions, or competing conceptions of the legal order, are perfectly illustrated by the judgments in *ProLife Alliance*. The willingness of the Court of Appeal to interpret the Broadcasting Act in the light of the fundamental principle of freedom of speech contrasted sharply with the House of Lords' insistence on an absolutist, non-contextual meaning, impervious to the demands of legal principle.[16] The BBC and other broadcasters had refused to transmit the Alliance's party election broadcast, at the time of the 2001 general election, on the ground that its images of aborted foetuses, though accurately and reasonably presented, would be offensive to viewers. It was alleged that transmission would breach the broadcasters' obligation under the Broadcasting Act 1990, section 6(1), to transmit nothing that 'offends against good taste or decency' (or the similar obligation under the BBC's agreement with the Secretary of State).

The Court of Appeal recognized that the case raised major issues of freedom of speech: it concerned the ability of a political party to present its message effectively, in exercise of its statutory right to a free broadcast in Wales, at the time of a general election. It was held that the broadcasters had exercised a censorship of political speech that could not be justified by reference to the Broadcasting Act, which must be read as subject to the fundamental principle of freedom of speech. Laws LJ explained how the court's enforcement of the protections of Article 10 of the European Convention marched hand in hand with the commitment of the common law to freedom of expression. The courts were ultimately trustees of the framework of democracy: 'as a matter of domestic law the courts owe a special responsibility to the public as the constitutional guardian of the

[15] *R (Daly) v Secretary of State for the Home Department* [2001] 2 AC 532, 548.

[16] *R (on the application of ProLife Alliance) v BBC* [2002] EWCA Civ 297, [2003] UKHL 23, [2004] 1 AC 185.

freedom of political debate'.[17] The court should decide for itself whether the censorship imposed was justified; and, in all the relevant circumstances, it was plainly not justified: it would be a rare case in which the considerations of taste and decency would prevail over freedom of speech by a political party at election time.

The House of Lords, by contrast, denied that the court could make its own assessment of the relative claims of free speech, on one hand, and protection from the distress caused by offensive material, on the other. In the view of the majority, Parliament had itself struck the balance by imposing its restrictions on broadcasts that offended good taste; the broadcasters were simply performing their statutory duty. Although the Alliance had made no direct challenge to the compatibility of the Broadcasting Act with Article 10, the 'thrust of its submissions', according to Lord Hoffmann, was that 'the statute should be disregarded or not taken seriously'.[18] The appropriateness of imposing the offensive material restriction on party broadcasts was not strictly an issue in the proceedings. The Court of Appeal (in Lord Nicholls's view) had rewritten the content of the statutory restriction: Parliament had already settled the question of justification that the court had sought to answer.

Few are likely to find such reasoning persuasive.[19] Had Parliament really tied the broadcasters' hands, and hence also the judges'? Or was the House of Lords merely less receptive to the Alliance's free speech claim (whether for good reasons or bad) than the judges in the Court of Appeal? Lord Hoffmann's surprising refusal to acknowledge the relevance of the general election to the context in which the Alliance's claim fell to be assessed—it was merely an additional opportunity to publicize its views—may be indicative of where his sympathies lay. His tone could hardly have differed more strongly from that of the judges below: 'The Alliance had no human right to be invited to the party and it is not unreasonable for Parliament to provide that those invited should behave themselves'.[20] For Simon Brown LJ, by contrast, the Alliance was pursuing a 'legitimate political programme', and their pictures were in a real sense their message: words alone could not convey the essentially human character of the foetus and the nature of its destruction by abortion.

The canonical terms of the Broadcasting Act could not settle the content of the broadcasters' duty, viewed from within the Constitution of Reason, without an analysis of the kind undertaken by the Court of

[17] [2002] EWCA Civ 297 [36]. [18] [2003] UKHL 23 [52].
[19] For a trenchant critique, see E Barendt, 'Free Speech and Abortion' [2003] PL 580.
[20] [2003] UKHL 23 [73].

Appeal. For we cannot know whether material infringes standards of good taste or decency until we have examined the reasons on both sides of the argument, and weighed them in the balance. A superficially 'offensive' broadcast may be redeemed by its countervailing social value. The reasons are always stronger than the language alone, whenever there is any scope for interpretative doubt; the words are only the servants of aims and assumptions that invite critical scrutiny in the light of concrete events. And there is scope for interpretative doubt whenever there is a serious threat to rights that enjoy a protected constitutional status. It is understandable that, seeking to evade controversy, judges may sometimes attribute their conclusions to the force of a statutory command they are obliged to obey; but the power of a cogent dissenting judgment will often provide a telling counterpoint.

As Lord Scott explained, a general provision to safeguard the demands of good taste and decency, applicable to every kind of broadcast, could not automatically determine the legality of the broadcasters' censorship of a party political broadcast in all the circumstances of a particular case. A far more nuanced question must be asked, suitably tailored to the facts in issue. The question was 'whether the rejection by the broadcasters of this particular programme, the purpose of which was to promote the cause of the Alliance at the forthcoming general election, was a lawful application by the broadcasters of the conditions by which they were bound'.[21] Material that might be unacceptable in one type of programme might be permissible in another. The nature of the broadcast and its intended audience were factors of critical relevance.[22] The broadcasters were required to interpret their obligations in the light of the specific context; and in the present context, their decision that the broadcast would be offensive failed to give proper weight to the resilience that must be shown by participants in political debate within a mature democracy.

It is important to see that conceptions of language, authority, and law fit together as interlocking elements of rival theories of public law. Crude notions of unqualified parliamentary sovereignty, in particular, assume straightforward distinctions between 'interpretation' and 'amendment': legislative instructions could not otherwise secure the requisite submission. A more subtle account of the idea of legislative intent, emphasizing its indeterminacy in the face of the most serious threats to basic individual rights, tends to blur the division of authority between lawmaker and judge. The notion that the application of rights in particular cases is determined by legislative intention, where the relevant 'intention' is

[21] ibid [92]. [22] Compare Simon Brown LJ at [2002] EWCA Civ 297 [56].

equated with the immediate political aims of those currently in charge of the legislative machine, reflects a view of the judges as mere servants of Parliament. As 'faithful agents' of the legislative will, the courts must interpret their instructions, but not revise them.[23] Within the Constitution of Reason, by contrast, the judges serve the constitution or the legal order; their submission to the legislative will is a reasoned and reflective one, attuned to all the circumstances.[24]

The assumption, indeed, that Parliament may give authoritative instructions about the interpretation of its own enactments, though widely accepted, is in fact open to question. If judges are merely servants of a fluctuating political will, they should no doubt be grateful for whatever guidance they are given as a means of interpreting it correctly. As servants, rather, of the constitutional order, however, they can scarcely avoid responsibility for developing a *theory* of legislative supremacy, along with the interpretative principles and presumptions that give such a doctrine its wider constitutional context and meaning. From this perspective, the application of general rules to particular cases is truly an independent judicial function. In a genuine constitutional regime, where the rule of law is not merely the temporary grant of the current political majority, a balance of power between lawmaker and interpreter is inherent in the concept of 'law'.[25] There are limits to the legislative power inherent in that constitutional logic: Parliament could hardly (without an infinite regress) give instructions on the correct approach to its interpretative instructions. The interpretative power of the superior courts is as fundamental as Parliament's legislative supremacy: shared sovereignty is intrinsic to constitutional government.

Those whose loyalty to orthodox notions of parliamentary supremacy remains undiminished ought, then, to share Geoffrey Marshall's scepticism about the 'supposed new interpretative obligation'.[26] He objected that once the old 'lynchpin of parliamentary intention' is removed, and the 'bounds and limits of possibility stretched', the statutory meaning becomes somewhat detached from the words it is supposed to reflect. This looks much like judicial disobedience: a strained meaning is, after all, a meaning that the specific language seems to contradict. If, as Lord

[23] See J Goldsworthy, 'Parliamentary Sovereignty and Statutory Interpretation', in R Bigwood (ed), *The Statute, Making and Meaning* (Wellington: LexisNexis, 2004).

[24] See T Allan, 'The Rule of Law as the Rule of Reason: Consent and Constitutionalism' (1999) 115 LQR 221. See also T R Hickman, 'Constitutional Dialogue, Constitutional Theories and the Human Rights Act 1998' [2005] PL 306.

[25] See further Allan, n 12 above.

[26] G Marshall, 'The Lynchpin of Parliamentary Intention: Lost, Stolen or Strained?' [2003] PL 236.

Millett has suggested,[27] the court can properly 'do considerable violence to the language and stretch it almost . . . to breaking point', it plainly has power to remould the provision in question. If what Lord Millett calls an 'unnatural or unreasonable' meaning may nonetheless be 'intellectually defensible', it draws inspiration from a broader constitutional morality than Marshall acknowledged. But the judicial language here is redolent of the Constitution of Will; for we cannot judge what is truly 'natural' or 'reasonable' in abstraction from the demands of justice that guide our interpretative efforts.

It does not follow that we should jettison the 'legislative intent' as irrelevant or meaningless. Jeffrey Goldsworthy is right to insist that, stripped of the intentions and purposes that a contextual reading elicits, the statutory words cannot provide the guidance or instruction that the idea of legislative authority requires.[28] A purely formal or literal reading is as apt to block a legislature's objectives as to serve them, leaving the interpretative choice unfettered. It is true, nonetheless, that 'Parliament . . . is sovereign only in respect of what it expresses by the words used in the legislation it has passed'.[29] Since, moreover, Parliament's 'intention' is distinct from the wishes of any of its particular members—especially government ministers—it cannot be determined (with or without a bill of rights) in isolation from the moral opinions and reasonable expectations of the citizen, or those that may reasonably be attributed to his elected representative. In short, the interpretation of enacted laws is as much a matter of *con*struction, to meet the exigencies of specific cases and particular contexts, as of *in*struction. Legal interpretation is always a subtle blend of reason and fiat, as Lon Fuller argued;[30] semantic constraints cannot operate independently of our substantive moral judgments.

It may be objected that words cannot be infinitely elastic; interpretation must have its limits. According to Lord Hope, section 3 'does not give power to the judges to overrule decisions which the language of the statute shows have been taken on the very point at issue by the legislator'.[31] But how may such decisions be identified? And who is the 'legislator' for the purpose of ascertaining a univocal legislative intent? Let us imagine a

[27] *Ghaidan v Godin-Mendoza* [2004] UKHL 30 [67].

[28] See Goldsworthy, above n 23, 4–9. See also J Goldsworthy, 'Legislative Intentions, Legislative Supremacy, and Legal Positivism', in J Goldsworthy and T Campbell (eds), *Legal Interpretation in Democratic States* (Aldershot: Dartmouth, 2002).

[29] *Black-Clawson International Ltd v Papierwerke Waldhof-Aschaffenburg AG* [1975] AC 591, 638 (Lord Diplock).

[30] See L L Fuller, *Anatomy of the Law* (Harmondsworth: Penguin Books, 1971) and, by the same author, *The Morality of Law* (2nd edn) (New Haven: Yale University Press, 1969).

[31] *R v Lambert* [2001] UKHL 37 [79].

representative member of the legislative majority who knows the ordinary meaning of the words enacted. When has he determined the 'very point at issue'? We must attribute to him a knowledge of at least the immediate statutory context; but how far should we assume an awareness of the potential conflict with Convention rights? (Presumably, the statute does not state, in terms, that such rights are simply to be ignored.) Perhaps an adaptation of the language to achieve compatibility would sharply alter his sense of what the statute means in practice? But the risk of such surprise is inherent in the operations of section 3; so it is merely a matter of degree. And the more serious the threat to fundamental rights, the greater our confidence that the representative legislator would accept a 'strained' or nuanced interpretation; or, at least, the weaker our assurance that, confronted by the full implications of an ordinary reading, he would nonetheless affirm it.

The truth is that statutory provisions owe their meaning as much to their interpreters as their authors; it is, after all, the interpreter who must decide what the statute's consequences are to be in the light of unfolding events, rarely foreseen with any clarity at the time of enactment. The cognitive and creative elements of interpretation are interdependent and intermixed: we can only locate what Parliament has done within the realm of what, as good citizens (or competent legal interpreters on their behalf), we think it reasonable for Parliament to do. The more dubious the consequences of adhering to the ordinary meaning, in present circumstances, the weaker the power of semantic constraints to control our interpretative conclusions. And it follows that repeated declarations that permissible 'interpretation' must be distinguished from unauthorized 'legislation' are little more than empty rhetoric; for these are ultimately labels to be attached to interpretative conclusions that one approves or disapproves, all pertinent considerations taken into account. It is in one sense plainly true that creative interpretation, sensitive to the demands of human rights, is a form of legislative revision. The separation of powers between courts and Parliament turns out to be a matter of degree; when the reasons for revision (or 'amendment') are sufficiently powerful, the 'ordinary' contextual meaning must yield.[32]

Speaking of 'revision' and 'amendment', however, suggests that a statute's one true meaning is ascertainable, in principle, at the time of its enactment. Then we treat judicial construction as involving the discovery

[32] The creative and evaluative features of judicial interpretation are also emphasized by Aileen Kavanagh: see A Kavanagh, 'The Elusive Divide between Interpretation and Legislation under the Human Rights Act 1998' (2004) 24 OJLS 259.

of a latent, if not patent, legislative intention adequate to resolve every case that falls within its literal terms. But it is more realistic to think of the statute as substantially inchoate, applicable straightforwardly only to the central or more obvious cases caught by its ordinary meaning—those cases where the statutory purpose plainly demands a particular outcome, if the ordinary meaning of the words allows it. Beyond this central core of meaning, the statute's application must be highly sensitive to context and circumstance: its true meaning must be *ascribed* rather than *discovered*. The cases that present a danger to human rights lie outside the core; they raise difficult questions of judgment about how best to reconcile the statutory purpose with the protection of fundamental values. Even if the outcome appears to contradict the ordinary meaning, entailing a significant qualification of the statute's general instructions, it need not be dubbed an 'amendment' or 'revision' of doubtful legitimacy. It can properly be considered a new 'development', attuned to the needs of the time and place—a legitimate adaptation to present conditions that no one could have foreseen in any great detail.

A statute's meaning, accordingly, will change as the surrounding law evolves. The lynchpin of legislative intent—in the sense of the meaning the canonical words most plausibly bore at the time of enactment—will give way to an interpretation that is better suited to contemporary conditions, just as judicial opinions enmeshed in the attitudes of an earlier age may not withstand scrutiny today. We are bound, as a matter of constitutional justice, to give an enactment the meaning its words most plausibly bear today—when its injunctions must be reconciled with other elements of the legal order, reflecting the moral and social imperatives of more recent law.[33] It is therefore no objection, as Lord Millett thought in *Ghaidan*, that the Rent Act was a 'statute framed in gender specific terms, and enacted at a time when homosexual relations were not recognised by law'.[34] A new interpretation is needed for a new era. Nor is the allegedly 'retrospective' nature of the change an insuperable objection; when a statute is properly integrated into the wider body of law it will inevitably share many of the characteristics of common law rules. The amendments made to the Rent Act in 1988 were poorly drafted to satisfy (what are now recognized to be) the requirements of justice: the unfair discrimination should be corrected by a suitably robust construction.[35]

[33] Cf William N Eskridge Jr, *Dynamic Statutory Interpretation* (Cambridge, Mass: Harvard University Press, 1994), esp ch 2.

[34] *Ghaidan v Godin-Mendoza* [2004] UKHL 30 [99].

[35] It follows that *Fitzpatrick v Sterling Housing Association* [2001] 1 AC 27, which denied same-sex partners the protection accorded to unmarried heterosexual survivors,

In *Lambert*, Lord Hope pointed to Parliament's imposition of an evidential, rather than legal, burden of proof on the accused in more recent legislation as a guide to the correct construction of the Misuse of Drugs Act 1971.[36] A 'dynamic' approach of this kind, moreover, does not depend entirely on the Human Rights Act; it is what the common law constitution, properly understood, in any case requires. If, by application of section 3, it is possible to construe the 1971 Act as imposing only an evidential burden as regards the defendant's knowledge of the substance found in his possession, it is legitimate to read it in that way without recourse to section 3. Even if the 'ordinary meaning' of the phrase 'it shall be a defence for the accused to prove' suggests a persuasive burden, the ordinary meaning is not decisive if there are strong considerations of principle against it. A 'possible' reading is simply one that the words permit when considered in context, including the constitutional context; and provided that the statutory purposes are not defeated, or too gravely impeded, such a possible reading may be taken as correct. Lord Clyde, accordingly, thought the statute should be read—with or without section 3—consistently with 'respect for the "golden thread" of the presumption of innocence'.[37]

At the heart of our perplexities over the bounds of legitimate interpretation lies a questionable view of the relationship between statute and the common law. If we think of a statute as having no effect on the common law beyond the specific changes it plainly enacts, it seems hard to justify its extension to analogous cases. Conversely, if we assume that the statute applies to every instance within the literal meaning of its provisions, a more nuanced or restrictive reading looks suspicious. When we recall, however, that the rule of law requires that discrimination between persons or classes of person must be properly justified—on grounds that meet the human rights standards we officially profess—we can see the importance of interpreting both common law and statute as a seamless and unified body of law.[38] Analogies may as legitimately be drawn from statutory rules as from rules of common law, where they are recommended by principle and where legislative policy permits—or even when, though specific policy commitments present a stumbling-block, the broader claims of general principle have (in all the circumstances) especial force.[39]

was wrongly decided (even before the Human Rights Act affirmed the proper interpretative approach). On any other view, moreover, *Ghaidan* has a questionable retrospective effect on vested rights: see D Mead, 'Rights, Relationships and Retrospectivity: The Impact of Convention Rights on Pre-existing Private Relationships following *Wilson* and *Ghaidan*' [2005] PL 459.

36 *R v Lambert* [2001] UKHL 37 [92]–[93]. 37 ibid [157].

38 See generally Allan, n 12 above, esp chs 5 and 8.

39 Cf R Dworkin, *Law's Empire* (London: Fontana, 1986).

The rights vindicated in *Ghaidan* were statutory rights, in the sense that they were granted by the Rent Act, appropriately revised. But in another sense they were common law rights, acknowledged as *entailed by* the statutory scheme—not dependent on any choice of statutory language but implicit in the sense of being *necessary* to complete a scheme which would be compatible with the Convention. The rights of the homosexual partner flowed, we might say, from the equity rather than the specific provisions of the statute; and such considerations of equity are quintessentially matters of judicial reason rather than explicit parliamentary stipulation. The tenant's rights derive from common law rights against Parliament—rights against unjustified discrimination. The lynchpin of legislative intent is therefore loosened; though the sovereignty of Parliament can still be affirmed, in a formal sense, by invoking Parliament's presumed desire (reflecting Britain's obligations under international law) to comply with the Convention.

It follows that the 'interpretative obligation' imposed by the Human Rights Act, section 3, is less novel than it may initially appear. If the true meaning of a statute is partly a function of its present context, rather than simply a matter of what its authors apparently envisaged, the old lynchpin of parliamentary intent was never fully determinative. That does not mean that the words of a provision are not entitled to the greatest respect; their natural or ordinary meaning always makes the first claim on our attention. But the ordinary meaning is only a gateway to the *true* meaning, which embodies the commands of reason alongside those of the relevant political will. We cannot shirk the continuing responsibility to bring the provision into harmony with present expectations and constitutional needs. It is always an inescapable interpretative task to determine how far—in what circumstances—the statutory purposes should surrender to competing moral imperatives. And since the European Convention on Human Rights was already part of the modern interpretative background, section 3 largely confirms the status quo: it is, in the last analysis, an acquiescence in the instructions of the common law constitution.

The Boundaries of Legitimate Interpretation

What, then, are the boundaries of legitimate interpretation? When must a provision be condemned as irredeemably incompatible with Convention rights? If the whole *raison d'être* of a provision violates the Convention, no interpretation can save it: a declaration of incompatibility (under section 4) will be the appropriate judicial response. The detention without trial of foreign terrorist suspects provides a recent example: the arbitrary discrimination between citizen and foreigner was intrinsic to the statutory scheme.[40] In the great majority of cases, however, section 3 is likely to be applicable; for the intention to comply with the Convention can normally be safely assumed and the necessary adjustments made to the statutory language—or a suitably charitable reading adopted—without any constitutional overreaching. Parliament can, after all, always alter the terms of its instructions if they have been seriously misunderstood; or at least it can do so within a wide jurisdiction to settle the requirements of the common good.

That last proviso is necessary because liberal democracy is not compatible with an infinitely elastic conception of the common good. Even if Parliament retains the power to repudiate decisions of the European Court of Human Rights, it cannot destroy the most fundamental elements of the unwritten constitution from which its own lawmaking power is ultimately derived. The presumption that Parliament intends to legislate in accordance with the Convention may be rebuttable; but the presumption that Parliament acknowledges the rule of law, as a sovereign ideal of individual freedom and human dignity, is surely more secure. Even if Article 6 is ultimately expendable, for example, the right to a fair trial is, in its essentials, an intrinsic part of the common law constitution. No declaration of incompatibility can be given in respect of a statute that threatens the rule of law, for no such statute—read as having that effect—could be acknowledged as truly law.

The revision, or restrictive reading, of the Youth Justice and Criminal Evidence Act 1999, section 41, in *R v A* was justified by the overriding importance of preserving the defendant's right to a fair criminal trial.[41] Article 6 of the Convention is matched by what may be viewed as an absolute common law right: the rule of law cannot countenance the state's prosecution of unfair proceedings against the accused. It was entirely legitimate, therefore, to reject any literal reading of a provision which appeared, on the face of it, to deny the admissibility of evidence of the complainant's sexual behaviour, in a trial for a sexual offence, even where it would be relevant to the defendant's case. Lord Steyn rightly explained that it was 'realistic to proceed on the basis that the legislature would not, if alerted to the problem, have wished to deny the right to an

[40] *A and others v Secretary of State for the Home Department* [2004] UKHL 56, [2005] 2 AC 68; see further below.

[41] *R v A (No 2)* [2001] UKHL 25, [2002] 1 AC 45.

accused to put forward a full and complete defence by advancing truly probative material'.[42] It is true that the judges doubted that they could achieve a similar result through 'ordinary methods of purposive construction', in the absence of the Human Rights Act; but their doubts seem misplaced. To deny Lord Steyn's presumption would be to impugn Parliament's good faith—to question its commitment to constitutional justice.

It is no answer to say that Parliament may have taken a different view of the requirements of a fair trial; there is little scope here for 'deference'. No general rule can determine conclusively all the cases that may fall within its ordinary meaning, let alone its literal (acontextual) reading. While it governs the standard case—where we can clearly discern the abuse or injustice for which it provides a remedy—we must rely more fully and squarely on own moral judgment elsewhere. The 1999 Act should be applied so as to suppress the 'mischief' at which it was directed: evidence of doubtful relevance should not be adduced as a means of embarrassing or intimidating the complainant. But truly relevant evidence must be admitted, however infelicitous the statutory wording, in order to prevent a miscarriage of justice. Lord Hope's denial that the court could read in a qualification that preserved the elements of a fair trial was hard to square with his approval of Lord Steyn's summary of the court's conclusions; it reflected his desire to preserve a sharp division of powers between judge and legislator—a division that, if applied with insufficient regard for the constitutional context, could threaten rather than sustain the rule of law.[43]

We are now well placed to appraise the House of Lords' decision in *Anderson*, which is widely thought to illustrate the limits of the interpretative function.[44] It was held that the Crime (Sentences) Act 1997, section 29, could not be read consistently with Article 6 of the European Convention (requiring sentencing to be performed by an independent and impartial tribunal rather than by a member of the executive). In Lord Bingham's view, it would have been 'not judicial interpretation but judicial vandalism' to read the section in a way that precluded the Home Secretary from setting the tariff for a mandatory life-sentence prisoner at a level in excess of that judicially recommended.[45] Such an interpretation would not be consistent with Parliament's intention. Lord Steyn thought that it 'would not be interpretation but interpolation inconsistent with the plain legislative intent to entrust the decision to the Home

[42] ibid [45].

[43] For detailed analysis, see A Kavanagh, 'Unlocking the Human Rights Act: The "Radical" Approach to Section 3(1) Revisited' [2005] EHRLR 259.

[44] *R (Anderson) v Secretary of State for the Home Department* [2002] UKHL 46, [2003] 1 AC 837.

[45] ibid [30].

Secretary, who was intended to be free to follow or reject judicial advice'.[46] But these assertions of judicial powerlessness are not persuasive; they invoke too crude a 'legislative intention', stripped too brusquely from its constitutional context. This is the sort of legislative intent that, in the view of the *dissentients* in *Venables* and *Pierson*, authorized the Home Secretary to have regard to public opinion as regards the deserts of a notorious offender, or to increase a tariff previously announced; for those judges held that the imposition of quasi-judicial constraints was contrary to Parliament's intention in granting the relevant powers to a government minister.[47]

As Lord Steyn reminded us, in *Pierson*, Parliament does not legislate in a vacuum: 'Parliament legislates for a European liberal democracy founded on the principles and traditions of the common law'.[48] The maintenance of the separation of powers between the courts and the executive is an important aspect of those traditions; and it followed that, construed in the light of the general 'principle of legality', the Home Secretary's powers in relation to the detention of life sentence prisoners were properly subject to quasi-judicial constraints. It would have been only a very small step further to insist that the minister should follow judicial advice, as regards the length of a tariff; the risk of arbitrariness could be eliminated only if the minister complied with a uniform judicial standard, applicable in principle to all comparable offenders. The European Court of Human Rights had held in *Stafford* that domestic law no longer supported a distinction between mandatory life prisoners, discretionary life prisoners, and juvenile murderers as regards the tariff: it was a 'sentencing exercise' in each case.[49] The House of Lords in *Anderson* acknowledged the cogency of that conclusion; so the requirements of Article 6 ran perfectly in tandem with common law principle.

If we suppose, as we should, that Parliament had no intention that the Home Secretary should be free to violate Convention rights, or to flout an essential precept of the rule of law, the literal words of the Crime (Sentences) Act 1997, section 29, could and should have been qualified accordingly. All that that 'not very perspicuous section'[50] expressly contemplated was the release of a convicted murderer on the recommendation of the Parole Board, after consultation with the judiciary. It was wholly silent on the subject of the tariff, or on its consequences for the

[46] ibid [59].

[47] See *R v Secretary of State for the Home Department, ex p Venables* [1998] AC 407; *R v Secretary of State for the Home Department, ex p Pierson* [1998] AC 539.

[48] [1998] AC 539, 587.

[49] *Stafford v United Kingdom* 35 EHRR 1121, 1143–4.

[50] *Anderson*, [30] (Lord Bingham of Cornhill).

legality of the minister's actions. A duty to refer the case to the Board before the tariff's expiry could readily be implied.[51] The Human Rights Act, section 3, could be invoked to convert the minister's discretion to follow judicial advice into a duty: he should exercise the power in accordance with the Convention, as section 6 of the Act requires. But the same conclusions can be drawn at common law. If we acknowledge a duty to interpret statutes in accordance with the rule of law, the relevant 'parliamentary intent' must be constructed, rather than discovered or surmised. It is a matter of forging the best reconciliation we can between the statute's literal provisions, on one hand, and the demands in that context of constitutional principle, on the other. And when those demands are urgent and pressing, adherence to an overly literal, or prima-facie reading can amount to *constitutional* vandalism. As Lord Steyn observed, the idea that punishment by imprisonment may only be ordered by a court is a 'principal feature of the rule of law on which our unwritten constitution is based'.[52]

The presumption that Parliament intends the rule of law to be upheld is a cornerstone of Britain's unwritten constitution; and it is a perfectly familiar principle that the requirements of the rule of law are not frozen as they were perceived at the date of a statute's enactment. They evolve as our grasp of the implications of liberal constitutionalism is deepened by reflection on experience. We do not think that administrative powers are only subject to judicial review on the basis of principles clearly identified when the powers were granted. We understand that the exercise of all powers must conform to the requirements of legality, rationality, and fairness that apply today. Such a view is implicit in the very notion of equality before the law, when 'law' is understood to encompass general principles as well as discrete 'laws' for particular purposes. If that means that the 'legislative intent' in question has been reconsidered, or rather reconstructed, we do not think we are thereby flouting the sovereignty of Parliament. We are, in effect, updating the statute to enable it to keep up with changes in the law that surrounds it and with the expectations of those subject to the powers it confers. From that perspective, we should be less troubled by Lord Hutton's view that the removal of the Home Secretary's power to determine

[51] Lord Bingham doubted 'whether it could ever be lawful to continue to detain a convicted murderer who had served the punitive term judged necessary to meet the requirements of retribution and general deterrence and whose release was not judged by the Parole Board to present any significant risk of danger to the public' (ibid, para 11). Could such restrictions on the minister's powers be circumvented by refusing to refer the case to the Parole Board?

[52] ibid [51]. cf *A and others v Secretary of State for the Home Department* [2004] UKHL 56 [97] (Lord Hoffmann).

the length of the tariff would amount to statutory amendment rather than interpretation.[53] It is an 'amendment' only in the sense that it alters the previous understanding—an understanding overtaken and outflanked by an evolution of legal principle.

The status of the ultra vires principle has come under challenge in recent years for similar reasons. It seems artificial to attribute the ordinary constraints of administrative legality to legislative intent when the nature and scope of those constraints vary with the evolution of the common law. But the rule of law is the rule of both common law and statute, appropriately interwoven. Since the practical application of common law principles must be sensitive to the administrative context, largely fashioned by the relevant Act, the court must seek to bring common law and statute into harmony. The statutory purposes must be reconciled with legal principle in the manner that does least harm to either: 'the justice of the common law will supply the omission of the legislature' while respecting the general purposes.[54] Neither parliamentary sovereignty nor the ultra vires doctrine needs to be abandoned to accommodate the realities of judicial review; but we do have to grant their largely formal, conclusionary character. For the constitution supplies (or assumes) an overriding, all-purpose legislative intention that executive powers should be exercised in accordance with the rule of law, and makes the courts the final judges, in particular cases, of what the rule of law requires.

It follows that the nature and scope of executive powers will depend on the statute's correct *constitutional* construction. Even the plainest words await interpretation because no statute, however precise its instructions or recent its enactment, exists in a constitutional vacuum. It awaits construction because it awaits integration into the tapestry of which it can only form a single thread. Moreover, its integration is, in substance, a matter of adaptation and adjustment, case by case; its requirements are ascertained by reasoned argument in the light of unfolding events. Whether or not, for example, the Home Secretary can deprive a prisoner of access to the news media, on the basis of his jurisdiction over prison administration, depends on all the circumstances—the grounds of the prisoner's desire to talk to a journalist, the stringency of the conditions imposed on such a meeting, and the likely impact on prison discipline, in particular.[55] What is lawful will depend on what is reasonable. The *meaning* of a statute—to summarize the argument—is a matter of its *application*

[53] ibid [81].
[54] *Cooper v Wandsworth Board of Works* (1863) 14 CB (NS) 180 (Byles J).
[55] See *R v Secretary of State for the Home Department, ex p Simms* [2000] 2 AC 115.

to the endless variety of circumstances that social and political life can devise. It is not a discrete matter of semantics; and it is not determined once and for all at the date of enactment.

Conclusion

I have argued that we can only determine the nature and limits of the interpretative duty imposed by the Human Rights Act, section 3, by reflection on the nature of statutory interpretation within the Constitution of Reason. When we acknowledge the creative and evaluative character of interpretation, performed by judges committed to the protection of the rule of law, we will abandon the attempt to distinguish, by means of some general formula, between 'interpretation' and 'amendment'. The distinction reflects a judgment about the proper limits of interpretative freedom within a specific context, where the importance of the rights affected and the scale of the threatened interference with them will exert a critical influence. To see this, however, is also to see that section 3 reproduces a fundamental feature of the common law constitution; for the common law also recognizes basic constitutional rights and requires their protection against unjustified encroachments. Since the European Convention rights are sometimes more demanding than basic common law entitlements, section 3 ensures that interpretative creativity encompasses their protection even if the presumption of respect for international law alone is insufficient. Within the substantial sphere of overlap between common law and Convention rights, however, section 3 adds little or nothing to constitutional law. It requires the courts to fulfil their common law obligation to interpret statutes in accordance with such basic rights—an obligation implicit in, or constituted by, the rule of law.

It is doubtful, therefore, whether Conor Gearty's paraphrase of subsection 3(2)(b) can provide much practical guidance: 'An interpretation of a provision . . . which substantially impairs its continuing operation or enforcement is not a possible interpretation for the purposes of section 3(1)'.[56] The degree of acceptable impairment is so much dependent on the context that any such general test is empty. For most purposes, it is no doubt true that 'it should in principle take much less than a total stifling of an Act's purpose under the weight of section (3)(1) before the proviso in section 3(2)(b) is permitted to come riding to the rescue'.[57] But how much less? The answer will depend on the consequences for human

[56] Gearty, n 2 above, 53. [57] ibid.

dignity and liberty of the measure in the circumstances arising. Moreover, any acceptable interpretation of section 3 must take account of its common law analogue. The view that judges must not 'rewrite' the Human Rights Act to achieve the power that Parliament 'consciously and quite deliberately withheld from them'[58] presupposes that the courts are subject to binding legislative instructions as regards their interpretative methods and assumptions; and I have questioned whether that is true.

In preserving the 'validity, continuing operation', and 'enforcement' of incompatible primary legislation, the Human Rights Act upholds a formal principle of parliamentary sovereignty. In substance, however, it acknowledges that the meaning of formally valid statutory provisions depends on considerations of justice, rooted in a legal tradition of respect for basic values of individual liberty and human dignity. By losing sight of the interdependence of legislative and judicial authority, and the close interaction of statute and common law, we mistake the Constitution of Reason for the Constitution of Will and condemn ourselves to incoherence and contradiction. The idea that legislation is superior to precedent as a source of law is accurate enough for everyday purposes; but it obscures the truth that, in the last analysis, a statute obtains its meaning from its context of application—a context of which the common law forms a fundamental part. It is wrong, therefore, to think of the common law as a merely residual backcloth—what is left once we have settled the statutory meaning independently. On the contrary, our common law principles and presumptions help us to refine and clarify that meaning in specific instances.

We cannot know, for example, what matters constitute 'exceptional circumstances', for the purpose of a statute that otherwise imposes a life sentence on someone convicted of a second 'serious' offence, until we review that purpose in the light of our basic principles of criminal justice.[59] If the youth of the offender at the time of the first offence, or the lapse of time between offences, or the different nature of the 'serious offences' involved, are matters relevant to the *justice* of the infliction of a life sentence, we should be slow to conclude that the court cannot take them into account. If, therefore, there are no adverse consequences for what appears to be the statutory purpose—to protect the public against truly dangerous offenders—such factors may properly be regarded as amounting to 'exceptional circumstances' within the contemplation of the rule.[60] Reason and authority are thus intertwined: the enactment's

[58] ibid, 52. [59] See Crime (Sentences) Act 1997, s 2.

[60] See *R v Offen* [2001] 1 WLR 253 (CA). See also *R v Drew* [2003] UKHL 25, 2 Cr App R 371 [20].

meaning is made sensitive to purpose and context. Although, in *Offen*, the court justified this result chiefly by reference to the Human Rights Act, it is clear that the common law supplied the same conclusion: earlier cases had adopted an unduly rigid conception of 'exceptional circumstances', overlooking the statute's rationale.[61]

Gearty is embarrassed to admit his concurrence with the judgment; for 'however it is dressed up or explained away, the *Offen* case has effectively disembowelled a particularly savage legislative intervention, passed at the height of a panic about crime and (if its words were to be believed) designed to inflict exactly the kind of punishment that was originally imposed on Offen and his fellow appellants'.[62] His confidence about the demands of justice, in the circumstances of Offen's case, however, shows that his embarrassment is an unnecessary hangover from a former allegiance to the Constitution of Will. When we understand the search for justice as a collective endeavour, treating legislative instructions as a contribution to that endeavour, we must repudiate 'savage' readings of such instructions as unforeseen and unintended. It is, then, the savage reading that is 'disembowelled' rather than the statute. There was no legislative intention in respect of Offen's case, or any case giving rise to similar apprehension; only the general rule was truly 'intended', or enacted, leaving its integration with the broader principles of criminal justice to the judiciary.

Gearty rejects my conception of the rule of law, in favour of a narrower principle of 'legality', on the ground that space for considerations of justice must be found within the legislative branch rather than outside it. Civil liberties are intended chiefly to strengthen the democratic process, so that debates about the justice of people's treatment must be settled 'at the stage of law-making rather than law-enforcing'.[63] Gearty denies the existence of objective values separate from the democratic process; he accepts and celebrates the inevitability of conflict in a free society. But he fails to acknowledge that the legal process is an integral part of the resolution of conflict as it arises in practical instances. A general rule cannot determine its own meaning or sphere of application: it requires interpretation as events unfold. If, therefore, the application of rules is to be properly respectful of the democratic process, it cannot prescind from the considerations of justice that provide the substance of parliamentary debate. If the legislative process should be understood as a deliberative forum, in which elected representatives seek to determine the requirements of justice, the judicial process must receive and interpret its enactments in the same

[61] [2001] 1 WLR 253, 269–72. [62] Gearty, n 2 above, 77. [63] ibid, 64.

spirit. Moreover, the open public appraisal of both legislative and judicial decision-making, which is a primary feature of genuine democracy, depends on the health of a public political culture that transcends current institutional attitudes and outcomes.

When the courts accept responsibility for an integration of statutory purpose and common law justice, along the lines I have defended, occasions of deadlock between the legislative and judicial branches are likely to be rare. When reasons of justice are compelling, the meaning and scope of legislative provisions can be adjusted to meet their demands. There remains a limited scope for the operation of the Human Rights Act, section 4: a declaration of incompatibility may be appropriate where, though the statute can be interpreted or applied consistently with common law justice, the requirements of the European Convention would remain unsatisfied. Although, in *Anderson*, for example, an appropriately robust construction would have secured the essential requirements of the separation of powers, the Convention (as interpreted in Strasbourg) appeared to preclude even the formal participation of the Home Secretary in sentencing an offender.[64] In the gravest instance of a challenge to constitutional justice, however, where Convention rights will match their fundamental common law counterparts, resort to the declaration of incompatibility would be mistaken; no court can, without self-contradiction, sanction a departure from the rule of law.

The indefinite detention, without trial, of persons suspected of endangering public safety tests the boundaries of fundamental justice.[65] The arbitrary nature of the distinction between aliens and British nationals, as regards those subject to the powers of detention under the Anti-terrorism, Crime and Security Act 2001, offended the common law principle of legal equality as much as Article 14 of the Convention; and the legal status of the relevant provisions must therefore be open to doubt as a matter of common law. The principle of legal equality denies the status of 'law' to acts (or 'bills') of attainder; but general legislation permitting detention at the hands of the executive, under certain conditions, may usually be saved by the imposition of procedural safeguards.[66] The appellate role of the Special Immigration Appeals Commission provided important quasi-judicial protection, even though the ordinary rules of natural justice, as regards notice of the grounds for suspicion, were heavily qualified. The Commission's independence from the Secretary of State may be

[64] See *R (Anderson) v Secretary of State for the Home Department* [2002] UKHL 46 [27]–[28].

[65] See *A and others v Secretary of State for the Home Department* [2004] UKHL 56, [2005] 2 AC 68.

[66] See Allan, n 12 above, chs 5 and 8.

thought to guarantee the essential minimum of rule-of-law protection, even if the House of Lords' attempt to limit this independence, in *Rehman*, threatened to undermine this essential minimum.[67]

Yet the discrimination against foreign nationals seems to have lacked any plausible justification: the House of Lords expressly rejected the relevance of the detainees' immigration status. In these circumstances, the provisions ought surely to have been challenged, and repudiated, as a violation of the rule of law—the declaration of incompatibility was too weak, leaving the violation unremedied. The gravity of the encroachment on the principle of legal equality, in the circumstances of the case, is underscored by Baroness Hale's suggestion that 'black', 'disabled', 'gay', or 'any other similar adjective' might (for purposes of illustration) be substituted for 'foreign' before 'suspected international terrorist'.[68] Could a common law judge, consistently with her oath to administer justice, enforce a provision that made such distinctions in the context of indefinite detention without trial? The limits of judicial cooperation with statutory purposes are set by the strength of the reasons that inform those purposes; there is no common law requirement to comply with demands that are judged to be arbitrary and irrational.

A competent analysis of the Human Rights Act 1998 must be rooted in a more general theory of British constitutionalism; and I have defended a critical and 'constructive' judicial approach to the interpretation of statutes as a requirement of the rule of law. Confronted by potential threats to fundamental constitutional rights, the judges cannot escape their own responsibility for legal outcomes by deference to supposedly unyielding statutory commands. There is almost always scope, in practice, for reasonable accommodation between statutory purpose and legal principle, according to the circumstances arising. But even when the scope for accommodation diminishes, or entirely disappears, the court must adhere resolutely to the rule of law. For the judge's duty is always to administer justice; and though the justice administered must be justice according to law, the law in a liberal democracy has its own intrinsic moral nature. Its deepest principles of legal equality and procedural fairness define the basic idea of government according to law.[69]

[67] *Secretary of State for the Home Department v Rehman* [2001] UKHL 47, [2003] 1 AC 153.
[68] *A and others v Secretary of State for the Home Department* [2004] UKHL 56 [238].
[69] See further Allan, n 12 above.

European Constitutionalism in the State Constitutional Tradition

Neil Walker

The Shadow of the State

Since the idea of the European supranational structure as a constitutional entity began to attract serious consideration in academic and political circles in the early 1990s, the vexed question of its relationship to the tradition of state constitutionalism that provides the topic of the present essay has never been far from the surface.[1] The reason is obvious. Although the term constitution, like much of our contemporary political vocabulary—including democracy, republicanism, federation, and citizenship—pre-dates the modern state, its mature conventional meaning has emerged from the social and political context of the modern state and bears its imprint. Accordingly, we should not be surprised that the question of the nature and viability of EU constitutionalism—and, in particular, in the current critical 'moment'[2] of 'big-C'[3] Constitutionalism, of the viability of a first documentary Constitution for the EU—is tied up with the question of its 'translatability' from the state tradition.[4]

This is no mere scholastic dispute. The fate of European constitutionalism cannot be reduced to an exercise in political epistemology concerning whether and under what conditions the delivery of the idea of constitutionalism from the state into the supranational context is or might become a meaningful object of knowledge. Both proponents and critics of the idea of an EU Constitution are typically motivated by considerations that are both more basic and more practically consequential. Yet political epistemology remains important in two senses. First,

[1] See eg J H H Weiler, *The Constitution of Europe* (Cambridge: Cambridge University Press, 1999), ch 6; N Walker, 'Legal Theory and the European Union: A 25th Anniversary Essay' (2005) 25 *Oxford Journal of Legal Studies* 581.

[2] N Walker, 'The Legacy of Europe's Constitutional Moment' (2004) 11 *Constellations* 368.

[3] N Walker, 'Big "C" or small "c"?' (2006) 12 *European Law Journal* 12.

[4] Weiler, n 1 above, 270; N Walker, 'Postnational Constitutionalism and the Problem of Translation' in J H H Weiler and M Wind, *European Constitutionalism Beyond The State* (Cambridge: Cambridge University Press, 2003), 27.

political epistemology does indeed constitute an important boundary consideration when weighing up different positions, for what is possible and desirable depends upon a threshold test of what can be meaningfully imagined. Secondly, in keeping with the high degree of symbolic power invested in the idea of constitutionalism,[5] many key protagonists in the current debate over the ratification of the 2004 EU Constitutional Treaty[6] remain attracted to the kind of rhetorical flourish that certain uncompromising judgments in political epistemology allow—that permit us to say that the idea of an EU Constitution is simply beyond contemplation, and so an absurd thought-object, or, alternatively, to declare or just assume that it is an entirely comprehensible successor to, or even within, the national constitutional tradition.

Clearly, then, the question of the EU's fit with a state-dominated constitutional tradition is an important one in both theoretical and practical-political terms, and indeed as regards the relationship between theory and practice. Let us begin to sharpen our appreciation of what is at stake by teasing out the range of different and mutually contested metatheoretical perspectives that it is possible to adopt on the relationship between state, constitution, and EU.

First, there is the 'miscategorization perspective'. According to this, EU constitutionalism cannot operate within the state constitutional tradition, and since the state tradition is the only viable constitutional tradition, this means there is no viable basis for European constitutionalism. The idea of European constitutionalism is simply a 'category error',[7] and to the extent that we nonetheless continue to apply the label, it is a pseudo-constitutionalism or a diminished constitutionalism of which we speak. European constitutionalism is either a nonsense—there is no adequate political epistemology to account for it and render it meaningful—or a pale imitation. It simply does not and cannot possess that attribute or combination of attributes without which the adequate realization of the distinctive normative potential proper to constitutionalism is deemed inconceivable.[8]

A second position, by contrast, sees no such difficulties. According to the 'continuity perspective', EU constitutionalism can operate within the

[5] eg S S Wolin, 'Collective Identity and Constitutional Power' in Wolin, *The Presence of the Past: Essays on the State and the Citizen* (Baltimore: Johns Hopkins, 1989); R Cotterrell, 'Some Aspects of the Communication of Constitutional Authority' in D Nelken (ed) *Law as Communication* (Aldershot: Dartmouth, 1995), 129.

[6] Hereafter 'CT'.

[7] G Majone, 'The Dilemmas of European Integration' (Oxford: Oxford University Press, 2005), 20; A Moravcsik, 'A Category Error' *Prospect* July 2006, 22.

[8] eg D Grimm, 'The Constitution in the Process of Denationalization' (2005) 12 *Constellations* 447.

state constitutional tradition with little or no adjustment. The EU polity is sufficiently 'state-like' that a form of normative discourse evolved in the context of the state can apply equally to it. Such a position, it must be emphasized, need not imply that the EU is already approximate to or is likely to become some kind of European superstate, although sometimes it will imply this,[9] and even where it does not it may well be caricatured by its opponents as so doing.[10] What it does presuppose, however, is that in respect of those aspects of political organization that constitutional discourse considers relevant—whether, and in whatever combination, the claim to and legal consolidation of sovereign authority, the rights of the citizen against government, the separation or balance of institutional capacities, the authority of the executive, the forms of legislation and the internal hierarchy of law-making, the power of judicial review or the mechanisms of popular accountability—the EU bears enough of a family resemblance to the state to be susceptible to the same kind of constitutional treatment as the state.

A third perspective likewise sees supranationalism as offering no fundamental challenge to the idea of constitutionalism, but for a quite different reason. On this view, it is a matter of indifference whether EU constitutionalism fits within the state tradition, since constitutionalism can mean whatever we want it to mean within the very broad framework of whatever may be considered desirable by way of the regulation of political authority. The 'nominalist perspective' enlarges the domain of applicability of constitutionalism, not by emphasizing the resemblance between state and non-state sites, but by insisting that there is no canonical set of problems or solutions to which constitutionalism must be faithful, and so no scope for the special privileging of the state and of the 'problem-solutions' appropriate to its context in the first place.[11]

A fourth and final position we may term the 'adaptation perspective'. This holds, with the miscategorization and the continuity perspectives and against the nominalist perspective, that the state constitutional tradition cannot be discounted as it remains the key contemporary frame of reference for meaningful discussion of constitutionalism. Yet, unlike the miscategorization perspective, it maintains that the limits imposed by this frame are not rigid, and that it is instead possible to imagine other

9 eg F Mancini, 'Europe: The Case for Statehood' (1998) 4 *European Law Journal* 29.

10 See Walker, n 4 above, 27–31.

11 For discussion, see N Walker, 'EU Constitutionalism and New Governance' in G De Burca and J Scott (eds), *Constitutionalism and New Governance in Europe and United States* (Oxford: Hart, 2006), 15. Many examples of nominalism are collected under the label of non-constituent constitutionalism below. See n 75 below.

types of polity, including post-state polities such as the EU, becoming successfully constitutionalized, even if that requires a level of adjustment not contemplated under the continuity perspective.

As already indicated, in so far as they supply the Manichean terms of much of the politico-rhetorical struggle over the CT, the first two positions are undoubtedly of practical importance. Theoretically, however, they provide unpromisingly partial understandings and accounts of the nature of constitutionalism. By denying that the move from the state to the supranational level is even possible in the one instance, or at all problematic in the other, each remains entirely under the shadow of the state, and neither, it follows, is prepared to pursue the possibility of an innovative understanding of constitutionalism appropriate to the supranational domain. The nominalist perspective is also conceptually unambitious. If constitutionalism can mean whatever we say it means, if it is a mere solipsistic indulgence or ideological headline-grabber, then why bother with it at all? Its currency or otherwise cannot explain anything, cannot make any difference other than in terms of the diverse other concepts through which it is explicated. On this view, the ideological struggle may present itself as one about ownership of the constitutional image but the real battle of ideas is elsewhere—in what we mean by justice, democracy, rule of law or whatever, and constitutionalism is reduced to no more than an attractive veneer for our pet ideas.[12]

The fourth perspective is the most promising in terms of a genuine extension of the 'discourse of conceptualization and imagination'[13] associated with the state constitutional tradition. It is the only one sufficiently grounded in conventional understandings yet also sufficiently flexible to hold out the prospect of providing us with explanatory purchase—and beyond that political purchase—on what is at stake in and beyond the current 'ratification crisis' of a new supranational species of the familiar genus of written constitutions. More specifically, the potential of the adaptation perspective lies in its sensitivity to opposing considerations concerning the social grounding of political concepts. On the one hand, it acknowledges the undeniable weight and path-dependency of conceptual and ideological history in human affairs, and of the material structures that lie behind these concepts and ideologies. This is particularly so in respect of an idea such as constitutionalism which has long had a double resonance—as both a meta-concept which seeks to explain and to evaluate affairs from an external vantage point and an object-concept which itself

[12] eg N Walker, 'The Idea of Constitutional Pluralism' (2002) 59 *Modern Law Review* 517–59, 531–3.

[13] Weiler, n 1 above, 223.

has significant discursive currency within the quotidian social and political world of entrenched interests and competing preferences and is regularly invoked as a form of practical reason that seeks to make a difference to how issues within that everyday world are addressed. On the other hand, the adaptation perspective does not conclude that nothing can change and we are fated merely to repeat the ideas and structures of the past; for it also acknowledges that just because of its significance as a politically resonant and practically consequential 'speech act',[14] constitutionalism remains a deeply contested concept, one whose meaning is inherently volatile and subject to persuasive redefinition.

In taking the state tradition seriously without being paralysed by its legacy, the adaptation perspective is most in line with what the study of the history of ideas suggests about both the scope and the limits of the transformability of historically embedded political concepts.[15] Ironically, however, the very practical contestability that underlies the plausibility of the adaptation approach also points us towards the resilience of the other perspectives discussed above. For precisely because so much is at stake ideologically, we will find that the meta-theoretical assumptions these other perspectives embrace with regard to the relationship between state, polity, and constitution may likewise be carried over and woven into constitutional argumentation in a self-fulfilling manner. So even if one can demonstrate that the meta-theoretical assumptions and insights about the nature of constitutionalism associated with one perspective are more compelling than those associated with other perspectives—more acute in their analysis of the social and historical conditions and limits of transformation of the constitutional idea—it does not follow that this position will in practice prevail against those other perspectives and against the structures of interests and preferences that sustain and are sustained by these assumptions.

All of this suggests that there are formidable burdens both of a theoretical and practical nature to discharge if the state constitutional tradition is to be successfully adapted to the supranational situation of the EU. It is one thing to proceed through a series of negative inferences to the point of intimation of a new and attractive sense of theoretical and practical possibility, and quite another to explore and exploit that new possibility. Too often, the discussion of the 'tradition-framed novelty' of European

[14] On the application of speech act theory to transnational politics, see W G Werner and J De Wilde, 'The Endurance of Sovereignty' (2001) 7 *European Journal of International Relations* 283.

[15] eg J Tully, *Strange Multiplicity: Constitutionalism in an Age of Diversity* (Cambridge: Cambridge University Press, 1995), 34–43.

constitutionalism, as indeed of the alternative claims as to its impossibility or seamless continuity or radical discontinuity, simply gets stuck at the declaration stage—in the awkwardly 'in-between' announcement that we must and can escape the shadow of the state while not dismissing its normative message.[16] The aim of this essay is to go further, and to provide a theoretical framework within which the question of the adaptability of the state constitutional tradition to the supranational site can be challengingly posed and an answer sought that is persuasive both in specifying the difficulties and optimal conditions of normative order in a post-state context and in its engagement with the rival conceptions of constitutionalism set out above. Its first priority lies in addressing the question of the in-principle mobility of the constitutional template in a manner that takes us beyond declarations of faith and prejudice, and so the main emphasis will be on the sketching of the theoretical framework itself, both in the abstract and in the context of the evolving structure of the EU. But in closing the essay also engages in some preliminary analysis of how that framework illuminates the current predicament of EU documentary constitutionalism, and in particular of how meta-theoretical disagreement on the proper conception of the relationship between state, polity, and constitution percolates through to and must be addressed in the real world of constitutional politics.

The Adaptation Perspective

In methodological terms, an adequate examination of the adaptation perspective requires us to move through the four stages of disaggregation, abstraction, modulation, and reintegration. We must begin by challenging the common assumption that constitutionalism, if not a one-dimensional matter, is a matter in which one or some dimensions are more important than and so can encapsulate or dominate the others, for it is precisely the selective narrowing of horizons entailed by this essentializing assumption that allows both adherents of the miscategorization perspective so readily to dismiss postnational constitutionalism and adherents of the continuity perspective so readily to accept it.[17] Rather, we should acknowledge

[16] eg A Verhoeven, *The European Union in Search of a Democratic and Constitutional Theory* (Dordrecht: Kluwer, 2002), parts I–III.

[17] For example, as explained below, those for whom the 'legal order' dimension dominates find it easy to adhere to the continuity perspective with regard to the EU, whereas those for whom the 'constituent power' dimension dominates, unless they are prepared seriously to contemplate its adaptation to the supranational level, are apt to fall back on the miscategorization perspectives or to turn to the nominalist perspective.

and separate out the various dimensional prerequisites of the state constitutional tradition, without making any prior assumptions of their relative importance or optimal combination. Secondly, we should seek to conceptualize these disaggregated dimensions and draw conclusions about their character at a level of abstraction that is not necessarily confined to the state, such that we are in a position to ask whether we can imagine constitutional arrangements for the EU performing a similar set of functions.

Thirdly, in posing that question and in seeking to resituate constitutionalism within the EU, we should be prepared to contemplate a modulated version of constitutionalism—in two senses of that term. On the one hand, there will be a change of key. In the sequence of abstraction and recontextualization there will inevitably be some shift in the quality of our understanding of the various dimensions of constitutionalism, and perhaps of the balance between them, but in the absence of an essentializing approach that would concentrate exclusively or primarily on one dimension of constitutionalism, such modulation is less likely to be fatal to the very idea of transferability of meaning from the state to the post-national domain. On the other hand, there may also be modulation in the sense of a tempering or 'toning down' of what we mean by constitutionalism in some of its dimensions, without this inviting the conclusion of the proponents of the miscategorization perspective that supranational constitutionalism is thereby falsified or categorically reduced. This second sense of modulation, which again is made easier to contemplate by an approach that does not privilege any particular dimension(s) of constitutionalism as essential or as of presumptively highest importance, is especially crucial to the development of the adaptation perspective in the context of the unfinished process of European integration. For unless we can contemplate constitutionalism as something of which there may be more or less, then not only are we unable as a matter of conceptual fiat to conceive of constitutionalism in a manner that is alert to the uneven strength and variable composition of its parts, but we also lose any sense of how to think about constitutionalism in a diachronic sense—of constitutionalism in transition and so in various provisional stages of transformation.[18]

Fourthly, and finally, however, we must rejoin the constitutional dots. We must acknowledge that it is one thing to be sceptical about constitutional dogmatism in any form—whether the idea of a narrow category of constitutional essentials or priority attributes, or of there being some kind

[18] eg Walker, n 11 above, 339–54.

of absolute threshold of constitutional status, or as to the existence of a single acceptable pattern of composition of its various parts—but quite another to think of the constitutional quality of a particular entity simply as the formless aggregation or accumulation of these various parts. The point of the initial disaggregation is to highlight the variety of dimensions of constitutionalism that are interlocked in the state tradition and to ensure that we are as open as possible to the ways in which these may be (re)combined, not to deny the necessity and significance of any such combination. The different dimensions of constitutionalism are not separate items in a check-list, but aspects that are as deeply as they are variably connected. In tracking the practical integration of these various dimensions of constitutionalism at postnational sites, we have to ask a key counterfactual question: whether, in the absence, diminished presence, or qualitative transformation of some of the dimensions recognized under the statist template, the new constitutional whole would be other than, and perhaps less than the sum of, its various parts. As we shall see, it is at this vital final stage that the basic viability of the adaptation approach is most sharply challenged, and the very coherence of the idea of supranational constitutionalism put most directly in question.

Disaggregating the State Tradition

Following this methodological scheme, we can begin by identifying and abstracting from five dimensions of state constitutionalism. These are legal order, the institutionalization of a specialized political system, self-authorization, societal integration, and reflexivity. Let us say something about each of these disaggregated dimensions of state constitutionalism in turn, in so doing seeking a level of conceptualization which stands above the state setting.

Legal Order

Legal order or legal system(ization) is both the most obvious and least remarked dimension of state constitutionalism. Every state has it own distinctive legal order or orders, and we often refer to as constitutional these features which we understand to be constitutive and definitive of the legal order *qua* legal order.[19] While the basic idea of legal order as a

[19] eg J Raz, 'On the Authority and Interpretation of Constitutions: Some Preliminaries' in L Alexander (ed), *Constitutionalism: Philosophical Foundations* (Cambridge: Cambridge University Press, 1998), 152–3.

bedrock component of state constitutionalism is uncontroversial, what precisely this entails is by no means settled, with positivists (pedigree rules), realists (behaviour), and natural lawyers (ideal norms) having their different views of the cornerstones of ordered legality. Nevertheless, certain general features are commonly agreed or assumed. Most abstractly, a legal order or system is normally deemed deserving of being so characterized to the extent that its own normative resources are sufficient both to its distinctive identity, or integrity, considered synchronically, and to its continuity, considered diachronically.[20] Typically, the resilient distinctiveness of any such entity is broadly understood as being tied up with the notion of normative self-containment or completeness. In turn, the measure of this tends to be taken by reference to more specific attributes such as autonomy, comprehensiveness, self-definition, and self-enforcement.

By autonomy we mean the normative independence of the order from any other normative order. Legal sovereignty or supreme normative authority is deemed by the key legal actors of the order to be located within the legal order itself, and in so far as other legal orders are recognized, such recognition does not compromise the supreme normative authority of the legal order itself. Comprehensiveness is the internal corollary of autonomy. For the systemic identity of the legal order depends not only on the authoritative foundations prevailing over external challenges, but also on these highest-order norms controlling the operation of the system generally. Two mechanisms of control are engaged here.[21] In the first place, provision should be made for the generation of norms such that there is no area within the self-defined ambit of the legal order that its normative authority is incapable of reaching. Secondly, higher-order norms should trump norms recognized as lower within the internal hierarchy in cases of potential conflict.

For its part, self-definition covers a number of different features of the 'momentary'[22] and dynamic authority of legal orders. In the first place, the legal order is the master of its own jurisdiction or ambit. Or in the language of German federal theory, it has *Kompetenz-Kompetenz*. This means not only the absence of dependence upon another system for the specification of the boundaries of the system, a facet of self-containment or completeness already covered by autonomy, but also the absence of a strict framework of autolimitation, or system rigidity. That is to say, the system should

[20] eg J Raz, *The Concept of a Legal System: An Introduction to the Theory of a Legal System* (2nd edn) (Oxford: Oxford University Press, 1980), chs 8–9.

[21] eg N Walker, 'Fundamental Law' in *The Laws of Scotland: Stair Memorial Encyclopaedia* (2nd edn) (Edinburgh: Butterworths, 2002), para 48.

[22] Raz, n 20 above, ch 8.

not be committed to stasis; rather, there should be mechanisms of definition and redefinition located within the system itself. In turn these typically take two forms, both of which are capable of embracing not only redefinition of boundaries but also changes which do not bear upon boundary questions. In the first place, there is the 'interpretive autonomy'[23] of the legal order—the location within the legal order of a judiciary or other category(ies) of privileged interpreters with the last word in deciding the meaning of the system's norms. In the second place, there is the power of self-amendment, the availability within the terms of the system itself of a procedure for changing the higher-order rules of the system.

Self-enforcement is a final feature of a self-contained system. Again we see external and internal dimensions in play. Externally, there should be no outside agency involved in its enforcement. Rather, all mechanisms and institutions involved in ensuring the application and vindication of the norms of the legal order should be authorized under the legal order itself. Internally, it implies that these internally authorized norms should be adequate to ensure that all forms of power enabled under the order, which importantly includes such power as accrues to those institutions created by the order as components of the government of that order, are also subject to the rule of (its) law.[24] Self-enforcement, in short, implies enforcement both 'by' and 'of' the collective 'self'.

Specialized Political System

Whereas the first building block of modern constitutionalism can be traced back to the Roman roots of civilian law, by contrast the second feature was one of the distinctively novel features of the modern state that emerged as a new form of political domination in continental Europe in response to the confessional civil wars of the sixteenth and seventeenth centuries.[25] What we are concerned with here is the establishment and maintenance of a system of specialized political rule, a development which achieved an early stylistic maturity in the form of the documentary constitutions of the late eighteenth century. A system of specialized political rule is a decisional framework that is autonomous rather than heteronomous. Neither its title to rule nor its ongoing purpose flows from

[23] T Schilling, 'The Autonomy of the Community Legal Order: An Analysis of Possible Foundations' (1996) 17 *Harvard International Law Journal* 389, 389–90.

[24] On the resilient centrality of the idea of 'government limited by law' to the modern idea of the rule of law, see B Tamanaha, *On the Rule of Law: History, Politics, Theory* (Cambridge: Cambridge University Press, 2004), ch 9.

[25] eg Grimm, n 8 above, 449.

prior and fixed economic or status attributes or concerns or from some notion of traditional or divine order external to the system itself, as in pre-modern constellations of political power. Instead, authority rests upon the very idea of a dedicated political domain, one that develops its own authoritative yardsticks for conflict-resolution and its own mechanism for collective decision-making.[26]

This development speaks to a new stage in the differentiation of social forms, one in which there is constituted for the first time a separate sphere of the public and political that in its operative logic is distinctive from the society over which it rules. Such a specialized system has the dual attributes of immanence and self-limitation. On the one hand, it purports to be self-legitimating, in that what justifies the continuing claim to authority of the autonomous political domain and the higher-order rules through which that authority is inscribed is nothing more or less than the operation of the political domain itself. On the other hand, and as the flip-side of this, there emerges a general sphere of purely private action and freedom that lies beyond either the specialist sphere of politics or the now redundant special mixed regimes of public and private right and obligation based upon prior forms of privilege or advantage.[27]

The regulatory structures of the new specialist political order echo its distinctive attributes. Positively, and reflecting the quality of immanence, they take the form of third-order institutional rules for making (legislature), administering (executive), and adjudicating (judiciary) the second-order 'legal system' norms through which the coordination of first-order action or the resolution of first-order disagreement within a population is secured. Negatively, and reflecting the quality of self-limitation, they take the form of formal or informal catalogues of rights aimed at demarcating and respecting a separate sphere of private individual or group freedom, one safe from incursions at the third-order level of public authority or infraction at the second-order level of the substantive norms of the legal system.

Self-Authorization

The institutionalization of a normatively separate and specialist sphere of political contestation and decision as a defining feature of a polity does not necessarily imply democratic operating procedures, still less a democratic

[26] eg M Loughlin, *The Idea of Public Law* (Oxford: Oxford University Press, 2003), ch 3.

[27] eg Grimm, n 8 above, 452–3; see also J Habermas, 'Constitutional Democracy: A Paradoxical Union of Contradictory Principles' (2001) 28 *Political Theory* 766.

founding or a continuing democratic warrant. The operational autonomy and specialist nature of the political sphere may be consistent with a set of arrangements in which the original authorization comes from beyond the system, as in many subaltern constitutions,[28] or where the original authority is located within the system but is presented as monarchical or aristocratic rather than popular. That is to say, the autonomy of the political need not imply that all those affected by the operation of the system participate or be represented in its institution or even its subsequent homologation. It need imply merely that a logic of political action should prevail, whether this be presented in terms of *raison d'état* or *salus populi* or some other version of the public good, that is adequate to its claim and character as a special sphere of political action—one where there is no transcendental or otherwise overriding external justification, freedom from special interests, and generality of scope.

Arguably, however, the autonomy of the political is a precarious achievement and one of obscure virtue unless and until it is joined by a claim of self-authorization. Within constitutional thought, such self-authorship is typically conceived in terms of the idea of constituent power, or the ultimate sovereignty of the people.[29] Again, the documentary form that centres modern state constitutionalism engages this dimension, with such texts typically claiming to be not only for the people but also of the people, and their drafting procedures—in particular, through the involvement of constituent assemblies and popular conventions—dramatizing a commitment to substantiate that claim of popular authorship.[30] So prevalent is the ethic of democratic pedigree in modern state constitutionalism—of democracy as a meta-value in terms of which other governance values are understood and articulated[31]—that debate tends to centre not on the question of its appropriateness but only on the adequacy of its instantiation. This may manifest itself in the critique of those constitutional settlements that lack a founding documentary episode, or at least a plausible narrative of subsequent popular homologation,[32] or in the claim that the constitution has betrayed its popular foundations, or in the criticism that for all its derivative concern with

[28] eg K C Wheare, *The Constitutional Structure of the Commonwealth* (Oxford: Oxford University Press, 1960).

[29] On the history of the concept of constituent power, see eg A Kalyvas, 'Popular Sovereignty, Democracy and the Constituent Power' (2005) 12 *Constellations* 223.

[30] eg A Arato, *Civil Society, Constitution and Legitimacy* (Lanham, Md: Rowman and Littlefield, 2000), ch 7.

[31] eg J Dunn, *Setting the People Free: The Story of Democracy* (London: Atlantic, 2005).

[32] In the British context, see A Tomkins, *Our Republican Constitution* (Oxford: Hart, 2005).

democracy at the level of the everyday framework of government, the constitution is not autochthonous, but instead remains dependent upon the 'constituted' power of another polity or polities.[33]

Societal Integration

Modern state constitutionalism is not only about the generation through an act and continuing promise of democratic self-authorization of the normative wherewithal for the operation of a self-sufficient legal order underpinned by its own institutional framework of political rule. Alongside these normative or juridical products, the state constitution typically also both presupposes and promises a degree of integration on the part of the social constituency in whose name it is promulgated and to whom it is directed.[34]

There is a close link between the normative and the integrative register, for the successful implementation of the normative products of the constitution requires that we step outside the hermeneutic circle of pure normativity and consider the question of social supports. Unless there is already in place some sense of common cause sufficient first, to endorse those interests or ideals that the constitutional text has identified as being well served by being put in common; secondly, to affirm and so vindicate the capability and appropriateness of the institutional means that the constitution deems instrumental to the pursuit of these common interests or ideals and to the generation and pursuit of other common ends; and thirdly, to assent to the constitution's normative expectation that such common ends be pursued and such common means be adopted in this rather than any other community, then the constitution is fated to remain a dead letter.

What this prior propensity to put things in common or basic sense of political community amounts to is of course an issue of much controversy, and in any event is something that is better conceived of as a matter of degree than in all-or-nothing terms. As a basic minimum, however, we are talking about a sense of common attachment or common predicament within the putative demos sufficient to manifest itself in three interrelated forms. First, it should be sufficient to ensure that each is prepared to trust the others to participate in the common business of dispute-resolution, decision-making, and rule-following on fair and

[33] eg N Walker, 'Europe's Constitutional Momentum and the Search for Polity Legitimacy' (2005) 3 *International Journal of Constitutional Law* 211, 213–22.

[34] eg D Grimm, 'Integration by Constitution' (2005) 3 *International Journal of Constitutional Law* 193.

equal terms. Secondly, it should be sufficient to ensure that each demonstrates the minimum level of sustained mutual concern or solidarity required to reach and respect collective outcomes which may work against their immediate interests in terms of the distribution of resources and risks. Thirdly, it should be sufficient to support a basic common idiom or political vernacular through which the diversity of individuals and groups can find the means to resolve some of their differences, and make common sense of and accept those that remain.[35]

Yet it would be wrong to suggest that just because it cannot supply the necessary social supports of trust, solidarity, and common political vernacular merely through normative enunciation, the constitution cannot do anything to influence the degree of social integration necessary to its effective application and must merely passively presuppose its prior existence. To begin with, its normative framework of political rule seeks to provide a settled template for living together in circumstances free from despotism or intractable conflict, and to that extent offers an incentive to all who are attracted by such a template to secure such a floor of common commitment as is necessary for its effective implementation. Secondly, the act of making the constitution may have a mobilization dividend that goes beyond agreement on the particular text in question. The value of the process is not exhausted by its textual product,[36] but may extend to the generation or bolstering of just these forms of political identity necessary to the successful implementation of the textual product. Thirdly, just because constitutions in the modern age are typically viewed as the expression and vindication of the constituent power of a 'people', the successful making of a constitution has come to assume a special symbolic significance as a totem of peoplehood. There may, of course, be a rational foundation to this conviction inasmuch as the very fact of a common accord affords some prior evidence of both the capacity and the motivation to put things in common. However, the extent to which and the manifold circumstances under which possession of a constitution is treated as a symbolic shorthand of peoplehood outstrip that rational foundation. So powerful is the chain of signification developed under the modern banner of popular, nation state constitutionalism, that

[35] eg M Canovan, *Nationhood and Political Theory* (Cheltenham: Edward Elgar, 1996); D Miller, *On Nationality* (Oxford: Oxford University Press, 1995).

[36] eg W Sadurski, 'Conclusions: On the Relevance of Institutions and the Centrality of Constitutions in Post-Communist Transitions' in I J Zielonka (ed), *Democratic Consolidation in Eastern Europe, Volume 1—Institutional Engineering* (Oxford: Oxford University Press, 2001), 455, 466–72.

regardless of how it came into existence, the very fact that a constitution exists is typically understood and widely portrayed as testimony to the achievement of political community. Fourthly, in so far as the constitution crystallizes such general common ends or values as are the subject of deliberation in the constitution-making moment and as may also be already present in the pre-constitutional ethical life of the relevant social constituency, it may have a 'double institutionalization'[37] effect. That is to say, the addition of the constitutional imprimatur may amplify the importance of and the extent of common subscription to these common values and ends, and in so framing or reinforcing a common political vernacular, strengthen the supportive relationship between common political vernacular, trust and solidarity through which political community is forged.

If these factors all speak to the importance of the constitutional event and its textual fruit, we may, fifthly and finally, also look beyond the founding moment of the constitution to see how it can become an ongoing source of intensification of the social foundations necessary to its effective implementation. This operates in at least two ways. First, the constitution may function as a reminder of community. In so far as common political identity often develops alongside and feeds off the collective memorialization of claimed common events, achievements, and experiences, constitutional history provides one such stream of sanctified tradition. The constitution, in other words, may write itself into collective history.[38] Secondly, the constitution may provide a resilient but flexible structure for political-ethical debate, an anchor for a continuing conversation about the meaning of political community which operates in a Janus-faced manner to strengthen that political community. Looking back, it is a token not only of the supposed depth and extension of common experience, but also of the weight of accumulated collective wisdom. Looking forward, the constitution may be sufficiently open-ended and sufficiently understood as a work of trans-generational authorship for its structures and values to be capable of being inflected in ways which retain the symbolic gravitas of accumulated wisdom yet are more suited to contemporary forms of political vernacular and contemporary understandings of the basis of trust and solidarity. In other words, the constitution may provide both a repository for and corroboration of the

[37] P Bohannan, 'The Differing Realms of the Law' in P Bohannan (ed), *Law and Warfare: Studies in the Anthropology of Conflict* (1967), 43, 45.

[38] eg A Margalit, *The Ethics of Memory* (Cambridge, Mass: Harvard University Press, 2002), 12.

settled ethical basis of political community as well as a vehicle for its continuous adaptation.[39]

Reflexivity

For something to be reflexive means that it is capable of bending or turning back on itself. In the case of a political institution *tout court*, reflexivity refers to the capacity of any communal contrivance for addressing collective problems to make normative demands of itself, and in the particular case of the ethically self-inscribed political institution of indeterminate duration and broad societal scope that is the documentary constitution, it speaks to the general commitment of a political community to the idea of responsible self-government on an ongoing and self-adjusting basis.[40] Accordingly, the idea of reflexivity captures the essential novelty of the species of constitutionalism that accompanied the emergence of the modern state.[41] Whereas the ancient constitution purported to be at one and the same time a description of social and political reality and a confirmation of the proper order of things,[42] the modern constitution, through the vehicle of the state, adds a dimension of normative aspiration. In so doing, it posits a gap between facts and norms. If a constitution is well described as a 'model'[43] of political community, it adds a second sense of model *qua* ideal and projected type to the old sense of model *qua* miniature representation of existing structure.

Crucially, reflexivity can be viewed as the glue that binds the other disaggregated features of modern constitutionalism; or more dynamically, as a characteristic that both depends on and reinforces these other features. In order for reflexivity to 'get going', we need; first, an idea of a collective self; secondly, a capacity on the part of that collective self to distance itself from how it is presently constituted and so articulate demands of itself; and thirdly, an ability to take measures that plausibly seek to meet these demands. The basic idea of the collective self is supplied by the third feature set out above, namely self-authorship. The articulation of demands is met through the second feature, namely the institutional norms of the

[39] eg J Habermas, 'On Law and Disagreement: Some Comments on "Interpretative Pluralism" '(2003) 16 *Ratio Juris* 187.

[40] eg J Bast, 'The Constitutional Treaty as a Reflexive Constitution' (2005) 6 *German Law Journal* 1433, 1448–51.

[41] eg Grimm, n 8 above, 452. On reflexive modernization more generally, see U Beck, W Bonss, and C Lau, 'The Theory of Reflexive Modernization: Problematic, Hypotheses and Research Programme' (2003) 20 *Theory, Culture and Society* 1.

[42] eg Tully, n 15 above, 40–2: C McIlwain, *Constitutionalism: Ancient and Modern* (rev edn) (Ithaca, NY: Cornell University Press, 1947).

[43] Walker, n 1 above, 600.

specialized political system. And the capacity to take effective measures depends both on the organized authority of the formal legal order, as captured in the first feature, and the 'battery'[44] of social power and 'compliability' provided through societal integration, as captured in the fourth feature. In turn, successful reflexivity underscores each of these features. It may vindicate the idea of formal order as a basic template of collective organization, sustain the special authority of the political domain as grounded in an immanent rationality, and transform self-authorship from an event into a sustained process. Moreover, in providing the very idea of the self-institution, adaptable self-maintenance, and open-ended normative unity of a collectivity, one whose efficacy depends upon the bonding properties of trust, solidarity, and common vernacular, it may reinforce these same social bonds.

Abstracting from State Constitutionalism

Before turning to the constitutional credentials of the EU, we can draw a number of general and closely related inferences from the above analysis. In the first place, it is not meaningful to talk of the final authority or the dominance of either the legal or the political when considering the deep structure of constitutionalism. Rather, the legal and the political are mutually constitutive or symbiotic.[45] The political requires a legal frame, most evidently in the case of the basic underlying legal order itself but also in the normative articulation of the specialized system of political rule and in the recognition and channelling of constituent power. But the legal also requires political imagination—the very idea of reflexivity of political community, as well as political will—punctual or retrospective popular support or initiative.

In the second place, and related to this symbiotic character, constitutionalism has to be considered in significant part if by no means exclusively in constructivist terms. That is to say, constitutional norms, whether the thin constitutional precepts of legal order or the framework rules of the political system, and whether or not contained in a written constitution with its self-inscription of constituent power, constitute many of the conditions of their own efficacy. In significant respects, the connection is a direct one, with many of the norms of the constitutional order themselves directed toward its operationalization. And crucially,

[44] Canovan, n 35 above, 80.

[45] eg B Van Roermund, 'Sovereignty: Unpopular and Popular' in N Walker (ed), *Sovereignty in Transition* (Oxford: Hart, 2003), 33.

even the final stage of constitutional efficacy, understood as the social basis of mobilization and implementation, is in some measure and through a complex of interlocking mechanisms susceptible to the indirect influence of constitutional norms in encouraging the requisite degree and forms of social integration.

In the third place, while modern constitutionalism, in identifying the key constituency and institutional and substantive norms in whose terms the polity should be framed, is by implication committed to the indefinite extension and stability of that frame, it is also committed to transformation through that frame. For as we have seen, modern constitutionalism differs from ancient constitutionalism not in discarding the latter's representational conception of a 'model', but in adding to that older descriptive register a new and aspirational register. The point of the constructive work of the constitution is foundational rather than conservative. It is not to freeze-frame and sustain a timeless ideal of social and political order, but to posit and pursue a secular ideal of social and political order.

In the fourth place, it is this element of projection that explains the importance of reflexivity, and the centrality of reflexivity in turn accounts for the holistic element of constitutionalism—the sense in which the whole must necessarily be seen as greater than the sum of its parts. The legal order and political systemic elements cannot operate in a fully reflexive manner without the constituent power of self-authorship, but, equally, the collective author requires the instruments of self-expression supplied by the legal order and the political system. Finally, to complete the web of supportive relations, the entire political imaginary under which the collective author is connected to the means of self-expression is meaningless without the fourth dimension—the affirmation of collective identity and plausible capacity for will-formation and implementation supplied by a measure of societal integration.

EU Constitutionalism

Against the statist backdrop of the five key constitutional dimensions and in light of the horizontal characteristics of legal-political symbiosis, constructivism, projection, and holism, how do we take the measure of EU constitutionalism? We should begin by acknowledging the simple but crucial point that EU constitutionalism is much stronger in the first two dimensions—distinctive legal order and specialist system of political rule—than in the other three—self-authorization, societal integration, and reflexivity. From the treaty foundations and early development of judicial and political institutions, Europe's supranational community has been marked by a highly elaborated framework of legal order and a well-developed regime of political decision-making.[46] Yet prior to the current documentary constitutional process, there had been no serious political initiative to affirm a distinctive constituent power for the EU. Even more crucially, and recalling our argument that widespread practical affirmation of any underlying constitutional perspective can lend a self-fulfilling force to its meta-theoretical assumptions,[47] the frequency and insistence with which it has been asserted from the sceptical perspective that the EU has 'no demos' distinct from the *demoi* of its constituent member states,[48] poses a serious question and introduces a significant doubt as to whether the EU's existing level and quality of preparedness to put things in common is adequate to support such a claim to constituent power, both at the initiative stage of constitution-making and in terms of any longer-term trajectory of integration and deepening of political community which might flow from that initiative. And, finally, in the absence of an explicit framework of self-authorship and the social supports necessary to the formation and implementation of collective political will, the EU patently lacks the means towards a developed political reflexivity.

But, how should we assess those two dimensions which have had to bear the entire developmental burden of EU constitutionalism? If the EU's constitutionalism is significantly truncated or short-circuited in comparison to its statist predecessors then, given the horizontal consideration of holism, it would seem that this cannot but affect and threaten to compromise its operation in those areas where it does possess constitutional pedigree. Is the EU's truncated constitutionalism nevertheless adequate to its appropriately modulated normative task? And to the extent that it is not, does the present documentary constitutional process, *pace* the sceptical perspective, hold out short-term or long-term prospects for a more adequate constitutional framing? Let us examine the first of these questions and then, by way of conclusion, introduce the second.

A Truncated Constitutionalism

Let us begin with the modulating influences. The distinctiveness of the twin planks of the EU's early constitutional register of debate and understanding—its legal order and it specialist system of political rule—rests on the interaction of two trends and of the structural tendencies that

[46] eg Weiler, n 1 above. [47] See 'The Adaptation Perspective' pp. 56–8 above.
[48] eg D Grimm, 'Does Europe Need a Constitution?' (1995) 1 *European Law Journal* 282.

those trends produce. Each of these trends and tendencies is bound up with the emerging situation of the EU within a plural or compound global order, although in keeping with the fluctuating and unsettled quality of that emergent order, they pull in quite different directions. A first trend stresses the heterarchical dimension of the new order. In the novel plural or compound configuration where states exist alongside a range of emergent post-state political sites of which the EU is only the most powerful,[49] unlike the simple or one-dimensional Westphalian configuration, the relevant 'units' are no longer mutually exclusive territories with mutually exclusive jurisdictions and citizenries. Rather, the new species of post-state polity in general, with the EU in the vanguard, increasingly overlaps the states in terms of geographical reach, competence, and the political identity of its citizens. It follows that the relationship between these different orders of polity is best conceived of as 'osmotic',[50]—as a generalized process of mutual infiltration—rather than as the negotiation and maintenance of clear boundaries as in the case of traditional inter-state relations. This first relational structural tendency, in turn, has implications both for how we understand and for how we assess the EU. In terms of understanding, it means that the orientation of the EU towards other polity sites is a key rather than a derivative characteristic—it becomes 'central at the margins'.[51] In terms of assessment, it means that in these new domains of overlap we cannot evaluate and assess any of the important measures of political 'health'—whether the adequacy of certain functional governance projects or the level of citizenship engagement or rights protection—except in terms of the overall relations between the implicated polities, and that in so doing we have to judge the contribution of the EU as only one part of a wider picture.

A second trend, by contrast, stresses the residue of state-centred hierarchy in the new global order. It reminds us of the ways in which we still must understand the EU in structural terms as a secondary polity, one that emerged from the Westphalian order and continues in significant measure to be defined and challenged by its conditions of emergence. Again, this has both explanatory and evaluative implications. It explains why the EU, as a still relatively recent addition to the scene,

[49] Alongside other regional organizations such as NAFTA and global organizations such as the WTO.

[50] U Preuss, 'The Constitution of a European Democracy and the Role of the Nation State' (1999) 12 *Ratio Juris* 417.

[51] Walker, n 4 above, 54.

continues both to be a 'polity-in-the-making',[52] and one whose evolution takes place in a political environment in which its state creators still wield considerable material and symbolic power. In turn, that material and symbolic power threatens to create an evaluative double-bind. On the one hand, we simply cannot understand either the truncated constitutional condition of the EU—its lack of constituent power, its fragile social bonds, and its limited reflexivity, or, as we shall see, many of the distinctive pressures that affect those two dimensions in which it has managed to develop a constitutional profile, other than in terms of its role as a secondary player in a struggle for political resources. On the other hand, the EU is nonetheless still prone to be judged by these very competitive state interests in accordance with the received constitutional standards of statehood—so alerting us to the fact that the resilience of the statist constitutional tradition has both ideational and ideological implications, speaking not only to the enduring relevance of these standards but also to the ability of entrenched interests to control the strategic terms of debate.

If we consider the relational and secondary tendencies together, we can begin to locate the points of tension within the EU's current truncated constitutional domain. The relational tendency means that the EU operates within a complex of closely interlocking normativity with state polities, while its secondary status means that in the negotiation and application of the terms of its relations with these state polities it is both subject to their competitive challenge and in some respects dependent upon and vulnerable to their resilient sources of power. Equally, the relational tendency means that in some measure we should assess the EU framework in partial terms, as a contribution to a broader set of governance projects, while its secondary status reminds us both of the ideological pressure and the genuine ideational challenge to continue to take seriously the totality of the constitutional terms of reference evolved under the Westphalian order. The first opposition, between interlocking normativity and boundary competition, is arguably the key distinguishing tension of the first dimension of EU constitutionalism—the legal order—while the second opposition between a partial institutional framework which complements a broader governance heterarchy and one that is subject to universal constitutional standards is arguably the key

[52] J Shaw, 'The Problem of Membership in European Union Citizenship' in Z Bankowski and A Scott (eds), *The European Union and its Order: the Legal Theory of European Integration* (Oxford: Blackwell, 2000).

distinguishing tension of its second dimension—the system of political rule. In turn, as we shall see, in a manner that dramatizes the difficulties of finding a *via media* between a constitutional sensibility that is bound by existing statist understandings and one which is entirely dismissive of them, these tensions threaten to encourage somewhat skewed responses within the two domains of the fledgling EU constitutional order. In the one case, that response is in danger of being unduly in thrall to the state tradition, while in the other it may attend too little to that tradition—and in so doing eloquently expose the limits of a truncated constitutionalism.

The EU Legal Order: Let us take, first, the question of legal order, for the idea of European supranationalism as comprising a new and distinctive legal order is perhaps the central facet of conventional wisdom amongst its legal practitioners and commentators. The founding pillars of that conventional wisdom can be found in the seminal early case-law of the Court of Justice on direct effect[53] and supremacy.[54] Beyond these classics, however, within the EU legal community broadly defined [55] and the vast primary and secondary literature that community has produced, it is striking how closely the intensification of an explicitly constitutional register of debate and the influence of a certain type of assertive constitutional self-understanding is bound up with the coming-of-age and sustained maturity of the EU legal order.[56] It is also telling, however, if we recall and briefly elaborate on the four sub-themes of legal order considered above—autonomy, comprehensiveness, self-definition and self-enforcement—to what extent understandings of the maturity of the EU legal order both require to be moderated in the light of considerations of interlocking normatively and remain subject to competitive challenge from national legal orders.

As regards autonomy, we observe two powerful claims made on behalf of the supranational legal order, but in each case with externally contested

[53] *Van Gend en Loos v Nederlandse Administratie der Belastingen* [1963] ECR 1.

[54] *Costa v ENEL* [1964] ECR 585.

[55] eg H Schepel and W Wesseling, 'The Legal Community: Lawyers, Officials and Clerks in the Writing of Europe' (1997) 2 *European Law Journal* 165.

[56] For the ECJ's own modest ventures into explicitly constitutional terrain, see *Parti ecologiste 'Les Verts' v Parliament* [1986] ECR 1339; *Opinion 1/91; Re Draft Agreement on a European Economic Area* [1991] ECR 6102. On the more general dominant narrative linking legal order maturity with constiutionalization, see eg Weiler, n 1 above, ch 6; B De Witte, 'Direct Effect, Supremacy and the Nature of the Legal Order' in P Craig and G de Burca (eds) *The Evolution of EU Law* (Oxford: Oxford University Press, 1999); P Craig, 'Constitutions, Constitutionalism, and the European Union' (2001) 7 *European Law Journal* 125; S Douglas-Scott, *Constitutional Law of the European Union* (London: Pearson, 2002), ch 15.

boundaries. Both the extent to which the EU is a normative order whose authority is not, or, at least, no longer, exhausted by its conditions of origin, and has achieved independence from the ultimate sovereignty of its constituent member states,[57] and, relatedly, the extent to which it can be considered as a 'self-contained regime'[58] that excludes the operation of the secondary rules of general international law, are issues where claims or assumptions internal to the system are subject to vigorous external challenge. As regards comprehensiveness of reach, whereas the norm-generative capacity of the EU legal order through the range of norm-making instruments available to it is wide-ranging,[59] the question whether such normative authority can or should be directly applicable in all national contexts and should trump conflicting national provisions depends on the fine detail of the direct effect and supremacy, or primacy,[60] doctrines respectively; and despite their venerable status, the scope of these doctrines, whose most basic remit is to penetrate the normative space of national legal orders, remains importantly restrained at the margins.[61]

[57] On the question of overlapping sovereignty claims and potential constitutional collision between the EU and member states, see N MacCormick, *Questioning Sovereignty: Law, State and Practical Reason* (Oxford: Oxford University Press, 1999); C Richmond, 'Preserving the Identity Crisis: Autonomy, System and Sovereignty in European Law' (1997) 16 *Law and Philosophy* 377; M Kumm, 'Who is the Final Arbiter of Constitutionality in Europe?: Three Conceptions of the Relationship between the German Federal Constitutional Court and the European Court of Justice' (1999) 36 *Common Market Law Review* 351; N Walker, 'Late Sovereignty in the European Union', H Lindahl, 'Sovereignty and Representation in the European Union', and M Maduro, 'Contrapunctual Law: Europe's Constitutional Pluralism in Action' in Walker, n 45 above, 3–32, 87–114, 501–38.

[58] eg *Amministrazione delle Finanze Dellostato v Essevi* [1981] ECR 1413; for a recent overview, see G Conway, 'Breaches of EC Law and the International Responsibility of Member States' (2002) 13 *European Journal of International Law* 679.

[59] Art. 249 EC.

[60] The term preferred by the CT (2004) *Official Journal of the European Union* C 310/01, Art I-6.

[61] In the case of direct effect, there are a number of contexts, perhaps most notably that of the horizontal direct effect of directives, where the scope of the doctrine remains unresolved and subject to oscillation; eg Case C-144/04, *Werner Mangold v Rudiger Helm* Judgment of 22 November 2005; discussed in 'Editorial Comments: Horizontal Direct Effect—A Law of Diminishing Coherence' (2006) 43 *Common Market Law Review* 1. In the case of supremacy, the main qualification is that EU law is treated as leading to the disapplication, in the particular case, rather than the general invalidation of inconsistent national law; see eg *Simmenthal SpA v Commission* [1979] ECR 777. These limitations clearly speak to a measure of acknowledgment of the inherently relational nature of the EU legal order and the need to find solutions other than those based on the simple principle of hierarchy. Perhaps one of the most insightful recent discussions of these aspects of the EU legal order from a relational perspective, however, comes not from the ECJ but from the Spanish Constitutional court in its Opinion 1/2004 of 13 December 2004 on the Treaty

As regards self-definition, while they are extremely potent devices, neither separately nor in combination do interpretive autonomy and the power of self-amendment of the EU provide unrestricted routes to full *kompetenz-kompetenz*. The interpretive autonomy of the EU is well established in the form of the ECJ's own boot-strapping labours of self-authorization,[62] but this remains a power of interpretation of a particular text which in the last analysis, and even allowing for the development of a generous doctrine of implied powers,[63] is bound by the competence limits set out in that text and by its failure to allocate the plenitude of political authority. And the power to amend that text through treaty amendment, while formally internal to the normative order, in substance is subject to the veto power of any one of the member states whose authority may be threatened by any extension of supranational competence.[64]

Finally, self-enforcement is subject to certain significant limits and areas of tension as regards both its freedom from external independence and its scope of internal coverage. Externally, while the EU has developed a powerful doctrine of state liability for breach of its provisions,[65] this stands out as an exceptional mode of intervention against a backdrop of continuing procedural autonomy on the part of the member states.[66] Indeed, here more than anywhere else, the conflict between self-sufficiency and effectiveness seems sharpest, underlined by the fact that for all the development of new competences in matters of internal and external security,[67] the EU lacks the basic control of the means of violence which has provided the traditional longstop guarantee of the legal enforcement powers of states. Internally, too, developments such as the Charter of Fundamental Rights, and ongoing debate and contestation over its status and effects, underlines the extent to which in an area of complex interpenetration of national, international, and the EU supranational jurisdiction, the scope and effectiveness of application of the fundamental

establishing a Constitution for Europe. The Spanish court makes much of the turn in the CT to the language of 'primacy' and away from that of 'supremacy' as a switch from an inappropriately and unnecessarily hierarchical language towards a more contingent sense of priority; see comment by F C de la Torre (2005) 42 *Common Market Law Review* 1171.

[62] See De Witte, n 56 above.

[63] See eg *Germany v Commission* [1987] ECR 3203; *Germany v European Parliament and Council* [2000] ECR I-8419.

[64] Art 48, TEU.

[65] *Francovich and Bonifaci v Italy* [1991] ECR I-5357.

[66] eg *Rewe-Zentralfinanz eG and Rewe-Zentral AG v Landwirtschaftskammer für das Saarland* [1976] ECR 1989; *Rewe-Handelsgesellschaft Nord mbH v Hauptzollamt Kiel* [1981] ECR 1805.

[67] See Titles V and VI TEU, and Title IV, EC.

principles of the legal order to the institutions of the legal order itself remain incomplete and unresolved.[68]

In summary, the 'constitutional' maturity of the EU legal order is complexly qualified with regard to two quite different sets of factors. On the one hand, a key aspect of the traditional statist idea of legal order maturity, namely normative completeness or self-containment, simply does not and cannot apply in the same pure form in the context of complexly interlocked normativity. In some aspects, as in the question of comprehensiveness of normative reach, the EU system inevitably overlaps and 'colonizes' its national counterparts, while in other aspects, notably procedural effectiveness, it must remain dependent upon them. Accordingly, relational adequacy demands an awareness and openness to interdependence, and an appreciation that the mutual articulation of heterarchically aligned legal orders is more conducive to their respective purposes than their monadic self-sufficiency. On the other hand, and recalling the secondary status of the EU legal order, some of the claims to systemic reach made on its behalf are subject to powerful national objection, resistance, and qualification, notably as regards the basic autonomy or 'sovereignty' of the EU legal order and as regards its powers of self-amendment. If we put these two sets of factors together, however, the danger arises that the logic or hierarchy and opposition may marginalize the logic of heterarchy and mutual coordination. Just because of and in response to the competitive dimension, there is a tendency for the attraction of the traditional state understanding of system maturity *qua* normative completeness as an appropriate model for the EU to be reinforced, and for imitation to be practised as the best form of defence and self-assertion.[69]

The EU's Specialized System of Political Rule: If we turn to the second dimension of EU constitutionalism, here the truncation of the EU constitutional domain poses a more direct challenge. Whereas the legal order

[68] For a recent discussion, see *Human Rights Proofing EU Legislation: Report with Evidence*, 16th report of session 2005–6, House of Lords papers 67 2005–6.

[69] On the temptation for the ECJ in the context of strategic interaction with national political players to seek to enhance its legitimacy by emphasizing its technocratic credentials and its distinctly legal pedigree, and to draw upon familiar conceptions of legal order, see variously, J H H Weiler, 'The Community System: The Dual Character of Supranationalism' (1981) *Yearbook of European Law* 267, and n 1 above, ch 2; A Burley and W Mattli, 'Europe before the Court: A Political Theory of European Integration' (1993) 47 *International Organization* 41; W Mattli and A Slaughter, 'Revisiting the European Court of Justice' (1998) 52 *International Organisation* 177. For a recent overview of the Court literature, see A Stone Sweet, *The Judicial Construction of Europe* (Oxford: Oxford University Press, 2004).

is one of pure, self-referential normativity, and as such its adequacy is only tested externally and indirectly in the form of the boundary challenges posed by other legal orders, the political system is subject to tests of adequacy in terms of empirically sensitive standards of political morality. It is, therefore, vulnerable to whatever deficiencies are exposed in these terms by the absence of a developed constitutional profile as regards the dimensions of constituent power, societal integration, and political reflexivity. As is well known, the EU political system, and in particular the Community method of Commission proposal and Council and European Parliament disposal, has long been criticized for its democratic deficit, and this critique can be linked to constitutional truncation in two main ways. First, and most obviously, the absence of a *pouvoir constituant* in the form of an inclusive process of constitutional initiation speaks to a lack of deep democratic foundations—to the lack of a democratic pedigree for the system of government itself. Secondly, the weak level of societal integration and the lack of a deep sense of political reflexivity, both of which may be abetted by the absence of the assertion of democratic pedigree through a process and act of self-authorship, may curtail the potential of those institutions and aspects of the system of government that themselves claim democratic credentials and whose quality and effectiveness depend upon a sense of belonging to and engagement with political community that we earlier associated with minimum levels of trust, solidarity, and common political vernacular.

We cannot understand the main line of arguments made in defence of the constitutional credentials of the EU political system except as a way of anticipating or addressing these lacunae and the criticisms they suggest. These arguments—what we may term non-constituent forms of constitutionalism—typically proceed in two stages. In the first place, in exploring the logic of political action peculiar to the EU, they either make a virtue of the apparently non-democratic pedigree and unfavourable democratic-constitutive prospects of the EU, and in a manner which typically draws on and seeks to reinforce its credentials as a distinctive and self-contained legal order;[70] or, at least, they hold that its origins in or homologation through a popular constituent act are of no or marginal relevance to the question of the ongoing democratic quality of the EU system of governance.

As regards the first of these possibilities, in their rather different ways, for instance, the ordoliberal tradition[71] and Hans Ipsen's idea of the EU

[70] ibid.

[71] eg E-J Mestmacker, 'On the Legitimacy of European Law' (1994) *RabelsZ* 615; see also D Chalmers, 'The Single Market: From Prima Donna to Journeyman' in J Shaw and

as a special purpose association[72]—perspectives that inspired or tracked political positions that were influential in the early years of integration[73]—saw the supranational as a domain of activity which could and should be shielded from direct expression or representation of popular political interest. For the ordoliberals, the Treaty of Rome supplied Europe with its own economic constitution, a supranational market-enhancing system of rights whose legitimacy depended precisely on the absence of democratically responsive will formation and consequential pressure towards market-interfering socio-economic legislation at the supranational level, a matter which should instead be left to the member states—and even there only in so far as compatible with the bedrock economic constitution. Ipsen's theory, to which Majone's work on the idea of a European 'regulatory state'[74] is a notable successor, shares with ordoliberalism the idea that supranationalism transcends partisan politics, but here the invisible hand of the market is supplemented by the expert hand of the technocrat. The scope of European law is no longer restricted to negative integration—to the market-making removal of obstacles to wealth-enhancing free trade—but also extends to certain positive measures of an administrative nature. In Majone's elaborately developed model, these regulatory measures are concerned not with macro-politically sensitive questions of distribution, but with risk-regulation in matters such as product and environmental standards where expert knowledge is paramount, and where accountability is best served by administrative law measures aimed at transparency and enhanced participation in decision-making by interested and knowledgeable parties rather than the volatile preferences of broad representative institutions.

If these approaches, whether through providing a form of rights-insulation and guarantor of predictability and calculability in market relations, or through developing and refining forms of governance which counteract received models of broad representative government, suggest a constitutional sensibility that treats democracy as something to be

G More (eds) *New Legal Dynamics of European Union* (Oxford: Oxford University Press, 1996), 55–72. On the continuities between the legal and political thought of the Weimar Republic and post-war thinking about supranationalism more generally, see C Joerges and N S Ghaleigh (eds), *Darker Legacies of Law in Europe* (Oxford: Hart, 2003).

[72] H-P Ipsen, 'Europaische Verfassung—Nationale Verfassung' (1987) *European Review* 195.

[73] C Joerges, '"Good Governance" in the European Internal Market: An Essay in Honour of Claus-Dieter Ehlermann', European University Institute Working Papers, RSC No 2001/29.

[74] G Majone, 'The Rise of the Regulatory State in Europe' (1994) 17 *West European Politics* 77; see also Weiler, n 1 above. On the connections between Ipsen and Majone, see Joerges, n 73 above.

contained or cordoned off, the second way of justifying the absence of an autonomous democratic pedigree instead places the nurturing of postnational democracy back in the frame. It does so, however, in a way that eschews or downgrades the value of a holistic conception of democracy. On this view, rather than nominal—'democracy'—the key index of value is adjectival—'democratic'. The worth of democracy is divorced from the development of an idea and a self-conception of common political community and located instead in certain disaggregated and mobile virtues of democratic arrangements. In particular, emphasis tends to be placed on democratic and deliberative practices in communities defined not in territorial terms but in functional, epistemic, or practical 'problem-solving' terms, with 'output' at least as important as, and inextricable from, democratic 'input' in the legitimation of such forms.

What the many and sophisticated variants of an adjectival conception of democracy in the European debate have in common is an emphasis on the special treatment at the transnational level of two of the mobile democratic virtues, namely the enhancement of decision-making capacity through building common knowledge and understanding and the articulate expression and adequate consideration of the diversity of particular interests. It is claimed, first, that democratic contestation is best located in domains of discrete engagement, where the necessary motivation and knowledge to put things effectively in common already exists and, secondly, that such discrete engagement is best realized through innovative institutional forms designed to nurture the relevant motivational and knowledge capacities and to respond to the particular voices in question.[75] The total sum of added value is not ignored, but capacity and pluralism are seen as optimally developed and recognized in a bottom-up mode and through mutual learning and exchange of good practice rather than as a function of a prior transnational political identity.

[75] To take two relatively recent examples, for all their differences, the influential defence of the Open Method of Coordination (OMC) in the name of democratic experimentalism on the one hand, and those forms of deliberative supranationalism that look to the complex of national, supranational, and sectoral interest representation and pooling of knowledge in EU 'comitology' or committee structures as paying an epistemic dividend on the other, share this adjectival conception of democracy. For OMC and experimentalism, see O Gerstenberg and C F Sabel, 'Directly-Deliberative Polyarchy: An Institutional Ideal for Europe?' in C Joerges and R Dehousse (eds), *Good Governance in Europe's Integrated Market* (Oxford: Oxford University Press, 2002); J Zeitlin, 'Social Europe and Experimentalist Governance' in G de Burca (ed), *EU Law and the Welfare State: In Search of Solidarity* (Oxford: Oxford University Press, 2005), 213–41. For deliberative supranationalism, see C Joerges, ' "Deliberative Supranationalism": Two Defences' (2002) 8 *European Law Journal* 133. See also, Walker, n 10 above.

As our term suggests, the significant mark left by the non-constituent approach to the justification of the EU political system, unlike the predominantly mimetic approach to the question of legal order, stands in stark contrast to the state-based constitutional tradition. Indeed, this is underlined by the ambivalent attitude by the partisans of the various approaches collected under the non-constituent banner to the very discourse of constitutionalism.[76] Yet, however packaged, such views are indubitably constitutional in nature insofar as they purport to provide an adequate normative theory for the EU political system—one based on the relational premise of the EU's partial contribution to a broader governance project. To the extent that they do not succeed, their implicit or explicit constitutional vision may be considered deficient.

The common vulnerability of the various species of non-constituent constitutionalism is exposed if we move to the second stage of their argument. For underlying the majority of the positions within the horizon of non-constituent constitutionalism, whether or not this is explicitly acknowledged, is a continued reliance on the indirect pedigree of national constitutional authority and democratic origins.[77] Whether couched in the language of delegation theory,[78] or national sovereignty,[79] or international law,[80] or realist or liberal versions of international relations,[81] or

[76] To the extent that we can discern a recent momentum in favour of constitutional language even in such unpromising quarters, this is surely not unconnected with the emergent standing of constitutional discourse as the master trope of normative discussion in the EU—a development both signalled and reinforced by the drafting of the Constitutional Treaty—and so is as at least in some measure strategic and tending towards a nominalist reading of constitutionalism; see n 11 above. For discussion of this strategic development, see N Walker, 'Europe's Constitutional Momentum and the Idea of Polity Legitimacy' (2005) 3 *International Journal of Constitutional Law* 211.

[77] The majority, but not all. Some versions of constitutional scepticism are deep rather than contingent, involving a critique of the very idea of constituent power as a meaningful or desirable way of thinking about political authority in any of the political sites of late modernity—national or postnational. Interestingly, such sceptical conclusions can issue from both ends of the ideological spectrum, from positions highly supportive of the efficiency and other dividends of markets and critical of a conditional steering mechanism that would too easily interfere with these dividends (eg K-H Ladeur, 'Towards a Legal Theory of Supranationality—The Viability of the Network Concept' (1997) 3 *European Law Journal* 33) as much as from positions highly critical of the injustices of the market and of constitutionalism's tendency to act as a handmaiden to neoliberalism (eg G Anderson, *Constitutional Rights after Globalization* (Oxford: Hart, 2005)).

[78] See P Lindseth, 'Delegation is Dead: Long Live Delegation; Managing the Democratic Disconnect in the European Market Polity' in Joerges and Dehousse, n 75 above, 139–63.

[79] Grimm, nn 8 and 48 above.

[80] eg J Klabbers and P Leino, 'Death by Constitution' (2003) 12 *German Law Journal* 1293.

[81] eg A Moravcsik, 'The European Constitutional Compromise and the Neofunctionalist legacy' (2005) 12 *Journal of European Public Policy* 349.

whether simply taken for granted, it is precisely the continuing employment of the idea of constituent power at the national level and its extension to cover the authorization of the transnational or supranational pooling of authority that accounts for the readiness of thinkers in this category to accept the redundancy of the idea of transnational constituent power. Crucially, at this final stage the necessity of constituent power and the secondary status of the EU polity reasserts itself. It is not the case that the majority of writers who accept the redundancy thesis reject the purposes and merits normally associated with the idea of constituent power as irrelevant to the supranational domain. It is just that they believe these purposes to be well enough served by the combination of indirect democratic legitimation from national means and whatever other first-stage arguments they rely on at the supranational level itself—whether rights insulation, technocratic expertise, or disaggregated and instrumentalized democratic benefits.

The argument that treats direct constituent power at supranational level as redundant, therefore, is at root empirically based. It arises in the context of an investigation of the application of a normative theory of constituent power directed towards the discovery of its optimal location, rather than in the questioning of that normative theory *per se*. Accordingly, it is only as convincing as the evidence it can muster in its defence. If that is so, however, there are in fact several developmental features of the supranational polity which appear to stretch the plausibility of the indirect legitimation thesis, and of those supranational constitutional positions that depend on that thesis, to breaking point.

To begin with, to return to the intrinsic normative claim of the pedigree argument, the idea of constituent power refers us to a general argument about the virtues of self-rule and the standing of democracy as a meta-value of modern politics, one that argues for a popular founding for those political systems that attain a certain threshold of authority and of autonomy. That threshold is reached in these systems that, in terms of their authoritative scope and the quotidian procedures through which such authority is translated into political decisions, are capable of significantly affecting the life-chances of those who are subject to them and of doing so in a manner that cannot be effectively counter-influenced at the level of any other political system. The relevance of this to the EU is palpable. The double movement, accelerating over the twenty years since the signing of the Single European Act, towards expanding the scope of the EU from internal market regulation to large areas of social and security policy combined with the reduction or sacrifice of national veto positions in legislative and other decisional procedures, suggests such a profound transformation of both the scope and autonomous capability of the EU as to undermine the claims for indirect legitimation and underline the demand for direct legitimation.[82]

What is more, if we move onto the consequentialist arguments associated with constituent power, those concerned with its causal relationship with societal integration and with political reflexivity, again the case has become more persuasive, albeit its tenor remains more speculative. This can be developed on at least three grounds, the first two of which mirror the arguments made by the proponents of the disaggregated democratic version of non-constituent constitutionalism. In the first place, there is the capacity argument. Just as at the state level,[83] we can distinguish between the formal legal competence and the effective political capacity of the EU polity. The notorious 'joint-decision trap'[84] of a contemporary decision-making constellation that seeks to track the different sites and multiple levels of collective action problems that we confront under conditions of economic, cultural, and political globalization, speaks to the ways in which the increase in competence at the EU level in matters such as monetary policy and positive regulation of various general social interests and against certain general social threats can reduce both competence and capacity at the state level without necessarily generating a compensatory, still less a surplus, measure of additional capacity at the EU level. Super-majoritarian decision rules and the residual veto positions they entertain are only part of the problem here. Much more important is the lack of shared political capital—and so the absence of the elements of trust, mutual concern, and common terms of reference of which such shared capital is comprised—necessary to put and keep things in common sufficiently to exploit European political capacity. The danger is of 'false negatives',[85] of the EU's inability to fulfil its formal democratic potential by effectively putting in political common those matters that cannot, or cannot any longer, be adequately addressed through the variety of national political agendas. The possible contribution of a theory of constituent power here is instrumental rather than intrinsic, not based upon the political morality of democratic pedigree *per se* but on how pedigree can help guarantee the continuing quality of democracy. It is, in short, based on the proposition that the political act of self-constitution

[82] N Walker, 'A Constitutional Reckoning' (2006) 13 *Constellations* 140.

[83] Loughlin, n 26 above, ch 5.

[84] F Scharpf, 'Problem Solving Effectiveness and Democratic Accountability in the EU', Max Planck Working Papers (2003).

[85] P Pettit, *Republicanism: A Theory of Freedom and Government* (2nd edn) (Oxford: Oxford University Press, 1999).

may contribute to the fostering of a sense of political community and the production of a common political capital sufficient to overcome the problem of false negatives.[86]

In the second place, and less obviously, there is the argument from pluralism. This holds that however much the European people want to put things in common, whether more so than presently, much the same, or perhaps even less, and wherever they want to strike the balance between national and supranational action, respect for diversity and responsiveness to the variety of internal opinion can only be enhanced by an increase in the resources of dedicated political capital available at the European level. The key to this argument is historical as well as normative. It lies in asserting that the idea of constituent power and of its relationship to a dedicated public or political sphere that we find in the enlightenment thought of such as Locke and Sieyès, and which inspired at least some of the protagonists of the English, French, and American revolutions, was not intended, as has often subsequently been misunderstood or misappropriated, simply as an assertion of the greater power and potential impact of a political authority founded in popular opinion rather than proprietary right.[87] Just as important a dividend of popular sovereignty as the empowerment of public authority in the name of the public good was that of the limitation or forbearance of government authority in that same name. For the idea of an indivisible collective that is foundational of government denies to any section of that collective, or to any government operating in the name of any section of that collective, final and unlimited exercise of constitutional authority. That is to say, if self-government properly rests in the constituent authority of the collective people, then any constitution based upon an image of collective self-government must be concerned as much with checking governmental factionalism or abuse of minorities as with democratic empowerment of majorities. This ambitious thesis, moreover, need not be dismissed as wishful thinking or pious hope. For the normative strength of the aspirational model of political community which has been contained in much of Western constitutionalism lies precisely in the promise, however imperfectly delivered, that investment in a shared political capital will engender a sufficient sense of a community of attachment and a sufficient fund of shared political

[86] eg J Habermas, 'Why Europe Needs A Constitution' (2001) 11 *New Left Review* 5, and n 39 above. See also, N Walker, 'Europe's Constitutional Engagement' (2005) 18 *Ratio Juris* 387.

[87] See B Yack, 'Nationalism, Popular Sovereignty, and the Liberal Democratic State' in T V Paul, J Ikenberry, and J A Hall (eds), *The Nation State in Question* (Princeton, N J: Princeton University Press, 2003), 29–50.

capital not only to make the idea of non-unanimous decision-making—of sometime winners and losers—fair and palatable to all in a longer perspective, but also, and reciprocally, to restrain what may legitimately be done to any part of the community by the sometime winners in the name of the whole.

In the third place, there is an argument more specifically concerned with political reflexivity. The undeniable fact that the quotidian regulatory structure of the EU inevitably contains many of the democracy-containing or constraining mechanisms applauded by the non-constituent constitutionalists is on close analysis an argument for, rather than against, a more general democratic cradling. The significant extent to which the primary regulatory structure of the European supranational political system emphasizes expert knowledge and the protection of core freedoms alongside and in some measure instead of democratic mechanisms makes it all the more important that a threshold sense of democratic collective subjectivity be fostered, sustained, and capable of political operationalization. This is for two reasons. First, and substantively, without such a threshold sense of collective subjectivity the overall direction of the policy agenda to be pursued through the semi-democratic primary regulatory structure will lack democratic articulation.[88] Secondly, and procedurally, without such a threshold sense of collective subjectivity, the very semi-democratic form of the primary regulatory structure lacks an ongoing monitor and guarantee of democratic approval.[89]

The Deep Structure of Supranational Documentary Constitutionalism

Coming finally to the politics of the present, we cannot understand the impetus behind the current documentary constitutional process without reference to the deep structure of the EU's truncated constitutionalism. For all the attention its contents have received, the CT is of only modest importance as a story of the sum of its detailed provisions, and not just because these detailed provisions look increasingly unlikely ever to enter into force. Largely a consolidating measure, the CT announces only limited substantive reforms, all of which could in principle have been provided by the regular process of Treaty amendment.[90] More so than as

[88] A Follesdal and S Hix, 'Why There is a Democratic Deficit in the EU: A Response to Majone and Moravcsik' (2005) *European Governance Papers* No C-05-02.

[89] Walker, n 82 above.

[90] See J H H Weiler, 'On the Power of the Word: Europe's Constitutional Iconography' (2005) 3 *International Journal of Constitutional Law* 173.

a text, the CT is significant as an event—one that has grown out of a cumulative sense of challenge to the overall 'polity legitimacy' of a post-state order of unprecedented jurisdiction.[91]

As an event, the CT dramatizes both the resilient creative potential of constitutionalism in the state tradition and its deep contestability. On the one hand, a powerful if often implicit concern of some promoters and supporters of the CT has been to address just these system deficiencies set out above by seeking to harness and to adapt the broader constructivist promise of the state-inspired constitutional tradition. From this perspective, a documentary constitutional act might repair the hole in the middle of EU constitutionalism, providing the absent ingredient of a democratic founding. It might also supply, in consequence, a mechanism for diffusing and regularizing political conflict, an occasion for a new and more intense mobilization of a sense of common political engagement, a token of community and an amplifier of common values, as well, in the longer haul, as a chapter in an identity-building common historical narrative and an anchor for a self-evolving sense of transgenerational constitutional multilogue. In so doing, it might engender the kind of socially integrative momentum that the current EU lacks and which undermines the capacity, pluralism, and collective reflexivity of its political community. [92]

Such an approach crucially pays equal attention to both the challenge and the opportunity presented by the horizontal characteristics of constitutionalism in the state tradition.[93] It recognizes the strength of the holistic requirement—of the unavoidable interdependence of all five dimensions of constitutionalism—and how this requirement means that for so long as EU constitutionalism is concentrated on just two dimensions, it is bound to remain a truncated and democratically diminished constitutionalism in the ways set out above. However, this approach also recognizes what our tendency to freeze and reify particular constitutional achievements often obscures, namely the deep sense in which constitutionalism under the sign of the modern state has always been constructivist in nature, and has always possessed the closely related and complementary attributes of legal-political symbiosis and projection. Constitutionalism has always been a way of actively developing as well as recording and consolidating the development of the political imaginary, and it is this 'cumulative open-endedness'—this quality as a 'palimpsest'[94] rather than

[91] See Walker, n 33 above.
[92] See Walker, n 86 above.
[93] See 'Abstracting from State Constitutionalism', above.
[94] As one writer has described the British constitution; see D Marquand, 'Pluralism v. Populism' (1999) 42 *Prospect* 27, 29.

a sacred text—that in the final analysis underwrites the translatability of its various dimensions to the postnational level.

On the other hand, as an event provoked by system deficiency, the constitutional debate must also be seen as much as a symptom of that deficiency and of the conundrums and conflicts that underpin it as a means of overcoming it. Indeed, what we observe in the simultaneous resort to and deep contestation of a constitutional discourse of reform is a double paradox. In the first place, and most obviously, as dramatically highlighted in the Dutch and French 'no' votes and in the polarized political atmosphere surrounding these votes,[95] debate over a first documentary Constitution has provided a vivid public frame within which latent disagreement over the type of polity the EU is or should be may be brought to the surface. Yet the potential for the sharpening and amplification of difference over the polity orientation of the EU is not just a matter of the heightened public profile that a self-styled constitutional event brings. It is also, in the second place, about the way in which disagreement is built into the evolution of the constitutional idea itself. As noted at the outset, each of the approaches to the translatability or otherwise of the state constitutional tradition raises fundamental questions about the intimacy of the link between state and constitution, and the answers they suggest closely track differences over the terms on which and the extent to which it is possible to imagine polities other than the state. The constitutional process, it follows, is no mere platform for disagreement over polity aspirations, but one that bears an internal, question-begging relationship to the terms of such disagreement.

Alongside the constructivist agenda with its ambitious adaptation of state constitutional ideas, we can observe other deep orientations at play in the constitutional debate. In particular, we may point to two broad attitudinal clusters or coalitions. One is of constitutional limitation, and maps onto the sceptical approach to EU constitutionalism. The other, an even broader tent, we may describe as an attitude of constitutional vindication,[96] and it maps onto both the continuity and the nominalist approach, while sharing some of the basic background assumptions of the sceptics. The immediate point is not to examine these complex groupings in depth,[97] but simply to indicate their potential to induce constitutional gridlock. Constitutional scepticism refuses to credit the possibility that the missing goods of constitutionalism that constructivism seeks to

[95] See W Pfaff, 'What's Left of the Union?' (2005) 52(12) *New York Review of Books* 26; Moravcsik, n 7 above.

[96] See Walker, n 33 above, 228–30.

[97] ibid.

supply through its postulation of supranational constituent power as an affirmation of democratic pedigree, and as the basis of reflexive construction and maintenance of political community, as well as an indirect stimulant towards an enhanced collective decision-making capacity and a pluralist respect for different communities of attachment and interest, are indeed better served by the diversification and multiplication of 'constituent' constitutional sites beyond the state. Rather, constitutional scepticism can be seen as the inverse image of constructivism, calculating that beyond current levels of integration of supranational political community there is a negative or at best zero-sum relationship between the simultaneous promotion of voice, capacity, and respect for pluralism at national and supranational levels. In turn, far from the tapping of unrealized potential in the relationship of heterarchically located political communities, the strategic dividend of scepticism is likely to be one of limitation in either of two senses. Negatively, this may take and often has taken the form of denying the validity of the very process of documentary constitutionalism beyond the state for fear that its efforts in creating positive-sum dividends effects succeed only in eroding the key indices of national political community. More positively, as we have seen in recent years when the momentum of documentary constitutionalism has threatened to consign to the margins anyone unprepared to frame their claims in such constitutional terms, it may take the form of drawing competence-delimiting or rights-protecting constitutional lines in the sand to minimize the prospect of such national erosion.[98]

The attitude of constitutional vindication has even greater internal complexity and is less directly in conflict with the constructivist perspective, but arguably it offers just as great a challenge to constructivism. By vindication we mean an approach which treats the conclusion of the constitutional episode and the nominal constitutional achievement itself as the symbolic key, rather than, as in the broader constructivist approach, only one element in a multi-faceted and progressive social technology associated with constitutionalization. The temptations of constitutional vindication are apparent. Its backward-looking bias—its sense of the constitutional act as a higher validation and celebration of something that already exists—resonates closely with the peculiarly truncated nature of EU constitutionalism. For in the absence of favourable conditions for the kind of social integration that state constitutionalism has typically assumed or sought, the

[98] For example, in the decision of the notoriously Eurosceptic *Economist* magazine to come out in favour of a power-limiting EU Constitution: *The Economist* 4 November 2000.

vindication approach falls back on the old supranational faithfuls of a mature and familiar legal order and a mature and unfamiliar specialized political system. As we have seen, there is a powerful strand of thought that views the constitutional strength of the EU legal system as lying precisely in its continuity with the state legal order. And there is another equally powerful and often complementary strand of thought that sees the strength of its political system as lying in its *sui genericity*—and so as relying on a nominalist understanding of constitutionalism as including those 'non-constituent' brands whose virtue in the postnational domain is at least partly dependent upon their acceptance in common with the sceptical position that there is simply no scope for democratic assertion of constituent power at different levels simultaneously. On this view, the CT becomes a kind of 'achievement constitution',[99] its very constitutional self-coding both confirming the venerable status of the EU's constitutional roots and vindicating its accumulated record. The deep difficulty with such an approach, however, is that it risks treating the problem as the solution. It tends towards closing down and treating as finally resolved[100] the very debate about constitutional possibility that the EU must keep open, and to do so in terms that explicitly authorize and reinforce the truncated tradition that such debate needs to put at issue.

As noted at the beginning of this essay, constitutional theory as an activity directed towards and implicated in the domain of practical reason always contains a self-fulfilling element—it operates by assuming the very social and political conditions of action of whose viability or inevitably it seeks to convince its audience. In the debate over the terms of supranational constitutional possibility we see the opposition between just such self-fulfilling assumptions—from adaptation on the one side through continuity and nominalist approaches to scepticism on the other side—and the danger of a deep impasse at the various points of mutual disconnection. Even if the current constitutional process is somehow revived or renewed, is the idea of constitutionalism beyond the state not fatally compromised by the very depth of contestation between different meta-theoretical understandings of the proper domain and purpose of the constitutional? More concretely, as these differences percolate through to the constitutional process, is such a constitutional project not vitiated by the inevitability of disagreement or blockage over the optimal balance of representation of national and postnational constituencies, interests, and aspirations, at various stages, whether at the point of initiative, in the

[99] C Mortati, *Le forme di governo* (Padova: Cedem, 1973), 393.
[100] See Walker, n 33 above, 231.

content of the text, in its wider symbolic ambition, or in the terms of its interpretation and revisability? On this view, the theoretical plausibility of the constructivist approach to the adaptability of the state constitutional tradition threatens to be of little value, defeated by the very conditions of action that it can only plaintively claim could have been otherwise.

The only possibility of avoiding this bleak prospect is to point to one final and more positive implication of the grounding of constitutionalism in the domain of practical reason. If practical reason, quite simply, is any reason aimed at a conclusion concerning what to do, then any 'constitutional' situation that cannot tell us what to do and how to go on displays a kind of performative contradiction. Arguably, the present constitutional situation is of that order. It is not only that the documentary constitutional initiative is blocked, but also that the circumstances of its blockage undermine any default solution. To the extent that the CT's failure not only thwarts the constructivist approach but also foils the vindication approach, it thereby also undermines the existing Treaty configuration that is the object of the failed vindication, while providing no positive mandate for any broader dismantling of those proto-constitutional features of the framework of legal and political integration that may be preferred by some brands of scepticism. In short, the tribulations of the CT tell us not what we can do in 'constitutional' common, but only what we cannot or cannot any longer do.[101]

The case for renewal of the constitutional debate and for the continuing exploration of the lessons of the state tradition, therefore, ultimately depends upon taking a step backwards in the face of the destabilizingly diverse manifestations of our common commitment to the very idea of constitutional commitment. It involves an additional reflexive turn whose purpose and very justification is none other than an examination of the limits or otherwise of the kind of political reflexivity inaugurated under the state constitutional tradition. In circumstances where the contemporary European peoples stand not only 'unavoidably side by side'[102] but ever more closely mutually implicated, we are faced with a situation of deep disagreement over the constitutional conditions under which and even the basic framework of constitutional frames with which we may optimize democratic voice, effective political capacity, and respect for diversity, but one of consensus that we must nevertheless seek to do all of

[101] See Walker, n 82 above.

[102] As in the famous Kantian formulation in the context of his advocacy of cosmopolitanism; H Reiss (ed), *Kant's Political Writings* (Cambridge: Cambridge University Press, 1970), 107–8.

these things. All we know in common in pursuit of these shared hopes and fears are: first, that we do indeed disagree over constitutional means; secondly, that there is no authoritative default for deciding and providing such means in the presence of disagreement, only our current capacity to face up to and resolve any such disagreement, and: thirdly, that according to our national experience, however we resolve our disagreement, its constitutional resolution under circumstances of inclusive deliberation may contribute to the very conditions of political community indispensable to the success of any such resolution.

However sceptical or otherwise we are over the available models of post-state constitutionalism, under circumstances of intimate interdependence we have no option other than to go back to the table with those with whom we are intimately interdependent to try to resolve the optimal conditions of our interdependence. In the final analysis, it is that deeper premise of collective reflexivity—the idea that we can only decide the terms and limits of our common action together and through some putative frame of collective subjectivity—rather than the particular set of candidate goods associated with collective reflexivity under the state tradition, that provides the most pertinent if also the most attenuated legacy of the state constitutional tradition. Proponents of this or any successor EU Constitution cannot succeed unless they can persuade their diverse audiences that the answer to the question of the viability and potential of a post-state constitutional frame of common political engagement and commitment is one we cannot afford not to address in common—that we must seek to be collectively reflexive 'all the way back' about our scope for collective reflexivity in the tradition inaugurated by state constitutionalism. Equally, such proponents do not deserve to succeed unless they insist that the terms on which such a question is posed are true to the best understanding of its motivation; that is to say, under the kind of open conditions of collective reflexivity where no candidate constituencies and no candidate solutions to the perennial but highly mobile problem of collective political action—whether or not so-called 'Constitutional'—are ruled out in advance.

Comparative Constitutional Law in the Courts: Is There a Problem?

*Cheryl Saunders**

Introduction

For more than a decade,[1] debate has raged in the United States about the use of foreign law by courts in the course of constitutional adjudication. Much of the criticism of the practice denies its legitimacy, although there is also a growing focus on the methodology that courts employ.[2] Controversy has been fuelled by occasional decisions of the Supreme Court often, but not always, involving application of the Bill of Rights, in which one or more Justices have included references to foreign legal experience in their reasoning and others have disputed their right to do so.[3] In one much-quoted rejoinder, for example, Justice Scalia described

* Faculty of Law, University of Melbourne, Australia. The chapter was written in the course of a year spent in the Faculty of Law, University of Cambridge as Arthur Goodhart Visiting Professor of Legal Science.

1 Both the practice of citing foreign law and debate about it have a much longer genealogy, which can be traced to the first part of the nineteenth century: Steven G Calabresi and Stephanie D Zimdahl, 'The Supreme Court and Foreign Sources of Law: Two Hundred Years of Practice and the Juvenile Death Penalty Decision' (2005) 47 *William and Mary Law Review* 743, 753–5. Calabresi and Zimdahl argue that the practice has increased in significant respects since *Trop v Dulles* 356 US 86 (1958). The current, intense, phase of the debate follows the use of foreign law in *Thomson v Oklahoma* 487 US 815 (1988); *Washington v Glucksberg* 521 US 702 (1997); and *Printz v United States* 521 US 898 (1997).

2 Richard A Posner, 'The Supreme Court 2004 Term Foreword: A Political Court' (2005) 119 *Harvard Law Review* 31, 85–8 combining both types of critique in his analysis of the 'cosmopolitan court'.

3 See in particular the following cases: *Thompson v Oklahoma* 487 US 815 (1988) (reference to the use of the death penalty in a range of jurisdictions by Stevens J, for the Court, at 830–1; rejected by Justice Scalia, with whom Chief Justice Rehnquist and White J concurred, at 868–9 and n 4); *Printz v United States* 521 US 898 (1997) (reference to foreign constitutional practice by Breyer J at 977, criticized by Scalia J at 921 n 11); *Atkins v Virginia* 536 US 304 (2002) (reference to the views of the 'world community' by Stevens J, writing for the plurality, at 316, rejected by Scalia J, with whom Rehnquist CJ and Thomas J concurred, at 347–8); *Lawrence v Texas* 539 US 558 (2003) (reference to decisions of the ECHR and those of 'other nations' by Kennedy J, writing for the plurality, at 576, rejected by

comparative analysis as 'inappropriate to the task of interpreting a constitution, although it was of course quite relevant to writing one'.[4]

The practice remains a topic of fierce debate among scholars in the United States[5] and among judges writing extra-judicially.[6] It has been the subject of critical comment in the press.[7] It has attracted the attention of Congress, spawning a series of proposed resolutions seeking, in one way or another, to discourage judicial reference to foreign constitutional experience, with impeachment a veiled threat in the background.[8] The legitimacy of referring to foreign law for the purposes of constitutional interpretation was raised with Justice John Roberts (as he then was) during his confirmation hearings.[9] His response was sharply dismissive of the practice, suggesting that the debate is likely to continue.

Scalia J, with whom Thomas J concurred at 598); *Roper v Simmons* 161 L Ed 2d 1 (2005) (reference to 'the opinion of the world community' by Kennedy J, writing for the plurality, at 26, criticized on methodological grounds by Scalia J, with whom Rehnquist CJ and Thomas J concurred, at 61–4, and also by O'Connor J, on methodological grounds, at 49–50, albeit specifically endorsing the potential relevance of foreign law). Of these four cases, *Printz* was concerned with federalism; *Atkins* and *Roper* with the understanding of 'cruel and unusual punishment' in the context of the Eighth Amendment and *Lawrence* with the application of the due process clause to the criminalization of homosexual conduct.

4 *Printz v United States* 521 US 898, 921 n 11 (1997).

5 For a sample of scholars who broadly support the practice see Vicki C Jackson, 'Constitutional Comparisons: Convergence, Resistance, Engagement' (2005) 119 *Harvard Law Review* 109; Harold Hongju Koh, 'International Law as Part of Our Law' (2004) 98 *American Journal of International Law* 43. Those critical of the practice include Roger P Alford, 'Misusing International Sources to Interpret the Constitution' (2004) 98 *American Journal of International Law* 57; Ernest A Young, 'Foreign Law and the Denominator Problem' (2005) 119 *Harvard Law Review* 148.

6 See eg Ruth Bader Ginsburg, '"A Decent Respect for the Opinions of [Human]kind": The Value of a Comparative Perspective on Constitutional Adjudication' (2005) 64 *Cambridge Law Journal* 575; see also Justice Stephen Breyer and Justice Antonin Scalia, 'A conversation between US Supreme Court Justices' (2005) 3 *International Journal of Constitutional Law* 519.

7 See eg Dana Milbank, 'And the Verdict on Justice Kennedy is: Guilty', *Washington Post*, 9 April 2005.

8 Reaffirmation of American Independence Resolutions, H Res 568, 108th Congress (2004); H Res 97, 109th Congress (2005), S Res 92 109th Congress (2005); see also H Res 468, introduced on 21 November 2003: 'Expressing disapproval of the consideration by Justices of the Supreme Court of the United States of foreign laws and public opinion in their decisions, urging the end of this practice immediately to avoid setting a dangerous precedent, and urging all Justices to base their opinions solely on the merits under the Constitution of the United States'. In addition, see Title II of the *Constitution Restoration Bill of 2005* that, if enacted, would have prohibited any court from 'rely[ing] upon any constitution, law, administrative rule, Executive order, directive, policy, judicial decision, or any other action of any foreign state or international organization or agency, other than English constitutional and common law up to the time of the adoption of the Constitution of the United States'.

9 United States Senate Judiciary Committee, Hearing on the Nomination of John Roberts to be Chief Justice of the Supreme Court, Transcript, Day Two, 13 September 2005,

It may be that the criticism has been exacerbated by certain features of the cases that have sparked the debate. In each case the issue at stake was one that was hotly contested in the United States of the late twentieth and early twenty-first century: the constitutionality of the death penalty for mentally impaired offenders[10] or for minors;[11] the constitutionality of the criminalization of homosexual relations between consenting adults;[12] the invalidation of congressional legislation on federalism grounds.[13] In each case also the judges used foreign law in a manner that was distinctive and potentially vulnerable. In *Atkins, Lawrence*, and *Roper*, in one way or another, the references to foreign law assumed the persuasive qualities of universalism. In these circumstances, comparative analysis was not necessary for the purposes of the argument, exposing the majority justices to accusations of merely 'counting . . . noses'.[14] In *Printz*, Justice Breyer's guarded attempt to use the administration of central laws by member states in Germany, Switzerland, and the European Union to cast 'empirical light'[15] on the constitutionality of the conferral of federal duties on state officials in the United States was open to attack on the ground that he failed adequately to take structural differences between the two types of federations into account.[16] It is clear from the tenor of the debate on the use of foreign sources in the United States, however, that these features of the cases are not the sole cause of the controversy. The criticisms are generalized and embrace all substantial references to foreign law.

The controversy that attaches to the use of constitutional comparison by courts in the United States is in marked contrast to the position elsewhere in the common law world,[17] where references to foreign law are freely made in all types of cases, without apparent concern about legitimacy and

in response to questions from Senator Kyl, <http://www.washingtonpost.com/wp-dyn/content/article/2005/09/13/AR2005091301210.html>, viewed 24 June 2006.

[10] *Atkins v Virginia* 536 US 304 (2002).

[11] *Roper v Simmons* 161 L Ed 2d 1 (2005).

[12] *Lawrence v Texas* 539 US 558 (2003).

[13] *Printz v United States* 521 US 898 (1997).

[14] Posner, n 2 above, 151, arguing that the methodology of 'including foreign jurisdictions in the denominator of noses that count accords *authoritative* weight to their choices' (emphasis supplied).

[15] *Printz v United States* 521 US 898, 977 (1997).

[16] His reasons acknowledge the possibility of 'relevant political and structural differences': ibid. In this instance, however, the structural difference is so deep that it threatens the relevance of the comparison altogether.

[17] There is a growing literature on the use of foreign law by courts in civil law countries also: see eg Guy Canivet, Mads Andenas, and Duncan Fairgrieve (eds), *Comparative Law Before the Courts* (London: British Institute of International and Comparative Law, 2004). The exclusive focus on common law courts in this chapter is justified by the broad similarity in the style of their reasons for decision.

with relatively little overt attention to method.[18] The purpose of this chapter is to explore the reasons for the contrast and the implications of it from the perspective of countries whose courts make reference to foreign law often enough for the practice to be considered unexceptionable. Using the twin concerns about legitimacy and method to organize the argument, the chapter focuses on two sets of questions in particular. The first seeks a better understanding of the attitude of most common law states towards the legitimacy of the use of foreign law in constitutional cases. Is it justified, and if so how and under what conditions? What insight, if any, does acceptance of the practice offer into the nature of constitutions and constitutional adjudication in such states: itself a potentially significant question for the purposes of comparative understanding? A second set of questions concerns the methodology employed by judges who make use of foreign law. Are there specific methodological concerns? If so, what is required? What, if anything, is the relevance of the debate on comparative method that is taking place within the discipline of comparative law,[19] with its primary focus on private law,[20] to the use of foreign law in constitutional adjudication?

The first part of the chapter is designed to scope the field of the inquiry. It justifies the exclusion of consideration of references to international, as opposed to foreign legal sources; explains the sometimes wavy line between constitutional and other forms of adjudication; and begins the laborious process of understanding the range of ways in which courts use foreign law. It introduces at this point a series of cases from a range of jurisdictions, to serve as concrete examples in the analysis that follows. The next two sections deal respectively with the challenges of legitimacy and methodology. The section on legitimacy considers not only legitimacy *per se*, but also certain aspects of judicial method that have the potential to raise the issue of legitimacy in another guise. The section on methodology thus can be confined to comparative method alone and

[18] For an examination of the practice in Australia, by reference to a series of cases in which the High Court of Australia held that the Constitution provided some protection for freedom of political communication, see Cheryl Saunders, 'The Use and Misuse of Comparative Constitutional Law' (2006) 13 *Indiana Journal of Global Legal Studies* 37. For an analysis of practice in England, Canada, and South Africa, as well as selected civil law countries, see Sir Basil Markesinis and Jörg Fedtke, 'The Judge as Comparativist' (2005) 80 *Tulane Law Review* 11 and the various commentaries on their article in the same issue.

[19] For a selection of recent works, see Pierre Legrand and Roderick Munday (eds), *Comparative Legal Studies: Traditions and Transitions* (Cambridge: Cambridge University Press, 2003); Mark Van Hoecke (ed), *Epistemology and Methodology of Comparative Law* (Oxford: Hart, 2004); Esin Orucu, *The Enigma of Comparative Law* (Leiden: Martinus Nijhoff Publishers, 2004).

[20] William Twining, *Globalisation and Legal Theory* (London: Butterworths, 2000), 185.

facilitates examination of the relevance of the debate on methodology in comparative private law. The final section draws some brief conclusions, noting that greater attention to questions of the methodology that courts employ in making reference to foreign constitutional experience may be timely, in order to preserve and enhance the practice itself.

Scoping the Field

Foreign, Rather than International Law

In order to clarify the issues raised by the use of foreign law, in terms of both legitimacy and method, references by courts to international law are excluded from the scope of the chapter.

In fact a case can be made, on various grounds, for including international law in a study of external doctrinal influences on constitutional adjudication. Most obviously, the dividing line between international and foreign constitutional law, never entirely distinct,[21] is becoming increasingly blurred. What Gerald Neuman has helpfully isolated as the 'suprapositive' aspect of international human rights norms is reflected in many contemporary constitutional systems, albeit sometimes at a level of considerable generality.[22] More significantly still, some Constitutions directly incorporate international human rights norms and may in addition specifically authorize recourse to them for the purposes of constitutional interpretation.[23] Further, in so far as the purpose of reference to external legal sources is to seek 'interpretative inspiration'[24] it may be met as well by international as by foreign domestic law.

[21] See eg Jeremy Waldron, in the context of a discussion of *ius gentium*: 'The distinction between international law and domestic law was much less crisp at the time Bentham was writing . . . than it was in the middle of the twentieth century, and it has become less crisp again with the emergence of human rights law': 'Foreign Law and the Modern Ius Gentium' (2005) 119 *Harvard Law Review* 129, 135.

[22] Gerald L Neuman, 'The Uses of International Law in Constitutional Interpretation' (2004) 98 *American Journal of International Law* 82, 84. Neuman distinguishes this aspect of rights from their consensual aspect (signifying acceptance and consent) and their institutional aspect (the extent and manner of implementation).

[23] South Africa is a case in point. The constitutional principles, on which the final Constitution was based, required 'universally accepted fundamental rights, freedoms and civil liberties' to be 'protected by entrenched and justiciable provisions': Interim Constitution, 1993, Appendix A, principle II. Courts are required to consider international law in interpreting the Bill of Rights: see Constitution of the Republic of South Africa, section 39(1)(b).

[24] Aharon Barak, 'Comparative Law, Originalism and the Role of a Judge in a Democracy: A Reply to Justice Scalia', a paper delivered to the Fulbright Convention, 29 January 2006 (copy on file with the author).

For these reasons, many courts and commentators refer to both foreign and international law, without clearly distinguishing between them.[25] This tendency is encouraged by the emergence of the phenomenon of supranational courts, with responsibilities for regional adjudication. Such courts necessarily are themselves practitioners of comparative constitutional law.[26] More relevantly for present purposes, they also have a dual character. From the standpoint of a member state they are effectively international courts, with consequences for the hierarchy of norms that depend on the detail of the particular regional arrangement. From the standpoint of other states, however, such courts are foreign courts whose jurisprudence technically has the status of foreign law, even though the law reflects the standards of multiple states.[27]

For present purposes, however, the case for excluding international law from consideration is stronger still. The extent to which legal norms can and should converge across national boundaries is a controversial issue in comparative law.[28] References by courts to international law necessarily assume a degree of convergence, within the limits of flexibility that international law itself allows.[29] At a level of generality, which varies between different aspects of constitutional systems, convergence may in fact have occurred, either historically, as the natural consequence of the common foundation of western constitutional systems or more recently, through the processes of internationalization and globalization. Even where this is so, however, it does not necessarily extend to the level at which particular questions arise for constitutional adjudication. Excluding international law from this study makes it possible to avoid prejudging the question of whether references to external legal sources automatically involve the convergence of constitutional norms at this point. If the influence of international norms on constitutional law continues to deepen, however, over time it will become increasingly impracticable to isolate it from the use of foreign law.

[25] See the discussion in Daphne Barak-Erez, 'The International Law of Human Rights and Constitutional Law: A Case Study of an Expanding Dialogue' (2004) 4 *International Journal of Constitutional Law* 611, 612.

[26] See eg the development of 'general principles of law' by the European Court of Justice from the constitutional traditions common to the member states: Anthony Arnull, *The European Union and its Court of Justice* (Oxford: Oxford University Press, 1999), 190–1.

[27] For an unusual example of a judicial exchange on this issue, in relation to a decision of the European Court of Human Rights, see *Al Kateb v Godwin* (2004) 219 CLR 562, 594, per McHugh J, 628 per Kirby J.

[28] Orucu, n 19 above, 195–202.

[29] Ian Brownlie, *Principles of Public International Law* (6th edn) (Oxford: Oxford University Press, 2003), 549–52.

Recourse by courts to international law also raises somewhat different questions from the perspective of both legitimacy and method. A state is bound by international law.[30] International law thus has a claim to the attention of the state, increasing its relevance to a court as a source of law, while making the manner in which the claim is made good a sensitive issue. Where a court unilaterally gives effect to an international norm, questions about separation of powers may be raised.[31] Ironically, no doubt, obligation-free references to domestic foreign law raise no concerns on this score, even where the foreign law itself reflects international legal standards. On the other hand, references to foreign law raise a range of methodological questions, directed to ensuring that the comparison is well-founded, which are quite different to those presented by international law.[32]

Constitutional Adjudication

A second preliminary observation concerns the concept of constitutional adjudication itself. The principal focus of the chapter is on the use of foreign law in the course of interpreting and applying formal written Constitutions. These constitute the core of constitutional law in most states. They also raise questions about legitimacy and methodology in their most acute form. It should be noted that, even thus confined, the study includes the full range of justiciable constitutional norms, dealing not only with rights, but also with the organization of public power. Different aspects of constitutional law present different challenges for effective comparison and it is sometimes necessary to distinguish between them for this purpose.

On the other hand, it is neither desirable nor necessary to confine the topic too rigidly to written Constitutions and in what follows the boundaries are extended in at least two respects.

First, in most common law states claims under the common law and statute may arise in the course of constitutional adjudication in a manner that closely intertwines them with constitutional questions.[33] Similarly,

[30] ibid 34. [31] Young, n 5 above, 163–5. [32] Brownlie, n 29 above, 52–3.

[33] This is most obviously the case when a question arises about the impact of the Constitution on relations in private law. See eg *Hill v Church of Scientology of Toronto* [1995] 2 SCR 1130; (1995) 126 DLR (4th) 129; *Lange v Australian Broadcasting Commission* (1997) 189 CLR 520; *Du Plessis v De Klerk* 1996 (3) SA 850 (CC). See generally D Friedman and D Barak-Erez (eds), *Human Rights in Private Law* (Oxford: Hart Publishing, 2001); Andras Sajo and Renata Uitz (eds), *The Constitution in Private Relations* (Leiden: Eleven International Publishing, 2005).

questions of process[34] and interpretative technique[35] may bear both a common law and a constitutional character. Indeed, the juxtaposition of the common law and constitutional law in common law states is part of the explanation for the extension to constitutional adjudication of the long-established common law practice of drawing on foreign legal experience.

Secondly, some states do not have a formal written constitution. The United Kingdom and New Zealand are examples, as was Israel, at least before the *Mizrahi Bank* case.[36] The experience of the courts of these states with the use of foreign law in determining questions that elsewhere would be likely to be covered by a formal constitution nevertheless is relevant to this study. This claim can be justified by reference to the United Kingdom as the most familiar, particularly challenging case.[37] In the United Kingdom, it has so far has been possible to avoid introducing a formal, written constitution because institutions, principles, and practices of a constitutional kind have developed organically over time, drawing their legitimacy in large part from that process. The result, in the early years of the twenty-first century, is a quintessentially national legal and political construct of a constitutional kind, embedded in the culture of the state and with a structural logic of its own. Thus understood, questions about the use of comparative constitutional law by courts in the United Kingdom are similar enough to those that arise elsewhere, even after allowance is made for the absence of any formal distinction between constitutional and ordinary law.[38]

Use

Finally, the manner in which, in practice, courts use foreign law also has profound implications for the topic and thus needs to be canvassed at this stage. The variety of usage is vast, making it impracticable to design a typology that is sufficiently precise to be useful. Nevertheless, it is possible

[34] For example, the issue of prospective overruling: see *National Westminster Bank v Spectrum Plus Limited* [2005] UKHL 41, and the cases there cited from the United States, India, Ireland, Canada, and Australia.

[35] For example, proportionality as a technique for evaluating the lawfulness of public action; or the use of preambles for the purpose of the interpretation of texts.

[36] *United Mizrahi Bank v Migdal Co-operative Village* (1995) 49 (4) PD 221. For a statement of the present position see Barak P in *Rubinstein v Minister of Defence* 52 (5) PD 481(High Ct, 1997) [31].

[37] See generally, David Feldman, 'None, One or Several? Perspectives on the UK's Constitution(s)' (2005) 64 *Cambridge Law Journal* 329.

[38] It may be that such a distinction is beginning to emerge: *Thoburn v Sunderland City Council* [2002] EWHC 195.

to begin to grasp the phenomenon by organizing some of the principal variations in different ways that may be useful for different purposes.

One possible variation, which should be noted at the outset, is the nature of the foreign source on which a court draws. It may be a conclusion of law[39] or a constitutional or legal norm, whether articulated by a court or otherwise.[40] Equally, however, it may be an argument,[41] a value,[42] a perception,[43] an interpretative approach,[44] or merely a happy turn of phrase.[45] The list is intended to be illustrative, rather than exhaustive.

A second type of variation is the stage in its reasoning at which a court refers to foreign experience. It may be used to assist to frame the question;[46] to identify options or more generally to survey the field;[47] to support a step in the argument;[48] to suggest an answer;[49] to test a

[39] A redefinition of Parliament cannot be disregarded by a succeeding Parliament: *Jackson v Attorney-General* [2005] 3 WLR 733, 761 per Lord Steyn, citing various Commonwealth authorities.

[40] The elements of qualified privilege in an action for defamation involving publication to an extended audience: *Hill v Church of Scientology of Toronto* [1995] 2 SCR 1130, referring to *New York Times v Sullivan* 376 US 254 (1964). The horizontal division of power in the German federation is an example of another kind, although justified by reference to the 'empirical light' that it cast on the question before the Supreme Court of the United States in *Printz v United States* 521 US 898 (1997), 976–7, per Breyer J.

[41] 'People cannot adequately influence the decisions which affect their lives unless they can be adequately informed on facts . . . ', Lord Simon of Glaisdale, *Attorney-General v Times Newspapers Ltd* [1974] AC 273, 315, to which Mason CJ referred in *Australian Capital Television v Commonwealth* (1992) 171 CLR 106, 139.

[42] 'the fundamental importance . . . of freedom of communication . . . in the modern system of representative government': *Australian Capital Television v Commonwealth* (1992) 171 CLR 106, 140, per Mason CJ.

[43] *McGinty v Western Australia* (1995) 186 CLR 140, 187 per Dawson J: 'The democratic traditions of both Canada and Australia find their origins in the English model rather than in rebellion against it as is the case in the United States'.

[44] The use of techniques of statutory interpretation to avoid invalidation of a statute: *Rubinstein v Minister of Defence* 52(5) PD 481(High Ct, 1997), Barak P, citing practice in the United States and Germany.

[45] The 'chilling effect' of libel actions, to which reference is made in eg *Australian Capital Television v Commonwealth* (1992) 171 CLR 106, per Mason CJ, drawing on *New York Times v Sullivan* 376 US 254 (1964).

[46] Laurie H Ackermann, 'Constitutional Comparativism in South Africa: A Response to Sir Basil Markesinis and Jörg Fedtke' (2005) 80 *Tulane Law Review* 169, 185.

[47] *Executive Council of Western Cape Legislature v President of the Republic of South Africa* 1995 (4) SA 877 (CC), available at <http://www.constitutionalcourt.org.za/site/thecourt/cases/wpcape.pdf> (viewed 17 July 2006)

[48] *Lange v Australian Broadcasting Commission* (1997) 189 CLR 520, rejecting the United States state action doctrine as irrelevant to Australian circumstances, as a step leading to the conclusion that the Australian Constitution did not directly override the common law.

[49] The goal of an electoral distribution might be to achieve 'effective representation' rather than 'equality of voting power': *Reference re Electoral Boundaries Commission Act* (1991) 81 DLR (4th) 16 La Forest, Gonthier, Stevenson and Iacobucci JJ, drawn on by Dawson J in *McGinty v Western Australia* (1995) 186 CLR 140, 186–7.

hypothesis;[50] to confirm a conclusion;[51] or to explore the consequences of a particular result.[52] Again, the list is not necessarily exhaustive.

A related variation concerns the nature of the impact of the foreign experience on the court's own deliberative processes. There is a distinction to be drawn here between constructive and reflective use. In the case of the former, the foreign experience is used for guidance, in ways that range from quantifying the experience of states[53] in order to determine universal or at least widespread practice,[54] to the somewhat more commonly held purpose of deriving 'the full benefit of others' experience . . . of solutions that have proved successful but also, scarcely less valuable, . . . of solutions that have for any reason proved unsatisfactory'.[55] Reflective use, by contrast, is well captured by observations of Aharon Barak, President of the Supreme Court of Israel, that comparative law 'awakens judges to the potential latent in their own system' and 'allows for greater self-knowledge'.[56] There is an incomplete parallel here with yet another mode of analysing the use of foreign law, by reference to the acceptance, adaptation, or rejection of the foreign experience in question. Reflective use may often involve an awareness of difference and rejection of the foreign experience, but it will not always do so.

This multiplicity of usages of foreign legal experience is sometimes described in terms of dialogue,[57] conversation,[58] or, more recently

[50] Ackermann, n 46 above, 185.

[51] *Australian Capital Television v Commonwealth* (1992) 171 CLR 106, 140: 'much the same view was taken in Canada . . . ', per Mason CJ.

[52] Arguably, the purpose of the reference to Germany, Switzerland, and the European Union by Breyer J in *Printz v United States* 521 US 898, 976–7 (1997). See also *Hill v Church of Scientology of Toronto* [1995] 2 SCR 1130, 1182, exploring commentary on the consequences of the adoption of the 'actual malice' standard in the United States.

[53] Posner, n 2 above; see also Young, n 5 above, at 153.

[54] See eg the references to the views of the 'world community' in *Atkins v Virginia* 536 US 304, 316 (2002) and in *Roper v Simmons* 161 L Ed 2d 1, 26 (2005).

[55] Lord Bingham of Cornhill, 'The Break with the United Kingdom and the Internationalisation of the Common Law' in Peter Cane (ed), *Centenary Essays for the High Court of Australia* (London: Butterworths 2004), 84.

[56] Aharon Barak, 'Foreword: A Judge on Judging: The Role of a Supreme Court in a Democracy' (2002) 116 *Harvard Law Review* 16, 111, 110. See also Laurie Ackermann: 'foreign law may stimulate "creative imagination"' (quoting Einstein), n 46 above, 185.

[57] Honourable Claire L'Heureux-Dubé, 'The Importance of Dialogue: Globalization and the International Impact of the Rehnquist Court' (1998) 34 *Tulsa Law Journal* 15. See also the work of Sujit Choudhry, who has identified the 'dialogical' approach to comparative references by courts as a middle course between particularism and functionalism: Sujit Choudhry, 'The *Lochner* Era and Comparative Constitutionalism' (2004) *International Journal of Constitutional Law* 1, 50–3; see also Sujit Choudhry, 'Globalization in Search of Justification: Toward a Theory of Comparative Constitutional Interpretation' (1999) 74 *Indiana Law Journal* 819.

[58] Sarah K Harding, *Comparative Reasoning and Judicial Review* (2003) 28 *Yale J International L* 409, 424 referring to 'cross-border judicial dialogue or conversation'.

'engagement'.[59] Such formulations are useful to convey the complexity of the practice and to contrast it with applications of it that are particularly vulnerable to criticism, including the borrowing or transplantation of principles or institutions from one system to another or references to foreign law that assume universalism. The typically mixed usage of foreign law does not necessarily make methodological questions irrelevant, however. For present purposes, a more precise focus is required on the particularities of use.

To assist in developing such a focus, three general propositions may be made. First, foreign legal experience is never treated as binding, at least in the legal sense. In the words of President Chaskalson of the Constitutional Court of South Africa: 'We can derive assistance from . . . foreign case law, but we are in no way bound to follow it'.[60] Even direct borrowing is relatively infrequent.[61] Secondly, foreign legal experience is rarely used as an exclusive source of law and more often than not may play a relatively small supporting role in the reasoning of a court, at least in quantitative terms.[62] Thirdly, references to foreign experience are less likely to be made when the domestic law is settled unless, at least, its suitability is questioned in some way.

At most, foreign law is treated as persuasive. And in some cases, both the manner in which courts refer to a foreign decision and the effect of doing so is virtually indistinguishable from the use of domestic persuasive authority save for the acknowledgement that the source is foreign and therefore carries lesser weight.[63] On the other hand, in many instances, references to foreign law cannot readily be equated to the use of persuasive authority, at least in the traditional sense. Not all references to foreign law are to principles of law formulated by courts, for example; and reflective use is more passive than the notion of 'authority' generally allows.

[59] Jackson, n 5 above.

[60] *State v T Makwanyane* (1995) (3) SALR 391 (CC), [39].

[61] In a survey of Canadian Charter cases between 1998–2003, for example, Bijon Roy has calculated that only one of the sixty references to foreign legal experience involved a direct adoption of a foreign solution: Bijon Roy, 'An Empirical Survey of Foreign Jurisprudence and International Instruments in Charter Litigation' (2004) 62 *University of Toronto Faculty of Law Review* 99, 130–1.

[62] For a close analysis by reference to an Australian case study see Saunders, n 18 above, 31.

[63] For an example see the reference to Commonwealth authorities in *Jackson v Attorney-General* [2005] 3 WLR 733, 761. See also Justice Sandra Day O'Connor, Remarks to the South Center for International Studies 1–2, 28 October 2003, 'conclusions reached by other countries . . . should at times constitute persuasive authority in American courts': available at <http://www.southerncenter.org/OConnor_transcript.pdf> (viewed 26 May 2006). See generally H Patrick Glenn, 'Persuasive Authority' (1987) 32 *McGill Law Review* 261.

Even where a court refers constructively to a principle of law enunciated by a court in another jurisdiction, any analogy that it seeks to draw must have at least two dimensions: the relevance to the case in hand of the issues before the foreign court and the relevance of the legal experience of the other jurisdiction to that of the domestic court. In the words of Patrick Glenn, such a foreign source 'attracts adherence as opposed to obliging it'.[64] Judges themselves often claim a role for foreign law far removed from the notion of persuasive authority. Thus Emeritus Justice Laurie Ackermann, formerly a Justice of the Constitutional Court of South Africa, has described the purpose of recourse to foreign law as 'seeking information, guidance, stimulation, clarification, or even enlightenment . . . [o]ne is doing no more than keeping the judicial mind open to new ideas'.[65]

For present purposes, it is possible to define the field further, by confining consideration to references to foreign law that play a not insubstantial role in the reasoning of a court or of a member of it. Within the broad area of constitutional adjudication that remains, however, the reality that the manner in which foreign law is used varies widely complicates the task of generalizing about the methodology that should be applied.

Selected Cases

The discussion of legitimacy and method in the remainder of the chapter will refer from time to time to a series of case studies that are outlined briefly in this section. The cases are drawn from different common law or mixed common law jurisdictions: Australia, Canada, Israel, South Africa, and the United Kingdom. Collectively, they span a range of constitutional issues encompassing, relevantly, questions about both institutions and rights. Individually and collectively, they also illustrate a variety of uses of foreign law in constitutional adjudication and of approaches to the use of foreign law. They are not otherwise distinctive, however. It would be possible to identify other cases within each jurisdiction, or cases in other jurisdictions, to perform a broadly similar role.

In *McGinty v Western Australia*,[66] the question for the Australian High Court was whether a wide disparity in the numbers of electors in State electorates, drawn pursuant to State law, was inconsistent with any limitation on State power that might be implied from principles of

[64] Glenn, n 63 above, 263.
[65] Ackermann, n 46 above, 183.
[66] (1995) 186 CLR 140.

representative democracy inherent in the Australian Constitution. In a two-step reasoning process, the Court considered first whether a principle of equality of Commonwealth electoral boundaries could be implied from the Australian Constitution. It was referred in argument to judicial decisions from both the United States and Canada. The former favoured relatively strict numerical equality; the latter allowed other factors also to be taken into account in the interests of securing 'effective representation'.[67]

The validity of the legislation was upheld.[68] While the majority justices differed to a degree in their conclusions about the scope of the protection for electoral fairness that the Constitution offered, none accepted a strict numerical standard. In the course of their reasoning, three of the four majority justices[69] referred approvingly to the observation of McLachlin J, as Chief Justice of the Supreme Court of British Columbia, that Canada had a tradition of 'evolutionary' democracy, in contradistinction to the position in the United States where 'democracy . . . sprang from a revolution ushering in a new regime'.[70] Seizing on the observation as applicable also to Australia, these judges rejected the United States approach.[71] Justice Gummow went further, drawing on Canadian principles to fashion a doctrine that, in his view, applied to the Australian Constitution.[72]

While categories of use of foreign law inevitably are blurred at the margins, *McGinty* represents a case in which the High Court drew on both principles and perceptions in foreign case law, to identify and evaluate options available to it, in a manner that tended to be reflective rather than constructive.

One issue before the Supreme Court of Canada in *Hill v Church of Scientology of Toronto*[73] was the consistency of the Canadian law of defamation with the principles of the Canadian Charter of Rights and Freedoms.[74] In argument about whether the common law should be modified to bring it into line with the Charter, the Court was referred to applicable legal principles in Australia, the United Kingdom, and the

[67] *Reference re Electoral Boundaries Commission Act* [1991] 2 SCR 158, 187–8, McLachlin J.

[68] Brennan CJ, Dawson, McHugh, and Gummow JJ, Toohey and Gaudron JJ dissenting.

[69] Dawson, McHugh, and Gummow JJ. Toohey J, in dissent, also preferred the Canadian approach, while drawing different conclusions from it: at 203–4.

[70] *Dixon v Attorney-General (British Columbia)* (1989) 59 DLR (4th) 247, 262–3.

[71] Dawson J at 186; McHugh J at 246–7; Gummow J at 266–8, 287–8.

[72] At 287–8.

[73] [1995] 2 SCR 1130; (1995) 126 DLR (4th) 129.

[74] An earlier argument that action by the respondent Crown Attorney was governmental action and thus directly subject to the Charter failed: at 1162–4.

United States, as well as to Canadian authority. In particular, the appellants urged the Court to accept the doctrine laid down by the Supreme Court of the United States in *New York Times v Sullivan*, [75] pursuant to which a public official must establish that a defamatory statement impugning his or her fitness for office was made 'with knowledge that it was false or with reckless disregard for whether it was false or not'[76] in order to succeed in the action.

The Court[77] refused to change Canadian law. In doing so, it used the United States experience in several ways. First, it identified some empirical consequences of the 'actual malice' standard in the United States, which had caused the doctrine to be criticized in that country and that made it undesirable in Canada also.[78] Secondly, it distinguished *New York Times* as the product of a particular social, political, and legal context that did not apply in Canada.[79] In this connection it noted that the actual malice standard had also been rejected in England and Australia.[80] Thirdly, it used the United States experience reflectively, to explore and explain the rationale for the differing standard in Canada, where greater weight is accorded to the reputation of the individual, thus reflecting 'the innate dignity of the individual, a concept which underlies all the *Charter* rights'.[81]

Rubinstein v Minister of Defence[82] concerned the validity of the use of executive discretion by the Israeli Minister for Defence to defer military service for full-time students in religious seminaries, pursuant to a general statutory authority to grant deferrals[83] and in circumstances in which 8 per cent of all those eligible for military service were granted a deferral on this basis.[84] The challenge raised the issue of the division of power between the legislature and the executive.[85] Barak P, with whom the other members of the Court agreed, restated the 'basic rule' that '"primary arrangements" that determine general policy and the guiding principles must be enshrined in statute ... whereas regulations or administrative guidelines must only determine "secondary arrangements"'.[86] In the

[75] (1964) 376 US 254. [76] At 280.

[77] Cory J, delivering the judgment of La Forest, Gonthier, Cory, McLachlin, Iacobucci, and Major JJ. L'Heureux-Dubé, who delivered a separate judgment, did not dissent on this point. [78] 1183.

[79] 1180–1, 1188. [80] 1185–6. [81] 1179. [82] HC 3267/97.

[83] Section 36 of the Defence Services Law conferred such a power for a range of specified 'or other' reasons.

[84] The distinction between 'administrative regulations' and an accumulation of 'individual acts' is not clearly drawn in the case, although see Barak P at [23] and in particular Cheshin J at [10]. [85] Barak P at [32].

[86] [19].

event, the Court held that the exercise of discretion required a 'principled decision' of the Knesset, and was invalid.[87]

Both the basic rule and its application drew extensively on Israeli case law and secondary sources. Foreign law played a substantial role, however, in a somewhat unusual way, which may be attributable to the unusual nature of the Israeli Constitution,[88] as a series of Basic Laws that underwent a process of 'constitutionalization' through judicial decision.[89] In his reasons for decision, President Barak linked the basic rule identified by the Court with the underlying constitutional principles of separation of powers, the rule of law, and substantive democracy.[90] He explained the relevance of these principles and drew conclusions from them about the boundary between legislative and executive power by reference to both Israeli and foreign sources; the latter comprising decisions from the United States, Germany, Canada, and the European Court of Human Rights.[91] Foreign sources thus provided constructive support for the legal doctrine developed by the Court as well as contributing to an understanding of the rationale for it.

In *Executive Council of Western Cape Legislature v President of Republic of South Africa*[92] the Constitutional Court of South Africa also was concerned with the scope of executive, *vis-à-vis* legislative, power. In this case, the question was provoked by legislation conferring authority on the President to amend the parent Act or any schedule to the Act. In purported exercise of this authority, the President had amended the principal Act. The substance of the amendments was contested by the Western Cape Legislature. If the delegation was not valid, under the new interim Constitution of South Africa, it followed that the amendments were invalid as well.

As is normally the case, the scope of legislative authority to delegate was not specified in the interim Constitution. Very wide delegations had been permitted under the apartheid regime.[93] The earlier cases could not be determinative, however, under the 'new constitutional order'.[94] In these

87 [43]. The operation of the order was, however, postponed for twelve months.

88 I owe this insight into a possible reason for the difference in the style of using foreign law in Israel to Professor Amnon Reichman, of the University of Haifa.

89 *United Bank Hamizrachi Ltd v Migdal Cooperative Village* PD 49 (4) 221.

90 See also Cheshin P: '. . . in a social framework government by the Rule of Law . . . ; in a society in which governmental powers and the power to coerce are divided between the legislative and executive branch; in a society in which human rights are at the pinnacle; in these social-governmental frameworks, first principles unequivocally instruct us that the broad exemption granted to Yeshiva students must be prescribed by statute. I unreservedly concur . . . '[7].

91 [20]–[22].

92 CCT 27/95.

93 Chaskalson P, at [52].

94 ibid.

circumstances, members of the Court explored options identified by the constitutional law of a range of other countries: the United Kingdom, the United States, Ireland, Australia, Canada, and, with some hesitation, India.[95] These options differed. The United States and Ireland drew a distinction between delegating power to make law and delegating power to make rules 'giving effect to principles and policies which are contained in the statute itself'.[96] Countries in the British constitutional tradition, on the other hand, tended to tolerate a wider delegation of legislative power. In the event, despite the broad structural similarity between the constitutional arrangements in South Africa and in other parliamentary systems, a majority of the Court favoured the United States and Irish approach, concluding that the interim Constitution at least precluded delegation to the executive of power to amend the Act by which the delegation was conferred.[97]

The fifth and final case, *(R) Jackson v Attorney-General*,[98] is a decision of the House of Lords. The issue in dispute was the validity of the Hunting Act 2004, enacted without passage through the House of Lords, in reliance on the procedure established by the Parliament Act 1911, as amended by the Parliament Act 1949. The 1911 Act had modified the composition of the Parliament in the circumstances to which it applied. The 1949 Act had modified the procedure prescribed by the 1911 Act, using that procedure for the purpose. The claimant attacked the validity of the Hunting Act through the validity of the 1949 enactment procedure. He argued, in essence, that the law-making process established by the Parliament Act 1911 was not a primary law-making process; that in consequence there were implied, as well as express limitations on its use; and that, in particular, the procedure could not be used to amend the 1911 Act itself.

The challenge failed. The Parliament Act procedure was held to have created a 'new way of enacting primary legislation',[99] which could be used to change the details of the enactment mechanism itself. In so deciding, the Court necessarily rejected an argument for the claimant that drew on

[95] The hesitation was caused by concern about the accuracy of the information about the Indian position that was available to the Court: Chaskalson [57]; cf Mahomed DP at [134].

[96] *Cityview Press Ltd v An Chomhairle Oiliuna* [1980] IR 381, 395, quoted in the *Western Cape* case at [54].

[97] Chaskalson P with whom Langa J concurred. Ackerman, O'Regan, and Kriegler JJ would have gone further to preclude any delegation of power to amend an Act of Parliament. Mahomed and Sachs JJ would have evaluated each delegation by reference to a range of factors. Madala J and Ngoepe AJ reached their decision on another point.

[98] [2005] 3 WLR 733.

[99] Lord Bingham, at 745.

Australian[100] and South African[101] cases to establish that a derivative law-making process, which on one view the 'controlled' constitutions of the former dominions represent,[102] could not be used to alter the terms in which it was conferred, without express authority to that effect. The argument failed, in part because the cases were distinguished on factual and constitutional grounds[103] and in part because the claimant failed to convince the Court that the cases established the proposition for which they were advanced.[104]

The outcome in *Jackson* has potentially deeper constitutional significance, however, causing at least two members of the House of Lords to use the foreign authorities in another way. *Jackson* establishes that the Parliament can redesign itself so as to provide an alternative primary legislative process that can be used for particular purposes. It raises a question whether Parliament can also redesign itself so as to provide an alternative primary legislative process that *must* be used for particular purposes; in effect providing a basis for the entrenchment of constitutional arrangements in the United Kingdom. Both Lord Steyn and Baroness Hale drew on the Australian and South African cases to provide a basis for such a conclusion[105] even though, in the words of Baroness Hale, the decision was 'for another day'.[106] The Commonwealth authorities are used constructively, as a form of persuasive authority, in a manner that, at least in the case of Lord Steyn, only lightly distinguishes them from domestic cases.

Legitimacy

Legitimacy and illegitimacy, as Joseph Weiler once remarked in the context of a discussion of the European Union, are 'notoriously elusive

[100] *Attorney-General for New South Wales v Trethowan* (1931) 44 CLR 394; *Taylor v Attorney-General of Queensland* (1917) 23 CLR 457; *Clayton v Heffron* (1960) 105 CLR 214; see also Owen Dixon, 'The Law and the Constitution', 51 LQR 590.

[101] *Harris v Minister of the Interior* 1952 (2) 428 (AD); *Minister of the Interior v Harris* 1952 (4) 769; see also D V Cowen, *Parliamentary Sovereignty and the Entrenched Sections of the South Africa Act* (Cape Town: G-VG Juta, 1951).

[102] In this context the term 'derivative' was used to distinguish law-making procedures the validity of the exercise of which is 'open to investigation in the courts' from procedures where this possibility is not recognized: Lord Bingham at 744. This analysis is preferable to the analogy that also was drawn with delegated legislation. Neither captures the conception of a different notion of parliamentary sovereignty that now prevails in the former dominions: see eg *Attorney-General (WA) v Marquet* (2003) 217 CLR 545, 570, Gleeson CJ, Gummow, Hayne, and Heydon JJ.

[103] [2005] 3 WLR 733, 750, Lord Bingham.

[104] At 162, Baroness Hale.

[105] Lord Steyn, 761–3; Baroness Hale, 783–4.

[106] At 784.

concepts'.[107] One of the causes of the difficulty is that legitimacy may be viewed objectively or subjectively and evaluated normatively or empirically.[108] In relation to institutions of government, including courts, democracy supplies a familiar normative measure and elite and public acceptance can be used for empirical purposes, however problematic these may be.[109] The normative rationale necessarily must take into account the role that courts play and are expected to play in a democratic society, in upholding the constitution and maintaining the rule of law.

It is not necessary for present purposes to engage in depth with the problem of judicial review in democratic theory. Whatever the basis on which judicial review is accepted and explained, the inquiry here is more narrowly confined to the question of whether recourse to foreign law makes a difference to its legitimacy. This section distinguishes two distinct ways in which the question of legitimacy might be raised by the use of foreign law. First, it may be argued that a court is never justified in considering foreign sources in the course of constitutional adjudication subject to, perhaps, minor exceptions. This form of difficulty is referred to here as the problem of legitimacy *per se*. Secondly, even if references to foreign law are acceptable in principle, questions about legitimacy may be raised indirectly by the way in which the foreign experience is used or, in other words, by judicial method.

Legitimacy *Per Se*

References to foreign law may automatically be denied legitimacy because the sources on which a court may draw for constitutional adjudication are regarded as closed. There are several possible explanations for a view of this kind.

One group of explanations denies the legitimacy of judicial recourse to foreign law by reference to considerations deriving from the domestic constitutional system that are deemed to preclude the practice. It has been suggested, for example, that restrictions on the use of foreign law might be inferred from the logic of the judicial appointment process, through which the legitimacy of the judicial role is reinforced by the democratic legitimacy of the elected branches.[110] It may be that this

[107] J H H Weiler, 'Epilogue' in Anne-Marie Slaughter, Alec Stone Sweet, and J H H Weiler, *The European Court and National Courts—Doctrine and Jurisprudence* (Oxford: Hart Publishing, 1998), 372.

[108] Christopher W Morris, *An Essay on the Modern State* (Cambridge: Cambridge University Press, 1998), 102.

[109] ibid.

[110] Posner, n 2 above, 88–9.

concern is tied to the use of foreign law to establish universal practice although, even in this context, it seems exaggerated.[111] It appears nevertheless to be shared by Chief Justice John Roberts who, in the course of his confirmation hearing, observed that:

> If we're relying on a decision from a German judge about what our Constitution means, no president accountable to the people appointed that judge and no Senate accountable to the people confirmed that judge. And yet he's playing a role in shaping the law that binds the people in this country.[112]

An alternative consideration, of a somewhat different kind, involves the authority for the Constitution itself. The sources on which a court may draw in the course of constitutional adjudication need not be considered closed merely because the Constitution is seen as an exercise of sovereignty on the part of the people of the state concerned. Popular sovereignty is a theoretical construct that serves to legitimize the status of a constitution as fundamental law and may have other, practical, implications for the attitude of the governors to the governed. It does not necessarily confine the sources to which a court may turn in interpreting the Constitution and developing the reasons for its decision. But a foundation in popular sovereignty that is coupled with an approach to law that understands it purely as an exercise of will,[113] or with an approach to constitutional interpretation that demands fidelity to the intention of the framers or to the expectations of the national community of the time,[114] may present impediments to the use of foreign sources, as well as confining the process of constitutional interpretation in other ways.

There is a second type of explanation that suggests another basis on which the sources for constitutional adjudication may be considered closed. In a recent article in the *Harvard Law Review*, Jeremy Waldron argues the need for a theory that positively justifies recourse by courts to all sources on which they draw and that identifies and explains the key features of the practice.[115] In relation to domestic law Waldron finds such

[111] 'To cite foreign decisions in order to establish an international consensus that should have weight with US courts is like subjecting legislation enacted by Congress to review by the United Nations General Assembly': ibid 89.

[112] United States Senate Judiciary Committee, Hearing on the Nomination of John Roberts to be Chief Justice of the Supreme Court, Transcript, Day Two, 13 September 2005, in response to questions from Senator Kyl, <http://www.washingtonpost.com/wp-dyn/content/article/2005/09/13/AR2005091301210.html>, viewed 24 June 2006.

[113] Waldron, n 21 above, 147.

[114] Barak, n 24 above, discussing both intentionalism and originalism.

[115] Waldron, n 21 above, 129. See also Mark Tushnet, 'The Possibilities of Comparative Constitutional Law' (1999) 108 *Yale Law Journal* 1225, seeking 'authority' for use of foreign law.

a theory in the doctrine of precedent.[116] In relation to foreign law, he suggests that a theory might be based upon a modernized conception of *ius gentium*. By analogy with scientific method, *ius gentium* might be perceived to represent 'the established deliverances of legal science . . . more than a sum of its parts . . . a dense and mutually reinforced consensus . . . '.[117]

Waldron's argument is directed specifically to the issues raised by references to the standards of the 'world community' in resolving the kinds of moral questions presented in *Atkins* and in *Roper*. He accepts that the actual practice in those cases does not conform to the standards that his theory prescribes.[118] Nor does his theory seek to cater for the significantly more diverse use of foreign legal experience that in fact occurs elsewhere. Thus, if there is a need for a theory to legitimize the practice of referring to foreign law more generally, the need is not satisfied by the possibilities of *ius gentium*. On the other hand, to the extent that Waldron's argument calls for a theory about how foreign law is used, as opposed to whether it can be used at all, he can be understood as raising concerns about judicial method, rather than about legitimacy *per se*.

The Perspective from other Common Law Countries

Many of the arguments against the legitimacy of the use of foreign law that have currency in the United States are unpersuasive elsewhere in the common law world, for reasons that are in large part to do with attitudes to law, including constitutional law, and to judicial reasoning.

The starting point is the nature of the common law itself. Over centuries, the common law has been developed by its judges drawing on ideas from both within and outside the home jurisdiction. As long as the ideas are used appropriately, with due regard to the hierarchy of domestic legal sources in accordance with the prevailing theory of precedent, common law states do not recognize any normative or empirical reason why judges should be confined in the sources from which ideas come. Patrick Glenn has described this process as 'law as inquiry' as opposed to 'law as national response'.[119] The distinction parallels Waldron's dichotomy between law as reason and law as will.[120] If law is conceived of as reason, he argues, we 'may well be willing to approach it in a scientific spirit that relies not just on our own reasoning but on some rational relation between what we are wrestling with and what others have figured out'.[121]

[116] Waldron, n 21 above, 130, 135. [117] ibid 143, 145. [118] ibid 146.
[119] Glenn, n 63 above, 284. [120] Waldron, n 21 above, 146.
[121] ibid at 147.

The origins of this approach to law lie in the history of the common law also recounted, for this purpose, by Glenn.[122] The habit of drawing on other legal sources, from both within England and outside it, was developed early by common law judges: 'for centuries . . . the common law existed in a kind of perpetual, institutional debate with other laws'.[123] The success of the practice, from the standpoint not only of the competitiveness of the common law courts but also, and more importantly, of the quality of the body of substantive law, underpinned its acceptance. Comparable sentiments were expressed by Edmund Burke, in 1790: 'We are afraid to put men to live and trade each of his private stock of reason; because we suspect that this stock in each man is small, and that the individuals would do better to avail themselves of the general bank and capital of nations, and of ages'.[124]

The practice survived the loss of flexibility that followed the introduction of the doctrine of precedent[125] and persisted in the face of the emergence of distinct nationalisms, with their associated demands.[126] Persistence was made possible by the continued reliance of common law states on judge-made law and by the independence of a common law judiciary, resisting nineteenth-century pressures to create national identity through law.[127] The United States emerged as an exception, for reasons that range from the conception of law itself to the volume of law generated by the multiple American jurisdictions.[128] The common law practice of drawing on foreign legal sources enjoyed a renaissance in the latter part of the twentieth century,[129] for reasons that almost certainly include the new and extraordinary ease of access to foreign legal experience by electronic means.[130]

A cynic might suggest the lingering effects of empire as a somewhat dismal alternative explanation for the ready recourse of common law courts to the legal experience of other Commonwealth countries.[131] It may also be that examination of patterns of foreign citation would suggest that this is closer to the truth than one might wish.[132] On the other hand, again

[122] H Patrick Glenn, *Legal Traditions of the World* (2nd edn) (Oxford: Oxford University Press, 2004).

[123] ibid at 256.

[124] Edmund Burke (J C D Clark ed) *Reflections on the Revolution in France* (Stanford, Calif: Stanford University Press, 2001), 251.

[125] J P Dawson, *The Oracles of the Law* (Ann Arbor: The University of Michigan Law School, 1968).

[126] Glenn, n 122 above, 247, 257.

[127] ibid at 248.

[128] ibid at 249. See also Glenn, n 63 above, 268.

[129] Glenn, n 122 above, 245.

[130] See also the suggestions in, eg Young, n 5 above, 156 that the phenomenon is due also to more frequent meetings between judges.

[131] Saunders, n 18 above, 25.

[132] It would be interesting to explore, for example, the extent to which emphases in patterns of citation reflect former colonial links between the United Kingdom, Australia,

following Glenn,[133] it is possible to see the imperial interlude as part of the same story. The second British Empire reached its zenith around the same time as the doctrine of *stare decisis* took hold, minimizing the effect of the latter development by providing a larger law area within which authorities carried binding force across jurisdictional boundaries. The typically gradual, evolutionary process by which the colonies acquired independence removed from Commonwealth courts the obligation to follow each other without depriving them of the authority to continue to draw ideas from each other; a practice that was extended, once the constraints of empire were broken, to the courts of other jurisdictions as well.

It is one thing to claim that courts have authority to refer to foreign legal experience in developing the common law and another to claim legitimacy for the practice in the more distinctively national context of constitutional adjudication.

For the purposes of considering this question it is convenient to put aside the growing number of instances in which a Constitution itself authorizes recourse to foreign law. An example of a provision that explicitly authorizes courts to 'consider foreign law' can be found in the Constitution of South Africa.[134] Significantly for present purposes, while the explicit constitutional authority is confined to the interpretation of the Bill of Rights, the practice of referring to foreign law in the course of constitutional interpretation in South Africa is familiar in relation to other parts of the Constitution as well.[135] Authority to consider external sources of law can also be inferred in relation to constitutions that prescribe the extent to which rights might be limited by law by reference to limitations that 'can be demonstrably justified in a free and democratic society'.[136]

Even in the absence of constitutional authority of these kinds, the prevalence of the practice of referring to foreign law in the course of constitutional adjudication in common law states suggests an absence of concern about legitimacy. Thus in none of the five cases identified earlier was the legitimacy of reference to foreign law an issue. The explanation

Canada, and New Zealand through the Privy Council. An affirmative answer would not conclude the question, however, given other similarities between these countries. For a veiled suggestion that citation practice also may reflect old assumptions of racial superiority, see Upendra Baxi, 'The Colonialist Heritage' in Legrand and Munday n 9 above, 46.

[133] Glenn, n 122 above, 257.

[134] Section 39(1)(c).

[135] The *Western Cape* decision illustrates the point. See also Ackermann, n 46 above, 175: 'I have not the slightest doubt that . . . the Court would have placed the same reliance on foreign law even had there been no such provision in the Constitutions'.

[136] Canadian Charter of Rights and Freedoms, section 1. See also Constitution of the Republic of South Africa, 1996, section 36(1).

lies in a combination of the pragmatism of the common law and of attitudes to both Constitutions and constitutional interpretation in most common law states. The advantages of treating law as inquiry or as a matter of reason apply no less in relation to constitutional law than to other forms of law. The extension to constitutional law of the technique whereby judges sometimes use foreign legal experience to inform their own understanding of national legal problems and solutions is encouraged by certain characteristic features of constitutions.[137] They are designed to last for lengthy periods notwithstanding changes in national circumstances, whether they in fact do so or not. Typically, as a consequence, they are written in general terms, leaving considerable discretion to the judiciary, as the final interpreter in systems that recognize judicial review. Self-evidently, they draw on a political philosophical tradition that is shared by others. Importantly, there is nothing about the conception of a Constitution in these states or about the manner of constitutional interpretation that acts as a bar to recourse to foreign constitutional experience, methodological objections apart. The evolutionary tradition of which they are part assumes a degree of constitutional evolution over time, through judicial interpretation and without formal change, although the extent to which this can properly occur is contested. Judicial techniques are adapted as necessary to the needs of constitutional adjudication, but there is no suggestion that these proscribe optional recourse to foreign legal experience.

Judicial Method

The legitimacy of judicial review itself, however, requires the judiciary to maintain a somewhat delicate balance between giving the Constitution appropriate effect through the process of adjudication and trespassing onto fields that belong to the elected branches of government. Exactly where the balance is struck varies between states. How it is struck is in large part the stuff of judicial method, on which there is greater agreement, at least at a general level. Judges are expected to act impartially; to provide public, reasoned, explanations for their decisions; and to administer justice according to law.[138] What 'law' requires for this purpose is contested. On any view, however, common law judges have considerable

[137] See also the suggestion by Aharon Barak that the approach to constitutional interpretation is itself a part of the 'common law of the system', offering another explanation of the legitimacy of appropriate use of foreign law in constitutional interpretation where foreign law can also be used in adjudicating non-constitutional cases: Barak, n 24 above, 7.

[138] A M Gleeson, 'Judicial Legitimacy' (2000) 20 *Australian Bar Review* 4.

discretion, which nevertheless is bounded by a range of presumptions and techniques emanating from the common law itself.[139]

One of the criticisms sometimes made of judicial use of foreign sources is that it alters the balance between courts and the other branches to a degree that affects the legitimacy of judicial decision-making. Broadly, the concerns are twofold. The first is that recourse to foreign legal experience expands and may serve to conceal expansion of the scope of judicial discretion beyond accepted bounds. The second is that it enables the outcome of a decision to be manipulated by unprincipled selection of foreign experience, in a manner sometimes described by the deceptively innocent term of 'cherry-picking'.[140] Thus again to quote Justice Roberts, in the course of his confirmation hearings:

> ... foreign precedent doesn't confine judges ... Domestic precedent can confine and shape the discretion of the judges. Foreign law, you can find anything you want. If you don't find it in the decisions of France or Italy, it's in the decisions of Somalia or Japan or Indonesia or wherever. As somebody said in another context, looking at foreign law for support is like looking over a crowd and picking out your friends .... And that actually expands the discretion of the judge. It allows the judge to incorporate his or her own personal preferences, cloak them with the authority of precedent ... and use that to determine the meaning of the Constitution.[141]

The charge that recourse to foreign legal experience unacceptably expands judicial discretion receives greater credence from the reality that judges often refer to foreign sources in dealing with novel cases or with cases in which previously settled national law is undergoing change. These are cases in which the discretion of a judge in any event approaches its outer limits. They are also cases that are likely to attract the most attention and, in some circumstances, controversy. Such cases must be determined, however, with or without the insights offered by comparative law. In at least some such cases, foreign experience can help to elucidate the issues and options for their resolution. It has potential to contain, rather than expand, the discretion of a judge, identifying directions that others

[139] Michael McHugh, 'The Judicial Method' (1999) 73 *Australian Law Journal* 37.

[140] Christopher McCrudden, 'A Common Law of Human Rights? Transnational Judicial Conversations on Constitutional Rights' (2000) 20 *Oxford Journal of Legal Studies* 499; Yash Ghai, 'Sentinels of Liberty or Sheep in Woolf's Clothing? Judicial Politics and the Hong Kong Bill of Rights' (1997) 60 *Modern Law Review* 459.

[141] United States Senate Judiciary Committee, Hearing on the Nomination of John Roberts to be Chief Justice of the Supreme Court, Transcript, Day Two, 13 September 2005, in response to questions from Senator Kyl, <http://www.washingtonpost.com/wp-dyn/content/article/2005/09/13/AR2005091301210.html>, viewed 24 June 2006.

have taken and enabling evaluation of their consequences, while leaving the judge free to craft a domestic solution. Emeritus Justice Laurie Ackermann has suggested further that a 'comparative legal approach' can give judges insight into their own prejudices and assist in eliminating personal preferences.[142]

The impact of the use of foreign law on judicial discretion can be explored further by reference to the five cases outlined earlier. Expansion of judicial discretion was not an issue in *Hill* or *McGinty*, in both of which foreign law was used reflectively and in neither of which did it contribute to significant doctrinal change. In *Rubinstein, Western Cape*, and *Jackson*, however, foreign law was used in circumstances capable of raising questions about judicial discretion. In *Jackson* the issue is *de minimis* in the sense that the constructive conclusion from foreign law[143] was drawn by only two of the judges and clearly represented *obiter dicta*. The conclusion heralded a significant legal development, however. Relevantly for present purposes, moreover, Lord Steyn did not consistently distinguish between the domestic and Commonwealth sources to which he referred, although the distinction is likely to be obvious enough to most of his readers.

In both *Rubinstein* and *Western Cape*, on the other hand, the manner of reference to foreign law followed a pattern that is more typical in such cases. Domestic authorities were examined first; foreign authorities were considered subsequently and were clearly identified as such. In *Western Cape*, moreover, the reasoning of the justices who considered foreign law was explicit about the purposes for which it was used and hence the weight to be accorded to it.[144] In *Rubinstein*, by contrast, there was no explicit reference to the authority of the foreign sources, leaving this to be inferred from their provenance.

If concern about the impact of comparative law on judicial discretion has any foundation at all, it can be alleviated in obvious ways. The first is by distinguishing foreign from domestic sources. In practice this is rarely a problem; the distinction is generally made by courts automatically, as part of the normal process of categorizing sources in the course of judicial reasoning.[145] The second is by more explicitly identifying the role that foreign law plays and the weight accorded to it. This is an aspect of a

[142] Ackerman, n 46 above, 192.

[143] That Parliament cannot disregard a redefinition of itself for a specific purpose: [2005] 3 WLR 733, 761.

[144] See for example Chaskalson P: 'This brief and somewhat limited survey of the law as it has developed in other countries is sufficient to show that . . . ', at [61].

[145] In some courts, of which the Supreme Court of Israel is an example, the list of cases cited also distinguishes between domestic and foreign sources.

court's reasoning that may demand particular attention where foreign law is used constructively, in a manner analogous to persuasive authority. The response need not be formulaic, however. The purpose of the reference to foreign law will generally appear readily enough from judicial reasons that are logically argued and clearly articulated, with their intelligibility in mind.

A second concern from the standpoint of judicial method is the greater potential for manipulative use of foreign law. Manipulation may occur in various ways, ranging from misstatement of the law to an unjustifiable selection of sources. It will be remembered that Justice Roberts' concern was that a judge might use foreign law 'to incorporate his or her own personal preferences'. From the standpoint of a judge seeking a more neutral application of foreign law the problem is compounded by the reality that the interests of the opposing parties lie in advancing the foreign authorities most favourable to their cause. In the absence of guidance about the appropriate selection of foreign sources,[146] their citation is not effectively controlled by reference to the obligation of barristers to 'assist the Court in the administration of justice'.[147] By contrast, all domestic authority is potentially relevant *ipso facto*; in this context, indeed, the obligation of a barrister is to 'ensure that the Court is informed of all relevant decisions . . . of which he is aware whether the effect is favourable or unfavourable towards the contention for which he argues'.[148] The extent to which this obligation applies to references to foreign sources necessarily is unclear.[149]

The selection of foreign sources in the course of constitutional adjudication is a question for both comparative and judicial method. For present purposes the principal focus is the latter. The former can be used to determine the criteria for selection, however, to assist foreign law to

[146] The *Practice Direction on the Citation of Authorities 2001* is not directed to this purpose, although its requirements might have the effect of encouraging greater attention to be paid to the purpose of referring to foreign authority and thus may indirectly affect the criteria used: <http://www.hmcourts-service.gov.uk/cms/814.htm> (viewed 11 July 2006).

[147] Code of Conduct of the Bar of England and Wales, 302: <http://www.barcouncil.org.uk/document.asp?languageid=1&documentid=2827#ParaLink> (viewed 11 July 2006).

[148] Code of Conduct of the Bar of England and Wales 710(c). Comparable obligations are recognized in common law jurisdictions elsewhere. See also *Glebe Sugar Refining Company Ltd v The Trustees of the Port and Harbour of Greenoch* [1921] Scots Reports 72.

[149] Although the *Practice Direction 2001*, n 146 above, suggests that it applies to some extent: para 4. And see also extra-judicial remarks by Lord Steyn, noting an expectation of 'a high standard of research and presentation from barristers' involving, in appropriate cases, 'comparative material from, say, Australia and New Zealand': 'The Role of the Bar, the Judge and the Jury' [1999] *Public Law* 51, 58. The rationale is also relevant for present purposes: to explore 'all available sources as to the shape of the arguments in the case being reviewed'.

contribute to a process of reasoned decision-making and to defend judicial choice, at least, from charges of 'sophistry'[150] or 'picking . . . friends'.[151] It is not possible to be prescriptive about such criteria in the abstract, because the rationale for the selection of foreign experience depends in each case on the purpose for which comparison is used. In considering the general approach that might be taken, however, it is possible to see that both a quantitative and a qualitative element may be involved.

The significance of the quantitative element depends on the claim that is made. A claim that all members of a group act in a particular way requires substantiation, whether the claim is explicit or implicit. A claim that they do not, equally obviously, requires only one, well-chosen example.[152] In broadly similar vein, a small number of examples can be used to identify alternatives to a single, powerful doctrine that is being urged upon the court, as in *Hill* and *McGinty*.[153] More difficult are cases in which a sample of jurisdictions is used to identify options as, for example, in *Western Cape*. Again, assessment of the adequacy of the selection, in quantitative terms, depends on the nuance of the argument in the particular case. Examination of each jurisdiction that meets the selection criteria, whatever they may be, generally is not necessary where the purpose is to prompt reflection, provide insight, assist to frame the question for the court, suggest options, or perform any of the multitude of functions of comparative law associated with the compendious concept of 'dialogue'. In *Western Cape* itself any residual difficulty was avoided by the relatively modest claims that were made for foreign law.[154] On the other hand, where another jurisdiction that clearly meets the selection criteria has relevant experience that runs counter to the view favoured by the court, the reasons of the court are weakened by omitting reference to this additional source. If the omission is deliberate or even clearly incautious, it is properly characterized as 'cherry-picking'. Indeed,

[150] See eg Scalia J in *Roper*: 'To invoke alien law when it agrees with one's own thinking and ignore it otherwise is not reasoned decision-making but sophistry': at 63.

[151] Transcript of hearing on the nomination of Justice John Roberts, n 112 above.

[152] See eg the critique in *Lawrence v Texas* 359 US 558 (2003) of Chief Justice Burger's references to the 'history of Western civilization and to Judeo-Christian moral and ethical standards' in *Bowers v Hardwick* 478 US 186, 196 (1986), which 'did not take account of other authorities pointing in an opposite direction': Kennedy J, for the Court.

[153] In both cases the applicants had urged US precedents. In *Hill* the Supreme Court of Canada pointed to their rejection in South Africa and Australia; in *McGinty* the High Court of Australia pointed to alternative Canadian experience. In both cases, reasons were given for preferring one course of action to another.

[154] See the judgment of Chaskalson P: 'While it seems to be accepted in most of the Commonwealth . . . ' and 'This brief and somewhat limited survey of the law as it has developed in other countries is sufficient to show . . . ' at [60], [61].

this is one context in which the obligation of counsel to refer the court to 'relevant decisions' necessarily extends to the use of foreign law.

The qualitative aspect of the selection of foreign legal experience for comparative purposes is more complex. Ran Hirschl has helpfully identified five principles of case selection that can be used for this purpose.[155] A version of his category of 'most similar cases' frequently is employed in judicial reasoning, apparently instinctively, although no doubt also on the pragmatic grounds that these are the jurisdictions with which both counsel and judges are most familiar. Importantly, they also have the advantage of lessening the challenge of comparative method.

In four of the cases used by way of illustration in this chapter, *Hill, McGinty, Western Cape*, and *Jackson*, relevant similarities in the legal systems, constitutional arrangements, and historical experiences of the jurisdictions to which reference was made suggest that the selection might be justified on the basis of similarity. The rationale for the selection of the United States, Germany, Canada, and the ECHR in *Rubinstein* is less obvious, however. As established western democracies, these four jurisdictions have enough in common to be useful to establish that there is a link between questions about the respective scope of legislative and executive power and the key constitutional principles of separation of powers, rule of law, and democracy, which was one of the purposes for which the Court used them. Given differences between the legal systems of these various jurisdictions and the design of the legislative and executive structures over which they adjudicate, however, they form a less rational group for the purpose of determining where the line is drawn in Israel between an exercise of legislative and executive power. The difficulty here overlaps with questions of comparative method and it is taken up in that context again below.

Courts do not necessarily articulate the rationale for referring to the legal experience of particular foreign jurisdictions and, by inference, for not referring to the legal experience of others. Articulated or not, however, the integrity of the judicial process requires that there be a rationale and that the conclusions drawn from foreign law are tailored to it. The more substantial a role played by foreign law in the reasoning process, the more useful it may be explicitly to state the criteria for selection on which the court relies.

[155] Ran Hirschl, 'The Question of Case Selection in Comparative Constitutional Law' (2005) 53 *American Journal of Comparative Law* 125, 133–52. His categories refer to 'most similar cases', 'most different cases', 'prototypical cases', 'most difficult cases', and 'outlier cases'.

Comparative Method

Does Comparative Method Matter?

It was argued in the preceding section that references to foreign law in constitutional adjudication complicate aspects of judicial method, requiring greater attention to be paid to the rationale for the selection of sources and care to be taken in the manner in which they are used and in the weight accorded to them.

The question in this section is whether there are other methodological demands that references to foreign law place on courts that might compendiously be attributed to comparative method. The challenge of comparative method may involve no more than getting the foreign legal experience right: a task that by definition is more complex in relation to foreign than to domestic law. But comparative method may involve broader factors as well, directed to ensuring that the comparison is apt and that the conclusions drawn from it are reliable.

Given the kinds of use often made of foreign law in constitutional adjudication it may be possible to argue that comparative method is relatively unimportant. If foreign legal experience is merely a general reservoir of ideas on which a judge draws during one or more phases of the adjudicative process for aid in reaching an essentially domestic solution, does it matter whether the foreign experience itself is fully understood? Does it matter whether a foreign practice or doctrine is still in use in its country of origin? Does it matter whether the source of the idea is a dissenting judgment or a decision that subsequently was overturned on appeal?

The answer to these questions necessarily depends in part on the particular use that is made of foreign law. In principle, however, both the quality of the reasons of a court and the advantages of referring to foreign law are enhanced by paying appropriate regard to these methodological questions.[156] Common law judicial method calls for reasoned judgment, which also serves to underpin the legitimacy of the judicial function at the higher appellate levels where the courts exercise considerable discretion in developing the law and where the potential for conflict with other branches is at its height. The quality of judicial reasoning arguably is more important, rather than less, in relation to the use of foreign law. This is

[156] Jackson, n 5 above, 125: '... the persuasive value of a foreign source will depend on ... the comparability of contexts ...'. But see also at 126: 'Determining comparability is a serious challenge ...'.

both because the practice of referring to foreign legal experience draws on a conception of judge-made law as an outcome of a reasoning process and because the usual safeguards of the adversary system are weakened in relation to foreign law.[157] Adequate attention to methodology may deflect criticism on legitimacy grounds.[158] Failure to pay due regard to comparative method, on the other hand, may unnecessarily expose a court's reasoning to criticism, inhibiting the utility of the reference to foreign law and, in extreme cases, reducing it to a rhetorical device.

If this is correct, the question that remains is what comparative method requires in the context of constitutional adjudication. A useful starting point is the insight that might be derived from comparative private law, where a vigorous debate on methodological issues has for some time been under way.

Insights from Comparative Private Law

The discipline of comparative law, with its almost exclusive focus on private law,[159] has a long history spanning the entire twentieth century.[160] Comparative scholars endorse the value of comparative law as offering 'a greater variety of solutions than could be thought up in a lifetime by even the most imaginative jurist who was corralled in his own system'.[161] But comparative law scholarship warns also of the difficulties inherent in drawing conclusions from the legal experience of different national jurisdictions. Every legal phenomenon forms part of a larger legal system; form and practical operation may differ; both, but in particular the latter, may be affected by the legal, political, economic, social, or cultural context in which the phenomenon is found; change, presently driven by the contradictory influences of localization and globalization, is likely over time;[162] and there are internal perspectives on legal systems, including assumptions and beliefs that insiders take for granted,[163] which outside observers will find it difficult, if not impossible, to fully grasp.

[157] Although cf Jackson, n 5 above, 126 noting that the deficiency may in part be supplied by other members of a multi-member court.

[158] See eg Young, n 5 above, 152: 'The hallmark of persuasive authority is engagement with the *reasons* for a practice or a decision rather than the counting of noses' (emphasis in original).

[159] K Zweigert and H Kotz, *An Introduction to Comparative Law* (3rd edn) (Oxford: Oxford University Press, 1998), 3, referring to 'comparative private law, the heartland of all comparative law'.

[160] ibid 2–3.

[161] ibid 15.

[162] Roderick Munday, 'Accounting for an Encounter' in Legrand and Munday n 19 above, 3, 20.

[163] James Whitman, 'The Neo-romantic Turn', in Legrand and Munday, n 162 above, 312, 315.

One influential solution to the difficulties of comparative law was, and to a lesser degree remains, the analytical technique of functionalism. Functionalism seeks to meet the reality that 'similar institutions can fulfil different functions in different societies . . . and . . . that similar functional needs can be fulfilled by different institutions'.[164] It thus takes function as the common or shared element between jurisdictions, comparing different ways in which similar functions are achieved. It claims the advantages of neutrality in pursuing the comparative project[165] and presents itself as a particularly useful technique for comparison between different systems of law.[166]

Functionalism necessarily assumes that legal systems perform functions that are sufficiently similar and sufficiently discrete to be used for comparative purposes in this way. In recent years these and other features of it have been the focus of criticism in the face of what has been termed the new critical comparative law.[167] Some of the criticisms have been directed at the claimed advantages of functionalism questioning, for example, its neutrality[168] and the utility for many comparative purposes of the very notion of functional equivalence, which chooses one function to the exclusion of others.[169] Other criticisms are directed at the assumptions of functionalism, with their seemingly universalist tendencies, suggested by the dependence of this methodological approach on the similarity of problems and its correspondingly weaker emphasis on other aspects of contextual difference. By contrast, some of the new theoretical approaches focus on difference, emphasizing and prioritizing the depth of diversity between legal systems for which functionalism cannot fully account.[170] Suspicion of functionalism is fuelled by observations by leading functionalist scholars that comparative law provides a means for identifying 'which solution of a problem is the best' and for 'the international unification of law'.[171]

[164] Ralf Michaels, 'The Functional Method of Comparative Law', 20, <http://eprints.law.duke.edu/archive/00001249/01/Functional_Method.pdf>, forthcoming in Mathias Reimann and Reinhard Zimmerman (eds), *The Oxford Handbook of Comparative Law* (Oxford:Oxford University Press).

[165] Zweigert and Kotz, n 159, 35.

[166] Michaels, n 164 above, 21: '. . . functionalist comparison should be able to overcome the epistemic/doctrinal difference between civil and common law by ignoring it as irrelevant'. See also Zweigert and Kotz, n 159, 37 ' . . . the Common Law, with its inductive and makeshift habits, produces low-level legal institutions specially adapted to solve particular concrete problems'.

[167] Orucu, n 19 above, 215.

[168] Michaels, n 164 above, 27.

[169] ibid 34.

[170] Legrand and Munday, n 19 above; Mark Van Hoecke (ed), *Epistemology and Methodology of Comparative Law* (Oxford: Hart, 2004); William Ewald, 'Comparative Jurisprudence (1): What Was It Like to Try a Rat?' 143 (1994–5) *University of Pennsylvania Law Review* 1889.

[171] Zweigert and Kotz, n 159, 8, 24.

The debate on methodology in comparative law is somewhat self-absorbed, but it has done a service to the discipline, challenging old ideas and encouraging new ones. For the most part, however, it has had relatively little impact on comparative constitutional law.[172] One reason for the gulf between the two branches of the discipline lies in the assumption about the desirability of the convergence of comparative private law, which was associated with functionalism, and which was deemed to be inapplicable to public law. Whether either assumption necessarily is correct is presently beside the point. Rejection of convergence as an ideal by the new critical approaches to comparative law in one sense offers a means for bridging this version of the public/private divide. At the same time, however, the new emphasis on diversity and on the difficulty of adequately understanding the other further complicates the methodological challenge for comparing constitutions, with their deep roots in history and political practice.

Comparative Method and Constitutional Law

Two questions in particular are raised by this brief survey of the debate on methodology in comparative private law for the comparative methodology of courts that refer to foreign law in the course of constitutional adjudication. The first is the applicability of functionalism. The second is the relevance of difference, including the extent to which contextual difference must be explored in drawing conclusions from foreign experience for domestic constitutional purposes.

Consideration of the function of particular legal phenomena is a useful tool in comparative constitutional law, as in other branches of comparative law. Arguably, for example, it informed the decision of the Supreme Court of Canada in *Hill* not to adopt the United States standard of actual malice for the purposes of defamation law. Cory J, for the Court, noted that the standard adopted in *New York Times v Sullivan* sought to protect the freedom of the press from attempts to inhibit it through defamation suits at a time when passions about desegregation ran high while 'a review of jury verdicts in Canada reveals that there is no danger of numerous large awards threatening the viability of media organisations'.[173] Function is not explicitly considered, however, and the reasoning of the Court might equally be understood as taking the social, political, historical, and legal context in which *Sullivan* was decided into account.

172 For an exception see Mark Tushnet's treatment of functionalism at n 115 above, 1225.

173 At 1181, 1188.

The usefulness of functionalism for the purposes of constitutional adjudication is limited, however, by the generality of some of the key functions that might be considered to be similar across jurisdictions in constitutional law. It can be assumed for the purposes of argument, albeit at the cost of ignoring important differences in detail,[174] that all western constitutional systems provide for the performance of broadly similar functions in terms of, for example, limiting the potential for abuse of power by distributing power between different branches of government; securing a rule of law; enabling democracy; and protecting human rights. At this level, however, the function is too general to provide the basis for a comparison that is likely to assist with most of the questions likely to come before a court. Different constitutional systems perform these functions in a multitude of different ways, through institutions and principles that in many cases have developed organically over time, which complement and compensate for each other.

The difficulty is illustrated by *Rubinstein*. On one view, the reasoning of the Supreme Court of Israel might be understood as a form of functional comparison, using separation of powers, the rule of law, and democracy as the functions that are common to all the jurisdictions to which the court referred. But the mixture of institutions and principles through which such purposes are served in the United States, Germany, and Canada respectively is too diverse to enable the point at which the line between legislative and executive power should be drawn in Israel to be readily elucidated by functional comparison at this level, in the way that the Court sought to do.[175] In this instance, comparative method required closer attention to be paid to the structural logic of the constitutional systems to which the Court referred to determine whether there were other relevant differences between them that would affect the conclusions that the Court drew from the comparison.

Justice Breyer's opinion in *Printz*[176] provides another possible example of a functional analysis with less than satisfactory results. The judge

[174] Thus in *McGinty* the High Court accepted the view of successive Canadian courts that there are differences between the 'evolutionary' democracy of Canada and Australia and the democratic arrangements born of revolution in the United States: eg Gummow J, (1995) 186 CLR 140, 287–8. The explanation may be contested; the reality of difference nevertheless remains.

[175] See eg the argument at [23], in which the Court uses decisions of the Canadian Supreme Court pursuant to the Canadian Charter of Rights and Freedoms to establish the link between human rights protection, democracy, and the notion that rights can only be limited by law; but also, less persuasively, uses the Canadian and other decisions taken pursuant to codified rights instruments to establish that the 'fundamental criteria' for administrative arrangements must be established by legislation.

[176] *Printz v United States* 521 US 898, 976–7 (1997).

identified as a 'common legal problem' the challenge of 'reconciling central authority with the need to preserve the liberty enhancing autonomy of a smaller constituent governmental entity'.[177] On this basis he turned to the federal-type arrangements of Switzerland, Germany, and the European Union to cast 'empirical light' on the consequences of tackling the problem by providing that 'constituent states, not federal bureaucracies, will themselves implement many of the laws, rules, regulations, or decrees' of the central authority. He used the comparison to support his view that the United States Constitution did not preclude the assignment of federal duties to State officials. In doing so, he acknowledged the possibility of 'relevant political and structural differences' between the American and European federations, but did not pursue them. Failure to do so diminished the force of the comparison. The horizontal division of powers is a systemic feature of European federations, supported by a range of institutions, principles, and practices directed to making the system work smoothly and to safeguarding the position of both the centre and the constituent units. These additional features also required consideration to determine whether the comparison was apt.

A second issue raised by consideration of the debate within comparative private law is the relevance of context. The textual and structural setting for the foreign legal experience on which the court draws are almost always relevant. Thus in *Jackson*, Lord Steyn's omission of any acknowledgement of the difference in the conception of sovereignty between the United Kingdom and its former dominions weakened the integrity of his argument; and also denied him the opportunity to use dominion experience reflectively, to evaluate the conception of sovereignty that so far has prevailed in the United Kingdom. For the most part, however, the essentially legal dimensions of context are taken adequately into account by courts, applying their customary legal techniques. A more difficult question is whether and when courts should take into account other dimensions of the context that might affect a more complete understanding of the foreign experience.

The somewhat unsatisfying answer must be that it depends on the circumstances including, in particular, the use that is made of foreign law. Where a court is urged to adopt a new rule, drawing on a foreign source, deeper consideration of context may be appropriate. Indeed, this occurred in *Hill*, where the Supreme Court of Canada considered both the socio-political context in which *New York Times v Sullivan* was decided and the practical consequences in the United States of adoption of the actual

[177] Ibid.

malice standard in deciding that it should not be applied in Canada. On the other hand, where foreign law is invoked less directly, as an aid to a court in developing its own view of the law, deep contextual inquiry may be less important. Thus in *Western Cape* foreign experience was used to identify a range of approaches that had been taken in other jurisdictions in order to identify any constitutional limits on the extent to which legislative power could be delegated to the executive branch. In evaluating these varying approaches, Chaskalson P took into account both structural differences in the systems of government of the several jurisdictions[178] and historical differences[179] that might account for some of the choices that had been made. The Court did not go further, however, to examine, for example, whether in any of these jurisdictions there were non-legal mechanisms by which excessive delegation might be controlled. In the circumstances, it was not necessary to do so. Foreign law had served its purpose of prompting reflection on the answer that the South African Court should give to the necessarily doctrinal question that was before it, which would be responsive to 'the language of the Constitution, construed in the light of the country's own history'.[180]

No doubt there is more to be said about comparative method in constitutional adjudication, both generally and in relation to these cases. Tentative conclusions nevertheless might be drawn as follows. First, counsel, judges, and constitutional scholars should at least be aware of the methodological issue. Secondly, courts should avoid what Justice Kate O'Regan has referred to as 'shallow comparativism'.[181] Thirdly, what amounts to shallow comparativism will depend on the use that is made of foreign legal experience, in addition to other factors. Where the role played by reference to foreign experience is not insubstantial, the appropriate method is likely to involve at least an accurate and up-to-date account of the foreign experience; sufficient contextual understanding of the foreign experience to enable it to be adequately evaluated for the purpose for which it is used; and an explanation of where the comparison sits in the reasoning of the Court, to enable others to learn from it and to evaluate it. Fourthly, however, on the other hand, O'Regan J's warning against excessive methodological demands also is relevant here: 'To forbid

[178] These included, importantly, the distinction between a presidential and a parliamentary system, the significance of which ultimately was dismissed by Chaskalson P for instant purposes: at 31.

[179] In particular, the continuing influence in many Commonwealth countries of the UK approach to the delegation of legislative power, forged in the context of parliamentary, as opposed to constitutional, supremacy: at 29–37.

[180] At 36.

[181] *N K v Minister of Safety & Security* 2005 (6) SA 419 (CC), 24–5.

any comparative review because of [the risks associated with comparative method] would be to deprive our legal system of the benefits of the learning and wisdom to be found in other jurisdictions'.[182]

Conclusion

In general terms, the response to the question raised in the title of the chapter may be summarized as follows.

In constitutional adjudication in common law states, necessarily excepting the United States, no problem of legitimacy is raised by the mere fact of reference to foreign legal experience of either a constructive or reflective kind. On the contrary, the practice is accepted as a valuable one that enables national constitutional systems to draw on a wider pool of experience and ideas without compromising their constitutional autonomy or their capacity for national self-development.

The methodology that courts employ for the purpose is potentially more problematic, however. The demands of method should not be exaggerated, given the nature of the uses typically made of foreign legal experience. On the other hand, as an often significant dimension of the reasoning of a court, the method employed in drawing on foreign sources must sustain the conclusions that are drawn. For the most part courts have handled these requirements instinctively in the past with results that, judging by the small sample of cases used here, are often reasonable but sometimes patchy. In this first decade of the twenty-first century, however, there is a range of reasons why references to foreign law in constitutional cases might begin to attract closer, and not necessarily friendly, scrutiny. These include the continuing fall-out of the debate on the use of foreign law in the United States; the impact of the new emphasis on difference in comparative private law; the growing nationalism that is a sign of the times, whether as a reaction against increasingly heterogeneous communities, threats of terrorism or globalization; and the mounting hostility of governments to what they perceive as judicial activism.

It has been argued in this chapter that this aspect of the constitutional adjudicative process deserves more conscious attention, in both the formulation and the articulation of reasons by courts. In essence, what is required is adherence to the familiar legal standards of accuracy, relevance, and justifiability, applied to the somewhat different circumstances of the use of foreign law. Often, a court can draw its conclusions by reference to

[182] Ibid.

legal context, including constitutional history and structure. In some cases, however, it is necessary to inquire further into the wider context from which the foreign experience emerged and within which it presently functions. Whether and when this is so will vary between cases, by reference to the purpose of the reference to foreign law.

One final complication is that the field necessarily is changing. The principal catalysts for change are supranational and international law and the forces of globalization. These both manifest and further encourage convergence of the broad conceptual foundations on which constitutions are based. If the process extends further into doctrine and institutional design it will force corresponding adjustment to comparative constitutional method.

Law and Order—A 20:20 Vision

Robert Reiner

Introduction—Law and Order 1984–2020

Twenty-one years ago Michael Freeman gave a *Current Legal Problems* lecture called 'Law and Order in 1984'.[1] It was an impressively knowledgeable and accurate analysis of the rise of law and order politics in Britain in the run-up to the 1979 Conservative Party victory under Margaret Thatcher, and in the early years of her government. It detailed the truncheon-rattling rhetoric of the 'New Right', and the Thatcher government's budget bonanzas for expenditure on policing and prisons at the same time as it culled social spending. It offered a detailed analysis of the Police and Criminal Evidence Act 1984,[2] depicting it as 'the cornerstone of contemporary "law and order" politics'.[3] There was discussion of the restrictions on the powers of trade unions, new public order legislation, expanded powers against terrorism, tougher penal policy, and a transformation of policing towards a more proactive social control style based on information-led surveillance and targeting. Freeman concluded that the law and order policies of the New Right threatened our liberties and set us in the direction of George Orwell's dystopian *1984*. He ended with a call to 'fight against current law and order policies', in favour of more socially just ones that paid at least equal attention to the crimes of the powerful as they did to the crimes of the powerless.[4]

Freeman's paper was and is a state-of-the-art representation of liberal and Left thinking about law and order in the early 1980s. But it now reads nostalgically as a memento of a bygone age of comparative innocence. Inspired by Orwell's dystopian vision, it nonetheless failed to anticipate the enormity of the crime and control changes, and broader social transformation, that were to come. This is not a criticism of Freeman's failure to acquire the mantle of 'Mystic Michael'. No analyses at the time provided any inkling of how profoundly the whole context for

[1] M Freeman, 'Law and Order in 1984' (1984) *Current Legal Problems* 175–231.
[2] Hereafter 'PACE'. [3] Freeman, n 1 above. [4] ibid 220.

discussions of crime and criminal justice was to change over the last two decades of the twentieth century.

The vision of 2020 I am going to offer is an even more pessimistic one, with only the most tenuous prospect of amelioration. It is based on a reading of current trends, but I very much hope that it will be refuted by events and turn out to be myopic rather than 20:20 vision. The account I will give examines six issues: (1) the rise of law and order politics; (2) what is crime?; (3) what has actually happened to crime trends?; (4) the development of contemporary crime control policies; (5) the explanation of trends in crime; and (6) how to explain and assess the new punitiveness in crime control policies? It will then conclude with a discussion of possible futures.

The Rise of Law and Order Politics

Until the late 1960s criminal justice policy had not been a partisan policy issue, at least since the early nineteenth century. According to Downes and Morgan's definitive study it did not feature in any political party's election manifesto between the Second World War and 1970.[5] Nor was crime an important issue to the public until the 1970s, at least as registered by opinion polls, although it has been a favourite theme in all branches of popular entertainment for centuries.[6] Some specific aspects of criminal justice policy were politically controversial, notably capital punishment, and competing penal policy lobbies campaigned vigorously.[7] Particularly spectacular or salacious crimes have always been regular topics of popular fascination, part of a perennial tendency for middle-aged, respectable opinion to bewail the supposedly declining moral standards of young people, which seemed to sag in line with the belts of the lamenters.[8] But the overall state of crime was not a widespread cause of concern, nor was criminal justice policy subject to political controversy and conflict. For example, the publication of new crime statistics, which

[5] D Downes and R Morgan, 'The Skeletons in the Cupboard: The Politics of Law and Order at the Turn of the Millennium' in M Maguire, R Morgan, and R Reiner (eds), *The Oxford Handbook of Criminology* (3rd edn) (Oxford: Oxford University Press, 2002).

[6] R Reiner, 'Media Made Criminality: The Representation of Crime in the Mass Media' in Maguire *et al*, ibid.

[7] M Ryan, *The Acceptable Pressure Group* (Farnborough: Saxon House, 1978); M Ryan, *The Politics of Penal Reform* (London: Longman, 1983); T Morris, *Crime and Criminal Justice in Britain since 1945* (Oxford: Blackwell, 1989).

[8] G Pearson, *Hooligan* (London: Macmillan, 1983).

now are regularly a stimulus to 'shock-horror' news headlines, only began to feature in newspaper reports in the 1970s, and then in a minor way.[9]

'Law and order' had first become politicized in the USA in the 1960s.[10] 'Law and order' itself is an old phrase, traditionally invoked as if it represented some unproblematic, linked perfect partnership, like Laurel and Hardy or 'bangers and mash'. But as it came to be used as a political slogan it became impregnated with controversial meanings. Classical social theory of all kinds had been explicitly or implicitly sceptical about the law playing a significant part in social order.[11] Order was the product of complex processes of social interdependence and informal control,[12] or of ruling class interests,[13] or of different types of power and authority.[14] The law was the expression or product of order, not its source.

Like much of the current dominant Right-wing policies that prevail in the USA today, the law and order trail was blazed by Barry Goldwater in his abortive but prophetic Presidential bid in 1964. In the hands of the political Right, the demand for law and order condensed a number of specific meanings—above all, that law could and should produce order—but that it failed to do so because of weak formulation and enforcement. Law's purpose was crime control, but it was shackled by excessive due process restraints.[15] The law and its front-line troops, the police, should be unleashed to restore order. Law and order became a successful campaigning slogan for Richard Nixon in his 1968 election victory, becoming a codeword for race, culture, and generational backlash. As we now know Nixon, Spiro Agnew, and the rest of the elite Republican cadre

[9] R Reiner, S Livingstone, and J Allen, 'From Law and Order to Lynch Mobs: Crime News since the Second World War' in P Mason (ed), *Criminal Visions* (Cullompton: Willan, 2003), 25–6.

[10] K Beckett, *Making Crime Pay* (New York: Oxford University Press, 1997), ch 3.

[11] R Reiner, 'Classical Social Theory and Law' in J Penner, D Schiff, and R Nobles (eds) *Jurisprudence* (London: Butterworths, 2002).

[12] E Durkheim, *The Division of Labour in Society* (Glencoe: Free Press, 1973).

[13] K Marx, *Capital Vol 1* (London: Penguin, 1976), ch 10.

[14] M Weber, *Economy and Society Vol 1* (Berkeley: University of California Press, 1978), 217–20.

[15] The distinction between 'crime control' and 'due process' models of criminal justice was suggested by H Packer, *The Limits of the Criminal Sanction* (Stanford, Calif: Stanford University Press, 1968). For discussion of whether these values do conflict see D McBarnet, *Conviction* (London: Macmillan, 1981); M McConville, A Sanders, and R Leng, *The Case for the Prosecution* (London: Routledge, 1991); D Smith, 'Case Construction and the Goals of the Criminal Process' (1997) 37(3) *British Journal of Criminology* 319; M McConville, A Sanders, and R Leng, 'Descriptive or Critical Sociology?' (1997) 37(3) *British Journal of Criminology* 347; D Smith, 'Reform or Moral Outrage?' (1998) 38(4) *British Journal of Criminology* 616; A Ashworth and M Redmayne, *The Criminal Process* (3rd edn) (Oxford: Oxford University Press, 2005); A Sanders and R Young, *Criminal Justice* (3rd edn) (London: Butterworths, 2006).

of 1968 knew what they were talking about in relation to law and order, mostly ending up on the wrong side of the bars a few years later.

The politicization of law and order was heralded in Britain in the 1970 General Election, when the Conservative Party manifesto said that 'the Labour Government cannot entirely shrug off responsibility' for rising 'crime and violence'.[16] It also linked crime with industrial disputes as instances of 'the age of demonstration and disruption'.[17] The Labour manifesto replied by attacking the Conservatives' attempt 'to exploit for Party political ends the issue of crime and law enforcement'.[18]

It was under Margaret Thatcher's leadership of the Conservative Party that the politicization of law and order really accelerated. During the late 1970s, in the build-up to her election victory in 1979, Mrs Thatcher blamed the Labour government directly for rising crime and disorder, pledging a 'ring of steel' to protect people against lawlessness. She promised to boost the resources and powers of the police to prevent and clear up crime, and to sharply toughen penal policy, reversing the softness on crime that was attributed to Labour. The Tories' law and order campaign was greatly helped by the emergence of the police as a political lobby, backing up the Conservative's agenda in a series of advertisements and speeches.[19] The issue was a major factor in Thatcher's 1979 election victory, according to polls monitoring the shifts in public opinion.[20] The police were directly rewarded for their open support when the Conservatives implemented in full a recommended pay rise as one of their first acts in office.

The party political gulf on law and order reached its widest point in the mid-1980s. The key conflicts were over the policing of the urban disorders and of the Miners' Strike of 1984–5—both results of the economic and social dislocation engendered by the Thatcher government's monetarist policies—the Police and Criminal Evidence Act 1984, and the campaigns for democratic police accountability. On all these issues Labour took a civil libertarian stance, attacking the Conservative government for violating the principles of the rule of law. Labour also attacked Conservative law and order policies for being counter-productive in increasing social divisions, and aggravating rather than reforming the

[16] Downes and Morgan, n 5 above, 288. [17] ibid. [18] ibid 289.

[19] R Reiner, 'Fuzzy Thoughts: The Police and Law and Order Politics' (1980) 28(2) *Sociological Review* 377; E McLaughlin and K Murji, 'Resistance through Representation: "Storylines", Advertising and Police Federation Campaigns' (1998) 8(4) *Policing and Society* 367; I Loader and A Mulcahy, *Policing and the Condition of England* (Oxford: Oxford University Press, 2003), ch 7.

[20] D Butler and D Kavanagh, *The British General Election 1979* (London: Macmillan, 1980), 163.

root causes of crime in social inequality and relative deprivation. Whilst this position may have had the support of the majority of criminologists, it was an electoral liability for Labour. In the 1984 and 1987 General Elections the Tories attacked Labour for being 'soft' on crime because of its concerns about civil liberties, 'permissiveness', links with trade unionism—associated with disorder—and failure to develop any short-term solutions to bolster public protection.

In the late 1980s signs appeared of a new cross-party consensus on law and order. The Conservatives began to offer a more nuanced approach, perhaps because of the apparent failure of toughness to stem rising crime. They began to emphasize crime prevention, proportionality in penal policy, and value-for-money—a major Thatcherite theme. The new tack culminated in the 1991 Criminal Justice Act. For its part, Labour began to try and repair some of the 'soft' law and order image that the Tories had successfully foisted on them, culminating in Tony Blair's legendary 1993 soundbite, 'tough on crime, tough on the causes of crime'.[21] This finely balanced the new realist recognition that crime really was a problem that needed short-run policies not just reliance on long-run reform, with a more traditional social democratic criminological concern with 'causes'. But the main departure was rhetorical: the double whammy of toughness packed into one short, sharp sentence.

Since 1993 there has developed a new 'second order' consensus on the fundamentals of law and order policy[22]—toughness, toughness, toughness—with frenzied partisan conflict on specifics—anything you can do, I can do tougher. Law and order politics has become a dominant discourse of the age: the 'culture of control'.[23] The reasons for this will be considered below.

What is Crime?

Crime and its control have become central concerns in public and political debate. The term 'crime' is usually tossed about as if its meaning is clear and unproblematic, yet many if not most arguments about it involve people talking past each other, with fundamentally different issues in mind.[24] At least the following five different constructions of crime and

[21] T Blair, 'Why Crime is a Socialist Issue' (1993) 29(12) *New Statesman* 27.

[22] D Downes and R Morgan, n 5 above, 287.

[23] D Garland, *The Culture of Control* (Oxford: Oxford University Press, 2001).

[24] S Henry and M Lanier (eds), *What is Crime?* (Lanham, Md: Rowman and Littlefield, 2001); N Lacey, C Wells, and O Quick, *Reconstructing Criminal Law* (3rd edn) (London:

the criminal can be distinguished, each itself signifying a complex web of concepts, practices, and values.

Legal Constructions

As Nicola Lacey has remarked, to 'anyone other than a specialist, the proposition that the intellectual concerns of criminology are intimately connected with those of criminal law would probably seem obvious to the point of banality'.[25] Probably most people would, if asked to define 'crime', invoke the criminal law as its basis. Yet there is considerable variation between legal and other social constructions of crime. There is also 'an enormous diversity among criminal laws: in terms of the style of their drafting; their scope; their construction of their subjects and objects; their assumptions about responsibility; their procedural requirements'.[26] Defining the scope of criminal law in substantive rather than formal or procedural ways is notoriously problematic because of the multitude of different kinds of function and character apparent in the vast, rapidly growing and shifting corpus of criminal law.[27]

Consequently, most criminal law texts define crime in a positivist, formal, and essentially circular way, following the arguments advanced fifty years ago in a celebrated *Current Legal Problems* lecture by Glanville Williams: 'crime is an act capable of being followed by criminal proceedings having a criminal outcome, and a proceeding or its outcome is criminal if it has certain characteristics which mark it as criminal'.[28] Article 6 of the European Convention for the Protection of Human Rights[29] on the right to a fair trial sets out various specific rights for those facing 'any criminal charge', notably the presumption of innocence, and adequate legal assistance with the preparation of a defence. There are further due process requirements specifically for criminal cases in Article 7

Lexis-Nexis, 2003), ch 1; L Zedner, *Criminal Justice* (Oxford: Oxford University Press, 2004), chs 1–2; P Hillyard, C Pantazis, S Tombs, and D Gordon (eds), *Beyond Criminology* (London: Pluto, 2004); W Morrison, 'What is Crime?' in C Hale, K Hayward, A Wahidin, and E Wincup (eds), *Criminology* (Oxford: Oxford University Press, 2005), are some recent discussions of the problems of defining crime.

[25] N Lacey, 'Legal Constructions of Crime' in Maguire *et al*, n 5 above, 264.

[26] ibid 281.

[27] L Farmer, 'The Obsession with Definition' (1996) 5(1) *Social and Legal Studies* 57; A Ashworth, 'Is the Criminal Law a Lost Cause?' (2000) 116(2) *Law Quarterly Review* 225; Lacey *et al*, n 24 above, 1–15; P Ramsay 'The Responsible Subject as Citizen: Criminal Law, Democracy and the Welfare State' (2006) 69(1) *Modern Law Review* 29.

[28] G Williams, 'The Definition of Crime' (1955) *Current Legal Problems* 107.

[29] Hereafter 'ECHR'.

and several Protocols. This has resulted in extensive ECHR jurisprudence on delineating the criminal/civil borderline.[30]

The leading case is *Engel*, [31] in which the Court formulated three criteria for determining whether proceedings are 'criminal'. These are: (i) the domestic classification of the offence; (ii) 'the very nature of the offence'; and (iii) the seriousness of the potential punishment. The ECHR has maintained an 'autonomous' definition of 'criminal', to ensure states cannot deny the rights necessary for a criminal trial by redefining the offence, so criterion (i) is asymmetric: an offence is criminal if it is so defined in domestic law, but it may also be held to be criminal even if not defined as such by a particular country. The second criterion, the substance of the offence, has not produced analysis of the principles characterizing behaviour as criminal. Rather, it has involved a set of essentially procedural issues: is there a punitive element to the sanction? Is the offence generally binding or restricted to a specific sub-group? Does the verdict require finding culpability? Are proceedings instituted by a public body? How are such matters defined in other jurisdictions? In most cases the third criterion, the severity of potential punishment, has proved decisive.[32] The ECHR case-law delineates the criminal/civil borderline in essentially formal and procedural terms, and does not offer a substantive theory of the nature of crime.

The issue of legal definitions of crime has become even more complex with the rise of hybrid offences whereby criminal sanctions attach to breach of orders that are initially determined by civil processes. The most significant of these is the Anti-Social Behaviour Order[33] that section 1 of the Crime and Disorder Act 1998 enables a magistrates' court to make in civil proceedings. Breach of this Order without reasonable excuse can attract a penalty of up to five years' imprisonment on indictment.[34] The ECHR principles outlined above would seem to suggest that this potentially severe penalty should make the proceedings as a whole, including the initial imposition of the Order, 'criminal', but against this the House of Lords has held that an ASBO is preventive not punitive in purpose.[35]

[30] These are reviewed in detail in B Emmerson and A Ashworth, *Human Rights and Criminal Justice* (London: Sweet and Maxwell, 2001), ch 4; S Treschel, *Human Rights in Criminal Proceedings* (Oxford: Oxford University Press, 2005), ch 2.

[31] *Engel v Netherlands* (1979–80) 1 European Human Rights Reports 647.

[32] Emmerson and Ashworth, n 30 above, 151–2.

[33] Hereafter 'ASBO'.

[34] A Ashworth, 'Social Control and "Anti-Social Behaviour": The Subversion of Human Rights' (2004) 120(2) *Law Quarterly Review* 263); P Ramsay, 'What is Anti-Social Behaviour?' (2004) *Criminal Law Review* 908.

[35] *Clingham v Royal Borough of Kensington and Chelsea; R v Crown Court at Manchester ex p McCann and others* [2003] 1 AC 787. For discussion, see S Macdonald, 'The Nature of the Anti-Social Behaviour Order' (2003) 66(4) *Modern Law Review* 630.

The imposition of an ASBO thus represents 'a position mid-way between the civil and the criminal paradigms',[36] in that the Lords have held it requires the criminal standard of proof because of the potential severity of penalties, but with the more relaxed civil rules of evidence, including hearsay. ASBOs have been controversial as an extension of criminal sanctions to vaguely defined behaviour, requiring judgements of value about what is 'reasonable' in specific contexts that are likely to vary according to the social position of the defendant,[37] and subject to procedures less rigorous than the criminal.

Andrew Ashworth has recently suggested that we can 'identify a principled core of criminal law',[38] comprising 'four interlinked principles'. The last three of these are procedural: equal treatment and proportionality in enforcement, the human rights protections of Article 6 of the ECHR for suspects, and proportionality in sentencing. The first, however, proposes a fundamental principle to delineate the ambit of criminal law: 'the criminal law should be used, and only used, to censure persons for substantial wrongdoing'. This claim certainly has bite and substance. For example, it would rule out the penchant of governments for hybrid offences like the ASBO, or the plethora of 'administrative offences' with diluted culpability requirements. However, it clearly raises the issue of whether there is or can be agreement on what constitutes culpable 'substantial wrongdoing', and Ashworth's explicit purpose is 'to re-kindle debate about the functions and characteristics that the criminal law ought to have'[39] if criminal law is to have principled coherence and integrity. As Tadros and Tierney argue, despite recent theoretical advances, 'fully coherent and well defended principles that could be used to identify and distinguish wrongs are yet to emerge, let alone principles that might govern incorporation of those distinctions into the criminal law'.[40]

This implicitly leaves to social scientists, historians, philosophers, and people on Clapham omnibuses, the task of explaining and evaluating its substantive scope. Some critical theorists of criminal law have sought to transcend this divide,[41] analysing the processes of criminalization 'as a set of interlocking practices in which the moments of "defining" and

[36] A Ashworth, n 34 above, 277. [37] Ramsay, n 34 above, 918.

[38] Ashworth, n 27 above, 253. [39] ibid 256.

[40] V Tadros and S Tierney, 'The Presumption of Innocence and the Human Rights Act' (2004) 67(3) *Modern Law Review* 411.

[41] D Nelken, 'Critical Criminal Law' (1987) 14(1) *Journal of Law and Society* 105; I Dennis (ed), *Criminal Law and Justice* (London: Sweet and Maxwell, 1987); I Loveland (ed), *Frontiers of Criminality* (London: Sweet and Maxwell, 1995); A Norrie, *Crime, Reason and History* (2nd edn) (London: Butterworths, 2001).

"responding to" crime can rarely be completely distinguished and in which legal and social extra-legal constructions of crime constantly interact'.[42] This points to the variety of alternative, often conflicting, conceptions of crime apart from, and often in conflict with, the legal.

Normative Constructions

Positivist or formalist legal definitions of crime open themselves to normative critique. Does criminal law proscribe and sanction behaviours that ought not to be punished, because they are acceptable or desirable, or even if regarded as wrong, because criminalization is for a variety of possible reasons not regarded as the appropriate means of control? Conversely, the scope of criminal law can be criticized normatively for failing to include behaviours that should be proscribed and punished.

There are many jurisprudential and criminological debates about the normative limits of criminal law. Perhaps the most familiar argument about alleged over-reach of criminal law is the claim from liberal political philosophy that 'private [im]moral behaviour' should not be subject to criminal law, for both principled and pragmatic reasons, the subject of the famous 'debates' between Mill and Fitzjames Stephen, and Hart and Devlin.[43] On the other hand, critical criminologists have frequently argued that criminal law fails to define as criminal very serious and wilful harm committed by the powerful, states, and corporations.[44] This has developed into the recent claim that criminology should be replaced by 'zemiology', the study of serious culpable harms, rendering as problematic whether or not they are proscribed by criminal law.[45] The definition of 'harms' is, of course, as socially contentious as notions of 'crime', but it explicitly involves normative evaluation, not authoritative declaration.

42 Lacey, n 25 above, 282.

43 J S Mill, *On Liberty* (Oxford: Oxford University Press, 1998); J F Stephens, *Liberty, Equality, Fraternity* (London: Elder, 1873); H L A Hart, *Law, Liberty and Morality* (Oxford: Oxford University Press, 1963); P Devlin, *The Enforcement of Morals* (Oxford: Oxford University Press; 1965); J Feinberg, *The Moral Limits of the Criminal Law Vols1–4* (New York: Oxford University Press, 1984–90); S Lee, *Law and Morals* (Oxford: Oxford University Press, 1987).

44 E Sutherland, *White-Collar Crime* (New York: Holt, Rinehart and Winston, 1949); H Schwendinger and J Schwendinger, 'Defenders of Order or Guardians of Human Rights?' in I Taylor, P Walton and J Young (eds), *Critical Criminology* (London: Routledge, 1975); G Slapper and S Tombs, *Corporate Crime* (London: Longman, 1999); S Tombs and D Whyte (eds), *Unmasking the Crimes of the Powerful* (New York: Lang, 2003); P Green and T Ward, *State Crime* (London: Pluto, 2004). For a discussion of the problems of defining and regulating white-collar or corporate crime, see D Nelken, 'White-Collar Crime' in Maguire *et al*, n 5 above; J Gobert and M Punch, *Rethinking Corporate Crime* (London: Lexis Nexis, 2003).

45 Hillyard *et al*, n 24 above.

Social/Cultural Constructions

Emile Durkheim's famous attempt to provide a sociological definition of crime suggested that 'Crime shocks sentiments which, for a given social system are found in all healthy consciences . . . an act is criminal when it offends strong and defined states of the collective conscience'.[46] This is as positivist, tautologous, and formal a definition as the standard criminal law textbook's, albeit emphasizing social/cultural rather than legal construction. Moreover, it is even more explicitly based on a consensus model of society. As Durkheim himself recognized, conceptions of the criminal vary considerably between and within societies, and over time. What is typically sanctioned as deviant will vary from the formal definitions of law, and also be hotly contested between different groups. An occupational hazard for a criminologist at parties is to deal with irate demands to explain why the police and courts harass the speeding motorist instead of 'real' criminals. Is drink-driving socially deviant? While it is in most circles nowadays, it was not in England until three decades ago, but it was even then in countries such as, for example, Scandinavia. Will driving under the influence of mobile phones go the same way? Who is 'really' criminal—the 'honest, victimized' householder Tony Martin, or the young burglar he was convicted of murdering?

Criminal Justice Constructions

Who gets formally processed by the criminal justice system as criminal, and for what offences, offers yet another construction of crime and criminality. Recorded crimes and criminals are a very small and almost certainly unrepresentative sample of all law-breaking. The official statistics and research evidence have been well summed up in the title of Jeffrey Reiman's critical classic *The Rich Get Richer and the Poor Get Prison*.[47] They are in prison mainly for a variety of street crimes, not suite crimes—car theft and burglary, not insider trading or pensions mis-selling. The imbalance starts with what is reported and gets more marked as cases go through each stage of the criminal justice process. The overwhelming majority of those in prison (and *a fortiori* those executed in the USA) are male and from economically underprivileged groups, with a huge disproportion of black and other ethnic minority people.[48]

[46] Durkheim, n 12 above, 73, 80.

[47] J Reiman, *The Rich Get Richer and the Poor Get Prison* (7th edition) (Boston: Allyn and Bacon, 2004).

[48] R Morgan, 'Imprisonment' in Maguire *et al*, n 5 above, 1132.

The pattern of offences for which people are processed and convicted is almost the obverse of the amount of space they get in typical criminal law books and journals. Most are charged with driving offences, thefts, and only a minority with the serious violent and sexual offences and homicide that occupy the attention of criminal law texts.

Mass Media and Policy Constructions

The constructions of crime offered by the mass media, those that inform most policy debates, are again a very different pattern. Mass media representations follow a 'law of opposites'.[49] They are the obverse of what official statistics on recorded crime and criminals portray—although neither are likely to be a 'true' picture of overall patterns of offending, most of which never comes to light at all.

The mass media—'factual', 'fictional', and hybrid forms—overwhelmingly focus on the most serious violent and sexual offences, above all murder, even though these are thankfully rare.[50] Victims and offenders portrayed in media accounts are disproportionately older and higher in the social scale than their counterparts in official statistics, although they share the common feature of being overwhelmingly male. The criminal justice system is primarily represented by the police, and is mainly presented as successful, law-abiding, and morally virtuous; negative portrayals have certainly increased over the last fifty years but they remain a small minority. In news and fiction stories the police almost invariably get their man, although in reality only a tiny proportion of crimes are cleared up.

It is this mass media picture that informs most contemporary public and policy debate. Politicians generally are highly sensitive to the sensational but rare crimes that are the focus of most media attention, and policy-making is often jolted by them. Increasingly the main attention is on the suffering of massively injured, vulnerable, and ideal-typically innocent victims, as reflected in the new tendency to name laws after them.

An Overlapping Core Construction?

I have distinguished between five different constructions of crime in contemporary discourse, all offering a very different picture: the legal; different moral views; the socially/culturally sanctioned; the criminal justice

[49] R Surette, *Media, Crime and Criminal Justice* (2nd edn) (Belmont: Wadsworth, 1998).
[50] For a summary of research on media representation of crime see R Reiner, 'Media Made Criminality' in Maguire, n 5 above. Changes since 1945 are analysed in R Reiner,

process; and the mass media/public policy focus. It is difficult to see any common core. Some ideal-typical cases may in Durkheimian fashion unite all 'healthy consciences', say the Jamie Bulger or Soham murders. These highly unusual crimes are clearly regarded as such on all dimensions. But there will be alternative views on the gravity and even the 'really' criminal nature of most other cases, even if there is no doubt about their legal status. So much policy and popular debate about crime and control involves people talking past each other.

What Happened?—Unravelling Crime Trends

As anyone who has studied even a week of criminology knows, official crime statistics have to be approached with extreme caution.[51] The key official national statistics, going back to the 1850s, are compiled from returns by police forces of crimes they have recorded as known to them. These are both an incomplete and a biased sample of all crimes that occur. There is a substantial 'dark figure' of unrecorded crime, constituting a variable multiple of the recorded rate. Many crimes are not recorded because victims do not report them, the police do not record them even if they are reported, or they have no individual victims and are not discovered by the police. Recorded trends and patterns must be interpreted sceptically because they may reflect changes in recording practices rather than criminals committing crimes. Officially recorded offenders are also a tiny and biased sample of all law-breakers, the lottery losers of the criminal justice process.

Having said this, very substantial steps have been taken in recent decades to alleviate these problems. The most important is the development of alternative ways of measuring crime and offending, above all the regular British Crime Surveys[52] since the early 1980s. There have also been two recent reforms of the police recording process, intended to make it more complete, reliable, and victim-oriented. The first was a revised set of counting rules issued to police forces by the Home Office in 1998, increasing the range of offences that had to be recorded, and specifying more tightly how to calculate the number of offences to record

S Livingstone, and J Allen, 'Casino Culture: Media and Crime in a Winner-Loser Society' in K Stenson and R Sullivan (eds), *Crime, Risk and Justice* (Cullompton: Willan, 2001); R Reiner, S Livingstone, and J Allen, 'From Law and Order to Lynch Mobs: Crime News since the Second World War' in Mason, n 9 above.

[51] For a comprehensive review of the issues see M Maguire, 'Crime Statistics: The "Data Explosion" and its Implications' in Maguire *et al*, n 5 above.

[52] Hereafter 'BCS'.

in particular cases. This had the expected and inevitable effect of increasing the recorded crime rate. The second reform, the 2002 National Crime Recording Standard, aimed to achieve greater consistency between different areas in recording practices, above all by requiring that incidents be recorded according to the victim's perception irrespective of the police view of its accuracy. Again this was expected to boost recording, as it restricted officers' discretion not to record offences if they doubted the victim's versions of events. These are desirable reforms but do make comparison over time more problematic, although the Home Office calculated the 1998 statistics using both old and new versions of the counting rules in order to estimate the effect of the changes.

The advent of the BCS twenty-five years ago has shed much light on reporting and recording practices, allowing statistics to be interpreted more confidently. Above all they offer two alternative measures of trends for offences covered by the survey, which gives greater confidence when they point in the same direction, as they did for most of the history of the BCS. However, in recent years the trends indicated by the police statistics and the BCS have begun to diverge, producing a politicization of the debate about their interpretation and the relative merits of different measuring instruments.

Putting together the different sorts of data available, what can be said about the trends in the last half century? The most apparent trend is the spectacular rise in recorded crime since the late 1950s. In the early 1950s the police recorded less than half a million offences per annum. By the mid-1960s this had increased to around one million, and by the mid-1970s to two million. The 1980s showed even more staggering rises, with recorded crime peaking in 1992 at over 5.5 million—a tenfold increase in less than four decades.[53] By 1997 recorded crime had fallen back to 4.5 million. The counting rule changes introduced in 1998 and 2002 make comparison of the subsequent figures especially fraught, but on the new rules, which undoubtedly exaggerate the increase, just under six million offences were recorded by the police for 2003–4—the highest on record—but this had fallen back to just over 5.5 million in 2004–5.[54] Until the 1970s there were no alternatives to the police statistics. Criminologists were wont to give cautionary warnings about whether crime really was increasing as the figures indicated, but it was impossible

[53] G Barclay and C Tavares, *Digest 4—Information about the Criminal Justice System in England and Wales* (London: Home Office, 1999), 2.

[54] S Nicholas, D Povey, A Walker, and C Kershaw, *Crime in England and Wales 2004/05* Statistical Bulletin 11/05 (London: Home Office, 2005), 13.

to know how much of any change was due to new patterns of reporting and/or recording crime rather than offending behaviour.

During the 1970s the General Household Survey[55] asked respondents about their experience of burglary. This allowed an estimate of changes in victimization and reporting patterns for this common offence, which was of crucial importance for public anxieties about crime and the politics of law and order. In the 1970s the increase in recorded burglaries was mainly accounted for by an increase in victims' propensity to report them to the police, not an increase in victimization by burglary. Between 1972 and 1983 recorded burglaries doubled, but victimization increased by only 20 per cent according to the surveys.[56] There was a considerable increase in the proportion of victims reporting burglaries to the police, and the reason is plain from the GHS. In 1972 the property stolen was insured in only 19 per cent of burglary incidents, but by 1980 this had increased to 42 per cent.[57] Thus, the first set of victimization statistics, from the GHS in the 1970s, reinforced criminological scepticism about how much of the huge increase in recorded crime statistics was really due to increased offending.

However, as the BCS came to be repeated in several sweeps during the 1980s and early 1990s the discrepancy in the trends recorded by the surveys and by the police figures began to lessen. Although there was still some increase in reporting and recording, most of the huge rise in recorded crime in the 1980s and early 1990s corresponded to an increase in victimization. Between 1981 and 1993, the number of crimes recorded by the police increased 111 per cent, whilst BCS offences rose by 77 per cent. The proportion of offences reported to the police by victims increased from 31 per cent in 1981 to 41 per cent in 1993 according to the BCS. In the most common types of property crime, such as car thefts and burglary with loss, reporting and recording rates had reached almost 100 per cent.[58] When there is almost complete recording by the police of victimization the trends in the BCS and police figures will of course be almost identical.

From the early 1990s, however, the two sets of statistics begin to diverge once more. Between 1992 and 1995 the police statistics begin to decline

[55] Hereafter 'GHS'.

[56] M Hough and P Mayhew, *Taking Account of Crime: Key Findings from the Second British Crime Survey* (London: Home Office, 1985), 16.

[57] P Mayhew, D Elliott, and L Dowds, *The 1988 British Crime Survey* (London: Home Office, 1989), 19–22; G Barclay, C Tavares, and A Prout, *Digest 3—Information on the Criminal Justice System in England and Wales* (London: Home Office, 1995), 7.

[58] Barclay *et al*, ibid, 6.

from their record height of 5.5 million. But the BCS continued to register increasing victimization in these years.[59] The 'missing crimes' in the police statistics are due to a reversal of the trend towards saturation reporting of the most common property offences. Paradoxically, the very high levels of crime set in train processes that led victims to report less, and the police to record fewer of the crimes reported to them.[60] Victims in higher risk categories faced more onerous conditions for insurance, reducing the incentive to report crimes. The police were coming under a tighter performance measurement regime, encouraging under-recording where possible.

After 1997 the divergence between the police and BCS statistics has continued, but in the reverse direction. The police figures increased from 1997 to 2003–4, slightly dropping in 2004–5. This is largely accounted for by the two changes in counting rules over this period. The BCS figures, however, show continuing declines in total victimization from 1995 to 2004–5.

It is hardly surprising that this has made the relative significance of the two sets of statistics highly politicized, with the Conservatives attempting to undermine the validity of the BCS in the 2005 General Election campaign, aided by publications from sympathetic think-tanks.[61] The official crime statistics show crime rising almost continuously from the late 1950s, until they begin to fall sharply during Michael Howard's period as Home Secretary, but then rise again to new record levels under New Labour. The GHS and BCS victimization statistics, by contrast, suggest that until the Thatcher government much of the rise in recorded crime was due to increased reporting.

The spectacular rise in the 1980s and early 1990s was a genuine increase in offending, confirmed by both measures. The apparent decline in recorded crime under Michael Howard, however, was again largely a product of changes in recording—BCS crime continued to rise. But the growth of recorded crime under New Labour is mainly due to recording changes attributable to the revised counting rules. Victimization as measured by the BCS has declined to its lowest level since 1979, when Mrs Thatcher defeated the previous Labour government.

So whether Michael Howard or Tony Blair wins the accolade of the most successful crime-buster since Batman turns on which figures are more reliable. The BCS cannot and does not claim to be a perfect

[59] Nicholas *et al*, n 54 above, 18.

[60] R Reiner, 'The Case of the Missing Crimes' in R Levitas and W Guy (eds), *Interpreting Official Statistics* (London: Routledge, 1996).

[61] N Dennis and G Erdos, *Cultures and Crime* (London: Civitas, 2005).

barometer of crime—this is not possible. Most criminologists would argue, however, that as a measure of trends it is more reliable than the police statistics, which are notoriously subject to the vicissitudes of victims' reporting and police recording behaviour. But then most criminologists are probably not fans of Mrs Thatcher, Michael Howard, or Tony Blair!

A New Leviathan? Crime Control Policies

During the 1970s and 1980s law and order was the exclusive slogan of the political Right.[62] David Downes vividly labelled this as the 'theft of an issue'.[63] As the emerging school of New Left Realism argued, the primary victims of crime were the poorest and most vulnerable groups in society, those that the Left had traditionally seen as its constituency.[64] Crime could also be explained by the social ethos and conditions of unbridled capitalism that the Left had traditionally attacked.[65] The missing link that New Left Realists urged was serious consideration by the Left of short-term crime control policies that might offer some protection whilst waiting for long-term reforms addressing the basic causes.[66]

In the early 1990s Labour tried in earnest to recapture the ground lost on the issue of law and order, especially once Tony Blair became Shadow Home Secretary. They began to attack the Tories not only with the old social democratic arguments about crime being produced by inequality, egoism, and exclusion, but by pointing to failures of Conservative criminal justice policies. Given the record increases in crime in the 1980s, despite burgeoning expenditure on policing and punishment, this was an open goal—as even Tory cabinet ministers privately conceded.[67]

The wrong-footing of the Tories on law and order came to a head in 1993, with Tony Blair's emblematic pledge to be 'tough on crime, tough on the causes of crime'—covering all bases at the same time.[68] Michael

[62] R Reiner and M Cross (eds), *Beyond Law and Order* (London: Macmillan, 1991); M Brake and C Hale, *Public Order and Private Lives: The Politics of Law and Order* (London: Routledge, 1992).

[63] D Downes, *Law and Order—Theft of an Issue* (London: Fabian Society, 1983).

[64] J Lea and J Young, *What is to be Done about Law and Order?* (London: Penguin, 1984).

[65] I Taylor, *Law and Order: Arguments for Socialism* (London: Macmillan, 1981).

[66] R Matthews and J Young (eds), *Confronting Crime* (London: Sage, 1986).

[67] K Baker, *The Turbulent Years* (London: Faber, 1993), 450.

[68] This celebrated soundbite was first aired in speeches and articles in early 1993 by Tony Blair as Shadow Home Secretary, outlining the Labour Party's approach to law and

Howard fought back vigorously with his 'prison works' speech to the 1993 Conservative Party Conference, and policies inspired by it. Nonetheless the game had changed dramatically. Having ditched its electoral 'hostages to fortune' such as exclusive association with civil liberties, trade unionism, and analysis of crime primarily in terms of social justice,[69] Labour was making the political running on what had been one of the Tories' most secure policy areas. As with the whole New Labour project, the ditching of old commitments was seen as a price worth paying for its electoral rewards.

The period 1992–3 was a decisive watershed for the politics of law and order, as for other policy areas. Whilst during the late 1970s and 1980s neo-liberal and neo-conservative political parties, ideas, and policies became dominant in Britain, the US and most of the Western world, they were fiercely if unsuccessfully contested. On a world scale the New Right's ascendancy was marked by the fall of the Soviet Union in 1989. But what really confirmed the global hegemony of neo-liberalism was the acceptance of the fundamentals of its economic and social policy framework by the erstwhile social democratic or New Deal parties of the West. The Clinton Democrats, New Labour, and their embrace of the 'third way'—neo-liberalism to a cool beat—marked a new, deep consensus, delivering the death-knell of the post-war mixed economy, Keynesian settlement that the conservative parties had accepted when they returned to power in the early 1950s: Blatcherism was Butskellism in reverse.

As argued earlier, in relation to crime the new 'second order' consensus, predicated on an auction of toughness,[70] had five core elements:

(i) Crime, disorder, and now terrorism, are *the* major threats to society and to individual citizens;

(ii) Crime is the fault of offenders, due to their free choice, individual or cultural pathology, or to intrinsic evil. It is *not* caused by social structural factors;

(iii) The victim is the iconic centre of discourse about crime, ideal-typically portrayed as totally innocent. Crime policy is predicated

order, in the wake of the national agonizing stirred by the tragic abduction and murder of the Liverpool toddler James Bulger by two older boys. See Blair, n 21 above. Its significance is discussed usefully in Downes and Morgan, n 5 above, 296–7; T Newburn, *Handbook of Policing* (Cullompton: Willan, 2003), 206–7; C Hale, 'The Politics of Law and Order' in Hale *et al*, n 24 above, 439–41.

[69] Downes and Morgan, n 5 above.

[70] ibid; R Matthews and J Young (eds), *The New Politics of Crime and Punishment* (Cullompton: Willan, 2003).

on a zero-sum game: concern for victims precludes understanding of—let alone any sympathy for—offenders;

(iv) Criminal justice *can* control crime provided it is tough *and* smart. Criminal justice controls crime through effective deterrence, prevention, and incapacitation. 'Prison works', as does 'zero tolerance' policing, and 'responsibilizing' citizens to take self-protective measures against victimization. Civil liberties are at best marginal issues, and deeper social causes of crime are denied; and

(v) Popular culture and the routines of everyday life are increasingly focused on crime risks; politics is dominated by fears about crime, disorder, and the threat of alien evil.

This new hegemonic 'culture of control'[71] has displaced the welfare/rehabilitative consensus that prevailed for most of the twentieth century in the Western world. This is part of a broader shift in politics and culture, the 'death of the social'.[72] The rise of neo-liberalism, individualism, and the 'risk society'[73] has eclipsed the Keynesian, mixed economy, welfare state consensus that prevailed for the first three post-war decades.[74] In the sphere of domestic politics this has been exemplified above all by the ascendancy of New Labour in the 1990s and early twenty-first century, with its promise of a 'third way' 'beyond Left and Right'.[75]

New Labour's crime control policies embodied this triangulation, epitomized by the flagship 1998 Crime and Disorder Act.[76] It was a characteristic 'third way' synthesis of the tough and the smart. It provided 'evidence-led', 'joined up' policy in the duties it placed on police, local authorities, and other relevant agencies to develop a coordinated 'strategy for the reduction of crime and disorder in the area', culminating in the ambitious Crime Reduction Programme launched in 1999. But it also offered tabloid-appeasing toughness: minimum mandatory sentences, ASBOs, and curfews.

The Janus-faced tough/smart policy combination is encapsulated above all in the restructuring of youth justice in the 1998 Act: systematic,

[71] Garland, n 23 above.

[72] N Rose, 'The Death of the Social?' (1996) 25(3) *Economy and Society* 327.

[73] U Beck, *Risk Society* (London: Sage, 1992).

[74] For economic analyses of the sources and implications see: M Blyth, *Great Transformations* (Cambridge: Cambridge University Press, 2002); G Dumenil and D Levy, *Capital Resurgent* (Cambridge, Mass: Harvard University Press, 2004); D Harvey, *A Brief History of Neoliberalism*, (Oxford: Oxford University Press, 2005); A Glyn, *Capitalism Unleashed* (Oxford: Oxford University Press, 2006).

[75] A Giddens, *The Third Way* (Cambridge: Polity, 1998); C Leys, *Market-Driven Politics* (London: Verso, 2003); M Bevir, *New Labour: A Critique* (London: Routledge, 2005).

[76] Hereafter 'the 1998 Act'.

evidence-based attempts to address and prevent offending by early prediction of risks and appropriate remedies, coordinated by inter-agency teams in the form of the local Youth Offending Teams, and centrally by the Youth Justice Board.[77] Alongside this, however, were a variety of new powers for the police and the courts to control youth crime and disorder, such as ASBOs, child curfew schemes, abolition of *doli incapax*, detention and training orders. The net result was an increase in the use of custodial penalties for young offenders.

Gradually 'tough on crime' has eclipsed 'tough on the causes of crime'. For example, there has been a remorseless growth of police powers. The legislative trend since 1993 has been extensions of police powers without corresponding safeguards, with the Human Rights Act of 1998 constituting the only exception. New powers to intercept communications, conduct covert operations, stop and search and arrest, and new public order offences were created in the early years of New Labour by the Police Act 1997, Crime and Disorder Act 1998, Regulation of Investigatory Powers Act 2000, Terrorism Act 2000, and the Criminal Justice and Public Order Act 2001. In 2002 the Home Office conducted a review of PACE, premised on the view that the regime of safeguards it had instituted created a regime of procedures adequately protecting suspects. The concern was to provide a 'useful tool supporting the police and providing them with the powers they need to combat crime'.[78] It was deemed necessary to 'simplify police procedures; reduce administrative burdens on the police; save police resources; speed up the process of justice'.[79] Accordingly the Review floated a number of proposals to dilute the safeguards of PACE. The Criminal Justice Act 2003 authorized detention for 36 hours for all, not just 'serious', arrestable offences, and added criminal damage to the possible grounds for stop and search. The Serious Organized Crime and Police Act 2005 created a power of arrest for all offences, ending the category of non-arrestable offences. It enhanced powers of search, and to take fingerprints. It also allowed for the creation of civilian custody officers, overturning the PACE requirement that they should normally be police sergeants. The clear trend is for enhanced police powers and reduced safeguards, reflecting the law and order politics that have prevailed since the early 1990s.

Contrary to the 1984 forebodings of Freeman and others cited at the start of this chapter, the regime of safeguards established since PACE had

[77] J Pitts, *The New Politics of Youth Crime* (London: Palgrave, 2001); T Newburn, 'Young People, Crime and Youth Justice' in Maguire *et al*, n 5 above, 559.

[78] D Blunkett and Lord Macdonald, 'Foreword' in *Report of the Joint Home Office/Cabinet Office: Review of Police and Criminal Evidence Act 1984* (Home Office, November 2002).

[79] ibid, para 8.

a substantial impact on police practice, inhibiting gross violations of suspects' rights. However, the pressures on the police to achieve results have intensified in the new crime control climate, and they are increasingly armed with new powers unfettered by safeguards. This is likely to reduce the legal accountability of the police, despite the welcome enhancement of the complaints process represented by the creation of the Independent Police Complaints Commission.

Prison numbers have risen to record-breaking levels. During the first half of the twentieth century the trend had been for the number of prisoners to fall. From the late 1950s to the early 1980s it doubled from around 20,000 to 40,000, and had grown to around 50,000 by the late 1980s. Following a short period of reduction in the wake of the Criminal Justice Act 1991, there has been a relentless, massive increase of around two-thirds since 1993. In 1993 the rate of imprisonment was 90 per 100,000 population, but it rose to 143 per 100,000 by 2003, and is now over 75,000. This is largely the result of tougher sentencing policy and practice. The proportion of offenders found guilty of an indictable offence that received custodial sentences increased from 15 per cent in 1991 to 25 per cent in 2001. A variety of changes in sentencing powers under New Labour, following in the wake of Michael Howard's 'prison works' approach, from the Crime and Disorder Act 1998 to the Criminal Justice Act of 2003, have resulted in large increases in the proportion and numbers of prisoners serving long sentences.[80]

New Labour has been repeatedly jolted into new 'tough' laws and initiatives by particular media-driven moral panics, and since 2001—and *a fortiori* 2005—the threat of terrorism. This has been epitomized by Tony Blair's 'street crimes summit' at Downing Street in March 2002, and the accompanying initiative pledging to get robbery 'under control' by September.[81] Michael Tonry has documented no less than 33 such get-tough-on-crime initiatives announced between June 2001 and May 2003 alone,[82] with thirteen 'crime summits' between 1999 and 2003.[83] It has been estimated that over 700 new criminal offences have been created by New Labour.[84]

These measures, and the law and order paradigm with its 'can-do' confidence about bringing crime under control by toughness, might get some superficial vindication from the overall fall in crime in the last decade that is indicated by the British Crime Survey, although less clearly

[80] A Ashworth, 'Sentencing' in Maguire *et al*, n 5 above; M Tonry, *Punishment and Politics* (Cullompton: Willan, 2004).
[81] For details, see Tonry, ibid 47.
[82] ibid 41–7.
[83] ibid 39–41.
[84] H Kennedy, *Just Law* (London: Vintage, 2005).

by the recorded crime figures. However, the fall has mainly been in the less serious 'volume' crimes, whilst robbery and more serious violent crimes have increased.[85] The role of criminal justice policy in explaining these crime trends is in any case complex and debatable.

Explaining Crime Trends

The predominant account offered by the media and by politicians of the rise in crime since the late 1950s has been the one advanced by the New Right.[86] This blames crime on the personal moral and other defects of offenders, that used to be held in check by effective social controls until post-war liberal social policies culminating in 1960s 'permissiveness' undermined them.

The theme of permissiveness as the basic cause of rising crime has been emphasized recently by Tony Blair, in a speech launching the Home Office's five-year Strategic Plan for law and order. Blair claimed it 'marks the end of the 1960s liberal, social consensus on law and order'.[87] He explicitly blamed the '1960s revolution' for encouraging 'freedom without responsibility', when 'a society of different lifestyles spawned a group of young people who were brought up without parental discipline, without proper role models and without any sense of responsibility to or for others'.[88]

Blair's speech represents the quintessential conservative analysis of rising crime. In this account, the Enlightenment values of personal liberty, autonomy, and self-realization were dangerously democratized by 1960s 'permissiveness'. As this spread to the masses it brought the destruction of family, responsibility, and self- control—the bulwarks of any civilization.[89] This narrative overlooks the ways in which the 'permissive' legislation of the 1960s embodied a restructuring rather than relaxation of control.[90] It cannot explain why tolerant and liberal cultures like those of Holland and the Scandinavian countries were not racked by crime, violence, and law and order politics[91]—though these are emerging

[85] D Rose, 'Violent Crime' *The Observer* 28 May 2006, 20–2.

[86] For a crisp demolition see S Hallsworth, *Street Crime* (Cullompton: Willan, 2005), ch 4.

[87] T Blair, 'A New Consensus on Law and Order', Speech launching Home Office Strategic Plan for Criminal Justice, 19 July 2004. Available via <www.labour.org.uk/news/tbcrimespeech>.

[88] ibid.

[89] Dennis and Erdos, n 61 above.

[90] T Newburn, *Permission and Regulation* (London: Routledge, 1991).

[91] D Downes, *Contrasts in Tolerance* (Oxford: Oxford University Press, 1998); H Tham, 'Law and Order as a Leftist Project—The Case of Sweden' (2001) 3 *Punishment*

with the impact of neo-liberalism and the weakening of social democracy since the 1980s.

There have been huge cultural changes since the 1950s in all Western societies—greater individualism, autonomy, concern with self-realization, more scepticism about authority, and less deference.[92] But whilst this 'desubordination'[93] may have reduced internalized controls restraining deviance, it cannot by itself explain rising crime. Other factors need to be examined, including shifts in motivation, opportunity, formal controls, and the labelling of offences.[94]

To understand why crime rates have increased over the last fifty years, in terms of both 'actual' crime and 'recorded' crime, we need to consider all the necessary ingredients both of offending, and of perceptions of crime—controls are only one part of the picture. There are at least four necessary conditions of existence for the occurrence of behaviour that is regarded and recorded as criminal.

Labelling

For behaviour to be treated as 'criminal' it is necessary first for there to be an authoritative construction of the general category of crime it falls under. If it is to be recorded as a crime, the behaviour must then be interpreted as such by victims and/or witnesses, and official criminal justice agents. Shifts in criminal law, and in patterns of reporting and recording incidents, can be major influences on apparent patterns and trends in crime for numerous possible reasons.

Motivation

Social, cultural, and economic changes affect the pressures and attractions of behaviour labelled as criminal, increasing or decreasing the numbers of people motivated to commit them. The most influential and plausible account of how macro-social structures can affect variations in

and Society 409; U Bondeson, 'Levels of Punitiveness in Scandinavia: description and explanations' in J Pratt, D Brown, M Brown, S Hallsworth, and W Morrison (eds), *The New Punitiveness* (Cullompton: Willan, 2005).

[92] A Giddens, *Modernity and Self-Identity* (Cambridge: Polity, 1991).

[93] R Miliband, 'A State of Desubordination' (1978) 29(4) *British Journal of Sociology* 399.

[94] R Reiner, 'Crime and Control in Britain' (2000) 34(1) *Sociology* 71; Hallsworth, n 86 above, part 2; R Reiner, 'Political Economy, Crime and Criminal Justice' in M Maguire, R Morgan and R Reiner (eds), *The Oxford Handbook of Criminology* (4th edn) (Oxford: Oxford University Press, forthcoming).

motivations to commit crime between cultures and over time is Merton's theory of anomie.[95] This suggests how cultures that emphasize material success, especially if this is defined primarily in monetary terms, and ones that encourage widespread aspirations in a context of structurally limited legitimate opportunities for achievement, generate strains towards deviance and crime.

Criminal Opportunities

Social and economic changes can increase or reduce the availability of criminal opportunities. These opportunities can be analysed in terms of targets for crime, and the capacity to commit offences. In this sense 'opportunity makes the thief'.[96] Criminal opportunities can be expanded by a proliferation of targets—for example, the spread of ownership of mobile phones—or shifts in 'routine activities'.[97]

Controls

People with motives and opportunities to engage in criminal behaviour may be more or less restrained by controls, both formal and informal. Changes in the efficacy of formal controls through, for example, more or less successful policing strategies, will alter the attractions or possibility of crime. Cultural trends such as liberalization may affect the operations of internalized restraints, 'conscience'—Eysenck's 'inner policeman'[98]—in the way that proponents of the 'permissiveness' thesis argue.

Explaining recent trends in crime requires us to consider how changes in political economy, social structure, and culture have impacted on all these elements of offending. To recap briefly, the pattern we have to explain is: rising recorded crime from the late 1950s to the early 1970s, when there was no alternative to the official police figures; rising recorded crime during the 1970s, but with the GHS burglary victimization statistics suggesting this was largely a product of more reporting by victims; rising recorded crime 1981–92 which was probably mainly due to increased offending, as it was supported by the BCS; falling recorded crime 1992–7, but with the BCS suggesting this was largely a recording phenomenon,

[95] R Merton, 'Social Structure and Anomie' (1938) 3 *American Sociological Review* 672.

[96] M Felson and R Clarke, *Opportunity Makes the Thief: Practical Theory for Crime Prevention* (London: Home Office, 1998).

[97] M Felson, *Crime and Everyday Life* (3rd edn) (London: Pine Forge, 2002).

[98] H Eysenck, *Crime and Personality* (2nd edn) (London: Granada, 1970).

and crime was still rising; rising recorded crime since 1997—but with the BCS suggesting this was mainly due to increased recording, largely because of the major changes in counting rules.

This suggests the following broad three sub-periods:

Late 1950s–1970s—Rapid Crime Rise: The rise in recorded crime was mainly a product of the new mass consumer society. The GHS figures for the 1970s suggest that some at any rate of the recorded increase was due to more reporting and recording of victimization by property crime, a plausible process in a society in which high value consumer goods were proliferating and increasingly insured against theft. However, the culture and social structure of mass consumerism would also plausibly generate higher offending levels. Most obviously this would result from the spread of tempting targets for crime: cars, radios, and other equipment in cars, television sets, videos, computers, mobile phones, and so on. These all increased the opportunities for relatively easy, lucrative thefts.

Although unemployment and inequality were at a historic low point and diminishing, and general living standards rising, Mertonian anomie may well have been increasing motivations to steal. The increasingly materialistic culture of mass affluence emphasized monetary success rather than the means of achieving it. The stimulation of consumption by advertising explicitly undermined norms of deferred gratification—'Live Now, Pay Later', 'Take the Waiting Out of Wanting'. This could have eroded inhibitions about illicit access and not just the legitimate use of credit cards.[99] The pervasive stress on the desirability of must-have consumer products for all would have increased the sense of relative deprivation amongst those sectors lacking in legitimate opportunities. All this was predicted by social democratic criminologists at the dawn of the era of mass affluence,[100] and doubtless continues to fuel crime.[101]

The beginnings of youth culture and broader aspects of de-subordination would have reduced internalized restraints against offending. As recorded crime began to rise, pressures on the police increased, leading to lower clear-up rates and hence a decline in the deterrence and incapacitation

[99] Access cards were the first commonly available credit cards in Britain, marketed under the slogan 'Take the waiting out of wanting'.

[100] R Reiner, 'Beyond Risk: A Lament for Social Democratic Criminology' in T Newburn and P Rock (eds), *The Politics of Crime Control* (Oxford: Oxford University Press, 2006).

[101] On consumerism and crime, see J Young, *The Exclusive Society* (London: Sage, 1999); J Lea, *Crime and Modernity* (London: Sage, 2002), 78–81; M Fitzgerald and C Hale, *Young People and Street Crime* (London: Youth Justice Board, 2002); K Hayward, *City Limits* (London: Glasshouse Press, 2004); Hallsworth, n 86 above.

effects of criminal justice. In sum, after the late 1950s a variety of interlinked consequences of mass consumerism fed rising crime rates. These increased the labelling of crime, opportunities and motivations for offending, and weakened both informal and formal controls.

1980s—Crime Explosion: All these processes continued in the 1980s and early 1990s, during which recorded crime reached historical record heights, and the new BCS confirmed that this was primarily a rise in victimization by crime not a recording change. The key change, however, was the brutal displacement of the consensus, Keynesian, welfare state policies of the post-war decades by neo-liberal monetarist policies. This produced the massive social dislocations of de-industrialization and resurgent mass unemployment—indeed long-term never-employment for increasing numbers of young men, especially amongst ethnic minorities and in inner-city areas. Inequality sharpened into a yawning chasm between the top and bottom of the economic hierarchy, and poverty began to rise after a long historical process of increasing social incorporation and inclusion. Industrial and political conflict was sparked on a scale not experienced for half a century or more, with much more violent disorders.

Informal social controls of all kinds were eroded as whole communities lost the material basis of settled life, with incomparably greater ramifications for stable or any family life and 'morality' than the 'permissiveness' that the Right railed against. Moral *laissez-faire* followed the economic. A culture of egoism, the 'me society', was stimulated under the guise of the ethic of individual responsibility. 'Greed is good' was the infamous watchword of a new Gilded Age. The unbridled turbo-capitalism of the Thatcher years had devastating consequences for order that far outweighed the strong state measures introduced to control it in a Canute-like effort to stem the social tsunami.[102]

[102] For evidence about the links between inequality, long-term unemployment, and crime and violence, see, for example, C Hale, 'The Labour Market and Post-War Crime Trends in England and Wales' in P Carlen and R Morgan (eds), *Crime Unlimited* (London: Macmillan, 1999); C Hale, 'Economic Marginalisation, Social Exclusion and Crime' in Hale *et al*, n 24 above; S Hall and S Winlow, 'Rehabilitating Leviathan: Reflections on the State, Economic Management and Violence Reduction' (2003) 7(2) *Theoretical Criminology* 139; S Hall and S Winlow, 'Crime and Violence in the Breakdown of the Pseudo-Pacification Process' in J Ferrell, K Hayward, W Morrison, and M Presdee (eds), *Cultural Criminology Unleashed* (London: Glasshouse Press, 2005); D Dorling, 'Prime Suspect: Murder in Britain' in P Hillyard, C Pantazis, S Tombs, and D Gordon (eds), *Beyond Criminology* (London: Pluto, 2004); R Wilkinson, *The Impact of Inequality* (New York: New Press, 2005), 47–51, ch 5; Reiner, 'Political Economy', n 94 above.

1992—Falling Crime, Rising Fear: The drop in recorded crime during 1993–6 was probably a recording phenomenon rather than a real decline in offending, as argued earlier. Michael Howard may not have succeeded in his aims to be tough on crime, but the 'business-like' police managerialism he sponsored was certainly tough on the recording of crime.

However, after 1997 the BCS points to a sustained and substantial fall in victimization, returning to the levels of the early 1980s. The rising recorded rates of crime overall since 1997 are primarily due to the new counting rules, and in any event have also reduced in the last year. This has not, however, been accompanied by a decline in fear of crime.[103] Falls in recorded crime, and often victimization statistics, are a world-wide phenomenon of the 1990s, not least in the USA and the much trumpeted New York miracle. In the next section we will consider the possible factors that explain the 1990s crime drop.

Tough on Crime? Assessing the New Punitiveness

Explaining 'Law and Order'

As seen earlier, since the late 1970s there has been greater public concern about crime, and increasing support for a tough, 'law and order' approach to it. Crime and criminal justice policy are couched within a 'culture of control'.[104] As David Garland's analysis shows, this had at least three principal sources.

First, is the greater reality of victimization. It is not just that crime has increased, but that it has victimized middle-class and elite groups that were previously relatively immune to risks of crime.[105] As has often been quipped, a conservative is a liberal who has been mugged.

Secondly, the crime drop of the mid-1990s[106] was used by the police, many politicians, and conservative criminologists, to refute the 'nothing works' pessimism of the 1970s and 1980s. They claimed that tough criminal justice policies can contain crime without addressing social root causes—if these existed at all. We shall consider the evidence for such claims below. Thirdly, however, the new public and political support for

[103] M Hough, 'Modernisation and Public Opinion: Some Criminal Justice Paradoxes' (2003) 9(1) *Contemporary Politics* 143.

[104] Garland, n 23 above.

[105] ibid 154–6.

[106] Both the recorded drop of the early 1990s, and the later fall in victimization, have been used in this way, albeit with somewhat different party political biases. The Conservatives emphasized the former, New Labour the latter.

tough law and order politics can at best only be explained to a very limited extent by a 'truth will out' narrative about its validity. Public support for 'law and order' in the USA has been shown to be much more closely tied to prior media and political campaigns than by objective changes in crime rates.[107] Media narratives—news and fictional—have increasingly been framed in 'law and order' terms since the 1970s.[108] As inequality and social divisions have been exacerbated in the last quarter of a century, politicians have found crime concerns to be a way of constructing consensus in limited areas through focusing attention on fear of criminal folk-devils.[109]

Assessing 'Law and Order'

To what extent, if any, can the 1990s crime drop, in Britain and the US, be attributed to the politics of law and order—tougher policing and the new punitiveness? The police, particularly in the US, and especially those associated with the crime drop in New York City, have not been slow to claim credit. As William Bratton, the NYPD Commissioner between 1994–6, unabashedly trumpeted, 'Crime is down: blame the police'.[110] Throughout the world this has stimulated a new 'can-do' confidence amongst the police, palpably relieved that after two decades in which 'nothing works' seemed to be the clear conclusion of research on policing and punishment, new policing tactics seemed at last to be vindicating their crime-busting credentials.[111] The broad coincidence of falling crime rates and record imprisonment levels, especially in the USA and Britain, also encouraged those who had claimed that 'prison works'.

Independent research suggests a much more complex and indeed enigmatic picture than the prophets of 'zero-tolerance' and toughness. Most do not question that substantial declines in crime have occurred in the USA and in Britain, but explaining this is far more problematic.[112] It is

[107] Beckett, n 10 above; J Roberts and M Hough, *Understanding Public Attitudes to Criminal Justice* (Maidenhead: Open University Press, 2005).

[108] Reiner *et al*, n 9 above.

[109] As anticipated in S Hall, C Critcher, T Jefferson, J Clarke, and B Roberts, *Policing the Crisis* (London: Macmillan, 1978).

[110] W Bratton, 'Crime is Down: Blame the Police' in N Dennis (ed), *Zero Tolerance* (2nd edn) (London: IEA, 1998).

[111] D Dixon and L Maher, 'Policing, Crime and Public Health' (2005) 5(2) *Criminal Justice* 115.

[112] Indeed, so puzzling is the crime fall at a time when the major supposed drivers of crime such as inequality and deprivation have not declined, and in many ways have got worse, that some experts have felt renewed scepticism about the measurement of crime

precisely the widespread character of the crime-drop that calls into question some of the most popular explanations, in particular 'zero-tolerance' policing. As many commentators have argued, crime fell in most parts of the USA despite the considerable variations in policing styles. Whilst the celebrated New York City drop was especially marked, crime declined to a comparable extent even in cities that did not pursue the same, or any, reform strategy.

Close analysis of the New York experience itself suggests problems in attributing most of the falls in homicide and other serious crime to policing changes, because of the timing of these.[113] Certainly some of the huge decline in New York City is plausibly due to policing changes, but there is considerable doubt about how much is attributable to the much-celebrated 'zero-tolerance' aspect of the changes. Even Bratton plays down the label of 'zero-tolerance' for his reforms, and most analysts see the much more rigorous and speedy analysis of crime, and the stricter local managerial accountability for crime trends, summed up as 'COMPSTAT', as the most important element in the NYPD's success.[114]

At the national level, the most rigorous assessment of the 1990s crime drop in America finds that socio-economic and demographic changes—particularly the more buoyant labour market, and the decline in the high-crime age groups in the population—made a more significant impact than criminal justice policies, although these played some part.[115] In Britain too, the success of New Labour in maintaining relatively low levels of unemployment, and reducing poverty to a limited extent, but not inequality, are probably key factors.[116] More intelligence-based assessments of risk underlying patterns of policing, prevention, and punishment have also played a part. Certainly, the marked reductions in the

even by victim surveys, eg R Garside, *Crime, Persistent Offenders and the Justice Gap* (London: Crime and Society Foundation, 2004).

[113] B Bowling, 'The Rise and Fall of New York Murder' (1999) 39(4) *British Journal of Criminology* 531; A Karmen, *New York Murder Mystery* (New York: New York University Press, 2000).

[114] D Weisburd, S Mastrofski, A McNally, R Greenspan, and J Willis, 'Reforming to Preserve: Compstat and Strategic Problem Solving in American Policing' (2003) 2(3) *Criminology and Public Policy* 421; M Moore, 'Sizing Up Compstat' (2003) 2(3) *Criminology and Public Policy* 469.

[115] A Blumstein and J Wallman (eds), *The Crime Drop in America* (Cambridge: Cambridge University Press, 2000).

[116] D Downes, 'New Labour and the Lost Causes of Crime' (2004) 55 *Criminal Justice Matters* 4; R Garside, 'Is it the Economy?' (2004) 55 *Criminal Justice Matters* 32; C Hale, 'Economic Marginalisation, Social Exclusion and Crime' in Hale *et al*, n 24 above.

highest volume property crimes such as car crime and burglary owe much to vastly improved prevention practices.

Whilst emphasizing that crime overall has been declining, New Labour and senior police officers have struggled to benefit from this, above all because of the evidence from surveys and from media discussions that public fears have not declined. This has been labelled the 'reassurance gap' by policy-makers, and stimulated the so-called 'reassurance policing' agenda to try and plug it.[117] A key concept is Martin Innes' and Nigel Fielding's notion of 'signal crimes',[118] that particular offences have special power to symbolize broader crime and disorder and stimulate anxiety, outweighing the general statistical decline in crime—not a million miles away from the old Marxist notion of false consciousness.

There may, however, be a rational kernel to the stubborn refusal of public anxiety to decline with the crime rate, beyond blaming the messengers of the sensationalist and bad news-addicted media, although they are very significant. Within the decline in overall crime, the most worrying serious violent crimes have continued to rise.[119] In so far as the decline in crime overall is due to what Garland has called the 'criminologies of everyday life'[120]—more successful adoption of protective equipment and preventive routines by crime-conscious citizens, rather than any reduction in the root causes of offending—the burden falls on potential victims above all. Whilst prevention tactics, burdensome as they may be, are preferable to victimization, they are a product of insecurity, and indeed may reinforce rather than reduce fear. What is required is not reassurance about crime but about the causes of crime.

Conclusion

The trends I have outlined are dystopian in the extreme: increasing inequality, social polarization, egoism, all fuelling more serious crime. These can be contained—if at all—in fragile ways, by exclusionary and

[117] A Millie and V Herrington, 'Bridging the Gap: Understanding Reassurance Policing' (2005) 44(1) *Howard Journal* 41; M Hough, 'Policing, New Public Management and Legitimacy in Britain' in J Fagan and T Tyler (eds), *Legitimacy, Criminal Justice, and the Law* (New York: Russell Sage Foundation Press, 2006).

[118] M Innes and N Fielding, 'From Community to Communicative Policing: "Signal Crimes" and the Problem of Public Reassurance' (2002) 7(2) *Sociological Research Online*, available via <www.socresonline.org.uk>; M Innes, ' "Signal Crimes": Detective Work, Mass Media and Constructing Collective Memory' in Mason, n 9 above.

[119] Hallsworth, n 86 above; Rose, n 85 above.

[120] Garland, n 23 above, 127–31.

preventive routines that reflect and exacerbate fear. Enhanced physical security—locks, fences, window-bars—may protect particular targets, but there is evidence that they divert some offenders to more serious crimes,[121] and may exacerbate fear by offering constant physical reminders of the threats they are intended to control.[122] The use of apparently neutral technological surveillance by CCTV largely reproduces the patterns of discriminatory suspiciousness of traditional policing culture, focusing on the socially disadvantaged.[123] The life of the respectable majority takes place increasingly in 'mass private property',[124] spaces that are legally private but cater to large numbers of people, such as shopping malls or amusement parks. The safety of such 'security bubbles' is largely achieved by the expulsion of people perceived as threatening, whether or not they have acted suspiciously.[125] In the long run such measures exacerbate social divisions and disadvantage, and are likely to increase the pressures driving crime as they accentuate the social exclusion that fuels anomie and resistance.[126]

Rosa Luxemburg's stark choice, socialism or barbarism,[127] remains apposite. But actually, existing socialism as practised in Eastern Europe was barbarism. Its collapse pulled down in its wake the more ethical democratic socialism in the West that had produced more peaceful and just societies, and the promise of further improvement. Whether there is any possibility of its revival, in the face of the globalizing tendencies that have made more difficult if not impossible the agenda of social democracy in one country, and the more individualistic ethos engendered by three decades of neo-liberal hegemony, is a crucial question, not least for crime and criminal justice.[128]

A major difficulty is that neo-liberalism has relinquished the tools available to social democratic states to try and remedy inequality and

[121] The growth of street robbery, for example, has been explained as in part a result of the better protection of cars and homes. See Hallsworth, n 86 above.

[122] L Zedner, 'Liquid Security: Managing the Market for Crime Control' (2006) 6(2) *Criminology and Criminal Justice* 267.

[123] M McCahill, *The Surveillance Web* (Cullompton: Willan, 2002); R Coleman, *Reclaiming the Streets* (Cullompton: Willan, 2004).

[124] C Shearing and P Stenning, 'Private Security: Implications for Social Control' (1983) 30(5) *Social Problems* 493.

[125] ibid. See also A Wakefield, *Selling Security* (Cullompton: Willan, 2003). Shearing and Stenning refer to this accentuation of social divisions as a 'new feudalism'.

[126] The classic demonstration of this is M Davis, *City of Quartz* (New York: Vintage, 1992).

[127] R Luxemburg, 'The Junius Pamphlet: The Crisis in German Social Democracy' in P Hindis and K Anderson (eds), *The Rosa Luxemburg Reader* (New York: Monthly Review Press, 2004).

[128] This argument is elaborated in Reiner, n 100 above.

exclusion. For example, greater mobility of capital flows, partly because of technological and cultural changes associated with globalization, but crucially because of liberalization of controls over financial movements, has weakened the regulatory and taxation capacity of individual governments in relation to corporations. However, the extent to which this has systematically and irretrievably weakened governments' abilities to tax for redistributive and welfare purposes is debatable, and the position still varies considerably between different countries.[129] There is considerable evidence that variations in the political economy of different states are associated with the character of their penal systems, and with their patterns of serious and violent crime.[130] The more neo-liberal states tend to be the most punitive, whilst more social democratic and welfare-oriented states have less harsh penal regimes.[131] There is also both historical and comparative evidence of links between serious violent crime, inequality, and social exclusion.[132] The combination of general economic prosperity, low unemployment, and some mitigation of the worst levels of poverty,[133] together with more effectively targeted crime prevention and policing, and the huge growth in imprisonment, have bought an overall reduction in crime during the late 1990s. But serious violent crime remains a growing threat, and the containment of volume crime is fragile in the face of the continuing resilience of its basic causes, in particular the anomie of a consumerist society that fuels egoistic aspirations whilst bracketing off issues of the legitimacy of means, and with widening

[129] R Goodin, B Headey, R Muffels, and H-J Dirven, *The Real Worlds of Welfare Capitalism* (Cambridge: Cambridge University Press, 1999); P Hall and D Soskice (eds), *Varieties of Capitalism* (Oxford: Oxford University Press, 2001); A Glyn (ed), *Social Democracy in Neoliberal Times* (Oxford: Oxford University Press, 2001); D Held, *Global Governance* (Cambridge: Polity, 2004); R Taylor, *Sweden's New Social Democratic Model* (London: Compass, 2005).

[130] Reiner, 'Political Economy', n 94 above.

[131] K Beckett and B Western, 'Governing Social Marginality: Welfare, Incarceration and the Transformation of State Policy' (2001) 3(1) *Punishment and Society* 43; M Cavadino and P Dignan, *Penal Systems: A Comparative Approach* (London: Sage, 2006); D Downes and K Hansen, 'Welfare and Punishment in Comparative Perspective' in S Armstrong and L McAra (eds), *Perspectives on Punishment* (Oxford: Oxford University Press, 2006).

[132] E Currie, 'Market, Crime and Community: Towards a Mid-Range Theory of Post-Industrial Violence' (1997) 1(2) *Theoretical Criminology* 147; S Hall and S Winlow, 'Barbarians at the Gate: Crime and Violence in the Breakdown of the Pseudo-Pacification Process' in J Ferrell *et al*, n 102 above; Hale, n 68 above; S Hall and C McLean, 'A Tale of Two Capitalisms: A Preliminary Comparison of Violence Rates in European and Anglo-American Market Societies' (University of Northumbria: Division of Sociology and Criminology, 2005); Reiner, 'Political Economy', n 94 above.

[133] J Hills, *Inequality and the State* (Oxford: Oxford University Press, 2004); J Hills and K Stewart (eds), *A More Equal Society?* (Bristol: Policy Press, 2005).

inequality.[134] Economic collapse, an ever present threat in market economies, with a return of mass unemployment and deprivation, would almost certainly trigger a repeat of the 1980s explosion of crime and disorder—or worse—and more authoritarian control efforts.

Certainly the regulative capacity of states to achieve social democratic ends has been undermined by globalization under the neo-liberal auspices of the 'Washington consensus'. But this could be seen as a challenge not a fatal conclusion.[135] The social democratic deficit of states could lead to a search to develop 'collaborative mechanisms of governance at supranational and global levels'.[136] Unless there is some mitigation of neo-liberalism, and the inequality and egoism it carries with it, there is no real hope of reversing the deep pressures that have driven crime up, and assured the ascendancy of law and order politics. Law and order in 2020 would realize the worst visions of 1984.

[134] J Young, *The Exclusive Society* (London: Sage, 1999).
[135] Lea, n 101 above; Hall and Winlow, n 102 above.
[136] Held, n 129 above, 15; Harvey, n 74 above, ch 7.

Identity Cards and Data Protection: Public Security Interests and Individual Freedom in Times of Crisis

Jörg Fedtke

Identity Cards in the United Kingdom

Few topics have attracted as much public attention in the United Kingdom over the past years as the ongoing discussion about identity cards. What started off as an initiative to combat benefit fraud—the project was initially launched under the less conspicuous heading 'Entitlement Cards'[1]—has by now metamorphosed into a scheme aimed at the establishment of a comprehensive national database and the gradual allocation of identity cards to every individual aged 16 and above legally resident in the United Kingdom for a period of at least three months.[2] This development is very much in line with the trend towards tougher security legislation in many European countries, the European Union, and the United States following the terrorist attacks on Washington and New York in September 2001. America took the lead with the Patriot Act and the creation of the equally Orwellian-sounding Department of Homeland Security, which was recently authorized to set nationwide standards for federally approved identity documents.[3] In France, there are indications that police authorities have moved towards a strategy of 'zero tolerance' involving increased surveillance of suspicious individuals, more frequent security checks on mosques, restaurants, and long-distance telephone shops suspected of giving shelter to extremists, and a tougher system of criminal justice.[4] The German legislator added to the country's already

[1] See Secretary of State for the Home Department, 'Entitlement Cards and Identity Fraud—A Consultation Paper' (July 2002), CM 5557.

[2] Identity Cards Act 2006, s 2.

[3] Real ID Act 2005. On the introduction of identity cards in the United States, see D J Steinbock, 'National Identity Cards: Fourth and Fifth Amendment Issues' (2004) 54 *Florida Law Review* 697 ff. It is worth noting that other forms of identity checks, such as the extensive use of the social security number in many unrelated contexts, perform a similar function.

[4] See eg 'The French Lesson', *The Economist* 13 August 2005, 31 ff.

substantial security legislation[5] in November 2001[6] and January 2002[7] two further measures aimed at countering international terrorism. And the European Union, finally, alongside other activities involving a higher degree of police and judicial cooperation, mandated both fingerprints and facial biometrics for Member States' passports within the Schengen area in 2004,[8] and entered into a controversial agreement with the United States concerning the transmission of extensive passenger information, so-called 'Passenger Name Records', of individuals flying across the Atlantic.[9] But while governments all over the world have introduced new measures to combat terrorism and organized crime, often involving more secure forms of identification, the idea of British citizens carrying ID cards and producing these documents to identify themselves to public authorities, the postman delivering a registered letter at the door, the teller in a high-street bank, or their general practitioner[10] on the occasion of a medical check-up, remains odd and very much in conflict with the collective memory of Clarence Henry Wilcock, the brave dry-cleaner from Finchley who stood up against Leviathan in the guise of Police Constable Harold Muckle in December 1950 by refusing to show his wartime identity card on the occasion of a routine traffic control. This event and its legal repercussions, eventually involving no less than seven High Court judges including the Lord Chief Justice and the Master of the Rolls,[11] may have influenced Winston Churchill's decision to scrap the relevant provisions of the National Registration Act 1939 two years later,[12] and identity cards have remained an emotionally charged issue ever since.

[5] A useful legacy or, depending on one's point of view, an overly harsh remnant of the struggle against left-wing terrorism in the 1970s.

[6] Gesetz zur Finanzierung der Terrorbekämpfung, 10 December 2001, so-called 'erstes Sicherheitspaket', BGBl I 2001, 3436 ff.

[7] Gesetz zur Bekämpfung des internationalen Terrorismus, 9 January 2002 so-called 'zweites Sicherheitspaket', BGBl I 2002, 361 ff, 3142 ff.

[8] EC Council Regulation No 2252/2004 13 December 2004 on standards for security features and biometrics in passports and travel documents issued by Member States, OJ 385, 29 December 2004.

[9] Council Decision 2004/496/EC 17 May 2004 on the conclusion of an Agreement between the European Community and the United States of America on the processing and transfer of PNR data by Air Carriers to the United States Department of Homeland Security, Bureau of Customs and Border Protection (OJ 2004 L183, 83, and corrigendum at OJ 2005 L255, 168). The European Court of Justice annulled this agreement on 30 May 2006 for lack of an appropriate competence to use personal data collected for commercial purposes in the context of public security measures; see Joined Cases C-317/04 and C-318/04 of 30 May 2006.

[10] Hereafter 'GP'.

[11] *Wilcock v Muckle* [1952] 1 KB 367.

[12] Identity cards were also used during the First World War (see the National Registration Act 1915) and abandoned in 1919.

Bearing this historical background in mind, it comes as no surprise that the Identity Cards Bill,[13] launched by the Home Office after consultation and pre-legislative scrutiny in the Home Affairs Committee,[14] has had an increasingly rough ride since its first introduction in the House of Commons in November 2004.[15] Presented as a core initiative of the Government in the Queen's Speech on 23 November, and set to tackle the legislative hurdles with the help of substantial public support and a comfortable Labour majority, the project suffered a first setback four weeks later when nineteen Labour rebels came out against the measure and a large number of MPs chose to avoid the controversial issue and simply not show up for the vote.[16] Due to the initial support of the Conservative Party under its former leader Michael Howard, the Bill nevertheless passed the Commons with an overwhelming majority of 292, but fell when Parliament was dissolved for the General Election in April 2005. Subject to minor amendments concerning, *inter alia*, the responsibilities of the envisaged independent watchdog, the 'National Identity Scheme Commissioner', and the devolved administrations, the Bill was re-introduced a month later by a Government enjoying substantially less Parliamentary support.[17] The House of Lords and House of Commons Joint Committee on Human Rights had already warned that the public aims set out in the Bill would not justify such a large amount of data to be compiled by the Home Office,[18] and a second rebellion of Labour backbench MPs, though failing to stop or substantially change the proposal, later demonstrated that the Home Office, now headed by Charles Clarke,[19] was indeed treading thin ice. The Bill scraped through the report stage in the Commons with a slim majority of twenty-five,[20] and subsequently suffered further turbulence in the House of Lords. The House of Lords Select Committee on the Constitution called for additional safeguards in October 2005, arguing that identity cards could

[13] Hereafter 'the Bill'.

[14] House of Commons Home Affairs Committee, Session 2003–2004, Fourth Report, 20 July 2004; Home Office press notice 331/2004, 27 October 2004, 'Home Secretary Sets Out Next Steps on ID Cards'.

[15] Identity Cards Bill, 29 November 2004 (Bill 8).

[16] See 'Party Leaders Humiliated by ID Card Revolt', the *Independent* 21 December 2004, 15.

[17] Identity Cards Bill, 25 May 2005 (Bill 9).

[18] See 'ID Cards "Threat to Human Rights"', *The Times* 3 February 2005, 24.

[19] Who had inherited the scheme from his predecessor David Blunkett and defended the plans in Parliament during his very first appearance as Home Secretary in December 2004.

[20] See 'Clarke Offers Concessions on ID Cards to Head Off Rebellion', the *Independent* 18 October 2005, 21; 'ID Card Rebellion Slashes Majority to 25', the *Independent* 19 October 2005, 19; 'Rebels Cut ID-Card Majority', *The Times* 19 October 2005, 2.

fundamentally alter the relationship between the individual and the state.[21] Peers do not, by convention, vote against bills at second reading, but opening comments made during the debate on the proposed legislation in the Lords in November 2005 already indicated that it would take some effort to sort out the substantial differences of opinion that existed between the two Houses on this issue. Unsurprisingly, the Bill was then passed back and forth between the Commons and the Lords when Parliament resumed its activities in early 2006,[22] forcing the Government to accept a compromise,[23] before the Lords eventually passed the beleaguered project on 20 March 2006. The Bill received Royal Assent ten days later, but the measure continues to divide the country. The Conservative Party, shifting gears after the Bill ran into trouble in the Lords,[24] has repeatedly vowed to review the Act should it win the next general election.[25] Identity cards are thus not only a very current legal problem; they are also likely to cause continued political debate in the years to come.

Views on the proposal could hardly lie further apart, and range from utter condemnation to full endorsement. Critics have called the initiative expensive, pointless, and dangerous, a folly, a threat to privacy, race relations, and traditional freedoms.[26] Richard Thomas, the Information Commissioner, has put on record that the identity cards scheme, in conjunction with other databases such as the Citizen's Information Project planned by the Office for National Statistics, various already existing fingerprint and DNA databases,[27] and four million CCTV cameras currently in operation throughout the country, might contribute to 'East German Stasi-style' snooping, and warned that the nation could 'sleepwalk into a surveillance society where much more information is collected

[21] See 'Peers Demand ID Safeguards', *The Times* 25 October 2005, 2.

[22] See 'ID Cards Plan in Crisis after Peers Inflict Defeat', the *Independent* 17 January 2006, 6; 'Government Fights On As Peers Inflict Defeats on ID Card Bill', the *Guardian* 17 January 2006, 12; and 'ID Card Stand-Off', *The Times* 14 March 2006, 2.

[23] Postponing, *inter alia*, the compulsory introduction of identity cards for individuals applying for a new passport.

[24] See 'Tories Change Tack Again to Oppose Identity Cards Plan', *The Times* 19 January 2006, 26.

[25] See the comments by the Shadow Home Secretary David Davis, *House of Commons Hansard Debates* 29 March 2006, col 1004: 'I will accept the Government's limited stay of execution, but I do not accept the Bill as a whole. It is still an unwarranted intrusion on the privacy of the individual. It is still ineffective, costly and potentially dangerous. It is still a massive reversal of the relationship between the citizen and the state. While I recommend that my party support the amendment, let there be no doubt that my first act when I take over as Home Secretary after the next election will be to do away with the Bill'. See also 'Tories Would Repeal ID Cards Law', the *Independent* 30 June 2005, 9.

[26] For a summary of these criticisms see House of Commons Research Paper 05/43, 13 June 2005, 43 ff.

[27] Such as the National Automated Fingerprint Identification System (Nafis) or the England and Wales National DNA Database (ND-NAD).

about people, accessible to far more people, and shared across many more boundaries, than British society would feel comfortable with'.[28] Supporters, on the other hand, maintain that identity cards will help tackle illegal immigration, unauthorized working and employment, organized crime, terrorist activity, identity theft, and fraudulent access to public services. They are also convinced that the cards will help citizens to deal with every-day transactions such as renting videos or opening bank accounts, and that they could simplify travelling, eventually replacing passports and driving licences.[29] Listening to this long list of advantages, it seems as if a personalized magic wand is in the works, or, in the words of Charles Clarke, writing for *The Times* in December 2004, a 'profoundly civil libertarian measure because it promotes the most fundamental civil liberty in our society, which is the right to live free from crime and fear'.[30]

To rehearse each of these arguments in greater detail would be tedious; suffice it to emphasize that the public discussion has, it seems, focused too much on four aspects of the scheme: first, the question whether IDs should be compulsory; secondly, whether they should be carried at all times and presented on request in the course of on-the-spot checks in the street; thirdly, the possible cost of single cards and the system as a whole, for both the individual citizen and the taxpayer in general; and, finally, the ability of the Government to efficiently cope with a high-tech project of this magnitude.[31] Less attention has thus far, on the other hand, been paid to what seems to be the keystone of the whole scheme: data protection. This contribution is devoted to a closer analysis of two issues: the amount of information which the so-called National Identity Register could eventually hold on each individual and the danger of creating one central database which is accessible by a number of very different public authorities and private bodies performing equally diverse functions. The reader is thereby invited to consider German experience as we go along, despite the warning of Baroness Thatcher, who in a private meeting denounced identity cards as a 'Germanic concept completely alien to this country'.[32] As explained earlier, this statement is certainly correct in the

[28] See 'Beware Rise of Big Brother State, Warns Data Watchdog', *The Times* 16 August 2004, 1–2.

[29] See eg Home Office, Identity Cards Briefing, May 2005.

[30] See 'ID Cards Defend the Ultimate Civil Liberty', *The Times* 20 December 2004, 14.

[31] See eg 'Make Your Identity Known—or Face a Fine of £1,000', *The Times* 30 November 2004, 26; 'Chaos as Police Fingerprint Database Fails', the *Independent* 3 December 2004, 19; 'ID Cards to Cost £300 per Person', the *Observer* 29 May 2005, 1; 'ID Cards will "Help Fraudsters"', *The Times* 13 June 2005; and 'ID Cards with New Passport to cost £93', the *Daily Telegraph* 14 October 2005, 10.

[32] See 'Identity Cards', *Guardian unlimited* 20 December 2004; 'Identity crisis over UK cards', the *Telegraph* 8 March 2005, via <www.telegraph.co.uk>.

sense that IDs have only featured as a wartime measure in the United Kingdom whereas Germany has relied on identity documents in one form or the other for centuries;[33] indeed, the 'emergency that was the occasion of the passing of this Act', referred to in section 12(4) of the National Registration Act 1939, was the threat posed by an authoritarian and centralized Germany, a regime which drew much of its strength from an unparalleled degree of internal surveillance and control. But this is, more than sixty years later, only one side of the coin. While identity cards are admittedly regarded as something perfectly normal by its citizens, Germany has at the same time pioneered the idea of data protection as a human right enjoying full constitutional status. Important court decisions on the matter were handed down as early as the late 1960s, and the worldwide first piece of specific legislation in this field of law seems to have been the Data Protection Act of 1970 in the State of Hessen.[34] This is no coincidence. As we shall see later, Germany experienced a substantial terrorist challenge some thirty years ago, a threat which first led to a powerful security response by the state, and then, in part perhaps a counter-reaction, the development of stricter standards for the protection of personal data. Due to this specific history, the German approach could thus provide some insight when it comes to balancing security interests and individual freedom in today's troubled times.

The Identity Cards Act 2006[35]

In short, this legislation is geared towards the creation of a central register and the establishment of powers to issue identity cards for everyone living permanently in the United Kingdom.[36] It will ensure that biographical checks can be made against other existing databases in order to confirm specified details of an identity on application.[37] Once in operation, the Register will enable public and, to a more limited extent, private sector

[33] For a detailed account of identification documents in Europe see V Groebner, *Der Schein der Person. Steckbrief, Ausweis und Kontrolle im Europa des Mittelalters* (Munich: C H Beck Verlag, 2004).

[34] Hessisches Datenschutzgesetz, 30 September 1970 (GVBl. I 1970, 625). On this early data protection law see H J Reh, 'Gegenstand und Aufgabe des Datenschutzes in der öffentlichen Verwaltung' in Hessischer Datenschutzbeauftragter (ed), *Beiträge zum Datenschutz*, Heft 2 (1974); S Simitis (ed), *Bundesdatenschutzgesetz* (6th edn) (Baden Baden, Nomos Verlagsgesellschaft, 2006), Einleitung no 1 (S Simitis). The United States enacted the Fair Credit Reporting Act, more specifically designed to protect the personal data of bank customers, only a few weeks later.

[35] Hereafter 'the Act'.

[36] Identity Cards Act 2006, ss 1–2.

[37] ibid, s 9.

organizations to verify a particular identity before providing certain services if the person concerned agrees.[38] More importantly, the Act defines the circumstances in which specified agencies such as the Secret Intelligence Service, the Government Communications Headquarters, the Serious Organized Crime Agency, or Her Majesty's Revenue and Customs can be provided with information without an individual's consent or even knowledge.[39] The Act also includes powers to link future access to specified public services such as education, healthcare, or state benefits to the production of an identity card, rendering IDs, in practical terms, a necessity for many, if not all, citizens, and provides the power to make entries for an individual with or without application or consent if information capable of being recorded is already available elsewhere and if the Secretary of State believes that the addition to the Register would be consistent with the statutory purposes of the scheme.[40] Linking identity cards to the provision of public services would thereby require the involvement of Parliament and approval by resolution of each House[41] while the latter measure is left to administrative discretion. The future compulsory registration of individuals as initially envisaged by the Government was dropped due to the opposition of the Lords.[42]

The amount of information which will be recorded in the Register is impressive. Schedule 1, sections 1 to 5 of the Bill mention the full name and any other names by which a person is or has been known, the date and place of birth, gender, the principal and any other place of residence in the United Kingdom, the image of the head and shoulders, the signature, fingerprints and other biometric information such as an iris scan, the nationality, details of any existing entitlement to enter or remain in the country, any national insurance number, the number of any UK or foreign passport that was issued, the number of any identity card issued by the authorities of a country or territory outside the United Kingdom, the number of any existing work permit, any driver number allocated by a driving licence, the date of expiry or period of validity of any of the above mentioned documents, as well as the particulars of changes affecting that information. The Register will also record the date of an individual's death. Any verification of identities based on this volume of information alone would already provide what the Home Office calls a 'gold standard'.[43]

[38] ibid s 12. [39] ibid s 17. [40] ibid s 13. [41] ibid s 14.

[42] Identity Cards Bill, 25 May 2005 (Bill 9), s 6.

[43] Government Reply to the Fourth Report from the Home Affairs Committee, Session 2003–04 HC 130, 14 at no 21.

Three further provisions of the Act are, however, of particular interest in our context. Schedule 1, section 5, authorizes the retention of any information once validly recorded in the Register, while section 7 extends the database to all information submitted and steps taken to verify the initial individual entry or subsequent changes. This substantial collateral information is supplemented by what is arguably the most powerful tool of the whole Act. Tucked away at the very end of Schedule 1 is an authorization to record the circumstances of every occasion on which information contained in the Register was provided, and thus facilitates indirectly the creation of an individual profile on the basis of all services used by a person which have led the relevant provider to check a citizen's identity or entitlement, and depending on the decision of the relevant bodies, occasions on which the Register was accessed by security authorities without the knowledge or consent of the affected citizen.[44] This access record, a feature not contemplated under the initial Entitlement Card scheme, will inevitably reveal a substantial number of sources where detailed personal information is held outside the National Identity Register. More importantly, the fact that the Register was used to verify a person's identity at a particular time and in a particular context will in itself allow inferences to be drawn with respect to the type of transaction involved and, consequently, provide important clues to the kind of life a person is living. Does he travel much, and if so, does he make use of car rentals? Does he rely on public services, and if so, of what nature? Does he watch videos or DVDs? Does he have a bank account, and if so, where? How often does he see his GP? Does he receive registered mail requiring identification or hold a post office box? Is he a student, and if so, where is he enrolled? Does he read books?

The density of this web of information, ranging from the seemingly harmless fact that someone applied for membership of a video rental or public library to the far more sensitive profiling of an individual's movements and habits on the basis of a long-term analysis of requests made to access the Register will, of course, depend on the number of compulsory checks eventually introduced by the Government and the success of the verification scheme in the private sphere. But even in its most basic form, entries to the Register will in all likelihood contain a substantial amount of personal information and indirect access data.

[44] Identity Cards Act 2006, Schedule 1 s 9.

The Potential of Modern Information Technology in the Light of German Experience

Reflecting on Schedule 1 of the Act, it seems as if the magic identity card could easily turn into a curse. Why is that? What is the danger of allowing the state to compile information already available, for the greater part, in separate sets of data held by separate public bodies? Two examples from Germany might serve as a useful illustration.

German police strategies have in the past shown how initially unrelated bits and pieces of information, combined with imaginative thinking, can be used to assemble the profile of and track down certain individuals.

When Hanns-Martin Schleyer, former Board Member of Daimler Benz and President of the German Employers' Association, was kidnapped in September 1977 by members of the left-wing terrorist organization Rote Armee Fraktion, who killed three security officers and the driver of Schleyer's car on the spot, police authorities combined knowledge about the geographical location of the kidnapping with a number of clever assumptions concerning the likely plan of the terrorists to eventually identify three flats in the wider Cologne area suspected of harbouring both the kidnappers and their victim.[45] The choice was based on six criteria. They predicted, first, the possible distance a car could travel before the risk of being caught by police road blocks set up shortly after the attack became too great— this area covered a distance of roughly fifteen kilometres in all directions; secondly, the likelihood of the kidnappers using a fairly anonymous council estate-type building to hide the victim; thirdly, the probability that this building would be conveniently located close to a highway in order to facilitate quick moves if so required by the further course of events; fourthly, that the location would probably feature a discreet drive-in garage with easy direct access by elevator in order to both hide the get-away car and bring the victim into the building without fear of discovery; fifthly, that the terrorists would probably pay their utility bills in cash rather than by direct debit in order to limit their paper trail; and, finally, that they would in all likelihood rent the flat under a false identity, and would probably have done so fairly recently. This last assumption was crucial.

[45] For a detailed account of the background of the Rote Armee Fraktion and, *inter alia*, the kidnapping of Hanns-Martin Schleyer, see S Aust, *Der Baader-Meinhoff-Komplex* (2nd edn) (Hamburg: Hoffmann und Campe Verlag, 1997); and H Breloer, *Todesspiel.*

After comparing the names of legitimate customers of utility and insurance companies operating in the area, the data held by local authorities with which Germans are required to register their place of residence, and names of property owners, registered, again, in a separate databank, very few flats with possibly illegitimate tenants remained. It later emerged on reconstruction of the tragic events that the local Cologne police, applying these six criteria, had actually found the hide-out where the terrorists were holding Schleyer less than forty-eight hours after the kidnapping; that a plain-clothes member of the police force had performed an initial check on the location, knocking on the correct door while the terrorists were standing on the other side, gun in hand; but that this information concerning the flat and its suspicious tenants, who had rented the property at very short notice and insisted on paying the deposit in cash, was lost in the vast amount of clues collected by the special unit charged with the investigation and thus ignored. The glitch had serious repercussions. Following the close call, the kidnappers moved to a different location outside Germany, and the hunt continued unsuccessfully for another forty-three days. The Government of Chancellor Helmut Schmidt, refusing to negotiate with the Rote Armee Fraktion, was taken to the Federal Constitutional Court by the son of the victim, who argued that the state was under a duty to save the life of Schleyer at all costs.[46] The Court rejected the application in what remains to the present day one of the hardest decisions that judges in Germany were required to make. Hanns-Martin Schleyer's body was found dead in an abandoned car three days later.

Two years after these events, the police were more successful. Rudolph Heißler, one of the terrorists involved in the Schleyer kidnapping, was arrested, this time with the help of a simple combination of personal information contained in four unrelated databases. Starting again with the assumption that the suspect would pay his electricity bills in cash, the investigators eliminated from a list of 16,000 customers of the Frankfurt municipal power provider living in fairly anonymous apartment blocks all those who had officially registered their place of residence, held a driving licence, had a vehicle registered under their name and address, or were receiving a children's allowance from the welfare authorities. Two apartments

Von der Schleyer-Entführung bis Mogadischu. Eine dokumentarische Erzählung (3rd edn) (Cologne: Kiepenheuer und Witsch Verlag, 1997).

[46] BVerfGE 46, 160 ff. For a summary of the decision see H-G Dederer, 'Grundrechtliche Schutzpflicht des Staates für das menschliche Leben bei terroristischer Erpressung des Staates: Freie Hand für die Staatsleitung' in J Menzel (ed), *Verfassungsrechtsprechung* (Tübingen: Mohr Siebeck, 2000).

remained on their list: one used by a drug dealer, the other a safe house of the Rote Armee Fraktion where Heißler was apprehended by special forces.

Both events prove the enormous potential of an intelligent selection and combination of personal data, and the technique has been further refined and is used by police authorities in Germany to the present day.[47]

Four observations should be made at this point.

The first is that these investigative techniques were developed thirty years ago with technological resources not even remotely comparable to those available to public authorities in this day and age. A central database with the potential of the envisaged National Identity Register would far exceed the surveillance and law enforcement capacity available to the German police in the late 1970s.

Secondly, these two examples from Germany illustrate the positive side of information held or acquired and then processed by public authorities. Tracking down terrorists and fighting organized crime are, no doubt, very legitimate aims. There are, however, arguments that militate against the accumulation of information which enables the state to assemble a detailed profile of individual citizens: personal information, patterns of behaviour, and lifestyles. Terrorists and criminals aside, critical and perhaps unconventional, but essentially harmless, individuals could easily fall victim to overly zealous security authorities, especially if public opinion calls for quick investigative successes in the aftermath of catastrophes such as the attacks on the World Trade Centre or the London bombings of July 2005. In Lower Saxony, police authorities searched for students possibly involved in the terrorist attacks on the United States, targeting individuals from twenty-three predominantly Muslim countries and collecting large amounts of information from immigration authorities, universities, and private employers for the purposes of profiling. The exercise did not result in a single investigative success, and the collected material was destroyed, as prescribed by law, eighteen months later. The State Data Protection Commissioner nevertheless expressed deep concern about the scrutiny of so many innocent residents, and criticized what he felt was police activity at the very limits, and in some cases clearly beyond the limits, of data protection law. The Federal Constitutional Court recently deliberated on the constitutional complaint of one of the individuals monitored by the police, and declared the measure unconstitutional for lack of an immediate threat to important public interests.[48]

[47] So-called *Rasterfahndung*; see P Gola and R Schomerus, *Bundesdatenschutzgesetz* (8th edn) (Munich: C H Beck Verlag, 2005), para 13, no 6a.

[48] Case 1 BvR 518/02, 23 May 2006.

The highly controversial case highlights the danger of abuse if techniques similar to those described above are deployed for preventive purposes rather than for the investigation of crimes already committed, as in the Schleyer situation.

A third observation, to which we shall return shortly, concerns the legal footing on which German police authorities based their investigations in the late 1970s. An unambiguous legal authorization to access and evaluate information held in different public and private databases was introduced only a decade later and under the pressure of an evolving system of constitutional data protection principles developed by the courts. Today, police laws across the country feature specific provisions allowing for access to personal data held in a variety of public and private registers in order to prevent the most serious of crimes, subject to the condition, *inter alia*, that these could not be prevented or efficiently investigated by other more conventional and less intrusive police strategies.[49] But there was substantial opposition to such rules on the part of the security establishment, which would rather have kept the old regime based on widely phrased general police powers. Even the existing police laws will have to be reviewed in the light of the judgment of the Federal Constitutional Court in the *Lower Saxony* case.

Finally, the two events highlight a statement made by the German Federal Constitutional Court a few years after the Schleyer kidnapping in its so-called *Volkzählung* decision of 1983,[50] a highly politicized case concerning the constitutionality of a comprehensive census of the German population and probably the most important German judgment on data protection thus far. In dealing with the amount and quality of the information German citizens were required to provide to the national statistical agency, the Court argued that modern technology had rendered the notion of 'insignificant' or 'harmless' data obsolete.[51] According to this view, any piece of information can be relevant, depending on the wider context of an inquiry and the technological potential to combine seemingly unrelated facts and give them a new meaning.[52]

[49] For summaries of the respective provisions found in the police laws of the States see T Groß, *Terrorbekämpfung und Grundrechte, Kritische Justiz* (2002), 1–3 ff; and B Pieroth, B Schlink, and M Kniesel, *Polizei- und Ordnungsrecht* (3rd edn) (Munich: C H Beck Verlag, 2005), 302 ff.

[50] BVerfGE 65, 1 ff.

[51] ibid 45; H Dreier (ed), *Grundgesetz* (2nd edn) (Tübingen: Mohr Siebeck, 2004), Art 2 I, no 80.

[52] For a recent evaluation of this decision in the context of new technological developments see H P Bull, *Zweifelsfragen um die informationelle Selbstbestimmung—Datenschutz als Datenaskese?, Neue Juristische Wochenschrift* (2006), 1617 ff.

The German and UK Approaches Compared

What conclusions then did Germans draw about the idea of data protection from their struggle against terrorism in the late 1970s and, more importantly, the incredible public opposition to the census law of 1982, which attracted over 1,300 individual constitutional complaints? And how could this experience be in any way relevant to the discussion concerning the introduction of identity cards in the United Kingdom over twenty years later? The answer, I believe, is threefold.

First, the right of the individual to control the use of any personal data,[53] according to German doctrine a facet of the general right to the protection of an individual's personality, the so-called *allgemeines Persönlichkeitsrecht*, is a human right worthy of substantial protection.[54] This does not mean that personal data may not be collected and used by the state, which has a legitimate and growing need for information in order to adequately fulfil many of its modern-day functions. As is the case with most human rights, sufficiently important public aims, from the provision of public services to the wider need to ensure the security interests of a country, may lead to a reasonable limitation of individual freedom.[55] Each limitation, however, requires a constitutional statutory basis which gives citizens a clear idea of the amount and nature of information held by a particular public authority at a particular point in time. This means that the German state does not exist as one single entity when it comes to personal data. Each public body at every level of government requires its own and specific legislative authorization to collect and use personal data for its own limited purposes, and any access to information held by other public bodies will require an equally specific statutory basis. In terms of personal data, the German state is thus highly 'compartmentalized', a concept which gives citizens a stronger position when dealing with single public authorities.[56] A very similar approach was adopted in

[53] So-called *Recht auf informationelle Selbstbestimmung*. This phrase appears to have been coined by M Hirsch in his dissenting opinion in BVerfGE 57, 170, 182 ff and 201 f.

[54] See A Podlech, 'Das Recht auf Privatheit' in J Perels (ed), *Grundrechte als Fundament der Demokratie* (Frankfurt am Main: Suhrkamp Verlag, 1979), 50 ff, 55; K Rogall, *Informationseingriff und Gesetzesvorbehalt im Strafprozeß* (Tübingen: Mohr Siebeck, 1992), 41 ff; Simitis, n 34 above, Einleitung nos 30 ff; P Gola and C Klug, *Grundzüge des Datenschutzrechts* (Munich: C H Beck, 2003), 1 ff; D C Umbach and T Clemens (eds), *Heidelberger Kommentar zum Grundgesetz*, Band I (Heidelberg: C F Müller, 2002), Art 2I nos 45 ff; BVerfGE 65, 1 ff, 43; BVerfGE 78, 77 ff, 84 ff; BVerfGE 96, 56, 61; BGH NJW 1991, 1532–3.

[55] See eg Umbach and Clemens, ibid, Art 2I no 54 ff.

[56] So-called *bereichsspezifischer Datenschutz*; see P Gola and C Klug, *Grundzüge des Datenschutzrechts*, 8 ff; H Wohlgemuth and J Gerloff, *Datenschutzrecht* (3rd edn) (Munich: Luchterhand, 2005), 7 ff.

the United Kingdom by the Data Protection Act 1998. The Second Data Protection Principle enshrined in Schedule 1 states that 'personal data shall be obtained only for one or more specified and lawful purposes, and shall not be further processed in any manner incompatible with that purpose or those purposes'. A good example of the practical consequences of this so-called 'purpose limitation principle' is council tax legislation, which is very specific about the purposes for which the information contained in these fairly comprehensive registers may be collected and used.[57]

Closely related to this point is a second consideration following from the principle of proportionality (*Verhältnismäßigkeit*). An uncodified constitutional standard for the exercise of any public authority in Germany, the principle requires that a particular measure be capable of promoting a particular public aim; that it is necessary in the sense that this aim cannot be reached by less restrictive or milder means; and that the burden placed on the individual citizen is, finally, not disproportionate to the advantages for the general public interest. This analysis requires each and every public act to be justified in the light of the specific purpose involved. In the field of data protection the approach sets different limits on the amount and quality of information which may be collected and used by different public bodies according to their very specific statutory functions.[58] A social security agency is unlikely to require knowledge about whether a particular individual holds a driving licence or a passport in order to perform its functions properly; and customs authorities will not need the social security number of citizens to perform theirs. Each public interest and each set of measures involving personal data will therefore have to be evaluated separately. The Data Protection Act 1998 again contains quite a similar requirement. The Third Data Protection Principle states that 'personal data shall be adequate, relevant and not excessive in relation to the purpose or purposes for which they are processed'. In his legal guidance for employers, the Information Commissioner elaborates that data controllers, when reviewing their responsibilities in the light of this provision, should seek to identify the minimum amount of information that is required in order properly to fulfil their purposes.[59] The same applies to public authorities.[60]

[57] On the Second Data Protection Principle see P Carey, *Data Protection* (2nd edn) (Oxford:Oxford University Press, 2004), 54 f.

[58] See eg Gola and Klug, n 56 above, 46.

[59] Information Commissioner, Employment Practices Data Protection Code, 35 f; S Gaskill and P Weinman, 'Information Requirements and Fair Processing' in P Carey, *Data Protection Handbook* (London: The Law Society, 2004), 117 ff.

[60] On the Third Data Protection Principle, see Carey, n 57 above, 55 f.

It is revealing to compare the Identity Cards Act 2006 with its German counterpart, the so-called *Personalausweisgesetz*,[61] in this respect. Section 1(4) of the UK Act names five very different interests for the purposes of which the National Identity Register is to provide a secure and reliable method for individual data to be ascertained or verified. These are national security; the prevention or detection of crime; the enforcement of immigration controls; prohibitions on unauthorized working or employment; and, finally, the efficiency and effective provision of public services.[62] In line with these comprehensive aims, a variety of bodies are envisaged to have potential access to the Register. Private entities aside, the Act specifically mentions the Security Service, the Secret Intelligence Service, the Government Communications Headquarters, the Serious Organized Crime Agency, police authorities, Her Majesty's Revenue and Customs, persons who provide a public service, and on the basis of a general clause contained in section 21 any other public authority by virtue of an order of the Secretary of State requiring approval by both Houses of Parliament.[63] Finally, it is important to bear in mind that the Data Protection Principles just mentioned and most of the key provisions of the Data Protection Act do not apply where exemption is required to safeguard national security.[64]

By contrast, section 2 of the *Personalausweisgesetz* restricts the purposes of the corresponding German Register to two very limited functions: first, to issue identity cards and determine their validity; and secondly, to determine the identity of the person holding the card. It is important to note that on-line access to information held on the Register is limited to border control authorities and the police when searching for individuals in the course of criminal law enforcement. Other public authorities or private entities do not have on-line access and must rely on the limited information immediately visible on the card itself.[65] The amount of information held on the German Register is, moreover, far less extensive than that envisaged for the National Identity Register in the United Kingdom. Its main function is to technically facilitate the production of identity cards, which themselves, in most cases, prove who the holder of the card is, and not to record personal information on one central database for a wide variety of public and, indirectly, even private aims.[66] A statement contained in an Identity Cards Briefing by the Home Office

[61] Gesetz über Personalausweise, 19 December 1950 (BGBl 1950, 807 ff) with subsequent amendments.

[62] Identity Cards Act 2006, s 1(4).

[63] ibid, ss 17–21.

[64] Data Protection Act 1998, s 28. See Carey, n 59 above, 133 f.

[65] Personalausweisgesetz, s 3a.

[66] Personalausweisgesetz, s 1.

clarifies the difference between these two approaches. According to the protagonists of the project in the United Kingdom, the 'ID cards scheme is more than just issuing pieces of plastic. It is about recording on a *central database* basic personal information.'[67] This critical point was also identified by the House of Lords Select Committee on the Constitution, which noted in its recent report that:

> [T]he Bill's primary significance lies in the creation of a national scheme for registering the identities [and associated personal details] of all persons within the United Kingdom . . . The Bill's title is therefore misleading, and it might more accurately be described as the *National Identity Register and Identity Cards Bill.* When the scheme is fully in place, the role of identity cards themselves will be secondary to the database of information recording the personal history on a life-long basis of every individual in the Register. It will be possible, once all the biometric information is recorded, for the authorities, by scanning anyone who is or should be on the Register, to check their identity and access the information about them without recourse to the identity card itself.[68]

The logic of the German scheme is quite the opposite.

Comparing these two approaches to identity cards and their necessary technical foundation, that is, databases containing information capable of issuing cards safely and verifying, if necessary, the identity of individuals, I would argue that it is preferable to identify and then pursue single public interests in separate pieces of legislation, applying the idea of proportionality separately in each and every case. But careful balancing, the essence of proportionality, is only possible if the interest of the state and the negative effect of a particular measure on the individual are precisely determined. To pursue the obvious and certainly legitimate need for a database to physically facilitate ID cards, on the one hand, and, on the other, the general need for information on persons living in a country for a variety of very different public concerns, muddies the waters. The House of Lords and House of Commons Joint Committee on Human Rights came to a similar conclusion in its recent report when it noted that the Bill's provision for the retention of extensive personal information relating to all or large sections of the population may be insufficiently targeted to be justified as proportionate to the statutory aims.[69]

To be fair, the Act contains elements of proportionality and data protection thinking. Section 21, for example, dealing with instances in

[67] Home Office, Identity Cards Briefing, May 2005, 3.

[68] House of Lords Select Committee on the Constitution, 5th Report of Session 2004–5, Identity Cards Bill, Report with Evidence, HL Paper 82, 4.

[69] House of Lords and House of Commons Joint Committee on Human Rights, Identity Cards Bill, 5th Report of Session 2004–5, HL Paper 35, 9.

which the ID Cards Register may be accessed without the individual's consent, forces the Secretary of State to satisfy himself that it would not have been reasonably practicable for the person to whom information is provided to have obtained that data by other means. Moreover, other conditions and personal as well as technical limitations may be introduced by regulation in order to safeguard personal data in that particularly sensitive context. Another example is section 15(3)(c) which allows for a selective use of information held on the Register in cases where regulations authorize persons providing a public service to check the identity of an individual. Access to personal information could be restricted to a smaller number of details, depending on the nature of the public service in question.

These limitations on the unqualified use of the Register are commendable but also highlight another difference between the German and UK identity card regimes. German constitutional law requires the legislator himself to decide issues which substantially impact on human rights by formal parliamentary legislation.[70] The UK Bill, by contrast, is described by the Home Office as 'an enabling measure, (...) not a detailed blueprint for the scheme. It sets out a legal framework in primary legislation within which the scheme will operate without being overly-prescriptive about the detail'.[71] Despite the safeguards established by countless 'affirmative' and 'super-affirmative' procedures imposed on the Secretary of State when making regulations on the basis of the envisaged Act, it would be preferable to create clear and precise statutory foundations by primary legislation in this highly sensitive area of modern human existence. In particular, the possible limitations on access to information held on the Register by various public and private bodies should be spelt out in each and every case. To my mind, the chosen approach does indeed bear a high risk of 'sleepwalk[ing) into a surveillance society', as the Information Commissioner put it so eloquently.

Finally, there is a third aspect to the compilation of personal information where the German approach to data protection could provide food for thought, an approach, I hasten to add, developed in the course of many heated battles between protagonists of efficient public authorities and their more sceptical critics. Indeed, the conflict surrounding the 1983 census, endorsed by all political parties represented in Parliament and eventually settled in court, threw Germany into a deep political crisis which could, arguably, even be dubbed a 'cold' civil war.

[70] On the basis of the so-called 'Wesentlichkeitstheorie'.
[71] Home Office, Identity Cards Briefing May 2005, 9.

What is this third and perhaps most important dimension? Put simply, data protection as a human right prevents the German state constitutionally from creating a comprehensive profile of single individuals by assembling vast amounts of personal information in one central and permanent database. 'Constitutionally' means that 'simple' legislation, that is any rule below the rank of the Basic Law, has to respect this final limitation. The approach has its roots in the notion of human dignity in Article 1 of the Basic Law and will allow no exceptions, whether in the interest of national security or any other public aim. As early as 1969, the Federal Constitutional Court declared it incompatible with human dignity if the state were to systematically create a personal profile, a catalogue containing extensive information on certain citizens or, worse, the whole population.[72] But where is the borderline? How extensive may a collection of personal data be, and what information would contribute to the creation of such a human profile?

Initially, the Court argued in terms of different spheres of life, categorizing information as belonging to the social, private, or intimate dimensions of a person's existence. This is again quite similar to the approach of the Data Protection Act 1998, which establishes stricter conditions for the use of particularly sensitive personal information, including data pertaining to the racial or ethnic origins, political opinions, religious beliefs, the physical and mental health condition, or the sexual life of a person.[73] But while the Data Protection Act 1998 names ten conditions under which information of this kind may nevertheless be processed, including the necessary use for the administration of justice or the exercise of functions conferred on a person by or under an enactment,[74] the German Court in 1969 acknowledged a core area of human life where the state may not collect data under any circumstances, and the distinction between information concerning different spheres of life, with a decreasing level of protection as data become less intimate, has become less easy to invoke by public authorities wishing to record seemingly harmless facts.[75] The German Government nevertheless won the case in question; the disputed information, again requested in the context of a census, concerned the way citizens spend their holidays, certainly an issue of fundamental importance to most Germans, but not sufficiently relevant to merit non-disclosure in the eyes of the Court.

How would the ID Cards scheme fare under this approach? Anxious to address the mounting criticism of its plans, the Home Office has

[72] BVerfGE 27, 1 ff. [73] Data Protection Act 1998, s 2.
[74] ibid, Schedule 3.
[75] BVerfGE 65, 1 ff, 45; H Dreier, *Grundgesetz*, Art 2I, nos 80, 88.

repeatedly pointed out that medical information or data concerning religious beliefs would not be recorded in the National Identity Register. It is not clear, however, whether excluding such particularly sensitive information from being recorded in an otherwise extensive database would in itself suffice in Germany today. In its 1983 decision, the Federal Constitutional Court was, as pointed out above, at pains to emphasize that 'harmless' data have simply ceased to exist in this day and age, in which vast amounts of information can be assembled, combined, and transferred with a few clicks of a mouse. It is not only the quality of the information, as under the Court's own previous doctrine, but also the amount of personal data which can be collected, possible combinations between various entries to a register, and the technical potential for electronic processing which determine the danger that a given database can pose to individual freedom. The Court justified this approach mainly out of concern for the autonomy of the citizen. If the individual cannot reasonably predict what the state might know about him in a particular context, there is a real danger that he will feel severely inhibited in his actions and may refrain from exercising valid rights.[76] This position was more recently modified by the Federal Data Protection Act of 2003,[77] which (under the influence of European developments and again similar to the current position in the United Kingdom) mentions a category of particularly sensitive data which may be processed but is subject to more severe safeguards.[78] It remains to be seen how the courts will interpret this new law, which marks a change in the German approach to data protection. Early decisions, however, already indicate that the more restrictive doctrine of the Federal Constitutional Court will continue to have a strong, if not decisive, influence. As a constitutional human right discovered, some would say invented, by the *Bundesverfassungsgericht* in 1983, this right, in its interpretation by the Court, would prevail if it ever came to the crunch.

The National Identity Register, and especially the idea of keeping access records as part of the individual entry, seems to me quite exceptional in this regard. Some citizens might, for instance, refrain from applying for social security benefits or other public services for fear that their application might leave an access trail on a database which would then be visible to a large number of other authorities for the rest of their

[76] For a summary of BVerfGE 65, 1, see A Peilert, 'Das Recht auf informationelle Selbstbestimmung als konkretisierung des allgemeinen Persönlichkeitsrechts' in J Menzel, *Verfassungsrechtsprechung*, 344 ff.

[77] Bundesdatenschutzgesetz, 14 January 2003 (BGBl I, 66 ff).

[78] Bundesdatenschutzgesetz, ss 3(9) and 4d (5).

lives. For the same reason, others might be reluctant to use internet resources requiring age verification if the provider were to demand an identity check based on information recorded in the Register. The House of Lords and House of Commons Joint Committee on Human Rights was again correct to say that: '[T]he retention of records of checks against the Register . . . is likely to build up a comprehensive picture of an individual's employment, use of public services and private transactions, which, over time, would amount to a considerable intrusion on the individual's private life'.[79]

It is interesting to note in this context that the German Anti-Terrorism Act of 2002, which also introduced, *inter alia*, the use of biometric information in passports and identity cards, specifically excludes the establishment of any central database, and that comprehensive information collected in the course of criminal investigations of the sort described earlier has to be destroyed, including any records of access to existing databases, once a specific search has been concluded.[80] Access data, whether resulting from a public or private application supplied with information, simply do not exist.

Conclusion

Intrigued by the remark of Baroness Thatcher concerning the Germanic origin of identity cards, this contribution has analysed the Identity Cards Act 2006 with the considerable assistance of foreign ideas. It seems that the approaches of German and English law when it comes to data protection are at times quite similar, if not identical, in principle; various provisions in Germany could easily be exchanged for rules contained in the Data Protection Act 1998, not least because of the common European legal framework created by the Data Protection Directive of the European Community ten years ago.[81] But some crucial differences nevertheless exist, if not in the general thrust, then certainly in the extent to which data protection features as a human right in both societies. One of the few more fundamental differences, however, is the angle from which both legal orders have developed their respective data protection rules. In Germany, 'informational self-determination' is regarded primarily as a human right which insulates the individual from overly oppressive state

[79] House of Commons and House of Lords Joint Committee on Human Rights, First Report, Session 2005–6, Identity Cards Bill, no 4.11.

[80] Gesetz zur Bekämpfung des internationalen Terrorismus, 9 January 2002, BGBl I 2002, 361, 366 f.

[81] Directive 95/46/EC.

measures in the classic sense; the emphasis is placed on protection against infringements. In the United Kingdom, far more thought is given to the equally important problem of individual access to information held by public or private bodies. Both dimensions are, of course, part and parcel of the same human right. It would seem, however, that in the case of identity cards and their corresponding registers we are in fact dealing with the *status negativus* of the citizen: his right to defend himself against the accumulation of too much information by the state. The German experience, it seems, is of more use in this particular context.

Where does this comparative analysis leave us when it comes to the Identity Cards Act? On balance, I believe that the criteria developed in Germany militate for the introduction of identity cards in the United Kingdom, but against the creation of a central register as envisaged by the Act. Fairly secure, if not foolproof, IDs are a useful tool in achieving many of the aims correctly emphasized by the Government in its quest to justify the scheme. The fight against identity theft and fraudulent access to public services, for example, is likely to benefit from more secure forms of identification than the notorious two utility bills currently used in so many everyday situations. I admit that I was fairly irritated when asked for these bills on application for a membership card in my local video rental some years back, then again on the occasion of opening a bank account, and, more recently, on application for a social security number. A computer and printer, together with a reasonably good colour photocopier, it seemed to me, could easily produce the necessary documents with a selection of different false names and addresses within half an hour. More importantly, the frequent warnings about utility bills being thrown in the bin and finding their way into the wrong hands, causing much despair to those affected by fraud, show that identity cards do have their merits. German video rentals, banks, and social security agencies do not accept such letters as proof of identity, and Germans do not usually throw their identity cards in the bin.

The state, on the other hand, will need a fair amount of data, including biometrical information, to issue the cards and, in specified cases, verify the identity of persons carrying them. A central database, however, with the potential to create a comprehensive profile of every citizen and accessible for a wide variety of public aims, does indeed change substantially the relationship between the citizen and the state, and is a measure which should at the very least be carefully considered and, in the light of German experience, better avoided. Separate registers, specifically designed to meet the needs of the public bodies involved, and accessible, where absolutely necessary, by intelligence services and the police, will suffice for the achievement of an adequate level of security. They would also limit the dangers of a so-called function creep, the modern term for a phenomenon already identified by Lord Justice Goddard in *Willcock v Muckle* so many years ago when he criticized the use, or rather the abuse, of special police powers envisaged to tackle wartime dangers such as espionage in the course of routine traffic controls years after the end of the Second World War. The inevitable shortcomings of a compartmentalized state, in which each unit enjoys only a limited, or better proportionate, amount of information, are a price worth paying for the sake of individual freedom.

German experience with security legislation suggests, moreover, that certain measures, once introduced in times of crisis, have the disquieting tendency to remain on the statute books long after the emergencies which they were designed to address have disappeared. The best example of this again dates back to the Schleyer kidnapping of 1977, when a special law allowing the complete isolation of single prison inmates in times of an immediate threat to the important interests of the state was enacted in the record time of just five days.[82] This provision, though dormant, is still contained in the Act on Criminal Procedure today,[83] a stark reminder that legislation should not be rushed through Parliament with undue haste and under the impression of an immediate threat.[84] The National Registration Act 1939, which introduced wartime identity cards in this country only two days after the outbreak of the Second World War, but remained in force well after the unconditional surrender of Germany in May 1945, is an equally striking example. The Identity Cards Act 2006, no doubt influenced by the global insecurity following 9/11, will hopefully not fall into the same category.

Finally, I suspect that the most important difference between societies may lie in a factor completely outside the realm of law, data controllers, or computer systems. It is mentality. Four million CCTV cameras cause little concern in this country; apparently, a person living and working in London is likely to be filmed about 300 times on an average day, and posters in buses recently proclaimed that passengers are secure 'beneath the watchful eyes of the Metropolitan Police' on four out of five vehicles. The same posters would probably have caused considerable concern in

[82] Kontaktsperregesetz, 30 September 1977 (BGBl I, 1877 ff).

[83] Einführungsgesetz zum Gerichtsverfassungsgesetz, ss 31 ff.

[84] The Federal Constitutional Court accepted this law as constitutional at the time (BVerfGE 49, 24 ff), though it is open to debate whether it would take the same view again if asked to revisit the issue in substantially changed circumstances.

Berlin, Munich, or Hamburg, where CCTV observation is still very much restricted by law, and citizens resent the idea of being watched all the time. Identity cards, on the other hand, equally part and parcel of security and data protection concerns, produce exactly the opposite reaction in both societies. This, I believe, is where Baroness Thatcher is on target. Identity cards are simply as alien to this country as CCTV cameras are to Germany.

Making Sense of *Mens Rea* in Statutory Conspiracies

*David Ormerod**

Introduction

The issue of *mens rea* in conspiracy provides a perfect current legal problem. It has prompted scholarly articles,[1] commentaries,[2] and an array of decisions from the appellate courts. Causing costly confusion in the courts,[3] it is currently poised for examination by the House of Lords[4] and the Law Commission. Unless resolved, the problem is likely to increase in significance since the shift to intelligence-led policing is likely to produce greater reliance on conspiracy and other inchoates. The advantages in relying on conspiracy charges also suggest that it will remain a firm favourite with prosecutors: it allows for earlier arrests, is easier to indict, allows for more evidence to be adduced, and most importantly for trial, allows the prosecutor to roll together the events of a continuing course of

* I am grateful for comments on earlier drafts and/or discussions on the subject matter from: Rudi Fortson, the members of 6 King's Bench Walk who attended a seminar on some of the issues in June 2005, in particular David Perry QC, and also members of 18 Red Lion Court Chambers, especially Tony Shaw QC, John Anderson, and Jonathan Fisher QC.

[1] See in particular: J C Smith, 'Conspiracy under the Criminal Law Act 1977' [1977] *Criminal Law Review* 598; D W Elliott, '*Mens Rea* in Statutory Conspiracy' [1978] *Criminal Law Review* 203; A C E Lynch, 'A Further Comment' [1978] *Criminal Law Review* 205; J C Smith, 'Some Answers' [1978] *Criminal Law Review* 210; D Hodgson, 'Law Com. No. 76—A Case Study in Criminal Law Reform' in P Glazebrook (ed), *Reshaping Criminal Law: Essays in Honour of Glanville Williams* (London: Stevens, 1978); G Orchard, 'Agreement in Criminal Conspiracy' [1974] *Criminal Law Review* 297; G Williams, 'Letters to the Editor' [1978] *Criminal Law Review* 251, 383.

[2] See J C Smith, commenting on *Taylor* [2002] *Criminal Law Review* 205; *El Kurd* [2001] *Criminal Law Review* 234; *Hussain* [2002] *Criminal Law Review* 407. See also my comments on *Sakavickas* [2005] *Criminal Law Review* 293; *Harmer* [2005] *Criminal Law Review* 482 and *Ali* [2005] *Criminal Law Review* 864.

[3] Cf A J Ashworth, *Principles of Criminal Law* (4th edn) (Oxford: Oxford University Press, 2003), 188: it is 'relatively unusual for the element of knowledge of circumstances to be contested in serious crimes'. While this is largely true of serious crimes requiring *mens rea*, it is unlikely to remain so as Parliament introduces more strict liability serious crimes, eg in the Sexual Offences Act 2003.

[4] *Saik* [2004] EWCA Crim 2936 was overturned by the House of Lords after this chapter was completed. [2006] UKHL 18, [2006] 2 WLR 993.

conduct into a single charge more easily packaged and presented to the jury. No wonder it is a charge often called the 'prosecutor's darling'.

This chapter's principal aims are to analyse the problem and offer intermediate workable solutions for the courts. The approach adopted is a doctrinal and practical rather than a philosophical one.

An Outline of the Problem

Hundreds of offences in English law can be committed without proof of any *mens rea* as to a material circumstance, or on proof of recklessness or suspicion as to the existence of that circumstance. For example, it is an offence:

1. intentionally to touch sexually a child under 13 years of age irrespective of one's (lack of) awareness as to the child's age. It must be proved that the child is under the age of 13, but liability is strict as to the circumstance of age;[5]
2. to launder the proceeds of crime, by transferring, converting them etc., if one suspects that the property is illicit;[6]
3. intentionally or recklessly to damage property belonging to another, with recklessness sufficing as to the circumstance of ownership or possession of the property.[7]

There are many other examples, not all necessarily as serious as these mentioned. When the charge is one of conspiring to commit such crimes, should it be sufficient for the prosecution to prove that D1 and D2 agreed to commit the offence and that D1 and D2 had the *mens rea* in relation to the proscribed circumstances that would be required for the substantive crime? Or, should the prosecution prove a greater degree of *mens rea*? The Criminal Law Act 1977, section 1, is supposed to provide the answer:

> (1) . . . [I]f a person agrees with any other person or persons that a course of conduct shall be pursued which, if the agreement is carried out in accordance with their intentions, either
> (a) will necessarily amount to or involve the commission of any offence or offences by one or more of the parties to the agreement, or
> (b) would do so but for the existence of facts which render the commission of the offence or any of the offences impossible,
>
> he is guilty of conspiracy to commit the offence or offences in question.

[5] Sexual Offences Act 2003, s 7.
[6] Proceeds of Crime Act 2002, ss 327–40.
[7] Criminal Damage Act 1971, s 1.

(2) Where liability for any offence may be incurred without knowledge on the part of the person committing it of any particular fact or circumstance necessary for the commission of the offence, a person shall nevertheless not be guilty of conspiracy to commit that offence by virtue of subsection (1) above unless he and at least one other party to the agreement intend or know that that fact or circumstance shall or will exist at the time when the conduct constituting the offence is to take place.

The difficult nature of the provision has been acknowledged by both academics and the courts.[8] The current legal problem under discussion lies in interpreting and applying that section, particularly section 1(2) in the context of conspiracy generally. Two important preliminary matters must be raised: the relationship of the conspiracy and the substantive crime and the need to view the *mens rea* of conspiracy holistically.

Conspiracy, *Mens Rea* and the Relationship to the Substantive Law

Interpreting section 1(2) presents problems of a technical nature: it is a difficultly worded section.[9] Interpreting section 1(2) also exposes one aspect of a more fundamental problem: identifying the true purpose of the conspiracy offence. In short, the more willing we are to treat conspiracy as a free-standing crime founded on the wrong of the act of agreement to commit crime, divorced from the substantive crime to which it relates, the more likely we are to require a stricter *mens rea* element. However, in practice, it is all too easy for the conspiracy to be viewed as a part of the substantive crime, and the practitioners' desire for a comprehensible offence, capable of explanation to a jury in concrete terms, tempts them into treating it as such.

It is well established that *mens rea* assumes a greater significance in inchoate offences which usually involve a less direct or obvious wrong than with substantive crimes.[10] As there is a lesser, or less obvious, wrong or as the wrongdoing appears more distant from the core harm, it seems sensible and desirable for the law to adopt special caution in ensuring

[8] See eg *Ali* [2005] EWCA Crim 87, [2006] QB 332, considered below.

[9] Described rather generously as 'inelegant'. See J R Spencer, 'Conspiracy and Recklessness' [2005] *Cambridge Law Journal* 279, 281, and as 'obscure' by G Williams, 'The New Statutory Offence of Conspiracy' [1977] *New Law Journal* 1164, 1165. See also the criticism in the debates on the 1977 Bill—Hl 20 January 1977, cols 144–62; 1 March 1977, cols 547–58.

[10] Although this is not always the case. For example, with attempted murder D might have shot V and caused very serious injury.

adequate fault of an accused. A stricter *mens rea* maintains a fair equilibrium in the criminal equation.[11] In addition, since the conduct of the inchoate offender might lack any 'manifest illegality', for example where it is merely an agreement or words of encouragement, *mens rea* requirements ensure that only the blameworthy are punished.[12]

Conspiracy is particularly problematical in this respect since the external elements of the wrongdoing are notoriously vague, being even further distanced from the core harm of the substantive crime than for attempts. In some jurisdictions, this fear of over-criminalization has led to conspiracy being restricted by a requirement to prove an overt act in pursuance of the illegal agreement.[13] That option was rejected by the House of Lords in *Churchill v Walton*.[14]

Following the *Churchill* case, the *mens rea* of conspiracy evolved such that a concise statement of the elements prior to the 1977 Act was uncontroversial.[15] The Law Commission explained that the common law definition of *mens rea* ought to remain. In particular:

> Both [conspirators] must *intend* that any consequence specified in the definition of the offence will result and both must *know* of the existence of any state of affairs which it is necessary for them to know in order to be aware that the course of conduct agreed upon will amount to an offence.[16]

Section 1 represents the statutory attempt to embody that proposal. It is possible to deconstruct the *mens rea* for ease of exposition—(i) an intention to agree, which is entirely uncontroversial;[17] (ii) an intention that the agreement should be carried out,[18] which caused the House of Lords difficulty in its only foray into the interpretation of section 1 in *Anderson*;[19] and (iii) intention or knowledge as to material circumstances. Only this final element of *mens rea* is of concern here.

It is well recognized that the academic's desire to deconstruct crimes into constituent elements for ease of exposition can too readily obscure

[11] *actus reus* + *mens rea* + (− defences) = guilt.

[12] See G Fletcher, *Rethinking Criminal Law* (Boston: Little, Brown and Company, 1978), 219.

[13] See eg the US Statute 18 USCA s 371. See also G Williams, *Criminal Law the General Part* (London: Stevens, 1953), 666.

[14] [1967] 2 AC 224. Hereafter 'the *Churchill* case'.

[15] See J C Smith and B Hogan, *Criminal Law* (2nd edn) (London: Butterworths), 151.

[16] *Report on Conspiracy and Criminal Law Reform* (Law Com No 76), para 7.2. Hereafter '*Report on Conspiracy*'. Emphasis added.

[17] See G H L Fridman, '*Mens Rea* in Conspiracy' [1956] *Modern Law Review* 276.

[18] *Report on Conspiracy*, n 16 above, paras 1.25–1.41. At common law, see *Mulcahy* (1868) LR 3 HL 306, 317 (Willes J).

[19] [1986] AC 27.

the true nature of the offence under examination.[20] Throughout the discussion special caution must be exhibited as the *mens rea* of crime of conspiracy, more than most, can be misunderstood: the crime must be viewed holistically with particular focus on the intentions of the parties as to the conduct they have agreed to pursue.

Section 1(2) of the Criminal Law Act 1977

Section 1(2) describes, awkwardly, a critical element of conspiracy. The crime is one of agreeing to pursue a course of conduct which will necessarily involve the commission of an offence. If D1 and D2 do not intend or know of the circumstances rendering their conduct criminal how can they be agreeing to pursue a course of conduct that will necessarily involve an offence?

If D1 and D2 agree to touch sexually X, how can that alone be a crime,[21] unless, applying section 1(2), they also know or intend that X will be under the age of 13? Without that knowledge they might to be agreeing only to touch sexually a consenting adult prostitute of youthful appearance.

If D1 and D2 agree to damage property, say they burn some papers, how can that amount to a conspiracy to commit criminal damage unless they also know or intend that the papers belong to someone else? If they are D1's papers their agreement may merely be to clear rubbish. If D1 and D2 conferred and were uncertain as to the papers' ownership, but agreed to burn them, they have an intention to cause damage and are reckless whether the property belongs to another. The substantive criminal damage offence requires that D intends or is reckless about causing damage (the result), and that D knows or is reckless as to whether the property belongs to another (circumstance). If D1 and D2 go ahead, their *mens rea* suffices for the substantive offence. As for conspiracy, in the circumstances that actually exist, carrying out the agreement 'will necessarily amount' to criminal damage; but on a natural reading of section 1(2), it is not a conspiracy to commit criminal damage. There would be no criminal damage in the circumstances which the parties intend, or know will exist. D1 and D2 are only reckless as to the circumstance of ownership. Recklessness as to that circumstance of the *actus reus* is not a sufficient

[20] See P H Robinson, 'Should the Criminal Law Abandon the Actus Reus–Mens Rea Distinction?' in S Shute, J Gardner, and J Horder (eds), *Action and Value in Criminal Law* (Oxford: Clarendon Press, 1993), arguing for the abandonment of over-simplistic categorization into *actus reus* and *mens rea*.

[21] Sexual Offences Act 2003, s 7.

mens rea on a charge of conspiracy to commit a crime even where it is a sufficient *mens rea* for the crime itself.

If D1 and D2 agree to transfer cash into an account: how can that constitute an agreement to pursue a course of conduct necessarily involving money laundering unless they also know, or intend, that the cash represents the proceeds of crime?

The Origins of Section 1(2)

The Churchill case: In 1967, in a welcomed decision,[22] the House of Lords in the *Churchill* case laid to rest uncertainty over the *mens rea* in conspiracy at common law.[23] Previously a series of Court of Criminal Appeal (CCA) decisions,[24] none conspicuous for its depth or clarity of reasoning, suggested that no *mens rea* was required over and above an intention to agree. Conspirators charged with agreeing to commit a strict liability[25] offence could be convicted on the mere intention to agree. Taking the example of the crime of intentional sexual touching of a child discussed above, proof of the agreement to touch a person sexually would be sufficient for conviction for conspiring to commit the offence even though the parties had no idea the victim was under the age of 13. Obviously, this represents an incredibly harsh approach particularly when the substantive crime is one of such severity and attracts such stigma.

The Court of Criminal Appeal had tended to confuse the lack of awareness of the relevant facts rendering the activity unlawful and the lack of awareness of the criminal law. Clearly, knowledge of the latter is not, and should not be, an element of *mens rea*. As for the former, as commentators observed, in principle conspiracy ought to require proof of *mens rea* even where liability is strict as to the unlawful act which forms the object of the agreement.[26] The Court's difficulties in identifying the *mens rea* of conspiracy stemmed partly from the explicit rejection of

[22] See J C Smith, [1967] *Criminal Law Review* 236 and Orchard, n 1 above, 335. See also the discussion in the *Report on Conspiracy*, n 16 above, paras 1.34–1.38.

[23] See G Williams, n 13 above, 263, para 73, suggesting that the matter is not settled.

[24] See especially *Clayton* (1943) 33 Cr App R 113; *Jacobs* [1944] KB 417; *Sorsky* (1944) 30 Cr App R 84. See also J C Smith commenting on the *Churchill* case in the Court of Appeal, [1966] *Criminal Law Review* 329, who described the decision as 'a very serious error' and J R Scott, 'Conspiracy and *Mens Rea*' [1966] *New Law Journal* 1595, 1596, who concluded it was not 'very satisfactory'.

[25] Or, as the CCA preferred to call them, 'absolute liability'.

[26] Williams, n 13 above. See also J W C Turner, *Kenny's Outlines of the Criminal Law* (19th edn) (Cambridge: Cambridge University Press, 1966), para 453.

the idea that conspiracy represents a separate 'wickedness'.[27] The Court preferred to see conspiracy as closely allied with the substantive offence involved,[28] and as noted, this failure to acknowledge conspiracy as a separate wrongdoing can lead to a misplaced focus on the *mens rea* of the substantive offence.

All these pre-*Churchill* cases involved relatively obscure war-time defence-quota offences criminalizing illegal supplies, and the *Churchill* case involved a strict liability offence relating to the differential tax liability on oils.[29] That substantive offence had no requirement of knowledge that the oil being supplied was of a particular type. As for the *mens rea* for conspiring to commit the offence the House of Lords held that:

> *mens rea* is only an essential ingredient in conspiracy insofar as there must be an intention to be a party to an agreement to do an unlawful act; that knowledge of the law on the part of the accused is immaterial and that knowledge of the facts is only material insofar as such knowledge throws a light on what was agreed.

Viscount Dilhorne went on to emphasize that knowledge of circumstances should not be artificially divorced from the other elements of the offence:

> In cases of this kind, it is desirable to avoid the use of the phrase '*mens rea*', which is capable of different meanings, and *to concentrate on the terms or effect of the agreement made by the alleged conspirators.* The question is: 'What did they agree to do?' If what they agreed to do was, on the facts known to them, an unlawful act, they are guilty of conspiracy and cannot excuse themselves by saying that, owing to their ignorance of the law, they did not realise that such an act was a crime. If, on the facts known to them, what they agreed to do was lawful, they are not rendered artificially guilty by the existence of other facts, not known to them, giving a different and criminal quality to the act agreed upon.[30]

The Law Commission Proposals and the Gestation of the 1977 Act

In Working Paper Number 50,[31] the Commission recommended adopting the *Churchill* case, but added that recklessness as to circumstances should suffice for conspiracy unless the *mens rea* of the substantive crime

[27] *Clayton*, n 24 above, 118.

[28] See also *Sorsky* (1944) 30 Cr App R 84 (Humphreys J).

[29] Customs and Excise Act 1952, s 200.

[30] See the *Churchill* case, n 14 above. Emphasis added.

[31] Law Commission Working Paper No 50, *Codification of the Criminal Law, General Principles: Inchoate Offences, Conspiracy, Attempt and Incitement* (London: HMSO, 1973), discussed by R Card, 'The Working Paper on Inchoate Offences: Reform of the Law of Conspiracy' [1973] *Criminal Law Reform* 674.

specifically required a higher level of *mens rea*, namely actual knowledge.[32] Subsequently, in Report Number 76,[33] the Commission preferred a strict application of the *Churchill* case requiring knowledge as to circumstances always to be proved.[34] This rejection of recklessness as to circumstances as a sufficient *mens rea* was welcomed by commentators,[35] although it has proved to be the Achilles' heel of the 1977 Act offence.

The Report's discussion of *mens rea* is less thorough than might be expected, but explicably so, as the Commission's principal focus was the preservation of common law conspiracies.[36] Indeed, the Commission's preparation of the Report was so controversial and turbulent that it formed the basis of a case study into the difficulties of law reform agencies.[37] That is not to say that the issue of *mens rea* was ignored: in fact three draft versions of the statutory formula for section 1 were produced.

The Two Problems Posed by Section 1(2)

Section 1(2) of the 1977 Act has prompted numerous appeals involving various crimes, but almost all of the decisions must be regarded as erroneous at least in part. Two broad categories of mistake have arisen: cases in which the court has reached the wrong conclusion in considering whether section 1(2) applies, and cases in which the court has reached the correct conclusion on applicability, but has then interpreted section 1(2) in ways that were certainly never intended.

Identifying when Section 1(2) Applies

Avoiding the Scandalous Paradox: The courts' interpretation of section 1(2) has occasionally produced what Professor Elliott[38] described as a 'scandalous paradox'. On a literal reading, intention or knowledge as to all the circumstances of the *actus reus* is to be required only where the

[32] Working Paper, ibid, paras 52–3.

[33] *Report on Conspiracy*, n16 above. See J Andrews, 'Conspiracy and Criminal Law Reform' [1976] *Criminal Law Review* 483.

[34] ibid, para 1.40.

[35] See Andrews, [1976] *Criminal Law Review* 486, who describes this as 'surely right'.

[36] See also the attention on squatting and forcible entry: Law Commission Working Paper No 54, *Offences of Entering and Remaining on Property* (London: HMSO, 1974).

[37] See Hodgson, n 1 above.

[38] D W Elliott, 'A Comment' [1978] *Criminal Law Report* 202. The issue was seen by Lord Hailsham in debates on the Bill, HL 20 January 1977, col 161.

agreement is to commit a crime which may be committed with recklessness or strict liability as to a material circumstance. On this reading, intention or knowledge would not be required where the substantive offence does require knowledge. Section 1(2) would therefore have imposed a more onerous *mens rea* for conspiracy to commit crimes of strict liability than for conspiracy to commit crimes which in substantive form require proof of knowledge or intention as to circumstances.

To avoid this 'scandalous paradox' learned commentators including Sir John Smith argued that section 1(2) must be read as applying to all conspiracies, irrespective of the *mens rea* of the substantive crime.[39] His view was that Parliament should be taken to be saying 'even where liability for any offence may be incurred without knowledge', knowledge or intent is required on a conspiracy charge.

Until very recently the courts avoided the scandalous paradox, but in the *Sakavickas* case,[40] the Court of Appeal seemed prepared to adopt precisely that reasoning. The appellants were convicted of a conspiracy to commit an offence contrary to section 93A of the Criminal Justice Act 1988, which prohibited[41] entering into or being otherwise concerned in an arrangement whereby the retention or control of another person's criminal proceeds were facilitated, when the defendant knew or suspected that that other person had been engaged in or had benefited from criminal conduct. In *mens rea* terms section 93A requires the prosecution to prove only that the defendant had 'suspicion' that the person whose property he was assisting with was engaged in criminal conduct.

The Court of Appeal, upholding the convictions, held that section 1(2) did not apply because *mens rea* in some form was needed in the substantive crime under section 93A. Kennedy LJ appears to read section 1(2) as applying only to conspiracies to commit strict liability offences. The Court was referred to numerous commentaries on the section, so it cannot be suggested that the effects of this interpretation were unknown. Indeed, Kennedy LJ observed that John Smith's view that section 1(2) applied to all crimes, including those where knowledge is required, as an element of the substantive, 'was not shared by all other academic commentators'.

Some commentators agree with the Court that section 1(2) has no application. James Richardson[42] suggests that section 1(2) does not apply

[39] See also A C E Lynch, [1978] *Criminal Law Review* 209, accepting this on slightly different grounds.

[40] [2004] EWCA Crim 2686, [2005] 1 WLR 857.

[41] Superseded by the Proceeds of Crime Act 2002.

[42] J Richardson, *Criminal Law Week*, 4 February 2006.

here because of the defence in section 93A(4) for a person to prove that he did not know or suspect the arrangement related to any person's proceeds of criminal conduct. His argument is that when section 93A is viewed as a whole, a conviction cannot arise if D has no knowledge as to the fact of the property being a person's proceeds of crime. But surely a conviction remains possible on proof of suspicion alone? It is necessary for the prosecution to prove that the property is in fact illicit,[43] but not to demonstrate knowledge as to the fact or circumstance, that property is the proceeds of A's crime.[44] Moreover, it is insufficient for D to seek to defend himself by adducing evidence that he had no knowledge as to that fact unless that also shows that he lacked any suspicion.[45] The offence can be satisfied without proof of 'knowledge' of that fact, and section 1(2) applies: 'where liability . . . may be incurred without knowledge . . . of any particular fact or circumstance necessary for the commission of the offence'. Whatever its merits as a technical argument, Richardson's claim turns on the form of the particular section 93A offence and sheds little light on the correct interpretation of section 1(2).

Overly Broad Application of Section 1(2)

Not only have the courts occasionally denied the application of section 1(2) when it was appropriate, but in some circumstances have applied the section when it was never intended to have any impact. This stems from a willingness to focus on the substantive offence and a failure to disentangle the separate conspiracy based on the act of agreement. Numerous examples can be offered.

Criminal Damage Cases: One example of the courts' overly broad application of section 1(2) is in relation to conspiracies to commit criminal damage being reckless as to whether life is thereby endangered.[46] The Court of Appeal has apparently held that section 1(2) requires that knowledge or intention is proved as to the circumstance of life being endangered.[47] The false premise on which the cases seem to be based is

[43] *Sakavickas*, n 40 above, [9].

[44] Counsel in *Sakavickas* may have erred in saying that it was enough that D suspected the proceeds to be illicit; that much is presumed unless rebutted under section 93A(4).

[45] Section 1(2) is inconsistent with any requirement that D proves lack of knowledge or intention. See *McGowan* [1990] *Criminal Law Review* 399 and commentary.

[46] This is an awkward offence potentially under-inclusive since the endangerment must be by the damage intended or about which D was reckless, not the damage caused, and over-inclusive since there need not be any life endangerment in fact.

[47] *Mir* 22 April 1994, *Browning* 1998, *Ryan*, *The Times* 13 October 1999.

that life endangerment is 'a circumstance' that needs to exist for the full offence under the Criminal Damage Act 1971 to be committed. Since it does not, it is unnecessary in a case of conspiracy to commit that offence for the prosecution to prove that D1 and D2 knew of or intended such a fact or circumstance.[48]

There is a more sophisticated argument arising from the trilogy of cases which deserves consideration. This underpinned the appellants' arguments in the *Mir and Beg* case but seems never to have been fully appreciated by the Court of Appeal then or subsequently.[49] Crucial to understanding this problem is that *Caldwell* recklessness[50] applied to the Criminal Damage Act 1971 offences at the time of the three appeals. The fact or circumstance that had to be proved to exist for the substantive offence was that either the defendants themselves saw the risk of life endangerment from the damage to property that they intended or were reckless about causing and nevertheless damaged property, or that a reasonable bystander would have realized there was a risk of life endangerment from the damage which the defendants intended or about which the defendants were reckless.[51] Under *Caldwell* the offence did involve an objective circumstance that had to be established: a reasonable bystander would have appreciated that there was a risk of life endangerment. So, the argument goes, for a conspiracy the defendants must be shown to have known or intended that circumstance: not knowing that a life would be endangered, not knowing that there was a risk to life, but knowing that there were circumstances that a reasonable bystander would have realized might pose a risk of a threat to life.

In *Mir and Beg* the appellants were alleged to have conspired to cause a fire and explosion at Mir's store in order to make an insurance claim. They had spread petrol and turned on the gas taps at the premises before being apprehended. Counsel for Beg submitted that the prosecution had to establish: that M and B knew of the gas being on and knew that it 'would create an obvious risk to life' by the risk of explosion, that they recognized that risk and still took it. These submissions were accepted in the Court of Appeal. Counsel succeeded in reversing the trial judge's direction which had sought to apply *Caldwell* recklessness to the conspiracy, but

48 If it is argued that the risk of life endangerment is a consequence not a circumstance, there is for a conspiracy, a need to prove an intention in relation to that consequence under section 1(1) of the 1977 Act, so that does not provide a neat avoidance of the issue.

49 All were too readily disposed to follow *Mir and Beg* and avoid having to deal with the complexity of the issue: eg in *Browning*: 'fortunately we do not have to become embroiled in the debate' (Mantell LJ).

50 *MPC v Caldwell* [1982] AC 341.

51 *Sangha* (1988) 87 Cr App R 88.

what did counsel succeed in persuading the Court of Appeal to accept? Was it, first, that the prosecution had to prove knowledge or intention of the circumstance that a life was endangered?[52] If so, it is clearly wrong. There is no requirement of life being endangered for the substantive crime and there is nothing on which section 1(2) can bite in conspiracy. A second interpretation is that the court imposed a requirement of proof of recklessness as to whether a life was endangered. This would be wrong on two counts: there is no requirement that a life is in fact endangered and secondly, section 1(2) requires proof of knowledge or intention, not recklessness.[53] The third interpretation is that the conspirators had to know of the circumstances which would cause a reasonable person to consider a risk to life was posed. That would, arguably, be a correct application of section 1(2) of the 1977 Act bearing in mind that *Caldwell* applied. In the substantive offence, it was sufficient *mens rea* that the defendants were negligent as to the existence of the circumstance: that a reasonable person would realize the risk of life. Therefore, 'liability . . . may be incurred without knowledge . . . of any particular fact or circumstance necessary for the commission of the offence': section 1(2) would apply.

Unfortunately, the decisions following *Mir and Beg* offer no elucidation of what was held. In *Browning and Dixon*, protestors had severed a railway line before providing a warning to the authorities. The trial judge directed that the Crown had to prove *Caldwell* recklessness as to whether a life was endangered: a doubly erroneous approach. The Court of Appeal held, ambiguously, that the Crown had to prove that 'as a subjective ingredient . . . the appellants intended or knew that the agreed course of conduct would or might create a risk that the life of another would be endangered'.[54] In *Ryan*, a case of arson involving bogus insurance claims, the judge, purporting to follow *Mir and Beg*, directed that D1 and D2 must be reckless whether life would be endangered. The Court of Appeal held that section 1(2) did not apply. This suggests the Court had seen the light, but the Court went on to confuse things by explaining that section 1(2) did not apply because 'arson reckless as to life requires knowledge of a risk to life' and cannot be committed 'without knowledge on the part of the person committing it of that risk'. This is difficult to understand. The substantive offence did not, under *Caldwell*, require knowledge of the risk of life endangerment. It required proof of negligence, and now

[52] Some commentators take the view that this is what the Court of Appeal held. See R Card, *Card, Criminal Law* (16th edn) (Oxford: Oxford University Press, 2004), para 17.27.

[53] Some commentators take this interpretation of the case: see C Clarkson and H Keating, *Criminal Law Text and Materials* (5th edn) (Sweet & Maxwell, 2003), 165.

[54] Mantell LJ.

requires only subjective recklessness, as to that circumstance. Moreover, a life need not actually be endangered. For these reasons, the Court was in error.[55]

The landmark overruling of *Caldwell* in *G*[56] adds a twist in the tail. Under the present law, the fact or circumstance which must exist under the substantive offence is that the defendants themselves perceived the risk of life endangerment from the damage to property that they intended or about which they were reckless. The circumstances relating to the risk of life endangerment are now purely *mens rea* elements of the substantive crime. On a conspiracy to commit aggravated criminal damage, section 1(2) can no longer have any role to play. To require proof of the defendants' knowledge or intention as to the defendants' own *mens rea* of the substantive crime was never envisaged. Section 1(2) of the 1977 Act applies where the fact or circumstance of the substantive crime is one of *actus reus*.[57]

Section 1(2) should have no application in relation to matters of *mens rea* in the substantive offence. If it did, it would require proof that D1 and D2 knew or intended that they would be reckless as to whether life would be endangered by the risk from that damage they intended to cause. Oddly, in the Criminal Damage Act offence, if section 1(2) did not apply the difference would seem to be practically non-existent: the conspiracy could be proved if D1 and D2 agreed that they would be reckless as to a life being endangered by the risk from that damage that they intended to cause. But this is merely a coincidence of the highly unusual nature of the aggravated criminal damage offence.[58]

Money Laundering cases pre-Montila: These criminal damage cases influenced the Court of Appeal's reasoning in recent money laundering cases: *Saik* and *Rizvi*. There are, it is submitted, a number of errors in the Court of Appeal's approach in these cases.

As an introductory point, it is worth noting the irony that as Parliament has made substantive money laundering offences easier to prove with *mens rea* requirements of mere suspicion, proving a conspiracy to commit them has become harder. In each of the cases to be discussed

[55] The court may have been misled by the Law Commission Working Paper, although not cited by the court, which provides a like example in para 50, example 3, but that was pre-*Caldwell*, pre-1977 Act, and pre-*Parker* [1993] *Criminal Law Review* 856, which acknowledged that no life need be endangered.

[56] [2004] AC 1034.

[57] See the *Churchill* case, n 14 above.

[58] Special thanks are due to Rudi Fortson, counsel for Beg, for his comments on this aspect of the chapter.

the substantive offences could have been readily established, but the prosecutor's preference was for conspiracy, illustrating the way that offence is used as a convenient *procedural* device by prosecution agencies.

The first error in the Court of Appeal's approach in these cases is that the Court consistently held section 1(2) to apply when it ought not to have done so. Prior to the decision in the House of Lords in *Montila*[59] the Court of Appeal[60] had held, *inter alia*, that for the substantive offences[61] the prosecution did not need to prove the fact or circumstance of the illicit nature of the property being transferred.[62] If the substantive offences could be committed even if the property in which the defendants were dealing did not represent the proceeds of crime, the substantive crime did not contain an element of 'fact' or 'circumstance' relating to the provenance of the property. Therefore, on a charge of conspiracy there was no need for the conspirators to have intention or knowledge in relation to that fact. There was nothing on which section 1(2) would bite. The correct approach for the Court in cases such as *Rizvi* and *Saik* should therefore have been to reject the application of section 1(2) on that basis. In *Montila* the House of Lords held unanimously that for the substantive charges the Crown were obliged to establish the illegal provenance of the property. Following *Montila* there was clearly a fact or circumstance in the substantive offence on which section 1(2) should bite.

The second error in the Court of Appeal's approach to money laundering conspiracies pre-*Montila* is that the Court was misled by the criminal damage cases to accept that the fact or circumstance about which the conspirators must have knowledge[63] under section 1(2) was either the fact (i) which would have caused a reasonable person to believe something, or (ii) of the conspirators' own states of mind.

Sufficiency of Knowledge of some Fact from which Knowledge of the Prohibited Circumstance Forming an Element of the Offence can be Inferred: This approach involves regarding the 'fact or circumstance' about which the conspirators are to have intention or knowledge in the substantive offence as something other than the 'fact or circumstance' of the illicit nature of the property being transferred.

[59] [2005] 1 Cr App R 425.

[60] *Montila*, [2004] 1 Cr App R 427. The CA had previously accepted counsel's concession on this issue in *El Kurd* [2001] *Criminal Law Review* 234 (CA).

[61] Under Criminal Justice Act, s 93C(2) and Drug Trafficking Act 1994 s 49(2).

[62] Other offences require proof of the property's illicit nature. See ss 49(1), 50, 51 Drug Trafficking Act and corresponding Criminal Justice Act offences.

[63] This is where a third error creeps in: the Court did not hold that 'knowledge' was required.

In *Rivzi and Chisti*,[64] R was convicted of conspiring to deal with the proceeds of drug trafficking and/or criminal conduct when handling monies in a foreign exchange bureau.[65] The substantive offence criminalized converting property knowing or 'having reasonable grounds to suspect' that the property is illicit. The Court of Appeal held that the conspiracy is committed if D knows or has reasonable grounds to suspect that the money is 'hot'.[66] The conspirators' knowledge, it was held, must be established only as regards the facts or circumstances on which his suspicion was formed, and not as to the fact or circumstance of the provenance of the money, that is the material circumstance of the substantive offence.

This was a heavily criticized decision.[67] This commentator observed in the *Criminal Law Review* that there is an enormous gulf between what section 1(2) requires on a natural reading, knowledge that the money is 'hot', and knowledge of a fact that gives rise to a suspicion that it is 'hot'. As the House of Lords observed subsequently in its consideration of the money laundering offences in *Montila*:[68]

> A person may have reasonable grounds to suspect that property is one thing (A) when in fact it is something different (B). But that is not so when the question is what a person knows. A person cannot know that something is A when in fact it is B. The proposition that a person knows that something is A is based on the premise that it is true that it is A. The fact that the property is A provides the starting point. Then there is the question whether the person knows that the property is A.

The decision in *Rizvi* would short-circuit this reasoning by treating D's knowledge of facts giving rise to a suspicion of the property being 'A' as equivalent to D knowing 'A'. Section 1(2) of the 1977 Act requires proof of knowledge of or intent as to the fact or circumstance 'A', not knowledge of some preliminary facts.

The position is distinguishable from the criminal damage cases noted above where on a substantive count, under *Caldwell*, it was sufficient to prove that circumstances existed which would cause a reasonable person

[64] *Rivzi and Chisti* [2003] EWCA Crim 3575.

[65] The substantive offences being laundering drug money under s 49(2) of the Drug Trafficking Act 1994 and laundering money from other criminal activity under s 93C(2) of the Criminal Justice Act 1988.

[66] See n 64 above, [13].

[67] See J Barnard, 'A Stupid Conspiracy' [2005] 2 *Archbold News* 5.

[68] [2005] 1 Cr App R 425 [27] (Lord Hope of Craighead). See also *Souter* [1971] 2 All ER 1151, CA holding that reasonable grounds for suspicion, an objective test, was not equivalent to suspicion, a subjective test, and neither was to be equated with knowledge. See also the helpful analysis by J Fisher and J Bewsey, 'Laundering the Proceeds of Fiscal Crime' [2000] *Journal of International Banking Law* 11, 16–18.

to appreciate a risk to the life of another by the damage. In a conspiracy, it should have been sufficient to prove that D1 and D2 knew of the circumstances that caused the reasonable person to appreciate that risk. With a charge under section 93C(2), the prohibited circumstance is the illicit provenance of the property. There is an additional requirement that there are reasonable grounds to suspect that the property is illicit. There cannot be a conviction under the substantive offence where the prosecution can only prove the reasonable grounds to suspect that the property is illicit but not that the property is illicit. This is the crucial difference from the criminal damage cases where the prosecution could, under *Caldwell*, succeed on proof of reasonable grounds to appreciate a risk to life, without also proving that there was a risk to life. Unfortunately the differences were not identified by the Court of Appeal in *Rizvi*.

Rizvi is not alone in seeking to adopt this approach. In *Sakavickas*,[69] the Court of Appeal accepted *obiter*,[70] that the position might be different if the substantive offence required proof that the offender had 'reasonable grounds for suspicion'. In that case the Court suggested that a conspirator would only have to have knowledge of the reasonable grounds on which a suspicion might be founded.[71]

This doubly erroneous approach of *Rivzi* was also followed by the Court of Appeal in *Saik*.[72] S was manager of a Bureau de Change which had been used to launder the proceeds of Colombian drug money, and had pleaded guilty to a conspiracy to commit an offence under section 93C(2)[73] on the basis that he had suspected the money was from an illicit source. The principal basis for appeal was that S had received erroneous advice as to plea, but the Court of Appeal dismissed the ground of appeal relating to *mens rea* for conspiracy since S had pleaded guilty, and because *Rizvi* seemed to be directly on point.[74]

In *Saik* the Court of Appeal again seemed willing to regard proof of the *mens rea* required for the substantive offence as a sufficient *mens rea* for the conspiracy:

> A person who suspects that property which he is converting or transferring represents the proceeds of criminal conduct will also, almost inevitably, realise (a) that there is a risk of a criminal prosecution being brought against those who

[69] *Sakavickas*, n 40 above.

[70] It was dealing with the quite separate s 93A offence.

[71] See n 70 above, [18].

[72] *Saik*, n 4 above.

[73] The substantive crime is committed if D has reasonable grounds to suspect the property's illicit nature.

[74] The court purported to follow *Sakavickas*, though that involved a different offence under s 93A with different *mens rea* and different material facts to be proved.

may be responsible for the criminal conduct in question and (b) that by converting or transferring the property he is helping to reduce that risk. It is not a big step from there to say that he realises that the purpose of the conversion or transfer is to assist others to avoid prosecution for the criminal conduct which *he suspects (though he does not know for certain)* has been committed. If that is the position, he has the *mens rea* of the offence under s. 93C(2).[75]

Oddly, *Saik* is the case appealed to the House of Lords to resolve the current legal problem. Surely their lordships can dispose of the appeal on the simple ground that it was decided pre-*Montila* and the central issue has since been dealt with in the House of Lords. If that were not enough to dispose easily with the appeal, there is also the fact that it failed to distinguish properly between the cases on sections 93C and 93A.

It is submitted that as a matter of principle, *Rivzi* and those decisions following it are wrong. At the time, the authorities held that the provenance of the property was not a fact or circumstance which needed to be established for the substantive offence. Section 1(2) of the 1977 Act should, at that time, have had no application. Secondly, even if section 1(2) was applicable, proof that conspirators knew the money they proposed to deal with might be illicit is not equivalent to knowledge of the fact that it would be or was illicit.

Knowledge of the Conspirators' own States of Mind as Sufficient for Section 1(2): The Court of Appeal has in some money laundering cases suggested that the fact or circumstance necessary for the commission of the offence, and about which D as a conspirator must have knowledge, is his own mental state.[76] This is clearly not how section 1(2) was intended to be interpreted.

In *Sakavickas*, the appellants argued that section 1(2) applied on a charge of conspiracy to commit an offence under section 93A, where liability might be incurred without knowledge of the fact that the money which was being laundered represented proceeds of another's criminal conduct. Applying section 1(2), it was argued that the appellant and at least one other conspirator had to know or intend that the money to be laundered was or would be the proceeds of another's crime. On a natural reading of section 93A, the relevant circumstance to be proved is that the retention of another's proceeds of crime was facilitated. Liability as to the retention appears to be strict. There is an additional *mens rea* requirement in the substantive offence of knowledge or suspicion as to the other's involvement in criminal activity. An orthodox application of section 1(2) would require that knowledge must be established for charges

[75] *Saik*, n 4 above [66]. Emphasis added.

[76] See *Sakavickas*, n 40 above.

of conspiring to launder such proceeds. However, the Court of Appeal dismissed the appeals, holding that section 1(2) did not apply.

The Court relied on the aggravated criminal damage cases discussed above to conclude that the relevant fact or circumstance of the substantive offence of which the conspirators had to know was their own suspicion of the provenance of the property. The Court regarded the conviction as safe because although a conspirator had to have knowledge of that suspicion inevitably he would have knowledge of his own state of mind.[77] This is a very surprising result and its full impact can be illustrated by a straightforward example taking the offence of simple, non-aggravated, criminal damage. The prosecution must establish that the property damaged belongs to another and that D was reckless as to that fact. Applying *Sakavickas*, on a charge of conspiracy to commit simple criminal damage, D1 and D2 would have to be shown to have knowledge of their own state of mind of recklessness as to the circumstance of ownership. The editor of *Archbold* describes this aspect of the decision as 'absurd'.[78]

Identifying what Section 1(2) Requires when it does Apply

The spate of money laundering appeals under the pre-Proceeds of Crime Act law are remarkable, not only because the Court of Appeal erred in applying section 1(2) when it had no application, but also because when the Court did apply the section it went on to misinterpret it in the dramatic fashions discussed. Following the House of Lords' decision in *Montila*, the Court of Appeal has adopted a more satisfactory approach to the application of section 1(2).

In *Harmer*,[79] the Court of Appeal made two significant steps forward. H and another were convicted of conspiracy to convert currency which they had reasonable grounds to suspect represented another person's proceeds of criminal conduct and/or drug trafficking. The Court of Appeal allowed the appeals, accepting that following *Montila*, the substantive offence requires the prosecution to prove that the money was in fact from an illicit provenance,[80] and that it is not enough that D believed or suspected or had reasonable grounds to suspect that the proceeds were illicit. The trial judge failed to direct the jury on that point, unsurprisingly

[77] ibid [17]. [78] *Criminal Law Week*, n 42 above.
[79] [2005] EWCA Crim 1.
[80] In addition, under s 93C(2), that it is from criminality other than drug dealing.

since he was following the Court of Appeal in *Montila*, which was subsequently overruled in the House of Lords. The Court of Appeal quashed the convictions.

The first significant step forward is in recognizing the impact of *Montila* on conspiracies. It is surely right to say that since the substantive requires proof of the fact of the provenance, in the conspiracy it is necessary to prove that the conspirators knew of that provenance. Indeed, it might be said that the circumstances that must be demonstrated for the substantive offence alleged in *Harmer* are: (i) that the money was illicit; (ii) that its origin is non-drug criminality; (iii) that it is someone else's money; (iv) that D is possessed of an awareness of facts relating to its provenance; and (v) if the *mens rea* for the substantive offence is objective, that the reasonable person would have formed the suspicion on those facts available to D. An orthodox application of section 1(2) therefore requires that on a charge of conspiracy, each defendant's knowledge must be established as to all five circumstances.

The second significant and positive step in *Harmer* was to endorse, albeit *obiter*, the natural meaning of section 1(2). The court relied on John Smith's commentaries to conclude that the fatal flaw in the prosecution's argument was that they had not established 'knowledge' as to the illicit provenance of property which the conspirators had agreed they would be dealing with:

> [the commentary] emphasises the statutory requirement that, where, as in the present case, the substantive charge would only be that the defendant had reasonable grounds to suspect that the money was the proceeds of crime (i.e. the offence would be incurred without knowledge on the part of the person committing it), he is not to be guilty of conspiracy unless he and at least one other party to the agreement intend or know that the money will be the proceeds of crime when the agreed conduct takes place.[81]

There is, however, a flaw in *Harmer*. The Court suggested that in a conspiracy it was necessary for the prosecution to prove not merely knowledge as to the illicit provenance of the monies but that the monies were in fact illicit. This conclusion stems from an argument that if 'knowledge' as a state of mind can only be possessed of things that are true,[82] then a

[81] *Harmer*, n 79 above [26]. The commentary referred to was that on *Hussain* in [2002] *Criminal Law Review* 407, 409. The commentary and that on *El Kurd* [2001] *Criminal Law Review* 234 dealt with the separate problem of conspiracy being to either commit offence A or B, ie launder property that was the product of drug related or non-drug related crime. This caused difficulties prior to the Proceeds of Crime Act when two separate offence regimes dealt with the two categories of provenance.

[82] *Harmer*, n 79 above [26].

requirement of knowledge would necessarily entail proof of the existence of the fact or circumstance. As the Court explained, 'if the prosecution cannot prove that the money was [from] the proceeds of crime, they cannot prove that the appellant knew that it was'.[83]

However, with a conspiracy it must be proved that at the time of the agreement, the conspirators' plan was to pursue a course of conduct that if carried out in accordance with their intentions would necessarily constitute an offence. There is no need to prove that the property that it was intended to deal with was in fact illicit if the conspirators intended to deal with or knew they were going to deal with illicit property. Unfortunately, on the facts of *Harmer* all that the prosecution could establish was that the conspirators suspected that the property would be illicit. The prosecution had neither shown that it was illicit nor that the conspirators intended to deal with illicit property.[84]

In part, this extreme level of technicality stems from the prosecution's use of conspiracy charges where the substantive offences have been completed in full. This is an effort to achieve the easiest presentational package of a course of alleged offending for the trial. However, in money laundering cases, reliance on conspiracy can back-fire spectacularly. If the Crown alleges the substantive offence, it will have to prove that the property was illicit, and that the accused suspected or that he or she had reasonable grounds to suspect that fact. Alternatively, the Crown can allege the conspiracy and need not establish that the property was illicit. Note, however, that where the offence has occurred in full, proof of knowledge of the illicit nature of the property necessarily entails proof that the property was illicit. A third alternative is that the prosecution allege a conspiracy and prove that the conspirators intended to deal with illicit funds. On the facts of *Harmer* that route was not pursued by the Crown. The fact that the monies were laundered is evidence that the conspirators intended to engage in that activity, but not evidence that the conspirators intended to launder *illicit* monies.

The subsequent decision of the Court of Appeal, *Ali*,[85] offers a further positive development, by acknowledging the error in *Harmer*. In *Ali* the appellants had been convicted of conspiracies to contravene the same substantive offences. For those substantive offences, liability arose where D 'knew' or had 'reasonable grounds to suspect' that the property was illicit. In *Ali* the indictment on which conspiracy convictions had been

[83] *Harmer*, n 79 above [26].

[84] This lies behind prosecution counsel's argument that the position is analogous to an impossibility case: ibid, para 24.

[85] *Ali*, n 8 above.

secured alleged that the conspirators had known or had reasonable grounds to suspect that the property was illicit. The appellants relied on *Harmer* and the House of Lords' decision in *Montila* to suggest that because they could not know that the property concerned was illicit when, in fact, it was not, it followed that an agreement to deal with that property would only necessarily amount to or involve the commission of the substantive offence and thus constitute a conspiracy where D1 and D2 knew that the property was illicit.[86]

A number of significant points flow from this important decision. First, it is submitted that the Court adopted the correct approach to the question of whether section 1(2) applied to money laundering offences. Developing the dictum in *Harmer*, the Court in *Ali* held that section 1(2) 'bit' on the requirement in *Montila* that the property concerned was, in fact, criminal property. Secondly, and equally welcome, was the Court's rejection of the erroneous aspect of *Harmer*. After a comprehensive analysis of the case law, Hooper LJ held that where D1 and D2 agree to transfer property which, in fact, was criminal property and which D1 and D2 suspected was criminal property at the time of agreement to transfer it, one of the substantive offences would necessarily be committed if the property was transferred. The same applied where the agreement was to deal with property should the opportunity present itself on a future occasion: if the prosecution proved that the property that was the subject of the agreement would, to the knowledge of the co-conspirators, be criminal property at the time when the conduct constituting the substantive offence was to take place, then the offence of conspiracy would be made out because section 1(2) referred to knowledge that the fact or circumstance should or would exist at the time when the conduct constituting the offence was to take place. Accordingly, section 1(1)(a) of the Act was satisfied.[87] Contrary to the suggestion in *Harmer*, it is not necessary in a conspiracy to launder criminal property for the prosecution to prove that the property is criminal. It is sufficient that the conspirators intend or know that it will be. If D1 and D2 agree to launder criminal proceeds of X's criminality should he offer them the opportunity, they have committed the conspiracy even if the property never materializes or exists.[88]

Thirdly, the Court in *Ali* rightly rejected the view in *Rizvi* that it was sufficient to establish the conspirators' knowledge only as to the facts which ought to have given rise to the suspicion that the property was illicit. As Hooper LJ pointed out, if that was so, it was difficult to see how a jury could be sure, as the substantive offences required, that the purpose

[86] ibid [23]. [87] ibid [99]–[110]. [88] ibid [98].

of the conspirators was to avoid any person's prosecution for a relevant offence.[89]

The only quibble with *Ali* is with an *obiter* where the Court seemed to equate 'knowledge' with 'belief' despite explicit recognition that a conspirator would only be guilty where he 'knew' that the property concerned was illicit, mere suspicion, be it objective or subjective, being insufficient: 'section 1(2) which refers to knowledge (belief would be a better word) that the fact or circumstance shall or will exist at the time when the conduct constituting the offence is to take place'.[90] This view is hardly surprising since it was one endorsed by eminent academic commentators including John Smith.[91]

This brings us to the next aspect of the current problem: how should section 1(2) be interpreted? That entails a number of interesting questions: Is it necessary to construe 'knowledge' as including 'belief'? Is it sufficient to regard knowledge as including 'wilful blindness'? Can the House of Lords adopt a workable solution to the section?

Possible Judicial Solutions

This section examines various options of construction of intention and knowledge. Neither word is ideally suited to describe a conspirator's *mens rea* as to the existence of future circumstances.

Knowledge Strictly Construed

On a literal interpretation, since the statute is explicit in its requirement of 'knowledge' that is how the courts should apply it. This prompts further questions: what does knowledge mean? And if knowledge is strictly construed does conspiracy become 'redundant' in practical terms?[92]

Knowledge Defined: By comparison with *mens rea* elements such as the notorious concept of intention and the infamous 'recklessness', knowledge has attracted comparatively little scholarship. Academic attention has focused on how knowledge plays a part in the general scheme of

[89] ibid [89]. [90] ibid [98].

[91] J C Smith and B Hogan, *Criminal Law* (10th edn) (London: LexisNexis UK, 2002), 304.

[92] As J C Smith suggested in n 1 above, 604. In subsequent commentaries he occasionally suggested that a strict construction of knowledge was required: eg *Siracusa* [1989] *Criminal Law Review* 712.

mens rea and to what extent it factors into negative fault elements, that is, mistaken beliefs, that displace *mens rea*. It is, however, a term deserving attention as it features in many statutes. It is usually considered to sit alongside intention in the *mens rea* hierarchy, but whereas intention is usually descriptive of state of minds as to consequences, for example, I intend to kill; knowledge is usually used in relation to circumstances, for example, importing a substance into England knowing it is prohibited.[93]

Knowledge is not the only legislative term to describe prohibited states of mind as to circumstances. Parliament has deployed a range of terms: 'knowledge', 'belief', 'suspicion', 'having reasonable grounds to suspect', and even 'recklessness'.[94] Parliament's use of these different terms clearly supports the view that they do not share the same meaning in law. The argument that these are not synonymous is strengthened considerably by the fact that the terms are used in many offences as alternative *mens rea* requirements.[95] Parliament's use of alternatives alongside knowledge may also indicate recognition of the difficulty that proof of knowledge poses. Judicial interpretation of the different terms in a variety of different offences[96] also makes clear that they are quite distinct. The difficult issue lies in identifying the respective boundaries of each concept. More light has been shed on the matter by recent academic scholarship, with Professors Shute and Sullivan[97] in particular seeking to identify essential conditions which must exist before a state of mind might legitimately be described as 'knowledge'.

As for what comprises knowledge, the orthodox view is that 'one cannot know a thing unless it is so',[98] and 'one cannot know a thing will be so unless it will be so'.[99] The critical feature is that the fact or circumstance 'is'.[100] As Shute acknowledges, 'there are good reasons why the law should

[93] See the clear discussion by Ashworth, n 3 above, 187–91.

[94] As in reckless rape with recklessness as to the issue of consent being a sufficient *mens rea*.

[95] See the comprehensive catalogue provided by S Shute, 'Knowledge and Belief in the Criminal Law' in S Shute and A Simester (eds), *Criminal Law Theory* (Oxford: Oxford University Press, 2002), ch 8. See also G R Sullivan, 'Knowledge, Belief and Culpability' in Shute and Simester, *ibid*, ch 9.

[96] See eg the interpretation of the concepts of knowledge and belief in handling stolen goods.

[97] Shute, n 95 above.

[98] Smith, n 1 above.

[99] ibid. See also G Williams, n 13 above, 133, and more generally writings on knowledge in philosophy, eg A J Ayer, *The Problem of Knowledge* (London: Macmillan, 1956), 35: 'I conclude that the necessary and sufficient conditions for knowing that something is the case are first that what one is said to know be true, secondly that one be sure of it and thirdly that one should have the right to be sure', cited by R Buxton, 'Complicity in the Criminal Code' (1969) *Law Quarterly Review* 252.

[100] This is clarified in *Hall* (1985) 81 Cr App R 260, knowing a fact 'might be' is not the same as knowing 'it is'.

decline to extend its definition of knowledge generally to include knowledge that [the disputed proposition] is possible, likely etc'.[101] Since it seems to be universally accepted that mere suspicion is not knowledge,[102] the crucial question lies in distinguishing knowledge from mere belief.[103] Shute suggests three distinguishing features:

> first the proposition forming the subject matter of the *belief must be true*, not just believed to be true; secondly, the person whose belief it is must be justified in holding that belief; thirdly, the belief holder must have a degree of commitment to the belief over and above the commitment required for beliefs *per se*.[104]

In short, Shute concludes that 'belief is . . . a necessary condition for knowledge. But it is not a sufficient condition'.[105]

In the context of the present discussion, the problem is whether conspiring money launderers can ever be said to have knowledge rather than belief of future circumstances. Shute considers an example of the likelihood that there will be daylight in New York tomorrow. Everyone believes that fact will materialize, but do they know it? On the basis of the criteria identified by Shute, it would seem they could not know it, the circumstance does not exist. But Shute, in an apparent qualification of his earlier definitions, concludes that in some cases a belief is no less than knowledge.[106] For Shute, the belief in daylight in New York tomorrow is no less true than and no less justified or lacking in commitment than if it were known.[107] This view is shared by Sullivan, who in his essay regards the proposition that one cannot know the future as a fallacy.[108] Two responses to this might be made. First, the conclusion can be challenged on the basis that the fact that daylight in New York is almost inevitably

[101] Shute, n 95 above, 195.

[102] 'Suspicion in its ordinary meaning is a state of conjecture or surmise where proof is lacking: "I suspect but I cannot prove" ': *Hussein v Chong Fook Kam* [1970] AC 942, 948. See also *Griffiths* (1974) 60 Cr App R 14 (CA).

[103] See *Hall* (1985) 81 Cr App R 260, 264 (Boreham J): 'Belief, of course, is something short of knowledge. It may be said to be the state of mind of a person who says to himself: "I cannot say I know for certain that these goods are stolen, but there can be no other reasonable conclusion in the light of all the circumstances, in the light of all that I have heard and seen" '.

[104] Shute, n 95 above, 185. Emphasis added.

[105] ibid. Shute regards knowledge as parasitic on belief. According to Shute, the six characteristics making up a 'belief' are: it must be about something, true or false, open to revision, fallible, to which there is commitment, and be dependent for its identity on a network of other beliefs.

[106] This must be right, since D might legitimately be described as knowing some facts, for example, the fact that either he will be alive tomorrow or not. I am grateful to Jeremy Horder for this example.

[107] Shute, n 95 above, 87.

[108] Sullivan, above n 95 above.

going to occur tomorrow does not mean that it is known.[109] On Shute's own analysis, arguably D only believes it, although he has the strongest bases for belief. The question whether it is 'true' or not cannot occur until it has happened. The same comment can be made about Sullivan's analysis, 'when we assert that D knows that Φ, we make a claim about the mental disposition of D and a claim concerning the state of the world. We assert both that D believes that Φ and that Φ obtains in fact'.[110] Secondly, and more importantly, even if it is possible to identify some cases, for example naturally occurring phenomena, in which knowledge of a future event might be accepted to exist, that cannot be extrapolated to suggest that it is possible to find knowledge as a matter of legal definition as to any future circumstance. In particular, it is difficult to see how one can know future circumstances where the possible existence of those circumstances is affected by the involvement of a human being who retains a distinct degree of control over whether the circumstance will materialize.

It is important to note also that none of these academic analyses deals directly with the question of knowledge in conspiracies. Their principal focus is to analyse the relationship between knowledge and belief when they are used as alternatives in the same offence.[111]

Should Knowledge be Interpreted Strictly in Section 1(2): The strongest argument for adopting a narrow interpretation of knowledge is that Parliament endorsed that term after the Law Commission had considered less onerous alternatives, including recklessness. The Commission's final recommendation was to require:

> . . . *full intention and knowledge* before a conspiracy can be established. What the prosecution ought to have to prove is that the defendant agreed with another person that a course of conduct should be pursued which would result, if completed, in the commission of a criminal offence, and further, that they both *knew* of any facts which they would need to know to make them aware that the agreed course of conduct would result in the commission of the offence.[112]

Strict interpretation is also supported by the fact that unlike other statutes, knowledge was not used in the alternative with belief. Furthermore, as a matter of principle, since the offence of conspiracy has the potential to over-criminalize, the strictest interpretation of *mens rea* in favour of the

[109] See G Williams, 'No-one can know the future' [1977] *New Law Journal* 1167. See also J Wigmore, *The Principles of Judicial Proof* (Boston: Little, Brown, 1913), 96.

[110] Sullivan, n 95 above, 222. [111] Shute, n 95 above, 195.

[112] *Report on Conspiracy*, n 16 above, para 1.39. Emphasis added.

accused ought to be adopted. As the Canadian Supreme Court explained in *USA v Dynar*:[113]

> Because it is not possible to know what is false, no one who converts money that is not in fact the proceeds of crime commits these offences. This is clear from the meaning of the word 'know'. In the Western legal tradition, knowledge is defined as true belief: 'The word "know" refers exclusively to true knowledge; we are not said to "know" something that is not so'.[114]

The Consequences of Adopting a Narrow Interpretation of Knowledge: Commentators on the Act warned that the requirement of knowledge may have disastrous effects on the prosecution's ability to utilize the offence. John Smith went so far as to say that it may be fatal to its usefulness. The requirement does present problems in many offences in which liability is strict, but it is not necessarily fatal. First, in some cases proof of knowledge will be straightforward because unless the prohibited circumstance existed D1 and D2 would, on the terms of their own agreement, be engaged in a futile exercise. Secondly, there are numerous other offences in which proof of knowledge is achieved. A danger in relying too heavily on this argument is that in some contexts knowledge is given a particularly wide interpretation, a stark example being in secondary participation. That is a particularly pertinent example because, like conspiracy, it is concerned with knowledge of future circumstances. In secondary liability, D must know the essential matters of the principal offence, including the principal's *mens rea*.[115] The courts have diluted this requirement to include belief because, as Professor K J M Smith points out,[116] 'to limit knowledge in its strict sense would be self defeating for an accessory cannot know the essential matters of an offence until it has been committed'.[117]

Arguably the secondary party example is distinguishable because the courts may have been more willing to dilute that *mens rea* requirement because it is imposed only by common law, than they would with conspiracy which is statutory. Moreover, in terms of proof, there is an important difference: in participation D's liability is derivative on the

[113] *USA v Dynar* [1997] 2 SCR 462.

[114] Williams, *Textbook of Criminal Law* (2nd edn) (London: Stevens, 1983), 160.

[115] *Johnson v Youden* [1950] 1 KB 544.

[116] K J M Smith, *A Modern Treatise on the Law of Criminal Complicity* (Oxford: Oxford University Press, 1991), 181.

[117] See also G Williams, 'Complicity, Purpose and the Draft Code' [1990] *Criminal Law Review* 98.

principal's, and the question of what D knew at the time of his act of assistance only arises if the principal performs the acts, by which time the prohibited circumstance must, by definition, have existed. It is, at least in practical terms, easier to suggest that D must have had 'knowledge' of that fact. In conspiracy, in contrast, the act of agreement is a sufficient trigger for D's liability, and the inquiry is forward-looking: the prosecution cannot necessarily point to the existence of the circumstance and suggest that D must have known of it.

A third argument that construing knowledge strictly will not render conspiracy unworkable is because proof of knowledge by inference is permissible provided the inference is compelling: 'one (and the only one) that no reasonable man could fail to draw from the direct facts proved'.[118] This is a narrow category and leads neatly into a discussion of 'wilful blindness'.

Wilful Blindness as Knowledge

One of the easiest solutions to the current problem might be to extend the meaning of knowledge to include 'wilful blindness'. The courts have for centuries[119] willingly interpreted knowledge as including 'shutting one's eyes to an obvious means of knowledge' or 'deliberately refraining from making inquiries the results of which the person does not care to have'.[120] Even the House of Lords controversially adopted this proposition:

> It is always open to the tribunal of fact, when knowledge on the part of a defendant is required to be proved, to base a finding of knowledge on evidence that the defendant had deliberately shut his eyes to the obvious or refrained from inquiry because he suspected the truth but did not want to have his suspicion confirmed.[121]

[118] *Kwan Ping Bang* [1979] AC 609, 615. It is submitted that this is still quite distinct from the position in *Rizvi*, that knowledge of the facts from which a person can reasonably suspect the existence of the prohibited circumstance, the illicit provenance, is knowledge of that circumstance. *Kwan* requires it to be the only inference available, not one that could reasonably be drawn.

[119] See the discussion of the early case law in J Edwards, 'The Criminal Degrees of Knowledge in Statutory Offences' in *Mens Rea in Statutory Offences* (London: Macmillan, 1955), ch IX, 194.

[120] *Roper v Taylor's Garage* [1951] 2 TLR 284 (Devlin J). See also eg *Warner v Metropolitan Police Comm* [1969] 2 AC 256, 279 (Lord Reid); *Atwal v Massey* 56 Cr App R 6, DC.

[121] *Westminster City Council v Croyalgrange Ltd* (1986) 83 Cr App R 155 164 (Lord Bridge).

Wilful blindness is not a panacea for the problem: a precise definition of wilful blindness or connivance[122] remains elusive,[123] and there are specific concerns about applying this extended definition to conspiracy.

The Conditions of an Extended Meaning Incorporating Wilful Blindness: Perhaps the best-known exposition of the concept is that of Devlin J in *Roper v Taylor Garages (Exeter)*. His lordship distinguished actual knowledge, wilful blindness or knowledge in the second degree, and constructive knowledge or knowledge in the third degree.[124] Actual knowledge has been considered above. As for wilful blindness, Devlin J emphasized:

> a vast distinction between a state of mind which consists of deliberately refraining from making inquiries, the result of which a person does not care to have [wilful blindness], and a state of mind which is merely neglecting to make such inquiries as a reasonable and prudent person would make [constructive knowledge].[125]

Other judicial definitions[126] have variously incorporated elements of: a deliberate or intentional refusal to investigate the circumstances suspected; an opportunity to investigate them; an absence of doubt as to outcome or at least an awareness by D of the likely outcome of investigation and that the outcome would not be one D desired if he investigated his suspicions; and a causal link between the refusal to investigate and the assumed likely outcome.[127]

The core elements appear to be a degree of awareness of the likely existence of the prohibited circumstances coupled with a blameworthy

[122] See *Winson* [1969] 1 QB 371, 383 (Parker LCJ). Old statutes often used the word 'connivance' but none recently use 'wilful blindness'.

[123] It seems this was owing to the confusion historically over its relationship with vicarious liability: Edwards, n 120 above, 196–8.

[124] More sophisticated subdivisions have been attempted including Peter Gibson J's five categories in the *Baden* case [1993] 1 WLR 509, para 250. While these were rejected as unhelpful by the House of Lords in the particular context of dishonesty in *Royal Brunei Airlines v Tan* [1995] 2 AC 378, they are worth noting: '(i) actual knowledge; (ii) wilfully shutting one's eyes to the obvious; (iii) wilfully and recklessly failing to make such inquiries as an honest and reasonable man would make; (iv) knowledge of circumstances which would indicate the facts to an honest and reasonable man; and (v) knowledge of circumstances which would put an honest and reasonable man on inquiry'.

[125] *Roper*, n 120 above, 288.

[126] See those discussed by Edwards, n 119 above, 199. The Draft Criminal Code also suggests that knowledge includes wilful blindness, cl 18(1)(a): a person acts knowingly 'with respect to a circumstance only when he is aware that it exists or will exist but also when he avoids taking steps that might confirm his belief that it exists or will exist'.

[127] See eg *Roper*; *Agip (Africa) v Jackson* [1990] Ch 265, 293: 'deliberately shutting eyes to facts he would prefer not to know'; and *Warner v MPC* [1969] AC 256, 279

conscious refusal to enlighten oneself. Academic opinion seems united in requiring proof of more than mere suspicion.[128] Williams described it in terms of suspicion 'plus' a deliberate omission to inquire.[129] More recently Sullivan described it in terms of 'suspicion coupled with deliberate failure to use readily available and effective means to resolve the suspicion'.[130] However described, the second limb of the test ensures that the defendant must have possessed more than a state of awareness of the risk: he must demonstrate a blameworthiness[131] that justifies treating his state of mind as akin to actual knowledge.[132]

The boundaries of 'wilful blindness' are imprecise. None of the core elements are defined with adequate precision. It is unclear what degree of awareness of risk D must hold. Is suspicion sufficient or must D hold a belief?[133] It is unclear how readily available the bases of enlightenment must be to D. Is he only wilfully blind if he can reasonably or immediately discover the truth, or is the matter one of proportionality depending on the degree of risk and the severity of the harm posed if the risk materializes? It is unclear how convinced of the outcome of investigation D must be. Must it be proved as Ashworth suggests that D refrained from making inquiries because he was virtually certain that suspicion would be confirmed?[134] Further, it is unclear what motivation or purpose D must have in seeking to avoid the enlightenment, for his refusal to constitute wilful blindness.

What are the Consequences of Applying the Wilful Blindness Doctrine in Conspiracy: In principle, there are strong arguments against adopting wilful blindness unless its elements can be defined with much greater

(Lord Reid): 'it is a commonplace that, if the accused had a suspicion but deliberately shut his eyes, the court or jury is well entitled to hold him guilty'. See also *Evan v Dell* [1937] 1 All ER 349, 353: 'deliberately refraining from making inquiries, the results of which [D] might not care to have'.

[128] Although that was not judicially accepted in the nineteenth century: see Edwards, n 119 above, 207.

[129] Williams, n 13 above, 127, para 41. In his article on *mens rea* in secondary liability, 'Complicity, Purpose and the Draft Criminal Code' [1990] *Criminal Law Review* 98, Williams described the element as 'an attempted fraud on the law', n 1 above.

[130] See Sullivan, n 95 above, 214.

[131] See generally, M Wasik and M P Thompson, 'Turning a Blind Eye as Constituting *Mens Rea*' (1981) 32 *Northern Ireland Law Quarterly* 324, 337–41.

[132] Described as 'purposeful avoidance' by W Wilson, *Criminal Law Doctrine and Theory* (Harlow: Longman, 2001), 167.

[133] Williams, n 13 above, 127, para 41, where Williams argued it should be 'realisation that the fact in question is probable, or at least possible above average'. Also, the Law Commission proposed a formula based on D having 'no substantial doubt'. See Wasik and Thompson, n 131 above, 333.

[134] Ashworth, n 3 above, 193.

precision.[135] Moreover, it is unlikely to provide a solution to the problem in conspiracy, at least not in the controversial money laundering cases where the prosecution can often only establish suspicion. Of itself that would not constitute wilful blindness; there would have to be proof of deliberate avoidance of enlightenment. In the money laundering context, the defendant might well have plausible explanations for such avoidance: it does not lie solely within his power to find out; asking would be a futile venture since he would be lied to; no opportunity exists for independent validation of the provenance of the property which would not either lose him his clients or his personal safety. In short, the whole purpose of money launderers is to render it difficult for people to determine the origins of their property.

It is noteworthy that the courts have rejected wilful blindness in the offence of handling where the statute requires knowledge or belief as to the stolen nature of the goods.[136] Handling may be distinguishable since Parliament has provided a lesser *mens rea*, that of belief. However, that ground of distinction could be used to support an argument against construing knowledge in conspiracy to include wilful blindness: handling already provides a lesser *mens rea* so the courts were right not to extend knowledge, but in conspiracy Parliament has not provided a lesser alternative, and hence the wilful blindness doctrine might be used. This argument could equally be inverted to support a narrow approach to knowledge in conspiracy, since wilful blindness has been rejected even where Parliament has provided a lesser *mens rea* so it ought to be even more forcefully resisted when Parliament has not done so.

Even if the courts were to apply the wilful blindness 'doctrine', it is important to note its limits in the conspiracy cases: constructive knowledge will not suffice. In *Roper*, whilst prepared to regard wilful blindness as sufficient, Devlin J regarded constructive knowledge as 'merely neglecting to make inquiries' as inadequate.[137] On this basis, wilful blindness is quite distinct from the position postulated in *Rizvi* that

[135] Many commentators regard the concept as having no part to play in the conspiracy context. See Card, n 52 above, para 17.25: this is 'almost certainly not the case [in conspiracy]'.

[136] See the cases on the requirement of knowledge or belief in handling stolen goods: *Forsyth* [1997] 2 Cr App R 299; *Moys* (1984) 79 Cr App R 72; *Harris* (1987) 84 Cr App R 75. It has been held to be wrong to instruct a jury that D closing his eyes amounted to a belief, let alone to knowledge: *Ismail* [1977] *Criminal Law Review* 557; see also *Pethick* [1980] *Criminal Law Review* 242.

[137] *Roper*, n 120 above, 289. This was regarded at the time as being contrary to much authority and was treated with 'reserve' by commentators. See Edwards, n 119 above, 190, 214. See also J Hall, *General Principles of Criminal Law* (Indianapolis: Bobbs-Merrill, 1947), 215.

D's knowledge of the facts from which a person can reasonably suspect the existence of the illicit provenance of monies is sufficient to constitute knowledge of that circumstance.

Knowledge Satisfied by Belief

Although Parliament, judges, and academics accept that 'belief' is a distinct state of mind from 'knowledge', there is a possibility that the courts may construe section 1(2) as including beliefs as to future prohibited circumstances. Eminent academic commentators suggested that this was necessary if the section was to work sensibly.[138] Furthermore, some commentators regard belief as a possible synonym for knowledge when the matter at issue is whether future circumstances will exist. In addition, as noted, the courts have slipped into the language of belief when dealing with money laundering conspiracies.[139]

The attraction of reading belief as a sufficient *mens rea* is obvious. It would be enough that the conspirator's state of mind was such that although he could not say 'I know for certain that the property I propose to transfer will be illicit', he would say 'but there can be no other reasonable conclusion in the light of all the circumstances, in the light of all that I have heard and seen'.[140]

Aside from obvious principled arguments for strict statutory interpretation, especially as to *mens rea*, there is a strong pragmatic argument against the courts accepting belief as sufficient *mens rea*. The money laundering crimes which have generated the most acute problems are satisfied by proof of suspicion or reasonable grounds to suspect.[141] Even if the prosecution could establish these states of mind, if they can be described as such, they would fall short of belief. Is it worth the courts making such a significant dilution of *mens rea* for conspiracy generally, contrary to unambiguous statutory wording, when doing so would not resolve these

[138] See G Williams, [1977] *New Law Journal* 1164, 1167: Smith, n 1 above. See also his formulation in Smith and Hogan, n 92 above, 304. But note that in more recent case comments Smith adopted a strict stance. Notably in the case which proved so persuasive with the CA in *Harmer*, he commented that 'a person who believes that there is a 50/50 chance that something is so can hardly be said to know that it is so'. See Smith, commentary on *Hussain* [2002] *Criminal Law Review* 407, 409. See also Card, n 31 above, 681, where Card uses the word 'belief'.

[139] As in *Ali*, n 8 above.

[140] *Hall* (1985) 81 Cr App R 260 (Boreham J).

[141] Ironically, there was a proposal in the House of Lords when the money laundering offences were being debated that suspicion should be replaced with belief. That was rejected by the government on the ground that Article 7 of the European Council Directive on Money Laundering was drafted in terms of suspicion. See *Hansard*, 10 December 1992, col 324.

most difficult cases? In policy terms, this would surely expose the courts to strong criticism for their willingness to adopt an approach favouring prosecution processes which it is not necessary to pursue to obtain a conviction. The prosecution could, in almost all these cases, easily secure convictions for substantive offences.[142] It is the desire to rely on conspiracy, the 'prosecutor's darling', with its procedural perks which precipitates the prosecution problems with *mens rea*.[143]

A Note on Recklessness

Some commentators[144] suggest that recklessness is akin to wilful blindness, but academic consensus seems to be that wilful blindness is a narrower category of *mens rea*.[145] It is narrower for several reasons including: (i) it assumes that D has the opportunity to avail himself of the facts or circumstances about which he has an awareness; (ii) that D's assessment of the likelihood of the fact is higher than foresight of a risk, as required for recklessness;[146] and (iii) he intentionally chooses not to enlighten himself. The distinction has been acknowledged in other jurisdictions, for example the Canadian Supreme Court recently observed:

> Wilful blindness is distinct from recklessness because, while recklessness involves knowledge of a danger *or risk* and persistence in a course of conduct which creates *a risk* that the prohibited result will occur, wilful blindness arises where a person who has become aware of the need for some inquiry declines to make the inquiry because he does not wish to know the truth. He would prefer to remain ignorant.[147]

[142] On the limitations to adding a count of conspiracy, see the *Practice Direction* originally introduced in [1977] 2 All ER 540, now in the *Consolidated Practice Direction* IV, 34.3; and see *John M Jones* (1974) 59 Cr App R 120 (CA).

[143] As the court in *Ali* observed, implementing the Domestic Violence Crime and Victims Act 2004, s 17, which despite its inadequacies would assist matters. It allows for a number of substantive counts to be laid with some being selected pre-trial to be dealt with by judge alone after a jury trial on the remainder. This would enable the Crown to prosecute the true criminality of the operation in terms of its duration and scale, as a conspiracy charge always does.

[144] I H Dennis, 'The Mental Element for Accessories' in P F Smith (ed), *Essays in Honour of J.C. Smith* (1987). See also Edwards, n 119 above, 203.

[145] See the characteristically forthright statements of E J Griew, 'Consistency, Communication and Codification Reflection on Two *Mens Rea* Words' in Glazebrook, n 1 above, 73.

[146] Especially when recklessness is construed in its subjective sense, following *G* [2004] 1 AC 1034 (HL).

[147] *R v Williams* [2004] 2 LRC 499 [27]. Quoting from *Sansregret v R* [1985] 1 SCR 570, 584 (McIntyre J). Emphasis added.

While there are strong arguments against the courts diluting the clear statutory requirement of knowledge to allow convictions for conspiracy on proof of recklessness as to the existence of prohibited circumstances, that course is open to Parliament.[148]

It is worth considering that in relation to attempts although the Criminal Attempts Act 1981 requires proof of intention as to circumstances, the courts have held that recklessness will suffice if that state of mind is an adequate *mens rea* for the substantive offence.[149] Why not then in conspiracy? One reason is because the dilution of *mens rea* for attempts proved controversial.[150] In addition, there are sufficiently significant differences between attempt and conspiracy to deter the courts from taking a similar approach. The principal differences are that in conspiracy *mens rea* as to circumstances is expressly provided for, section 1(2) requires knowledge; there is no equivalent provision in the Criminal Attempts Act.[151] Furthermore, conspiracy is distinguishable from attempt because although they are both inchoate crimes, attempt is more firmly anchored to the substantive crime to which it relates. The acts involved must be more than preparatory to that crime, whereas in conspiracy the freestanding act of agreement is sufficient to establish liability.[152] The greater remoteness from the substantive crime and the identifiable harm it protects against, the stricter the *mens rea* of the offences should be.

Most commentators reject the idea that section 1(2) could be satisfied by proof of recklessness to circumstances. As Professor Sullivan puts it, it would be 'unfortunate' if the attempt cases were read as endorsing a

148 Williams suggested that this ought to be the *mens rea*. See Williams, n 13 above, para 159. Note also its endorsement in general terms by law reform agencies, eg the Canadian Law Reform Commission, *Re-Codifying Criminal Law* Report No 31 (1987), cl 2(4), recommended that reckless as to circumstances suffice for any crime with a fault element of purpose or knowledge.

149 See *Khan* (1990) 91 Cr App R 29. The decision in *A-G's Reference No 3 of 1992* [1994] 1 WLR 409 seems to go further. See Smith and Hogan, *Criminal Law* (11th edn) (London: Oxford University Press, 2005), 404.

150 See eg the comments by G Williams, 'Intents in the Alternative' [1991] 50 *Cambridge Law Journal* 120; and see R A Duff, 'The Circumstances of An Attempt' [1991] 50 *Cambridge Law Journal* 100, and J C Smith, [1990] *Criminal Law Review* 519.

151 Thus the courts were able to construe the requirement of 'intention' as applying only to the consequences, although it is clear that the Law Commission intended full knowledge as to circumstances should be proved for attempts. See Law Commission Report No 102, *Attempt and Impossibility in relation to Attempt, Conspiracy and Incitement* (London: HMSO, 1980) paras 2.14–2.15. The Law Commission Working Party (1973), para 3, also recognized that attempt and conspiracy were different forms of inchoate offence to which different considerations apply.

152 *Bolton (Roger John)* (1992) 94 Cr App R 74, 80 (Woolf LJ): 'in the case of conspiracy as opposed to the substantive offence, it is what is agreed to be done and not what was in fact done which is all important'.

doctrine that where 'intent or knowledge is specified in the *mens rea* for an offence, recklessness will suffice as to circumstantial elements provided intention/knowledge is present as to other constituent parts of the offence'.[153]

Oblique Intention

A further solution to the current problem is to place greater reliance on the concept of intention.[154] Again, this will not produce a panacea for all the problems identified. Section 1(2) can be satisfied by proof of intention, and in some cases this offers the most natural description of the conspirators' *mens rea*, as where D1 and D2 agree on a course of conduct and they can control the occurrence of circumstances necessary for the substantive crime to occur. In other cases, where they have no control over the future circumstances, this alternative *mens rea* element would seem rather nonsensical.[155] Some eminent commentators described the use of intent in this context as being 'not a very sensible description'.[156]

Even in such cases, it can be argued that 'intention' might have a role to play. This entails discussion of a number of issues.

The Meaning of Intention: Despite a turbulent period at the end of the last century with no fewer than four visits to the House of Lords in just over twenty years, the definition or description of intention in criminal law[157] seems settled. Intention has the meaning attributed to it in *Woollin*[158] as applied in *Matthews and Alleyne*:[159]

(1) A result is intended when it is the actor's purpose to cause it.
(2) A court or jury may also find that a result is intended, though it is not the actor's purpose to cause it, when –
 (a) the result is a virtually certain consequence of that act, and
 (b) the actor knows that it is a virtually certain consequence.

Intention as to Circumstances in Section 1(2): Both 'direct' and 'oblique' intention can properly be used to describe *mens rea* in relation to

[153] Sullivan, n 95 above, 218.

[154] We are not concerned with the controversial decision in *Anderson* [1986] AC 27, described as 'amazing' by Card, n 52 above, para 17.26, and 'extraordinary' by Ashworth, n 3 above, 464. See also P W Ferguson, 'Intention Agreement and Statutory Conspiracy' (1986) 102 *Law Quarterly Review* 26.

[155] See Smith, n 1 above, 604–5.

[156] ibid.

[157] This is strictly an exaggeration since the House of Lords in *Woollin* [1999] 1 Cr App R 8 (HL) expressly restricted their comments on intention to the law of murder.

[158] ibid.

[159] *Matthews* [2003] 2 Cr App R 30 (CA).

circumstances as well as consequences. D could be said to have a direct intention as to circumstances where the existence of the circumstance is part of the package of results he desires. These will be rare cases, as for example where paedophiles agree to have intercourse with a person who, to satisfy their perversion, must be under the age of 13.

Of course, since conspiracy is complete when D1 and D2 agree on a course of conduct which would be criminal if carried out in accordance with their intentions, they can be liable where the crime is impossible. This is put beyond doubt by the Criminal Attempts Act 1981, section 5. Thus, D1 and D2 who agree to have intercourse with a person intending her to be under the age of 13 are guilty of the conspiracy even if the victim in mind turns out to be older. D1 and D2 who agree to transfer monies which they hope will be illicit are guilty of conspiracy even if the monies turn out not to be illicit.[160]

Oblique intention describes the *mens rea* as to circumstances where D knows the circumstance is virtually certain to exist and nevertheless pursues his course of conduct and the existence of that circumstance is irrelevant to the success or failure of D's action.[161] Where D1 and D2 agree to transfer monies through their *bureau de change* and foresee that it is virtually certain that the monies will be illicit, but they agree to transfer the monies anyway, they have such an intention.

Is this mere Recklessness?: The discussion above concluded that reckless is not a sufficient *mens rea* in section 1(2). It is submitted that an oblique intent test does not deviously reintroduce that same idea; oblique intention as to circumstances is narrower than recklessness. As Simester and Chan observe:

> . . . what is necessary . . . is that the defendant shall think that the relevant circumstances exist with probable certainty. The crucial feature is acceptance. The defendant must accept or assume or have no serious doubts at the time he [agrees] that the circumstance is [will be] present . . . It is not enough for him to believe there is a possibility or likelihood [of the circumstance].[162]

160 See Card, n 52 above, para 17.25, who argues that knowledge has to include belief because otherwise it would be impossible to convict in cases of impossibility. This overlooks the requirement of intention. If D1 and D2 agree to kill x, and unknown to them x is dead, they have conspired to commit murder. Clearly they cannot know that x will be alive at the time they propose to kill him, but they intend to kill a live human being and have agreed on a course of conduct that will necessarily amount to or involve the commission of an offence if carried out in accordance with their intentions.

161 R A Duff, *Criminal Attempts* (Oxford: Clarendon Press, 1996), 21.

162 W Chan and A Simester, 'Intention Thus Far' [1997] *Criminal Law Review* 704, 716.

The *mens rea* involves not merely foresight of a risk, but foresight of the material circumstance as virtually certain. As with distinctions between intention and recklessness as to consequences, fine lines must be drawn, but the two remain distinct concepts. If anything, oblique intent as to circumstances is closer to wilful blindness: D has awareness of the circumstance, indeed, he thinks the circumstance is virtually certain to exist and proceeds anyway, which is similar to D suspecting and deliberately choosing not to enlighten himself. Codes of criminal law commonly treat this state of mind as a form of knowledge,[163] and the Law Commission have previously recommended knowledge be defined in these terms: 'Did the person whose conduct is in issue either know of the relevant circumstances or have no substantial doubt of their existence'.[164] Intention does however seem slightly wider than wilful blindness, since as Ashworth observes, 'one can intend something which does not come to fruition, one cannot know something which is not in fact (or in law) true'.[165] This is an important distinction in conspiracy where the focus is always as to future circumstances.

The Consequences of Applying Oblique Intention in Section 1(2): Oblique intention will not solve many of the problem cases in section 1(2). It offers no substantial extension of liability beyond the wilful blindness. Indeed, it may be that it is narrower since it requires foresight of virtual certainty, not mere suspicion.[166]

Rethinking Intention

Viscount Dilhorne was at pains to point out in the *Churchill* case that the wrongdoing in conspiracy must be viewed as a whole. This remains true under the 1977 Act. The section 1(2) problem cannot be viewed in isolation; section 1(1) also includes *mens rea* elements. Is it possible that in seeking a solution to the *mens rea* problem the focus has been too exclusive, looking only to section 1(2), ignoring section 1(1)? As Glanville Williams advised at the time of enactment, 'the overriding purpose of section 1(1) is to make a person liable for conspiring on the basis of his intention'.[167]

[163] Eg US Model Penal Code 2.02(7): 'when knowledge of the existence of a particular fact is an element of the offence such knowledge is established if a person is aware of a high probability of its existence, unless he believes that it does not exist'.

[164] Law Commission Report No 89, *Mental Element in Crime* (London: HMSO, 1978), 58.

[165] Ashworth, n 3 above, 188.

[166] ibid 143.

[167] [1977] NLJ 1165.

The *mens rea* question for the offence as a whole could be unpacked as follows: D1 and D2 have to be proved to have a direct or oblique intention, or knowledge, including wilful blindness, that the circumstances will be such that when they perform their agreed conduct in accordance with their intentions, it will necessarily involve the commission of a criminal offence. Can section 1(2) be satisfied by the proof that D1 and D2 share an intention that the material prohibited circumstances of the substantive offence will exist if they carry out their plan as they intend? Such intentions seem to be a species of conditional intention, and that concept deserves brief examination.

Distinguishing Types of 'Conditional' Intentions

Academic writing has produced a diverse range of classifications and terminology in this area, but three broad categories are accepted. In examining each, it is convenient to use the example of our putative money launderers.

We Will do 'x' if 'y': Kenneth Campbell in his useful analysis of the concepts describes these as 'non-comprehensive conditional intentions'.[168] The defendant's state of mind is declared only in relation to one possible eventuality.

If D1 and D2 declare 'we will transfer the money if it is clean money', there is no declared intention about what course of conduct they would adopt if the money is illicit. This is not a sufficient state of mind to constitute an intention to launder money. D1 and D2 have implicitly seen the risk that the money will be illicit, but have not declared an intention to deal with criminal money. It cannot be said that D1 and D2 have agreed on a course of conduct that will necessarily involve them in the commission of an offence if carried out in accordance with their intentions. In fact, acting in accordance with their declared intentions, all we can assert is that they will not commit a money laundering offence.

If the statement is 'we will transfer money if it is criminal', clearly this is a sufficient intention to constitute a conspiracy to launder money. The other eventuality, what they would do if the money is legitimate, is neither here nor there. D1 and D2 have declared an intention to pursue a course of conduct which if carried out in accordance with their intentions, which here must be taken to mean including those circumstances

168 K Campbell, 'Conditional Intention' [1982] 2 *Legal Studies* 77, 84–5.

that they anticipate and accept,[169] will necessarily involve a criminal offence. There will be few such cases.[170]

We Will do 'x' only if 'y': Campbell calls these 'comprehensive conditional intentions'.[171] They differ significantly from the previous category because D1 and D2 have declared intentions as to their course of conduct in both eventualities: where *y* materializes and where it does not.[172]

The money laundering duo might say: 'we will transfer the money only if the money is clean, if it is not we will not transfer it'. There is no intention to pursue a course of conduct that will necessarily involve the commission of an offence. There can be no liability for conspiracy. Alternatively, the duo might say 'we will transfer the money only if the money is criminal'. This would obviously constitute an intention to launder. D1 and D2 would have agreed on a course of conduct which if carried out in accordance with their intentions will necessarily involve them in the commission of a criminal offence. These will be rare, in the money laundering context at least. It may be that they are more frequent in other examples such as the paedophile who might say 'I will touch the girl sexually only if she is under the age of 13';[173] or the thief, 'I will steal only if there is something worth stealing'[174]

Such examples do feature in conspiracy case law. It seems settled that there will be a conspiracy where the parties' objective is to commit a crime, but not if it proves too difficult or too dangerous, as where D1 and D2 agree that they will abandon their intention to commit burglary if they find the house surrounded by police. They agree to commit the burglary only if it is safe. If they go through with the agreed conduct as intended they must, of necessity, commit burglary. The fact that an

[169] According to Smith, n 1 above, 603 this must include 'the relevant circumstances which the parties expect to exist at the time of performance of agreement'.

[170] See J Gardner and H Jung, 'Making Sense of *Mens Rea*: Anthony Duff's account' (1991) *Oxford Journal of Legal Studies* 568, who describe reason-giving conditions as those 'which identify what an agent now intends to do in the future should certain contingencies arise in the future and these being bare or future intentions have no role to speak of in the criminal law'.

[171] ibid.

[172] Conditional intentions provide that 'if A then B, if not-A then C'. See A Lynch, 'A Further Comment' [1978] *Criminal Law Review* 205, 207.

[173] Even that is unlikely. It is more likely that he will say 'I will touch her only if she looks under the age of 13'.

[174] The courts got muddled with this in the theft and burglary cases in the 1970s, in particular *Easom* [1971] 2 QB 315. See also L Koffman, 'Conditional Intention to Steal' [1980] *Criminal Law Review* 463; J Parry, 'Conditional Intents: A Dissent' [1981] *Criminal Law Review* 6; and see the cogent criticism by K Campbell, [1981] *Criminal Law Review* 78.

agreement to commit a crime is subject to express or implied reservation does not necessarily preclude liability for conspiracy.[175]

In *Reed*[176] D1 and D2 were guilty of conspiring to aid and abet suicide where they agreed that D1 would visit suicidal individuals and either discourage or actively help them, depending on his assessment of the appropriate course of action. This could be constructed in the form: 'we intend to assist only if the person is a suitable suicide'. D1 and D2 have agreed on a course of conduct which if carried out in accordance with their intentions will necessarily involve an offence.

In *Jackson*,[177] D1 and D2 agreed with D3 that D3, if convicted of the burglary for which he was on trial, should be shot in the leg so that the court would sentence him more leniently. They were guilty of conspiring to pervert the course of justice. This is an agreement that D1 and D2 intend to shoot him only if he gets convicted. D1 and D2 have agreed on a course of conduct which if carried out in accordance with their intentions will necessarily involve an offence.

In *O'Hadhmaill*,[178] it was held that an agreement by IRA members during the period of the IRA ceasefire to make bombs with a view to causing explosions, if, but only if, the ceasefire came to an end, was a conspiracy to cause an explosion. This is a case where D1 and D2 agreed to pursue a course of conduct which would definitely involve the commission of a crime, but only if it is necessary to perform the acts at all because the ceasefire had failed.[179]

In each case the Court of Appeal found a sufficient intention. The decisions may be criticized on the basis that the satisfaction of the condition may be too dependent on D's own subsequent evaluation of the circumstances to be said to represent a true intention. For example, in *O'Hadhamaill*, the question arises whether the ceasefire could be regarded as a fact or circumstance that was clearly determinable without reverting to D's opinion.[180]

[175] *Mills* (1963) 47 Cr App R 49, [1963] Criminal Law Review 181, CCA, and commentary. See *Hussein* [1978] *Criminal Law Review* 219 (CA).

[176] *Reed* [1982] *Criminal Law Review* 819 (CA).

[177] *Jackson* [1985] *Criminal Law Review* 442 (CA).

[178] *O'Hadhmaill* [1996] *Criminal Law Review* 509.

[179] Sullivan suggests that the decision is useful in 'refut[ing] any notion that, in legal discourse, one can never be found to have knowledge of facts relating to the future'. But, does this overlook the fact that the decision is more readily if not equally explicable on the basis of future intentions without detracting from the orthodox view that one cannot know the future? See Sullivan, n 95 above.

[180] See also J Parry, 'Conditional Intents: A Dissent' [1981] *Criminal Law Review* 6. I am grateful to Dr Jeremy Horder for comments on this section. He should not be taken to endorse the views advanced.

To do 'x' even if 'y': Campbell calls these unconditional intentions. They are generally regarded as a form of direct intention. Taking the money laundering duo as an example, let us imagine that D1 and D2 say 'we know that the monies involved in our business might be criminal, we do not know for sure that they will be, but our business is transferring money and we agree that we will pursue such conduct even though some of the monies we transfer are criminal'. Their agreement could be reconstructed as one which includes a confirmed intention: 'we intend to pursue a course of conduct (transferring money) which is not criminal money and if certain circumstances transpire (the money is criminal), we intend nevertheless to pursue a course of conduct (transferring money)'. The agreement will, if completed in accordance with one of their intentions, necessarily involve the commission of a crime.

How would this approach work with other problems postulated above:

(1) D1 and D2 agree to pursue a course of conduct, touching a person in a sexual manner; they foresee that the victim might be under the age of 13. They agree to continue if she is under that age. This could be seen as an agreement to touch a person even if she is under the age of 13 if that circumstance arises. On that agreement they will necessarily commit an offence: their agreements include one to touch a child sexually if she is under the age of 13.

(2) D1 and D2 agree to pursue a course of conduct, damaging property; they foresee that the property might not belong to D1. They agree to continue even if that may be the case. Their agreements include one intentionally to damage property if it belongs to another.

The Implications for Section 1(2)

Section 1(2) requires that D1 and D2 'intend or know' that the fact or circumstances shall or will exist at the time when the conduct constituting the offence takes place. The wording implies the 'knowledge and intention' is separate from the *actus reus*, the conduct constituting the offence. The conditional intention approach requires the concept of intention to perform a double duty: D1 and D2 intend to pursue a course of conduct (section 1(1) intent), and intend that the circumstances necessary for the commission of the crime will exist if they carry out their plan (section 1(2) intent), and the circumstances necessary for the commission are those that they intended. In section 1(1) the intention is to pursue a course of criminal conduct. Foresight of the prohibited circumstances arising, coupled with a present declared intention to go ahead with the plan assuming and accepting that they will materialize, is sufficient. In section 1(2), D1 and D2 must be regarded as intending the circumstance that is necessary for the commission of the offence on the basis that since they have agreed to intend to pursue the enterprise even if that circumstance is present they have intended it.

These are not, it is submitted, states of mere recklessness. D1 and D2 have a present declared intention. If D1 and D2 had said simply 'we will transfer monies', realizing that the money might be criminal, that would be a state of recklessness,[181] they would not have declared what they would do if the prohibited circumstance materialized. If the circumstance did materialize, it would be necessary to return to them to confirm their plans. Where D1 and D2 have declared an 'even if' intention, there would be no point in returning to them to clarify their state of mind, if the circumstance materialized: they have already declared it. At the time the 1977 Act was enacted, Professors Smith and Williams clearly thought that reliance on a conditional intent approach would be a recklessness formula in disguise. Williams wrote that: 'conditional intention must not be applied so widely as to efface the distinction between intention and recklessness, but there is no reason why it should not extend the concept of intention to cases where the criminal intends to do something if it is necessary to effect his purpose'.[182]

Discussion of conditional intents in commentaries on the Act was brief, focusing largely on the issue of D1 and D2 agreeing to perform a second criminal course of conduct only if it became necessary because the first planned criminal agreement failed. John Smith in his article gave a series of examples, one being[183] where D1 and D2 agree to burgle and carry arms so that if necessary they will use violence against anyone who intervenes. His conclusion, subsequently rejected by the courts, was that they have only conspired to burgle. Glanville Williams doubted Smith's conclusion,[184] arguing that D1 and D2 have conspired not merely to burgle but also to wound. This is surely right. In a case where D1 and D2 agree to pursue course of conduct A, which will necessarily involve a crime, and if the circumstances necessitate, to perform crime B as well, they are guilty of two conspiracies. For example, if conspirators agree they

[181] Williams was particularly sceptical of this sort of approach taken by Lords Cross and Hailsham in *Morgan* [1976] AC 203, where their lordships spoke in terms of D 'intending' that the victim was not consenting to the intercourse where D saw it as possible that she would not consent but did not care whether she did or not. Williams subsequently confessed to having changed his mind on this topic generally. See Williams, 'Intents in the Alternative' [1991] 50 *Cambridge Law Journal* 120.

[182] Williams, n 9 above.

[183] Smith, n 1 above.

[184] See also J C Smith, [1977] *New Law Journal* 1164, 1165.

will steal a particular item and they will, if necessary, commit either burglary or robbery to obtain it, that will amount to an agreement to commit the offences of theft, burglary, and robbery.[185]

More pertinent for this discussion is Smith's other example. D1 and D2 having been invited by E to have sex with his wife, V, confer and being uncertain whether V will consent, agree that they will have intercourse with her. The view that the difficulty posed by section 1(2) might be ameliorated by the use of conditional intentions was reluctantly rejected by Smith who regarded this example as not comprising a conspiracy to rape.[186] He did concede that conditional intention may be enough and acknowledged that it would be better if it were.[187] On the analysis above, D1 and D2 could be said to have agreed: to intend to have intercourse with V if she consents and to intend to have intercourse with V even if she does not consent. The latter will necessarily involve them in the commission of the offence if the conduct is pursued in accordance with one of their intentions.[188]

Judicial Acceptance of Conditional Intents in Conspiracy?

Arguably, despite the dangers that it poses in terms of diluting the requirement of intention into one of recklessness, this conditional intent approach has already met with some judicial approval. Perhaps this is what Auld LJ was espousing in *Singh*:[189]

If two or more people intend and agree to commit an act that they know to be unlawful, then knowledge or mistake as to a fact critical to the success of the conspiracy is immaterial to its proof; *the intention is proxy for, or more correctly an alternative to, knowledge of such a fact*. And, it follows, gradations of knowledge, such as 'reasonable grounds to suspect' it are irrelevant.[190]

Conclusion

In 1977 it was noted that there were:

two principal motives for the reform of the common law of criminal conspiracy. First because . . . it led to much litigation on appeal and tended to give an undesirable complication to the criminal law. Secondly, there was a popular feeling

185 *A-G's Ref (No 4 2003)* [2004] EWCA Crim 1944 [14]; *Hussain* [2002] 2 Cr App R 26 [27].

186 Smith, n 1 above, 601.

187 J C Smith, [1978] *Criminal Law Review* 212.

188 Smith has regarded this precise example as a conditional intention. See Smith, 'Intention in Criminal Law' [1974] *Current Legal Problems* 93, 115.

189 *Singh* [2003] EWCA Crim 3712.

190 ibid [31]. Emphasis added. It has been seriously doubted as an authority by academics and by the Court of Appeal in *Ali*, n 8 above. It was decided before *Montila* in the House of Lords.

against it, in the belief that it was a means by which the prosecuting authorities were unjustifiably extending what constituted a crime and increasing penalties that could be awarded.[191]

One could be forgiven for having a sense of *déjà vu*. The *mens rea* for conspiracies is giving rise to an undesirable complication and to many appeals. The use of conspiracy in money laundering cases where the offence has been completed in full raises again the question of whether prosecuting authorities are seeking to extend the scope of the criminal law further than is appropriate.

Although the House of Lords may supply a solution to the immediate problem in money laundering conspiracies, it is unlikely that any judicial solution would be regarded as ideal. In short, Parliament needs to act. By way of conclusion, three pleas to Parliament are offered, in the hope that future legislative reform is focused on the correct issues to provide a permanent and principled solution to the *mens rea* in conspiracy.

Assess the True Rationale of Conspiracy

Only when Parliament has addressed this question can it properly answer the *mens rea* issue. There is considerable antipathy, at least in some quarters,[192] to the desirability of inchoate offences in general, and of conspiracy in particular. The principal concern is that the conduct will often be far removed from the prescribed harm that would constitute a substantive offence. These are not 'ivory towered' anxieties: when the Law Commission began its study of the subject in 1970, one of the first questions posed to Glanville Williams was 'Do we need an offence of conspiracy at all?'[193] In short, should the mere agreement to perform a crime be subject to the criminal sanction, given that such conduct represents a different 'wrong' or 'harm' from the commission of the crime itself?[194]

There are numerous academic arguments which cannot be dealt with here, save only to offer a flavour of the diversity and ingenuity of the objections to what is an offence of considerable pedigree,[195] and

[191] T Aldridge, *The Criminal Law Act 1977* (London: Butterworths, 1978), para 12.

[192] Not all; for calls for a wider offence see D Fitzpatrick, 'Variations on Conspiracy' [1993] *New Law Journal* 1180.

[193] See Hodgson, n 1 above in Glazebrook, n 1 above.

[194] In England, see I Dennis, 'The Rationale of Criminal Conspiracy' (1977) 93 *Law Quarterly Review* 39; and in the USA, see P Marcus, 'Conspiracy: The Criminal Agreement in Theory and in Practice' (1977) 65 *Georgetown Law Journal* 925, 950; P E Johnson, 'The Unnecessary Crime of Conspiracy' (1973) 61 *California Law Review* 1137, 1141.

[195] W S Holdsworth, *History of English Law*, vol III (London: Methuen, 1923), 400 ff; R S Wright, *The Law of Criminal Conspiracies and Agreements* (London: Butterworths, 1873); R Spicer, *Conspiracy* (London: Lawrence and Wishart, 1981).

significant practical value. It has been argued, for example, that: conspiracy criminalizes conduct before it has been confirmed to constitute a harm or real threat of harm, even earlier than an attempt in which an act of more than mere preparation is required; it allows for the punishment of conduct by two which would not be criminal if performed by a sole actor; it allows each conspirator to be punished for the acts of others; and procedurally, it allows the Crown to avoid specificity in the case and carries with it the disadvantages inherent in joint trials.

Judicial opinions on the true nature of conspiracy are also illuminating. As the US Supreme Court has observed:

> For two or more to . . . combine together to commit . . . a breach of the criminal laws is an offence of the gravest character, sometimes quite outweighing, in injury to the public, the mere commission of the contemplated crime. It involves deliberate plotting to subvert the laws, educating and preparing the conspirators for further and habitual criminal practices. And it is characterized by secrecy, rendering it difficult of detection, requiring more time for its discovery and adding to the importance of punishing it when discovered.[196]

There are equally respectable counter-arguments defending the need for conspiracy. For example, that it allows for earlier law enforcement intervention, which better protects society; that it reflects a unique and distinct harm involved in collaboration in criminal activity; that it deters not only the substantive crimes but the planning and collaboration in criminality generally,[197] acknowledging that such collaboration may increase the likelihood of commission of the offence and perhaps even an increased level of harm if committed;[198] that it allows the prosecution to focus on the true nature of the criminality of a group of individuals; and along with other inchoates, it better respects the principle of fair

[196] *Pinkerton v US* 328 US 640, 644 (1946), quoting from *US v Rabinowich* 238 US 78, 88 (1915). This is not a novel claim: 'The general principle on which the crime of conspiracy is founded is this, that the confederacy of several persons to effect any injurious object creates such a new and additional power to cause injury as requires criminal restraint; although none would be necessary were the same thing proposed, or even attempted to be done, by any person singly'. See Criminal Law Commission, *Seventh Report* (1843), 90.

[197] This differs from attempt liability where no distinct harm, and hence no distinct deterrence, is involved in the performance of an act more than merely preparatory to the offence.

[198] This must surely depend on the type of crime. Counter-arguments are that the collaboration may also render conspiracies weaker since they are more susceptible to a disclosure of information or one party reneging. On the psychological and economic strengths of conspiracies, see N Katyal, 'Conspiracy Theory' (2003) 112 *Yale Law Journal* 1307.

labelling since the description of D's conduct accurately reflects his personal behaviour.[199]

The respective merits of the debate are not the focus of this chapter but they demonstrate that there is not even a consensus on the underlying rationale for the offence: Is the 'wrong' criminalized really that of an inchoate offence? Is there a distinct and qualitatively different wrong of 'collaborating' in crime sufficiently serious to warrant criminalization? The lack of clear rationale impacts on the crime by impeding certainty and clarity in definition. To what extent can the offence be seen as representing a distinct harm, capable of definition on its own terms? To what extent must the definition be reliant on the terms of the substantive offence?

Address whether a Section 1(2) or Equivalent is Needed at all?

At present, a stricter *mens rea* for conspiracy than for the substantive is felt to be necessary because it is categorized as a different type of wrong from that prescribed in the substantive offence. Strict liability crimes are, traditionally at least, not about blameworthiness, and on that basis it is not appropriate to have strict liability conspiracies. Strict liability conspiracies would involve neither the harm caused, the core of the substantive offence, nor any blameworthiness in terms of *mens rea*. But, arguably, since strict liability is now applied across a much wider field of conduct including offences of a serious nature, it can be suggested that some strict liability conspiracies might fairly be entertained in a criminal code. If strict liability applies to 'real' or 'serious' crimes, D, who agrees to perform such actions, is likely to know that the performance of the agreement will necessarily involve him in criminal conduct. This argument is at its strongest if the strict liability serious crimes also have explicit moral elements. Where the substantive offence, even if strict liability, involves some morally obvious harm, D should be more alert to the possibility that he is agreeing to do something which is criminal.[200]

199 See the discussion of the Law Commission proposals in respect of secondary liability, Law Commission Consultation Paper No 131 (London: HMSO, 1993); and see J C Smith, 'Secondary Participation in Crime—Can we Do Without it?' (1994) 144 *New Law Journal* 679.

200 It is notable that Viscount Dilhorne treated the *Churchill* case as an exception and opposed s 1(2) in debates on the 1977 Act as unnecessary. See Hansard, HL 1 January 1977, cols 144–62; 1 March 1977, cols 547–58.

Avoid Allowing Money Laundering to Corrupt the Law of Conspiracy

There is a danger that the high-profile money laundering cases, with so much at stake financially, will encourage dilution of *mens rea* requirements for conspiracy generally. But the problem of a conspirator knowing the provenance of monies is not new;[201] the prosecution of such individuals has been achieved before, and under the much maligned powers in the Proceeds of Crime Act 2002 can now be achieved more easily than ever if the prosecution relies on substantive offences. It is the prosecutors' preference for conspiracy which presents the problem. In 1977, discussing the quite separate problem of the added conspiracy count, Glanville Williams noted that although conspiracy might be regarded as the prosecutor's darling 'it has long been doubtful whether the attentions lavished upon the damsel were worthwhile'.[202]

The creation of a workable principled conspiracy offence is surely not beyond the wit of Parliament and its operation is not beyond the capability of the courts.

Addendum: After the submission of this chapter for publication, the House of Lords addressed the current legal problem in *Saik* [2006] UKHL 18. Their lordships acknowledged the assistance that this chapter (cited to them in draft form) had provided in their deliberations. However only Baroness Hale was fully persuaded by the conditional intention argument advanced above at pp. 221–6. For further consideration of the effects of the decision see D Ormerod, [2006] *Criminal Law Review* 1000–4.

201 In *Pollman* (1809) 2 Camp 20, a banker was charged with conspiracy when he took a deposit of illicit funds from three parties to a conspiracy.

202 G Williams, 'The Added Conspiracy Count' [1977] *New Law Journal* 24.

Undue Influence: Vindicating Relationships of Influence

*Mindy Chen-Wishart**

Introduction

Individual freedom has a sacred status in modern liberal democracies. I was born in a different place, where the superiority of obedience to parents, teachers, authority figures, and elders went largely unquestioned. Any deviation was not only foolish and sure to end in tears, but also morally delinquent and deserving of swift punishment. When my dad, an Olympic gymnastics coach amongst other things, said 'Jump', I did—literally! One day, I wandered into his coaching clinic just as he was claiming to be able to teach elephants to do somersaults. He called me over as the least athletic of his four daughters and said 'I can get her to back somersault on the trampoline after three tries'. This elephant did. Arriving in New Zealand at the age of 10 I saw a different set of norms and, although my parents will tell you that I was their most challenging daughter, my own three sons outdo my bids for freedom by a power of ten.

Freedom worthy of the name cannot be unconstrained. The subject of my lecture is the constraint on our freedom of transaction that goes by the name of undue influence.[1] What is it, and why is it bad? The answers to these questions are of widespread interest:

(1) Transactions procured by undue influence are unenforceable and restitution must be made of any benefits obtained pursuant to it. Hence, undue influence is of interest to contract, property, and unjust enrichment lawyers.

* My thanks to those who have allowed me to think out loud on this subject: Richard Sutton, Alan Bog, Jenny Payne, Kate Blackmon, Jonathan Herring, Laura Hoyano, Michael Spence, Sue Bright and, especially, Jane Stapleton. Thanks also to Shalini Perera for invaluable last minute research assistance.

[1] This lecture represents the second part of a two-part project, the first of which appears as M Chen-Wishart, 'Undue Influence—*Beyond* Impaired Consent and Wrong-Doing Towards a Relational Analysis' in A S Burrows and A Rodger (eds), *Mapping the Law: Essays*

(2) Undue influence regulates transactions made in the context of relationships involving high levels of trust and confidence and so, is also of interest to family and probate lawyers. Dr Harold Shipman, the infamous serial killer,[2] first came under scrutiny because he took a suspiciously large benefit under the will of one of his victims.

(3) The invocation of the language of 'abuse of influence', 'betrayal of trust', and 'failure to protect' implies a duty to protect that attracts the attention of trust and tort lawyers.

(4) Recently, even the criminal law has got in on the act. The House of Lords held in *R v Hinks*[3] that the recipient of consensual transfers could nevertheless be guilty of theft. Hinks, a single mother, became very friendly with a mentally slow, naive, gullible, middle-aged man, Mr Dolphin, a month after his father died. She effectively took over the running of his life. He withdrew sums to give her, often the daily maximum from cash machines. After seven months, she had haemorrhaged £60,000 out of his account and into her account. This was almost all of his money left to him by his father. The House of Lords' conclusion of theft sparked controversy: If the transfers are not voidable in civil law, the verdict is tantamount to convicting someone of stealing their own property.[4] The conundrum is more apparent than real in this particular case. If undue influence had been put, the likelihood of the transactions being vitiated is high. Whether approached from the criminal law or the civil law, our instincts seem remarkably uniform that the situation offends the standards of 'ordinary decent people'.[5] The question is how to explain or justify this instinct.

In the first section I will sketch the structure of undue influence law and explain the stalemate in the current debate about the normative basis of the doctrine, whether the claimant's defective consent or the defendant's reprehensible procurement of that consent. The second section will suggest that the origin of the stalemate lies in an overly

in Memory of Peter Birks (Oxford: Oxford University Press, 2006), 201. With expansion on some points, the lecture is published here substantially as it was delivered on 2 March 2006.

[2] He was convicted of fifteen murders and found by an Inquiry headed by Dame Janet Smith to be responsible for at least 215 deaths but suspected of about double that. He was also convicted of forging the will of his wealthy last victim.

[3] [2001] 2 AC 241 (HL); S Gardner, 'Appropriation in Theft—The Last Word' (1993) 109 *Law Quarterly Review* 194; S Gardner, 'Property and Theft' [1998] *Criminal Law Review* 35; A L Bogg and J Stanton-Ife, 'Protecting the Vulnerable—Legality, Harm, and Theft' (2003) 23 *Legal Studies* 402.

[4] J Beatson and A Simester, 'Stealing One's Own Property' (1999) 115 *Law Quarterly Review* 372.

[5] [2001] 2 AC 241 (HL) 262.

simplistic and inaccurate paradigm of the person whose exercise of transactional freedom is being assessed. Replacing this with a more accurate paradigm is the first step towards generating a more accurate story of undue influence. The third section adds the lessons from Hart and Raz which help us to confine the role of consent and legitimize the perfectionist action of the state in enhancing and preventing harm to the conditions in which individuals exercise positive autonomy. The fourth section shows that the new relational theory generates a better fit with the case law than either the claimant or defendant-sided theories. I will conclude by endorsing the view that the two traditional classes of undue influence are much closer than they first appear. In essence, they are but points on a common spectrum.

The Structure of Undue Influence Law

The two traditional ways of proving or committing undue influence remain substantially intact after the refinement by the House of Lords in *Royal Bank of Scotland v Etridge*.[6] A brief sketch suffices to anchor our discussion at this stage. First, the claimant can prove active undue influence by evidence that the defendant coerced her consent. This has been known as 'actual' or 'class 1' undue influence. For example, in *Clarke v Prus*[7] old Mr Clarke was befriended by a younger Mrs Prus. He gave her gifts totalling £1.9 million over some twenty years. The Court held that 'what started out as Mr Clarke's folly . . . finished up as Mrs Prus' victimization at the end of his life' when her requests turned into increasingly vehement demands made by verbal onslaughts and oppressive harassment. In *BCCI v Hussain*,[8] the husband of Benazir Bhutto's sister often subjected his wife to public humiliation verbally and physically, slapping her and pulling her hair. She did not like him much, nor did she trust him. He put her head in a sink, turned on the hot water and told her she had better accompany him to his lawyer where she guaranteed his debt. In *Langton v Langton*,[9] the son and daughter-in-law moved in with a man after he was released from prison for murdering his wife. They knew he was terrified of further institutionalization and they threatened to stop caring for him as his health failed unless he signed his property over to them.

It is often said that proof of a relationship of influence and an unfair outcome are unnecessary,[10] but subsequent discussion will show that

[6] [2001] 4 All ER 449 (HL). Hereafter '*Etridge*'. [7] [1995] NPC 41 (Ch).
[8] [2000] EWCA Civ 395. [9] [1995] 2 FLR 890 (Ch).
[10] *Chitty's Law of Contract* (29th edn) (London: Sweet and Maxwell, 2004), paras 7-053–7-054; J Beatson, *Anson's Law of Contract* (28th edn) (Oxford: Oxford University

both propositions require significant qualification.[11] The second way for the claimant to proceed is to ask the court to draw an inference of undue influence from proof that the claimant was in a 'relationship of influence' with the defendant, and the transaction is one which 'calls for explanation'.[12] Such a transaction is voidable unless the defendant rebuts the inference of undue influence by showing that the claimant gave 'full, free and informed'[13] consent, usually by showing that the claimant received independent advice. This has been known as 'presumed' or 'class 2' undue influence.

The first requirement of a 'relationship of influence' takes some well-recognized forms. It is automatically presumed in certain so-called 'class 2A' relationships, such as: parent and child, doctor and patient, solicitor and client, and religious adviser and follower. Other relationships require specific proof of the requisite influence, this is the old 'class 2B'. But, again, they fall into familiar, and usually familial, types. So, the requisite influence is conventionally found by husbands over their wives,[14] adult children over their parents,[15] and between more extended family members, either between siblings or, more commonly, by a nephew or niece over an elderly, increasingly frail, and often childless uncle or aunt.[16] There are also cases of friendship coloured by romance or dependency because of physical or mental deterioration.[17] Similar dependency and trust may be placed in an employee carer.[18] Conversely,

Press, 2002), 286–7; G Treitel, *The Law of Contract* (11th edn) (London: Sweet & Maxwell, 2003), 408–9; *Etridge*, n 6 above, [103].

[11] See text accompanying nn 164–9 below.

[12] *Etridge*, n 6 above, [28]–[29].

[13] *Zamet v Hyman* [1961] 1 WLR 1442 (CA), 1446.

[14] eg *Bank of Credit & Commerce International SA v Aboody* [1990] 1 QB 923 (CA), and the numerous wife guarantee cases where undue influence was found.

[15] eg *Humphreys v Humphreys* [2004] EWHC 2201 (Ch), [2005] FCR 712; *Mortgage Agency Services Number Two Ltd v Chater* [2003] EWCA Civ 490, [2004] 1 P & CR 4; *Greene King Plc v Stanley and others* [2001] EWCA Civ 1966, [2002] BPIR 491; *Wright v Cherrytree Finance Ltd and Others* [2001] EWCA Civ 449, (2001) 82 P & CR DG10; *Meredith v Lackschewitz-Martin and another* [2002] EWHC 1462 (Ch), [2002] WTLR 1451. But, the parent's influence over the child is accepted as generating an automatic presumption of a relationship of influence under the old class 2A.

[16] eg *Vale v Armstrong and another* [2004] EWHC 1160 (Ch), [2004] WTLR 1471 (nephew over aunt); *Cheese v Thomas* [1994] 1 WLR 129 (CA) (great-nephew over great-uncle); *Williams v Williams* [2003] EWHC 742 (Ch), [2003] WTLR 1371 (brothers); *Watson v Huber* (Ch 9 March 2005) (half-sisters); *Pesticcio v Huet* [2004] EWCA Civ 372, [2004] WTLR 699 (sister over brother); *Randall v Randall* [2004] EWHC 2258 (Ch), [2005] WTLR 119 (nephew over aunt); *Jennings v Cairns* [2003] EWCA Civ 1935, [2004] WTLR 361 (niece over aunt).

[17] *Hammond v Osborn* [2002] EWCA Civ 885, [2002] WTLR 1125; *Wright v Hodgkinson* [2004] EWHC 3091 (Ch), [2005] WTLR 435.

[18] *Re Craig* [1971] Ch 95 (Ch) (a companion-housekeeper); *Re Morris (deceased), Special Trustees for Great Ormond Street Hospital for Children v Rushin and Others* (Ch 19 April

the claimant may enter a transaction under the undue influence of an employer.[19]

The second prerequisite for raising the inference of undue influence, a transaction 'calling for an explanation', the preferred label to 'manifest disadvantage',[20] tends to entail transactional outcomes which are catastrophic for the claimants. The inference of undue influence can be rebutted but the nature of the rebuttal has been the source of some debate: what exactly is it trying to disprove? It suffices here to note its instability and to observe that the presence or absence of independent advice is not determinative.[21]

Three examples illustrate the inference of undue influence. First, in *Hammond v Osborn*,[22] an elderly and frail Hammond was befriended by Osborn, a neighbour, who helped him in various ways over 18 months as he became increasingly infirm. Osborn claimed that Hammond told her to cash in all his investments, some £300,000 worth, and to keep the proceeds. In inferring undue influence, the court emphasized that the sum represented 92 per cent of Hammond's liquid assets, leaving him only £27,000 and an income of £14,000 per year—insufficient to meet the costs of his care as he became more infirm—while making him liable for capital gains tax of £50,000. Secondly, in *Greene King v Stanley*,[23] elderly parents agreed to a charge on their home to secure their son's borrowing although they needed the property to be free of encumbrances in two years' time to enhance their pension. The son had business acumen while his parents were financially naïve; they and their adviser were ignorant of the extent of his indebtedness, the amount of the loan, and the loan period. Thirdly, we should note the venerable old case of *Allcard v Skinner*,[24] often offered as the classic example of undue influence. There, a young woman took a vow of poverty, chastity and obedience and eventually joined the convent as a full member. She later gave her very substantial inheritance to the Mother Superior of the convent. The rules of the convent imposed the most absolute submission by the nuns to the Mother Superior who was to be regarded as the 'voice of God'; they could not seek outside advice without her permission. Years later, she decided to leave. The court found undue influence and would have given

2000) (housekeeper); *Goldsworthy v Brickell* [1987] Ch 378 (CA) (farm manager); *O'Sullivan v Management Agency and Music Ltd* [1985] QB 428 (CA) (manager of a pop singer).

19 *Crédit Lyonnais Bank Nederland NV v Burch* [1997] 1 All ER 144 (CA); *Steeples v Lee* [1998] 1 FLR 138 (CA).

20 *Etridge*, n 6 above, [22], [24], [28]–[29].

21 See further, text accompanying nn 143–51 below.

22 *Hammond*, n 17 above.

23 [2001] EWCA Civ 1966, [2002] BPIR 491.

24 (1887) LR 36 Ch D 145.

her back what was left of her gift if she had not let her claim go stale through the lapse of time.

The Current Debate

The debate about the nature of undue influence has ossified into bipolar form.[25] The law intervenes, it is argued, either because the claimant's consent was defective or because the defendant behaved badly. The question is reduced to that of: undue influence, 'claimant-sided' or 'defendant-sided'? But, despite each side's appeals to the law, the war turns out to be one of attrition, a battle with no decisive winner. Two immediate problems can be identified, one relating to the use of precedents and the other to the instability of language.

Appeals to support by precedents can be made at three distinct levels. First, at the most general level of statements of principle, each side can claim victory because each can line up a collection of dicta supporting the defective consent[26] or the unacceptable behaviour[27] view. Confusingly, some cases are called in aid by both sides.[28] Similarly, no clear outcome emerges from the second and more detailed level of 'the law', namely the formal burden of proof. Each side can offer an explanation that is consistent with its favoured interpretation. The defendant-sided view would require wrongdoing to be proved or inferred. Substantive unfairness is

[25] P Birks and N Y Chin, 'On the Nature of Undue Influence' in J Beatson and D Friedman (eds), *Good Faith and Fault in Contract Law* (Oxford: Oxford University Clarendon Press, 1995), 57, hereafter 'Birks and Chin'; P Birks, 'Undue Influence as Wrongful Exploitation' (2004) 120 *Law Quarterly Review* 35; R Bigwood, 'Undue Influence—"Impaired Consent" or "Wicked Exploitation"' (1996) 16 *Oxford Journal of Legal Studies* 503; R Bigwood, *Exploitative Contracts* (Oxford: Oxford University Press, 2003); R Bigwood, 'Contracts by Unfair Advantage—From Exploitation to Transactional Neglect' (2005) 23 *Oxford Journal of Legal Studies* 65.

[26] Examples of recent cases include: *Commercial Bank of Australia Ltd v Amadio* (1983) 46 ALR 402, 461, 474; *Drew v Daniel* [2005] EWCA Civ 507 [36], [2005] 2 FCR 365; *Turkey v Awadh* [2005] EWCA Civ 382 [11], [36], [38], [39], [2005] 2 FCR 7; *Hammond*, n 17 above, [31]–[32], [55], [61]; *Randall*, n 16 above [36]; *Macklin v Dowsett* [2004] EWCA Civ 904 [10], [2005] WTLR 1561; *Jennings*, n 16 above, [34]–[35], [40]; *Pesticcio*, n 16 above, [1]–[2], [4], [20], [23]; *Papouis v Gibson-West* [2004] EWHC 396 (Ch) [26], [2004] WTLR 485.

[27] *Etridge*, n 6 above, [6]–[8], [32], [93]; *Mortgage Agency Services Number Two Ltd*, n 15 above, [27], [38]; *Attorney-General v R* [2003] UKPC 22, 21, 24, 27–8; *Leader v Stevens* [2005] EWCA Civ 50 [17], [19]; *Turkey*, n 26 above, [15], [119]; *Hughes v Hughes* [2005] EWHC 469 (Ch) [93], [2005] 1 FCR 679; *Rosenfeld v Ransley* [2004] EWHC 2962 (Ch) [90]; *Wright*, n 17 above, [131], [137], [138], [140]–[141]; *Eid v Al-Kazemi (No 1)* [2004] EWHC 2129 (Ch), [44], [55]; *National Commercial Bank (Jamaica) Ltd v Hew* [2003] UKPC 51 [28], [29], [32], [33]; *Randall*, n 16 above, [72], [82], [85], [86].

[28] *Turkey*, n 26 above; *Wright*, n 17 above; *Randall*, n 16 above; *Attorney-General v* R, n 27 above; *Etridge*, n 6 above.

relevant only as evidence of wrongdoing.[29] The claimant-sided view says real defendant coercion cases should go into duress;[30] the rest is about the claimant's inability to give meaningful consent. She lacks the capacity for self-management because of her morbid dependency on the defendant. Substantive unfairness is just evidence of this diminished capacity or it acts as a policy restrictor to prevent too much restitution.[31]

We are stuck in a loop with seemingly no way out. The 'either or' approach has the attraction of conceptual simplicity, clarity, and easy marketability. These approaches are even plausible in the 'unclean' cases which involve quasi-incapacity, where the claimants are mentally or physically dependent,[32] or quasi-duress, where the defendant's coercion is clear.[33] However, neither theory can explain the 'clean' cases like *Allcard v Skinner*,[34] where the Court found no diminished capacity by the claimant and no wrongdoing by the defendant, but still inferred undue influence from the relationship of influence between the parties, and the transaction which 'called for an explanation'.

The third, and most promising, level of appeal to 'the law' is in the messy detail of the cases. This invites us to begin 'at the bottom' rather than 'from the top down'[35] to identify the substance behind the justificatory language of defective consent and wrongdoing. But, as soon as we attempt the task of accurately describing the phenomenon that we are trying to explain, the case law, we encounter the second complication. Namely, the problem of language that lies at the heart of undue influence: its key concepts do not mean what they appear to mean in four distinct respects. First, words like 'impropriety', 'abuse', 'betrayal', 'wrongdoing', 'stigma', 'reprehensible', 'fault', are standardly invoked in the cases. But neither bad conduct nor bad faith is required and this is expressly confirmed by several recent cases.[36] The judges in *Allcard* were

[29] Bigwood, n 25 above, 391–3, 455, 472–7.

[30] Further discussed below at text accompanying nn 150–63 below.

[31] Birks and Chin, n 25 above, 82.

[32] eg *Pesticcio*, n 16 above; *Williams*, n 16 above; *Simpson v Simpson* [1992] 1 FLR 601 (Ch) and *R v Hinks*, n 3 above.

[33] eg *Hussain*, n 8 above, and *Langton*, n 9 above; see text accompanying nn 8–9 above. In *Woolwich plc v Gomm* [2000] 79 P & CR 61 (CA), the husband coerced his wife, who was 'vulnerable, dependant and impressionable' and from whom he had long separated, to guarantee his debt by threatening not to pay her maintenance.

[34] See also, *Cheese*, n 16 above; *Hammond*, n 17 above, [32]; *Jennings*, n 16 above, [33]; *Randall*, n 16 above, [36]–[39].

[35] P Cane, 'The Anatomy of Private Law Theory—A 25th Anniversary Essay' (2005) 25 *Oxford Journal of Legal Studies* 203, referring to J Coleman, *Risks and Wrongs* (Cambridge: Cambridge University Press, 1992), 8–9; J Coleman, *The Practice of Principle* (Oxford: Oxford University Press, 1998), 5–6.

[36] eg *Re the Estate of Brocklehurst* [1978] 1 Ch 14, 19, and see n 26 above.

at pains to acquit the Mother Superior of any wrongdoing or selfish motive. She was the model of rectitude. Indeed, true to the aspirations of the Order, she would have thought it best for the nun to divest herself of her worldly trappings. But still, there was undue influence. The claimant-sided camp highlights this in support of its interpretation.

However, and this is the second point, although courts sometimes use the justificatory language of defective consent, *Allcard v Skinner* cannot realistically support a claimant-sided story. There is ample finding that the nun knew what was expected of her before she joined the sisterhood, when her mother and barrister brother advised her against this action. The judges recognized that everything she did was referable to her own willing submission and enthusiastic devotion to the life and work of the sisterhood.[37] She 'chose it as the best for herself'. But this does not mean that she was 'unable to take care of herself or to manage her own affairs'.[38] She is perfectly free to act on her religious commitment in disposing of her property. 'Persons of this kind are not dead in law.' Indeed, Lord Nicholls admits in *Etridge* that courts merely 'deem' the claimant's consent to be 'defective when the defendant's conduct is reprehensible'.[39] So, we are thrown back to the first puzzle about the content of this bad behaviour.

Thirdly, the claimant must show that the transaction 'calls for an explanation' in that it is 'not to be reasonably accounted for on the ground of friendship, relationship, charity, or on the ordinary motives on which ordinary men act'.[40] But once we accept that someone can choose to be a nun, her decision to give her worldly possessions, as she has given herself, to the service of God is perfectly explicable. The fact that it was nevertheless held to 'call for an explanation' in *Allcard* shows that the formulation masks an implicit judgment about the normative acceptability of the transaction, and is not a straightforward inquiry into the reality of the claimant's consent.

Fourthly, the court found the inference of undue influence unrebutted because the Mother Superior could not show that the nun was free to get, and to follow, independent advice if she wanted. But, this seems purely formalistic when Kekewich J recognized, at first instance, that any advice against the gift however plainly and strongly given, would have been

[37] *Allcard*, n 24 above, 184.

[38] ibid 178 and at 181, 'although the Plaintiff was a religious enthusiast, no one could treat her as in point of law *non compos mentis*'.

[39] *Etridge*, n 6 above, [7]; in the context of duress see *Universe Tankships Inc of Monrovia v International Transport Workers Federation* (*the Universe Sentinel*) [1983] 1 AC 366 (HL) 384.

[40] *Etridge*, n 6 above, [22], [24], [28]–[29].

rejected as 'a temptation of the evil one'.[41] Thus, the malleability of both the law and of language at the level of statements of principle and burden of proof means that undue influence is equally susceptible of a claimant- or defendant-sided explanation. Yet neither can explain the 'clean' cases at the level of fact-finding and outcomes.

Even more disturbing is the fact that the current bipolar debate sets up a false dichotomy. Both are really about defective consent. The only difference between the two versions is the source of the claimant's supposed impairment, either the defendant's exercise of influence or the claimant's own susceptibility to influence. Hence, both versions can be presented in terms of the claimant's impaired consent.[42] This explains why Birks and Chin regard even duress, which requires the undoubtedly defendant-sided finding of illegitimate pressure, as claimant-sided.[43] In sum, our normative reasoning is totally consent-bound even as consent runs out of explanatory power. We can have any size so long as it is extra small, even if it does not fit most cases. How did we get in this position? To escape this impasse we first need to understand our obsession with consent and its ailments. We need to start at the beginning.

Autonomy: Detached or Relational?

Personal freedom or autonomy is recognized as valuable morally, politically, and economically. Its preservation is a ready justification for state action. Its core idea is that of self-authorship; that there is something intrinsically valuable in pursuing freely chosen goals and relationships. It is a fundamental feature of personhood, and respect for it is not just one value amongst many in human life, it is an absolutely fundamental value which must always trump any other.[44]

[41] *Allcard*, n 24 above, 159, 184. Lindley LJ required proof that the nun knew 'she would have been allowed to obtain [outside] advice if she had desired to do so . . . [and that] she was free to act on the advice which might be given to her', but any suggestion that the nun would have done something different had she been better advised seems quite fictional on the evidence before the court.

[42] This focus on causation or inducement, ie, whether the defendant's conduct caused the claimant's consent, means that even misrepresentation and unconscionable conduct can be described as 'claimant-sided'.

[43] Birks and Chin, n 25 above, 88–9, argue free consent is impaired only when it is distorted by an alien or illegitimate pressure so although pressure must be illegitimate, duress is a 'claimant-sided phenomenon, so that relief flows from the impairment of the claimant's decision-making capacity, not from unconscientiousness on the part of the other'.

[44] See eg J Rawls, *A Theory of Justice* (Cambridge, Mass: Harvard University Press, 1971).

Detached Autonomy

The problem lies in the very stripped-down, biased or skewed, but dominant, conception of the person whose exercise of freedom we value. The paradigm autonomous person is the rugged individualist. He is self-sufficient, self-knowing, and rationally self-interested. He is not Superman, but we can call him 'Super-Detached Man'. He is anonymous and atomistic; he exists without connection with others. His diversity and complexity are pared away and he is reduced to an interchangeable sameness behind John Rawls's 'veil of ignorance'. Behind this veil, his stance towards other similarly constituted individuals is competitive: he has rights to protect him from their self-interested pursuits. John Rawls's device of the 'original position' rests on this assumption.[45] This picture is reinforced by the biology of natural selection and the survival of the fittest. It is also reflected in Sir Henry Maine's famous proposition that 'the movement of the progressive societies is one "from status to contract" '.[46] We are self-made and we are constantly exhorted to be ourselves, told that we are 'worth it' and 'can do it', and should 'just do it'.

The Super-Detached Man is an iconic figure who has coloured the way we think about the law's legitimate role in regulating transactions. Four linked concepts are relevant here:

(1) We tend to see freedom in negative terms. That is, we think of freedom as freedom from undue interference with individual choices. It is autonomy in a negative sense. It assumes that freedom is good and the more of it the better.

(2) This freedom is manifested in the individual's consent. This elevates consent to a pivotal position in a way which tends to shut out other considerations.

(3) Objectionable transactional conduct which interferes with that consent is judged for its likely impact on the Super-Detached Man. That is why the 'pressure, emotional blackmail or bullying'[47] of class 1 undue influence is described in Chitty as 'relatively innocuous',[48] and led Birks and Chin to dismiss it as legally insignificant.[49]

[45] ibid, and see S Mulhall and A Swift, *Liberals and Communitarians* (2nd edn) (Oxford: Blackwell Publishing, 1996), 1–35.

[46] J Murray, *Ancient Laws, Its Connection with the Early History of Society and Its Relation to Modern Ideas* (reprinted edn) (Arizona: Tucson University of Arizona Press, 1986), 141.

[47] *Etridge*, n 6 above, [160].

[48] *Chitty's Law of Contract*, n 10 above, para 7–049.

[49] Birks and Chin, n 25 above, 77, 95. See further, discussion in text accompanying nn 150–63 below.

(4) The conception of Super-Detached Man is associated with the demand for small or minimalist government. The State should provide the necessary framework for making and upholding transactions, but it cannot and should not evaluate the choices made by individuals. Its stance should be one of 'hands off'. The idea is captured by the various labels of 'neutrality', 'value subjectivism', 'value scepticism', and 'anti-perfectionism'.

Relational Autonomy

Imagine a world where everyone behaves like Super-Detached Man. What would our dealings with our spouses, children, parents, friends, lovers, even colleagues, be like? To subject such beloved and close relations to detached inspection buys protection at a cost of oddness, awkwardness, a lingering sense of the unnatural, mechanical, and disrespectful. It empties all that is meaningful from such relationships since trust, dependency, and commitment are the very stuff of such relationships.

Super-Detached Man is far from life as we know it. He is a fiction and he provides a distinctly wobbly basis for normative reasoning. For a start, are we really rational? We have known since Freud and Nietzsche that the psyche is conflict ridden, often self-deluded, fundamentally opaque to itself, and driven by archaic desires of which it may not even be aware, let alone be able to master.[50] But, we need not go that far to grant the more qualified claim that it is simply delusional to view human beings as detached and self-sufficient.[51] Persons are embedded in society and only become persons in relations with others, many of whom will not have been acquired contractually or voluntarily. Four points can be made.

First, autonomous individuals are causally relational. Biologists have long shown bonding to be instinctual and attachment to be an essential drive. Baby monkeys prefer a cloth-covered dummy—to which they can cling—over a wire one that supplies milk.[52] Anyone who makes it does so with the help of others. Development from infancy necessitates dependency on others. What enables people to be autonomous is not isolation,

[50] C Mackenzie and N Stoljar, *Relational Autonomy* (Oxford: Oxford University Press, 2000), 10.

[51] See M A Fineman, *The Autonomy Myth: A Theory of Dependency* (New York: New Press, 2004); Mulhall and Swift, n 45 above, Part I Communitarian critiques 37–160, discussing the work of Sandel, McIntyre, Taylor, and Walzer; C Gilligan, *In a Different Voice* (Cambridge, Mass: Harvard University Press, 1982); Mackenzie, and Stoljar, n 50 above; S Sevenhuijsen, *Citizenship and the Ethics of Care* (London: Routledge, 1998).

[52] H F Harlow and R R Zimmermann, 'Affectional Responses in the Infant Monkey' (1959) 130 *Science* 421–32. Attachment theory, largely an elaboration of the research of John Bowlby, has become an important strain of contemporary psychotherapy.

but relationships with parents, teachers, friends, and loved ones that provide support and guidance.

Secondly, autonomous individuals are conceptually relational; we forge our identities in the social context in which we are embedded. We are persons with attachments. We commit ourselves to projects, relationships, and causes that make our lives worth living. We need society and its recognized social forms[53] in order to act autonomously because they provide the stock of options for us to choose from and give meaning to our choice. We learn how to be parents, friends, spouses, and whatever we choose in our careers, personal relations, and interests through continuous observation of and participation in the social form. Although each puts his personal stamp on the chosen form, its working out must fall within a range recognized as constituting that chosen form for the pursuit to have succeeded.

Third, relationships have obvious instrumental values. They provide vital and ready sources of the 'basic goods' or 'aspects of authentic human flourishing' that John Finnis identifies in *Natural Law and Natural Rights*,[54] as commonly yielded by anthropological surveys. These are: life, including all aspects of health and reproduction; knowledge; play; aesthetic experience; and 'religion', including all inquiries about human nature and its place in the universe.

Last, relationships are of intrinsic value. They imply attachment, interdependence, and generosity, a sphere of comfort in which we can be ourselves, let down our guard, communicate undefensively and experiment. To feel connection with those who mean most to us is to feel vitality, clarity, worth, meaning, and fulfilment. It is the stuff of great music, literature, and movies. Hence, the pathos of Simon and Garfunkel's lyrics 'I am a rock, I am an island . . . a rock feels no pain, and an island never cries',[55] and the exaltation in Dr Iannis's characterization of his relationship with his wife in *Captain Corelli's Mandolin*,[56] 'we had roots that grew towards each other underground, and when all the pretty blossom had fallen from our branches we found that we were one tree and not two'.

Striving for connection with others is a worthy goal. In contrast to Super-Detached Man, our Relational Hero throws himself into his significant relationships. He is willing to please; he gives generously, defines

[53] J Raz, *The Morality of Freedom* (Oxford: Oxford University Press, 1986), 161–2, 319.
[54] J Finnis, *Natural Law and Natural Rights* (Oxford: Clarendon Press, 1980), 64, 86–90.
[55] P Simon and A Garfunkel, *Sounds of Silence* (California: Columbia Records, 1966).
[56] L de Bernière, *Captain Corelli's Mandolin* (London: Secker & Warburg, 1994), 281.

himself partly in terms of his relationships, and takes pride in their continuity. Such behaviour, while admirable, exposes him to the danger of exploitation by his significant others and exposes them to the temptation to exploit him. Many are eaten alive in the name of relationship. Worse than unprotected sex may be unprotected commitment. Undue influence provides that protection. But, what is its normative basis?

The Normative Basis for Undue Influence

Defective Consent—The Thin Approach

From the Super-Detached reference point, the justification for undue influence rests on the claimant's defective consent. Such claimants are 'impaired in their judgmental capacity... arising from their morbid dependence on another'.[57] 'The relevant weakness... is that, within the relationship, by reason of excessive dependence on the other person, he or she lacks the capacity for self-management which the law attributes to the generality of adults'.[58] Her 'autonomy' or the 'integrity of her judgment' is 'markedly sub-standard' or 'impaired to an exceptional degree'.[59] This is unrealistic and insulting as a general description of undue influence claimants. It denigrates the values of attachment. What does it imply about Mother Teresa? An alternative view is that when the novice nun gave her worldly possessions to the Mother Superior she did not lack autonomy—she exercised it.

Defective Consent—The Thick Approach

A more relational approach can be posited which remains within defective consent reasoning. The argument would be that the current test of consent is too thin; it takes a 'snapshot' of one moment in time and looks for a minimal threshold of consent, such as the signature. As Stewart Macaulay says, it gives us, essentially, the duck test. 'If it looks like a duck, waddles like a duck and quacks like a duck, it is a duck!'[60] It is the law of 100 per cent on-off consent. Instead, a more nuanced approach to consent should be applied, analogous to Ian Macneil's relational approach to determining the content of contracts beyond the express written terms.

[57] Birks and Chin, n 25 above, 85. [58] ibid 67. [59] ibid 67, 68, 81, 87.

[60] S Macaulay, 'The Real and the Paper Deal—Empirical Pictures of Relationships, Complexity and the Urge for Transparent Simple Rules' in D Campbell, H Collins, and

He suggests that it is more like eating a Scotch egg in a haggis. The egg tastes different from an ordinary boiled egg since it will take its flavour from its thick coating which is, itself, seasoned by the surrounding haggis.[61] The question, then, becomes whether the claimant has really consented despite meeting the minimal threshold of consent.

Two objections can be raised against this 'thick' approach to consent. First, it is simply unworkable. It is impossible to determine, in principle, how thick is thick enough, and, in practice, whether a particular claimant's consent is thick enough. Secondly, it ultimately runs into the same problem of denigrating the claimant's agency and relational motives for acting. It effectively accuses the undue influence claimant of false consciousness: 'You think you know what you are doing, but you really don't'. Our discussion of the good of attachment shows that we should be entitled to trust our family and friends in a way that we are not with relative strangers. To do so is not pathological, it shows a healthy ability to connect with significant others.

Autonomy is not inconsistent with values like love, friendship, care, loyalty, and devotion that concern us all. A legal framework which protects people from relational exploitation whilst showing proper regard for the relational motivations can be achieved in two broad moves. First, putting consent in its proper place so that it is not the be all and end all of transactional liability, thus secondly, making room for the law's normative judgment on relational abuse.

Hart—The Defeasibility of Transactional Consent

Hart helps us with the first move to put consent in its proper place. In *The Ascription of Responsibility and Right*[62] he describes the line of reasoning that since consent gets you in, only lack of consent will get you out[63] as 'a disastrous over-simplification and distortion' of the law governing the vitiation of transactions. It fails to recognize: (i) that consent is a necessary but not sufficient condition of transactional liability; and (ii) that the validity of a transaction is a two-stage inquiry, so that even when the

J Wightman (eds), *Implicit Dimensions of Contract: Discrete, Relational and Network Contracts* (Oxford: Hart Publishing, 2003), 51, 56.

[61] I R Macneil, 'Reflections on Relational Contract Theory after a Neo-classical Seminar' in Campbell *et al*, ibid, 207, 209.

[62] H L A Hart, 'The Ascription of Responsibility and Rights', *Proceedings of the Aristotelian Society* (1948) 49; also in A G N Flew (ed), *Logic and Language—First Series* (Oxford: Blackwell Publishing, 1960), 145, 173.

[63] ibid 183.

language of consent is used in determining both the formation and vitiation stages, they deal with qualitatively different concerns. Hart writes:[64]

When the student has learned that in English law there are positive conditions required for the existence of a valid contract... his understanding of the legal concept of a contract is still incomplete... For these conditions, although necessary, are not always sufficient and he has still to learn what can defeat the claim that there is a valid contract, even though all these conditions are satisfied. That is the student still has to learn what can follow on the word 'unless' which should accompany the statement of these conditions... the law has a word which with some hesitation I borrow and extend: This is the word 'defeasible' used of a legal interest in property which is subject to termination or 'defeat' in a number of different contingencies but remains intact if no such contingencies mature. In this sense then, contract is a defeasible concept.

Hart surveys the range of vitiating factors and concludes that they are 'irreducibly defeasible in character and to ignore this is to misrepresent' them. This is obscured by the theorist who takes the language of impaired consent as suggesting 'that there are certain psychological elements required by the law as necessary conditions of contract and that the defences are merely admitted as negative evidence of these', rather than as 'a compendious reference to the defences with which claims in contract may be weakened or met'.[65] This distinction between factual or psychological and legal or in the eye of the law consent[66] is supported by Lord Nicholls's statement in *Etridge* that whenever the defendant's procurement of the claimant's consent is judged improper, that consent will not be deemed an expression of the claimant's will.[67] Thus, talk of consent here is conclusory, not explanatory; it is merely short-hand for the variety of factors rendering a transaction defeasible. It is a mistake to reason from the vitiating factors that:[68]

... the definition of contract requires as necessary conditions that the mind of the parties should be 'fully informed' and their wills 'free'... [T]he defence, e.g., that

[64] ibid 174–6 (emphasis in the original).

[65] ibid 177, 180, Hart explains 'the logical character of words like "voluntary" are anomalous and ill-understood. They are treated in such definitions as her words having positive force, yet, as can be seen from Aristotle's discussion in *Book III of the Nicomachean Ethics*, the word "voluntary" in fact serves to exclude a heterogeneous range of cases such as physical compulsion, coercion by threats, accidents, the stakes, etc, and not to designate a mental element or state; nor does "involuntary" signify the absence of this mental element or state.'

[66] The analogy is to the factual and legal benefit distinction in the context of the consideration doctrine post *Williams v Roffey Brothers & Nicholls (Contractors) Ltd* [1991] 1 QB 1 (CA).

[67] *Etridge*, n 6 above, [7].

[68] Hart, n 62 above. Also in Flew, n 62 above 145, 177–8.

B entered into a contract with A as a result of the undue influence exerted upon him by A is not evidence of the absence of a factor called true 'consent'... [N]o party attempting to enforce a contract is required to give evidence that there was 'true, full and free consent'... Of course, the theorist could... [ascribe] the actual procedure of the courts to the practical difficulties of proving 'mental facts'; and it is sometimes said that it is merely a matter of practical convenience... that the onus of proof is usually upon the defendant to prove the non-existence of these necessary elements... But to insist on this as the real explanation of the actual procedure of the courts in applying the defeasible concept of a contract would merely be to express an obstinate loyalty to the persuasive but misleading logical ideal that all concepts must be capable of definition through a set of necessary and sufficient conditions.

Hart's counsel allows us to detach the basis for vitiating transactions from the basis for enforcing them. Space is then opened up to consider values at work other than consent. The question is whether, in view of the relevant circumstances bringing the case within a recognized head of exception, a claimant should be relieved of responsibility for the transaction, despite her consent to it.[69] This resonates with rejection of the 'overborne will' explanation of duress. Lord Scarman said:[70] 'The classic case of duress is... not the lack of will to submit but the victim's intentional submission arising from the realization that there is no practical choice open to him'. Where this results from the defendant's illegitimate pressure, the law does not ascribe the normal responsibility it would to the victim's consent. As with undue influence, the claimant's consent is deemed to be vitiated.[71] This view avoids the fiction that the claimant gave no effective consent despite acting knowingly and intentionally. Rather, it takes the realistic and respectful view that the claimant engages with reason in consenting to the transaction, but should nevertheless be excused from responsibility in the circumstances. A similar analysis of undue influence would avoid the unrealistic and insulting characterization of a claimant who chooses to trust the defendant's judgment as thereby 'impaired'.

Raz—Preventing Harm to Positive Autonomy

Once consent is no longer the be all and end all of transactional validity, the way is cleared for asking why, at stage two, the claimant should be relieved of her transactional liability despite her consent, in particular, for undue influence. Joseph Raz's work provides the critical context in which

[69] ibid 174
[70] *Universe Tankships Inc of Monrovia*, n 39 above, 400.
[71] ibid 384.

to develop that understanding. In *The Morality of Freedom*[72] he gives us an ingenious version of personal autonomy which is at once pluralistic and consistent with both the harm principle and with perfectionist state action. For our purposes, the reasoning can be set out in six steps.

(1) Positive autonomy: The only freedom worthy of the name is a positive one. It is less about the right to be free from interference, and more about the freedom to pursue 'acceptable and valuable projects and relationships'.[73] Without worthwhile choices, autonomy is hollow.

(2) Perfectionism: The role of the state is less to hold people to their choices than to create the conditions of positive autonomy: 'it is the goal of all political action to enable individuals to pursue valid conceptions of the good and to discourage evil or empty ones'.[74] Hence, 'the autonomy principle is a perfectionist principle... [it] permits and even requires government [read law] to create and support morally valuable opportunities, and to eliminate or discourage repugnant ones'.[75]

(3) Plurality: Nevertheless, we must give a wide margin of tolerance to our conceptions of the worthwhile for three reasons. First, the value of autonomy itself requires options and/or room to choose. 'It admits a large number of differing pursuits among which individuals can choose';[76] '[V]aluing autonomy leads to the endorsement of moral pluralism'.[77] Secondly, the state may make mistakes on the margins and may act oppressively.[78] Thirdly, further tolerance is warranted by the pragmatism of not getting people's 'backs up';[79] '[t]he pursuit of full-blooded perfectionist policies, even of those which are entirely sound and justified, is likely... to backfire by arousing popular resistance leading to civil strife. In such circumstances compromise is the order of the day... [which] will confine perfectionist measures to matters which command a large measure of social consensus'. Nevertheless, eliminating the worst choices and most abusive social forms increases people's chances of living good autonomous lives, whilst still leaving them plenty of sub-optional options to choose from.

(4) Social forms: The point was made above that social forms are foundational to the worthwhile exercise of autonomy.[80] Raz argues

[72] Raz, n 53 above. [73] ibid 417. [74] ibid 133. [75] ibid 417.
[76] ibid 381. [77] ibid 399. [78] ibid 419, 427. [79] ibid 429.
[80] See text accompanying nn 52–5 above.

that 'a person's well-being depends to a large extent on success in socially defined and determined pursuits and activities';[81] 'i.e. on forms of behaviour which are in fact widely practiced in his society'[82] and that give meaning to his activities.[83] The state's perfectionist action to promote autonomy includes action to sustain such social forms as will promote autonomy, as well as responding, more predictably, to an individual's incapacity or reprehensible harm to another's interests. Raz cites monogamous marriage as an example of a cherished social form the survival of which would be undermined without the state's institutional support: [84]

> Supporting variable forms of life is a social rather than an individual matter. Monogamy, assuming that it is the only morally valuable form of marriage, cannot be practiced by an individual. It requires a culture which recognizes it, and which supports it through the public's attitude and through its formal institutions... [P]erfectionist ideals require public action for their viability. Anti-perfectionism and practice would lead not merely to a political stand-off from support for valuable conceptions of the good. It would undermine the chances of survival of many cherished aspects of our culture.

Elsewhere, Raz explains the whole institution of contract in analagous terms. The law supports the activity of voluntarily undertaking obligations because it creates special relationships between the parties to them. This is valuable because it enables people to make their own arrangements, to shape their own lives—it is autonomy-enhancing. Thus:

> [t]he purpose of contract law should be not to enforce promises, but to protect both the practice of undertaking voluntary obligations and the individuals who rely on that practice... One protects the practice of undertaking voluntary obligations by preventing its erosion—by making good any harm caused by its use or abuse.[85]

Here, the law acts in a supportive role, recognizing and reinforcing confidence in the reliability of existing practices. As such, it 'acts as a conservative force, hindering influences that tend to undermine

[81] Raz, n 53 above, 309. [82] ibid 308. [83] ibid 312.

[84] ibid 161–2. That this example is controversial does not detract from the thrust of his argument.

[85] Review of P Atiyah, *Promises, Morals, and Law* (Oxford: Oxford Clarendon Press, 1981) in J Raz, 'Promises on Morality and Law' (1982) 95 *Harvard Law Review*, 916, 937: 'To enforce voluntary obligations is to enforce morality through the legal imposition of duties on individuals. In this respect it does not differ from the legal proscription of pornography.'

the practices it reinforces. In addition . . . the law serves to extend such practices. But for the support of the law, contracts between complete strangers would not be as numerous and common as they are.'[86]

Relationships of influence can be seen in like terms, as patently valuable social forms which warrant the law's support. This is elaborated in the next section.

(5) Prevention of harm: Now we can apply Mill's harm principle,[87] but with a Razian twist. Consistent with the preceding discussion, the harm that perfectionist state action can justifiably prevent includes not only harm to individuals but also to social forms and to legal institutions which enhance positive autonomy. Raz explains that 'a government whose responsibility is to promote the autonomy of its citizens is entitled to . . . [make laws that] merely reflect and make concrete the autonomy-based duties of its citizens . . . [F]ailure to comply harms others and the harm principle is satisfied'.[88]

In this context, undue influence can be understood as the law's justifiable response to autonomy harms in three distinct senses that do not require denigrating the claimant's consent. First, undue influence responds to harm to the autonomy-enhancing social form of relationships of influence. Close relationships such as marriage, romance, family, care, and friendship trigger implicit relational norms about how people in such relationships treat each other. They determine the appropriate range of behaviour and of outcomes that is implicit in the distinction between 'due' and 'undue' influence. As Kekewich J said in *Allcard* v *Skinner*,[89] the law 'recognises influence as natural and right. Few, if any, men are gifted with characters enabling them to act, or even think, with complete independence of others, which could not largely exist without destroying the foundations of society. But the law requires that influence, however natural and however right, shall not be unduly exercised'. Consistently, courts speak of parties owing each other 'duties of fair dealing and honesty' which have 'no place as between strangers',[90] and of undue influence as 'failure to protect' the claimant's interests.[91] For example, friendship implies a certain

[86] ibid 934.

[87] J S Mill, *On Liberty* (New York: J B Alden, 1885). The broad assertion is that it is only justifiable for the state to coerce a person to prevent harm to others.

[88] Raz, n 53 above, 417.

[89] *Allcard*, n 24 above, 157–8.

[90] *Gray v Binny* (1879) 7R 332, 342.

[91] *Etridge*, n 6 above, [9].

attitude of goodwill. It involves acting for the sake of one's friends' purposes. In friendship one is not thinking of one or other's vantage point, but from the third, unique perspective from which one's own good and one's friends' good are equally 'in view' and 'in play'.[92] Although no two friendships will be alike, they will constitute variations of the same basic form in order to be recognizable as a friendship.

Secondly, undue influence prevents harm to the legal institution supporting voluntary transfers,[93] contractual or not, when it withdraws support from the defendant who seeks to use it to validate his harm to the relationship of influence. Thirdly, undue influence eliminates the harm to the claimant's personal autonomy when he makes a transaction that seriously jeopardizes his chance of leading an autonomous life.[94] This is consistent with the law's opposition to contracts of slavery and unreasonable restraints of trade. It explains why undue influence deals with transactions that have catastrophic, and not just sub-optimal, consequences for the claimant's substantive welfare.[95]

(6) The Legal Response: How should the law support social forms and protect from harm in the name of enhancing positive autonomy? Respect for autonomy entails a minimal use of coercion. In general, perfectionist action should not involve a coercive imposition of a style of life.[96] Consistently, the undue influence doctrine does not enforce the implicit norms of the relational context, as relational contract theory[97] would imply; it does not take the parties forward to their expected positions, even if that were sufficiently identifiable. Neither does the doctrine impose liability on the defendant to compensate the claimant's loss flowing from the transaction, including loss of opportunity, which a wrongdoing view of undue

[92] Finnis, n 54 above, 143; Raz, n 53 above, 211–12.

[93] See text accompanying nn 84–5 above.

[94] To the same effect, see D Kimel, *From Promises to Contract—Towards a Liberal Theory of Contract* (Oxford. Hart Publishing, 2003), 133; S Smith, 'In Defence of Substantive Unfairness' (1996) 112 *Law Quarterly Review* 112.

[95] Elaborated below, see text accompanying nn 106–24 below.

[96] Raz, n 53 above, 161.

[97] I Macneil, 'Contracts—Adjustments of Long-Term Economic Relations under Classical, Neoclassical and Relational Contract Law' (1978) 72 *North Western University Law Review* 854; I Macneil, 'Relational Contract—What We Do and Do Not Know' (1985) *Wisconsin Law Review* 483; H Collins, *Law of Contract* (4th edn) (London: LexisNexis UK, 2003), 33; and see more generally, Campbell *et al*, n 60 above.

influence would imply.[98] These options would be coercive. The former, by transforming relational obligations into legal ones and the latter, by making the defendant underwrite the claimant in what is essentially a joint venture. They are inappropriate in the relational context.

The law could refuse to get involved at all in transactions made in social or domestic contexts. The law should be wary of involving itself in private life because it should leave room for people to act for the 'right' reasons, which are expressive of the relationship, rather than because of the fear of state coercion.[99] Any problems should be settled by compromise or informal social sanctions. However, the value of autonomy demands that even parties in close relationships be able to invoke the institution of state-supported voluntary transactions. So, the law's response must be more nuanced. Its stance against involvement is qualified and stops at the level of a rebuttable presumption.

The law's primary response, via the undue influence doctrine, is to selectively decline to enforce transactions, and require restitution of values transferred, where it encounters harm in the senses described to social forms, to legal institutions upholding transactions, and to individual autonomy. As Zipursky explains, the private nature of private law means that: '[t]he law does not impose civil liability. The law empowers private parties to have other private parties held liable to them, if they choose'.[100] Power is conferred[101] on individuals who satisfy certain conditions to obtain

[98] Birks cautions against this, although he concedes that it may be appropriate in cases of 'aggravated' undue influence. He therefore prefers to interpret the 'equitable compensation' awarded in *Mahoney v Purnell* [1996] 3 All ER 61 (QB) as monetized rescission for 'innocent' undue influence, in P Birks, 'Unjust Factors and Wrongs: Pecuniary Restitution for Undue Influence' [1997] *Restitution Law Review* 72. See Birks, n 25 above. See also R Goff and G Jones, *The Law of Restitution* (6th edn) (London: Sweet & Maxwell, 2002), paras 11-012–11-013.

[99] Kimel, n 94 above, 135–42; Collins, n 97 above, 48. Contractual regulation of relationships risks reducing them to measurable obligations, shutting out the more open-ended obligations arising from trust and friendship, and subverting the values of the relationship.

[100] B C Zipursky, 'Philosophy of Private Law' in J Coleman and S Shapiro (eds), *The Oxford Handbook of Jurisprudence and Philosophy of Law* (Oxford: Oxford University Press, 2002), 623, 655 (emphasis added).

[101] H L A Hart, *The Concept of Law* (Oxford: Clarendon Press, 1961), 27–38, designates legal rules that recognize private plaintiffs as having rights of action as 'power-conferring rules'.

state assistance to coerce another individual to do something—perform a contract, pay damages. Since the state is essentially involved in private actions, the paradigm is one of state subsidization of a worthwhile activity. But, there is no reason for the state, via the law, to subsidize in an unqualified way. It can and should refuse to support something unworthy. Broadly speaking, the law should not implicate itself in, be complicit with, or collude in 'that sort of thing'.[102] The same reasoning underlies the unenforceability of contracts which are illegal or contravene public policy. Shiffrin[103] speaks of the law's avoidance of complicity with exploitation; Dalton[104] refers to the restraint on self-interest necessitated by norms of decency and equality; Smith[105] argues that contracts at non-normal price disrupt individuals' planning and ability to lead self-directed, autonomous lives. It amounts to saying that the law will not help the undue influence defendant exploit his relationship with the claimant. This can be seen as neutrality in a different sense, a selective refusal to help, rather than an indiscriminate subsidization of, the defendant.

Understanding the Case Law of Undue Influence

We now descend from the giddy heights of legal theory to territory more familiar to black letter lawyers. An examination of the case law on undue influence demonstrates a remarkable fit with the relational autonomy account of the doctrine and displays its workings in greater magnification.

The Relationship of Influence

We have already mentioned that the recognizable social forms which amount to relationships of influence are those which trigger the overlapping motivations of trust, commitment, and dependency—love, loyalty, friendship, care, reliance—on the claimant's part.[106] The claimant does

[102] Raz, n 53 above, ch 14.

[103] S Shiffrin, 'Paternalism, Unconscionability, and Accommodation' (2000) 29 *Philosophy and Public Affairs* 203.

[104] C Dalton, 'An Essay in the Deconstruction of Contract Doctrine' (1985) 94 *Yale Law Journal* 997 1024–38.

[105] Smith, n 94 above.

[106] See text accompanying nn 14–20 above.

not consciously self-protect, she 'lets her guard down', believing that the defendant will safeguard her interests in the transaction, and her decisions will be coloured by a concern to maintain or develop her relationship with the defendant. There is nothing wrong with such relational motivations; indeed, the causal relationship generates an obligation on the defendant's part to restrain his self-interest and to have regard to the claimant's interests. The defendant should observe these obligations because he not only knows of the dynamics of the relationship, but he will usually have actively participated in its creation.

The relationship calibrates the substantive and procedural norms against which harm is to be judged. Although there is a wide margin of tolerance in deference to autonomy, there is a limit. The defendant must stay within the boundaries which are constitutive of the relationship. Going beyond the boundaries puts him 'off-side' and tips him into the territory of worthless choices which cause harm to an autonomy enhancing social form and legal institution, and usually also to the claimant's future autonomy. The law will respond, not by coercing the defendant to keep high standards, but by refusing to empower him to coerce the claimant.

We can track the two ways of proving undue influence, starting with the rebranded inferred undue influence, the old class 2.

Transactions 'Calling for an Explanation'—Failure to Protect the Claimant's Welfare

Recall that undue influence is inferable from a relationship of influence and a transaction 'calling for an explanation', if the inference is not rebutted by the defendant. This is concerned with harm to the claimant's substantive welfare. A defendant in such a case cannot enforce or retain the benefits of a transaction 'calling for an explanation' even if he has not actively procured the claimant's consent, and even if he has not consciously set out to exploit her. In the context of a relationship of influence, the defendant cannot always enforce a transaction just because the claimant agrees, and even if she offers. He certainly cannot do so unless, and sometimes even if, he takes additional steps to protect the claimant by independent advice. He can only enforce an apparently unfair transaction if he can show that he has successfully shifted his obligation to protect the claimant to someone else, namely the independent adviser, and thus rebut the inference of undue influence.

What qualifies as a transaction 'calling for an explanation' is not a simple matter of disproportionate exchange measured against some objective market price. This is clearly meaningless in the case of gifts or exchanges with a gift element. In general, the abnormality of the transaction depends on three overlapping considerations: (i) its impact on the welfare of the claimant in her particular circumstances, (ii) its appropriateness for the type and specific nature of the parties' relationship, and (iii) the nature of transaction: whether contract, gift, guarantee, or will. Consistent with the value of autonomy and plurality there is a large margin of tolerance. But, these three considerations reflect the deeper concerns about future autonomy, social forms, and legal institutions.

(i) The claimant's future autonomy: The most obvious class of transactions 'calling for an explanation' are those of such extreme improvidence that they threaten the claimant's future autonomy. This was the real problem with the transaction in *Allcard v Skinner*. Labelling the nun's gift as one which 'calls for explanation' is misleading[107] shorthand for saying that it is objectively inappropriate. It is so because it failed to provide for the contingency that she might later choose a different life, outside the convent, and need financial resources. The gift substantially undermined her future autonomy. Even if it was unobjectionable for the Mother Superior to accept the original gift, her refusal to release the nun and return what is left of the gift, when the parties' assumption at the time it was made no longer holds, subverts the relevant social form. Her obligation to have regard to the nun's interest is a continuing one[108] and must take account of the radical change in the claimant's circumstances and the parties' relationship. As Cotton LJ remarked:[109]

> Such [charitable] work to be effectual must be done with a willing mind, and in my opinion it would be productive of evil to attempt to retain in such a society as the sisterhood, by the pressure of loss of property, those whose hearts and will are no longer in the work, and who desire to exercise their legal right of withdrawing.

In other undue influence cases involving gifts or guarantees by elderly claimants, the courts have repeatedly observed that the transactions would leave the claimant without adequate resources to meet the contingencies of old age.[110] The same concern explains

[107] It is misleading because it is in a significant sense perfectly explicable, see text accompanying n 39 above.

[108] I am indebted to Professor Tan Yock Lin of the National University of Singapore for this point.

[109] *Allcard*, n 24 above, 172.

[110] In *Cheese*, where the claimant, an 88-year-old man contributed £43,000 towards his great-nephew's purchase of a home for the claimant to live in until his death. While the claimant stood to gain very considerable benefits from the arrangement, these were

why most undue influence cases involve the loss of the claimant's home or of the vast proportion of the claimant's wealth.[111]

Consistent with a relational approach, courts also judge the propriety of the transaction in the context of the claimant's web of relationships with significant others who may have claims on the claimant's bounty.[112] If the transaction has left the claimant unable to provide for them then the situation 'calls for an explanation'.[113]

(ii) The parties' relationship: The question, according to the House of Lords, is whether the transaction is 'readily explicable by the parties' relationship'.[114] A relationship of influence does not bar transactions between parties to it; to presume undue influence by the trusted party without more would be 'too far-reaching'. It would taint 'every Christmas or birthday gift by a child to a parent', 'every transaction between a client and his solicitor or between a patient and his doctor' and that would be 'absurd'. So, 'something more is needed before the law reverses the burden of proof, something which calls for an explanation. When that something more is

outweighed by the drawbacks since he had paid over everything he had in exchange for a right which was seriously insecure, as revealed when the great-nephew's failure to keep up the mortgage payments triggered a mortgagee's sale of the house; the arrangement would also have tied C to that house when he might well have needed to move for health reasons. *Hammond* (n 17 above), and see text accompanying n 21 above: 'no consideration was given as to whether those assets [left to the donor] would be sufficient to satisfy his future needs'. *Randall* (n 16 above), [85]: 'here was the deceased, in the twilight of her life, increasingly frail, increasingly physically dependent on others. And yet... she would have been left with nothing... where was the money to come from... to pay for the deceased's care in her old age? Was she not entitled to have her assets utilised for the best possible care available to her and for little extra luxuries? She should, surely, not have been confined to such minimum standard of care as the state would provide for her. Was she not entitled, over however many years might remain to her, to have her assets utilised to ensure that she entered a more luxurious (and hence more costly) nursing home (than the minimum provided by the state)?'

[111] *Re Craig*, n 18 above; *Hinks*, n 3 above; *Allcard*, n 24 above; *Hammond*, n 17 above; *Re Morris*, n 18 above, *Clarke*, n 7 above; and *Macklin*, n 26 above.

[112] Most notably children. See *Humphreys*, n 15 above, [95]: 'Mrs Humphreys had seven children and it seems to me that there is much to be said for the view that it would be fair for her to retain at least part of... her free estate', but it may be other relatives; see mother in *Pesticcio*, n 16 above, or even a donkey in *Randall*, n 16 above, [71]: 'The deceased loved her home, loved her property and loved her donkeys. She would have required substantial persuasion to give away any of her property and the most considerable persuasion to do anything that would prejudice the position of the donkeys.'

[113] See also, *Meredith*, n 15 above; *Padgham and Another v Rochelle and Another* (Ch 1 November 2002); *Simpson*, n 32 above; *Watson*, n 16 above; *Vale*, n 16 above. Such explanation might be forthcoming and be acceptable, eg Campbell *et al*, n 60 above; *Davies v Norwich Union Life Insurance Society* (1999) 78 P & CR 119; see text accompanying nn 127–9.

[114] *Etridge*, n 6 above, [28]–[29].

present, the greater the disadvantage to the vulnerable person, the more cogent must be the explanation before the presumption will be regarded as rebutted.'[115]

A transaction 'calls for an explanation' if it entails a disadvantage that would 'have been obvious as such to any independent and reasonable person who considered the transaction at the time with knowledge of all the relevant facts'.[116] For example, *Portman Building Society v Dusangh*[117] shows that guarantees by parents to support loans to their children, while improvident for the parents, are regarded as unexceptional and 'capable of reasonable explanation on the basis of parental affection'. Analogously, a wife's guarantee of her husband's debts does not usually 'call for an explanation'.[118] In contrast, Swinton Thomas LJ observed in finding undue influence in *Crédit Lyonnais v Burch* that:[119] 'it would cause a bank manager to raise his eyebrows more than a little when he was engaged in entering into a contract with a young employee which involved guaranteeing her employer's indebtedness in the sum of £270,000, and mortgaging her home to the bank'. An unreasonably large gift that is disproportionate to the gratitude, love, or affection evinced by the evolution of the party's relationship[120] will also 'call for an explanation'. Recall *Hammond v Osborn*,[121] where an elderly and frail man's gift of £300,000 to a helpful neighbour was set aside for undue influence. Ward LJ commented that the gift was:

> an act of generosity wholly out of proportion to the kindness shown to him. Looking at the matter objectively, it was an irrational decision, not a good one. The very scale of the gift with the disadvantageous consequences that ensued serves only, in my judgment, to heighten the anxiety which founds this presumption, namely that pressure was operating on his mind.

(iii) The nature of the transaction: The nature of the transaction also colours when the law will consider a disadvantageous transaction

[115] ibid, [24]. [116] *Aboody*, n 14 above, 965.

[117] [2000] 80 P & CRD 20.

[118] See further text accompanying nn 133–8 below.

[119] *Hammond*, n 19 above, 158. Moreover, the bank only granted a small extension of the primary debtor's overdraft facilities, £26,000.

[120] eg *Randall*, n 16 above.

[121] *Crédit Lyonnais*, n 19 above, [58]; and see text accompanying n 21 above. See also *Randall*, n 16 above, [72], where the court found the gift to be so large that 'it cannot be reasonably accounted for on the grounds of relationship, charity or other ordinary motives

for the claimant as 'calling for explanation'. With respect to wills, 'influence, in order to be undue... must be an influence exercised either by coercion or by fraud', albeit widely interpreted.[122] Sir JP Wilde explains in *Hall v Hall*[123] that not all influences are unlawful: 'Persuasion, appeals to the affections or ties of kindred, to a sentiment of gratitude for past services, or pity for future destitution or the like—these are all legitimate, and may be fairly pressed on a testator'.

Contracts which were not obviously unfair at the time of formation are unobjectionable although made between people in close relationships.[124] This is also the case if, whatever the paper deal, the real deal gives the claimant substantively what she wants and is not unfair.[125] The case against relief is even stronger if the transaction is made in a business context.[126] But these are subject to the discussion above on (i) The claimant's future autonomy and (ii) The parties' relationship so that contracts which would leave the claimant unable to provide adequately for himself or his significant others[127] or which are disproportionate to the type and nature of the relationship[128] could 'call for explanation'.

Gifts which seriously jeopardize the claimant's future autonomy or are widely incompatible with the parties' relationship also 'call for an explanation'. But acceptable explanation may be forthcoming to eradicate the suspicion that the defendant has abused his relationship with the claimant. For example, undue influence was denied in *Re Brocklehurst's Estate*[129] where the claimant gifted a 99-year lease of the shooting rights over his estate in order to reduce its value to

on which ordinary men act. Particularly is this so granted the characters of the 'donor and donee.'

122 *Boyse v Rossborough* (1857) 6 HLC 2 (HL) 48–9.

123 (1868) L R 1 P & D (Courts of Probate and Divorce) 481, 482.

124 eg in *Hughes*, n 27 above (mother/son); *Dailey v Dailey* [2003] UKPC 65, [2003] 3 FCR 369 (separating husband and wife); *Eid*, n 27 above (couple secretly married).

125 eg in *Papouis*, n 26 above (aunt/niece); see text accompanying n 153 below; *Popowski v Popowski* [2004] EWHC 668 (Ch), [2004] 2 P & CR DG10 (parents/son); *Turkey*, n 26 above (father/daughter).

126 *Rosenfeld*, n 27 above; *National Commercial Bank (Jamaica) Ltd*, n 27 above; *Irvani v Irvani* [2000] 1 Lloyd's Rep 412 (CA); *AG v R*, n 27 above.

127 eg *Padgham*, n 112 above; *Humphreys*, n 15 above; *Vale*, n 16 above; *Cheese*, n 16 above; *Macklin*, n 26 above.

128 *Naidoo v Naidu* (Ch 1 November 2000); *Tufton v Sperni* (1952) 2 T L R 516 (CA); cases in the previous category can also be included.

129 *Re Brocklehurst's Estate*, n 36 above.

his nephew who would inherit it. Similarly, there was no undue influence in *Campbell v Campbell*[130] where the claimant gifted her house to one of her children who she believed to have been imprisoned unjustifiably. Again, in *Glanville v Glanville*[131] the claimant transferred property to his second wife, effectively disinheriting the children from his first marriage. Parke J said it was explicable on the basis of the claimant providing for his wife.

Guarantee cases are dealt with in much the same way. There is no suspicion of undue influence, or any such suspicion is eradicated, where the apparently non-commercial guarantee is in substance a bargain between the claimant and the primary debtor,[132] occurs in a business context,[133] or is acceptably explained by the parties' relationship.[134]

Wife guarantee cases have generated much litigation in recent years. The main difficulty is in trying to decide whether, in a typical case, a wife who guarantees her husband's business debts is sufficiently disadvantaged to raise an inference of undue influence by her husband. The error, as Lord Nicholls identifies in *Etridge*,[135] is in going to either extreme; that is, of treating such transactions as never bad for her—the response pre-*Barclays Bank v O'Brien*, [136] on the reasoning that the fortunes of husband and wife are ordinarily bound up together, particularly if his business is the source of the family income—or of treating such transactions as always bad for her—the post-*O'Brien* response, on the reasoning that she undertakes an onerous financial obligation while personally receiving nothing in return. The correct question, according to the House of Lords,[137] is whether the transaction is 'not readily explicable by the parties' relationship'. Dicta from *Etridge* inhibit inferences of undue influence[138] since wives' guarantee of their husbands' debts is readily explicable; not only does her affection and self-interest run

[130] *Campbell v Campbell* (Ch 21 February 1996).

[131] *Glanville v Glanville* [2002] EWHC 1587 (Ch).

[132] *Banco Exterior v Thomas* [1997] 1 WLR 221 (CA); *Allied Irish Bank v Byrne* [1995] 2 FLR 325 (Ch); *Butigan v Negus-Fancey* [2000] EGCS 67 (QB).

[133] *National Westminster Bank v Morgan* (1985) AC 686 (HL); *Mashreq Bank Plc v Tulsiani and another* (Ch 2 May 2001); *Bank of Credit and Commerce International (Overseas) Limited v Gokal and others* (Commercial Court 21 December 1999); *Johnson v EBS Pensioner Trustees Ltd and another* [2002] EWCA Civ 164, [2002] Lloyd's Rep PN 309; *Hudson v Cobetts* [2005] All ER (D) 258.

[134] *Portman Building Society* (n 117); see text accompanying n 117 above.

[135] *Etridge*, n 6 above, [28]–[29].

[136] [1995] 1 All ER 438 (CA).

[137] *Etridge*, n 134 above.

[138] Noted in *Chitty*, n 10 above, para 7–075.

hand-in-hand, but her action is natural and admirable in a healthy marriage.[139] Moreover, we are urged to be slow to infer undue influence where the husband's conduct does not go beyond what could be expected of a reasonable husband in the circumstances;[140] a somewhat question-begging notion.

Nevertheless, while the presumption against 'inexplicability' would appear to be strong, the cases do not all go one way. Judge Chambers QC in *McGregor v Michael Taylor*[141] found scope for relief in the so-called 'trust me' cases. He interpreted *Etridge* as preventing a husband, in a relationship of influence with his wife, from charging her interest in the matrimonial home to support his business, however soundly based at that time, where she does not have the necessary information, especially where the charge is unlimited in both time and amount.

In some cases, the wife's compliance with the husband's wishes is culturally constructed or demanded.[142] The same can be said of cases involving religion[143] or the military.[144] We should not destroy social forms which are not autonomy-enhancing, because they provide support for members of their community, but we can still refuse to uphold autonomy-reducing transactions.[145]

Rebuttal—Shifting the Obligation to Protect Claimant Welfare

Logically, the rebuttal denies whatever is inferred and so should identify the gist of undue influence. The transaction must be shown to be 'the spontaneous act of the donor under circumstances which enabled him to exercise an independent will'.[146] Birks and Chin point to *Allcard v Skinner* to press the point that it is not enough to deny the defendant's bad behaviour.[147] Indeed, it may be impossible to rebut the inference of

[139] *Etridge*, n 6 above, [28], [30].

[140] ibid, [31]–[32], [159]: 'Statements or conduct by a husband which do not pass beyond the bounds of what may be expected of a reasonable husband in the circumstances should not, without more, be castigated as undue influence. Similarly, when a husband is forecasting the future of his business, and expressing his hopes or fears, a degree of hyperbole may be only natural. Courts should not too readily treat such exaggerations as misstatements.'

[141] [2002] 2 Lloyd's Rep 468 (QB).

[142] *Aboody*, n 14 above; *Hussain*, n 8 above; *Barclays Bank v Coleman* [2002] 2 AC 773 (HL).

[143] *Allcard*, n 24 above; *Morley v Loughan* [1893] 1 Ch 736.

[144] eg *Attorney-General v R*, n 27 above.

[145] Raz, n 53 above, 423.

[146] *Allcard*, n 24 above, 171; *Re the Estate of Brocklehurst*, n 36 above, 36.

[147] Birks and Chin, n 25 above, 67–76.

undue influence even if the defendant does all he realistically can to emancipate the claimant. Advice against the gift would have been futile in *Allcard v Skinner*;[148] it would have been shunned as the voice of the devil. The same can be said of *Bank of Montréal v Stuart*,[149] and *Crédit Lyonnais v Burch*.[150]

But, while the rebuttal undermines a defendant-sided view of undue influence, it does not support a claimant-sided view. Recall that in *Allcard*, the inference was not rebutted although there was ample evidence that the nun fully consented. The point is that neither the presence of the claimant's consent nor the absence of the defendant's active wrongdoing lets the defendant off the moral hook.

The proper function of the rebuttal is to ask whether, once the inference is raised, the defendant has successfully shifted his obligation to protect the claimant to a third party—the independent adviser. If so, the paradigm will have changed; from a relational to an arm's length one, leaving the defendant free to deal self-interestedly with the claimant. This makes sense of the requirement of 'adequacy' of the independent advice. Comprehension of the transaction is necessary, but not sufficient. The question is whether the claimant is successfully emancipated; whether the independent advice freed her from the relational paradigm to the arm's-length one.[151] What will suffice depends on the relational dynamics and its appropriate range of outcomes. The greater the disadvantage to the vulnerable person, the more she needs help, the more cogent must be the explanation.[152]

In practice, the courts sometimes merge two analytically separate issues: the raising of the inference and its rebuttal. Recall *Re Brocklehurst's*

[148] *Allcard*, n 24 above, 159, 184. Lindley LJ required proof that the nun knew 'she would have been allowed to obtain [outside] advice if she had desired to do so . . . [and that] she was free to act on the advice which might be given to her', but any suggestion that the nun would have done something different had she been better advised seems quite fictional on the evidence before the court.

[149] [1911] AC 120 (PC) 137, it was said of the wife, who was 'absolutely cleaned out' by acting as surety for her husband: 'She says she acted of her own free will . . . and that she would have scorned to consult anyone . . . Her declarations . . . shew how deeprooted and how lasting the influence of her husband was'.

[150] *Crédit Lyonnais*, n 19 above, 156–7. Millett LJ said that the transaction was voidable even if she had received advice because while a party is 'normally entitled to assume that the solicitor has discharged his duty and that the complainant has followed his advice . . . he cannot make any such assumption if he knows or ought to know that it is false'. The latter was so because, in the light of the staggering burden she was assuming, the lender 'must have known that no competent solicitor could advise her to enter into a guarantee in the terms she did'; and see M Chen-Wishart, 'The *O'Brien* Principal and Substantive Unfairness' (1997) 56 *Cambridge Law Journal* 60.

[151] *Etridge*, n 6 above, [20].

[152] *Allcard*, n 24 above, 157–8, 'The more powerful influence or the weaker patient alike evokes a stronger application of the safeguard'.

Estate,[153] where an elderly aristocrat, without independent advice, gave a garage proprietor a 99-year lease of the shooting rights over his estate. The court found no relationship of trust and confidence between the parties and that, anyway, any presumption was rebutted since the gift was a 'spontaneous and independent act', explicable by the parties' friendship and by the donor's desire to deliberately reduce the estate's value before it was inherited by a detested nephew after his death. Similarly, in *Papouis v West*,[154] an elderly woman exercised her right to buy her council house at a substantial discount with a 50 per cent contribution from her niece. She then executed a deed of trust in favour of her niece on the understanding that she, the aunt, could live there rent-free for life. The Court rejected undue influence on the basis of the aunt's robustness and independence of mind, the lack of improvidence to her, and the adequacy of the advice she received.

Thus, the rebuttal may take the form of showing that, despite first appearances: (i) the claimant did have an acceptable explanation for the transaction, and so the defendant did not fail to, that is did, protect the claimant's welfare; or (ii) the claimant did actively exercise her judgment in relation to the transaction, rather than simply choosing to trust the defendant, so that no relationship of influence was operative and the defendant owes her no obligation to start with; or (iii) the claimant had adequate independent advice, so that the defendant has successfully shifted his obligation to another, the independent adviser, leaving the defendant free to deal at arm's-length, self-interestedly, with her. In substance, (i) and (ii) simply deny the conditions for raising the inference in the first place.

Harm to Specific Transactional Autonomy, Social Form, and Legal Institution

What are we to make of the old class 1 'actual' undue influence cases premised on the defendant's coercive procurement of the claimant's consent to the transaction? Birks and Chin argue that 'all cases of pressure should be treated as duress'.[155] Exporting out the defendant-sided cases advances their argument that undue influence is, or really should be, reserved for claimant-sided 'relational' cases.[156] This view is unconvincing. First, it is notable that even the 'non-relational' cases involve exploitation of the claimant's known relationship of love and affection, albeit

[153] *Re Brocklehurst's Estate*, n 36 above, and see text accompanying n 124 above.

[154] *Papouis v West* (n 26).

[155] Birks and Chin, n 25 above, 63.

[156] ibid 67.

with a third party rather than with the defendant. The relationship makes the claimant vulnerable to the defendant's threat to harm the third party by prosecution[157] or disclosure.[158] The analogy with 'duress to the person' is relatively clear. A looser analogy can be drawn with the 'three-party non-commercial guarantee' cases: the creditor's implicit threat to 'harm' the debtor, by controlling the flow of the debtor's finance, with whom the claimant shares a caring relationship, is practically relievable only by the claimant's willingness to act as guarantor.[159]

Secondly, pressure which occurs in the context of a relationship of influence should continue to be litigated under undue influence rather than under duress. Birks and Chin concede this[160] on the basis that the defendant's pressure is subsidiary to the claimant's impaired consent. This is unconvincing. The claimant gives valid consent because she knows what she is agreeing and she means to do it. The better interpretation is that the defendant's coercion violates an implicit procedural norm of his relationship of influence with the claimant. His conduct should not be endorsed not only because it reduces the claimant's autonomy, without negating his consent, in relation to the specific transaction, but also because it abuses the social form of intimate relationships and the facility of voluntary transactions.

What amounts to improper coercion depends on the nature of the relationship and the character of parties. The conduct may seem 'relatively innocuous',[161] although not necessarily so;[162] it may well be less than is necessary to register on the radar of duress between strangers.[163] But, it is an error to trivialize the sort of defendant conduct impugned by the Courts—'excessive pressure, emotional blackmail or bullying'.[164] Its legal

[157] *Williams v Bayley* (1866) LR 1 LH 200 (HL), threat to prosecute the claimant's son.

[158] *Mutual Finance Ltd v John Wetton & Sons Ltd* [1937] 2 KB 389 (KB), threat to disclose distressing information to the claimant's very frail father.

[159] Of course, considerations of administrative convenience have radically lowered the threshold for potential relief, a non-commercial guarantor receiving no direct benefit from the lender, and the creditor's obligation to safeguard the enforceability of the guarantee, to make minimal disclosure and ensure certification of legal advice to the guarantor. 'Equity, it is said, is not past the age of child-bearing.' *Etridge*, n 6 above, [89].

[160] Birks and Chin, n 25 above, 77, 95.

[161] *Chitty*, n 10 above, para 7–049.

[162] The conduct may be more serious as in *Hussain*, n 8 above; see text accompanying n 8 above, *Langton*, n 9 above; and text accompanying n 9 above. In *Woolwich Plc*, n 33 above, the husband coerced his wife, who was 'vulnerable, dependant and impressionable' and from whom he had long separated, to guarantee his debt by threatening not to pay her maintenance.

[163] Birks and Chin, n 25 above, 77.

[164] *Etridge*, n 6 above, [160]. Other behaviour castigated includes isolation of the claimant from others as in *Re Killick (deceased), Killick v Pountney and Another* [2000] WTLR 41 (Ch); see text accompanying n 166 below, and attempts at 'cover up' once questions are asked, *Hammond*, n 17 above, [32].

significance must be understood in the context of the parties' relationship of influence. In that context, the law imposes a procedural disability on the defendant: he cannot behave as he might towards an arm's-length stranger, on whom, anyway, such relatively innocuous pressures would have minimal impact, because the effect of such conduct is magnified when directed towards someone over whom the defendant has abnormal influence.

The examples of reprehensible coercion show the defendant exploiting the claimant's relational motivation for consenting. One group of cases involve threats to abandon. This is highly coercive to someone who cares enormously about the relationship and its continuity. For example, in *Bank of Scotland v Bennett*,[165] the husband used wounding and insulting words to accuse his wife of disloyalty. She agreed to guarantee his debt after he told her she would be a 'waste of rations' if she refused and that she would be splitting up the family. To the suggestion that his conduct was innocuous, she replied: 'that was how he put pressure on, was to go out a lot and not to speak to me'.[166]

In other cases, the defendant exerts excessive control, is secretive, and keeps others away who might dilute his influence. For example, in *Re Killick*,[167] the testator became the defendants' lodger when he was 32 years old and stayed there for forty years. As his health failed and he moved into a nursing home, the defendants took over his possessions and papers. They banned him from contact with his relatives on threat of not allowing him to come home, which terrified him. Given his bitterness towards the defendants, the judge concluded that highly coercive influence must have been required to induce his generous provision for them in his will.

Other cases involve bullying, confrontation, and harassment. For example, in *Drew v Daniel*,[168] the claimant agreed to confer a significant benefit on her nephew at the expense of her own son. The nephew coerced his aged aunt to agree in a distressing and lengthy conversation, coupled with a threat to sue her, and then concealed his dealings from her son and her solicitor. Ward LJ judged the defendant's conduct to be

[165] [1997] 1 FLR 801 (Ch); see also *Langton*, n 9 above, accompanying text above, and *Re Craig*, n 18 above, where an old man gave or spent on his companion housekeeper three-quarters of his wealth over six years. Absent direct evidence of pressure the court still found active undue influence because of the amount of the gifts, the claimant's vulnerability to pressure by the defendant, the evidence of the direct exercise of that pressure on other occasions and for other purposes, the parties' knowledge of the claimant's utter dependence on the defendant, and the whole history of the relationship.

[166] ibid.

[167] *Re Killick*, n 164 above, and *Re Craig*, n 18 above.

[168] [2005] EWCA Civ 507 [28], [2005] 2 FCR 365; see also *Clarke*, n 7 above.

'unacceptable' in view of his aunt's vulnerability, naiveté in business and fear of confrontation, and the nephew's forceful personality, although he said it may be too harsh to call him 'unscrupulous' and 'aggressive'. His coercion leaves no room for rebuttal, that is, for arguing that the unfair transaction was the product of arm's-length bargaining.

Now, of course, we can say of these claimants: 'Poor saps! Get a spine!' but that would be Super-Detached Man talking. A relational approach refuses to support the coercive defendant.

Conclusion

Are there one or two classes of undue influence post-*Etridge*? In one sense, this is a sterile semantic debate. In another, it touches on the coherence of the basis for undue influence. Four points are worth making. First, the two classes are much closer in their essence than they first appear. Whenever undue influence is alleged, the Court's inquiry inevitably gravitates around the same features, namely:[169] (i) the motivation of the claimant in view of her personality and her relationship with the defendant; (ii) any independent advice the claimant received; (iii) the defendant's conduct in view of his relationship with the claimant; and (iv) the resulting transaction.

While it is now conventional to say that the claimant proves undue influence either actually or with the benefit of an evidential inference which remains unrebutted, it is more precise to say that undue influence may be exercised by acts—actively, by overt unfair persuasion—or by omissions—passively, by failure to inform, advise, or otherwise 'deal fairly with her and have proper regard to her interests'.[170] Both classes are manifestations of the defendant's subversion of the implicit norms of the relationship of influence he shares with the claimant. Both respond to autonomy harms, to the claimant's future autonomy, the social form and the facility of voluntary transactions. This is consistent with the position in *Etridge* that there is only one class of undue influence[171] but two ways of committing or proving it. As Lord Clyde explains:

> [a]t the end of the day, after trial, there will either be proof of undue influence or that proof will fail and it will be found that there was no undue influence. In the former case, whatever the relationship of the parties and however the influence was exerted, there will be found to have been an actual case of undue influence. In the latter there will be none.[172]

[169] *Etridge*, n 6 above, [13]. [170] ibid, [107]. [171] ibid, [24], [16], [93].
[172] ibid, [93].

It would, therefore, be illogical to deny the existence of actual undue influence but find presumed undue influence.[173]

Secondly, it is perfectly understandable that the presence of active coercion should be highlighted in any justification for rescinding the transaction. But, it is important to note that while coercion may be sufficient for undue influence, it is unnecessary. In *McGregor v Michael Taylor*,[174] Judge Chambers QC described the case as a classic betrayal of trust: the husband did not need to actively coerce when he could get everything he wanted from his wife without resorting to such means. The two classes of undue influence may appear incompatible; the claimant willingly submits in class 2, but is forced to do so in class 1. But, 'It's a thin line between love and hate'.[175] The traditional categories are merely points on the spectrum.

Thirdly, and accordingly, even class 1 actual undue influence is premised on a relationship of influence; that is what makes otherwise low level coercion legally relevant. But, the presence of active coercion can compensate for less decisive evidence of the parties' relationship of influence than might be necessary to establish undue influence by inference.

Fourthly, an improvident outcome is practically indispensable even in class 1 coercion cases. It is true that an unfair outcome is not enough in itself to vitiate a transaction and, that it is sometimes evidence of the relationship of influence or of coercion. But, contrary to the predominant view, substantive unfairness is of the essence of undue influence. If we diminish its importance in the story of undue influence, we risk distorting the judicial decisional process, and losing rather than gaining a degree of consistency. Given that influence is not bad in itself, it is quite impossible to tell whether the influence operating was 'due' or 'undue' without reference to the outcome. There is a world of difference between a mother pressuring her children to do their homework and her pressuring them to hand over their savings.

The simplistic paradigm of Super-Detached Man led us down the path of negative autonomy, consent obsession, exploitation myopia, value scepticism, and anti-perfectionism. Replacing him with a more realistic or relational autonomous actor and adding a state which can act to prevent harm to the conditions for the exercise of positive autonomy, allows us to generate a more appealing and accurate theory of undue influence. Accordingly, undue influence intervenes to prevent harms to the claimant's future autonomy, and to autonomy-enhancing social forms and legal facilities.

[173] ibid, [219].

[174] *McGregor*, n 140 above, [53]; and see text accompanying n 135 above.

[175] A Lennox, *Medusa* (London: BMG Records (UK) Ltd, 1995).

This relational theory of undue influence is the fruit of cross-pollination between black letter law and legal theory. It (i) is a celebration of the complexity of life over the modern tendency to search for one-dimensional explanations which are simple, but usually deceptively so; (ii) shows why undue influence is and should be concerned with outcomes as much as with processes; (iii) explains the inextricable link between the parties' relationship and the substantive and procedural pathologies of a transaction vitiated for undue influence—the nature of that relationship determines when transactions 'call for an explanation',[176] and what 'counts' as improper active pressure and adequate rebuttal;[177] and (iv) vindicates relationships of influence. Relationships of trust and confidence are good. Acting relationally is not pathological. But going beyond the procedural or substantive boundaries which are constitutive of the relationship is pathological. The defendant enters the territory of unworthy choices which cause harm to an autonomy-enhancing social form and legal institution, and invariably also to the claimant's future autonomy.

[176] See text accompanying nn 68–77 above.

[177] eg in *Etridge*, n 6 above, [32], Lord Nicholls cautions against being too ready to find undue influence in husband and wife cases. In contrast, *Allcard*, n 24 above, 157–8, 183: 'the law requires that influence, however natural and however right, shall not be unduly exercised, that is, shall be exercised only in due proportion to the surrounding circumstances and the strength of the person submitted to it. The more powerful influence or the weaker patient alike evokes a stronger application of the safeguard . . . of all influences religious influence is the most dangerous and the most powerful'.

Equitable Rights and Wrongs

*Charles Mitchell**

Primary and Secondary Rights

Since we are at UCL, let us start with John Austin, who was appointed to a Chair in Jurisprudence when the institution was founded as the University of London in 1826.[1] Austin gave his first lecture-series in 1829, after three years of preparation, including a trip to Germany, where he visited Heidelberg and stayed in Bonn for six months to study German law. When he finally began, Austin was full of enthusiasm for his task, and urged his pupils to 'demand explanations and ply me with objections—turn me inside out'.[2] But many of them found his approach too abstract, and his lecturing style dispiriting: he wrote out his lectures in advance and read them aloud from start to finish, with all their many subtleties and repetitions. Numbers fell off as the students abandoned his classes for the lecture-room of his colleague, Andrew Amos, and in 1833 he discontinued the course. Nor did things go better the following year when he gave a course at the Inner Temple: his introductory lecture attracted between two and three hundred listeners, but his delivery was so poor that few of them could hear what he said. According to one report, 'The audience stared at each other, and looked extremely foolish: altogether the scene was truly ludicrous'.[3] Again, numbers dwindled and the course was abandoned. Discouraged by his failure, Austin resigned his Chair in 1835. But whatever may have been his shortcomings as a lecturer, and however detached he may have been from the mundanities of legal practice, his work on legal philosophy was a great intellectual achievement. His analytical methodology strongly influenced the study of legal theory in

* My thanks go to Robert Chambers, James Edelman, and Lionel Smith for their thoughtful comments on a draft of this lecture, but they are not responsible for what follows, and the opinions expressed here are my own.

1 Details of Austin's life come from J MacDonell, 'Austin, John (1790–1859)' in *Dictionary of National Biography* compact edn (Oxford: Oxford University Press, 1975), 62; W E Rumble, 'Austin, John (1790–1859)' in *Oxford Dictionary of National Biography* (Oxford: Oxford University Press, 2004).

2 Quoted in MacDonell, n 1 above.

3 *The Legal Examiner and Law Chronicle* 2 (1833–4) 416, quoted in Rumble, n 1 above.

England for at least a century after his death in 1859,[4] thanks in part to the work undertaken by his widow, Sarah Austin, who sorted and edited his papers, and arranged for the publication of posthumous editions of *The Province of Jurisprudence Determined*[5] and *Lectures on Jurisprudence*.[6]

It is to the latter work that we must direct our attention, and more specifically, to Lecture 45. Here, Austin gave an account of the law of obligations in which he drew a central distinction between 'primary' and 'secondary' rights and duties. Primary rights were 'those which exist *in* and *per se*', and secondary rights those which 'arise out of violations of primary rights'.[7] Thus, Austin considered that:[8]

> The events which are causes of rights and duties may be divided in the following manner: namely, into acts, forebearances, and omissions, which are violations of rights or duties and events which are not violations of rights or duties.

In drawing this distinction, Austin was influenced by William Blackstone's *Commentaries*, where the law was divided up into rights and wrongs consisting in the infringement of rights.[9] In Blackstone's scheme, a citizen has various rights, the violation of which constitutes a wrong, for which the law will give him an action, through the pursuit of which he can obtain a remedy. Like other members of Jeremy Bentham's circle, Austin generally tended to attack the *Commentaries*, but in this respect he thought that Blackstone had got it right. Indeed, he considered that Blackstone's approach was superior to the classificatory schemes proposed by the Roman jurists, because it enabled him to distinguish between 'those obligations arising from contracts and quasi-contracts which are *primary*' (treated in the first part of the *Commentaries* under the heading of 'personal property') and 'those obligations growing out of contracts or quasi-contracts which arise from breaches of those primary ones' (treated in the second part under the heading of 'wrongs').[10]

[4] Writing in 1954, Herbert Hart considered that 'within a few years of [Austin's] death it was clear that his work had established the study of jurisprudence in England, and that his influence on the development of legal theory in England had been 'greater than that of any other writer': H L A Hart (ed), J Austin, *The Province of Jurisprudence Determined* (London: Weidenfeld & Nicolson, 1954), xvi.

[5] S Austin (ed), J Austin, *The Province of Jurisprudence Determined* (2nd edn) (London: John Murray, 1861–3). An edition had previously appeared in Austin's lifetime, published by Murray in 1832.

[6] (London: John Murray, 1863).

[7] R Campbell (ed), J Austin, *Lectures on Jurisprudence or the Philosophy of Positive Law* (4th rev edn). (London: John Murray, 1879), 789. Hereafter page citations will be to this edition of the *Lectures*.

[8] ibid 788.

[9] W Blackstone, *Commentaries on the Law of England*, 4 vols, vol 1 (Oxford: Clarendon Press, 1765–9), 117–18.

[10] Austin, *Lectures* in Campbell (ed), n 7 above, 796–7.

In a paper written some twenty years ago, Peter Birks argued that Blackstone did not really deserve this compliment, because the classificatory scheme of the *Commentaries* broke down when discussion of secondary rights crept into the first part, and discussion of primary rights into the second. The root of the trouble was 'too great a reliance on the social contract as a means of explaining obligations imposed by law': this dissolved 'the line between voluntary and involuntary obligations and thence between primary and secondary too'.[11] More recently, in his 1999 Blackstone Lecture at Oxford University, Birks made the further point that although Austin endorsed and adopted Blackstone's two-tier conceptual scheme, he went further than Blackstone (who thought that rights existed only at a primary, super-structural level) in holding that the infringement of (primary) rights could generate further (secondary) rights.[12] In this respect Austin may well have drawn on the precepts of German law which he had studied in Bonn, according to which duties imposed in an obligational relationship (*Leistungspflichten* and *Verhaltungspflichten*) were distinct from those imposed in the event that performance of a primary duty had been 'disturbed' (*Leistungsstörungen*).[13] It seems likely that he had also read the work of the French jurist Robert-Joseph Pothier, whose *Traité des Obligations*[14] exerted a powerful influence on the thinking of English contract lawyers in the first half of the nineteenth century.[15] In Pothier's work a 'primary obligation' was said to be 'that which is contracted principally in the first place and on its own account' and a 'secondary obligation' to be 'that which is contracted in case of the non-performance of a primary obligation'.[16]

[11] P Birks, 'Obligations: One Tier or Two?' in P G Stein and A D E Lewis (eds), *Studies in Justinian's Institutes in Memory of J A C Thomas* (London: Sweet & Maxwell, 1983) 18, 23–4. In this paper Birks defended the Roman jurists from Austin's criticism that they had erred in collapsing primary and secondary rights into a single series. In Birks's view the division between primary and secondary rights was not needed in Roman law, because Roman actions 'each operated on a single plane. So, even though it was not always the same one, there were no choices to be made and no confusions to be avoided by observing that the single series really consisted in fragments of two'. ibid 37.

[12] P Birks, 'Rights, Wrongs, and Remedies' (2000) 20 *Oxford Journal of Legal Studies* 1, 4–5.

[13] B Dickson, 'The Contribution of Lord Diplock to the Law of Contract' (1989) 9 *Oxford Journal of Legal Studies* 441, 449.

[14] W D Evans (tr), J Pothier, *A Treatise on the Law of Obligations or Contracts* (London: Joseph Butterworth, 1806).

[15] As discussed in D J Ibbetson, *A Historical Introduction to the Law of Obligations* (Oxford: Oxford University Press, 1999), ch 12, *passim*; B Rudden, '*Pothier et la Common Law*' in J Monéger (ed), *Robert-Joseph Pothier, d'hier à aujourd'hui* (Paris: Economica, 2001) 91.

[16] W D Evans (tr), J Pothier, *Treatise*, n14 above, para183. Arianna Pretto notes that Evans's translation of Pothier's original '*obligations primitives*' into 'primary' rather than

We are now familiar with the concept of primary and secondary rights because Lord Diplock used this idea to expound various principles of contract law in a series of well-known cases running from the 1960s to the 1980s. Most famously, he held in *LEP Air Services Ltd v Rolloswin Investments Ltd* that where a contract is terminated for breach, the contract breaker's 'primary obligations' are replaced by:[17] 'a secondary obligation to pay to the other party a sum of money to compensate him for the loss he has sustained as a result of the failure to perform the primary obligations'. Judges and legal scholars continue to speak about contractual obligations in this way.[18] Similar language has been used by legal scholars,[19] and, less often, by the courts,[20] to explain obligations to pay tort damages. Other writers again have sought to characterize the duty to make restitution of an unjust enrichment as a secondary obligation, a controversial view which ultimately requires the receipt of an unjust enrichment to be misclassified as a wrong.[21] However, the ins and outs

'primitive obligations' 'better captures the ranking of the two categories of obligations in the way envisaged by Pothier': A Pretto, 'Primary Rights and Rights *in Rem*' in P Birks and A Pretto (eds), *Themes in Comparative Law: In Honour of Bernard Rudden* (Oxford: Oxford University Press, 2002) 65, 67.

17 [1973] AC 331 (HL) 350. See also *Photo Productions Ltd v Securicor Transport Ltd* [1980] AC 827 (HL) 849–50; and other cases discussed in Dickson, n 13 above, 448–51. Whether Lord Diplock himself drew upon Austin, Pothier, and/or German writers for these ideas is an open question: B Rudden, 'Correspondence' (1990) 10 *Oxford Journal of Legal Studies* 288.

18 eg *Law Debenture Trust Corp v Ural Caspian Oil Corp Ltd* [1995] Ch 152 (CA) 170 (Beldam LJ); *A-G v Blake* [2000] UKHL 45, [2001] 1 AC 268, 297–8 (Lord Hobhouse); *Alfred McAlpine Construction Ltd v Panatown Ltd* [2000] UKHL 43, [2001] 1 AC 518, 595 (Lord Millett); *OBG Ltd v Allan* [2005] EWCA Civ 106, [2005] QB 762 [47] (Peter Gibson LJ). See also G H Treitel, *The Law of Contract* (11th edn) (London: Sweet & Maxwell, 2003), 850–5; A Jolly. 'Is It Useful—or Even Possible—to Distinguish Primary from Secondary Liabilities Arising from Contractual Obligation?' [2003] *European Business Law Review* 57, giving an affirmative answer.

19 eg J Goldberg, 'Duty and the Structure of Negligence' (2000) 149 *Kansas Journal of Law and Public Policy* 149; J Goldberg and B Zipursky, 'The *Restatement (Third)* and the Place of Duty in Negligence Law' (2001) 54 *Vanderbilt Law Review* 657; N J McBride, 'Duties of Care—Do They Really Exist?' (2004) 24 *Oxford Journal of Legal Studies* 417; A Beever, 'A Rights-Based Approach to the Recovery of Economic Loss in Negligence' (2004) 4 *Oxford University Commonwealth Law Journal* 25.

20 eg *Walters v Babergh DC* (1983) 82 LGR 235 (QB) 241 (Woolf J); *Matthews v Ministry of Defence* [2002] EWHC 13 (QB), [2002] CP Rep 26 [21] (Keith J), reversed on liability: [2002] EWCA Civ 773, [2002] 1 WLR 2621; [2003] UKHL 4, [2003] 1 AC 1163.

21 eg P A Butler, 'Viewing Restitution at the Level of a Secondary Remedial Obligation' (1990) 16 *University of Queensland Law Journal* 27; K Barker, 'Rescuing Remedialism in Unjust Enrichment Law: Why Remedies are Right' (1998) 57 *Cambridge Law Journal* 301, critiqued in Birks, n 12 above, 28–31. On the same theme, see S A Smith, 'The Structure of Unjust Enrichment Law: Is Restitution a Right or a Remedy?' (2003) 36 *Loyola of Los Angeles Law Review* 1037.

of this interesting controversy will not be explored here. Instead, this lecture will look at equitable obligations, and more specifically, at the personal obligations owed by trustees to their beneficiaries in cases where the beneficiaries have been caused a loss by the trustees' breach of duty. The courts' treatment of such cases will be explained in the language of primary and secondary rights. Before embarking on this project, however, we must first clarify the relationship between rights and remedies, and consider why this relationship is sometimes misunderstood.

Rights and Remedies

In his Blackstone Lecture, Birks made the point that English lawyers use the word 'remedy' in several different senses, and have the bad habit of sliding between these different senses of the word with confusing results. Birks identified five separate senses, but for present purposes we need only focus our attention on two. First, it is sometimes said that if a defendant commits a wrong against a claimant, then the claimant's remedy lies in the fact that the defendant's breach of primary duty generates secondary rights against the defendant which can be enforced through legal proceedings. Lord Atkin used the term in this way in *United Australia Ltd v Barclays Bank Ltd*, when he said that where a tortfeasor receives money from his victim as a result of the tort, the victim can claim restitution, but also has 'the remedy of claiming damages'.[22] He meant that where a tort victim has been caused a loss, he acquires a secondary right to compensation which can be realized through a court order directing the tortfeasor to pay compensatory damages. Austin also used the word 'remedy' in this way, when he described 'secondary rights' as 'remedial rights', writing, for example, that:[23] 'Acts, forebearances, and omissions, which are violations of rights or duties, are styled delicts, injuries, or offences. Rights and duties which are the consequences of delicts are sanctioning (or preventative) and remedial (or reparative).'

Secondly, the term 'remedy' is frequently used to mean a right born of a court order or pronouncement. Lord Hobhouse used the term in this way when he remarked in *Arthur J S Hall & Co (a firm) v Simons* that

[22] [1941] AC 1 (HL) 28. See also *Telephone Rentals Plc v Burges Salmon & Co* (CA 9 April 1987) (Dillon LJ): if a contract-breaker prevents the other party from performing then he 'will be unable to earn the payments under the contract and so will in law have no remedy but to treat the contract as at an end and claim damages'.

[23] Austin, *Lectures* in Campbell (ed), n 7 above, 788.

claimants who bring civil proceedings invariably seek a remedy which is 'normally a monetary remedy but sometimes a remedy of declaration of right or specific implement'.[24] He meant that a claimant will only bring legal proceedings because he wants the court to realize his rights by making an order or pronouncement in his favour, which in turn will give him a new right to bring the enforcement mechanisms of the justice system to bear against the defendant.[25] Blackstone also used the term 'remedy' in this sense, although he avoided saying that a successful claimant acquires new rights when a judgment is made in his favour.

A significant insight of Birks's lecture was that although their terminology differed, Austin and Blackstone fell into the common error of thinking that the courts concern themselves solely with wrongs. Austin explicitly said that 'every right of action arises from a wrong',[26] which can only mean that the sole business of the courts is to give effect to secondary rights generated by breaches of primary duties. Blackstone would have put the point differently, saying that judgments follow from causes of action which are born of wrongs. But he would also have said that a claimant's cause of action crystallizes at the moment when a defendant commits a wrong against him, and that from this moment on the claimant is entitled to judgment. It follows that Blackstone's position and Austin's position were substantially the same.[27] They were also mistaken for the same reason, namely that they failed to allow for the possibility that the courts might make orders to realize primary as well as secondary rights.[28] As Birks wrote in a slightly earlier paper, it is 'a serious taxonomic error ... to suppose that liability attaches only to wrongs' when in fact the law often 'enforces primary obligations directly'.[29] Obvious examples of the English courts' ability to do this are orders (at common law) to pay an agreed sum and orders (in equity) for specific performance of a contract.

[24] [2000] UKHL 38, [2002] 1 AC 615 (HL) 744.

[25] Cf P Birks, 'Personal Property: Proprietary Rights and Remedies' (2000) 11 *King's College Law Journal* 1, 3: the process of realizing rights through litigation falls into three phases: (1) 'the assertion of a right capable of being entertained and realised by a court'; (2) the making of an order by the court to realize the right; (3) the enforcement of the order.

[26] Austin, *Lectures* in Campbell (ed), n 7 above, 793.

[27] Birks, n 12 above, 15–16, citing Blackstone, n 9 above, vol III, 396.

[28] Austin recognized that the English courts had a declaratory jurisdiction, but considered that when exercising this jurisdiction the courts were not 'acting as such': Austin, *Lectures* in Campbell (ed), n 7 above, 793.

[29] P Birks, 'Equity in the Modern Law: An Exercise in Taxonomy' (1996) 26 *University of Western Australia Law Review* 1, 11; prefigured in P Birks, 'The Concept of a Civil Wrong' in D G Owen *Philosophical Foundations of Tort Law* (Oxford: Oxford University Press, 1995) 31, 46–51.

Recognizing the truth that the courts can make orders and pronouncements whose purpose is to realize primary rights will be made no easier if we make the word 'remedy' do too much work. In particular, this truth will become obscured if we use the word remedy to denote a claimant's secondary rights, and also use it to denote the orders and pronouncements which are made by the courts to realize a successful claimant's rights, whether these are secondary or primary. For this reason, Rafal Zakrzewski has urged that we should confine ourselves to the latter usage in his stimulating new book on the subject, *Remedies Reclassified*.[30] He has also helpfully brought out the difference between a secondary ('substantive') right to damages which exists prior to a court order, and a right to damages arising out of a judicial command that damages should be paid. He writes:[31]

> The difference [between the two] is sometimes overlooked as both are indiscriminately called 'damages' in practice. The distinction . . . is very fine because courts give effect to secondary rights by restating them in the court order. But there is also a subtle difference apart from their origin. The former are unliquidated but the latter are usually liquidated. This means that secondary rights to damages are usually rights to compensation, restitution, or punishment in the abstract with the actual amount due being unassessed but rights to damages recast in a court order are usually assessed at a sum certain. The former are substantive rights, not remedies [as that term should be used].

Primary Duties of Trustees

Settlors create trusts for various reasons, including tax planning, efficiencies of scale (where many assets are held for multiple beneficiaries), flexibility (where beneficiaries' needs are met by the exercise of a discretion), and control (where beneficial interests are made contingent on the happening of a future event). These advantages, and others, derive from the fact that trusts can extend over time. Hence the whole point of many trusts is that the trustees should take responsibility for the trust assets, and the income which they generate, over an extended period. Consistently with this, the courts have said that the trustees' 'paramount obligation' is 'recovering, securing and duly applying the trust fund':[32] they must get in the trust assets where the trust deed requires them to do so,[33]

30 R Zakrzewski, *Remedies Reclassified* (Oxford: Oxford University Press, 2005), esp ch 4.

31 ibid 50.

32 *Re Brogden* (1888) LR 38 Ch D 546 (CA) 571 (Fry LJ).

33 *Maitland v Bateman* (1843) 13 LJ Ch 273; *Coppard v Allen* (1864) 4 Giff 497; *M'Donnel v White* (1865) 9 HLC 570, 585 (Lord Westbury LC).

'properly . . . preserve the trust fund', and 'pay the income and the corpus to those who are entitled to them respectively'.[34] If trustees retire while the trust is still on foot, then they must 'hand [the trust assets] over to their successors intact, that is, properly invested and without diminution, according to the terms of the mandate contained in the instrument of trust'.[35] When handling the day to day administration of trust business they must 'exercise the same care as an ordinary, prudent person of business would exercise in the conduct of that business were it his or her own',[36] and when investing the trust assets they must 'take such care as an ordinary prudent man would take if he were minded to make an investment for the benefit of other people for whom he felt morally bound to provide'.[37] They must also 'give all [their] *cestuis que trust* on demand information with respect to the mode in which the trust fund has been dealt with, and where it is'.[38] These are all primary duties, and the beneficiaries have corresponding primary rights,[39] to have the trust assets collected, maintained, and disbursed in accordance with the trust instrument,[40] to have these assets managed with an appropriate degree of care, and to gain access to the information which they need to ensure that the trustees are acting properly.[41]

[34] *Low v Bouverie* [1891] 3 Ch 82 (CA) 99 (Lindley LJ).

[35] *Head v Gould* [1898] 2 Ch 250 (Ch) 268 (Kekewich J).

[36] *Breen v Williams* (1996) 186 CLR 71, 137 (Gummow J). This proposition derives from various well-known authorities, eg *Speight v Gaunt* (1883) 9 App Cas 1 (HL); *Learoyd v Whiteley* (1887) 12 AC 727; *Austin v Austin* (1906) 3 CLR 516; *Fouche v The Superannuation Fund Board* (1952) 88 CLR 609.

[37] *Re Whiteley* (1886) 33 Ch D 347, 355 (Lindley LJ). Note the Trustee Act 2000, ss 1–5; and on the standard of care see too *Wight v Olswang (No 2)* [2000] EWCA Civ 310, (2000) 2 ITELR 689, applying *Saif Ali v Sydney Mitchell & Co (a firm)* [1980] AC 198 (HL) 218 (Lord Diplock).

[38] *Low v Bouverie* [1891] 3 Ch 82 (CA) 99 (Lindley LJ). See also *Kemp v Burn* (1863) 4 Giff 348, 349–50 (Stuart V-C): the trustee's duty is 'to keep proper accounts, and to have them always ready when called upon to render them'; *Lloyd v Attwood* (1859) 3 De G & J 614, 649 (Turner LJ), indicating that this duty extends to telling the beneficiaries when a breach of trust has been committed.

[39] In practice, settlors often write exemption clauses into their trust deeds, cutting back the trustees' duties, but there are limits to this; unless the trustees owe an 'irreducible core' of duties, there is no trust at all: *Armitage v Nurse* [1997] EWCA Civ 1279, [1998] Ch 241 (CA) 253 (Millett LJ). See also D J Hayton, 'The Irreducible Core Content of Trusteeship' in A J Oakley (ed), *Trends in Contemporary Trust Law* (Oxford: Clarendon Press, 1996) 47; J Penner 'Exemptions' in P Birks and A Pretto (eds), *Breach of Trust* (Oxford: Hart Publishing, 2002) 241.

[40] *Target Holdings Ltd v Redferns* [1996] AC 421 (HL) 434 (Lord Browne-Wilkinson).

[41] *Spellson v George* (1987) 11 NSWLR 300, 315–16 (Powell J); *Armitage v Nurse* [1997] EWCA Civ 1279, [1998] Ch 241, 261 (Millett LJ); *Foreman v Kingstone* [2004] 1 NZLR 841, esp [82] (Potter J), considering the impact of *Schmidt v Rosewood Trust Ltd* [2003] UKPC 26, [2003] 2 AC 709, on this principle. Note that the beneficiary's 'right to know what the trust property is and how it has been and is being administered by the trustee . . . is not conditioned on any purpose to investigate breaches of trust and to enforce the trust against the trustee': *Randall v Lubrana* NSW Sup Ct (Eq Div) (31 October 1975) (Holland J).

Some of these primary duties possess the characteristic that when they are breached, and the breach causes the beneficiaries a loss, there is only one practicable way for the courts to give content to the beneficiaries' corresponding primary rights, namely by holding that the trustees' breach of duty gives the beneficiaries a secondary right to compensation which the court can then realize by ordering the trustees to pay compensation to the beneficiaries. Thus, for example, when trustees cause their beneficiaries a loss by breaching their duty to take care when investing the trust funds, the only way for the courts to give effect to the beneficiaries' corresponding primary right is to hold that breach of this right generates a secondary right to compensation. It is too late for the courts to order the trustees to act carefully, and it cannot be known for certain what reasonable trustees in their position would have done, where they might have taken a number of different steps, all of them equally reasonable.

However, this is not true of *all* the primary duties owed by trustees. Consider the trustees' duty to maintain and disburse the trust funds in accordance with the trust deed. Suppose that trustees breach this duty, and thereby cause the beneficiaries a loss, by making an unauthorized investment, or by paying trust funds to a person who is not entitled to them. In principle, the courts *could* resolve this situation by holding that the trustees' breach of duty generates secondary rights to compensation, but this is not their *only* practicable way forward. They could also proceed differently, by allowing the beneficiaries to ignore the fact that the trustees have committed a wrong, and to ask for a court order directing the trustees to perform their primary duty to account for the trust property and to hold whatever sums are thereby found to be due for the beneficiaries. Allowing the beneficiaries to proceed in this way would be to treat them in the same way that claimants are treated at common law, when they are permitted to bring actions of debt to recover money lent to defendants, ignoring the fact that the defendants have committed a breach of contract when they have failed to repay the sum due.[42]

It follows that the primary duties owed by trustees vary in quality. Where trustees have caused a loss to the beneficiaries by breaching a primary duty, the range of the law's possible responses may be limited, depending on the nature of the duty which has been breached. Some of the beneficiaries' primary rights can only be realized through the creation of secondary rights which can then be realized by court order. Others could be realized in this way, but could also be realized through court orders which give direct effect to the beneficiaries' primary rights. Where

[42] *White and Carter (Councils) Ltd v McGregor* [1962] AC 413 (HL).

duties of the first kind are breached, the law has only two choices: leave the beneficiaries without a remedy, or create secondary rights which are then realizable by court order. Where duties of the second kind are breached, there are more choices to be made, because there is more than one way to put a remedy within the beneficiaries' reach.

Rights of Beneficiaries

Before moving on to consider what choices the courts have actually made, it is worth stressing a point which is sometimes overlooked in accounts of the law in this area, namely that the Chancery courts have had the power to make compensatory awards for breaches of equitable duty since the medieval period.[43] This fact ceased to be obvious when they developed procedures and terminology in breach of trust cases which made no explicit mention of compensatory awards, such as the taking of accounts on the footing of wilful default, and the orthodoxy developed that damages cannot be awarded for breach of trust.[44] Nonetheless, if they had wished to do so, the Chancery courts could have decided right from the start that they would give effect to a beneficiary's primary rights only where these had been breached, generating secondary rights to compensation in cases where the beneficiary had been caused a loss. Had they chosen to proceed in this way, the practice of the Chancery courts would have coincided with the accounts of the law given by Blackstone and Austin.

But of course they did not. Just as the Chancery courts have been able and willing to make orders and pronouncements *in personam* and *in specie* to give direct effect to a claimant's primary rights at common law,

[43] A point well made in J Edelman, 'Equitable Torts' (2002) 10 *Torts Law Journal* 64, 67–70, tracing the origin of this jurisdiction back to a statute of 1393 which empowered the Chancellor to make compensatory awards: 17 Ric II c 6. See also P M McDermott, 'Jurisdiction of the Court of Chancery to Award Damages' (1992) 108 *Law Quarterly Review* 652, reprised in P McDermott, *Equitable Damages* (London: Butterworths, 1994), 5–26; J Edelman and S B Elliott, 'Money Remedies against Trustees' (2004), 18 *Trust Law International* 116, 120, making the further point that damages were historically associated with common law causes of action because until the nineteenth century damages were conceived as jury relief and Chancery judges did not sit with juries; K Mason, 'Fusion: Fallacy, Future or Finished?' in S Degeling and J Edelman (eds), *Equity in Commercial Law* (Pyrmont, NSW: Lawbook Co, 2005) 41, 67–9.

[44] *Corporation of Ludlow v Greenhouse* (1827) 1 Bligh (NS) 18, 57–8; *ex p Adamson* (1878) 8 Ch D 807 (CA) 819; *Leeds Industrial Co-operative Soc v Slack* [1924] AC 851 (HL) 868; *Metall und Rohstoff AG v Donaldson Lufkin & Jenrette Inc* [1990] 1 QB 391 (CA) 473.

when acting in their auxiliary jurisdiction, so too have they been prepared to make such orders when acting in their exclusive jurisdiction, to give direct effect to a claimant's primary rights in equity. For example, they have made—and they continue to make—declarations setting out the nature of a beneficiary's interest,[45] or a trustee's duty;[46] orders directing trustees to make their accounts available for inspection by the beneficiaries,[47] or to give the beneficiaries an authority enabling them to obtain information about the trust assets from a third party;[48] orders directing trustees to exercise an obligatory discretionary power of appointment;[49] orders directing trustees to transfer trust assets to absolutely entitled beneficiaries;[50] and prohibitory injunctions, restraining trustees from acting inconsistently with their primary obligations.[51] It is axiomatic that beneficiaries who wish to obtain orders and pronouncements of this kind need not assert that the trustees have committed a breach of duty. Their claims resemble a claim for specific performance of the primary obligations owed under a contract, rather than a claim for damages for breach of contract or tort.[52]

[45] *Smith v Acton* (1858) 26 Beav 210. The courts now have an unfettered discretion to make binding declarations under CPR rule 40.20, but they will not normally entertain theoretical questions with no practical application: *Padden v Arbuthnot Pensions and Investments Ltd* [2004] EWCA Civ 582, [2004] CP Rep 36 [24] and [31]. The proper form of a declaration of equitable interest under rule 40.20 is discussed in *Powell v Wilshire* [2004] EWCA Civ 534, [2005] 1 QB 117 [39]-[45] (Arden LJ). The Trusts of Land and Appointment of Trustees Act 1996 s 14(2)(b) enables a person with an interest in property that is subject to a trust of land to obtain an order declaring the nature or extent of his interest, as in eg *Oxley v Hiscock* [2004] EWCA Civ 546, [2004] 3 WLR 715.

[46] *Cowan v Scargill* [1985] Ch 270 (Ch).

[47] *Re Fish* [1893] 2 Ch 413 (Ch); *Templeton Insurance Ltd v Penningtons Solicitors LLP* [2005] EWHC 2885 (Ch). Cf *Re Wells* [1962] 1 WLR 874 (CA).

[48] *Re Tillott* [1892] 1 Ch 86 (Ch).

[49] *Re Locker's ST* [1977] 1 WLR 1323 (Ch).

[50] *Re Knox's Trusts* [1895] 2 Ch 483 (CA); *Re Sandeman's WT* [1937] 1 All ER 368 (Ch). See also the Trustee Act 1925, ss 44(vi) and 51(1)(d), and cf *Quinton v Proctor* [1998] 4 VR 469; *Mok Chi Keung v Mok Chi Hoi* (2003) 215 HKCU 1; *Davis v Williams* [2003] NSWCA 371 [41].

[51] *Fox v Fox* (1870) LR 11 Eq 142 (improper distribution of assets); *Buttle v Saunders* [1950] 2 All ER 193 (sale of assets at an undervalue); *George v Macdonald* NSW Sup Ct (Eq Div) (6 February 1992) (sale of assets at an undervalue). It is no bar to the issue of an injunction restraining the unauthorized disposal of trust assets that the trustees have entered a binding contract with a third party: *Fouche v The Superannuation Fund Board* (1952) 88 CLR 609; and see too *Ord v Noel* (1820) 5 Madd 438; *Dance v Goldingham* (1873) LR 8 Ch App 902. On the question whether the trustee can claim an indemnity out of the trust fund for contract damages paid to such a third party when an injunction is awarded, see *Fitzwood Pty Ltd v Unique Goal Pty Ltd (in liq)* [2002] FCAFC 285.

[52] Note, however, that a court can order trustees to perform their obligations without regard to the adequacy of other remedies, whereas an order for specific performance of a contract will be made only where common law damages are an inadequate remedy. Note also that a claim for specific performance may succeed even though it is issued before the

But what of the situation where trustees commit a breach of duty which causes loss to the beneficiaries? Could the Chancery courts not have dealt with all of these cases, at least, by holding that the trustees' breaches of duty generate secondary rights to compensation which the courts can then realize by making compensatory awards? The answer, as Lord Millett stressed in a well-known article in the *Law Quarterly Review*,[53] and as Steven Elliott subsequently explained in detail in his brilliant study of the law in this area,[54] is that the courts could have dealt with all of the cases in this way, that in fact this is how they dealt with some of the cases, but that they treated one significant group of cases differently—namely the cases where the relevant breach of duty was a duty to maintain and distribute the trust funds in accordance with the trust deed. Here the courts allowed the beneficiaries to rely on their primary rights, to realize which the courts would order the trustees to produce a set of accounts which omitted no relevant incomings and which only recorded authorized outgoings, and they would then order the trustees either to transfer the assets which were thereby found to belong to the beneficiaries, or more usually to continue holding them on trust for the beneficiaries. In the event that there was a shortfall, the trustees would have to make this up out of their own pockets, and their obligation to do this was a primary rather than a secondary obligation. Thus, as Lord Millett wrote of these cases:[55]

> It is misleading to speak of breach of trust as if it were the equitable counterpart of breach of contract at common law; or to speak of equitable compensation for breach or fiduciary duty as if it were common law damages masquerading under a fancy name.... It is tempting, but wrong, to assume that a trustee is... under a primary obligation to perform the trust and a secondary obligation to pay equitable compensation if he does not. The primary obligation of a trustee is to

date when contractual performance is required, so that by definition no breach of contract can yet have occurred: *Hasham v Zenab* [1960] AC 316 (PC), noted R E Megarry, (1960) 76 *Law Quarterly Review* 200.

[53] Sir P Millett, 'Equity's Place in the Law of Commerce' (1998) 114 *Law Quarterly Review* 214, 225–7. See also Birks, n 29 above, 15 and 42–8; C E F Rickett, 'Equitable Compensation: Towards a Blueprint?' (2003) 25 *Sydney Law Review* 31.

[54] Elliott's work is most fully elaborated in his Oxford DPhil thesis: Compensation Claims against Trustees (2002). Parts of this have been published as: S B Elliott, 'Restitutionary Compensatory Damages for Breach of Fiduciary Duty?' [1998] *Restitution Law Review* 135; S B Elliott, 'Fiduciary Liability for Client Mortgage Frauds' (1999) 13 *Trust Law International* 74; S B Elliott, 'Remoteness Criteria in Equity' (2002) 65 *Modern Law Review* 588; S B Elliott and C Mitchell, 'Remedies for Dishonest Assistance' (2004) 67 *Modern Law Review* 16, esp 23–34; S B Elliott and J Edelman, 'Money Remedies against Trustees' (2004) 18 *Trust Law International* 116.

[55] Millett, n 53 above, 225.

account for his stewardship. The primary remedy of the beneficiary—any beneficiary no matter how limited his interest—is to have the account taken, to surcharge and falsify the account, and to require the trustee to restore to the trust estate any deficiency which may appear when the account is taken.

Unauthorized Disbursements

Looking a little more closely at these cases, we find that if a trustee cannot perform his obligation to account for and deliver a trust asset *in specie*, for example because he has lost or misapplied it, then the court can order him instead to pay money as a substitute for performance of his duty.[56] In this situation, the trustee may well have committed a breach of trust, but even so the beneficiaries need not plead or prove any breach in order to obtain their remedy. The reason is that the beneficiaries' claim is still a claim for performance of the trustee's primary obligation to deliver the asset, but with the difference that it is a claim for *substitute* performance of this obligation by the payment of a money sum.[57] It is not a claim for money to compensate the beneficiaries for any harm which they may have suffered as a consequence of the trustee's failure to perform his obligation *in specie*. Hence the amount payable is measured by the objective value of the property which the trustee should have delivered: the award 'looks not so much to the loss suffered as to what is required to restore the trust fund'.[58]

[56] Cf *Head v Gould* [1898] 2 Ch 250 (Ch) 266 (Kekewich J): 'As against a trustee who, on the accounts being taken, is shewn to have improperly applied part of the trust estate, the right of a *cestui que* trust is to have those accounts set straight—that is, to compel the trustee to pay such a sum as will make them balance'. See too *Wiglesworth v Wiglesworth* (1852) 16 Beav 269, 272 (Romilly MR); *Chaplin v Young* (1864) 33 Beav 330, 343 (Romilly MR).

[57] Damages awarded in lieu of specific performance under the Supreme Court Act 1981, s 50, should also be awarded on this basis, as the Supreme Court of Canada held in *Semelhago v Paramadevan* [1996] 2 SCR 415, discussed in L Smith, 'Understanding Specific Performance' in N Cohen and E McKendrick (eds), *Comparative Remedies for Breach of Contract* (Oxford: Hart Publishing, 2005), 221. Megarry J took a similar line in *Wroth v Tyler* [1974] Ch 30 (Ch), as did Cumming-Bruce LJ in *Malhotra v Choudury* [1980] Ch 52 (CA) esp 78–9, relying by way of analogy on *General & Finance Facilities Ltd v Cooks Cars (Romford) Ltd* [1963] 1 WLR 644 (CA) 648–9, where Diplock LJ observed that damages in detinue are assessed at the date of judgment because they are awarded in lieu of specific restitution of the claimant's chattel. It may be doubted whether these English cases survived Lord Wilberforce's speech in *Johnson v Agnew* [1980] AC 367 (HL), but for an interesting attempt to reconcile the authorities, see *Inmet Mining Corp v Homestake Canada Inc* (2003) 24 BCLR (4th) 1 [163]–[169].

[58] *New Cap Reinsurance Corp Ltd v General Cologne Re Australia Ltd* (2004) 7 ITELR 295 (Eq) [55] (Young CJ). See also *Re Anglo-French Co-operative Soc* (1882) 21 Ch D 492, 506; *Re Windsor Steam Coal Co (1901) Ltd* [1929] 1 Ch 151 (CA), 166–7; *Knight v Haynes Duffell, Kentish & Co (a firm)* [2003] EWCA Civ 223 [36]–[39]. It is often

Authorities supporting this analysis include *Bacon v Clark*,[59] where a trustee received assets out of which he was bound to pay money to the beneficiaries, the beneficiaries never received the money, and Lord Cottenham LC held that:[60] 'whether a breach of trust was committed or not . . . [the trustee's] estate must remain liable to pay what is due in respect of that sum, unless payment or a sufficient excuse for non-payment can be shewn'. A century later, in a Privy Council appeal from Singapore, *Ahmed Angullia bin Hadjee Mohamed Salleh Angullia v Estate and Trust Agencies (1927) Ltd*,[61] the defendant trustee contended that he should be chargeable with money spent for an unauthorized purpose only if the beneficiaries pleaded that this money had been spent in breach of trust. Lord Romer rejected this, ruling that the trustee owed the beneficiaries a duty to account for the trust assets, that 'it was incumbent upon [the trustee] to justify his payments, and those that he could not justify would necessarily have to be disallowed' from the account, leaving him under a primary duty to pay over the outstanding balance.[62]

The courts have often said that claims of this sort resemble claims for 'an equitable debt' and that the trustees' liability is a 'liability in the nature of a debt'.[63] The point of this comparison is that the beneficiaries' claim is not founded on an assertion that the trustees have committed a wrong, and so it makes no difference whether they have been caused a loss by the trustees' actions or omissions.[64] Nor does it matter whether the

said that the trustee must effect 'restitution' or 'restoration' of the trust assets which he has improperly withheld, or their money equivalent: eg *Re Dawson* [1966] 2 NSWR 211, 216; *Bartlett v Barclays Bank Trust Co Ltd (No 2)* [1980] Ch 515 (Ch) 543; *Target Holdings Ltd v Redferns* [1996] AC 421 (HL) 433; *Re French Caledonia Travel Service Pty Ltd (in liq)* (2003) 59 NSWLR 361 [64]; *Alexander v Perpetual Trustees (WA) Ltd* (2004) 216 CLR 109 [104] and [116]; *Waxman v Waxman* (2004) 7 ITELR 162 [663]. See also Pensions Act 1995, s 14.

[59] (1837) 2 My & Cr 294.

[60] ibid 298–9.

[61] [1938] AC 624 (PC). See also *Green v Weatherill* [1929] 2 Ch 213 (Ch) 222–3.

[62] ibid 627, citing *Re Stevens* [1898] 1 Ch 162 (CA) 172 (Cotton LJ): 'on taking the common account of their receipts, executors can properly be, and are often, charged with a devastavit arising on the accounts themselves . . . they stand charged with their receipts; and if they seek to discharge themselves by unlawful payments, their discharge is disallowed'. See also Lindley MR's comment in *Re Stevens* above, 170, that: 'A wrongful payment is one thing, and can be set right by disallowing it when the executor brings in his account. But if it is sought to charge him with loss attributable to some other breach of duty, call it wilful default or by any other name, such breach of duty must be proved'.

[63] *ex p Adamson* (1878) 8 Ch App 807 (CA) 819 (James LJ); *ex p Kelly & Co* (1879) 11 Ch D 306 (CA) 311 (James LJ); *Wickstead v Browne* (1992) 30 NSWLR 1, 14–5; *Armstrong v East West Airlines (Operations) Ltd* NSW Sup Ct (Eq) (3 February 1994) (Brownie J); *Turner v TR Nominees Pty Ltd* NSW Sup Ct (Eq) (3 November 1995) (Santow J).

[64] *Cocker v Quayle* (1830) 1 Russ & M 353; *Salway v Salway* (1831) 2 Russ & M 215; *Magnus v Queensland National Bank* (1888) 37 Ch D 466 (CA) 471–2 (Lord Halsbury

trustees have behaved negligently or dishonestly.[65] Nor do the concepts of remoteness[66] and contributory negligence[67] have any bearing on their claim.[68] Claims of this kind are mediated through proceedings for a common account, an order for which:[69]

> is made for the taking of accounts of money received and disbursed by the person who is responsible for the administration of a business enterprise or fund or other property, and for payment of any amount found to be due by that person upon the taking of the accounts... In such a case the making of the order need not imply any wrongdoing by the defendant.

When accounts in common form are taken, the court will scrutinize the entries on the credit side of the ledger, to check whether the trustees' receipts are all properly recorded, and the entries on the debit side of the ledger, to determine whether these record all the trustees' outgoings, and whether all the entries should be allowed. Obviously, the court will allow debit entries where these relate to authorized disbursements—such as distributions of trust assets, purchases of new assets with trust money, and payments of the trustees' own fees where permitted—and as a general rule they will disallow unauthorized disbursements, leaving the trustees with a shortfall in their accounts which they must make up out of their own pockets.[70] However, there are some exceptional cases where unauthorized disbursements are allowed, and the trustees exonerated from

LC); *British American Elevator Co v Bank of Bank of North America* [1919] AC 658 (PC) 663–4 (Viscount Haldane); *Re Dawson* [1966] 2 NSWR 211, 214; *Island Realty Investments Ltd v Douglas* (1985) 19 ETR 56, 64; *Youyang Pty Ltd v Minter Ellison Morris Fletcher* (2003) 212 CLR 484 [63] and [69].

65 *Caffrey v Derby* (1801) 6 Ves 488; *Clough v Bond* (1838) 3 My & Cr 490, 496–7 (Lord Cottenham LC), endorsed in *Target Holdings Ltd v Redferns* [1996] 1 AC 421 (HL) 434.

66 *Clough v Bond* (1838) 3 My & Cr 490; *Magnus v Queensland National Bank* (1888) 37 Ch D 466 (CA); *Re Dawson* [1966] 2 NSWR 211, 214; *Re Duckwari plc (No 2)* [1998] EWCA Civ 1795, [1999] Ch 268 (CA) 272; *McCann v Switzerland Insurance Australia Ltd* (2000) 203 CLR 579, 621–2.

67 *Nationwide BS v Bulmer Radmore (a firm)* [1999] PNLR 606 (Blackburne J): 'contributory negligence has never been a defence open to a trustee sued by his beneficiary for breach of trust in wrongfully paying away the trust fund' (NB this passage of Blackburne J's judgment is not reproduced in the report).

68 Cf *Jervis v Harris* [1996] Ch 195 (CA) 202–3: 'The plaintiff who claims payment of a debt need not prove anything beyond the occurrence of the event or condition on the occurrence of which the debt becomes due. He need prove no loss; the rules as to remoteness of damage and mitigation of loss are irrelevant.'

69 *Glazier Holdings Pty Ltd v Australian Men's Health Pty Ltd* NSW Sup Ct (Eq) (22 January 2001) [37] (Austin J), reversed but not on this point in *Meehan v Glazier Holdings Pty Ltd* (2002) 54 NSWLR 146.

70 *Ultraframe (UK) Ltd v Fielding* [2005] EWHC 1638 (Ch) [1513]–[1515].

performance of their primary duty to hold the relevant property for the beneficiaries.

One such is where the beneficiaries elect to adopt the trustees' disbursement and ask the court to treat their expenditure as though it had been authorized all along. Beneficiaries would wish to do this where their trustees have bought an unauthorized investment which has increased in value,[71] or where their trustees have wrongfully sold trust assets whose current value is less than the value of the sale proceeds in the trustees' hands.[72] The courts may also relieve trustees from performance of their primary duty where they consider that enforcement of this duty would be inequitable. For example, in *Jones v Lewis*, Lord Hardwicke LC held that:[73] 'if a trustee is robbed, that robbery properly proved shall be a discharge [in an action of account], provided he keeps [the trust assets] so as he would keep his own'.

Robert Chambers has concluded from the fact that trustees need not account for stolen trust property which they have kept with reasonable care that the courts will never require trustees to reach into their own pockets unless the trustees are proved to have committed a breach of trust.[74] However, this runs counter to the many cases which establish that proof of wrongdoing is unnecessary in claims to enforce the trustees' primary duty to account. Nor is it borne out by *Eaves v Hickson*,[75] where Romilly MR declined to relieve a trustee who had made unauthorized distributions on presentation of a forged document. No finding was made by the Master of the Rolls that the trustee had failed to examine this document carefully, and although counsel cited *Jones* and other robbery cases,[76] his Lordship concluded that the trustee was still 'bound to pay the trust fund to the right person'.[77]

[71] *Re Patten* (1883) 52 LJ Ch 787; *Re Jenkins* [1903] 2 Ch 362 (Ch); *Wright v Morgan* [1926] AC 788 (PC) 799. If the beneficiaries choose to adopt the investment, they cannot also demand that the trustees pay the difference between the current value of the investment and the (higher) current value of an authorized asset that was sold to make the purchase: *Thornton v Stokill* (1855) 1 Jur 751; *Re Lake* [1903] 1 KB 439.

[72] *Watts v Girdlestone* (1843) 6 Beav 188; *Shepherd v Mouls* (1845) 4 Hare 400, 504.

[73] (1750) 2 Ves Sen 240, 241. See also *Morley v Morley* (1678) 2 Ch Cas 2; *Jobson v Palmer* [1893] 1 Ch 71 (Ch). And cf *ex parte Belchier* (1754) Amb 218, 219 (Lord Hardwicke LC) (trustee not answerable for funds lost on banker's bankruptcy); *Job v Job* (1875) 6 Ch D 562, 563–4 (Jessel MR) (laying down a similar rule for executors).

[74] R Chambers, 'Liability' in P Birks and A Pretto (eds), *Breach of Trust* (Oxford: Hart Publishing, 2002) 1, 9.

[75] (1861) 30 Beav 136. See also *Ashby v Blackwell* (1765) 2 Eden 299; *Bostock v Flyer* (1865) LR 1 Eq 26; *Sutton v Wilders* (1871) LR 12 Eq 373.

[76] ibid 139.

[77] ibid 141.

Negligence

None of this is to deny that beneficiaries can also sue their trustees for negligence—and claims of this kind certainly do depend on the assertion that the trustees have committed a wrong, namely breach of their primary duty of care.[78] In cases where the beneficiaries successfully assert that the trustees have committed a breach of primary duty—whether a breach of their duty of care or some other primary duty—the award made is 'not readily distinguishable from [compensatory] damages except with the aid of a powerful legal microscope'.[79] It is calculated by reference to the loss actually suffered by the beneficiaries,[80] including the loss of a chance to avoid a detriment or make a gain.[81] The beneficiaries must prove that their loss has been caused by the trustees' breach of duty, using a 'but-for' causation test in all cases, regardless of whether the breach was innocent, negligent, or fraudulent.[82] Canadian authorities also indicate that the beneficiaries' claims are subject to the principle of *novus actus interveniens*,[83] and that where they have become aware that their trustees are not to be trusted, losses flowing from clearly unreasonable behaviour by the beneficiaries thereafter will be judged to have been caused by this

[78] *Partington v Reynolds* (1858) 4 Drew 253, 255–6; *Dowse v Gorton* [1891] AC 190 (HL) 202; *Re Stevens* [1898] 1 Ch 162 (CA) 170.

[79] *Bartlett v Barclays Bank Trust Co Ltd (No 2)* [1980] Ch 515 (Ch) 545 (Brightman LJ). See also *Bristol & West BS v Mothew* [1996] EWCA Civ 533, [1998] Ch 1 (Ch) 18 (Millett LJ), adopting *Permanent BS v Wheeler* (1994) 11 WAR 187, 237 (Ipp J); *Bank of New Zealand v New Zealand Guardian Trust Co Ltd* [1999] 1 NZLR 664 (NZCA) 687; *Hilton v Barker Booth & Eastwood (a firm)* [2005] UKHL 8, [2005] 1 WLR 567 [29] (Lord Walker).

[80] *Elder's Trustee and Executor Co Ltd v Higgins* (1963) 113 CLR 426, 453; *Fales v Canada Permanent Trust Co* [1977] 2 SCR 302, 320. Confusingly, claims of this kind are also often described as 'restitutionary', as in eg *Hodgkinson v Simms* [1994] 3 SCR 377, 440; *Re Mulligan* [1998] 1 NZLR 481, 507; *Swindle v Harrison* [1997] EWCA Civ 1339, [1997] 4 All ER 705 (CA) 733. However, this usage is best avoided, as in this context the word 'restitution' simply means 'compensation': *Bartlett v Barclays Bank Trust Co Ltd (No 2)* [1980] Ch 515 (Ch) 545 (Brightman LJ).

[81] *Sanders v Parry* [1967] 1 WLR 753, 767; *Nestle v National Westminster Bank plc* [1993] 1 WLR 1260 (CA) 1269; *Colour Control Centre Pty Ltd v Ty* NSW Sup Ct (Eq) (24 July 1995); *Bank of New Zealand v New Zealand Guardian Trust Co Ltd* [1999] 1 NZLR 664 (NZCA) 685–6; *Chirnside v Fay (No 2)* [2005] 3 NZLR 689 (NZCA) (reconceptualized as a gain-based liability on appeal: [2006] NZSC 68).

[82] *Target Holdings Ltd v Redferns* [1996] AC 421 (HL) 436; *Collins v Brebner* [2000] Lloyds Rep PN 587 (CA); *Hulbert v Avens* [2003] EWHC 76 (Ch), [2003] WTLR 387 [56]; *Gwembe Valley Development Co Ltd v Koshy (No 3)* [2003] EWCA Civ 1048, [2004] 1 BCLC 131 [147]. However, cf *Bairstow v Queen's Moat Houses plc* [2001] EWCA Civ 712, [2001] 2 BCLC 531 [53]–[54]. On the question whether such claims are subject to a remoteness cap, see S B Elliott, 'Remoteness Criteria in Equity' (2002) 65 *Modern Law Review* 588; also *Olszanecki v Hillocks* [2002] EWHC 1997 (Ch), [2004] WTLR 975.

[83] *Hodgkinson v Simms* [1994] 3 SCR 377, 443 (La Forest J); *Waxman v Waxman* (2004) 7 ITELR 162 [663].

behaviour and not by the breach.[84] Claims of this sort are mediated through proceedings for an account of the basis of wilful default, an order for which is:[85] ' "entirely grounded on misconduct", the defendant being required to account not only for what he or she has not received, but also for what he or she might have received had it not been for the default'.

Target Holdings v Redferns

In *Target Holdings Ltd v Redferns (a firm)*,[86] the claimant agreed to lend money to a borrower to purchase property. Repayment of the loan was to be secured by a charge on the property. The money was placed with the defendant solicitors on trust for payment to the borrower's order, once a duly executed charge over the property and supporting documents of title were delivered. The solicitors paid the money over to the borrower's order without first obtaining the charge or other documents, although these were later delivered. The borrower defaulted on the loan and it then transpired that the property had been fraudulently over-valued, so that the claimant was left substantially out of pocket after it had exercised its power of sale. The Court of Appeal held that the solicitors had committed a breach of trust by releasing the money before receiving the documents, and that at this moment there had been 'an immediate loss placing the trustee under an immediate duty to restore the moneys to the trust fund'.[87] The court concluded that the solicitors were liable for the full amount of the money, but to prevent double recovery the claimant was required to give credit for the amount realized by the sale of the property. On appeal, the House of Lords agreed that there had been a breach of trust, but disagreed that the clock should be stopped at the date of breach for the purpose of quantifying the solicitors' liability. Their Lordships held that the relevant date was the date of judgment, that is after the

[84] *Canson Enterprises Ltd v Boughton & Co* [1991] 3 SCR 534, 554 (McLachlin J), endorsed in *Corporaçion del Cobre de Chile v Sogemin Metals Ltd* [1997] 1 WLR 1396 (Ch) 1403–4. See also *Lipkin Gorman v Karpnale Ltd* [1992] 4 All ER 331, 361 (Alliott J) (not considered on appeal).

[85] *Glazier Holdings Pty Ltd v Australian Men's Health Pty Ltd* NSW Sup Ct (Eq) (22 January 2001) [39] (Austin J), reversed but not on this point in *Meehan v Glazier Holdings Pty Ltd* (2002) 54 NSWLR 146. See also *Re Tebbs* [1976] 1 WLR 924 (Ch); *Bartlett v Barclays Bank Co Ltd* [1980] Ch 15; *Armitage v Nurse* [1997] EWCA Civ 1279, [1998] Ch 241 (CA) 252; *Iliffe v Trafford* [2001] EWHC 469 (Ch) [9]. The phrase 'wilful default' is misleading in this context, as it encompasses negligence as well as fraud: *Walker v Symonds* (1818) 3 Swans 1, 69; *Re Chapman* [1896] 2 Ch 763 (CA) 776 and 779–80.

[86] [1996] AC 421 (HL).

[87] [1994] 1 WLR 1089 (CA) 1103 (Peter Gibson LJ).

transaction had been completed, and that the solicitors would be liable only if the claimant could prove that its loss would not have occurred but for the early payment of the money without taking any security. Hence the case was sent back to the High Court for determination of this point.

Unfortunately, Lord Browne-Wilkinson's leading speech is hard to follow, essentially because he failed to distinguish between claims by beneficiaries to enforce their primary right to insist that the trust property be maintained or disbursed in accordance with the terms of the trust, and claims by beneficiaries to enforce their secondary rights to compensation for loss caused by a breach of duty by the trustees.[88] He clearly thought that the claimant should have to prove a causal link between its loss and the solicitor's breach. Yet, as Lord Millett later observed extra-judicially in the *Law Quarterly Review*,[89] the claim was for performance of the solicitor's primary duty to hold and disburse the trust money in an authorized fashion, and so the question whether the claimant had suffered a loss as a result of the solicitor's breach was beside the point. In Lord Millett's view, the case should have been decided on the different basis that the solicitor's payment without taking the documents was a breach of trust, but that where a trustee has misapplied trust assets, his:[90] 'obligation to restore the trust property is not an obligation to restore it in the very same form in which he disbursed it, but an obligation to restore it in any form authorized by the trust'.Hence, when the solicitor acquired the title deeds and delivered them to the claimant, it performed its obligation to restore the trust property, not *in specie*, but in the form of an authorized substitute. Hence the solicitor should not have been liable.

This rationalization of the case leaves intact Lord Browne-Wilkinson's finding that the quantum of the liability owed by a trustee who misapplies trust property is not determined at the date of breach, even though he comes under an immediate liability to restore the property.[91] However, this does not mean that the court can look at events occurring after the breach to see whether the beneficiaries would ultimately have suffered the same loss anyway.[92] Instead, its significance lies in the fact that the court can look to see whether the trustee has rectified matters in an authorized

[88] As explained in J Edelman and S B Elliott, 'Money Remedies against Trustees' (2004) 18 *Trusts Law International* 116, 122–5, the source of this confusion was the Supreme Court of Canada's decision, and especially McLachlin J's minority judgment, in *Canson Enterprises Ltd v Boughton & Co* [1991] 3 SCR 534.

[89] Millett, n 53 above, 225–7.

[90] ibid 227.

[91] See also *Youyang Pty Ltd v Minter Ellison Morris Fletcher* (2003) 212 CLR 484 [35].

[92] *Cocker v Quayle* (1830) 1 Russ & M 535.

fashion since the date of breach. Also, if the trustee has not done this, then the value of his obligation to hand over the property will vary according to its current market value, or, where the property is money, according to the amount of (compound) interest accrued on the money between the date of breach and the date of judgment.

Where Do We Go From Here?

In the latest edition of his book, *Remedies for Torts and Breach of Contract*,[93] Andrew Burrows accepts that 'historically' the account of the law presented here 'has much to commend it', but he argues that the courts should now desist from letting beneficiaries enforce their primary right to an account, and should now require them to proceed against defaulting trustees in cases where they have been caused a loss by enforcing their secondary rights to compensation.[94] Burrows concedes that it would have been preferable for the House of Lords in *Target Holdings* to have cited all the cases which tell us that beneficiaries can ignore their trustees' breach of duty and enforce their primary rights, in order to overrule them. But he argues that the court 'impliedly' rejected them,[95] and considers that the court was right to do this in policy terms, for the following reasons:[96]

> A trustee does not contract to pay a particular sum to the beneficiaries and, if the beneficiaries would have suffered the loss even if the trustee had performed its fiduciary duties, it is hard to see why, as a matter of policy, they should have redress against the trustee for that loss. Put another way, to regard the trustees as being liable to a distinct account remedy appears to impose on them an unwarranted absolute duty to pay back into the trust fund the value of the moneys that, in breach of trust, have been paid out from it and not recovered.

Taking each of these points in turn, *Target Holdings* certainly seems to be inconsistent with earlier authorities standing for the proposition that beneficiaries who seek to enforce their primary rights need not prove a breach of trust, nor that this breach has caused them a loss. However, it may be doubted whether Lord Browne-Wilkinson clearly recognized *Target Holdings* as a case of the same kind, and meant to overturn centuries of authority to hold that henceforth beneficiaries should be prevented from proceeding in this way.

93 3rd edn (Oxford: Oxford University Press, 2004).
94 ibid 605.
95 ibid 605–6.
96 ibid 605.

Does it matter that 'a trustee does not contract to pay a particular sum'? Probably not, since even the common law recognizes primary contractual obligations to pay sums whose amount is unspecified at the time when the contract is entered,[97] and agreements of this kind are more akin to a trustee's undertaking to hold for the beneficiaries whatever sums are found to be due on the taking of an account.

Is it 'unwarranted' to make a trustee pay to replace missing trust assets that would have been lost whether or not the trustee did anything wrong? Undoubtedly it is severe, although we should not forget that the courts can excuse trustees from the performance of their duties in hard cases, nor that there is scope for trustees to escape the consequences of these rules by insisting on the insertion of an exclusion clause in the trust deed. More fundamentally, we should also take note of the reasons that have frequently been advanced by the courts for the severity of the treatment meted out to trustees. As Arden LJ recently stressed in *Murad v Al-Saraj*:[98] 'any rule that makes a wrongdoer liable for all the consequences of his wrongful conduct or for actions which did not cause the injured party any loss needs to be justified by some special policy'. But as she also stressed, 'in the field of fiduciaries there are policy reasons which have for a long time been accepted by the courts'.[99] The reasons boil down to this. Trustees control other people's property, in circumstances where their opportunities for abuse of power and neglect of duty are many, where their opportunities for suppressing evidence of such wrongdoing are many, and where their beneficiaries' opportunities to monitor their activities are few. Hence they must be held to a stringent performance standard, as a deterrent measure: in Lord Eldon's words, anything less 'would be an encouragement to bad motives; and it may be impossible to detect undue motives'.[100]

Is deterrence a convincing rationale for the tough treatment of trustees? Lionel Smith has argued that it is not.[101] In his view, deterrence reasoning comprises an undesirable incursion of public law into the private law sphere: because it looks outside the relationship between the claimant and defendant, and the conduct giving rise to the litigation, it disrupts the internal rationality of private law. Moreover, some awkward questions arise if the need for deterrence is said to derive from the special vulnerability of beneficiaries: what of beneficiaries who are not peculiarly vulnerable, but stand on an equal footing with their trustees, as in many

[97] Consider the Supply of Goods and Services Act 1982, s 15.

[98] [2005] EWCA Civ 959, [2005] WTLR 1573 [75].

[99] ibid.

[100] *Caffrey v Darby* (1801) 6 Ves 488, 496.

[101] L Smith, 'The Motive, Not the Deed' in J Getzler (ed), *Rationalizing Property, Equity and Trusts* (London: LexisNexis/Butterworths, 2003) 53, 60–1.

commercial trusts; and why does the law not also give special treatment to other peculiarly vulnerable claimants, such as pedestrians on road crossings at risk from drivers? John Langbein has also questioned the continued validity of the evidence-based rationale for the stern treatment of fiduciaries, observing that the strict rules governing fiduciary liability were developed two hundred years ago when shortcomings in the fact-finding processes of the Chancery courts set a premium on rules that avoided fact-finding. The fusion of the Chancery and common law courts, and successive reforms of civil procedure, have left the courts far better equipped in this respect, and at the same time, 'improvements in the standards, practices and technology of trust recordkeeping, as well as enhanced duties of disclosure . . . have largely defused the old concern that a trustee operating under a potential conflict could easily conceal wrongdoing'.[102]

In the end, then, perhaps Burrows is right, and the rules governing the compensatory liability of trustees need to be rethought, or at least recast in a more nuanced form. But we need to work through all the arguments before we can safely reach this conclusion—and that must be a project for another day.

[102] J H Langbein, 'Questioning the Trust Law Duty of Loyalty: Sole Interest or Best Interest?' (2005) 114 *Yale Law Journal* 929, 932.

Locating Disability Law

*Peter Alldridge**

Thirty years have seen significant developments in the relationship between disabled people and law. Thirty years ago the process of registration as disabled and the 3 per cent quota scheme, a genuine affirmative action provision, but one that did not work, were in force.[1] There were no anti-discrimination provisions, and if buildings or transport facilities presented obstacles, then no legal redress was available. Some things have changed, but disabled people still constitute a disadvantaged minority. In 2005, disabled people of working age were 30 per cent less likely to have jobs.[2] People with disabilities: '. . . remain more likely to live in poverty, to have fewer educational qualifications, to be out of work, and to experience prejudice and abuse.[3] They still routinely find themselves experiencing poorer services.'[4]

Prejudice against disabled people continues.[5] A recent survey found that only 62 and 37 per cent of employers in one pilot area, recruiting benefit claimants, said they would take on an employee with a physical or mental disability respectively. Disabled people also form an increasingly large proportion of the population, and that proportion will increase as

* This essay is a revised version of a Current Legal Problems Lecture delivered on 13 October 2005. I am grateful to Anna Lawson for helpful comments. Errors and omissions that remain are mine.

1 The Disabled Persons (Employment) Act 1944 (repealed from 1996 by the Disability Discrimination Act 1995 c 50, sch 7, para 1) included a series of provisions entitled: 'Provisions for enabling registered disabled persons to obtain employment or to undertake work on their own account'. On quota schemes, see L Waddington and M Diller, 'Tensions and Coherence in Disability Policy: The Uneasy Relationship between Social Welfare and Civil Rights Models of Disability in American, European and International Employment Law' in M Breslin and S Yee (eds), *Disability Rights Law and Policy: International and National Perspectives* (Ardsley, NY: Transnational Publishers Inc, 2002).

2 Department of Work and Pensions, *Delivering Equality for Disabled People* (Cm 6255, 2004), para 3.4.

3 One quarter of all disabled people say they have experienced hate crime or harassment. Cabinet Office Strategy Unit, *Improving the Life Chances of Disabled People* (London: The Stationery Office, 2005) (hereafter *COSU*), Executive Summary.

4 T Blair, *COSU*, Preface.

5 P Miller, S Parker, and S Gillinson, *Disablism: How to Tackle the Last Prejudice* (London: DEMOS, 2004).

the Baby Boom generation moves into its sixties and as medical care improves. The statistics on disadvantage work both ways. Disability causes poverty and lack of qualifications and poverty cause disability.[6]

Partly at least with a lead from the legislature,[7] consciousness has changed among people with disabilities and others. There has been a thirty year time-lag between legislative developments on race and gender[8] and equivalent disability legislation. After much debate[9] the Disability Discrimination Act 1995 was enacted, not to everyone's satisfaction. The Act made it unlawful for employers and providers of services to discriminate on the grounds of disability. There were exceptions; most significantly the provision of education,[10] and public transport,[11] and the omission of a body to be proactive about its enforcement was soon felt and remedied. The Disability Rights Commission[12] was established by the Disability Rights Commission Act 1999, has a broad remit,[13] and has done an excellent job. The Special Educational Needs and Disability Act 2001 extended the duty not to discriminate to schools[14] and education authorities and institutions of further and higher education. Oddly perhaps, it seems to have had more effect in institutions of Higher Education than the 1995 Act. The activities of the Disability Rights Commission are to be subsumed into the more general Commission for Equality and Human Rights.[15] Under the new regime there is a separate Office for Disability Issues reporting to the Minister,[16] but neither it nor the CEHR has the power the DRC has exercised to good effect to support individual

[6] C Barnes, *Disabled People in Britain and Discrimination: A Case for Anti-discrimination Legislation* (London: Hurst, 1991), ch 2.

[7] *COSU*, para 1.3, sets out the most important post-1997 changes.

[8] eg Race Relations Acts 1965 and 1968, Equal Pay Act 1970, and Sex Discrimination Act 1975.

[9] Barnes, n 6 above.

[10] Disability Discrimination Act 1995 s 19(5)(a). Part IV of the Act made limited provision in respect of education: Disability Discrimination Act 1995 ss 29–31.

[11] ibid, s 19(5)(b). Part V of the Act made limited provision in respect of taxi, PSV, and rail vehicles: Disability Discrimination Act 1995 ss 32–49.

[12] Hereafter 'the DRC'.

[13] '2.—(1) The Commission shall have the following duties—

(a) to work towards the elimination of discrimination against disabled persons;
(b) to promote the equalisation of opportunities for disabled persons;
(c) to take such steps as it considers appropriate with a view to encouraging good practice in the treatment of disabled persons; and
(d) to keep under review the working of the Disability Discrimination Act 1995 (referred to in this Act as 'the 1995 Act') and this Act'.

[14] See n 10 above, s 28A, inserted by Special Educational Needs and Disability Act 2001, s 11.

[15] Equality Act 2006, Part 1.

[16] For an indication of how this is intended to work see Blair, n 4 above, para 8.4. Information on the Office, which was established in 2006, can be found at <www.officefordisability.gov.uk>.

litigation. International efforts have grown in recent years. Increased concern in the EU for social policy has given rise to an Action Plan and the Framework Equal Treatment Directive (FETD).[17] In August 2000 the United Nations put in place a Convention on the Rights of Disabled People.[18]

The Disability Discrimination 2005 Act was enacted in the flurry of activity before the May 2005 General Election.[19] It had been the subject in the previous Parliamentary session of the pre-legislative scrutiny procedure.[20] The combination of the attenuated debate in 2005 and the benefits of the Scrutiny procedure mean that greater attention was paid by people with greater expertise during the scrutiny procedure, and that on the occasions where the Act departs from the recommendations of the Scrutiny Committee, such as in respect of the Armed Forces,[21] we should look closely at the reasons. The most recent Government statement on disability is the latest Cabinet Office Strategy Unit prescription for the period until 2025.[22] This is an important and wide-ranging document, which does the sort of joined-up thinking for which the enlarged Cabinet Office was created. Much of it is to be welcomed. We should certainly welcome thinking based upon a sufficiently long period of time to make a fundamental difference.

The Scope of Disability Law

This essay is an invitation to consider disability law. It will take 'disability law' to cover any interface of law and disability, and consequently to be a far wider area of legal study than simply discrimination law in the context primarily of employment, together with help from human rights law. The reason for casting the net so wide is that rights and the discourse of rights,

[17] Communication from the Commission to the Council, the European Parliament, the European Economic and Social Committee and the Committee of the Regions, *Equal Opportunities for People with Disabilities: A European Action Plan*, COM(2003) 650 final. See A Lawson and C Gooding (eds), *Disability Rights in Europe: From Theory to Practice* (Oxford: Hart, 2005); D Mabbett, 'The Development of Rights-Based Social Policy in the European Union: The Example of Disability Rights' [2005] *Journal of Common Market Studies* 97.

[18] <http://www.un.org/disabilities/convention>.

[19] Royal assent was granted on 7 April 2005.

[20] Lord Carter (Chair), Joint Committee on the Draft Disability Discrimination Bill Scrutiny Committee Report (HC 352-I HL 82-I), May 2004. See *Government Response to Report of Joint Committee on Draft Disability Discrimination Bill* (Cm 6276, DWP), 15 July 2004.

[21] See *Welfare to Work*, at <www.Sheffield.ac.uk/welfaretowork>.

[22] *COSU*. Some responses are at <http://www.strategy.gov.uk/work_areas/disability/final_response.asp>.

whilst tremendously important in the political battle, should not be given overriding significance in the range of laws that impact upon the lives of disabled people. A false picture of the disabled legal subject is generated by reading only anti-discrimination laws and decisions. Discussion only of the question of discrimination, the usual, but not the only 'rights question',[23] is usually bilateral, considering, for example, the employer and employee or would-be employee, or the service provider and client. This excludes the third party in the economics of disability, the extent to which a claim to support can be made against the State or the taxpayer. It also diverts attention from other legal approaches than anti-discrimination law. Whereas the standard legal response to discrimination on the basis of gender or sexuality or age or race or ethnicity is anti-discrimination legislation, it does not follow that anti-discrimination legislation is the only or the optimal legal response to discrimination on the basis of disability.

On this broader account of disability law, there are many areas of law that impact upon disability. There are, for example, several major areas of interface between medical law and disability law.[24] There are 'right to die' decisions, usually arising amongst people with degenerative conditions, where the person involved wants help in dying.[25] There are treatment and non-treatment decisions in respect of neonates.[26] There has been a range of cases that puts in issue the whole notion, in the context of some impairment, of 'life worth living'.[27] In the area of criminal law there are questions about: the use of cannabis for pain relief,[28] the availability of Anti-Social Behaviour Orders against people with mental impairments, particularly the neurodiverse,[29] and the treatment of and taking of

[23] The European Court of Human Rights (ECHR) gives little purchase, but has been used under Articles 3 and 8. See n 115 below.

[24] And see A Lawson, 'Mind the Gap! The Danger of Disablement through Law' in Lawson and Gooding, n 17 above, 265, 273–8.

[25] *R v DPP ex p Pretty* [2001] UKHL 61, [2002] 1 AC 800; *Pretty v United Kingdom* (2002) 35 EHRR 1. D Morris, 'Assisted Suicide under the European Convention on Human Rights: A Critique' (2003) 1 *European Human Rights Law Review* 65–91; E Wada, 'A Pretty Picture: The Margin of Appreciation and the Right to Assisted Suicide' (2005) 27 *Loyola Los Angeles International and Comparative Law Review* 275; *R (on the application of Burke) v General Medical Council* [2005] EWCA Civ 1003, [2005] 3 WLR 1132.

[26] See also J Read and L Clements, 'Demonstrably Awful: The Right to Life and the Selective Non-Treatment of Disabled Babies and Young Children' (2004) 31 *Journal of Law and Society* 482.

[27] *Jepson v Chief Constable of West Mercia* [2003] EWHC 3318. No proceedings were brought. See <http://www.cps.gov.uk/news/pressreleases/117_05.html>.

[28] See *R v Quayle* [2005] EWCA Crim 1415 [2005] 1 WLR 3642.

[29] People with varieties of autism such as Asperger's and Tourette's syndrome. See R Edmunds and T Sutton, 'Who's Afraid of the Neighbours?' in L Cooke (ed), *Modern Studies in Property Law* (Oxford: Hart, 2001), 133; N Cobb, 'Patronising the Mentally

evidence from victims with disabilities.[30] Even speech about disability can sometimes involve consideration of criminal law. Disabled people do not constitute a race or an ethnicity, so that when people advocate the mass killing of disabled people[31] they do not incite racial hatred, and so long as they do not actually incite murder, they do not commit a crime at all.[32] The law of torts supplies a jurisprudence of 'wrongful life'[33] but is also to a large extent part of the economic law of certain privileged disabilities. If an impairment is occasioned by negligent driving, the plaintiff recovers; if from genetic causes he does not.

A fuller account of specific areas of legal study that should be included would include parts of land law, mental health law, charity law, local government law, employment law, social security law, discrimination law, and environmental law. This essay will not deal in detail with all those matters. It will set out the context and method of disability law, and then identify and address three major issues that run through much or all of the interaction of disability and law. They are:

1. The claims that are made about disability rights and regulation: how should we describe the claims made for disabled people and what kinds of legal structures are needed to give them appropriate effect?
2. The economics of disability: a discussion of the allocation of economic burdens accompanying the claims of individual and collective rights is crucial to an understanding of the disabled legal subject.
3. The significance of the duty to promote equality imposed by the Disability Discrimination Act 2005: what difference will the new duty make?

This account requires a context and a perspective. Before turning to these major questions, therefore, the essay will briefly examine the context for disability law, in the growing discipline of disability studies, and then the possible perspectives that can be brought to bear on the study.

Disordered? Social Landlords and the Control of "Anti-Social Behaviour" under the Disability Discrimination Act 1995' (2006) 26:(2) *Legal Studies* 238.

[30] A Sanders, J Creaton, S Bird, and L. Weber, *Victims with Learning Disabilities—Negotiating the Criminal Justice System* (Oxford: University of Oxford, Centre for Criminology, 1997).

[31] The Deputy Mayor of Swindon, Dr Owen Lister, resigned in September 2005 after recommending the guillotining of disabled children. See S de Bruxelles, 'Uproar at "Kill Disabled Children" Remark' *The Times*, 24 September 2005.

[32] This is not to suggest there should be such a crime. See E Heinze, 'Viewpoint Absolutism and Hate Speech' (2006) 69(4) *Modern Law Review* 543–82.

[33] See also Lawson, n 24 above, 268.

Context—Disability Studies

There has grown up over the last twenty years a discipline called Disability Studies, which provides the context for disability law.[34] There are now undergraduate and postgraduate degree courses,[35] journals,[36] Centres,[37] and professional organizations in Disability Studies.[38] To some extent it is developing a corpus of essential texts,[39] and a core belief in the 'social model' of disability.[40] Several disciplines provide sources for Disability Studies. In the humanities, in particular, Cultural Studies, History, and Philosophy have been influential. So far as concerns Cultural Studies, Film, TV, and newspapers retain a fascination with disability, and film in particular figures large in accounts of disability in popular culture.[41]

Consider the range of depictions of disability in film. The analogy with Women's Studies is strong. There is a passage in *The Female Eunuch* in which Greer denounces the presentation of women in Bond films.[42] It is not only women who are maligned. Every Bond villain has a disability. That is how we know they are evil. Frequently their henchpeople do too.[43] This is not to claim that every representation of disabled people in

[34] D Johnstone, *An Introduction to Disability Studies* (2nd edn) (London: David Fulton, 2001); M Oliver, *Understanding Disability from Theory to Practice* (Basingstoke: Macmillan, 1996); M Oliver, *The Politics of Disablement* (London: Macmillan Education, 1990).

[35] S J Taylor and R Zubal-Ruggieri, 'Academic Programs in Disability Studies' 1(1) *Review of Disability Studies*. Access this article via <www.rds.hawaii.edu>.

[36] eg *Disability and Society* (formerly *Disability, Handicap, and Society*), *Disability Studies Quarterly*, *Review of Disability Studies*.

[37] eg The Leeds Centre, headed by Colin Barnes, is the prime mover in the UK <www.leeds.ac.uk/disability-studies>.

[38] eg The (American) Society for Disability Studies was founded in 1982; The (UK) Disability Studies' Association was founded in 2003.

[39] The Leeds Centre maintains a rich archive of writing in the area at <http://www.leeds.ac.uk/disability-studies/archiveuk/>. There is a useful, mainly American, bibliography on disability and law at <http://www.law.uga.edu/cgi-bin/faculty/new_disdb/dynddb.pl=20>.

[40] C Barnes, G Mercer, and T Shakespeare, *Exploring Disability: A Sociological Introduction* (Malden, MA: Polity Press, 1999); B Hughes and K Paterson, 'The Social Model of Disability and the Disappearing Body: Towards a Sociology of Impairment' (1997) 12 *Disability and Society* 325–40; M Priestley, 'Constructions and Creations: Idealism, Materialism and Disability Theory' (1998) 13 *Disability & Society* 75.

[41] See T Shakespeare, 'Cultural Representation of Disabled People—Dustbins for Disavowal' (1994) 9 *Disability and Society* 283.

[42] G Greer, *The Female Eunuch* (London: Palladin 1971), 13.

[43] On crime fiction, see I Zola, ' "Any Distinguishing Features?"—The Portrayal of Disability in the Crime-Mystery Genre' (1987) 15 *Policy Studies Journal* 485.

popular culture is negative, simply that too frequently and without reflection stereotypes are used so as to identify disability with one of a range of negative characteristics, and that it is the task of Disability Studies to draw attention to those matters.[44] Disability history includes the treatment of neonates in ancient Sparta,[45] freak shows,[46] village idiots,[47] the hearing impaired on Martha's Vineyard,[48] the history of the invalid carriage,[49] and Roosevelt's 'splendid deception'.[50] Political and moral philosophy have dealt with many difficult issues surrounding impairment and disability.[51] Why, if at all, are people with disabilities entitled to different treatment? What makes needs special?[52] In social sciences, there is a sociology of disability[53] and anthropologists have made their contributions.[54] Social Psychology has shown that attitudes to disabled colleagues in the workplace have ameliorated over the years, but still leave much scope for further improvement.[55]

[44] See M F Norden, *The Cinema of Isolation* (New Brunswick, NJ: Rutgers University Press, 1994); A Pointon and C Daview (eds), *Framed: Interrogating Disability in the Media* (London: BFI, 1997).

[45] M Huys, 'The Spartan Practice of Selective Infanticide and its Parallels in Ancient Utopian Tradition' (1996) 27 *Ancient Society* 47.

[46] R Bogdan, *Freak Show: Presenting Human Oddities for Amusement and Profit* (Chicago: University of Chicago Press, 1988); R Garland Thomson, *Extraordinary Bodies* (New York City, NY: Columbia University Press 1997).

[47] N E Groce, ' "The Town Fool": An Oral History of a Mentally Retarded Individual in Small Town Society' in P M Ferguson, D L Ferguson, and S J Taylor (eds), *Interpreting Disability: A Qualitative Reader* (New York: Teachers College Press, 1992), 175.

[48] N E Groce, *Everyone Here Spoke Sign Language: Hereditary Deafness on Martha's Vineyard* (Cambridge, Mass and London: Harvard University Press, 1985).

[49] See <www.disabilitymuseum.org>.

[50] H Gallagher, *FDR's Splendid Deception* (Arlington, Va: Vandemere Press. 1994).

[51] R Arneson, 'Disability, Priority, and Social Justice' in L A Francis and A Silvers (eds), *Americans with Disabilities: Exploring the Implications of the Law for Individuals and Institutions* (London: Routledge, 2000); R Arneson, 'Equality and Equal Opportunity for Welfare' (1989) 56 *Philosophical Studies* 77–93; H Brighouse, 'Can Justice as Fairness Accommodate the Disabled?' (2001) 27 *Social Theory and Practice* 537; J Wolff, 'Disability Among Equals' in K Brownlee and A Cureton (eds) *Philosophy and Disability* (Oxford: Oxford University Press, forthcoming); R Dworkin, 'Equality of Welfare' and 'Equality of Resources' in *Sovereign Virtue: The Theory and Practice of Equality* (Cambridge, Mass: Harvard University Press, 2000), 11–64 and 65–119 respectively.

[52] S Vehmas, 'What Makes Needs "Special"?', Disability Studies Association Conference, Lancaster 2004.

[53] Barnes *et al*, n 40 above.

[54] R Murphy, 'The Body Silent' (New York City, NY: Norton, 2001); D Kasnitz and R Shuttleworth, 'Engaging Anthropology in Disability Studies' in L Rogers and B Swadener (eds), *Is there a Culture of Disability?* (Albany, NY: State University of New York Press, 2001); S Linton, *Claiming Disability: Knowledge and Identity* (New York: New York University Press, 1998).

[55] I Grewal, S Joy, J Lewis, K Swales, and K Woodfield, *'Disabled for Life?' Attitudes Towards, and Experiences of, Disability in Britain* (Department for Works and Pensions, Research Report no 173, 2004).

Drawing upon all these sources, Disability Studies has grown up around the 'social model of disability'. This is the application of social constructionist ideas in the context of disability. The social model is described, for example, by the British Council of Disabled People, thus:

> [S]tudy of the economic, environmental and cultural barriers encountered by people who are viewed by others as having some form of impairment—whether physical, sensory or intellectual. The barriers disabled people encounter include inaccessible education systems, working environments, inadequate disability benefits, discriminatory health and social support services, inaccessible transport, houses and public buildings and amenities, and the devaluing of disabled people through negative images in the media—films, television and newspapers. The social model of disability can also be used to understand the family lives and personal relationships of disabled people. This is because the cultural environment in which we all grow up usually sees impairment as unattractive and unwanted.[56]

The barriers confronting disabled people are formed by attitudes, policies, and disempowerment as much as by physical geography.[57] Acceptance of the social model does not always mean that we can never say that the disabled person should behave or should have behaved otherwise. There will be cases in which we might want to ascribe fault or at least causality or even just say, 'I'm sorry, there is nothing I can do'. Commitment to the social model does not compel a particular solution in the case of the alcoholic co-worker or the obese aircraft passenger. The social model draws attention to the barriers. What must be done is another question. If the social model is an article of faith in Disability Studies, the enemy is the 'medical model'. The 'medical model' holds that impairment is a problem and that it is the task of medicine to take it away, or at best to help the person in question put up with it.[58] The medical model is blamed for the segregation of disabled people and for their being presented as passive. As Lawson writes: 'If they cannot be made normal, they must remain abnormal outsiders unable to cope with the real world'.[59]

In the legal context, the 'social versus medical model' question is manifest from the outset in debates as to how disability is to be defined.[60] There are several definitions of disability for the purposes of English law.

[56] British Council of Disabled People website; <www.wbcodp.org.uk>.

[57] *COSU*, Executive Summary.

[58] See S Wendell, *The Rejected Body: Feminist Philosophical Reflections on Disability* (New York and London: Routledge, 1996).

[59] A Lawson, 'The EU Rights Based Approach to Disability: Strategies for Shaping an Inclusive Society' (2005) 6 *International Journal of Discrimination and the Law* 269, 282.

[60] D Mabbett, ' "Some are More Equal than Others": Definitions of Disability in Social Policy and Discrimination Law in Europe' (2005) 34 *Journal of Social Policy* 215.

To take an example, the original basic definition of disability in the Disability Discrimination Act 1995 was as follows:

> 1.—(1) Subject to the provisions of Schedule 1, a person has a disability for the purposes of this Act if he has a physical or mental impairment which has a substantial and long-term adverse effect on his ability to carry out normal day-to-day activities.[61]

There were two main levels of criticism of this definition.[62] The first is that it was insufficiently wide: some cancers and AIDS and HIV were not necessarily included in 1995. That was dealt with in the 2005 Act.[63] The more fundamental criticism is that if we adopt the social model of disability, the same medical condition may or may not be disabling, depending upon the societal response. It follows from the social model that the definition of disability for any legally relevant purpose ought not to be a list of medical conditions. It should be a list of reactions.

Compare the DDA to the definition in the important Cabinet Office Strategy Unit policy document, 'Improving the Life Chances of Disabled People', which defines disability as:[64] 'disadvantage experienced by an individual resulting from barriers to independent living or educational, employment or other opportunities that impact on people with impairments and/or ill health.'[65] This clearly embraces the social model. Does it make that much difference whether or not statutory definitions reflect a particular model or not? One case where there might be a conflict is the case where a potential employer believes incorrectly that an applicant for a job has an impairment. On the face of it the person will not benefit from the DDA, but would from the Cabinet Office definition. It is always possible to tweak the statute to deal with such specific cases, but beyond that the use of the social model in the construction of definitions shows a way of thinking, and much of the project is about changing thinking. A commitment to a coherent programme of change should involve the adoption of appropriate starting definitions, and in 'Disability Studies' the social model supplies them.

Perspective and Method

As with any other area of law, a range of perspectives can be brought to Disability Law. It can and should be addressed by traditional doctrinal

[61] Disability Discrimination Act 1995, s 1 and sch 1.

[62] eg C Barnes, 'What Next? Disability, the 1995 Disability Discrimination Act and the Campaign for Disabled Peoples' Rights' (The Walter Lessing Lecture, 1996).

[63] Disability Discrimination Act 2005, s 18. [64] *COSU.* [65] para 3.1.

legal scholarship. It can be addressed by comparative law methods. The further question is the extent to which Disability Law should be informed by cognate disciplines and approaches to legal scholarship. Disability Studies shares much with areas such as Women's or Gender Studies, Critical Race Studies and Queer Studies, to the extent that a recent article in the *Village Voice* pronounced:

> Anyone who's taken a women's studies class or read Edward Said will be familiar with the terms of the field. The study of disability, like that of gender, race, and sexual orientation, is rooted in bodies perceived as 'other.' All of these disciplines use the language of critical theory.[66]

As for Women's Studies, Gender Studies, Critical Race Studies, Queer Studies, all of which have informed the law curriculum and the way we think about law, we should have regard to the insights that Disability Studies can offer Law, but we should also be careful about pushing the analogy with race, gender, and sexuality too far.

In the second edition of Roger Cotterrell's *Politics of Jurisprudence* there is a chapter entitled 'A Jurisprudence of Difference: class, gender and race'.[67] It deals with feminist jurisprudence and critical race theory and what those things have brought to the study of law, but it does not mention disability. That is no criticism of the book. I look forward to a time when there is more to write about in the area of disability. What can Disability Law learn from the emphases of the 'jurisprudence of difference' in cognate disciplines? I think there are at least four possibilities, only one of which I shall emphasize here.

First, there is work to be done on the corporeal as a site of legal struggle, drawing on work, for example, in Queer Legal Studies that emphasizes bodies rather than the metaphysical self.[68] Secondly, just as elements of autobiography in 'outsider scholarship' are to be seen in the work of critical race theorists like Patricia Williams[69] or Richard Delgado[70] there

[66] R Tuhus-Dubrow, 'Body Politics: The Wheel World: Is Disability Studies Academia's Next Frontier?' *Village Voice*, 2 August 2005.

[67] R Cotterrell, *The Politics of Jurisprudence* (2nd edn) (London: LexisNexis, 2003), 209 ff.

[68] See M Cole, 'In/Ensuring Disability' (2003) 77 *Tulane Law Review* 839, which draws upon Queer Theory to deal with the effect of *Doe v Mutual of Omaha*, and other insurance rules in the USA in driving some disabilities into 'the closet'.

[69] P Williams, *The Alchemy of Race and Rights* (Cambridge, Mass: Harvard University Press, 1991).

[70] R Delgado, 'Storytelling for Oppositionists and Others: A Plea for Narrative' (1989) 87 *Michigan. Law Review* 2411; A M Coughlin, 'Regulating the Self: Autobiographical Performances in Outsider Scholarship' (1993) 81 *Vanderbilt Law Review* 1229; R Delgado, 'Coughlin's Complaint: How to Disparage Outsider Writing, One Year Later' (1996) 82 *Vanderbilt Law Review* 95.

may be a place for the narrative and even the autobiographical. Jenny Morris wrote:

> Disabled people—men and women—have little opportunity to portray our own experiences within the general culture, or within radical political movements. Our experience is isolated, individualised; the definitions which society places on us centre on judgements or individual capacities and personalities. This lack of a voice, of the representation of our subjective reality, means that it is difficult for non-disabled feminists to incorporate our reality into their research and their theories, unless it is in terms of the way the non-disabled world sees us.[71]

The standard objection to be made here is that no matter how fervently the belief is held that only the members of the 'outsider' group really know what it is like, by its very nature the claim is not susceptible to falsification. The epistemological questions arising fall outside the scope of this essay.

Third, one theme that Disability Studies might take from the other fields of the 'jurisprudence of difference' is identity politics. Again, this needs to be approached with care. I am sceptical when people use expressions like 'celebration of identity'[72] in the context of disability.[73] Let us by all means explore the analogies with race, gender, sexuality, and so on, but still be aware that, as Tom Shakespeare wrote: '... the analogy between disability and gender/race/sexuality can be misleading. Disability may be more like poverty: not an identity to be celebrated.'[74] That is, impairments that detrimentally affect mobility or senses are more like an absence than a difference. Celebrating them is more like celebrating the difference between rich and poor than between gay and straight. The overwhelming preponderance of people with impairments would rather not have them. So let us not celebrate them as part of a diversity we treasure.[75] Let us celebrate where appropriate the individuals who have those impairments, but 'Black is beautiful' and 'Glad to be Gay' may have no direct equivalent in disability, and we should not strive artificially to generate one.[76]

71 J Morris, *Pride Against Prejudice: Transforming Attitudes to Disability* (London: The Women's Press, 1991), 8.

72 Sandra Fredman uses this expression in Lawson and Gooding, n 17 above, 214.

73 *From Exclusion to Inclusion* (London: Disability Rights Task Force, December 1999). See also the Government's response in *Towards Inclusion—Civil Rights for Disabled People*, Department for Education and Employment, March 2001.

74 Correspondence to the author. Shakespeare criticizes a branch of the British Disability movement that is sceptical about attempts to prevent or treat impairments.

75 Consequently, I am dubious about the effort of the Strategy Unit (*COSU*, 22) to embrace the 'diversity' approach to equality.

76 See also Wendell, n 58 above.

The final insight of the 'jurisprudence of difference' is to the 'neutrality' of laws, rules, and legal practices. Much feminist jurisprudence is directed to show that rules which, when abstracted from their context, appear neutral and impartial, in fact comprehend a history and a social context such that; 'When [the law] is most ruthlessly neutral, it will be most male; when it is most sex blind, it will be most blind to the sex of the standard being applied'.[77] Just as writers have demonstrated, for example, the gendered nature of the notion of reasonableness in the law of negligence,[78] or the 'excited utterance' rule in evidence,[79] so too the 'neutral' rule can frequently be shown adversely to affect people with disabilities. The search that has been conducted in feminist jurisprudence for 'gendered' concepts and rules is one that could easily be carried into disability law to seek 'disabling' laws. On this account, law is one of the things that establish the barriers to which the social model of disability draws attention.

In a search for 'disabling' laws, a starting point could be many 'reasonableness' requirements. Anna Lawson[80] draws attention to a neat example provided by the Scottish servitudes case of *Drury v McGarvie*.[81] The traditional view of rights over the land of another is that they impinge only to the minimum extent necessary upon the property over which they are held.[82] In this case the pursuers were an elderly couple with some impairments access to whose cottage was by a right of way over the field. It could only be exercised by opening and closing a gate that the farmer had installed. The couple averred that it was high and difficult to reach, and that their inability to open it rendered them virtual prisoners in their own cottage. In the Inner House of the Court of Session, the Lord President (Lord Hope) reasoned by analogy to stiles:

That some inconvenience is permissible without constituting an obstruction in the sense required for its removal is clear in the case of stiles. A stile must be climbed if the person who uses the way is to get over it. This may be inconvenient,

[77] C MacKinnon, 'Feminism, Marxism, Method, and the State: Toward Feminist Jurisprudence' (1983) 8 *Signs* 635, 658.

[78] M Moran, *Rethinking the Reasonable Person: An Egalitarian Reconstruction of the Objective Standard* (Oxford: Oxford University Press, 2003), 199; C A Forell and D M Matthews, *A Law of her Own: The Reasonable Woman as a Measure of Man* (New York: New York University Press, 2001).

[79] A Orenstein, ' "My God!": A Feminist Critique of the Excited Utterance Exception to the Hearsay Rule' (1997) 85 *California Law Review* 159.

[80] A Lawson, 'How the Law of Property creates Disability' in A Hudson (ed), *New Perspectives on Property Law, Human Rights and the Home* (London: Cavendish Publishing, 2004), 92, 120.

[81] *Drury v McGarvie* (1993) SC 95, 1993 SLT 987.

[82] The position in English law is apparently not so clear. See Lawson, n 80 above.

but the authorities show clearly that if the stile can be crossed by a person of normal physique and agility it does not amount to an obstruction of the right of way.[83]

So in determining whether the gate constituted a violation of the right of way, the court was not entitled to have regard to the pursuer's disability.[84]

Another example is the US case of *Doe v Mutual of Omaha Insurance*, which has significantly detracted from the value to disabled people of the Americans with Disabilities Act.[85] The plaintiff, who had HIV, challenged AIDS caps or limits on the amount of money that would be payable in respect of HIV and AIDS, that Mutual of Omaha had imposed on its health insurance policies. The company did not try to justify this by reference to actuarial principle, but simply said that it did not offer policies without AIDS caps and that that failure was simply a market-focused decision, rather than a failure to make reasonable accommodations for disabled people. The Federal Court of Appeals for the Seventh Circuit, with the lead judgment by Chief Judge Posner, held for the insurer, relying on the distinction between access to a service and the content of the service. He said that the insurer had to take steps to ensure that disabled people had access to the products they supply, but that they had no obligation to change the product. He used the analogy of the camera shop: a camera shop has an obligation, he said, to provide access to disabled people to any camera that it sells, but it does not have an obligation to provide modified cameras. A healthcare policy without an AIDS cap was like a unmodified camera. This has been the subject of criticism.[86] If the product is defined sufficiently narrowly to include the cap then the Act does not apply. However, the product could be defined more broadly as healthcare insurance, in which case it would not. Take, for example, the case of the obese airline passenger. If the airline is able to say: 'the content of what we provide is travel in seats of whatever width: if that is of no value to you, then don't buy it', then the ADA is seriously diminished in effect. The 'access/content' distinction is 'disabling'.[87]

[83] 1993 SC 102.

[84] Lawson, n 80 above, suggests the adoption of a test of the strength and agility of the average 70 year old would at least help, but that seems inconsistent with the idea that the obligation of the owner of the servient property should be fixed.

[85] *Doe v Mutual of Omaha Insurance Co* 179 F 3d 557 (1999). The Americans with Disabilities Act (42 USC 12101–12213 and 47 USC 225) was enacted in 1990 and is the high-water mark both for group interest theory of disability rights, and for the idea that the conferment of individual rights, without corresponding adjustments in the welfare system, is the best way to deal with disability claims.

[86] eg S R Bagenstos, 'The Future Of Disability Law' (2004) 114 *Yale Law Journal* 1, 45 ff.

[87] See Cole, n 68 above.

Further rules that impact differentially upon disabled people may be found in the identity cards legislation.[88] There will be those, Abu Hamza being one,[89] without fingertips and iris to provide the biodata. Then there will be those, whether because of aural or visual or cognitive impairment, to whom it is difficult to communicate the instructions to produce the card. There will also be those for whom it is difficult to actually produce the card on demand. These issues can be dealt with in the controlled circumstances of the immigration hall, but on the street the position will be different. The UK Passport Service Biometric enrolment trial had 750 or more disabled subjects. This group did significantly worse than the control in enrolling their biometrics, both in terms of accuracy and time taken to attempt enrolment and verification.[90] These problems relate only to enrolment. Use will be more difficult. Examples can be multiplied, but the point is simply that a significant task for disability law is to interrogate rules and their applications for disabling aspects, and that in doing this it should draw upon the other strands of the 'jurisprudence of difference'.

The Nature of the Claims Made by Disabled People

The history of political activism by disabled people is a history of rights being fought for, claimed, and exercised. In those struggles welfarism, leaving it to the State, was the enemy. It is easy to see why a welfarist perspective can cause irritation to people with disabilities:

> It is the agency of welfare, not the recipient, who decides what life goals are to be followed, what ambitions are to be entertained, what services are appropriate, what wants are to be recognised, what needs may be budgeted and what funds allocated to each. In short, the recipient is told what he wants as well as how much he is wanting.[91]

Rejecting welfarism from the 1960s forward, disability rights activists sought 'rights not charity'. They regarded the latter as paternalistic,

[88] Identity Cards Bill, before Parliament at the time of writing.

[89] Convicted of incitement to racial hatred and incitement to murder in February 2006. Throughout the pre-trial period popular newspaper coverage of the defendant concentrated much attention upon his prosthesis. Terminology such as 'Hook handed hate cleric . . . '. was typical. See T Worden and C Rae, 'A Cancer on the Name of Islam', the *Sun*, 4 May 2003.

[90] UK Passport Service, 'Biometrics Enrolment Trial Report', May 2005, 8–9, at <http://www.passport.gov.uk/downloads/UKPSBiometrics_Enrolment_Trial_Report.pdf>.

[91] J tenBroek and F Matson, 'The Disabled and the Law of Welfare' (1966) 54 *Southern California Law Review* 809, 831.

oppressive, and arbitrary. Broadly speaking, the complaint was that welfare is a legitimation strategy to 'buy off' disabled people. '... [S]uperficial indications of sympathy, and even pity, for the plight of disabled persons frequently conceal a deeper sense of discomfort and resistance that has perpetuated [their] segregation and inequality.'[92] So the major claim of the activists was for rights for people with disabilities.[93] This political focus has achieved much and we should applaud those involved. There is, however, a limited position deriving from the historical provenance of the movement for disability rights, that the achievement and exercise of individual rights is the only way forward. 'Nothing about us without us' as a political slogan has the legal corollary that conferring rights upon disabled people is the only solution. The Government's view was that 'change depends upon disadvantaged people enforcing their rights, rather than on bodies [ie the bodies that are regulated] ensuring that they meet their responsibilities'.[94] The 'rights-based' approach is also central to the EU's Action Plan.[95] In this section I shall contest that claim.

Sandra Fredman identifies three ways, in legal and political discourse, of making 'rights' arguments for disabled people.[96] The first is to deal in terms of individual rights, in this case a claim to equal treatment. On this account, equal opportunities provisions are means of ruling out irrelevant difference, and disability, just as much as race or gender, is sometimes an irrelevant difference. We should not forget the relatively recent time when this kind of discrimination, denying equal access, was commonplace. The formal equality claim is, however, limited, in that frequently disability is a relevant difference and the question will be how fairly to deal with it. Disability discrimination claims challenge the assumption made in the other 'other' cases that a fairly limited formal notion of equality is sufficient. While it is relatively easy to work out what equality would mean in cases of discrimination on the basis of gender, sex sexuality, race, or age, because people want the same thing as the comparator, the claimant in disability cases usually wants something different. The role of the

[92] H Hahn, 'Antidiscrimination Law and Social Research on Disability: The Minority Group Perspective' (1996) 14 *Behavioural Science and Law* 41, 43.

[93] See also L Waddington, 'Evolving Disability Policies: From Social-Welfare to Human Rights: An International Trend from a European Perspective' (2001) 19 *Netherlands Quarterly of Human Rights* 141.

[94] Department of Work and Pensions, *Delivering Equality for Disabled People* (Cm 6255, 2004), para 3.2.

[95] European Action Plan, n 17 above; and see Framework Equal Treatment Directive (2000/78/EC). The right to be consulted in advance about the standards to be applied is recognized in the EU approach. D Mabbett, 'The Development of Rights Based Social Policy in the European Union: The Example of Disability Rights' (2005) 43 *Journal of Common Market Studies* 97.

[96] Fredman in Lawson and Gooding, n 17 above, 206.

comparator, if any, is diminished in disability law.[97] In *Archibald v Fife Council*, the only case in which the House of Lords has considered the Disability Discrimination Act, Baroness Hale said:

[In the cases of the SDA and RRA] men and women or black and white, as the case may be, are opposite sides of the same coin. Each is to be treated in the same way. Treating men more favourably than women discriminates against women. Treating women more favourably than men discriminates against men. Pregnancy apart, the differences between the genders are generally regarded as irrelevant. The 1995 Act, however, does not regard the differences between disabled people and others as irrelevant. It does not expect each to be treated in the same way. It expects reasonable adjustments to be made to cater for the special needs of disabled people. It necessarily entails an element of more favourable treatment. The question . . . is when that obligation arises and how far it goes.[98]

The second way of characterizing disability rights is as a set of minority group rights. An individual aggrieved person may be saying: 'I, and those like me, are detrimentally affected in particular ways because of the way in which such-and-such a thing impacts upon us'. It might be a claim to parking spaces, hearing loops, to the exclusion from educational assessment procedures or from employment appointing procedures of criteria that impact differentially upon people with particular impairments, or one of a multitude of other things. The minority group analysis has been enormously fruitful politically, yet it is strange to see it embedded in a legal text.[99] Fixing it in its epoch, however, the preamble to the Americans with Disabilities Act 1990 states:

. . . individuals with disabilities are a discrete and insular minority who have been faced with restrictions and limitations, subjected to a history of purposeful unequal treatment, and relegated to a position of political powerlessness in our society, based on characteristics that are beyond the control of such individuals and resulting from stereotypic assumptions not truly indicative of the individual ability of such individuals to participate in, and contribute to, society.[100]

The question remains whether there is really much in common between the experience of a wheelchair user, someone with a visual impairment, and someone with chronic depression, or between people with visible

[97] However, see Disability Discrimination Act 1995, s 3A (inserted by the Disability Discrimination Act 1995 (Amendment) Regulations (SI 2003/1673), Pt 2, Reg 4(2)), which does cover indirect discrimination.

[98] *Archibald v Fife* [2004] UKHL 32, [47], [2004] 4 All ER 303.

[99] Sandra Fredman probably overstates the case when she says that all developments have come through that approach. See Fredman in Lawson and Gooding, n 17 above, 206,

[100] Americans with Disabilities Act 1990, 42 USC 12101–12213 and 47 USC 225.

disabilities such as facial disfigurement and invisible disabilities such as diabetes. These groups cannot easily be aggregated into anything a Marxian might take to resemble a class. Even if they could, it would not mandate the ADA position. It need not follow from the fact that mobilizing people in groups has been politically successful that enforcement need be done by groups, or by disabled people at all.

Arising, then, from doubts over the groups analysis, the third way of thinking about the political claims of disabled people is to portray a universal, to say that disability is not, as the ADA has it, 'discrete and insular', but part of normalcy. This is a position developed by Irving Zola.[101] The idea is that 'disability policy is not policy for some minority group, it is policy for all'.[102] The UN ad hoc Committee on the Rights of Persons with Disabilities said 'disability is a normal aspect of life'.[103] Lawson takes up this universalist theme, quoting Bickenbach: 'Eventually . . . we shall all joyously realise that we are all abnormal, disabled, impaired, deformed and functionally limited, because truth be told, that is what it means to be a human being.'[104] This is the complete reversal of the medical model. It reconfigures the normal rather than attempting to reconfigure the disabled person. In this context, a system of universal 'rights' need not mean more than a system of universal minimum standards. There are many areas of disability law where the optimal way in which to proceed is by the imposition of such standards. In those areas, contrary to the Strategy Unit's claim, change should not 'depend upon disadvantaged people enforcing their rights, rather than on bodies ensuring that they meet their responsibilities'.[105] Change depends upon decent standards being agreed and enforced. What is of critical importance, both politically and practically, is that disabled people should play a central role in the formulation of these standards. The identity of the enforcer does not matter so much.

This is a microcosm of a more general debate that arises in many fields as to rights and regulation; whether desirable objectives such as access to

[101] I K Zola, 'Towards the Necessary Universalising of a Disability Policy' (1989) 67 (Supp 2, Pt 2) *Millbank Quarterly* 401.

[102] J E Bickenbach, S Chatterji, E M Badley, and T B Uestuen, 'Models of Disablement, Universalism and the International Classification of Impairments, Disabilities and Handicaps' (1999) 48 *Social Science and Medicine* 1173, 1182.

[103] Fredman in Lawson and Gooding, n 17 above, 207.

[104] A Lawson, 'How the Law of Property Creates Disability' in A Hudson (ed), *New Perspectives on Property Law, Human Rights and the Home* (London: Cavendish Publishing, 2004), 92, 120, citing J E Bickenbach, 'Minority Rights or Universal Participation: The Politics of Disablement' in M Jones and L A Brasser-Marks (eds), *Disability, Divers-ability and Legal Change* (Leiden: Nijhoff, 1999), ch 7.

[105] Department of Work and Pensions, n 2 above, para 3.2.

public transport or housing can be better secured by conferring rights on individuals or groups or everybody or whether some other regulatory scheme should operate. My general claim is that neither the government nor the disability rights movement should be inflexibly wedded to the empowerment of individual disabled people by granting them rights but rather that they should pragmatically adopt whatever course works best.

Take two concrete examples, decided by the Court of Appeal in 2004. In *Roads v Central Trains*,[106] the plaintiff wheelchair user wanted to travel from Norwich to Thetford by train and then, apparently, get the train straight back. There is a footbridge at Thetford Station, but the only other way round is about 800 metres long and involved a busy road with no footpath. The plaintiff claimed to be the victim of discrimination.[107] There was at the relevant time no suitably adapted taxi in Thetford. A taxi from Norwich would have cost £45. The plaintiff was also offered free rail travel on to Ely, where there is an elevator, and back for no charge, but at the cost of an extra hour on trains. For some unknown reason[108] the station owner conceded that the cost of getting the taxi to come from Norwich was not to be taken into account,[109] so the case was argued on the bizarre assumption that a taxi from Norwich would have cost nothing. On that basis, the court had to say that it was unreasonable and consequently discriminatory not to supply the taxi, but made it clear that if the taxi fare had been taken into account, the position would probably have been different.[110]

In *Ross v Ryanair & Stansted Airport*[111] the plaintiff objected to Ryanair trying to get him charged for use of wheelchairs at Stansted Airport. Both Ryanair and the airport were the suppliers of a service, the airport, the

[106] *Roads v Central Trains* [2004] EWCA Civ 1541.

[107] Although there was no general duty under the Disability Discrimination Act 1995 to provide accessible trains, the effect of section 21 is that reasonable steps must be taken to provide a reasonable means of avoiding a feature (in this case the footbridge), or to provide a reasonable alternative method of making the service in question accessible. It was not explained why one would want to do what the plaintiff said he was being denied access to do, ie arrive at Thetford and then just get a train back. One suggestion is that the passenger might have gone to sleep and missed the previous station, but then he would not have been in a position to give the sort of notice that would make the claim to a taxi make sense.

[108] See n 106 above, Sedley LJ (9–10).

[109] It could have been under the relevant Code of Practice.

[110] The case is of some importance for the interpretation of the Act. Sedley LJ adopted a statement by Mynors Ch in *Re Holy Cross, Pershore* [2002] Fam 1 (Cons Ct) [32], [2001] 3 WLR 1521: '... [T]he policy of the [1995 Act] is not a minimalist policy of simply ensuring that some access is available to the disabled: it is so far as reasonably practicable, to approximate the access enjoyed by disabled persons to that enjoyed by the rest of the public'.

[111] *Ross v Ryanair and Stansted Airport* [2004] EWCA Civ 1751, [2005] 1 WLR 2447.

shopping mall, Stansted because they owned and licensed it, Ryanair because it issued the boarding passes.[112] Ryanair's original position was that if a person did not own a wheelchair and bring it to the airport, then he could not really say that he needed it at an airport. Ryanair did eventually concede that there are people who normally use sticks or crutches but might need a wheelchair at airports because of the distance involved, but then tried to place the responsibility on the airport.[113]

Both plaintiffs were successful. As to the substance of the cases, it is far less important that the owners of Thetford station have to provide a taxi to take wheelchair users from the east to the westbound platform than that wheelchairs should be provided at no cost at airports for people who have good reason to require one. As it happens, each of these cases was resolved within a framework of individual anti-discrimination rights. But each case could have been dealt with as a regulatory matter. There could be a set of binding rules about facilities at stations and at airports for people with disabilities[114] and there could be an inspector charged with their enforcement, and if such a system worked, it would probably be more effective than bringing DDA actions. Whether or not Central Trains have to supply the taxi service at Thetford should not depend upon the serendipity of the appearance of the individual aggrieved wheelchair user, but upon nationally applicable standards. There are enough wheelchair users that questions relating to wheelchair access at stations and airports and even beaches[115] ought not to be dealt with on a case-by case basis. Today it is not patronizing or offensive to put in place general regulations dealing with those issues and to expect someone else to enforce them. The disability rights movement should be mature enough to welcome that. It is a quite unnecessary imposition to expect a disabled person to become aggrieved and to bring proceedings.

I suggest that effective regulation within a paradigm of disability as normalcy is the best mechanism for securing accessible public transport. Public Transport was, in effect, exempted from the Disability Discrimination Act 1995.[116] Public transport was said by the Strategy

[112] See n 10 above, s 19(2)(b).

[113] The reason wheelchairs users avoid queues at airports is not that the person in the wheelchair is granted priority. It is because that is the only way the people who push the chairs can do their jobs.

[114] There are voluntary codes of practice and non-binding international agreements about airports. See *Ross* above, [2004] EWCA Civ 1751 [15–16].

[115] *Botta v Italy* [1998] ECHR 12, [1998] IIHRL 14.

[116] See n 10 above, s 19(5). Neither *Roads* nor *Ross* are cases about access to transport *per se*. *Ross* is about the provision of access to services at the airport shopping mall. *Roads* is about the Disability Discrimination Act 1995, s 19.

Unit to be the principal challenge identified by disabled people,[117] and the Scrutiny Committee referred to the effect of inaccessible public transport upon employment rates of disabled people.[118] It would have been possible to do something about the accessibility of taxis, buses, trains, and the London Underground by saying that from a given date they were fully subject to the DDA and obliged not to discriminate and obliged to accommodate. The early litigation would have dealt with the question of justification, and it would have led, for example, to lists of stations at which it was justifiable and those at which it was not, for the company operating the railway or the underground to deny access to people with each of a long list of impairments. In fact, the mechanism by which the DDA is to be extended to public transport is to be by giving the Secretary of State for Transport the power to extend Part 3 of the DDA to cover public transport and then rather complex manipulation of exceptions[119] and differential compliance dates as between various sectors of the Transport industry, ultimately leading to compliance notices and administrative fines.[120] In other words, the decision to move over a long period to step-free access to trains is to be implemented by classic regulatory means. In addition to step-free access, tactile markings, guidance systems for visually impaired people, and induction loops at ticket offices are being installed.[121] This is neither patronizing nor disempowering: it works.

There are other areas in which regulation can work. Among the most significant sets of rules for many disabled people are the rules laying down standards for the built and unbuilt environment. Physical geography—handrails, ramps, lifts, tactile markings, and so on matter a great deal. So far as public space is concerned, none of these matters is best dealt with by waiting for individual litigants. There is a range of Acts of Parliament, Statutory Instruments, British standards, DRC Guidelines, Building Regulations, and Codes of Practice dealing with the built environment. For example, from 1 May 2004 Part M of the Building Regulations was amended to provide that taps in public lavatories should be operated by levers and not spindles, and since 2002 the cubicle size for wheelchair accessible lavatories has been required to be 2200 mm, 10 per cent longer than before.[122] The fact that this has nothing to do with discrimination legislation or litigation does not make it any less disability law.

[117] *COSU*, Executive Summary.

[118] Lord Carter, n 20 above, para 122.

[119] See also House of Commons Transport Committee, *Disabled Person's Access to Transport* (6th Report Session 2003–4 HC 439).

[120] See DDA, s 5.

[121] See the Transport for London website at <http://www.londontransport.co.uk/tfl/ph_underground.shtml>.

[122] BS 8300 (2002) superseding BS 5810 (1956).

The arguments for a rights-based approach[123] to the treatment of people with disabilities are more to do with the politics and the rhetoric than with the immediate practical effect it has. It is said to be valuable that Roads and Ross, disabled persons themselves, are the instruments of the change they bring about and valuable that they be seen to be bringing it about. At some points in the struggle for equality, visible standard bearers are valuable. This, it is suggested, is not that point. The benefits claimed for the regulatory approach are that it does not wait for a breach before reacting[124] but puts the standard in place at the outset clearly and in the necessary detail; that it is universal as it applies to all stations, airports, and so on without waiting for the particular detrimentally affected person to come forward; that it is cheaper; and that it is clearer and more consistent and more effective. Moreover, reliance upon an individual aggrieved will always favour the vocal and the articulate and will not be so helpful to those with intellectual impairments. In short, the advantages are the advantages of legislation over case law.

It might be argued that if we use universal *minima* for our standards, then there is a danger that the *minima* will prove too low. The answer to that is that in the provision of transport there ought not to be a difference between the standard that is required by a court in a case such as *Roads*, having regard to the test laid down by the DDA, and the standard that would be chosen by a properly conducted legislative exercise. The regulatory approach has benefits in the economics of disability.

So is a 'rights-based approach' that important? Is it still necessarily central to a strategy for the empowerment of people with disabilities?[125] I suggest it is not. We should not be doctrinaire: whatever works. The political significance of claiming rights and the direct involvement of organizations of disabled people[126] ought not to conceal from us the practical benefits of regulation, in particular the specificity of the rules and the relatively low costs of enforcement. If a justification needs to be advanced for this in political theory it would be by reference to a social justice theory. Behind a Rawlsian veil of ignorance, we would agree that taps in

[123] See Mabbett, n 17 above, 98: 'From this perspective, rights may be transmitted or implemented through two main processes: judicial processes which utilize the hierarchy of the legal system to create a consistent interpretation of rights, and programmatic processes in which rights express goals which political actors at different levels (primarily the national level) agree to pursue. In both senses, rights can be seen as establishing foundational standards with which the Member States are expected to comply.'

[124] This is one of the evils that Colm O'Cinneide finds in the current voluntary schemes. See C O'Cinneide, 'A New Generation of Equality Legislation? Positive Duties and Disability Rights' in Lawson and Goodman, n 17 above, 221–4.

[125] See also Lawson, n 59 above.

[126] ibid 277 ff.

public lavatories should be operated by levers not spindles, and that access to trains should be step-free.[127] Indeed, the Strategy Unit gives social justice as its principal reason for the strategy it advocates.

Social justice requires the government to take steps to extend opportunities, choice, and empowerment for disabled people, to promote diversity and improve standards of living for all.[128] That does not mean there is no place for the claims by individuals, particularly individuals asking for specific accommodations within the context of employment. It does mean, however, that there are some areas of disability law, especially relating to public transport, where regulation works best, so long as the regulations are well informed by the needs of disabled people. They can be empowering. This can be accomplished by putting in place mechanisms under which regulation is done in a manner that is properly responsive to their needs. That is to be supplied in the duty to promote equality, to be considered later.

The Economics of Disability

This essay has suggested that disability law should be considered more broadly than as a species of anti-discrimination law. An holistic view of disability law also requires consideration of the economics of disability. Discourse confined to rights, or regulation, can obscure difficult economic realities:

> Anyone who thinks that there is an easy way of achieving a sensible, workable and fair balance between the different interests of disabled persons, of employers and of able-bodied workers, in harmony with the wider public interests in an economically efficient workforce, in access to employment, in equal treatment of workers and in standards of fairness at work, has probably not given much serious thought to the problem.[129]

Many disabilities adversely affect the economic status of the people affected. Impairments may, for example, take them out of the labour market, reduce their power within it, or compel expenditure that would not otherwise be incurred, whether in the context of employment or otherwise. There is in place a complex system of benefits, concessions,

[127] Similar conclusions will follow from the adoption of a communitarian perspective, eg see C A Ball, 'Looking for Theory in All the Right Places: Feminist And Communitarian Elements of Disability Discrimination Law' (2005) 66 *Ohio State Law Journal* 105.
[128] *COSU*, Executive Summary.
[129] *Clark v Novacold Ltd* [1999] EWCA Civ 1091 (Mummery LJ), [1999] ICR 951.

and tax breaks available to people with disabilities.[130] Some benefits are subject to means testing, and some are not.[131] Much of the law is highly technical, and the distinctions the law makes can appear disabling.[132] Even if the benefits have clear objectives, it is impossible perfectly to assess and meet the needs of every person affected. The usual kinds of arguments about targeting, means testing, and intrusiveness apply.[133]

The Strategy Unit policy on jobs is extremely ambitious: 'Future government policy should be designed to ensure that in twenty years time any disabled person who wants a job and needs support to get and keep a job anywhere in the country should, wherever possible, be able to do so'.[134] Achievement of this objective will require significant investment. Of the three justifications for government involvement given by the Strategy Unit for state intervention in the area of the treatment of disabled people the two economic reasons[135] given for trying to improve the lot of disabled people are: net benefits to the economy, widening the skills base and an increase in productivity; and increased tax revenues and lower spending on incapacity benefits.[136] As to the first, it is clear that there will be benefits to the economy from the widening of the skills base and an increase in productivity, but whether or not they are net benefits depends upon how much it costs to bring about that widening. There is no reliable information upon which to make the decision. It is also evident that for every disabled person in employment who would otherwise be receiving benefit, there will be increased tax revenues and reduced expenditure on incapacity benefits,[137] if this could be accomplished at no cost. However, whether it is a net benefit will turn on how much it would cost, and what it will cost depends upon the other effects of securing a job for the disabled person.[138] So the economic arguments are weak compared to the social justice argument.

Although economic conditions are now propitious for improving the lot of disabled people, this need not continue. Just as the 1960s were

130 The relevant disabilities are not necessarily the same as those under the Disability Discrimination Act, but the differences do not matter for present purposes.

131 See *Disability Rights Handbook* (30th edn) (London: Disability Alliance, 2005).

132 *eg Moyna v Secretary of State for Work and Pensions* [2003] UKHL 44, [2003] 1 WLR 1929.

133 N Wikeley, 'Social Security and Disability' in Neville Harris (ed), *Social Security Law in Context* (Oxford: Oxford University Press, 2000), 363.

134 *COSU*, Executive Summary. Much hangs on the meaning of 'where possible'. The major limiting criterion of possibility will be the financial resources needed.

135 The other, and principal reason, was social justice. ibid.

136 ibid.

137 Numbers claiming which have been falling since 1995. ibid, para 2.6.

138 See ibid, para 3.6 ff, for a more detailed account of how the Strategy Unit proposes to pay.

a good time for proponents of legislation on abortion and family planning,[139] because those legislative steps had the effect of increasing the number of women in the workforce at a time of full employment, so now is a time of relatively full employment. If the additional costs involved in getting disabled people into the workforce were to include the costs of making someone else unemployed, then the calculation would alter radically. The Government initiatives in respect of those on incapacity benefit,[140] alarming though they are to many disabled people, will, if successful, have the effect of increasing the labour force and probably would not be occurring if unemployment were higher.[141] To assume that there will be few or no costs incurred in the implementation of the Cabinet Office prescription would be naïve. In principle, how ought the costs to be allocated? The three distinct ways outlined above to make the claims for disabled people might generate different conclusions as to the power of the claim and also as to where the associated burdens are to fall.

So far as employment is concerned, which is the critical case, there are three obvious sources of resources to pay for the additional costs involved in the implementation of the Cabinet Office plan. The costs might be imposed upon the disabled person or the employer and hence his customer, or the taxpayer. A program genuinely directed towards social justice would not impose the costs on individual disabled people. Anti-discrimination legislation interferes with freedom of contract and the market.[142] In the case of discrimination on the basis of race the interference is such that we are happy to compel the employer to bear the costs. Even if the market would allow an employer to pay one group of workers more than another on racial grounds, or men more than women who do the same work, we all agree that the employer should not be allowed to do that and that he should bear the costs. The only significant cases where there might be extra costs is the case of maternity leave, and here, to some extent, the State pays.[143] In the case of disability, the moral responsibility of the employer is not so clear. If there is any cost following from a failure in respect of the formal equality right, the employer should be fixed with it. Disabled people should not be used as cheap labour and there should be no blanket bans on disabled people.

[139] J Clarke, *National Deviancy Conference: Permissiveness and Control* (London: Macmillan, 1980).

[140] *COSU*, ch 7.

[141] Department for Works and Pensions, Green Paper, *A New Deal for Welfare: Empowering People to Work* (Cm 6730, January 2006).

[142] M Kelman, 'Market Discrimination and Groups' (2001) 53 *Stanford Law Review* 833.

[143] See Fredman in Lawson and Gooding, n 17 above, 208–10.

Costs following from the way in which the workplace environment is regulated, the 'universal rights', will not be additional costs. A workplace should have a minimum level of accessibility whether or not there are disabled employees. These costs should not necessarily lead to any commercial advantage or disadvantage as against competitors.[144] The problem case is the costs following from the equality as fairness claims. This is the case where it would seem to cost an employer more to employ a person with a disability than one without. The employer might legitimately say: 'If I have to employ this person, then, because of his impairment, I would have to pay more to get them to do their job, and that would endanger my market position. I might, for example, have to modify buildings to accommodate wheelchairs or employ readers for a visually impaired worker'.[145] The Framework Equal Treatment Directive clearly permits the financial position of the employer 'unless such measures would place a disproportionate burden upon [it]'.[146] There is really no principled approach to the allocation of burdens in this area. It should be shared between the State and the employer or service provider, in such a way as to be broadly acceptable. Access to Work[147] is a programme of State intervention designed to fill in those, albeit limited, cases to which it applies. This gives the following allocation of legal activity and burdens.

		Political Claim	Legal Claim	Who pays?
1.	Formal equality: 'Disabled people should be granted (identical) access or pay or other benefits.'	Individual discrimination	Individual discrimination	Discriminator
2.	Fairness claims: 'I, and those like me, are detrimentally affected...' Grant disabled people equivalent access.	Group discrimination	Individual discrimination (*Roads*, *Ross*)	Burden allocated between enterprise and State
3.	Claims about universals: '... disability policy is not policy for some minority group, it is policy for all'. All workplaces should have wheelchair ramps, accessible lavatories.	Universalized policy	Enforcing obligations laid down in regulation	Regulated body

[144] Save to the extent that regulation tends to favour larger enterprises who can deal with it with economies of scale not available to smaller companies.

[145] Employers typically overestimate the costs of workplace adjustments. See *COSU*, 139.

[146] Framework Equal Treatment Directive (2000/78/EC), Art 5, paras 20–1.

[147] Hereafter 'AtW'.

Under the DWP plan, AtW[148] is to be reformed so that the support is more effective and targeted. Much of this will simply take the form of better organization. For example, movable equipment such as IT support will under the reformed scheme follow the employee so that new applications will not need to be made upon a change of jobs. Under the general duty to promote equality, AtW funding will at some point be withdrawn from authorities who are subject to the duty, on the grounds that the infrastructure questions should have been resolved already and the public authorities and bodies exercising functions of a public nature should build that into their own costs.[149] The idea is that more AtW money can then be deployed into small and medium-sized private sector businesses. So if there are alterations to infrastructure that large public sector bodies need to get done, now is the time. The deployment of AtW resources away from the public towards the private sector forms part of the Strategy Unit's response to the concern that the public sector might become the repository of disabled people in work. The whole enterprise depends upon assumptions as to how it will work out in practice that should be monitored closely,[150] but in principle, this is to be welcomed.

The Government initiative as to Incapacity Benefit[151] raises matters of considerable sensitivity. Nonetheless, if work is to be changed so that more people with impairments are able to take part in it, it will follow that fewer people are unable to work, and that numbers claiming Incapacity Benefit should fall. Legislation to introduce the 'employment and support allowance' is included in the Welfare Reform Bill, introduced into Parliament in July 2006.[152] What is not to be welcomed is the rhetoric, during the period in which the changes to Incapacity Benefit were announced, of 'crackdowns'[153] on benefit fraud. Rates of benefit fraud are at an historical low.[154] If the government wants more disabled people to have jobs, then this could be achieved without raising the spectres of scrounging and fraud.

[148] *COSU*, para 7.4. [149] *COSU*, paras 7.3–7.4. [150] See n 22 above.

[151] The plan is to replace incapacity benefit with an 'Employment and Support Allowance' (ESA), the new name indicating that there will be efforts to help those on incapacity benefit to find work. Claimants will be split into two groups, those deemed permanently incapable of work and those capable of work with help. The latter will be pressed to undertake work-focused interviews, or face benefit cuts. The gateway to the benefit will be tightened, with central monitoring of sick notes by GPs. See Department of Works and Pensions, Green Paper, n 141 above. [152] Bill 208.

[153] P Hennessy, 'Doctors Told to Clamp Down on Sick Notes' *Daily Telegraph*, 22 January 2006.

[154] D Hencke, '£500m Saved in Benefits Fraud Crackdown' the *Guardian*, 8 March 2005.

The Duty to Promote Equality

One major innovation in the Disability Discrimination Act 2005 is the imposition of a positive duty on public authorities to promote equality. This is the analogy in disability discrimination law to the duty in respect of race equality, introduced by the Race Relations (Amendment) Act 2000.[155] If the target of the first was institutional racism,[156] the target of the second is institutional discrimination against disabled people. The idea is mainstreaming by proactive and compulsory means, forcing public authorities to think about disability.[157] Fredman claims that this sort of duty: '. . . potentially bridges the gap between the two traditional approaches to tackling inequality: the legal strategy, via anti-discrimination legislation, and the social welfare strategy, which is sometimes seen as patronising and disempowering'.[158] Under the Disability Discrimination Act 1995 section 49B,[159] a general duty is to be placed upon a public authority in carrying out its functions:[160]

> 1) Every public authority shall in carrying out its functions have due regard to-
>   (a) the need to eliminate discrimination that is unlawful under this Act;
>   (b) the need to eliminate harassment of disabled persons that is related to their disabilities;
>   (c) the need to promote equality of opportunity between disabled persons and other persons;
>   (d) the need to take steps to take account of disabled persons' disabilities, even where that involves treating disabled persons more favourably than other persons;
>   (e) the need to promote positive attitudes towards disabled persons; and
>   (f) the need to encourage participation by disabled persons in public life.

155 Commission for Racial Equality, *Towards Race Equality: An Evaluation of the Public Duty to Promote Race Equality and Good Race Relations in England and Wales* (London: CRE, 2003). See also Audit Commission, *The Journey to Race Equality: Delivering Improved Services to Local Communities* (London: Audit Commission, 2004).

156 W MacPherson, *The Stephen Lawrence Enquiry* (London: The Stationery Office, 1999).

157 L Barnes and S Ashtiany, 'The Diversity Approach to Achieving Equality' (2003) 32 *Industrial Law Journal* 274.

158 Fredman in Lawson and Gooding, n 17 above, 214. This paper suggests that in some areas at least there is no such dichotomy as is suggested: regulation runs between.

159 Inserted by Disability Discrimination Act 2005, s 3.

160 ibid, see s 49B(1)(a) ' "public authority"—(a) includes any person certain of whose functions are functions of a public nature'.

The duty was the subject of specific pre-legislative consultation[161] and is now the subject of a Code of Practice, published by the Disability Rights Commission[162] that will come into force late in 2006. The 'duty to promote' that kind of approach has strong support among theorists of equality.[163]

There is a list of public authorities subject to general and specific duties.[164] All functions of public authorities[165] are under consideration: for example, in policing, the exercise of powers of arrest, detention, stop and search, in granting licences, so that a licensing authority might, in the exercise of its powers under the Licensing Act 2003,[166] have regard to the accessibility of the premises, in the publication of reports and in the conduct of prison and probation services. In the making of planning decisions, for example, when giving permission to build housing units with limited parking, regard will have to be had to disabled parking. There is also an anticipatory duty of reasonable adjustment on a public authority.[167] This is more proactive than the duty on employers generally, but it is not likely to make much difference to the authorities to whom it applies because they will generally have been obliged to put the measures in place anyway. This duty will certainly deal with the question of the station and the airport. The authorities responsible would be obliged to think in advance about the accommodation of disabled people,[168] and it is difficult to see how the obligation would be discharged otherwise than by having in place binding regulations of the nature to which I have referred. There are some exclusions, the most irksome being military recruitment and service.[169]

The advent of this duty will be a positive development in the critical area of employment law. It has been well considered by Colm O'Cinneide.[170] As the Strategy Unit Report and the DWP work both

[161] Department of Work and Pensions, n 2 above.

[162] Disability Rights Commission, *The Duty to Promote Disability Equality* (London: The Stationery Office, 2005).

[163] B Hepple and C Barnard, 'Substantive Equality' (2000) 59 *Cambridge Law Journal* 566.

[164] See Disability Discrimination Act 2005, s 3, inserting s 49A–49F in the Disability Discrimination Act 1995.

[165] Defined in Disability Discrimination Act 1995, s 21B(2)–(3); also, 'functions of a public nature exercised otherwise than by public authorities'.

[166] Licensing Act 2003, ss 5–9.

[167] Disability Discrimination Act 2005, s 21E.

[168] Ryanair performs 'functions of a pubic nature' so would still be covered.

[169] See Disability Discrimination Act 1995, s 49C(3).

[170] C O'Cinneide, 'A New Generation of Equality Legislation? Positive Duties and Disability Rights' in Lawson and Gooding, n 17 above, 219.

recognize, the question of employment is central to any improvement in the conditions of disabled people. There have been a number of voluntary 'mainstreaming' exercises within the employment field.[171] Various appellations—'Investors in People', 'equal opportunity employer', 'working towards equal opportunities', or 'positive about disabled people'—have been held out to employers who make various promises as to the employment practices, and in particular as to appointing practices—how jobs are to be advertised, shortlisted, interviewed for, and the appointment made. There is currently little to tie the employer to the promises and the effect they have depends to a large extent upon the commitment of the managers in the particular enterprise, the extent to which those managers, and especially human resources managers, think about disability. As O'Cinneide puts it: 'A persistent problem with mainstreaming policies has been the failure to ensure sustained attention, and sufficient focus, upon disability issues. Effective mainstreaming usually occurs when the necessary ingredients of political goodwill, organisational capacity, sustained leadership and expert advice are all in place'.[172]

What, then, will be the position when the duty is in force? Under regulations drawn up under the Act and the Code of Practice, an authority has to put in place a Disability Equality Scheme showing how it intends to fulfil the general duty and also the specific duties under the Act.[173] Disabled people are going to have to be involved in the formulation of the Code of Practice. That scheme will have to include statements of a number of points, and how they are to be monitored, including:[174] (d)(i) the effect on the recruitment development and retention of disabled employees.

All that will be to the good. There is one reservation about the duty on public authorities, and that is as to its effect upon the labour market. The government is right to set itself up as the exemplar employer,[175] but it must also avoid being a repository for people who cannot get private sector jobs. The AtW scheme, and changes to it, together with the DWP plans, will be critical in this endeavour and they must be monitored closely.[176]

[171] See also J Shaw, 'Mainstreaming Equality and Diversity in European Union Law and Policy' [2005] *Current Legal Problems* 255.

[172] O'Cinneide, n 170 above, 225.

[173] Disability Discrimination (Public Authorities) (Statutory Duties) Regulations 2005 (SI No 2966), paras 2–3.

[174] Disability Rights Commission, n 162 above, 63.

[175] *COSU*, Recommendation 7.18.

[176] See n 22 above.

Some Conclusions

Much has been achieved in thirty years. There is now for the first time widespread resolve to achieve the sorts of results set out as objectives in the Cabinet Office paper, and the economic conditions are right for the incorporation of more disabled people into the workforce. There is still profound resistance in some quarters. The rejection, after the bringing to bear of some influence by the Ministry of Defence, of the Scrutiny Committee's strong and considered recommendation[177] that military recruitment be covered by the Act is one indicator of how much work remains to be done.

Disability Law, in the widened sense outlined above, cannot provide all the answers to the appropriate treatment of people with disabilities. But it is a very important and dynamic area of law. It needs a context and it needs further analysis of the relationship with the other 'other' disciplines. While anti-discrimination legislation is central to the response, for example, to discrimination on the basis of race or gender, it need not be for discrimination on the grounds of disability. This essay has suggested that the universalizing thesis, in which disability is treated as part of the normal, is both the most intellectually satisfactory and the most effective, and that it has the consequence that anti-discrimination legislation might not always be the most effective legal response to disability discrimination. Nonetheless, every legal means available must be brought to bear.

[177] 'As nothing in the DDA (Disability Discrimination Act) requires the employment of any person who is not capable of doing the job the Committee can see no valid reason for maintaining this exception.' Scrutiny Committee Report, n 21 above, paras 118 and 120.

Creating New Commons: Recognition of Communal Land Rights within a Private Property Framework

Alison Clarke

Introduction

For many legal systems where the predominant form of land ownership is private ownership, there are real difficulties in accommodating communal land usage. The problems are particularly acute in jurisdictions where a private property system was imposed, via colonialization or conquest, on indigenous populations who made communal use of natural resources.[1] Different problems arise in countries such as England and Wales, where successive stages of land reform have concentrated on rules of private ownership, sidelining communal land usage. In such a system, as we have found to our cost, property law principles come to be articulated increasingly in private property terms, and the law struggles to find appropriate legal structures for the recognition and efficient regulation of land that is communally used. This causes difficulties not only when the objective is the preservation of ancient agricultural and recreational commons, which still exist throughout the United Kingdom, but also where the legal system is required to respond to the creation of new *de facto* commons. These come in diverse forms ranging from deliberately created common areas of

[1] See eg the difficulties of recognition and assimilation successively revealed in the Australian land rights cases, *Milirrpum v Nabalco Pty Ltd* (1971) 17 FLR 141, where the question of whether pre-colonial land users could be said to have property rights in the land was addressed by applying criteria appropriate only to private property: inevitably, the question was answered in the negative; *Mabo v State of Queensland (No 2)* (1992) 175 CLR 1, where it was held that, on the contrary, pre-existing usages, whether approximating to private property or communal property, gave rise to rights surviving annexation and still subsisting within the modern, predominantly private property, states of Australia; and *Wik Peoples v Queensland* (1996) 187 CLR 1 and *Yorta Yorta Aboriginal Community v Victoria* [2002] HCA 58, where, after these rights had been enshrined by statute, the Native Title Act 1993, subsequently amended, the courts had to consider how to reconcile post-colonial private property rights granted over land now found to be already subject to pre-existing communal aboriginal land rights.

commercial developments designed to serve multiple residential or commercial units, to land acquired by social or mutual self-interest groups, to land *de facto* used communally by families or local communities.

These new commons are not well served by English property law. By an accident of history our modern law, founded on the Commons Registration Act 1965,[2] focuses on the preservation of ancient commons. It fails to provide adequate mechanisms by which new commons might come into existence and evolve in response to changing social and economic pressures and preferences. New *de facto* commons nevertheless do come into existence all the time, in England and Wales as in other jurisdictions. Here, however, they have to be clothed in legal forms designed for other purposes. The use of these inappropriate legal forms tends to work against the development of viable new commons. They encourage (at worst impose) property holding structures and forms of governance and regulation which are unlikely to produce the conditions under which communal resource holding tends to flourish.

At the time when the principles underlying the 1965 Act were being formulated, there was little empirical or theoretical literature available on the workings of modern commons. Now, however, the situation has changed radically. The publication in 1967 and 1968 of Harold Demsetz's 'Towards a Theory of Property Rights'[3] and Garret Hardin's 'The Tragedy of the Commons',[4] presenting contentious analyses of the social and economic consequences of communal ownership of natural resources, marked the start of a wide-ranging academic debate. Since then ideas about the nature and function of the commons in modern society have been refined by commentators and analysts drawn from a variety of disciplines and working within a broad range of legal cultures. As a result, we now have a much clearer idea of what makes communal resource holding work, even if there is no consensus as to its function or social desirability.

But for English law, all this came just a few years too late. By the time 'The Tragedy of the Commons' was published in 1968, radical decisions about the structure of the modern law of the commons in this country had already been made, and legislation putting this new structure in place, the Commons Registration Act 1965, had been enacted. The 1965 Act was based on assumptions about the function, organization, and economic effect of commons that would probably not be made now if we were to start all over again the process of modernizing the law of commons. There have been significant judicial and legislative developments

[2] Hereafter 'the 1965 Act'.
[3] (1967) 57 *American Economic Review* 347.
[4] (1968) 162 *Science* 1243.

of the law since the 1965 Act, up to and including the recently enacted Commons Act 2006,[5] but these have been no more than developments upon the basic structure put in place by the 1965 Act. The more recent developments have been the product of a protracted series of consultation exercises, but none of these has challenged the basic assumptions underlying the 1965 Act. As a result, the overriding concern of the 2006 Act, as of the 1965 Act it will replace, is the recording and management of long-established communal land use that had survived into the 1950s, and the preservation of that use in the public interest. The question of providing a structure within which communal resource use might arise in the future, and might adapt and develop, is simply not on the agenda. *De facto* communal resource use consequently remains largely outside the legislation intended to govern the commons.

The first section of this chapter attempts to assess what the post-1967 literature can tell us about successful commons, that is, what makes communal resource holding work in a modern society. The following three sections then measure English law against these criteria, looking first at the very different way in which the modern English legislature views the commons, by examining the implicit and articulated assumptions underlying the recommendations of the Jennings Committee in 1957 and subsequent legislation. The following two sections then examine first the modern law of commons put in place by the 1965 Act and then the alternative legal forms that modern communal resource holdings are obliged to adopt, to consider how well they give legal recognition to *de facto* communal resource holding and allow it to adapt and function effectively.

What Makes Communal Resource Holding Work?

The 'Tragedy of the Commons' Debate

The contemporary debate about the viability of the commons was famously initiated by the articulation of the 'tragedy of the commons',[6] the thesis that a communally used resource will inevitably be destroyed by over-consumption and under-maintenance once the population of users passes a critical point. This put in train at least two sets of responses and counter-responses. The first consisted of defences of the commons.

[5] Hereafter 'the 2006 Act'.

[6] Most famously by G Hardin (1968) 162 *Science* 1243, more rigorously, in economists' terms, at any rate, a year earlier by H Demsetz (1967) 57 *American Economic Review* 347.

The second consisted of attempts to refine the basic thesis so as to produce a more sophisticated and credible justification of private property as the means of averting the tragedy of the commons in an economically efficient way.

Terminological Confusion

As an essential first step in both sets of responses, however, it was necessary to clear up a critical confusion in Hardin's terminology. In his formulation of the thesis Hardin failed to distinguish between three distinct categories of resource holding, each of which can loosely be referred to as 'commons'.[7]

The first, more accurately described as 'no property', is where everyone in the world is free to use the resource but no person has a right to do so. No one has a right not to be excluded from use of the resource, so no person's right is infringed if the resource has been used up, or spoilt, or monopolized by someone else who got there first. Hardin's examples of a river, or the atmosphere, into which everyone is free to pour pollutants, fall within this category. So too do leaves fallen from trees in the autumn.

The second, 'open access common property', is where everyone in the world has a right to use the resource, in the sense of a right not to be excluded from it. Hardin's examples of an unregulated public right of access to Yellowstone Park, and an unregulated right for humans to breed, probably both come within this category. Roads and paths over which there are public rights of way provide other examples.

The third is 'limited access communal property' where the only people entitled to use the resource are members of a community: in limited access communal property, all members of the community have a right to use the resource, and a right not to be excluded from it, and a right to exclude all non-members from it.

The distinction between the three categories matters, to both defenders and attackers of the 'tragedy of the commons' thesis. The possibility of averting the 'tragedy', the ways in which this might be done, and their effect, all vary depending on which category we are talking about.

Specifically, resources subject to a 'no-property' regime *will* inevitably suffer the tragedy of the commons once the resource becomes scarce,

[7] Out of many clarifications of the confusion, see eg, C M Rose, 'The Several Futures of Property: Of Cyberspace, and Folk Tales, Emission Trades and Ecosystems' (1998) 83 *Minnesota Law Review* 129, J Waldron, *The Right to Private Property* (Oxford: Oxford University Press, 1988), R Ellickson, 'Property in Land' (1993) 102 *Yale Law Journal* 1315, G G Stevenson, *Common Property Economics* (Cambridge: Cambridge University Press, 1991), and Y Barzel, *Economic Analysis of Property Rights* (Cambridge: Cambridge University Press, 1997).

but arguably this can be averted by the imposition of *any* property rights regime, that is, by reducing the resource to private ownership, or to state ownership, or to open access communal property subject to state regulation, or to limited access communal ownership. The success of the chosen regime in averting the tragedy then depends on the detailed workings of the regime, and the argument shifts to the question of which regime is capable of producing the most successful, and/or socially or politically desirable, outcome at the least cost. As Ostrom puts it:

> A clear prediction can be made in situations where no one has a property right related to the flow of benefits from a resource. If the benefits are greater than the costs of obtaining them, open-access resources [by which she means what is described here as 'no-property' resources] will be overexploited and may well be destroyed. When property rights exist—whether private property, state property, or common property—overexploitation and destruction depend on how well the property-rights regime copes with problems of allocating the costs and benefits of managing and governing a particular resource. In other words, property rights defining who has access, how much can be harvested, who can manage, and how rights are transferred are a necessary but not sufficient condition for avoiding overexploitation of a resource.[8]

As far as open access communal property is concerned, the destruction of a scarce resource so held is similarly real and inevitable *if use is unregulated*, but a total absence of regulation is difficult to conceive. The very idea of universal rights, as opposed to mere liberties, to use the resource presupposes some form of property regime, the most likely form of which would involve the recognition of an underlying 'owner' of some description who is charged with the responsibility of permitting, preserving, or protecting public access and correspondingly clothed with the authority also to regulate it. Again, the argument then shifts to the question of which regime is likely to do so most efficiently, and at what social and political cost.

The same applies in the case of limited access communal property. Whilst the inevitability of the tragedy of the commons is as convincing in the case of *unregulated* limited access commons as it is for unregulated open access commons, and for much the same reasons, again it is difficult to conceive of a wholly unregulated limited access commons. The very idea of limited access presupposes the existence of a community which recognizes the rights of insiders and the need to repel outsiders. The fact that the limited access use exists at all suggests some degree of success in doing both, which in turn suggests some level of organization and regulation.

[8] E Ostrom, 'The Rudiments of a Theory of the Origins, Survival, and Performance of Common-Property Institutions' in D W Bromley, *Making the Commons Work: Theory Practice and Policy* (ed) (San Fransisco: Institute for Contemporary Studies, 1992), 293.

Also, it is difficult to think of any real-life examples where the resource is not dedicated to a particular use. Even in Hardin's classic example of the pasture open to all herdsman in a community, the community appears already to have allocated the land to pasture use, which in itself suggests a certain level of cooperation and self-regulation. This brings us to the other significant distinction. Some limited access commons may be regulated from outside the community, perhaps by Government, or by state agencies or non-government organizations, and this will usually be where there is some public interest in the preservation or exploitation of the communal resource, or where the communal purpose is to provide a benefit to outsiders. Others, however, are mutual self-interest commons, and in practice mutual self-interest commons tend to be self-governing. Commons of this type exist to serve the interests of their members. In this respect limited access communal property is much closer to private property than to open access communal property (which more closely resembles public property, to be regulated in the interests of the public). In this type of limited access commons the real 'tragedy of the commons' issue becomes whether the community can regulate its resource use as efficiently (here meaning in its own selfish best interests) as a private owner would.

The focus of this chapter is on this last type of limited access commons, the mutual self-interest commons.

Defences of the Commons

As Stuart Banner pointed out in his review of the contemporary debate,[9] the defences of the commons which emerged in reaction to the Demsetz/Hardin analysis came in a variety of different, but sometimes overlapping, forms. So, for example, one form of reaction was to challenge the orthodox historical view of the medieval Northern European agricultural commons. The orthodox historical view was that these old commons were a relic of feudalism, and that they had died out because they were inefficient, wiped out by a series of agricultural revolutions that swept across the United Kingdom and Europe, replacing outmoded communal resource use with modern, efficient private ownership, producing the wealth that was to fuel the industrial revolutions that followed.[10]

[9] S Banner, 'The Political Function of the Commons: Changing Conceptions of Property and Sovereignty in Missouri, 1750–1850' (1997) 41 *American Journal of Legal History* 61. See also H Dagan and M Heller, 'The Liberal Commons' (2000–1) 110 *Yale Law Journal* 549.

[10] Banner cites H L Gray, *English Field Systems*, (Cambridge, Mass: Harvard University Press, 1915), 8–9; E C K Gonner, *Common Land and Inclosure* (London, Macmillan & Co, 1912), 302; G Slater, *The English Peasantry and the Enclosure of the Common Fields*

In defence of the commons, social and economic historians began to argue that, on the contrary, these long-established commons had persisted for centuries because they had provided highly efficient and sophisticated systems of resource use within their own contexts, some of them actually supplanting pre-existing private ownership systems. Their decline or extinguishment in the eighteenth, nineteenth, and twentieth centuries was not obviously attributable to inefficiency, but more likely to a complex of social, political, and technological developments.[11]

Another challenge to the accuracy of the tragedy of the commons hypothesis came in a series, still continuing, of empirical enquiries into the genesis and workings of 'successful' past and present commons.[12] What emerges from these studies is that communal resource use has occurred and continues to occur in various forms and in a variety of different historical and geographic locations. These studies remove the commons out of their 'feudal' box, demonstrating that communal resource use is a versatile and endemic phenomenon, not a relic of past or primitive societies. They have also produced valuable data on the ways in which communal resource use has been and is regulated so as to prevent over-consumption and under-maintenance. It is this data which has provided the foundation for theoretical and analytical defences of the commons. These have variously attempted to construct a synthesis of the conditions under which a commons might be a viable means of exploiting

(London, Constable, 1907), 262–3; F W Maitland, *Domesday Book and Beyond: Three Essays on the Early History of England* (Cambridge: Cambridge University Press, 1897), 337; P Vinogradoff, *Villainage in England: Essays in English Mediaeval History* (Oxford: Clarendon Press, 1892), 237; T E Scrutton, *Commons and Common Fields* (Cambridge: Cambridge University Press, 1887), 115.

[11] See eg C J Dahlman, *The Open Field System and Beyond: A Property Rights Analysis of an Economic Institution* (Cambridge: Cambridge University Press, 1980) and B C Field, 'The Evolution of Property Rights' (1989) 42 *Kyklos* 319. Banner, n 9 above, gives other examples at n 5.

[12] From amongst many, see those contained and referred to in Bromley, n 8 above; E Ostrom, *Governing the Commons* (Cambridge: Cambridge University Press, 1990); M McKean, 'Management of Traditional Lands in (Iraichi) Japan' in Bromley, n 8 above, 533–89; National Research Council, *The Drama of the Commons* (Washington, DC: National Academy Press, 2002); Banner, n 9 above; Stevenson, n 7 above; J Umbeck, 'A Theory of Contract Choice and the California Gold Rush' (1977) *Journal of Law and Economics* 421–37 (American West gold rush); M Chakravarty-Kaul, *Common Land and Customary Law: Institutional Change in North India over the Past Two Centuries* (Oxford: Oxford University Press, 1996); R Ellickson, 'A Hypothesis of Wealth-Maximising Norms: Evidence from the Whaling Industry' (1989) *Journal of Law, Economics and Organization* 83; Ellickson, n 7 above; T Eggertsson, 'Open Access versus Common Property' in T L Anderson and F S McChesney (eds), *Property Rights: Cooperation, Conflict, and Law* (Princeton: Princeton University Press, 2003), ch 3; and L De Alessi, 'Gains From Private Property: the Empirical Evidence' in ibid, ch 4.

and/or conserving a resource, and to subject the concept of viability to closer scrutiny, in particular to give consideration to the benefits that might accrue from communal resource holding that would not necessarily be identified by an economic analysis of efficiency.[13]

Refinement of the Hardin Thesis

Banner also charts the progress of the counterpart to these formidable defences of the commons, the development of restatements of the Hardin/Demsetz thesis, in what Banner describes as a 'much more intricate and qualified form' by neo-economists and political scientists. He cites Ellickson's 1993 *Yale Law Journal* article, 'Property in Land'[14] as the 'most complete version' of this kind of work to date, at least on the political science front.[15] Ellickson is concerned with the land rules (not just rules of law but also and primarily customary norms enforced through diffuse social sanctions) that 'close-knit' groups generate. He describes a 'close-knit' group as 'a social entity within which power is broadly dispersed and members have continuing face-to-face interactions, that is, where the conditions are conducive to cooperation in that they provide members with 'both the information and opportunities they need to engage in informal social control'.[16] His efficiency thesis is that, contrary to what others such as Libecap have argued,[17] land rules within a close-knit group do evolve so as to minimize its members' costs, because 'people on the ground recognize that property in land is a positive-sum game and play it cooperatively'.[18] Consequently, he concludes, 'a traditional village's grazing commons is unlikely to be tragic'.[19] In other words, Ellickson by no means rules out efficient communal land use. However, he sees it as occupying a relatively small place in the spectrum. More importantly, he questions whether this is a place where a liberal society would wish to find itself. He distances himself from Demsetz by, amongst other things, adding into his own efficiency equation 'other vital human concerns conventionally regarded as non-economic: liberty, privacy, equality, and

[13] Primarily amongst those recognizing that cooperation is a social good in itself: Dagan and Heller, n 9 above, 572–4, and the works cited there, to which can be added the many analyses of US common interest communities such as L Fennell, 'Contracting Communities' (2004) *University of Illinois Law Review* 829, P A Franzese, 'Building Community in Common Interest Communities (2003–4) 38 *Real Property Probate and Trusts Journal* 17, W S Hyatt, 'Common Interest Communities: Evolution and Reinvention' (1997–8) 31 *John Marshall Law Review* 303, A Lehavi, 'Property Rights and Local Public Goods: Towards a Better Future for Urban Communities' (2004) 36 *Urban Law* 1.

[14] (1993) 102 *Yale Law Journal* 1315.

[15] For the current state of play on the economics front, reference can usefully be made to Anderson and McChesney, n 12 above.

[16] Ellickson, n 12 above, 1320.

[17] Anderson and McChesney, n 12 above.

[18] ibid 1320.

[19] ibid.

community'.[20] He sees the choice between different forms of land use as involving, perhaps inevitably, choices between these virtues:

Classical liberals . . . regard private property in land as an essential instrument for promoting political freedom, privacy, and self-determination . . . In practice, a human group must make trade-offs between individual liberty and privacy on the one hand and community and equality on the other . . . [21]

And later, talking specifically about modern land communes, he says:

The social environment of a commune differs significantly from that of a parcelized land regime. A commune that succeeds in promoting equality and thick social ties simultaneously impinges upon the classical-liberal values of individual liberty, privacy, and self-determination. Anyone who prizes both community and individuality has to be perplexed by this trade-off.[22]

This view exemplified by Ellickson has in turn provoked its own reaction, moving the debate on to the question of whether a liberal commons is a viable concept, or whether communal resource holding can work only within a highly cohesive society, where altruistic behaviour is bought at the expense of severe social repression and the interests of the individual are sacrificed to the interests of the group.[23]

What Makes Commons Work?

These defences of the commons have succeeded in establishing that new *de facto* commons come into existence all the time, some relating to land holding or land use, others not, and that some succeed and some fail, for all kinds of social, political, and economic reasons. Unsurprisingly, they have not produced a blueprint for success. Nevertheless, it is possible to extract from the literature an indication of the conditions which are likely to be propitious.[24] Some of these relate to the circumstances in which the

[20] Demsetz, n 6 above, 1321. [21] ibid 1345. [22] ibid 1352.

[23] See Dagan and Heller, n 9 above, arguing that successful commons can exist in a liberal society if participants have appropriate (that is, not self-defeating), exit rights. Ellickson himself refers to some counter-examples of liberal societies which have chosen to hold some of their resources communally and others privately and which do not fit within his 'illiberal' pattern. There are others: see eg the English and Welsh commons described in I Jennings, *The Report of the Royal Commission on Common Land 1955–1958*, Cmnd 462 (hereafter 'the *Jennings Report*'). See also, the Swiss mountain pastures documented by Stevenson, n 7 above, and the Early American settlements discussed by Banner, n 9 above.

[24] A considerable body of work has been published on this. See eg R J Oakerson, 'Analysing the Commons: A Framework' in Bromley, n 8 above; E Ostrom, n 8 above, ch 13; and generally n 12 above; the factors listed by A Agrawal, 'Common Resources and Institutional Sustainability' in NRC, n 12 above; and also, in relation to specific studies, amongst many others, Banner, n 9 above, and Stevenson, n 7 above.

community finds itself: we know, for example, that because group ownership can operate as a risk-spreading device, it is often preferred to private property in high-risk environments.[25] Others, of more interest for present purposes, relate to the nature of the communities themselves, and the ways in which they regulate themselves. Of these, the following appear likely to be significant.

Exclusion of Non-members

It should go without saying that the success of limited access resource holding, whether or not for mutual self-interest, is dependent on the ability to exclude outsiders, at least where the resource is scarce. The tragedy of the commons is averted by communal holding only if the resource is controlled by a group which is small and cohesive enough to permit members, at a sufficiently low cost, to communicate between themselves and devise and enforce rules regulating their own use of the resource. But group control depends on being able to keep out non-members, or, what amounts to the same thing, on all resource users being subject to the social norms of the group regulating use.[26] In particular, the viability of the commons may be threatened by public access to the resource, if this weakens the community's will and/or ability to regulate the resource use. If communal resource holding is to work, it appears that outsiders have to be excludable from the resource in just the same way, and for just the same reasons, as they have to be excludable from private property. So, for example, a rule of law conferring public rights of access over land which is communally held is justifiable and workable only in the circumstances in which it would have been equally justifiable and workable in relation to the equivalent land if privately owned. There is nothing special about communally held land that warrants rights of public access that would have been inappropriate if the land had been privately held.

Public Interest

The glue that holds mutual self-interest communities together is the pursuit of that mutual self-interest. A confusion between this and the public

[25] Ellickson makes this point in n 7 above, 1341–4. He argues it might explain why early colonists in the high-risk environment of Jamestown, USA, in the early seventeenth century retained collective land ownership longer than colonists from the same origins headed for Jamestown who, diverted by rough weather, ended up settling in the low-risk environment of Bermuda instead. The Jamestown community was reportedly highly inefficient, its members unproductive and poorly motivated, in classic 'tragedy of the commons' style. The same was not true of the Bermuda community: 'In short, the unusually deadly environment at Jamestown not only decimated the labour force, but also helped perpetuate institutions that spread risks but put less food on the table'. De Alessi makes the same point in n 12 above, 110.

[26] See Ostrom, n 8 above, 310.

interest is similarly likely to threaten the community's ability to survive. There is no obvious reason why communities should have a higher duty to respect or promote the public interest in the use or management of their resources than private owners. So, for example, there is nothing special about communally held land that warrants imposing additional requirements on the rights holders to preserve the physical environment, or to take into consideration other aspects of the public interest. There are well-documented examples of scarce resources in fragile environments that have been conserved for centuries only because of the conservative patterns of use imposed by communal property regimes.[27] But all that that shows is that communal resource use might in appropriate cases serve the public interest better than any other pattern of resource use. It does not follow that it should carry with it a moral or legal duty to do so. In order to be viable, communal resource holding probably has to be just as private to the community as private property is to the private property owner.

Homogeneity of Interest

Also for obvious reasons, homogeneity of interest is a useful characteristic for members of a mutual self-interest community to have. Although Ostrom and others have demonstrated that disparate communities can work,[28] or at least noted examples of those that have done so, it is difficult to deny that communal property holding becomes more difficult to sustain as the level of homogeneity in the interests of the rights holders falls. If too many disparate and conflicting interests have to be accommodated, agreement will be difficult to sustain. Successful communal resource holders tend to be cohesive when they have a sufficient level of common interest.

Cohesive Community

This appears to be of even more significance than homogeneity of interest, in providing both the means (development and observance of social norms, clear lines of communication) and the motive (interdependence in the use of resources, desire for the social benefits of cooperation) for

[27] Most notably the use by aboriginal Australian peoples of desert and wilderness lands documented in the aboriginal land rights cases referred to in n 1 above. Similar examples appear in McKean's study of past Japanese commons, n12 above. Note, however, De Alessi in n 12 above, 110, who makes the necessary point that there is no inevitable correlation between communal resource use and conservation of natural resources (in this case beavers): 'The perception of [North American] Indians as ideal environmentalists is a myth . . . Indians behaved like any other group subject to the same constraints'.

[28] See Ostrom, n 8 above.

promoting mutual self-interest. This often entails or results from geographic proximity or isolation, but as Ellickson's study of social norms in the international whaling industry in the eighteenth and nineteenth centuries demonstrates,[29] even a group of individuals of disparate nationalities and in scattered geographical locations can form a sufficiently cohesive community if they share an area of sufficient mutual self-interest, however little else they have in common.

Idiosyncratic Regulation

Successful mutual self-interest communities typically have regulations, often complex and elaborate, about precisely who is allowed to use the resource, and when and how, and about the level of commitment required from members, and the procedure for enforcement. More significantly, the regulations tend to be self-generated rather than imposed from the outside, and highly specific, tailored to the particular needs and circumstances of that community. Empirical studies have revealed no common patterns of regulation: it appears that there is no single form of governance or organization that works for all mutual self-interest communities in all conditions. Successful communities seem able to (and perhaps even have had to in order to survive) evolve and enforce their own rules in their own way to meet their own particular circumstances. This might involve democratic decision-making, but it might not,[30] just as it might not involve equality in the distribution of risks, benefits, or burdens. Whether as cause or effect, the governance structure will reflect whatever hierarchical or egalitarian social form the community takes.

Sanctions

Nevertheless, there are two respects in which enforcement rules tend to converge. First, Ostrom notes that successful commons tend to involve mutual enforcement of regulations, in the sense that individual members regard themselves as entitled and required to police the behaviour of each other, reinforcing enforcement by an enforcing authority within the community.[31] Secondly, although methods and levels of enforcement vary, characteristically the ultimate sanction is exclusion, either from use of the resource or from membership of the group, for example by

[29] Ellickson, n 13 above.

[30] McKean, n 12 above, 74, notes that in the Japanese commons she has studied, the household and not the individual was the smallest unit of accounting, and that not all households had, or had equal, political rights within the community organization.

[31] Ostrom, n 8 above, 304.

expulsion, banishment, or ostracism,[32] rather than an appeal to an outside enforcement system. In this respect, mutual self-interest commons tend to see themselves as inherently private groups, who expect to police themselves, ultimately expelling anyone who is not willing to keep to the rules.

It has already been noted that these characteristics are, at best, descriptive rather than predictive of a successful commons. Nevertheless it is instructive to bear them in mind when considering the legal regime introduced into this jurisdiction by the Commons Registration Act 1965.

Background to the Modern English Law

In the mid-1950s, pre-empting the start of the tragedy of the commons debate by just over a decade, and so in this sense prematurely,[33] a Royal Commission on Common Land was set up to undertake a radical reappraisal of the law relating to communal land use in this country. It published its Report, 'the *Jennings Report*', in 1958, and the Commons Registration Act 1965 was enacted as what was intended to be the first stage in implementing its recommendations. The 1965 Act introduced a registration system for all pre-existing 'rights of common',[34] and for the land, 'common land',[35] over which these rights were exercisable. The second stage was intended to provide for public access to all common land and also for schemes for the management and improvement of common land. The recommendations for public access were subsequently implemented, in all essentials, by the Countryside and Rights of Way Act 2000,[36] and the recommended provision for schemes of management and improvement is now to be provided, following further extensive

[32] The instances of ostracism in Japanese traditional commons given by McKean, n 12 above, are just extreme examples of a phenomenon noted elsewhere in similar communities where physical expulsion is, for one reason or another, not feasible.

[33] But probably not premature in any other sense: the impetus for reform came from a general feeling that, following wartime disruption of land use, urgent action was essential to prevent the extinction of pre-existing ancient commons. See the *Jennings Report*, para 63.

[34] ie the limited class of communal land rights recognized as such in English law.

[35] For these purposes 'common land' includes but is not confined to town and village greens, whose use is primarily recreational. The use of other common land is a mix of agricultural and recreational.

[36] Section 2 of the Countryside and Rights of Way Act 2000 gives the public a right of access 'for the purposes of open-air recreation' to various categories of land, including registered common land. It was brought into force, as far as common land is concerned, on 14 December 2004 by the Countryside and Rights of Way Act 2000 (Commencement No 6) Order 2004 3088.

Government consultation exercises,[37] by the recently enacted Commons Act 2006.

As will be apparent from this narrative, our present law of the commons is set firmly within the template formulated by the authors of the *Jennings Report*. They were a noticeably cross-discipline committee of twelve, chaired by a constitutional lawyer but including also Professors of Social Geography and Agricultural Botany, a fellow of the Royal Institution of Chartered Surveyors and Past President of the Town Planning Institute, historians, land agents and other lawyers, with additional assistance provided by a couple of other legal historians and geographers. Had their deliberations taken place fifteen years later, at least some of them could have been expected to have been familiar with the idea of the tragedy of the commons, and to have been alive to the range of arguments as to the viability or otherwise of the commons as a system of land holding in a modern society. As it was, their perspective was essentially pragmatic.

As a matter of observable fact, in the 1950s ancient commons were in decline. The Commission did not see this as a matter of inherent economic inefficiency, nor did they share the assumption of contemporary English historians, noted earlier, that this marked the final stages in an inevitable historical progression from communal to private property. Indeed, they saw the commons as providing a method of land usage that was potentially productive. Nevertheless, they had no doubt that the decline was real and that the commons faced extinction. They attributed this to a number of factors, but most importantly for present purposes they identified the root problem as the extinction of the administrative machinery which had provided for the identification and regulation of rights of common, a process exacerbated by the dislocation precipitated by the widespread requisition of common land in the Second World War:[38]

163. Taking common land as a whole we are left with the impression that it is the relic of an ancient system of land management which has caused it to lag well behind other land in agricultural production. To a large extent, the commoners have remained outside the scope of recent agricultural legislation, ineligible for either its benefits or penalties, and incapable, as commoners, of contributing to

[37] See in particular the Department for Environment, Food and Rural Affairs (DEFRA), *Final Report: Consultation on Agricultural Use and Management of Common Land* (DEFRA, February 2005), reporting on the response to its August 2003 *Consultation on Agricultural Use and Management of Common Land*, which in turn put forward proposals about management made in the *Report of the Stakeholder Working Group: Agricultural Use and Management of Common Land*, published by DEFRA in April 2003.

[38] See the *Jennings Report*, para 116. The problem was not so much the requisition as the difficulties in deciding what to do with the land on de-requisition.

the industry's increased productivity. The administrative machinery through which their use of the land might have been adapted to modern conditions has mostly disappeared, and they themselves have in consequence become increasingly uncertain of their rights and unable to co-operate. Lacking vitality locally, the whole system which legislation over the last century aimed at preserving has tended to ossify instead. The result has all too often been the neglect of the land with the loss of production to the commoners and of amenity to the public.

165 . . . We have had impromptu talks with [some . . . groups of commoners whom we met informally on our journeys in England and Wales] . . . One lesson that this has taught us is that no two commons—or groups of commoners—however close geographically are exactly alike.

166 . . . for every common on our route where the commoners have been successful in creating some form of organisation, however sketchy, there were perhaps two or more where they have failed or never tried. The present state of some of the latter commons borders on the chaotic . . . .

In other words, whilst what the Commission saw around them was predominantly failed commons, they perceived the problem as essentially one of organization rather than of inherent unsustainability. They considered that their function was to put in place a structure within which these threatened ancient commons might be restored to productive use. This did not rule out changes in the law so as to enable existing commons to change and develop to adapt to modern conditions, but this was not where the focus lay. Still less was there any attention given to whether, and if so how, new commons might be created. The primary objective was the preservation of pre-existing communal land holdings, not the creation of new ones or the development of new forms of communal resource use.

Considerable attention was, however, given to other issues which have proved to be significant in the subsequent development of the law. The first concerns the form of management appropriate for commons. As already noted, even without the benefit of post-Hardin empirical research, the Commission was in no doubt about the importance of governance of the commons. Equally, its findings foreshadowed the works of commentators who were later to point out the importance of idiosyncratic management.[39] The Report remarks on the diversity of arrangements commoners had devised for themselves and emphasized at several points that the imposition of a single uniform management system would not be appropriate:

164. And yet, as we have endeavoured to show [in paras 165–6 above] it is almost impossible to generalise about common land. One common will be kept grazed

[39] ibid.

and well-managed alongside another which has been abandoned. The commoners, restrained by legal scruples and perhaps mutual suspicion in one place, will, in another, have undertaken schemes of improvement which would do credit to the most progressive owner-occupier . . . Any future legislation will need to take account of these wide differences: an attempt to impose a single uniform system of management would be doomed to failure.[40]

However, whilst later empirical findings as to the importance of idiosyncrasy were foreshadowed in the Report, those relating to exclusion and heterogeneity[41] most certainly were not. There was a strong conviction expressed in the *Jennings Report* that the way in which commoners managed their commons was not a private matter for the commoners to decide on for themselves without reference to other interests. The Report identified two significant sets of 'outside' interest here.

First, in English law there is always and necessarily the interest of the landowner over whose land communal rights are exercisable. In English law communities cannot own land, or indeed anything else, but only hold user rights over it. The implications of this are considered later,[42] but for present purposes the significant point is that the Commission took the pragmatic stance of assuming that where the interests of the underlying landowner diverged from those of the commoners, they would have to be accommodated. The idea that structural changes might be made to the law to transfer underlying ownership to the commoners themselves does not appear to have been contemplated.

Secondly was the public interest. The Commission took the view that there was a compelling, arguably even overriding, public interest in the preservation and management of the commons. This is of crucial importance. The Commission failed to mark the distinction between limited access and open access commons, in much the same way as Hardin had done, and as a result of this lack of clarity our modern law of the commons is founded on the assumption that communal property is a public resource. The Commission noted that there were public rights of access for recreational purposes of uncertain extent and origin over pre-existing commons, probably covering most but not all common land. The Report recommended they should be extended to all common land, partly to simplify the law and in recognition of the factual *status quo*[43] but also because they saw it as a valuable means of preserving the inviolability of pre-existing common land.[44]

40 ibid, para 176. 41 The *Jennings Report*, n 23 above. 42 ibid.

43 In practice no steps were taken to exclude the public from most areas of common land because of the difficulty in ascertaining whether or not the public had access over it.

44 The *Jennings Report*, ch 3, and paras 178, 221, and 312–17. The idea was that even if use as common land had to be suspended temporarily for management purposes, public

Moreover, the Commission saw the public interest as going further than public access. Because of their unique nature, pre-existing commons were of special importance to what was described in the Report as 'archeology and . . . the natural sciences'.[45] As explained in the Report:

> . . . the statutory restrictions imposed on the development of common land over the last century have given the land a unique character. Most of it has come to enjoy an immunity from man-made change . . . Common land has . . . become, as one of our witnesses described it, virtually the country's 'last uncommitted reserves of land'.[46]

Any decisions affecting commons, including management decisions made by the commoners themselves, must therefore take these interests into consideration, in the view of the Commission.

All of this made sense in the context of pre-existing commons. Those that could not survive public access had long since disappeared, and through historical accident they had indeed acquired a unique cultural and environmental importance. However, it makes the emergence of viable new commons highly problematic.

Two other features of our modern law, legacies of strategic decisions made at the time of the enactment of the 1965 Act, contribute towards the difficulties of accommodating new commons within the appropriate legal framework.

First, the substantive law of the commons, the precise nature and extent of the rights, powers, and duties held by the holders of communal land rights, has never been systematically reviewed. The *Jennings Report* did not envisage legislation providing for a modern re-formulation of the ancient law concerning the substance of the rights which were to be made registrable. As a result, the 1965 Act provided only for the registration of ancient town and village greens, common land, and rights of common: there was no accompanying (or subsequent) legislation modernizing or rationalizing the law relating to the substance and structure of any of the substantive rights. Consequently, the machinery for the registration and management of these ancient commons, added by the Commons Act 2006, is superimposed on a curious mixture of ancient and obscure common law rules.

interest in restoring public access would persist even if there were no surviving commoners. See ibid, para 315: 'In a sense, the interest of the vanished commoners in keeping the land open would be bequeathed to the public by virtue of the latter's possession of a right of access'.

45 ibid, para 222.

46 ibid, para 219 and see also para 223 on commons providing valuable reservoirs of species of plants and animals lost in the surrounding country.

Substantive reform would certainly have been a formidable undertaking (the law is *very* ancient and obscure)[47] but it is difficult to see how the Commission thought the registration system could work without it. When private property law was reformed in England and Wales in 1925 it was considered essential that the substance and structure of private property rights should be unified, clarified, and simplified before comprehensive registration of title could be introduced.[48] This was done by the Law of Property Act 1925, which came into effect immediately before the Land Registration Act 1925 introduced the new land registration system.[49] No such exercise was carried out in relation to communal land rights, either in 1925 or in 1965. Consequently we have no clear idea of the nature or extent of the rights which must be registered under the 1965 Act, nor do we know what effect, if any, registration or lack of registration has on their nature or quality or continued existence. The very act of superimposing registration machinery has inevitably had *some* effect on substantive rights, as subsequent litigation has demonstrated, but it is not at all clear what those effects are, and it is all too clear that some that have emerged were not intended.

So, for example, it was not until the North Oxford Trap Grounds case reached the House of Lords in *Oxfordshire County Council v Oxfordshire City Council*[50] in June 2006 that it was finally established that registration of land as a town or village green has the effect of *giving* the land that status.[51] Even more importantly, it took this House of Lords decision to finally establish that where a community's use of land as a green (that is, for recreational purposes), over a number of years has given rise to the right to have that land registered as a green, the effect of registration is

[47] The four most recent House of Lords decisions on the 1965 Act (*R v Oxfordshire County Council, ex p Sunningwell Parish Council* [2000] 1 AC 335 (HL), *Bettison v Langton* [2001] UKHL 24, [2002] 1 AC 27, *R (Beresford) v Sunderland City Council* [2003] UKHL 60, [2004] 1 AC 889, and *Oxfordshire County Council v Oxford City Council*, [2006] UKHL 15, [2006] 2 WLR 719) more than adequately illustrate the technical difficulties.

[48] As R Megarry and R M Wade, *The Law of Real Property* (5th edn) (London: Stevens & Son, 1984), 1145: 'It became [by 1911] the accepted truth that "to legislate for the registration of title without, as a preliminary step, simplifying the titles to be registered is to begin at the wrong end"', quoting from A Underhill, 'The Line of Least Resistance', Appendix to Cmnd 424 (1919), 34.

[49] The 1925 legislation made no formal distinction between communal and private property rights, but since it made private fee simple ownership the central organizing principle for all land, the inevitable emphasis was on private property rights, and few, if any, of the provisions had any effect on the substantive rights of communal land users or on the mechanisms for creating or transferring such rights.

[50] *Oxfordshire County Council*, n 47 above, 25.

[51] In other words, land cannot become a green unless and until registered: registration confers identity and validity on the interest, not just, as in some systems, enforceability against purchasers and trespassers.

actually to give the community an enforceable *right* to go on using it. Up until this point, the prevailing judicial view was that the only thing the community acquired when they succeeded in getting the land registered was the modest satisfaction that anyone else who interfered with its use as a 'common' would be committing a criminal offence.[52] Even now it remains unclear precisely what it is that the community will be entitled to do on their new green. In the *Oxford Trap Ground* case, the majority in the House of Lords rejected the argument that registration gave the community no more than the right to go on using the land precisely in the way that they had been using it. Instead, the court said, the effect of registration is to give the community the right to use the land 'generally for sports or pastimes'—in other words, possibly for wider or different purposes than before.[53] Lord Scott in the minority pointed out the difficulties this might give rise to between landowner and community, for example, in a case such as Bittacy Green in Barnet, registered as a village green on the basis of long-standing use for a bonfire every Guy Fawkes night.[54] Lord Hoffmann's optimistic response was that: 'There has to be give and take on both sides'.[55]

The second legacy of strategic decisions made in the 1950s is that *de jure* communal land rights are not fully integrated into the structure of private land rights: communal rights and private rights each have their own separate registration system, run by different bodies and on different principles.[56] When the decision was made in the 1950s to provide for registration of communal land rights, it seems to have been taken for granted

[52] It was Lord Denning in *New Windsor Corporation v Mellor* [1975] Ch 380 (CA) who first pointed out that this appeared to be the effect of the 1965 Act if read literally. This literal interpretation was adopted by the Court of Appeal in the *Oxford Trap Ground* case as a means of limiting the harm they considered to result from the creation of new greens, which they thought had never been intended by the 1965 Act. See *Oxfordshire County Council* [2005] EWCA Civ 175.

[53] Lord Hoffmann at paras 49–50: for the very good reason that there is no provision within the 1965 Act registration system for recording the nature of the user that gave rise to registration of the land as a green. In other words, if post-registration user was limited to the user giving rise to registration, registration would be virtually useless since it would not perform the function of telling the world precisely what rights are exercisable over the land.

[54] paras 84–90 and para 80.

[55] ibid, para 51.

[56] Specifically, the system set up by the Commons Registration Act 1965 and continued by the 2006 Act provides for there to be separate Commons Registers of communal rights or rights of common and of the land over which registrable rights are exercisable, as explained below. It was always intended that the title of the underlying owner of the land registered in the Commons Register would be registered in the Land Register, the register of all titles to land, when practicable, and this is being done: s 12 of the 1965 Act and para 8 of schedule 3 to the 2006 Act. However, it was never intended that the rights registered in the Commons Register should appear on the Land Register, and this is now expressly provided by s 3(7) of the 2006 Act.

that this would have to be done by creating a separate register, rather than by integrating them into the Land Register created by the Land Registration Act 1925 which caters for all other land rights. It is true that, in the 1950s and 1960s, there would have been logistical problems in requiring rights of common and common land to be registered on the Land Register, not least because it had yet to be extended to cover the whole of the country at that time.[57] Nevertheless, it is significant that it was decided to give the task of setting up and operating commons registers to local authorities rather than to the Land Registry. Whilst this may have been dictated largely by practical considerations, it is difficult to escape the conclusion that it was also influenced by a sense of what was appropriate. Our land registration system, unlike those in most other European jurisdictions, does not have cadastral origins or functions.[58] Its primary function is, and has always been, to ensure free marketability of private property rights by facilitating private conveyancing.[59] Until recently, the Land Registry did not regard itself as performing any public function beyond that.[60] Local authorities, on the other hand, are public bodies discharging public functions, including, via their role as planning authorities, the public regulation of land use in the public interest. Commons were seen to fall within the latter sphere, not the former. Consequently there is no clear interface between private and *de jure* communal land rights.

[57] Registration of title under the Land Registration Act 1925 did not become compulsory in all parts of the country until 1 December 1990.

[58] The cadastre (a systematic catalogue of land holdings compiled by the state for public purposes, originally fiscal but now also typically for land use regulation) formed the basis of most modern continental land registration systems. See R B Roper, C West, M Dixon, D Fox, S R Coveney, S Wheeler, and P Milne, *Ruoff and Roper on the Law and Practice of Registered Conveyancing* (2nd edn) (London: Sweet & Maxwell, 2003), paras 3.003–3.004, for an assessment of the significance of the differences between cadastral-based systems and the essentially 'private' registration systems developed in common law jurisdictions.

[59] The long battle to introduce registration of title, in the face of opposition from the conveyancing professions, is chronicled by A Offer, 'The Origins of the Law of Property Acts 1910–1925' (1977) 40 *Modern Law Review* 505. For a broader perspective, see J S Anderson, *Lawyers and the Making of English Land Law 1832–1940* (Oxford: Clarendon Press, 1992), *passim*, but especially ch 3, where he traces the emergence of questions about the extent, if any, to which registration of title might serve the public interest, during the formative period of 1844–75.

[60] The register was not even open to public inspection until December 1990, when the Land Registration Act 1988 came into force, and until very recently did not share its information with other government departments. See Land Registry, *Annual Report and Accounts 2002–2003*, putting the achievement of this as item 6 of their business objectives.

The Modern Law

Registrable Commons

As already noted, the primary purpose of the 1965 Act was to provide for the systematic registration of all communal land rights and the land over which they were exercisable. However, the focus on pre-existing ancient commons is reflected in the narrow terms used to define precisely what it is that can be registered. The intention was that all commons falling within the statutory definitions *must* be registered. The incidental effect is that *de facto* commons *not* falling within these terms *cannot* be registered, and so fall outside the system.

Registrable Rights: Rights of Common

The 1965 Act provides for the registration of 'rights of common'. This is a limited class of right: the ancient common law definition of rights of common—a right to 'take or use some portion of that which another man's soil naturally produces'[61]—probably applies, in the absence of a modern comprehensive statutory definition.[62] Such rights to participate in the natural produce of the land (technically, profits a prendre), run from grazing, shooting, and fishing rights to rights to take timber or extract sand or gravel. The 'rights of common' category is riddled with anomalies, not the least of which is that, although all are registrable under the 1965 Act, not all are communal rights. The sole right to take produce from someone else's land is as much a 'right of common' as a right to do so in common with others. Conversely, rights to make a particular use of someone else's land (technically, easements), such as a right of access over a path, or a right of drainage, are not rights in common, even though they may be exercisable in common with others. Also, the distinction between easements and profits a prendre, and hence between private rights and 'rights of common', is historically rather than logically determined. So, for example, rights to take water from someone else's land are easements

[61] G W Cooke, *Cooke's Inclosure Acts* (4th edn) (London: V & R Stevens Sons & Haynes, 1864), 5.

[62] Section 22(1) of the 1965 Act provides that, 'unless the context otherwise requires . . . "rights of common" includes cattlegates or beastgates (by whatever name known) and rights of sole or several vesture or herbage or of sole or several pasture, but does not include rights held for a term of years or from year to year'. The definition in s 61(1) of the 2006 Act is essentially the same.

(and not rights of common, even if exercisable in common with other members of a community), and not profits.[63]

New rights of common can be created,[64] but only in strictly regulated circumstances. They must be deliberately created: acquisition by long use (prescription) was long possible only by using the fiction of a lost grant, and is now to be made impossible.[65] Also, they cannot now be created over land that is already registered as common land or as a town or village green. This is to avoid the danger of over-exploitation,[66] and for the same reason, there are detailed regulations as to the variation of pre-existing registered rights of common, including in particular a provision to the effect that the commons registration authority can veto a variation which it considers would increase the burden on the land.[67] In other words, control over the level of use of the resource is taken away from the community of rights holders: they cannot decide for themselves the optimum level of exploitation. Of equal significance for present purposes, it is provided that any new right must be 'attached' to land. In other words the right must benefit other land privately owned by the right holder.[68] This means that new rights cannot be acquired by communities other than those defined by reference to individual landholding.

It follows that under this head there is little scope for creating new self-governing mutual self-interest commons which would have the hallmarks of a successful commons. So, if for example a group was to plant itself an orchard, or a community vegetable garden, the land could become eligible for registration as common land, and the user rights registrable as rights of common. But this is only if membership was defined by reference to individual landholding,[69] and the result would be that the state would then step in to ensure that there was no over-exploitation. Further, there might well then be public rights of way over it under the Countryside and Rights of Way Act 2000. And if the members chose to form themselves into a 'commons council' of the kind to be provided by the 2006 Act, they would be required to have regard to the public interest in managing and using the resource.

[63] For a succinct authoritative account, reference may be made to Megarry and Wade, n 48 above, 900–12; and see also Lord Mackay of Clashfern *Halsbury's Laws of England* (London: LexisNexis Butterworths, 2005), vol 6, 'Commons'.

[64] This was probably true under the 1965 Act: see Commons Registration (New Land) Regulations 1969, made under s 13 of the 1965 Act. Specific provision is now made by s 6 of the 2006 Act.

[65] This is the combined effect of s 6(1) and 6(2) of the 2006 Act.

[66] See the *Explanatory Notes* to the 2006 Act, para 42.

[67] See s 7(5) of the 2006 Act.

[68] ie the right must be appurtenant, not 'in gross': s 6(3)(b).

[69] ie the criterion for membership of the group would have to be ownership of land which demonstrably benefited from the right.

Registrable Land: Common Land and Town or Village Greens

All land over which rights of common are exercisable is registrable, and so too is land that is categorized as 'waste land of a manor', which may or may not be subject to rights of common.[70] These two types of land were referred to in the 1965 Act as 'common land'.[71] New common land will come into existence only when and if new rights of common are granted by the process noted above:[72] there is no scope for land to become common land by the creation or emergence of any other use rights. So if, for example, our group was to decide to use their land as a boating lake, or a rainwater reserve for watering their gardens, or a communal car and machinery repair yard, the land could not be registered as common land and the members' user rights could not be registrable as rights of common.

In addition, and of far greater significance, land which constitutes a 'town or village green' must be registered (in a separate register of town and village greens). Some of the uncertainties about the legal effect of registration of land as a green have already been noted above, but it must be appreciated that one of the root causes of the confusion has been controversy over what a town or village green actually is. Broadly, according to the 1965 Act, it is land which has come, by strictly circumscribed routes, to be used by the inhabitants of a locality for communal recreational purposes. The land must be subjected to limited access rather than open access communal use (as a result of the locality test in section 22 of the 1965 Act). Although the Jennings Committee's proposed definition of a green would have limited new greens, that is, those not already established by statute or since time immemorial, to 'uninclosed open space [in a rural parish] which is wholly or mainly surrounded by houses or their curtilages'[73] this never found its way into the legislation, and the House of Lords has now confirmed by a majority in the *Oxford Trap Grounds* case[74]

[70] See s 22(1) of the 1965 Act. For registration of 'new' common land see now s 6(5)(b) and paras 2 and 4 of sch 2 to the 2006 Act.

[71] ibid. Some ancient forests, including the New Forest, Epping Forest, and the Forest of Dean, and urban commons which, in effect, already had their own functioning local laws in 1965, are excluded from the provisions of the 1965 Act by s 11 of that Act and by s 5 of the 2006 Act.

[72] Or under the technical provisions contained in the 2006 Act for, amongst other things, rectifying mistakes in the register, s 22, allowing common land to be deregistered and new land registered as common land in exchange, ss 16–17, and allowing for the registration of manors which should have been registered under the 1965 Act but were not because of the restrictive definition adopted in *Box Parish Council v Lacey* [1979] 1 All ER 113 (CA). The decision was later overruled in *Hampshire County Council v Milburn* [1990] 2 All ER 257 (HL), but too late for the reinstatement of applications that had been abandoned or rejected as a result of the *Box Hill* decision.

[73] *Jennings Report*, para 43.

[74] *Oxfordshire County Council*, n 47 above, 25.

that *any* land can become a town or village green if used for general or specific recreational purposes by inhabitants of a locality, even purposes as specific as horse-racing on arable land,[75] mooring pleasure boats on rocks in Llanabadrig, spreading fishing nets to dry on someone else's land during the fishing season,[76] or annual hare-coursing through stubble fields, all examples given by Lord Hoffmann or Lord Scott in *Oxford Trap Grounds*. This was against the opposition of Lord Scott and, to a lesser extent, Baroness Hale in the minority in the House of Lords, who would have confined the status of 'town or village green' to something more in line with its popular meaning, that is, essentially grassy, and in a town or village.[77] The Trap Grounds themselves, nine acres of mixed wetland and rubble-strewn scrubland, bounded by a canal and a railway, of which considerably less than 25 per cent was 'reasonably accessible to the hardy walker', probably would have failed to qualify as a green under this minority test. However, it would have succeeded under the majority test, as did the development site near the town centre of Washington in Tyne and Wear, held to have become a green in *R (Beresford) v Sunderland City Council*.[78]

Two out of the three routes prescribed by statute for land to become registrable as (and hence to become) a green have now been closed. One was where, in 1965, land 'had been' allocated by statute 'for the exercise or recreation of the inhabitants of any locality', and the other was where the inhabitants of any locality had, in 1965, a 'customary right to indulge in lawful sports and pastimes'.[79] Since customary rights have to have existed since 'time immemorial',[80] and all had to have been registered by a cut-off date of 1 January 1970, no new greens can come into existence through either of these routes.

New town or village greens can, however, and do come into existence by the third route. These are what are called class *c* greens, and they come about where, 'for not less than twenty years a significant number of the inhabitants of any locality, or of any neighbourhood within a locality, have indulged in lawful sports and pastimes as of right' over the land in question.[81] Where the twenty years elapsed before 1 January 1970, the land had to be registered as a class *c* green by that date. These pre-existing greens are sometimes referred to as 'historic greens'. However, the statutory

[75] *Mounsey v Ismay* 1 H & C 729.

[76] *Mercer v Denne* [1904] 2 Ch 534 (Ch).

[77] Lord Scott at para 77 and Baroness Hale at para 145. See below for the similar views expressed by Lord Walker in *Beresford)*, n 47 above.

[78] [2003] UKHL 60.

[79] See s 22 of the 1965 Act and now s 15 of the 2006 Act.

[80] As to which see *New Windsor Corporation*, n 52 above.

[81] See s 22 of the 1965 Act as amended by s 98 of the Countryside and Rights of Way Act 2000 and now s 15 of the 2006 Act.

provisions also open up the possibility of 'modern' greens, that is, where the twenty years' recreational use arose after the 1970 cut-off date.

In so far as they allow for the creation of new greens, these provisions have attracted considerable hostility, particularly from the courts. Doubts have been expressed as to whether the Royal Commission or Parliament ever intended that new greens could be created in this way. In the Court of Appeal decision in the *Trap Grounds* case,[82] Lord Justice Carnwath said:

> Historic class *c* greens, as a concept, were a natural extension of the common law, and consistent with the objectives of the 1965 Act. Modern class *c* greens are neither; and it seems likely that they were an unintended consequence of the statutory definition. Although they are now firmly embedded in the law, there is no policy reason for giving them a substantive significance beyond that expressly or impliedly required by the statutory wording.[83]

The reason for the hostility is well put by Lord Walker in *R (Beresford) v Sunderland City Council*,[84] (the town centre development site case already referred to), concurring in the unanimous decision of the House of Lords that local residents had acquired the right to use local authority land awaiting development as a sports and recreational area through more than twenty years user as of right post-1970, but adding:

> I reach this conclusion with mixed feelings. The campaigning group named Washington First may feel that they have won a famous victory, and saved an important public amenity from being built on. That seems to be the likely consequence of this case. But the campaigners have achieved that end by a route which has bypassed normal development controls, and in a way which may be thought to stretch the concept of a town or village green close to, or even beyond, the limits which Parliament is likely to have intended.[85]

As Lord Justice Carnwath hinted, the response of the judiciary has been to interpret the statutory provisions so restrictively that at one point this route towards the creation of new commons was all but closed off, making it necessary for Parliament to intervene.[86]

82 [2005] EWCA Cir 175.
83 ibid, para 28.
84 *Beresford*, n 47 above.

85 ibid, para 92. Other commentators share these views: see eg M Ellis, 'The Commons Registration Act 1965 and New Town and Village Greens: Harmless Maypoles or a Trap for the Unwary?' (2003) *Journal of Planning and Environment Law* 1503.

86 The Court of Appeal in *Oxfordshire County Council* held that the twenty years user as of right necessary to support a claim for registration as a town or village green had to continue up until the time when registration of the land is completed. Since the landowner can stop user being 'as of right' at any time simply by putting up a sign either prohibiting or permitting it, this would have ruled out registration whenever it was opposed by the landowner. This has been reversed by the House of Lords (unnecessarily, as it happens, since s 15(2) of the 2006 Act will do the same thing). In the House of Lords decision in *Oxfordshire County Council*, paras 24 and 27, Lord Hoffmann gave other examples of judicial obstructionism.

More significantly for present purposes, class *c* greens are of limited interest here because the only communal land use they provide for is recreational. Under the 1965 Act,[87] a community defined by reference to a locality, but not by reference to any other factor, can hold in its own right an exclusive right to make recreational, but not any other, use of the land. In the early days of registration under the 1965 Act, the courts seemed inclined to allow any long-standing customary use by inhabitants of a community to qualify, for example, the drying of fishing nets noted above. But now that the House of Lords has established that the consequence of registration is that the inhabitants will become entitled to use the land for *any* sports or pastimes, it may be that stricter criteria can now be expected.

Finally, paradoxically, and in contrast to rights of common, these rights can come into existence only through long use, not as a matter of positive decision. I cannot make my back garden registrable as a green, whether by giving my local community the right to come and picnic or play football there or by simply declaring they may do so, or by any other means: it can only become registrable as a green if they take it into their heads to do so, and if I acquiesce in that without positively giving them permission to do so. In other words, if a community defined by reference to a locality builds up a pattern of recreational use of land over a period of years, the law will legitimize the use and the community will effectively acquire the right to continue that pattern of usage indefinitely. This idea of legal allocation of resources following *de facto* use which has persisted over time openly, peacefully, and without objection from those who are free to object, is familiar legal territory in this country and in most other jurisdictions in the world. However, at present we are living through a time of unprecedented hostility towards the acquisition of land rights by long usage. The courts in particular are increasingly on the attack against what they see as the injustice of extinguishing pre-existing rights, albeit long unasserted, in favour of the claims of *de facto* users.[88] Echoing this, the Land Registration Act 2002 has drastically reduced the circumstances in which titles to land can be lost through adverse possession, and first an English court at first instance and then the European Court of Human Rights have held that the long-established law of adverse possession that the 2002 Act replaced was incompatible with Article 1 of the First Protocol to the European Convention on Human Rights and

[87] As amended by s 98 of the Countryside and Rights of Way Act 2000.

[88] See generally A Clarke, 'Use, Time and Entitlement' (2004) 57 *Current Legal Problems* 239.

Freedoms.[89] At present it seems unlikely the same thing will happen to prescriptive rights, but this is by no means out of the question. Possible Human Rights Act challenges have been judicially discussed in town and village green cases.[90] Lord Hoffmann firmly rejected them in the House of Lords in the *Trap Grounds* case,[91] but necessarily without concluding the matter. A right that can come into being only through prescription therefore cannot be said to rest on very secure foundations in present English law.

Management of Commons

As noted above, the major concern of the Jennings Commission, and the impetus for the Commons Act 2006, was the need to provide for the management of surviving ancient commons. The management provisions of the 2006 Act apply only to registered commons, and so are not of central concern here since the scope for bringing new commons on to the register is so limited. It is nevertheless instructive to look at the extent to which the management model provided by the Act conforms to the criteria for successful commons considered above.

On the positive side, the model acknowledges the importance of allowing commons to develop their own idiosyncratic rules. It is true that the Act introduces a standardized form of governing body for registered commons,[92] the 'commons council', whose constitution and functions will be largely prescribed by statute and by statutory regulations. However, its use is not mandatory. The government is committed to allowing commoners to retain their own pre-existing governance structures if that is what they want to do, and care is taken to ensure that the statutory form is not imposed unless there is 'substantial support' for it.[93] A commons

[89] In, respectively, *Beaulane Properties Ltd v Palmer* [2005] EWHC 817 (Ch), [2006] Ch 79, and *J A Pye (Oxford) Ltd v United Kingdom* (2006) 43 EHRR 3 (ECHR). In the latter case, the ECHR was concerned only with the way adverse possession operated in registered land, and then only before the severe restrictions introduced before the Land Registration Act 2002 came into force.

[90] Most persuasively in *R (Laing Homes Ltd) v Buckinghamshire CC* [2003] EWHC 1578, [2004] 1 P & CR 36, paras 156–63, where however the judge declined to express a view, having decided in favour of the landowner that the land in question should not be registered as a town or village green, and by Lord Scott in *Oxfordshire County Council* in the House of Lords, paras 86–90.

[91] *Oxfordshire County Council*, n 47 above, paras 58–9.

[92] See s 26 of the 2006 Act: the commons council can also be used for the governance of a registered town or village green, but only if there are rights of common exercisable over it, ie only if there is agricultural as well as recreational use. See s 26(2)(b) of the 2006 Act.

[93] See s 27(4) of the 2006 Act.

council can only be established by order of the Secretary of State, and then only after a draft order has been published, representations invited, and if necessary, a local enquiry held. In deciding whether there is 'substantial support', the Secretary of State must take the representations and the findings of any enquiry into account, and pay particular regard to the representations of anyone who has an interest in or occupies the land, and any body with statutory functions relating to the maintenance or management of the land,[94] as well as the representations of the commoners themselves.[95] There is also some care taken to ensure that the rules of a commons council are tailored to particular circumstances. Exhaustive standardized rules governing function and management are provided by sections 29–35 and by statutory regulations, but to a certain extent these are only default rules: the order establishing the commons council may disapply, supplement, or replace any of them.[96] Whilst this is by no means a mechanism for allowing a community to develop its own rules as it goes along, it does at least allow for initial idiosyncratic preferences to be given effect.

On the negative side, this flexibility is limited by the emphasis put throughout the legislation on the public interest, and the need to have regard to the heterogeneous interests of landowners, commoners, and public bodies. All of this is evident from the procedure just described for setting up the commons council in the first place: no special weight is to be given to representations made by the commoners themselves where they differ from those made by the underlying landowner, or by an interested statutory authority. It is then made absolutely clear by section 31(6) of the Act, which provides that a commons council:

> *must* discharge its functions having regard to—
>
> (a) any guidance given by the [Secretary of State]; and
> (b) the public interest in relation to the land . . . .[97]

The 'public interest' is defined as including the public interest in:

> (a) nature conservancy;
> (b) the conservation of the landscape;
> (c) the protection of public rights of access to any area of land;
> (d) the protection of archeological remains and features of historic interest.[98]

These public functions have led the Government to acknowledge that a commons council will be a public authority within the meaning of

[94] Over half of registered common land in England is designated as Sites of Special Scientific Interest.
[95] See s 27(4)–(5) of the 2006 Act.
[96] ibid, s 29(3)–(4).
[97] Emphasis added.
[98] See s 31(7) of the 2006 Act.

section 6 of the Human Rights Act 1998, and subject to the duty in section 6(1) of the 1998 Act not to act in a way which is incompatible with Convention rights.[99]

All in all, then, it is clear that commons councils are not intended to be, and will not be, appropriate vehicles for the management of mutual self-interest commons.

De Facto Commons

The legislation resulting from the *Jennings Report* then, offers little scope for the creation of new mutual self-interest commons. New *de facto* commons can be created by utilizing other legal structures provided by the law, and this is what happens all the time, but there are problems. In the case of long-established vehicles such as the trust and the company this is hardly surprising given that they evolved for other purposes. In the case of new institutions specifically designed for group property holding, in particular the commonhold association examined below, serious thought has gone into the design of procedures that will work, but there are equally serious doubts as to whether this is going to be achieved.

Legal Structures for Communal Resource Holding

The Ownership Problem

The first problem in English law is that only a legal entity can have direct *ownership* of a resource, and communities are not legal entities, whether defined by reference to a locality or by reference to some other distinguishing characteristic such as neighbouring landholding or sharing of a particular interest. If all the residents of my part of Lambeth were to decide collectively to collect rain water in strategically placed rainwater butts, so they could use the water for watering their gardens, it would not be possible for them, as a group, to own the land on which the butts stand, or the butts themselves, or the water in them.

Communal Use Rights over Privately or Publicly Owned Land

Communities can have legally enforceable *rights* over resources which are owned by someone else, at least where the resource is land. As already noted, this is how common land and town and village greens work in England and Wales. A legal entity is the underlying owner of the land,

[99] See the *Explanatory Notes* to the 2006 Act, para 109.

over which the community (whatever it is) has enforceable rights. In some cases the underlying owner is an artificial entity, a company or trust, deliberately created by or for the community with the sole purpose of holding this ownership of the land and managing it for the benefit of the community. In other cases, the underlying owner is a quite separate individual, perhaps the Crown, the local authority, or a private landowner, whose interests might diverge from those of the community rights holders, and who may or may not have the right, power, or duty to manage the land for the benefit of the community.

Where the underlying owner is just a vehicle created for that purpose, the problem is the style of governance dictated by the legal nature of the vehicle. Each of the different forms of legal entity which might constitute the vehicle (for example, a company limited by guarantee, a trustee, a cooperative, or a commonhold association), has a prescribed constitution, generally highly regulated by statute. Whichever form is chosen, the function of the vehicle (the underlying owner), is to hold and manage the land for the benefit of the community rights holders. Nevertheless the way in which this is done, and the degree of control that the community has over the vehicle, is dictated by its form, as is the nature and level of its accountability, both to the community and to other interest groups. In other words, in such cases the community cannot choose the form of governance appropriate to its circumstances, as we have seen most successful communal resource holders do: the form of governance is dictated by the legal form the underlying owner happens to take.

Where the underlying owner is a separate individual in its own right, the fundamental problem is the complexity introduced by the existence of a separate interest holder whose interests are not the same as those of the communal users. Again as we have seen, this heterogeneity of interests is a factor threatening the viability of communal resource holding. Traditional English agricultural commons and town and village greens often suffer from this problem, where the land is owned by a private landowner but commoners have perpetual agricultural or recreational rights over the land. In these cases, the nature of the commoners' rights over the land, and the fact that they are perpetual, leaves the underlying owner with only vestigial ownership rights in the land, sometimes potentially quite valuable, and sometimes not. If the underlying owner was the community itself, it would balance the value of ignoring or exploiting the potential of these vestigial ownership rights and the consequent enhancement or decrease in value of its use rights. But when these vestigial ownership rights are held by an outsider, this balancing exercise has to be achieved by costly negotiation or through elaborate dispute resolution procedures.

Individual Use Rights Exercisable in Common with Others over Privately or Publicly Owned Land

Members of a community defined by reference to something like neighbouring landholding can each hold individual rights to make use of land in common with each other. As we have seen, rights of common come within this category. So too do the rights over common parts that unit holders in modern developments often have. In form, these rights are categorized as private particular use rights: easements (in so far as they permit positive use of the communally used land), or covenants (in so far as they restrict the user of the communally used land). There are two limiting factors. The first is that, unless there is a leasehold or commonhold nexus between the communal users and the owner of the communally used land, the range of rights that can be created is small. This is because only a relatively narrow range of rights qualify as private easements,[100] and covenants are generally enforceable only in so far as they do not impose a positive burden on the owner of the communally used land.[101]

However, the most important limiting factor again is that there has to be an underlying owner of the communally used land. The commoners cannot own it themselves directly, either as a community or as co-owners.[102] They can own it indirectly, by using a company or trust vehicle as described above, or it can be (and in practice frequently is), owned by a separate individual with separate and divergent interests in its own right.

Other Methods of Communal Resource Holding

The only other way for a community to hold resources, and the only one available where the resource is something other than land, is for the resource to be owned by a corporation or by trustees, with the members of the community being the members of the corporation or the beneficiaries under the trust. Sometimes they might have contractual rights to use the resource in addition to their 'membership' rights to control the behaviour of the resource owner, but sometimes not.

[100] See *Re Ellenborough Park* [1956] Ch 131 (CA).

[101] The long-standing rule that positive covenants are not enforceable, except between the original contracting parties, was reaffirmed in *Rhone v Stephens* [1994] 2 WLR 429 (HL).

[102] This kind of co-ownership is not recognized in England and Wales. It is however in other jurisdictions. In Hong Kong, for example, the common law is adapted to allow workable direct co-ownership of commercial and residential multi-unit developments: see S Nield, *Hong Kong Land Law* (2nd edn) (Hong Kong: Pearson Education Asia, 1997), ch 16. For other jurisdictions see D Clarke, 'Occupying "Cheek by Jowl": Property Issue as Arising from Communal Living' in S Bright and J Dewar, *Land Law: Themes and Perspectives* (Oxford: Oxford University Press, 1998), ch 15.

Ownership Vehicles

It follows from all this that, except in the relatively narrow range of circumstances where new commons can arise through long usage, a group of people who come together in order to administer a resource in their mutual self-interest will have to create a legal entity to hold the underlying ownership of the resource.[103] The two basic forms of vehicle remain the trust and the company. Recent government initiatives are taking seriously the promotion of community resource holding via new or revitalized legal forms. In addition to the commons councils already noted, there are new legal forms such as the commonhold associations considered below and community interest companies designed as a vehicle for not-for-profit organizations using their assets 'for the community interest',[104] as well as revamped legal regimes for cooperatives and industrial and provident societies.[105] However, they are all variations of the company format, and it currently looks as if they will not succeed in transcending the limitations of the corporate form.

Companies

There are several aspects of the corporate form that make it inappropriate—although not necessarily unworkable—for communal resource holding. Arguably, the fundamental characteristic of limited liability for members comes within this category. The basis for all modern companies is limited liability; even in companies limited by guarantee,[106] the corporate form traditionally used for not-for-profit organizations, the guarantee is invariably limited to a notional £1. The limited liability form evolved in the

[103] If, as often happens, they do not appeciate this, they will become an unincorporated association, an informal association whose existence is not recognized by law (except for taxation purposes). The legal analysis of property holding in an inadvertently created unincorporated association is unclear. As a matter of form, its property will almost always be held by one of its officers on trust, but the network of rights and control between the trustee and members, and between the members as between themselves, is an unsatisfactory and not wholly understood amalgam of private ownership, agency, and contract, in which, in theory at least, no legal recognition is given to the common purpose of the association: see A Clarke and P Kohler, *Property Law* (Cambridge: Cambridge University Press, 2005), 599–604.

[104] Created by the Companies (Audit, Investigations and Community Enterprise) Act 2004, following the publication of a Cabinet Office Strategy Unit Report, *Private Action, Public Benefit*, published in September 2002. For further details see the DTI guide, *An Introduction to Community Interest Companies*, published in December 2004, available from <www.dti.gov.uk/cics>; and see, more critically, S Cross, 'Community Interest Companies: A Tangled Corporate Web' (2003) 19 *Scots Law Times* 157.

[105] See Co-operatives and Community Benefit Societies Act 2003.

[106] Commons councils and commonhold associations are in form companies limited by guarantee.

industrial revolution to allow individuals to ring-fence a proportion of their wealth to be made available for a specific commercial project. Communal resource holding may require a greater commitment than that from its members. It cannot operate as a risk-spreading device[107] if the liability of each member is limited to its own share. Also, limited liability provides no solution to the problem of shortfall. No individual member of the community wants to pay more than their share, nor to devote a disproportionately large part of their private wealth to the communal purpose. But unless they do so, the commons will collapse whenever a defaulting member cannot or will not pay their share, or the company encounters unexpected costs or disasters.

There are other problems. Complying with the formalities for setting up and running a company requires a certain amount of expertise, even for a not-for-profit company: there are still requirements to file accounts, make tax returns, and make annual returns to Companies House, none of them particularly apt for small scale, non-trading, mutual self-interest communities. Idiosyncratic rules are possible, but it is not likely that they will be made initially, and most unlikely that they will emerge over time. This is because the rights and duties of the directors and shareholders as against each other and as against outsiders are prescribed by the relevant statute, and in exhaustive detail. Generally these are default provisions only, but varying them requires expert advice, and is likely to be difficult once rights have become entrenched.

Accountability of directors to shareholders may also cause difficulties. The duty of directors is to manage the assets of the company in the interests of the shareholders, but that does not mean that they have to act in accordance with their wishes, and that may not accord with the way in which the community wants to organize itself.[108] In short, companies are not natural vehicles for self-government: the basic structure is of one group of people, the directors, managing a business for another group of people, the shareholders.

Finally, there is the question of terminating the commons. There is an argument that a community is more than the sum of its present members, and that its present members should not be free to take the communal resources for themselves, free from any obligations towards past and future generations. This is a difficult question. It is a serious criticism of commons registered under the 1965 Act that traditionally, once

[107] See n 25 above.

[108] See generally, B Cheffins, *Company Law: Theory, Structure and Operation* (Oxford: Clarendon Press, 1997), esp ch 10.

they have come into existence, no one has the power to end the commons or vary the terms on which they are held.[109] On the other hand, complete freedom for present members to take the resources for themselves may not be acceptable either. Nevertheless, this is what they will have if the communal property is held by a company: the requisite majority of present members can always wind up the company for any or no reason, and take the company's assets for themselves.

New Corporate Models—The Commonhold Association

The commonhold association is a variation on the company format. Over the last twenty or so years it has become increasingly common for trusts and companies to be used as vehicles to hold the freehold interest in leasehold developments on behalf of the leaseholders. This is common in the case of long residential leases, where statutory rights conferred on leaseholders[110] have (intentionally) stripped the landlord's interest of market value. The leaseholders are made the members of the company or the beneficiaries under the trust. In other words, in a reversal of the classic economic progression of a resource being taken out of the common into private ownership as it becomes susceptible to economic exploitation, reversions on residential leases are now moving back from private ownership into the commons as this potential recedes.

The object of commonhold is to build on this development but to remove the artificiality of the leasehold device, and allow each unit holder to own its own unit. The development as a whole is then managed by a company of which the unit holders are the sole members, and which also holds the common parts of the development. A commonhold is therefore a classic limited access mutual self-interest commons, governed by a form of company specially designed for the purpose: the commonhold association, created by the Commonhold and Leasehold Reform Act 2002. Disappointingly, it does not seem likely to transcend the limitations of the standard form of company as a communal resource-holding vehicle, and in some respects is even less satisfactory.[111]

[109] The point was made by Lord Denning in *New Windsor Corporation*, n 52 above. Some limited scope for variation is now made in the 2006 Act. see eg ss 7 and 13.

[110] ie the enfranchisement statutes, now also conferring rights of management and, most significantly, control over service charges, starting with the Leasehold Reform Act 1967 and encompassing Part V of the Housing Act 1985, the Landlord and Tenant Act 1987, the Leasehold Reform, Housing and Urban Development Act 1993, and the Commonhold and Leasehold Reform Act 2002.

[111] For a detailed account of commonhold, see D N Clarke, *Commonhold* (Bristol: Jordans, 2004).

The commonhold association is basically a company limited by guarantee, but with a prescribed form of constitution. The limited liability problem is tackled by requiring the association to levy charges (essentially, service charges), on its members to recover the association's costs in carrying out its function of managing the common parts. Shortfalls can be made good by the association levying an additional charge to cover them, but if this is not done there is no default liability for members. This problem was foreseen and considered in the deliberations leading up to the commonhold legislation, and indeed the Aldridge Report[112] made quite radical recommendations to increase liability in certain circumstances, but these were rejected, and the legislation that emerged explicitly provides that no member can be made liable for more than their own share.[113]

There are other problems. There is a danger that commonholds will be too heterogeneous to operate effectively. It is envisaged that they will be used for mixed developments comprising public and private residential units, and/or retail and public service units such as, for example, schools, each of which will have voting rights. Voting rights need not be equal, but they must be allocated in advance by the developer setting up the commonhold. It seems plausible that the allocation as between different types of user will be based on the need to market the units initially, rather than by reference to achieving a workable balance between heterogeneous neighbours (if indeed such a balance is achievable). There are also worries that the developer may, for one reason or another, want to retain some level of control over the commonhold, and succeed in doing so.[114] Whatever the merits or demerits of this, it does mean that there will be yet another disparate interest to be taken into account in making community decisions.

The worst problem, however, seems likely to be over-prescriptiveness. Detailed provisions governing the rights and duties of the unit owners and company officers are prescribed,[115] and these provisions are nearly all mandatory. The few that can be varied—the percentage of liabilities to be borne by each unit, and the voting rights attached to each unit—must be

[112] T Aldridge, Report of a Working Group, *Commonhold: Freehold Flats and Freehold Ownership of other Interdependent Buildings*, Cm 179 (1987). This was the most significant of the consultation papers preceding the 2002 Act.

[113] Hence the inclusion of detailed (and not wholly satisfactory), provisions for the solvent and insolvent winding-up of commonhold associations: see further J Farrand and A Clarke, *Emmet & Farrand on Title* (London: Sweet & Maxwell, 2005), ch 28A.

[114] C G van der Merwe and P F Smith, 'Commonhold Development Rights—A Comparative Assessment' (2005) *The Conveyancer and Property Lawyer* 53.

[115] Commonhold Regulations SI 2004/1829.

settled by the developer *before* the individual units are sold off, and thereafter can be varied only with great difficulty. There is therefore no possibility of a commonhold community selecting or developing its own regulations to suit its own circumstances.[116] The enforcement provisions provide a good illustration of the level of detail and the inflexibility of approach. There is elaborate mandatory dispute resolution put in place, every step of which *must* be followed: even the circumstances in which the directors of the commonhold association need not take action on default by a unit-holder are spelt out,[117] and the sanctions that can be imposed on default are prescribed. The development of inventive sanctions appropriate to a particular community, which is characteristic of successful commons, is therefore ruled out. Also ruled out is mutual self-enforcement, the characteristic of successful commons noted above: individual unit-holders cannot enforce the obligations of other unit-holders except via the directors. Self-enforcement is further distanced by making provision for, in effect, appeal to an outside source, in the form of a specialized commonhold ombudsman scheme.[118]

It may also prove to be significant that expulsion, also characteristic of successful commons, is ruled out. Unit ownership may not be forfeited, however extreme the unit-holder's default.[119] There are good reasons for this, and for the general lack of flexibility. The prime objective of the legislation is to ensure commonhold units are as marketable as freeholds, and uniformity of terms and security of holdings was thought essential to persuade lenders to make mortgage finance available on equal terms. Whether it is also compatible with effective management of all types of commonhold remains to be seen.

Finally, and probably also for the same reason, the directors are in effect prohibited from taking into consideration any interests broader than those of the immediate members: by section 35(1) they are required to exercise their powers so as to permit or facilitate so far as possible:

(a) the exercise by each unit-holder of his rights, and
(b) the enjoyment by each unit-holder of the freehold estate in his unit.

[116] Compare the growing realization in the United States of America that common interest communities may need looser structures within which to develop their own regulations: see eg Hyatt, n 13 above, and Franzese, n 13 above.

[117] Section 35(3) of the 2002 Act provides that they need not take action 'if they reasonably think that inaction is in the best interests of establishing or maintaining harmonious relationships between all the unit-holders, and that it will not cause any unit-holder (other than the defaulter) significant loss or significant disadvantage . . .'.

[118] See s 42 of the 2002 Act.

[119] ibid, s 31(8).

In other words, there is no question of a commonhold being treated as being more than the sum of the interests of the present members.

Trusts

The other traditional vehicle for communal resource holding is the trust. This, especially in its American public trust form, has tremendous potential as a vehicle for holding and managing resources on behalf of disparate, potentially conflicting interests, especially inter-generational interests, and especially where the public interest has to be balanced against the interests of other beneficiaries. However, the American public trust is not a device for holding resources on behalf of a mutual self-interest community. For these purposes, the only available model is the private trust.

There is an initial technical problem that, whereas companies can continue in existence indefinitely, private trusts cannot. If trustees are to hold resources on behalf of a community, that means holding it on behalf of present and future members of the community. Their power to hold on behalf of future members is however limited by the perpetuity rule, so the trust must end (and all the resources must then be distributed to the then current members of the community) at the end of the appropriate period,[120] unless the current members can be persuaded to start the trust all over again.

However, the fundamental problem is that the trust is not a device for self-government. Management and control of the assets are sharply divorced from benefit. The trustees may not take any benefit from the trust, and whilst there is no difficulty with a trustee also being a beneficiary, rigorous accounting is necessary to prevent any mixing of the trust assets with the trustee's own personal assets. More importantly, the duty of the trustees is to act in the interests of the beneficiaries, not in accordance with their directions.

Also, the trust is essentially an investment device, designed for communal *wealth* holding, not the communal utilization of a specific resource. Unless the trust documents provide otherwise, the trustees are under a duty to invest the trust assets to produce the best return for the beneficiaries as a whole. This means that individual beneficiaries have no right to insist on being able to use the resources originally put on trust—they might have to settle for a share of the income produced instead.

Unlike commonhold associations and other companies limited by guarantee, trusts are highly flexible in form. There are virtually no

[120] Up to eighty years. The perpetuity rule does not apply to public (ie charitable) trusts.

mandatory statutory provisions. Legislation provides fairly rudimentary default provisions but mostly they are freely variable.[121] This means that trusts can be drafted so as to give the trustees and the beneficiaries virtually any rights and powers *vis à vis* each other.[122] The only problem is that all this requires expert legal drafting at the time when the trust comes into existence, which may not be forthcoming. Also, subsequent variation is difficult,[123] so the chances of appropriate regulation evolving are small.

However, there are other ways in which a trust might be more appropriate than a company for holding communal resources. Unlike companies, trusts are wholly private institutions. Trustees have no duties to make returns to anyone or to account to anyone other than their beneficiaries, and beneficiaries can ratify any action of the trustees, whether or not in breach of trust. The only limit on this flexibility is the need to take into account the interests of *all* beneficiaries: in the case of trustees holding on behalf of future generations this may considerably restrict the trustees' freedom of action.

Also, in a trust for the benefit of present and future members of the community, the present members cannot end the trust prematurely[124] and take the resources for themselves, as they could if the resource-holding vehicle was a company. There is an absolute rule that the beneficiaries of any trust, acting unanimously, can always end the trust and take the trust assets for themselves,[125] but this cannot be done when the class of beneficiaries includes future generations.

All in all, then, it is possible to adapt a trust to make it work reasonably well as a vehicle for communal resource holding, at least for a limited period, but it is not designed for that purpose, and the adaptation requires sophisticated professional advice. It is not therefore usually feasible for small communities, especially those who have not yet worked out exactly what regulatory form they want, and would prefer to work things out as they go along.

[121] See Trusts of Land and Appointment of Trustees Act 1996 and the Trustee Act 2000.

[122] But not in such a way as to get over the perpetuity problem.

[123] There is a limited jurisdiction for variation by the court under the Variation of Trusts Act 1958, and scattered powers in other legislative provisions such as ss 53 and 57 of the Trustee Act 1925.

[124] ie before it is naturally brought to an end by the expiration of the perpetuity period. The exception would be if they formed themselves into an unincorporated association, and then terminated the association, so cutting off the supply of future generations (but taking care to end the trust before the association ends, otherwise they will make themselves disappear, leaving their assets *bona vacantia*).

[125] The rule in *Saunders v Vautier* (1841) 4 Beav 115.

Conclusion

Successful modern commons undeniably do exist, consciously or unconsciously governed by the inappropriate legal mechanisms described above. This may just illustrate that legal rules are not that important in the self-generation and operation of the social norms that really govern the relationships within a mutual self-interest commons. Nevertheless, it is hard for a lawyer to accept that the content of the legal rules is wholly irrelevant. As Dagan and Heller put it:[126]

> Law should be understood to work as a set of background rules, always in operation, but seldom overly manifest in the daily life of commons resource management. Formal law is often not powerful enough, by itself, to establish directly the trust, cooperation, and mutual reliance that any successful commons requires for the day-to-day routines of self-governance. Commoners generally will not deploy law on a regular basis with each other, both because it would be costly and because people often perceive recourse to law as unnecessary, unneighbourly, or even hostile in ongoing relationships of trust and cooperation . . . Social norms and other modes of social organisation and structure, not formal law, govern most daily interactions.
>
> With that caveat, well designed background legal rules are nevertheless crucial for the success of the liberal commons . . . .

Legal rules have the potential both to facilitate and to discourage the development of successful commons. We need to look more closely at our legal institutions to ensure that they are doing the former and not the latter.

[126] Dagan and Heller, n 9 above, 578.

The Tax Avoidance Culture: Who is Responsible? Governmental Influences and Corporate Social Responsibility

*Judith Freedman**

Introduction

The Anglican Bishop of Liverpool has been reported as stating that 'In this country, we have created a culture of tax avoidance'.[1] Press coverage and the activities and statements of various lobby groups support this perception that there is a considerable loss of revenue arising from 'aggressive' tax avoidance by business and individuals.[2] In contrast, the increasing attacks on this 'tax avoidance culture' have been accompanied by complaints from business that the UK is becoming uncompetitive, not only due to higher rates of tax than elsewhere but also because of uncertainty and the rate of change in the tax system.[3] This clash of perceptions feeds a debate that is becoming progressively more polarized and unsatisfactory.

The UK government and revenue authorities have introduced many specific anti-avoidance provisions[4] and new mechanisms such as disclosure requirements[5] to regulate the situation. At the same time, these authorities argue that taxpayers have a responsibility to change their

* KPMG Professor of Taxation Law, University of Oxford. The author has benefited from discussing this issue with academic colleagues as well as members of the tax profession and government revenue departments and thanks them for their assistance but the views expressed here represent her views alone.

1 N Mathiason, 'Super-Rich Hide Trillions Offshore', the *Observer*, 27 March 2005.

2 The activities of the Tax Justice Network account for much of this increased interest. See <http://www.taxjustice.net/cms/front_content.php?idcat=2> and particularly The Tax Gap Limited, *Mind the Tax Gap* (London: 2006) at <http://www.richard.murphy.dial.pipex.com/MindtheTaxGapFinal.pdf>. See also A Missbach, *Tackling the Tax Avoidance Culture*, at <http://www.taxjustice.net/cms/upload/pdf/tax_avoidance_culture.pdf>.

3 See eg KPMG/Lighthouse Global Survey, *The Times*, 13 March 2006; CBI, *Recommendations for the 2006 Budget*, March 2006.

4 For the most recent examples see Finance Act 2006 ch 8.

5 ss 19 and 306–19 of the Finance Act 2004, as extended by the Finance Act 2006.

culture and to comply with the spirit of the law as well as the letter in order to steer clear of 'abusive tax avoidance' and ensure that they contribute their 'fair share' of revenue.[6] It is suggested that the corporate social responsibility (CSR) movement has relevance to the tax responsibilities of large corporates. Both the revenue authorities and the lobby groups favour this approach and some businesses and professional advisers have also taken steps towards embracing it, perhaps in the hope that it will reduce the threat of further and more radical statutory regulation.[7] The CSR movement is creating a group of advisers who have taxation firmly in their sights as part of the CSR agenda.[8]

It is against this shifting background that discussions of tax avoidance must take place. It is notoriously difficult to assess levels of tax avoidance, especially given the problems encountered in defining this term and determining which aspects of it are to be included in any assessment of revenue loss or 'tax gap', and which are part of a normal functioning tax system.[9] This chapter focuses on business taxation although many of the points made are of more general application. It argues that if there is a 'tax avoidance culture' in the UK, it is in part the consequence of governmental attitudes to taxation and inadequacies in our tax system. Naturally taxpayers will do what they can to minimize their tax bills, but their attitude to the lengths to which they should go to do this depends not only on the level of tax payable, and whether it is perceived to be fairly levied, but also on general attitudes to tax-paying, which are themselves affected by the structure of the tax system and the approaches to tax-paying taken by government and public bodies more generally.

There is an apparent change in behaviour taking place in the direction of less exposure to the risks of highly artificial tax schemes, at least at the

[6] This is contentious wording to which we shall return. See eg Inland Revenue Press Release, 9 January 2003; D Hartnett, Deputy Chairman of the Inland Revenue to the Wyman Debate at the Institute of Chartered Accountants on 15 March 2003 at <http://www.inlandrevenue.gov.uk/news/wyman_debate_05-03.htm>; C Tailby, 'Combating VAT Avoidance', the *Tax Journal*, 2 December 2002, 6.

[7] KPMG, *Tax in the Boardroom* (London: 2004); Ernst & Young, *Tax Risk Management* (London: 2004); Pricewaterhouse Coopers, *Total Tax Contribution Framework* (London: 2005) HMRC, *Tax Law in the Boardroom* (London: 2006); HMRC, Partnership Enhancement Programme, *Tax in the Boardroom Agenda: The Views of Business* (London: 2006).

[8] See eg Henderson Global Investors, *Responsible Tax* (London: 2005); SustainAbility, *Taxing Issues—Responsible Business and Tax* (London: SustainAbility, 2006); J Conley and C Williams, 'Engage, Embed and Embellish: Theory Versus Practice in the Corporate Social Responsibility Movement', *University of North Carolina Legal Studies Research Paper* No 05–16. <http://papers.ssrn.com/s013/papers.cfm?abstract_id=691521>.

[9] The UK Treasury and Her Majesty's Revenue and Customs (hereafter HMRC) have not published an estimate of the tax gap although they are known to have working figures—see *Treasury Minutes on the First and Second Reports from the Committee of Public Accounts 2003–2004*, Cm 6130 (London: The Stationery Office, 2004). On the US, see J Slemrod, 'The Economics of Corporate Tax Selfishness' (2004) 57 *National Tax Journal* 877.

corporate level, as a result of the combination of legislative change and other pressures being exerted on companies in the tax arena. There is, however, also a resentment building up from businesses, which feel that they are being asked to make tax decisions in a climate of uncertainty and undue complexity. The attempts being made to reduce avoidance by companies through persuasion, and appeals to corporate governance and CSR arguments, will only go a certain way towards achieving their aims, however effective the current campaign may be.

It will be argued here that care needs to be taken by the revenue authorities not to place too much faith in the CSR 'solution' without more, since CSR has limits of its own. Companies will engage in CSR only to the extent that it makes business sense for them and may even come to use CSR for their own presentational purposes rather than actually changing their behaviour.[10] In the end it is the task of Government to define what kind of behaviour is 'acceptable' or 'fair' and to do this through law rather than negotiations and media pressure. This is not to suggest that it is possible to draw a bright line between what is 'abusive' or 'unacceptable' and what is not. Clearly this presents severe difficulties and there will always be borderline cases. There is no simple solution, but in order to modify the tax avoidance culture at root a range of solutions is needed, ranging from changed Government behaviour to clearer signalling in the legislation. This will require changed attitudes to taxation from politicians and officials across Government since currently, as will be shown, mixed messages are given. In addition there is a need for improvements in the approach to specific legislation. Further, as this author has proposed elsewhere, a general anti-avoidance provision would send out valuable signals,[11] but if this is to operate usefully and fairly it requires not only an appropriate legislative background[12] coupled with an administrative and regulatory framework to support it, but also cultural and attitude changes on the part of Government as well as taxpayers.

What is Tax Avoidance? The Definitional Quagmire

In much of the tax avoidance literature there is a strong focus on categorization. Clearly the fact that the lines are hard to draw is the key problem

[10] D Vogel, *The Market for Virtue—The Potential and Limits of Corporate Social Responsibility* (Washington, DC: Brookings Institution Press, 2005); Conley and Williams, n 8 above.

[11] J Freedman, 'Defining Taxpayer Responsibility: In Support of a General Anti-Avoidance Principle' [2004] *British Tax Review* 332–57.

[12] Discussed further in J Freedman, 'Interpreting Tax Statutes: Tax Avoidance, Judicial Doctrines and the Intention of Parliament' (2007) 123 *Law Quarterly Review* 53.

in this area but some analysts and commentators, including the judiciary, give the impression that the creation of more categories and new language to describe the position will help in tackling the problem, whereas in fact this often merely creates more difficult borders to negotiate. It is not the purpose of this chapter to add to the existing extensive definitional debate but it is necessary to provide a framework for the discussion that follows, particularly for the non-specialist reader. Although the intention is that the framework given here should be relatively standard, it will nevertheless be contentious because this is an exceptionally contentious area. Statements found in recent literature from Her Majesty's Revenue and Customs (hereafter HMRC) will be used to illustrate the definitional failure and lack of common language that bedevils this area.

The starting position for any discussion of avoidance remains its differentiation from evasion.[13] Evasion is illegal and involves non-disclosure or concealment, be it fraudulent or not.[14] If it is discovered by the revenue authorities, not only will it be ineffective to save tax but it will also result in penalties for the taxpayer and perhaps even criminal prosecution. The conventional wisdom describes avoidance as legal, and that remains the case despite some attempts to muddy the picture.[15] The principle in the *Duke of Westminster's* case[16] remains (ie that a taxpayer is entitled to arrange his affairs so that the tax attaching under the appropriate Acts is less than it otherwise would be), although there are increasing attempts by the revenue authorities to change the culture of taxpayers and their advisers. On this view, avoidance is reprehensible where the legal analysis deviates from the economic substance and this is the case regardless of the wording of the legislation in question. The difficulty faced by HMRC is that the UK case law does not establish, and never has held, that economic substance overrides legal form as a general rule. Even when the judicial approach to tax avoidance was at its firmest, following the decisions in *WT Ramsay Ltd v IRC*[17] and *Furniss v Dawson*[18] (sometimes referred to as the 'new approach') there was never a blanket substance over form rule in the UK.

If an avoidance scheme is held by the courts to be effective it may still be considered highly artificial and 'unacceptable' by the revenue authorities

[13] For a full discussion see J Tiley, *Revenue Law* (Oxford: Hart Publishing, 2005), 84–5 and 93–5; J Kessler, 'Tax Avoidance Purpose and Section 741 of the Taxes Act 1988' [2004] *British Tax Review* 375–409; Freedman, n 11 above, 332–57.

[14] Freedman, n 11 above, 347–50.

[15] Revenue officials have been keen to stress that 'aggressive' avoidance may stray into evasion. See eg the then Chairman of Customs and Excise, R Broadbent, 'VAT Compliance in the 21st Century' (2003) *British Tax Review* 122, 128.

[16] *Inland Revenue Comrs v Duke of Westminster* [1936] AC (HL) 1.

[17] [1981] STC (HL) 174.

[18] [1984] STC (HL) 15.

but their only real remedy will then be to advise ministers to change the law, unless they can show concealment and fraud. They may, however, consider the taxpayer in question to be a high risk and pay special attention to that taxpayer's affairs in future and this in itself could be a considerable deterrent. This approach to risk management by the HMRC is now its published strategy and is being used forcefully to control avoidance.[19]

Sometimes avoidance is divided into sub-categories—acceptable or unacceptable. Others now prefer to use the word avoidance only for behaviour that is not acceptable. Of course the question arises, acceptable to whom? Clearly the final arbiters must be the courts, construing the will of Parliament, but at times, disconcertingly, the HMRC literature seems to substitute acceptability to ministers, or to the revenue authorities. Other phrases used are 'abusive'[20] or 'aggressive' but these are no more precise.[21] Names such as tax mitigation or tax planning are given to schemes that fall on the acceptable side of the line.[22] However, all formulations of that distinction are circular. Lord Templeman, in *Challenge*,[23] defines mitigation as a case where there is a reduction in income, or expenditure is incurred in circumstances that reduce the taxpayer's assessable income or entitle him to a reduction in his tax liability. The problem with this is that, as seen most recently in the case of *Barclays Mercantile Business Finance Ltd v Mawson*,[24] whether there has been a reduction of income, or expenditure has been incurred, for the purposes of the statute in question is precisely the question which has to be addressed in tax avoidance cases and so this formulation does not assist at all. Another formulation of the test is that the distinction between what is avoidance and planning depends on the 'evident' intention of Parliament.[25] Again, since

[19] HMRC, *Working with Large Business—Providing High Quality Service—Improving Tax Compliance* (London: HMRC, 2006). Risk indicators defined in this document include 'Complex structures and intra group transactions that generate tax benefits unrelated to economic substance of commercial activity, where the projected tax benefit is a vital part of the costing of the scheme' (Process Four, 20).

[20] This is entering the avoidance taxonomy largely through the European Court of Justice (hereafter ECJ) which has introduced the concept of abuse of law into the VAT avoidance cases—see *Halifax plc, Leeds Permanent Development Services Ltd, County Wide Property Investments Ltd, v Commissioners of Customs and Excise* Case C-255/02 21 February 2006.

[21] For a recent addition to the descriptions see the references to 'extreme tax avoidance' by the Institute of Directors in their Tax Policy Comment, *Tax Avoidance* (London: 2006).

[22] Lord Templeman, *CIR v Challenge Corporation Ltd* [1986] STC 548 (PC) 554–5. (References will be to Simon's Tax Cases throughout this article where possible since these are the specialist tax reports containing full cross-references to other tax cases, some of which are not reported elsewhere.)

[23] n 21 above.

[24] *Barclays Mercantile Business Finance Ltd v Mawson* [2004] UKHL 51, [2005] STC 1 (HL).

[25] *IRC v Willoughby* [1997] STC (HL) 995, 1004 (Lord Nolan).

what is the intention of Parliament is the very question at stake, which has to be discovered by applying the rules of statutory construction evolved by the courts, this terminology is not at all helpful. A better analysis is provided by Lord Hoffmann who states that 'the fact that steps taken for the avoidance of tax are acceptable or unacceptable is the conclusion at which one arrives by applying the statutory language to the facts of the case. It is not a test for deciding whether it applies or not.'[26]

If the interpretation contended for by the taxpayer is contrary to the intention of Parliament and held to be so by the courts as a matter of statutory construction, then the avoidance will not be effective and tax will be payable although it remains the case in the UK—at least for now—that there is no penalty for entering into an avoidance scheme.[27] In deciding on the intention of Parliament, the courts apply a purposive approach to tax as to any other area of law. According to the House of Lords in the case of *Barclays Mercantile Business Finance Limited*,[28] this was the only effect of the *Ramsay* decision.[29] In the early years following that decision, the *Ramsay* principle[30] was considered to apply a new approach to the interpretation of tax statutes where there was a pre-ordained series of transactions (also referred to as a composite transaction) and where steps were inserted which had no commercial (business) purpose apart from the avoidance of liability to tax. If those two ingredients existed, it seemed that the inserted steps were to be disregarded for fiscal purposes. There are real problems in describing how far that new approach now takes us, given the decision in *Barclays Mercantile*[31] that the only issue is one of statutory construction and that there is no judicial anti-avoidance doctrine. The *Scottish Provident* case,[32] however, decided by the same House of Lords, at the same time as *Barclays Mercantile*, suggests that something more survives, given the importance their Lordships placed in that case on the existence of a composite transaction. It seems from *Scottish Provident* that, in some circumstances, a series of transactions constitutes a composite transaction as a matter of law. This then has implications for the application of the relevant statute so that, whilst statutory construction is highly relevant, the substantive analysis of the transaction in question is also of importance.[33]

26 *MacNiven v Westmoreland Investments Ltd* [2001] UKHL 6, [2001] STC 237 (HL), 257.

27 Although there may be interest payable for late payment of tax.

28 *Barclays Mercantile*, n 24 above, [33].

29 *Ramsay*, n 17 above.

30 As developed particularly in *Furniss v Dawson*, n 18 above.

31 *Barclays Mercantile*, n 24 above.

32 *Inland Revenue Commissioners v Scottish Provident Institution* [2004] UKHL 52, [2005] STC 15 (HL).

33 The position reached by the case law is discussed in more detail in Freedman, n 12 above.

None of this recent case law assists in the definition of avoidance; indeed it removes some of the guidance that earlier was thought to exist. We are left, as before, with a spectrum of behaviours which need further examination in order to decide to what extent they should be controlled or limited and, if limitation is desirable, what techniques should be used to achieve this. At one end of the spectrum will be evasion in the true sense which all are agreed should be prevented and at the other, tax planning within the intention of Parliament, which all are agreed should be permitted. Between these activities, difficult as they are to define, is the grey area of activity which some consider to be completely legitimate and even desirable for the proper functioning of the tax system and others consider reprehensible. It is this grey area upon which the rest of this chapter will focus.

The 'Grey Area'

In the circumstances described above it is wise not to become too far engaged in terminology. What matters, it might be thought, is whether a court will hold that a scheme is effective or not. HMRC appear to have a slightly different view of the situation. Take, for example, the *International Tax Handbook*, written to train inspectors.[34] This suggests, entirely correctly, that the current dividing line might be impossible to define. The Handbook then goes on to state that 'In any event, distinctions between mitigation and tax avoidance are of less concern to the Government than the effect on the yield to the Exchequer'.

No doubt this is true, but it is a surprising statement to find in a technical training manual, which it might be thought should focus on proper application of the law. If it is intended to suggest that the schemes which should be targeted are not those which the courts might find to be ineffective but those which Government would like to be ineffective (and note the reference to Government rather than Parliament) then this is cause for concern. The latter is a matter on which HMRC should advise Government to legislate but it is not the basis on which it should be determined how to handle individual cases. Whatever is meant by acceptable and unacceptable avoidance, it is surely not this. The taxpayer's responsibilities and duties must be governed by the law and not simply by the

[34] HMRC, *The International Tax Handbook* ITH101, para 1, see (<http://www.hmrc.gov.uk/manuals/ithmanual/html/1ithcont/01_0001_ITHCONT.htm>). The purpose of this book is described as being to provide Inspectors of Taxes in the network with a basic understanding of the problems posed by international tax planning.

effect on the yield to the Exchequer of certain behaviour. The Handbook continues as follows:

Within the Revenue we do not categorise avoidance in quite the narrow way that the Courts have done. Of course we make a distinction between mitigation and avoidance. However, if a taxpayer takes advantage of the law to get a tax advantage which is not, in our understanding, within the spirit of the legislation, we tend to look on that as avoidance.

This alarming statement is at least modified by the recognition that 'unless the prerequisites of the new approach are present such avoidance can only be countered by legislation brought in for the purpose'. The passage then goes on:

As already noted, fine distinctions between 'tax planning' and 'tax avoidance' are seen as being of less consequence than the overall effect on the yield to the Exchequer. This is particularly so where the apparent result is not in accordance with Parliament's intentions or which would not have been had Parliament addressed itself to the particular issue. Where cross-border avoidance schemes are involved International Division will always consider the possibility of using the 'new approach' although, as will become apparent later in the book, the appropriate remedy is often by way of legislation.

This is a little more reassuring because it talks about Parliament's intentions (rather than Government's) and it recognizes the need for legislation and examination of the case law in the form of the 'new approach' (whatever that may now be). There remains, however, a potential gap between what the courts will find to be ineffective and what HMRC see as 'unacceptable' avoidance. Thus there exists a grey area of activity, not only in the international arena, but more generally, in which a question mark hangs over acceptability. We see reference to this again in the guidance on the latest regulations on disclosure of tax avoidance schemes where there are references to what is acceptable to HMRC as though this in itself was a test of avoidance in the pejorative sense.[35] It is in this area that morality, ethics, and CSR are sometimes called in aid and where companies in particular are asked to go beyond pure compliance with the law and to abide by its 'spirit'. 'Spirit' is equated by the revenue authorities with what is acceptable to them in some of this literature, but HMRC's view of Parliamentary intention is not the final arbiter of the meaning of tax

[35] HMRC, *Guidance. Disclosure of Tax Avoidance Schemes* (London: June 2006). Under these regulations schemes that have certain hallmarks need to be disclosed to HMRC. Disclosability is not synonymous with avoidance. The guidance states (6.1) 'The absence of a hallmark should not be regarded as an indication that tax arrangements not caught constitute practices that are acceptable to HMRC'.

legislation. Only a court decision has that status, and the courts do not always decide in favour of HMRC's view of acceptability.

The *Barclays Mercantile* case,[36] referred to above, is a good example of this. It was highly complex and also circular. The main benefit derived by the parties was the securing of capital allowances that would not have been available without some complexity although, arguably, the circular elements were not essential to the tax scheme but were designed to prevent any element of real risk arising on the part of the taxpayers. At the same time, this was a transaction involving parties at arm's length, within the context of a commercial financing transaction arranged by a lease finance company and relying upon legislation designed to provide a tax incentive for leasing. Whilst HMRC took the view that what was done was highly artificial and reprehensible, as did certain sectors of the media, the company considered that it was operating within the legislation in a proper commercial fashion and the courts were completely split, with a final decision for the taxpayer. In the High Court, Park J, upholding the court of first instance, the Special Commissioners, considered that the scheme in this case was not a tax avoidance scheme but was careful tax planning. Nevertheless, looking at the scheme as a whole, he considered that it was not 'standard commercial finance leasing' and so he did not consider that the capital allowances should be forthcoming.[37] Reversing him, Peter Gibson LJ in the Court of Appeal considered this to be an ordinary finance leasing transaction and found it 'difficult to understand what was thought by the Special Commissioners and the judge not to be commercial about it'.[38] The House of Lords reiterated the view that the transactions were undertaken for the purpose of the taxpayer's finance leasing trade and the additional elements, whether circular or not, were not necessary in creating the entitlement to capital allowances and so could be ignored.[39]

This illustrates perfectly the dilemma in which a taxpayer finds itself, particularly a corporate taxpayer pursuing business opportunities in a competitive environment which abounds with tax-linked incentives. In these circumstances the grey area on which this chapter is focused will always have uncertain boundaries that can be resolved only by further legislation or by court decisions. Improvements could be made to the boundaries by better legislation, as will be discussed below, but a grey area will remain. This is a particularly complex regulatory task because law

[36] *Barclays Mercantile*, n 24 above.
[37] *Barclays Mercantile Ltd v Mawson* [2002] STC 1068 (Ch D) [38] and [46].
[38] *Barclays Mercantile Ltd v Mawson* [2003] STC 66 (CA) [32]–[36].
[39] *Barclays Mercantile Ltd v Mawson*, n 24 above, [41]–[42].

enforcement has to be integrated with law reform as the boundary is constantly tested and re-drawn.[40] There will always be some taxpayers who will operate closer to the boundaries than others[41] but the way to regulate behaviour within this grey area, and the extent to which it is reasonable to castigate businesses operating close to the borders and to expect business to self-regulate, remains a key issue for business, the professions, and the revenue authorities.

Governmental Influence—Mixed Messages and Confused Structure

If taxpayers, businesses in particular, are to be expected to operate responsibly within the 'grey area' described above, and to steer clear of the boundaries, whatever they may be, then Government and the revenue authorities need to create a mind-set in which tax-paying is marked as a positive contribution and a clear obligation. There is a considerable amount of discussion in ministerial statements and HMRC and Treasury literature about the importance of taxpayers paying their 'fair share'.[42] Leaving aside for the time being how that fair share is to be judged, there is a problem in the way this language sits with the constant attempts to encourage certain behaviour by tax reduction, which might be thought to give the contrary message that tax-paying has negative connotations.

There is a tendency for politicians to think in terms of tax breaks whenever they wish to encourage an activity. This is not surprising since giving tax reliefs and incentives is one of the few actions that politicians have the power to take, but it is also not surprising that this encourages taxpayers in turn to think in terms of tax breaks. References to CSR from ministers are as likely to be linked with a tax break for behaving responsibly as they are with the notion of paying a full share of tax.[43] Use of taxes rather than other devices to penalize certain types of behaviour dilutes the concept of

[40] J Braithwaite, 'Large Business and the Compliance Model' in V Braithwaite (ed), *Taxing Democracy: Understanding Tax Avoidance and Evasion* (Aldershot: Ashgate, 2003), 177–99, 199.

[41] For an analysis of the different attitudes of taxpayers see V Braithwaite, 'Dancing with Tax Authorities: Motivational Postures and Non-complaint Actions' in Braithwaite (ed), n 40 above.

[42] Examples abound. For a recent one, see HMRC Press Release, *Major Tax Avoidance Scheme Closed Down* 20th January 2006, in which the Paymaster General, Dawn Primarolo, states 'The use of avoidance schemes such as this which get around the intention of Parliament is unacceptable and unfair to the majority of taxpayers who pay their fair share'.

[43] For an example, see the speech of Stephen Timms MP when Minister for Corporate Social Responsibility in 2002 explaining how governments can provide fiscal incentives for

tax as a revenue-raising device and confuses its objectives and thus taxpayers' attitudes to taxation generally. It is natural for taxpayers to think in terms of tax minimization in any event, as a matter of human nature, but this attitude of governments exacerbates the problem and sends out mixed messages to taxpayers.

If the aim is to encourage citizens to see tax as the price they pay for that citizenship, cutting the price for good behaviour will not encourage them to pay the full price. This encourages the impression that they should always look for savings, much as constant sales in the shops dissuade anyone from paying the recommended retail price. It would be better by far to have a lower, more transparently fair tax for all with fewer special breaks. The tax price should be cut if there is a real cost which genuinely reduces the taxpayer's ability to pay, such as expenditure on investment, but this should be done in a straightforward and transparent way and only to the extent necessary to compensate for that cost. Unless there is a real case of market failure then there is a strong case for the tax system to be as neutral as possible, leaving market forces to give rise to sensible commercial decision-making. Even if there is market failure, direct subsidies or payments may well be better targeted or more efficient than tax breaks.[44] Not only do tax breaks complicate the tax system and create opportunities for avoidance in themselves, but they also influence attitudes to taxation and support the tax avoidance culture in this way.

Many examples could be given: two recent ones will suffice to illustrate the point. These are the recent débâcle over tax breaks for incorporation, now happily terminated but not until much damage had been done, and salary sacrifice schemes, terminated only in part. Both give mixed signals and create groups of taxpayers, many at the start of their business careers, who have been persuaded to think about tax as an important part of setting up their initial arrangements by virtue of these tax reliefs.

Tax-Driven Incorporation

A very obvious example of this kind of confused message can be seen with the introduction of the nil rate of corporation tax, introduced in the

socially responsible behaviour through credit and similar. <http://www.dti.gov.uk/ministers/archived/Timms131202.html>. See also the DTI's Business Links page on corporate social responsibility which states, 'CSR can help you improve your business performance . . . You avoid unnecessary costs such as wasted energy or paying landfill tax on your waste collection.' See <http://www.businesslink.gov.uk/bdotg/action/detail?r.l3=1075408468&r.l2=1074446322&r.l1=1074404796&r.s=m&type=RESOURCES&itemId=1075408480>.

[44] For a simple discussion of the advantages of tax neutrality, see J Kay and M King, *The British Tax System* (5th edn) (Oxford: Oxford University Press, 1990), 19–20 and 162–3.

Finance Act 2002 for companies with profits of £10,000 or less, and known as the 'corporation tax starting rate'.[45] This was finally removed by the Finance Act 2006 after a very unhappy history: a brave recognition of a bad mistake but one that should not have been necessary and came too late to prevent harm from being done. Not only was there an attempt to use the tax system to reward entrepreneurship but it was one which was bound to distort decisions and encourage a climate of artificiality for tax purposes. Although the nil rate has now gone, many new business owners were inducted into this system and it will take a while to remove the misleading lesson it seemed to convey.

It was already the case in 2002 that one of the first issues small business owners faced when setting up was their choice of legal form as between a partnership or sole tradership and a company.[46] This decision has never been revenue neutral and many business owners therefore start their careers with the impression that decisions in commercial life are tax driven. This is fertile ground for a tax avoidance culture. The nil rate band was a deliberate attempt to encourage entrepreneurship through the tax system, which being targeted on corporations to the exclusion of unincorporated businesses created an obvious distortion or non-neutrality.

The problem was pointed out by the Institute for Fiscal Studies[47] and others and highlighted in the Standing Committee Debates on the 2002 Finance Bill.[48] Nevertheless the government persisted with this policy. Speaking in the House of Commons Standing Committee on introducing the measure, the Paymaster General explained the thinking.

> The measure recognises that businesses growing beyond a certain size will often be companies. We believe that cutting corporation tax is an effective way of targeting support at small and growing businesses . . . Surely small businesses will not look a gift horse in the mouth. We want to create growth and economic activity, and to sustain entrepreneurial activity.[49]

Small businesses did not look the gift horse in the mouth but they and their advisers took on board what they thought was the message they were

[45] Income and Corporation Taxes Act 1988 s 13AA. For a fuller discussion of the history of this discussion see J Freedman, 'Why Taxing the Micro-Business is Not Simple—A Cautionary Tale from the "Old World" ', (2006) 2 *Journal of The Australasian Tax Teachers Association*, <http://www.atax.unsw.edu.au/atta/jatta>.

[46] J Freedman and M Godwin, 'Legal Form, Tax and the Micro-Business' in K Caley, E Chell, F Chittenden, and C Mason (eds), *Small Enterprise Development* (London: Paul Chapman Publishing Ltd, 1992).

[47] L Blow, M Hawkins, A Klemm, J McCrae, and H Simpson, *IFS Budget 2002: Business Taxation Measures*, IFS Briefing Note No 24 (London: IFS, 2002).

[48] House of Commons Standing Committee F 16, May 2002.

[49] n 48 above, cols 114–15.

supposed to be imbibing. Small businesses of all kinds, entrepreneurial and not,[50] began to use the relief in a perfectly rational and entirely predictable way, incorporating their firms whether or not this was desirable for non-tax purposes in order to obtain the tax breaks. Incorporations rose from 222,000 in 2001 to nearly 397,000 in 2003.[51] At this point Government became concerned about loss of revenue and the use of the relief for tax and national insurance advantages without any change of economic activity.[52] It therefore introduced a complex anti-avoidance provision to counter the incentive effect of the zero tax rate for all those distributing their profits, which most very small businesses needed to do simply to be able to pay their bills. This measure, the non-corporate distribution rate,[53] was not a success and its repeal, together with that of the zero rate band, was announced in the pre-Budget report in December 2005 as a measure to 'better target tax incentives'. The Regulatory Impact Assessment for this change comments that

> [T]he benefits of existing incentives are being eroded by increasing numbers of new incorporations, who do not have growth ambitions, but are still able to take advantage of these incentives. The Government's objective is to refocus growth incentives so that the support for and the benefits of reinvestment go to businesses with growth ambitions and it is concerned that any incentives should be perceived as fair. Use of incentives by people being encouraged to incorporate and reduce their tax and national insurance contributions erodes that fairness.[54]

Any suggestion of abuse is carefully aimed at advisers rather than taxpayers themselves, but the above statement is still a clear recognition that setting up this incentive has encouraged tax-driven behaviour. This is a direct example of government encouraging a culture of tax avoidance, the word avoidance being used here in the 'grey area' sense described above as behaviour that is unacceptable to Government although entirely within the legislation and thus the intention of Parliament as it would be construed by the courts. At least the Treasury has now had the sense and courage to reverse these provisions, but it is unreasonable to blame taxpayers for having utilized them and the effect will remain influential on

[50] The majority of small businesses are very small indeed and have no intention of growing and this should have been very clear to government at the time of legislating; see Freedman, n 45 above.

[51] DTI, *Companies in 2004–5*, (London: The Stationery Office, 2005), table A4.

[52] HMRC, *Regulatory Impact Assessment Corporation Tax: The Non-Corporate Distribution Rate*, 6 April 2004.

[53] Finance Act 2004 s 28 and Schedule 3 (now Income and Corporation Taxes Act 1988 s13 AB and Schedule A2) noted in S Ball, [2004] *British Tax Review* 459–65.

[54] HM Treasury, *Regulatory Impact Assessment for Changes to the Corporation Tax Structure*, 16 March 2006.

all those who have received advice from their accountants to choose a legal form for tax reasons. Interestingly there does not seem to have been a major outcry from small business over the removal of this relief.[55]

Salary Sacrifice

A second example of a confusing Governmental message is a continuing scheme currently in place to encourage certain types of behaviour that Government favours: 'salary sacrifice'. At the time this chapter was first delivered as a lecture, the author predicted that the scheme might well be curtailed in future years, if and when it is used by people for whom it was not intended. One way in which the scheme was being used, linked to the home computer initiative, has now been terminated,[56] though this was not an attack on the salary sacrifice principle as such, and generally the scheme survives. Salary sacrifice involves both the high and the low paid and illustrates well how the tax avoidance culture, encouraged by Government, is permeating throughout our society. Even though this would not be treated as avoidance by Government to the extent that it achieves social ends which Government wishes to encourage, it has the hallmarks of an avoidance scheme and could lead taxpayers to consider this type of action to be acceptable in other contexts. Under this scheme, some part of an employee's salary can be transmuted into a non-taxable transfer if his contract is varied in such a way as to achieve a formal reduction of salary entitlement, albeit that there is substituted an alternative form of transfer that is of some value. The rationale is that the replacement benefit is not paid in salary so it is only taxable if it is easily convertible back into cash salary or is caught under the benefits in kind provisions. In reality, the employee would almost certainly describe this new arrangement as part of his or her salary package. What is really being given is a tax relief for certain expenditures but it is done by a formalistic variation of contract in a way that does not reflect the underlying economic substance. If this could be done in a more straightforward way it would be much less objectionable, and much less likely to encourage a view of taxation as complex, artificial, and almost inviting the taxpayer to engage in schemes. The convoluted way in which it is done encourages the tax avoidance culture across all levels of employee and in the corporate world.

[55] Indeed these changes had been proposed by several small business organizations, including the Forum for Private Business, which pointed out that the compliance cost of the anti-avoidance provision outweighed the savings from the nil rate—*The FSB's Key Recommendations within the pre-Budget Report* (November 2004), available at <http://www.fpb.co.uk/YZVgDTZo51MmUA.html>.

[56] Finance Act 2006 s 61.

In its governmentally approved form, the savings from this type of scheme are intended to go to taxpayers with expenditure that is considered socially desirable. In these cases this device is 'acceptable', albeit highly artificial, but in other cases it might not be considered 'acceptable' by Government, although there may be little difference in legal terms in the form of the transaction. In practice the schemes can be operated so that they result in savings for employers as much as for employees. This might be considered satisfactory, in that it enables employers to provide employees with help at no extra cost to the business but, in form, these schemes are pure tax avoidance in the sense of being highly artificial, complex, and often achieving no economic saving other than the tax saved. Again, Government gives out a confusing message by condoning this.

As explained above, salary sacrifice operates by an employee agreeing to forgo the future right to part of his or her salary in exchange for a benefit in kind.[57] If this can be done in such a way as to ensure that there is a genuine modification as a matter of law, so that the employee has a right only to the reduced salary and cannot revert back to the higher salary within the period of assessment, then there will be no tax payable on the salary forgone qua salary. This is so even though in terms of economic substance all parties will consider that the employee simply receives his salary in another form (the benefit in kind). The benefit in kind might be taxable at its full value under the benefits legislation, in which case the scheme will not be worthwhile, but if there is a relief available in respect of that benefit in kind, or if the taxing provision catching it does not achieve taxation at its full value, there will be a tax saving. There is twofold Governmental encouragement for this kind of scheme, therefore: first the relief available in respect of a particular benefit in kind, which is at least transparent and straightforward, but secondly there is this further possibility of a substitution of this benefit for wages, which arises from a detailed and arguably formalistic reading of contract and case law backed up in some cases by statute.

To give an example; if in substitution for £2,000 per month the employee receives £1,800 plus £200 in childcare vouchers, the vouchers may be exempt if they satisfy certain conditions.[58] The salary is reduced, thus tax and national insurance contributions, including employers' national insurance contributions, are reduced. The employee does not lose and the cost to the employer is not increased apart from the addition of compliance costs (which can be considerable for a small business

[57] For a full description see HMRC, *Employment Income Manual* EIM 42750 ff. (<http://www.hmrc.gov.uk/manuals/eimanual/EIM42700.htm>) (hereafter EIM).

[58] Income Tax (Earnings and Pensions) Act 2003 s 270A .

though they are probably less troublesome for a larger organization).The scheme is most often used in connection with special statutory tax reliefs, such as those for workplace car parking, provision of cycles, childcare vouchers, mobile phones, and some forms of childcare[59] but it can also work with other types of benefit such as approved retirement benefits schemes which are not taxable benefits,[60] and living accommodation, which may be under-taxed as a benefit in kind.[61] Until the Finance Act 2006, the scheme was also available for the home computer initiative but the relief for these benefits in kind has now been removed following evidence that, unsurprisingly, the relief generally and the salary sacrifice scheme in particular, have been exploited and abused.

> The exemption has been applied beyond the scope of its original intention. Some Home Computer Initiative providers have offered packages that include game consoles and MP3 players and allow employees to buy equipment through salary sacrifice arrangements rather than borrow it—an essential factor in determining whether the tax exemption applies.[62]

A search of the Internet shows that many organizations, including most universities and many Government departments, participate in salary sacrifice schemes. Interestingly, many unions and the lower incomes tax reform group issue warnings about these schemes because they contain traps for the unwary, particularly those on lower levels of pay.[63] Due to the decrease in what is described as salary resulting from the scheme, future state and employer benefit entitlement might be reduced. There is also a complex interaction with the tax credit system, which can mean that employees on low salaries can lose through salary sacrifice schemes. None of these traps needs to exist and would not do so if instead of using salary sacrifice a simple tax deduction from salary were permitted to be made by the employees for these socially desirable expenditures. Such a deduction would also be available across the board and not limited to employees with employers prepared to operate the scheme (normally larger employers). A straightforward deduction would also not need to rely on jumping through hoops to ensure the contractual arrangements were correct. Presumably Government prefers the salary sacrifice scheme because most employees do not complete tax returns and so to allow

[59] EIM 42755; Income Tax (Earnings and Pensions) Act 2003 s 237, s 244, s 270, s 318, s 318A, and s 319, as amended.

[60] EIM 42785.

[61] P Fisher, ' Sacrificial Lambs' *Taxation*, 19 May 2005, 182–5.

[62] Explanatory Note to Finance (No 2) Bill 2006 cl 61.

[63] Low Incomes Tax Reform Group, 'Childcare Vouchers Warning... Again' (10th April 2006). <http://www.litrg.org.uk/news/index.cfm?id=354&printpage=1>.

them to make deductions themselves would add complications, but the cost is the use of this scheme which results in complexity, lack of equity as between employees and confusing messages from Government to taxpayers.

Despite these potential problems, salary sacrifice has been widely taken up by larger employers, and has entered into the reckoning of many ordinary taxpayers. Once such a scheme is available and publicized then the natural reaction is for taxpayers to question why they should pay full tax when others are not doing so. It is a rational response to want to be treated as favourably as possible, and certainly no less favourably than others. If the route to achieving this seems artificial, then taxpayer attitudes will be accepting of that, not least because the tax system is so complex that it will just be thought of as one of the oddities of the system. In this way the unreality of the tax system is compounded and reinforced. If salary can be treated differently for tax purposes if it is received in a different form the message is conveyed that other schemes based on paying remuneration in different ways start to seem more 'acceptable'.[64]

This consequence is entirely Government and HMRC induced, as it is they who have decided to help make these schemes work through legislation and through guidance on how to apply and, one might even say, manipulate, the case law in those instances they consider 'acceptable'. They cannot then be surprised if the same methodology is adopted where it seems less 'acceptable' to them. It is true that the use of the schemes in the special cases referred to above is expressly facilitated by legislation passed through Parliament in the normal way, so that is not 'avoidance'. Simply creating such incentives is itself an encouragement to think of non-payment of tax as a reward. This strange scheme goes well beyond that in terms of its complexity and artificiality. Instead of producing straightforward relief, it relies upon a legal arrangement, which generates tax benefits unrelated to the economic substance of the transaction and where the projected tax benefit is a vital part of the costing of the scheme,[65] thus having the hallmarks of an avoidance scheme in terms of its structure.

[64] Some of the most 'extreme' tax schemes in recent years have related to employee remuneration, leading to a warning from the Government that it will legislate retrospectively in this respect: Paymaster General's statement appended to Inland Revenue Technical Note on Avoidance and Employment-Related Securities (December 2004). Though there was no evidence that they had been condoned by parliament, unlike salary sacrifice schemes, they had not been expressly prohibited.

[65] This wording here deliberately uses the description by HMRC itself of cases where there is likely to be avoidance in the pejorative sense—see *Working with Large Business*, n 19 above.

Normally an application of salary by the employer continues to be taxed as salary, but the effect of the salary sacrifice part of these schemes, which are not contained in legislation, is to remove that part of income from taxable salary. The employer can provide these benefits with no cost to himself because he deducts them from the salary and the entire benefit of the exercise is a tax benefit. Worker A, who does not use the salary sacrifice scheme, and worker B, who does, will have exactly the same level of economic benefit from the employer, but worker A will pay more tax. The employer will make a saving of national insurance contributions on worker B and maybe also have reduced pension contributions to pay whilst at the same time painting itself as being socially responsible in providing this benefit for its employees, derived entirely from the coffers of the Government (ie from other taxpayers).

The salary sacrifice scheme requires that the employee has genuinely given up a right to salary. Under general principles, if the employee has the right to give up the benefit at any time and revert to the original, higher, cash salary then the non-cash benefit may be taxable under the leading case of *Heaton v Bell*[66] and section 62 of the Income Tax (Earnings and Pensions) Act 2003 as 'money's worth'. Even if the employee does not have this right, however, so that he is not taxable under *Heaton v Bell*, he has clearly only exchanged his right to remuneration for some other benefit. Given that this other benefit must be worth the equivalent of the salary sacrificed, otherwise the employee would not have agreed to it, a finding that this is not taxable because it is not convertible into money's worth does look very like a case of legal form over economic substance. *Heaton v Bell* was decided as a question of construction of the relevant contract. Its findings are not very clear and legislative clarification should have been forthcoming. Arguably the current interpretation of it, relying on obiter statements in judgments based on a variety of reasoning, is not consistent with its spirit. In that case, an employee who gave up part of his cash remuneration in exchange for a car was held taxable on the full amount of the salary as earnings because under the contract he was still entitled to the salary. The reduction in respect of the car was, therefore, simply to be treated as a deduction by the employers in application of the wages. Had the contract been construed differently as a genuine reduction in wages the only question would have been whether the car was taxable as a benefit in kind. For many years *Heaton v Bell* was applied strictly, and taken to mean that a reduction of salary in this way would usually be impossible as a matter of contract. On this basis it would give problems

[66] [1970] AC 728 (HL).

for salary sacrifice schemes. It is now excluded by statute, however, in the case of mobile phones, workplace car parking, provision of cycles, and some kinds of childcare provision.[67] In respect of other types of case, the HMRC website now contains advice on how to modify the contract so as to escape the result in *Heaton v Bell* by relying upon what some might say is an over-literal reading of the case in a way which is entirely reminiscent of the kind of tax schemes which are so criticized by HMRC as being artificial and not having real economic substance.

Lord Upjohn in *Heaton v Bell* seemed well aware of this possible development and he stated

> It was suggested that a decision on these grounds could easily be circumvented by clever draftsmanship to make it clear that in fact the wage of the employee was reduced . . . and that in lieu he received a perquisite . . . .Of course one has to look at the real nature of the transaction[68] and not merely at its substance. That was decided in *IRC v Duke of Westminster*. But having ascertained the real nature of the transaction one cannot, in my opinion, disguise it by using camouflaged clothing. Here the whole essence of the employment of the taxpayer was as a machine minder at a weekly wage. If he so wished he could have part of the wages applied in providing for his own personal use a motor car, that was terminable by employers of taxpayer on short notice. Dress that up how you will, I hope a court would not be deceived by the disguise.[69]

Despite Lord Upjohn's warning, it appears that careful draftsmanship can achieve the desired tax saving. It must not be a sham but, provided there is a genuine agreement to take a lower wage, notwithstanding that in addition there is a benefit of value, that benefit will be taxable only if caught by benefits in kind legislation and not in general terms as earnings. The HMRC Employment Income Manual picks up the point that in *Heaton v Bell* the scheme was terminable on short notice and the suggestions in the case that had the variation to the contract prevented conversion back to cash for a whole year of assessment the scheme might have been effective.[70] For this reason the manual states that *Heaton v Bell* will not apply if the variation of the contract lasts more than 12 months.[71] This seems open to question, as it should always be a matter of construction. Nevertheless HMRC appears to sanction this convoluted and artificial scheme and to be prepared for it to become formalistic. It is backed up by legislation but it is not straightforward legislation and it does not apply in all cases where salary sacrifice is used. It is complex and costly to get the agreements right: the HMRC website itself has an example of how

[67] See n 59 above. [68] By this his Lordship must mean legal nature.
[69] *Heaton v Bell*, n 66 above, 749. [70] ibid 754. [71] EIM 42767.

easy it is to get it wrong and the importance of the form of the agreements.[72] The methodology used is exactly that which in another context HMRC would find unpalatable and contrary to the 'spirit' of the law.

The *Employment Income Manual* reiterates that it is important to recognize that employers and employees have a right to arrange the terms and conditions of their employment and to enjoy the statutory tax and national insurance treatment that applies to each element in the remuneration package. 'Arrangements, which are designed to make use of [the specific] exemptions, should not be regarded as avoidance.'[73] Clearly Parliament has intended that salary sacrifice should be available where it has made specific statutory provision to this effect but this convoluted approach, and the adoption of the very concept of salary sacrifice, encourages similar 'game-playing' in contexts of which government will not be so approving.

The mixed messages may be seen in action in a memorandum submitted to the House of Commons Select Committee on Treasury in 2003 on tax planning by government departments. Having stated that it is not good value for money for departments to seek to minimize their tax liability through transactions or activities for which there is no genuine justification in economic terms, the memorandum goes on to say that departments should not be deterred from taking advantage of arrangements in the tax system aimed at supporting good employment practices.

> In particular, where departments find that the use of salary sacrifice arrangements genuinely help to support the Government's objectives through childcare support *as opposed to acting as a tax saving device*, then salary sacrifice arrangements are permissible.[74] [Author's italics].

This suggests a distinction between two uses of the same methodology based on Government views of acceptability rather than legislation. There are some types of salary sacrifice schemes which are not, apparently, acceptable and it will not be surprising to see them attacked as unacceptable avoidance at some time in the future.

In summary, the salary sacrifice scheme has been sanctioned by HMRC as a way of achieving certain ends which are currently considered socially desirable but, in choosing to do this through salary sacrifice rather than a more straightforward approach,[75] the Government and revenue

[72] EIM 42790. [73] EIM 42752.

[74] Treasury Officer of Accounts, 22 May 2003, 'Guidance Issued to Departments on Tax Planning and Tax Avoidance', *Minutes of Evidence, Select Committee on Treasury* (2003), Annex B; emphasis in original.

[75] As hinted above, the reasons for this may be connected with the desire to ensure that any such schemes are operated through employers and thus compatible with the PAYE

authorities have once again given the signal that the tax system is open to manipulation of this kind and this notion is injected into the culture of tax-paying to encourage similar behaviour in contexts which Government may find less acceptable. The differential factor is that Parliament intends one kind of behaviour and not the other to work for tax purposes but if the words of the legislation do not differentiate then it may not be reasonable to expect taxpayers to make that differentiation for themselves and indeed may be quite unreasonable in some cases.

Corporate Social Responsibility and the Tax Avoidance Culture

Against the background of complexity, artificiality, and lack of clarity described above, we now turn to the responsibilities of taxpayers with a focus on corporate taxpayers. As has been noted above, there is considerable pressure on corporations to pay their 'fair share' of tax but the key question is how that share should be defined.

On one view, the fair share can only be what it is *essential* to pay by law, having exploited any scheme available which uses the law to the extent permitted by legislation (as construed by the courts) to minimize taxation. At the other end of the spectrum, it might be argued that companies should go beyond the law and look to the 'spirit' of legislation or even further in paying what is fair. This might be considered to be the true meaning of CSR, which has been defined by the European Commission as 'enterprises deciding to go beyond minimum legal requirements and obligations stemming from collective agreements in order to address societal needs',[76] but it will then be very hard to decide where to draw the line. Between these two points are many shades and variations, which in the case of businesses tend to focus around risk.

In the tax context, the issues at stake are the relationship between the corporate taxpayer and the revenue authorities and government. This differs from other areas of CSR such as the environment or labour issues where natural or human resources are concerned, because the very subject matter, tax-paying, is entirely centred on and arises from the relationship with Government, and therefore legal regulation must be the starting point as it defines the duty in question. There is no commonly accepted

system under which most employees do not complete tax returns. Apart from the resulting complexity, this also results in unfairness as the schemes are not made available to all, but depend on the employer participating.

76 European Commission Communication COM(2006) 01136.

norm for tax levels as there might be for other types of behaviour. As Honoré has written, apart from the law no one has a moral obligation to pay any particular amount of tax. This is an area where law is needed to back up morality. He is not saying that morality and law have nothing to do with each other—far from it. But he is saying that in a complex society a viable morality around tax must have a legal component.[77]

> Taxpayers cannot settle the amount they should pay for themselves as people can, within limits, settle for themselves, say, the proper way of showing respect for the feelings of others. Apart from the law no-one has a moral obligation to pay any particular amount of tax. An obligation to pay an indeterminate amount is not an effective obligation; it requires only a disposition, not an action. So apart from law no one has an effective obligation to pay tax.

Thus it is not surprising if businesses fix their tax-paying policies to what is required by law rather than trying to look beyond the law, although looking at the spirit rather than the letter of the law could be justified where that spirit is clear. Sometimes this will be a matter for dispute that it is legitimate to litigate. Businesses will naturally incline towards profit maximization and therefore tax minimization, but profit maximization may well be viewed in a longer-term context so that short-term profit is worthwhile only if the risk of entering into tax schemes at the boundaries is not too great in terms of potential cost and loss of reputation. A corporate taxpayer may be prepared to agree a policy of not engaging in a tax scheme that HMRC considers to be unacceptable, even if this has not been tested in the courts, because to challenge this view would be to increase the risk of investigation and take up management time and might also have reputational repercussions. However, businesses are more likely to have their own definition of what is acceptable, which will normally focus around the scheme having a commercial end purpose and not being wholly artificial, although, as we have seen, what amounts to a commercial purpose may be a matter for dispute. This is sometimes expressed as requiring that 'all tax structures and transactions should be aligned with the "real world" activities of the organisation's underlying business'.[78] But again, there may be differing views as to which transactions are so aligned, as we have seen in the *Barclays Mercantile* case.[79] Companies may apply a test of whether they would feel comfortable explaining the scheme to the media or authorities. These policies represent good corporate governance,

[77] T Honoré, 'The Dependence of Morality on Law' (1993) 13 *Oxford Journal of Legal Studies* 1, discussed in more detail in Freedman, n 11 above.

[78] Henderson Global Investor, n 8 above, 6. This is similar to the HMRC test in the Large Business Service report, n 19 above.

[79] n 24 above.

since these are considerations that all sensible boards will bear in mind, but they have little to do with CRS in the sense of voluntarily going beyond the law. There is some evidence of increased concerns amongst corporates about borderline activity but this seems likely to be the result of a steady tightening of legal disclosure requirements, although this may be coupled with a worry about reputational risk should it be shown that those legal requirements have been breached.[80]

Many boards now have written and published tax policies. These are set out as strategies with a business case. An example can be found in Vodafone's Tax Code of Conduct.[81]

> The objective of the Vodafone tax department is to maximise shareholder value in relation to the taxation consequences of all aspects of the Group's business activity:
>
> - Within the overall Group strategy;
> - In compliance with relevant laws, disclosure requirements and regulations; and
> - While protecting Vodafone's reputation and brand.
>
> Vodafone is not able to determine the 'fair' amount of tax for it to pay, overall, or in any particular territory. It believes its obligation is to pay the amount of tax legally due in any territory, in accordance with rules set by Governments.
>
> The maximisation of shareholder value will generally involve the minimisation of taxation. It will also involve choices as to the jurisdiction in which to locate capital and/or business activity. Such choices will take account of all the business consequences, including the taxation consequences, of operating in that location . . .
>
> The commercial needs of the Group are paramount and all tax planning will be undertaken in this context. Where alternative routes exist to achieve the same commercial result, the most tax efficient approach should be recommended.

The maximization of shareholder value involves taking due account of long-term considerations and risks including the maintenance of corporate reputation and relationships with Governments. It also requires the management of other risks, including the possibility of, and consequences of, disagreements with tax authorities over the application of the

[80] For surveys of US firms, see S. Morse, 'The How and Why of the New Public Corporation Tax Compliance Norm' 15 May 2006 <http://ssrn.com/abstract=905746>. She concludes that it is increased regulation, tax based and other such as Sarbanes–Oxley, which is resulting in such changes of attitude as are emerging.

[81] <http://www.vodafone.com/assets/files/en/code_of_conduct_290605.pdf>.

law. The management of risk will take all related issues and stakeholder interests into consideration.

Some companies go further than this, declaring that they will observe the law in spirit as well as letter.[82] This is consistent with the OECD Guidelines for Multinational Enterprises but it is notable that the OECD's examples of abiding by the spirit of the laws (full disclosure of information and conforming transfer pricing practices to the arm's length principle) are arguably something that any company abiding by the letter would also feel obliged to do.[83]

It has been noted more generally that companies will engage in CSR only to the extent that it makes business sense for them to do so and this marks the limits of CSR.[84] Whilst the corporate world is keen to embrace CSR publicly for reputational reasons, it would be unwise for government and revenue authorities to place too much weight on this as a controlling mechanism in the tax context. CSR may have the effect of changing the strategies firms pursue to maximize shareholder value but, unlike government regulation, it cannot force companies to make unprofitable decisions, even if they are socially beneficial in a wider sense.

Companies will present their policies within a CSR framework but will continue to enter into tax schemes which HMRC might dislike if they believe that they are within the law and if they consider that they need to do so in order to maintain their profitability and competitiveness and can do so without undue risk. They will consider schemes at the border carefully, and maybe more carefully than in the past, due mainly to increased disclosure requirements of various kinds,[85] but the question for them of where to draw the line is a more difficult one than the Government and revenue authorities give credit for, given the primary duty of directors to their shareholders and other stakeholders. If only because of the reputational risk referred to above, most listed companies at least will wish to be broadly compliant with law but can be expected to evaluate issues beyond the law only on the basis of the business case. This is recognized even by those who argue strongly for the application of CSR to the tax agenda.[86]

[82] The Henderson report, n 8 above, cites the HBOS Corporate Responsibility Report 2004, the HSBC Statement of Business Principles and Values, and the ICI Code of Conduct. Note, however, that all these are documents which are general in nature rather than specifically tax related.

[83] OECD, *Guidelines for Multinational Enterprises* (Paris: OECD, 2000), chapter X.

[84] Vogel, n 10 above.

[85] See Morse, n 80 above.

[86] See the report by SustainAbility, n 8 above, which recognizes in its foreword that 'While there are examples of reputational implications beginning to enter the frame . . . there is almost no evidence of companies taking decisions under the influence of corporate responsibility'.

The focus of this chapter is the UK tax avoidance culture, but clearly for large multinational companies, this cannot be divorced from the international climate. Given that shareholders will be international, and that duties to pay tax will be owed by the group to a multiplicity of revenue authorities, the picture is very much more complex. Jurisdictions may have competing calls on profits and allocation may be an issue. The point has been made already that CSR in relation to tax is a question of the relationship with governments rather than problems of natural or human resources where a norm can be established without government involvement. In the case of tax, governments define the essence of the duty in question. This makes CSR in relation to international tax a very difficult argument because more than one government may be involved and taxpayers may be caught in between two or more governments who have failed to reach sensible agreements between themselves or who are arguing over profit allocation under transfer pricing rules.[87] Most companies will take the view, like Vodafone, cited above, that it is perfectly legitimate to take tax into account just like any other cost when deciding where to locate activities. In this context the most that can be expected is transparency in reporting.[88] Allocation issues as between jurisdictions and the problems of profits being sheltered in low tax jurisdictions are issues for the international community and it cannot be expected that voluntary behaviour of the corporate sector can be relied upon in the international sphere.[89]

HMRC seems to have realized the defects of an argument based on ethics or morality and has moved the agenda onto reputational risk in their latest documents as we have seen. This is safer ground and more progress is likely to be made on this front, as it is in the enlightened

[87] For example companies are caught up in the failure of the European Union member states to harmonize their corporate tax rules—see especially *Marks and Spencer plc v Halsey* (Case C-446/03), [2006] STC 237 (ECJ).

[88] As required under the Global Reporting Initiative to which many multinational companies have signed up—<http://www.globalreporting.org/guidelines/062002guidelines.asp>.

[89] This does not prevent criticism of corporate taxpayers in this context. See eg J Plender, 'Counting the Cost of Globalisation: How Companies Keep Tax Low and Stay Within the Law', *Financial Times*, 21 July 2004; J Plender and M Simons, 'A Big Squeeze for Governments: How Transfer Pricing Threatens Global Tax Revenues', *Financial Times*, 22 July 2004; Tax Justice Network, n 2 above. This is on the basis both that they are locating activities into low tax areas and that they are paying insufficient tax to developing countries where they are based. It is not of course intended here to condone attempts to deprive locations where activities are based of their proper share of profits if this involves evasion, non-disclosure, or double non-taxation, but merely to point out the difficulties of arguing that CSR can do any more than support transparency and abiding by the law of the jurisdiction in question and internationally agreed double taxation agreements.

self-interest of companies to steer away from entering into tax schemes which will be attacked by HMRC and stand a high chance of being unsuccessful. It is unclear how much further this will take HMRC, however, and it will not operate well unless companies feel they have sufficient guidance. In particular it will not play well in a climate where Government itself is encouraging complexity and artificiality by the introduction of incentives. The two examples given above are widely applicable and easily understood and were chosen for that reason but in a business context others could be given, for example the whole area of finance leasing which was at the heart of the *Barclays Mercantile*. Leasing arrangements now have a whole hallmark to themselves under the new disclosure provisions[90] and are perceived to be a major cause of revenue loss recently tackled by a new legislative regime,[91] but of course all the schemes used arise out of legislation designed to provide incentives and a whole industry has grown up around them which, in its own terms, is commercial, so 'acceptability' in this context is a very subjective matter.

It is interesting to note that there has been no outcry from business against calls to apply CSR to tax and professional advisers have been largely supportive. Recent scholarship suggests that this is not surprising. Conley and Williams[92] have argued (in relation to non-financial performance) that the CSR movement has created subtle but significant opportunities for corporations to manage criticism and to enhance their power. Vogel adds that the claim that the business community will provide itself with incentives to change its social behaviour is very seductive and appeals to business as a way of saying 'we don't need additional government controls'. But ultimately, although something can be achieved by CSR, it is limited by the profit system that underlies capitalism. 'That is to say, the market provides some incentives for corporate responsibility, mostly around reputation, and it also provides a discipline, with constraints on corporate responsibility'.[93]

Corporate responsibility has a role to play in managing the tax behaviour of corporate taxpayers, especially in a situation in which it is impossible to draw bright lines. It cannot, however, remove liability from

[90] HMRC, n 35 above.

[91] As is clear from the need for the hallmark—see also The Tax Gap, n 2 above, where the author argues that excessive corporate tax allowances for plant and machinery unrelated to the underlying economic substance of the transactions taking place is a major contributor to the tax gap. Changes to the way long funding leases of plant and machinery are taxed have been introduced in the Finance Act 2006.

[92] Conley and Williams, n 8 above.

[93] D Vogel, *Corporate Social Responsibility and Government*, Transcript of Press Briefing, The Brookings Institution, 2 November 2005.

Government for the ultimate responsibility for creating a tax system which gives content to the obligation to pay tax and which gives clear messages to taxpayers about the role of the tax system and the way in which it is to function.

Tackling the Avoidance Culture

This chapter recognizes that there is a clash of perceptions about tax avoidance. Government and revenue authorities see a tax gap arising from the willingness of the corporate sector to engage in schemes that exploit tax legislation by ignoring what Government sees as its spirit or underlying economic reality. This they see as 'unfair', in that it reduces the tax available for Government expenditure or increases the tax that must be levied on other taxpayers. At the same time, Government offers tax reductions for certain types of behaviour as a method of attempting to micro-manage the economy and introduces legislation which itself creates distortions, sometimes based on purely legal distinctions. Business taxpayers receive a confused message. They see a complex tax system, resting at times on these legal distinctions not always grounded in economic reality, and Governmental creation of tax incentives based on technical provisions and legal form. Reductions of tax may be a reward for good behaviour or an encouragement to behave in a different way, detracting from the central message that the function of taxation is to raise revenue. This can make the spirit of tax legislation a matter for debate. The courts see their task as purposive and to construe legislation according to Parliament's intention, but the manner in which tax legislation is drafted and the confusion of objectives sometimes apparent may mean that there is a gap between the outcome of the proper application of legislation and its statutory construction by the courts on the one hand and what Government and the revenue authorities consider to be acceptable on the other. This gap is the grey area, defined above, upon which this article has focused. At its boundaries there might be widespread agreement that a transaction or scheme is 'unacceptable' but within the grey area there will be genuine room for different opinions.

Not all business taxpayers set out to be compliant in a tax context—some will lean more towards compliance than others and some will push the boundaries of the grey area more than others.[94] John Braithwaite's work on large corporations in Australia suggests that most of those

[94] Braithwaite, n 41 above.

taxpayers intend to comply with the letter of the law or at least to have a 'reasonably arguable position' that they have done so most of the time. However he also concludes, based on the amount of tax paid by these corporations, that there are many who do not intend to comply with what the Australian Tax Office regards as the policy purposes of the parliament's tax laws.[95] They operate within the grey area. Whether this is non-compliance at all is the question at issue.

Any revenue authority needs to administer the tax system in order to collect tax in a fair way, by the use of varying techniques depending on compliance levels, ranging from increased penalties and better enforcement for the genuinely non-compliant through additional disclosure requirements and down to increased consultation and tax reform for those in the grey area.[96] Where the issue is one of not abiding by what the revenue authorities perceive to be the spirit of the law, which at its borders may not be non-compliance at all, modifications to the way law is created or interpreted will need to be part of the package if that behaviour is to be changed, although persuasion and education about the risks of coming close to borderlines may also have some impact. The Treasury and HMRC are already using the work on compliance models pioneered by the Braithwaites and their team at the Centre for Tax System Integrity in Australia, which recommends the use of different levels of response, ranging from education and service delivery for the essentially committed taxpayer through to prosecution at the other extreme.[97] As John Braithwaite has argued, it is important not to place too much reliance on any single strand of a web of controls.[98]

As part of and beyond these compliance-enhancing techniques, the tax avoidance problem needs to be tackled by better signalling from Government to taxpayers and the judiciary. Some progress can be made by educating corporate taxpayers about the risks of pushing the boundaries and coming too close to the edge of the grey area but it cannot be expected that corporate taxpayers will go further than that which can be justified on the basis of a good business case. Beyond that it is for the Government to erode the tax avoidance culture using the tools at its disposal and not for corporate taxpayers to fill in the gaps left by faulty signalling.

[95] Braithwaite, n 40 above, 179. 'The evidence for this is that half of them pay no tax, some for many years, which is certainly not parliament's intention.'

[96] For a full discussion of the different techniques see Braithwaite, n 40 above and J Braithwaite, *Markets in Vice, Markets in Virtue* (Annandale, NSW: The Federation Press, 2005), 208.

[97] See nn 40, 41, and 89 above and see also K Murphy, 'Moving Forward towards a More Effective Model of Regulatory Enforcement in the Australian Tax Office' [2004] *British Tax Review* 603–19, esp n 5.

[98] Braithwaite (2005), n 96 above.

Government has a responsibility to create the right conditions and culture for a generally tax-compliant system which would benefit the entire legitimate business community in keeping costs down and spreading tax burdens fairly. This means not merely responding to tax avoidance schemes by shutting them down when they are discovered or increasing the chances of their discovery through disclosure (important though it is for these actions to be taken also). Government bears a responsibility for having created through legislation, actions, and language the conditions for the avoidance culture in which the reduction of taxpaying by the use of technical devices is seen as a reasonable activity by many taxpayers. From the first day of setting up a business or becoming employees, taxpayers are presented with choices driven by taxation. Only two examples were given here but many more could have been chosen. It is not surprising that business taxpayers come to think in these terms in other contexts. Government, in its political role, needs to review its own objectives and terminology when creating incentives and depicting tax reliefs as rewards for good behaviour. CSR should not be spoken of as a means of tax saving but as a way of encouraging tax-paying. This should be the message not only from the revenue departments but also across Government. This could have a real impact on the tax avoidance culture, by leading from the front in attitudes to taxation. To exhort taxpayers to pay the price of citizenship on the one hand and to provide rewards for good citizenship in terms of tax breaks on the other involves a confusion which spills over into taxpayer thinking.

In this way, changes to attitudes could be helpful. Public views on what is acceptable in relation to 'tax avoidance' will affect the perception of business about acceptability via risk evaluation. But this approach has its limits. Changes to the way tax law is created and communicated to the judiciary are also needed. The ideal would be to move to fundamental reform of the tax system to create a structure more clearly aligned with economic substance and less dependent on technicalities and distinctions ripe for exploitation. This is the only true solution to the problem and should be a long-term objective but it is not without its difficulties. Some would argue that tax systems will always be based on some level of artificiality.[99] Distinctions of a legal nature will persist because tax is not a natural phenomenon but must be made to conform to the underlying legal structures which may differ from economic structures. In fact there is much that can be done to move away from artificial distinctions such as

[99] J Prebble, 'Why is Tax Law Incomprehensible?' [1994] *British Tax Review* 380–93.

that between capital and income,[100] for example, which creates so many possibilities for avoidance. Generally, the creation of boundaries and different treatment for different kinds of assets, which provides opportunities for avoidance, could be reduced. However, complete elimination of all boundaries is impossible and reduction will be a long-term process, if it can happen at all.

Short of desirable but elusive fundamental structural reform, valuable steps would be a move towards principles-based drafting wherever possible.[101] This would force the legislators to consider their objectives on each occasion. Some tax legislation in Australia is now moving towards this basis and this will be an experiment well worth watching.[102] It might even be possible to insert some overriding tax principles into the legislation which might guide the judiciary in giving full effect to Parliamentary intention by ensuring that the judiciary has the tools it needs to work with to implement proper purposive interpretation. The author has argued elsewhere[103] for a general anti-avoidance provision to achieve this end. Critics of this idea argue that such a provision will not be successful if the underlying objectives of specific tax legislation are unclear because it will not assist the judges to go any further than normal principles of purposive construction could do.[104] Evidence from other jurisdictions suggests that a general anti-avoidance rule or principle may work, but only if it contains adequate instructions to the judiciary, which must include objective rules which can modify the specific legislation in line with the overriding intention of Parliament. Ideally such a general rule needs to be coupled with better, principles-based drafting of specific rules and possibly even some general tax principles to guide the judiciary.

[100] G Macdonald and D Martin, *Tax and Accounting: A Response to the 2003 Consultation Document of Corporation Tax Reform* (London: IFS, 2004).

[101] This approach was suggested by J F Avery Jones in 'Tax Law: Rules or Principles?' (1996) *British Tax Review* 580. See also J Braithwaite, 'Making Tax Law More Certain: A Theory' (2003) 31 *Australian Business Law Review* 72; D Weisbach, 'Formalism in the Tax Law' (1999) 66 *University of Chicago Law Review* 860. For a further discussion see Freedman, nn 11 and 12 above.

[102] Principles-based drafting is the subject of an experiment in Australia—see G Pinder, 'The Coherent Principles Approach to Tax Law Design', Australian Treasury 2005, <http://tofa.treasury.gov.au/content/downloads/coherent_principles.pdf>, discussed further below.

[103] Freedman, nn 11 and 12 above.

[104] For a judicial expression of this view in relation to the Canadian general anti-avoidance rule, see *The Queen v Canada Trustco Mortgage Co* 2005 SCC 54 and for a very cogent comment supportive of this view see M Gammie, 'Barclays and Canada Trustco: Further Comment from a UK Perspective' (2005) 53 *Canadian Tax Journal* 1047. For an alternative view see J Freedman, 'Converging Tracks? Recent Developments in Canadian and UK Approaches to Tax Avoidance' (2005) 53 *Canadian Tax Journal* 1038.

Government attempts to shift attitudes to what is acceptable in terms of tax behaviour are having an effect on the corporate sector. However, there remains a grey area which can present policy difficulties and an element of frustration is building up amongst the corporate sector and their advisers as the costs of disclosure and compliance build up for those who are generally compliant in any event.[105] Corporate taxpayers will evaluate their tax policies in terms of risk, and this will incorporate consideration of the likely reaction of HMRC, the media, and the public to their activities, but they do feel a need for criteria to guide them and it is not unreasonable to take those criteria from legislation as interpreted by the courts. Given that the courts have not laid down a judicial anti-avoidance doctrine, HMRC and the corporate taxpayer are pushed back to ordinary principles of statutory construction. Although HMRC may feel certain behaviour is clearly unacceptable, if it is not also clearly contrary to statute, corporate taxpayers may conclude that they are entitled to rely on what appears to be a reasonable interpretation of the statute, especially if they feel that their competitors would take up such opportunities and that their stakeholders would benefit from such action. A recent example can be seen in the Debenhams credit card handling fee VAT case (a scheme utilized by many leading retail stores). Debenhams won as a matter of contract law in the High Court[106] only to lose in the Court of Appeal.[107] HMRC considered the scheme to be clearly unacceptable but it was considered acceptable by a High Court judge. In these circumstances, should a board of directors have sanctioned this scheme or not? As a matter of CSR, though there was a loss to the exchequer and the Government clearly found it unacceptable and was determined to attack the scheme, there has been little outcry from the media or from customers about the participation of household names in this kind of transaction. The arguments for a corporate taxpayer are finely balanced and in the end can only be decided on their business merits. In the VAT context, the balance may have shifted and the grey area shrunk by the introduction of a judicial concept of abuse of law by the European Court of Justice.[108]

105 See eg the evidence on behalf of the Chartered Institute of Taxation given to the House of Lords Select Committee on Economic Affairs 6th Report HL 204-II Q235; KPMG, Report of Symposium, 'From Debate to Action—Drawing the Lines and Finding the Balance—legislation, Principles and Codes', May 2006, <http://www.kpmg.co.uk/>.

106 *Debenhams Retails plc v Customs and Excise Commissioners* [2004] EWHC 1540 (Ch); [2004] STC 1132 (HC).

107 [2005] EWCA Civ 892 (CA); [2005] STC 1155.

108 In *Halifax plc, Leeds Permanent Development Services Ltd, County Wide Property Investments Ltd, v Commissioners of Customs and Excise*, Case C-255/02 21 February 2006.

It remains to be seen whether Government will see fit to legislate to back this up and extend it to the area of direct tax. This would not be welcomed immediately by business but it would put weight behind the notion of following the spirit of tax legislation, although in many cases that spirit would still require improved drafting techniques to make it properly discoverable.

Conclusion

Governments and corporate taxpayers could work together to improve the tax-paying culture in the UK but neither side should expect too much. Business cannot expect Government to provide perfect certainty, or simple provisions, in an economy of great complexity, but improvements could be made in the thinking behind taxation and the mode of implementing it through legislation. The judiciary could be given legislation with a clearer purpose, so that purposive construction could be given a more substantial role. Government cannot expect business to pay tax on a voluntary basis where there is no legislative foundation, simply on the basis that the revenue authorities think that the tax should be paid, but it can expect full disclosure and cooperation and, if the purpose of legislation is made clear by the techniques referred to above, and if that purpose sends out messages which remove rather than create confusion, it can expect that the principles established by Parliament will be respected, that technical challenges will be reduced, and that the tax avoidance culture will be diminished.

Laws, Foreign Laws, and Facts

Richard Fentiman

Introduction

Conflicts lawyers take for granted that one country's courts can apply another country's laws. But the application of foreign law begs intensely difficult questions, which have yet to be satisfyingly answered—and which may be unanswerable. Sometimes problems arise when foreign law conflicts with the interests or mores of the forum. When should English public policy override the application of foreign law?[1] Sometimes difficulty arises because it may be inappropriate (or impossible) for the forum to jettison its rules of practice and procedure, even when applying foreign law. But which matters are substantive, governed by foreign law, and which procedural, regulated by English law?[2] Alternatively, the problem may be conceptual, as when a foreign legal system classifies an issue differently from that of the forum. How should issues and rules be characterized in the conflicts process?[3] How can, say, English law's choice of law rules in tort govern liability under foreign law which in English law would not be tortious? And what if under the applicable law, identified as such by English law, the relevant rule belongs to a different category? What if under the law governing an issue in tort, the relevant rule is regarded as belonging to the law of contract?

Again, what we mean by the applicable law may be uncertain, as the timeless debate about *renvoi* confirms.[4] If the applicable law is foreign, do we apply the domestic law of the system concerned, or its private international law (which may consider the applicable law to be different)? This in turn begs questions about our aspirations for the conflicts process. Should we aspire to apply foreign law precisely as a foreign court would, conflicts rules included? Or should we accept that the conflicts process is

[1] As required eg by the 1980 Rome Convention on the law applicable to non-contractual obligations, Art 16.

[2] See eg *Harding v Wealands* [2006] UKHL 32.

[3] E Lorenzen, 'The Qualification, Classification or Characterisation Problem in the Conflict of Laws' (1941) 50 *YLJ* 743.

[4] A Briggs, 'In Praise and Defence of *Renvoi*' (1998) 47 *ICLQ* 877.

not really about applying foreign law in a literal sense, but about resolving disputes in the way English law considers most effective and appropriate? Suppose that Utopian law governs an issue under the relevant English choice of law rule, but a Utopian court would apply another law. If the object is to mimic the foreign court, that other law should be applied. But to English eyes, to apply *renvoi* in such a case (or any case) might create uncertainty, or defeat the parties' likely expectation that foreign internal law will be applied. To what extent, then, should English law's control of the conflicts process qualify the operation of foreign law?

Such difficulties concern the appropriateness of domesticating foreign law when it applies in English courts. How far should the application of foreign law be compromised by considerations of practicality or principle? How far should the application of foreign law be viewed through the lens of English norms and English practice? How far is it necessary or possible to apply foreign law as a foreign judge would apply it?

These persistent questions are most pressing when an English court is required to establish the content of foreign law.[5] Here the domestication of foreign law is apparently complete. Issues of foreign law are traditionally treated as issues of fact, not law, in English practice.[6] Orthodoxy has it that establishing foreign law is a matter of evidence. The proof of foreign law depends on a court's assessment of expert opinion introduced by the parties. And if such evidence is absent, or inadequate, a rule of evidence deploys. Foreign law is then presumed to be the same as English law.

But this evidential approach is starkly at odds with the legal character of foreign law, which manifests itself in two particular ways. However much a court's knowledge about foreign law must depend upon expert opinion, a judge's skill and experience as a lawyer inevitably intrudes upon the process of proof. Uniquely amongst matters dependent upon expert opinion, an English judge has something legal to contribute. So is it appropriate to regulate the proof of foreign law strictly according to the rules of evidence? Would it be right if a judge were unable to interpret a foreign statute without expert testimony, where the parties request it, or where the expert evidence is insufficient or tied? Again, if foreign law

[5] R Fentiman, *Foreign Law in English Courts: Pleading, Proof and Choice of Law* (Oxford: Clarendon, 1998); L Collins (gen ed), *Dicey, Morris and Collins: Conflict of Laws* (London: Sweet & Maxwell, 2006) (14th edn), ch 9; T Hodgkinson, *Expert Evidence: Law and Practice* (London: Sweet & Maxwell, 1990), ch 16; A Layton and H Mercer, *European Civil Practice* (London: Sweet & Maxwell, 2004) (2nd edn), ch 8; T Hartley, 'Pleading and Proof of Foreign Law: The Major European Systems Compared' (1996) 45 *ICLQ* 271.

[6] *Bumper Development Corpn v Comr of Police of the Metropolis* [1991] 4 All ER 638, 643ff (CA).

applies in a given case, it governs the rights and liabilities of the parties—whatever its formal status. Is it then right to treat it as a fact? If the evidence is scant, but uncontradicted, is that sufficient evidence of foreign law? Is it right to assume, improbably, that its content is that of English law, because of some defect in the evidential process?

The tension between law and fact in establishing foreign law is the concern of the following remarks. As we shall see, in opposition to the traditional account, a cluster of recent cases, in England and Australia, have endorsed a non-evidential approach to foreign law. By doing so, they beg important questions about how foreign law should be established: how far, if at all, must a court mimic a foreign court's treatment of foreign law; how far must the treatment of foreign law reflect the realities of litigation in an alien forum?

It is useful to consider separately the juridical status of foreign law, then the role (if any) of the presumption that English law and foreign law are the same.

The Status of Foreign Law

To ask whether foreign laws should be treated as facts or laws, or neither, or something between, or something of both, may seem an arid question of taxonomy. But taxonomy matters, if it means that the law is properly stated—an important consideration, given that it is far from clear that 'foreign laws are facts', as often supposed. And labels have implications. The juridical nature of foreign law determines how foreign law is established in English courts. It dictates in particular how far adherence to the normal rules of evidence is required, and how foreign law is handled on appeal. Effective access to justice is also in question. If the applicable law is foreign, foreign law governs the parties' rights and liabilities, making it important to handle it correctly. And so is procedural efficiency. If foreign laws are facts in the usual sense, the time-consuming and costly process of assessing expert evidence is unavoidable.

Preliminaries

Before examining the nature of the foreign law problem, some preliminary observations are required.

First, the traditional view that issues of foreign law are merely issues of fact has always been insecure. Wolff considered that 'the foreign law which a court has to apply remains law'.[7] More recently, a leading work on international civil procedure states that the treatment of foreign law in English courts 'is closer to that of a question of law and to regard it merely as a question of fact may therefore be misleading'.[8] Again, the fact doctrine, in essentially its English form, has been almost universally disparaged in the United States,[9] condemned as anachronistic, impractical, even 'primeval'.[10] Rule 44.1 of the Federal Rules of Civil Procedure abolishes the characterization of foreign laws as facts in federal practice, and provides instead that establishing foreign law is not a matter of evidence.[11]

Secondly, the durability of the fact doctrine may owe much to some persistent theoretical assumptions. Dicey's vested rights theory long ago proclaimed that English courts do not apply foreign law but merely recognize rights created thereunder, a theory which itself reflects the limitations on state competence imposed by Dicey's preferred theory of national sovereignty.[12] Again, the traditional view that an English judge is an impartial umpire in a contest fought by the parties on their own terms, dictates that a judge is formally ignorant of everything except English law.[13] Combined, both lead naturally to the position that foreign laws are facts, beyond a court's knowledge and comprehension without expert assistance. More precisely, they ensure that foreign laws are facts of which judicial notice cannot be taken.[14]

Yet neither theory has stood the test of time, and neither need ordain how foreign law is seen today. Dicey's view—'inadequate as an explanation'[15]—does more to conform the conflicts process with his distinctive conception of state power, than to illuminate that process. And the image of the judge as a passive arbiter has been replaced by the more interventionist model of case management required by the Civil Procedure Rules.[16]

Thirdly, this theoretical perspective distorts the reality that even foreign law has an inherently legal aspect. Certainly, to state that English

[7] ibid. [8] Layton and Mercer, n 5, para above 8.003.

[9] A R Miller, 'Federal Rule 44.1 and the "Fact" Approach to Determining Foreign Law: Death Knell for a Die-Hard Doctrine' (1967) 65 *Mich L Rev* 615–750, 628; C A Wright and A R Miller, *Federal Practice and Procedure: Civil 2d*, (St Paul, Minn: West, 1995), para. 2441. [10] Miller, n 9 above, 628; Wright and Miller, n 9 above, para 2441.

[11] Wright and Miller, n 9 above, para 2441 ff.

[12] A Dicey, *Conflict of Laws* (2nd. edn) (London: Sweet and Maxwell, 1908), 23.

[13] Classically expressed by F Pollock, *The Expansion of the Common Law* (London: Stevens and Sons, 1904), 33–4.

[14] S Sass, 'Foreign Law in Civil Litigation: A Comparative Survey' (1968) 16 *AJCL* 332, 342.

[15] P North and J J Fawcett, *Cheshire and North's Private International Law* (13th edn) (London: Butterworths, 1999), 22. [16] CPR, r 1, (1).

courts do not apply foreign law, but only rights found as fact to exist under that law, is not itself a statement of fact. It is merely an assertion of a theoretical position. As the experience of many other jurisdictions attests, it is plausible and defensible to treat foreign law as law. Moreover, to assert that English courts do not strictly apply foreign laws, at best expresses the self-evident truth that an English court, not being a foreign court, does not stand in the same relation to foreign law as such a court. It does not have the same public duty as a foreign court in relation to its law. But it may have a duty to the parties before it to determine their rights and duties accurately. In a case governed by foreign law, foreign law still has normative effect.

Again, all contested questions of law—even foreign law—are inevitably questions of interpretation, in a broad sense. They concern the construction of written laws, and the analysis of judicial decisions. In cases involving English law, these are incontrovertibly questions of law. Sometimes such matters are governed by rule, where canons of statutory interpretation, or the rules of precedent, are involved. But more often they are matters of general legal method, of a court's inherent (if acquired) skill and expertise.

In cases involving foreign law such questions of interpretation are in principle matters of expert opinion. They belong to the realm of fact, not law. But it is unrealistic to claim that an English court's inherent skill and expertise in matters of legal reasoning is disabled in cases involving foreign law, so that a court becomes merely a passive arbiter of the evidence. Rather, an English court's legal experience is actively engaged. Indeed, in some cases it may come to the fore, as in cases involving conflicting or unsatisfactory expert evidence, or the review of a trial court's findings on appeal. In this sense, it is often counter-intuitive, even impossible, to regard foreign laws as anything but laws. In this respect, it should be noted, establishing foreign law is distinct from other technical areas dependent upon expert opinion. Judges are unlikely to have the same inherent feel for the issues, or be able to employ relevant skill and experience, in cases involving, say, scientific processes, building techniques, or maritime practice.

Fourthly, to ask after the status of foreign law is not an existential enquiry. It is not a matter of discerning the characteristics of issues of foreign law to see whether they belong properly to the genus law, or the genus fact. On the contrary, in English law, issues tend to be placed in the category of fact or law because of the practical consequences of doing so. Historically, the reason why foreign laws came to be treated as facts was practical: 'The way of knowing foreign laws is by admitting them to be proved as facts'.[17] An English court knows nothing of foreign law, so must be informed of its content. The only available means to do that is to require the parties to lead evidence of foreign law, and because foreign law is established by evidence, it becomes a matter of fact. Certainly, the only theoretical justification for calling foreign laws facts—or facts of which notice cannot be taken—is that establishing foreign law is a task beyond a court's knowledge and comprehension. To adopt such an instrumental approach to characterization clears the air conceptually, by avoiding fruitless meditation about the 'nature' of foreign law. And it has an important consequence: if foreign laws are facts because otherwise a court cannot know their content, they are not (or need not be) treated as facts where evidence of foreign law is not required.

Finally, it is important to register that to ask whether foreign laws are facts or laws is misleading. It implies that all issues of foreign law must belong to one category or the other, when there is no reason why different issues—or different types of issue—might not belong to different categories. More importantly, it conceals the real question, which is whether foreign law can be established (or reviewed on appeal), without strict adherence to the rules of evidence. Differently put, it is whether the determination of foreign law can ever be a matter for the knowledge and competence of an English judge. Clearly, foreign law could be established without evidence in so far as foreign law is law. But the same is true if foreign law is fact, provided it is a fact of which the court may take judicial notice. The issue, then, is not whether foreign laws are facts, but whether a court makes judicially noticed foreign law.

Of Facts, Special Facts, and Laws

As we shall see, English courts have sometimes taken a fundamentalist view of the fact doctrine, insisting that a foreign law is a fact like any other. But they have tended more often to recognize the legal quality of foreign law, loosening the fact doctrine's grip. Confusingly, however, they have conceptualized the particular nature of foreign law in different ways, and not always consistently. They have done so, opaquely, by describing foreign laws as special facts. But, more recently, they have both equated foreign law with English law, and speculated that foreign laws may be facts of which English courts may take judicial notice.

[17] *Mostyn v Fabrigas* (1774) 1 Cowp 161, 174 (per Lord Mansfield).

Foreign Laws as Special Facts

English courts have been reluctant to take judicial notice of foreign law, still less to characterize foreign laws as anything but facts. But they have been prepared to view them as facts of a special sort.

First, the Court of Appeal has consistently refused to treat foreign laws as ordinary facts, by considering appeals on questions of foreign law.[18] It is unclear, however, whether this has implications for the treatment of foreign law generally, or whether it responds only to the particular circumstances which arise on appeal.

Certainly, the treatment of all laws not of domestic origin on appeal begs questions special to the appeal process. There are sound reasons of policy and principle why findings of foreign law cannot sensibly be treated merely as findings of fact in such cases. Where the witness evidence is provided by experts, as in cases involving foreign law,[19] questions of credibility or reliability are unlikely to be an issue. In such cases, an appeal court need not display its customary reluctance to overturn the trial judge, who may be in a better position to assess such matters. Again, any limit on an appeal court's ability to review findings on foreign law may inhibit the parties' access to effective justice. This might be so if the scope for review is less than that which might be available in the courts of the country whose law is in issue. Indeed, the factual nature of foreign law findings, and the risk that appellate review might be diminished, has sometimes caused English courts to doubt that they are the appropriate forum for resolving complex questions of foreign law.[20]

Secondly, there are cases in which the courts have dispensed with strict adherence to the rules of evidence when handling foreign law at trial. They have relied instead on their expertise in English law, particularly in cases involving the construction of foreign statutes. But, again, the status of such decisions is uncertain. The flexible, 'legalist' tendency[21] has always been answered by a powerful trend in the opposite direction. Certainly, courts have been as willing to cleave strictly to the fact doctrine as they have been to subvert it.[22]

This tension between the legalist and factual tendencies arises whenever it is suggested that establishing foreign law in a given case is within

[18] Fentiman, n 5 above, 201–2.

[19] An in other cases involving expert testimony.

[20] *The Eleftheria* [1970] p 94; *The El Amria* [1981] 2 Lloyd's Rep 119 (CA); *The Sennar (No 2)* [1985] 1 WLR 490 (HL).

[21] Sometimes called 'constructionist': Hodgkinson, n 5 above, 306–9.

[22] And commentators: see, Hodgkinson, n 5 above, 294, 306–9.

the knowledge or experience of the court, and so exempt from the usual rules of evidence. It is sharply revealed in two conflicting lines of authority, concerning whether a court may legitimately establish foreign law by construing foreign primary sources, unaided by expert opinion. The problem arises in two situations: where the parties invite the court to establish foreign law without expert guidance;[23] and where the court considers that the expert evidence is unsatisfactory.[24] In such cases, courts have sometimes been prepared to assess for themselves such primary sources as are in evidence, either instead of expert opinion,[25] or to contradict it.[26] But there are powerful dicta denying that this is possible in either situation.[27]

Again, there is a similar difference in view between decisions which accept, and those which deny, that a proposition of foreign law may be treated as a notorious fact, as such not requiring proof.[28] It may be unlikely that foreign law would often be sufficiently notorious, but the interest of such cases is that some would deny that foreign law can ever be established other than by evidence, given the potency of the fact doctrine. The same difficulty arises in principle in cases where a judge claims a knowledge of foreign law when 'general principles of law' are involved (although criticism of this practice has been muted).[29]

As this suggests, the legal status of foreign law has long been confused. But there are clear indications that foreign laws are facts of a special kind, although the courts have been hesitant to admit that issues of foreign law may in truth be issues of law.

Foreign Law as Law

More recently, the Court of Appeal has approved the 'legalist' trend in the authorities, and has indicated that the distinctive treatment of foreign law on appeal is merely a reflection of its special status. In doing so, it has suggested (paradoxically), that establishing foreign law may exceptionally involve recourse to English law.

[23] Fentiman, n 5 above, 257–62. [24] ibid 195–9.

[25] *Stafford Allen & Sons Ltd. v Pacific Steam Navigation Co* [1956] 1 Lloyd's Rep 629 (CA); *Jabbour v Custodian of Israeli Absentee Property* [1954] 1 WLR 139; *Krajina v Tass Agency* [1949] 2 All ER 274 (CA); *Re Cohn* [1945] Ch 5.

[26] Fentiman, n 5 above, 196.

[27] *Rossano v Manufacturers Life Insurance Co* [1963] 2 QB 352, 381; *Re Banque des Marchands de Moscou* [1958] Ch 182, 202; *Lazard Brothers v Midland Bank* [1933] AC 289, 298 (HL); *Buerger v New York Life Assurance Co* (1927) 96 LJKB 930, 940 (CA); *Nelson v Bridport* (1845) 8 Beav 527, 541. [28] Fentiman, n 5 above, 248–51.

[29] ibid 247–8.

The juridical character of foreign law is inevitably exposed when a trial court's findings are subject to appeal. An appeal court has no choice but to characterize the nature of the foreign law problem, which determines both the extent to which appellate review is possible, and the nature of such review. Whether an appeal from a finding on foreign law is possible at all is not in doubt, even if such findings are characterized as finding of fact.[30] But for some time it was unclear how any review should be conducted. If such findings are treated as findings of law, an appeal court may revisit the issue and reach its own conclusions. It 'exercises its own judgment, independently of, though not uninfluenced by the views of the trial judge'.[31] But if such findings are regarded as findings of fact, the court's approach is circumscribed. The question is whether there was evidence which entitled the court below to reach its conclusions.

It has long been recognized that issues of foreign law are factual issues 'of a peculiar kind' for appeal purposes.[32] But the consequences of this delphic description were only fully explored by the Court of Appeal in *MCC Proceeds Incv Bishopsgate Investment Trust plc*, [33] a case concerning an appeal from the trial court's interpretation of the New York Uniform Commercial Code. There the correct handling of foreign law on appeal was directly in issue. The appellants sought (unsurprisingly) to approximate the question to one of law, inviting the Court of Appeal to interpret for itself the relevant New York provisions. In reply, the respondents urged a 'factual' approach to the issue, and invited the Court of Appeal to enquire merely whether the evidence justified the trial judge's conclusions. The Court of Appeal accepted the appellant's view. They revisted the question of interpretation afresh, and took an independent view of the relevant provisions of New York law. They did not confine themselves to assessing the consistency of the judge's findings with the evidence. In that sense they treated the question as if it were one of law, not fact.

The Court of Appeal seems to have accepted that a judge is always entitled to employ his or her legal skill and experience in resolving questions of foreign law.[34]

> He is entitled and indeed bound to bring that part of his qualifications to bear on the issue which he has to decide, notwithstanding that it is an issue of foreign law.

[30] *MCC Proceeds Inc v Bishopsgate Investment Trust plc* [1999] CLC 417 (CA).

[31] ibid, para 6.

[32] *Parkasho v Singh* [1968] p 233, 250; *Dalmia Dairy Industries Ltd v National Bank of Pakistan* [1978] 2 Lloyd's Rep 233, 286; *Bumper Development Corp v Comr of Police* [1991] 1 WLR 1362, 1370.

[33] [1999] CLC 417 (CA).

[34] ibid, para 19.

There is a legal input from him, in addition to the judicial task of assessing the weight of the evidence given.[35]

This is not so much a matter of deploying English canons of interpretation, as of bringing to bear their skill and expertise in English law in establishing foreign law. In this sense, the task of establishing foreign law does not depend upon evidence, but experience. It is a matter of technique, not knowledge, and thus within the province of the English court—just like a question of English law.

Bishopsgate is significant in two respects.

First, the judgment of the court explictly refers to the legal nature of the question at issue. In such a case, 'the trial judge's "finding" is essentially a conclusion as to statutory interpretation, and as such it should properly be regarded as an issue of law'.[36] Previously, even judges inclined to the same view have expressed themselves more cautiously, preferring the useful but elusive compromise that foreign laws are facts of a peculiar kind.[37]

Secondly, the court recognized that the proper treatment of foreign law may depend upon the circumstances, and indeed may vary from issue to issue in a given case. The correct approach 'varies according to the nature of the issue which arises in the particular case'.[38] The nature of the question in *Bishopsgate*, concerning the interpretation of a statute written in English from a common law jurisdiction, made it appropriate to handle it as if it were a question of English law. But it is implicit that in other cases it might be apt to treat the question more strictly as one of fact, where the conceptual fabric of the foreign system is clearly different.

The analysis begun by the Court of Appeal in *Bishopsgate* was refined in *Morgan Grenfell & Co Ltd v SACE*.[39] There somewhat different questions of foreign law were involved, concerning an insured party's duty of disclosure to an insurer under Italian law. The law in question was complex, and the conceptual structure of Italian law unfamiliar. By contrast with *Bishopsgate*, there was 'less room here than there was in that case for the judge to apply his own legal training and experience... because Italian law deploys principles and concepts which are in some respects different from those of the common law'.[40] Importantly, however, the court recognized that even in such a case 'it seems to us to be appropriate for us to have at least some regard to our own experience and training'.[41]

[35] para 13. [36] ibid, para 20.
[37] As did Evans LJ earlier in the judgment: see para 9.
[38] ibid, para 13; see also para 19.
[39] Judgment, 21 December 1999 (unreported), and [2001] EWCA Civ 1932.
[40] paras 51, 57. [41] ibid.

And the court again articulated the view that questions of foreign law, where they can be resolved by reference to general principles of legal reasoning, are in effect questions of law. As Evans LJ said, echoing *Bishopsgate*:

In the result, it seems to me that the situation with regard to appeals from the learned judge's findings of fact as to foreign law is little different, if at all, from the approach of this Court when findings of English law are sought to be appealed.[42]

SACE and (more explicitly) *Bishopsgate* thus endorse the flexible, 'legalist' approach, long visible in the cases, in preference to the rival 'factual' approach. But the Court of Appeal's approach begs two questions.

The first question is practical. What difference does this approach make? More, perhaps, than might be supposed. The Court of Appeal clearly thought that the approach they were endorsing was not confined to the treatment of foreign law on appeal. They were dealing at the appeal stage with a general question about establishing foreign law.[43] Indeed, they took for granted that trial judges are always free to deploy their training and experience in English law. The only question was whether the Court of Appeal could do the same.

The second question is theoretical. If the interpretation of foreign law is in principle a matter of law, is it a matter of English law, or foreign law? In neither *Bishopsgate* nor *SACE* was it suggested that the court should apply English principles of construction because the relevant foreign principles had not been proved. English law did not apply by default on the basis of any presumption of identity. Instead, the discussion proceeded on the basis that evidence of foreign law is sometimes unnecessary. Indeed, if an issue is to be treated as an issue of law in an English court, this can only be an issue of English law, fact and English law being the only categories available. There seems little doubt that English law applied in *Bishopsgate* because, in the circumstances, it was the applicable law.

The lesson to be drawn from these developments is simple but important. In principle, an issue before the courts can only be one of fact or *English* law. But this does not mean that all issues of foreign law must belong to one category or the other. Nor does it mean that every issue arising from the proof of a single proposition of foreign law must have the same character. As *Bishopsgate* confirms, the existence and formulation of a foreign rule are almost inevitably factual matters, in so far as they

[42] Judgment, 21 December 1999 (unreported), para 46.
[43] See eg *Bishopsgate*, para 13.

depend upon a knowledge of foreign law which can only be supplied by evidence. But the nature of the issue, and thus its juridical character, changes in so far as the construction of that rule is within the skill and competence of the judge. It becomes a matter of law—of *English* law.

So an issue of foreign law is not always one of fact, not even one of a peculiar kind. It can be a mixed question of fact and law, a question of fact which to some extent will be answered by an English judge using English legal methodology. The nature of the mix may vary from case to case, as the Court of Appeal has noted. Sometimes, as in *Bishopsgate*, the latter may have a prominent role in establishing foreign law. Sometimes, as in *SACE*, it may not. But, as the court in *SACE* recognized, it is unlikely to have no role at all.

Judicial Notice of Foreign Law?

The Court of Appeal has gone further, however, in re-imagining the foreign law problem, and has suggested a different and bolder analysis. A prolonged discussion of the tension between the 'factual' and 'legal' approaches in *Sace* ends with the following striking passage:

> We may perhaps be permitted to add that we hope that the time may not be far off when it will be permissible for the English courts to take judicial notice of decisions of foreign courts, including those in the European Union, (and perhaps academic writing) in deciding what the relevant foreign law is in cases of this kind.[44]

To say that a court has judicial notice means that it has, or is deemed to have, knowledge of that matter. An English court has judicial notice of English law, and of certain facts which are assumed to be within a judge's knowledge.[45] But the concept has a broader meaning with particular resonance in this context. To say that a court has judicial notice of a matter does not merely refer to a court's actual or presumed knowledge. It means that the task of establishing that matter is within a court's province, and so does not depend upon rules of evidence. It means that a fact may be 'noticed after inquiry'.[46] It refers not only to information, but to the court's control of the adjudicatory process. It is 'a method of ascertainment free from the strict rules of formal proof'.[47]

If we assume that foreign laws are always facts in the strict sense, the Court of Appeal's suggestion is arresting. But this has never been the case,

[44] para 53.
[45] H Malek (gen ed), *Phipson on Evidence* (London: Sweet & Maxwell, 2005) (16th edn), para 3.02.
[46] ibid.
[47] S Sass, 'Foreign Law in Civil Litigation' [1968] 16 *AJCL* 332, 342.

and the court's suggestion is less novel than might be supposed. English courts already take judicial notice of foreign law.[48] Most obviously, statute provides that they have judicial notice of European Union law.[49] But English courts have also tended to take judicial notice of the laws of other Commonwealth jurisdictions, even if strictly they are foreign.[50] They have also treated foreign law as within their province without invoking the doctrine of judicial notice. They have sometimes deployed a knowledge of a particular foreign law on the basis that it is a notorious fact,[51] although to do so is controversial.[52] They have sometimes done so on the basis that it reflects a universal legal principle.[53]

Presumably, the Court of Appeal contemplated that legislation should in future authorize the courts to take judicial notice of foreign law in all cases. They would, it seems, approximate all laws to the position of EU law. Certainly, in the absence of such authorization, the range of cases in which a court could judicially notice foreign law would be small. At common law, notice may be taken only of clearly established facts,[54] which is unlikely to include technical aspects of foreign law. Moreover, it has been suggested that only clear statutory authority could permit a court to take judicial notice of foreign law.[55]

But the design of such a rule involves more difficult issues than the Court of Appeal might have thought. As the experience in other common law jurisdictions confirms, intricate issues of principle are involved.[56] Should judicial notice of foreign law be mandatory, or at the court's discretion? Should notice be taken only of pleaded foreign law? Where judicial notice is taken, does this replace or augment the evidence of experts?

That experience also suggests, however, that the implications of any such change for current English practice might be less than dramatic. In many American states, courts may take judicial notice of foreign law, and, although the concept is not explicitly referred to, this is effectively the position in US federal courts.[57] But the consequence has been to alter

[48] Fentiman, n 5 above, 244 ff.

[49] European Communities Act 1972, s 3, Sch 1, Pt I.

[50] *A-G for New Zealand v Ortiz* [1984] AC 1 (HL); T Hartley, 'Pleading and Proof of Foreign Law: The Major European Systems Compared' (1996) 45 *ICLQ* 271, 280.

[51] *Saxby v Fulton* [1909] 2 KB 208, 211.

[52] *El Ajou v Dollar Land Holdings plc* [1993] 3 All ER 717.

[53] *Di Sora v Phillipps* (1863) 33 LJ Ch 129 (HL); *The Tolten* [1946] p 135, 148 (CA); *Adams v Cape Industries plc* [1990] 2 WLR 657, 714.

[54] ibid.

[55] *Re Helbert Wagg & Co* [1956] Ch 323, 356.

[56] The US experience is especially instructive. See, especially: CA Wright and AR Miller, *Federal Practice and Procedure*, vol 9 (St Paul, Minn: West Group, 1995), 634 ff.

[57] Federal Rules of Civil Procedure, Rule 44.1.

the courts' approach to the assessment of foreign law, more than their approach to how information about foreign law is provided.[58] In practice, such information is generally still provided by means of expert reports supplied by the parties.

But the concept of judicial notice has an important role, even if the supply of information about foreign law remains (or remains largely) the responsibility of the parties, and if information is generally delivered through expert testimony. It detaches the process of establishing foreign law from the strict rules of evidence, and provides a conceptual warrant for the informal, non-evidential approach which courts sometimes take to foreign law. In particular, it has two consequences. First, it permits a court to establish foreign law on the basis of foreign legal materials, even in the absence of expert testimony, thus avoiding the delay and expense of formal proof. Secondly, it affects the assessment of such information concerning foreign law as the parties may have introduced. It allows a court to deploy its inherent legal expertise when establishing foreign law. As *Bishopsgate* and *SACE* confirm, to resort to English principles of construction does not depend upon taking judicial notice of foreign law. But judicial notice offers a different route to the same result. It suggests that the task of establishing foreign law does not depend purely on rules of evidence, and that a court may deploy its own knowledge and expertise to that end.

As this suggests, to legislate to give courts judicial notice of foreign law may not substantially change existing practice. It merely confirms the practice of the courts in exceptional cases. But it means that such cases, even if exceptional, can no longer be dismissed as heterodox.

Foreign Law as . . . Foreign Law

It is difficult to insist that foreign laws are facts in the normal sense. Even if categorized as facts, their legal quality is inescapable. Unlike most facts, courts may have the technical competence to handle them without expert assistance. And, although any finding of fact may affect the outcome in a dispute, to establish foreign law is to establish directly the parties' legal rights and duties. This requires special attention to be paid to its normative character, and imposes on courts a particular obligation not to denature those rights and duties.

English courts have tried to adjust the conceptual structure of the foreign law problem accordingly. Elusively, they have been ready to concede

[58] S Sass, 'Foreign Law in Federal Courts' (1981) 29 *AJCL* 96, 107 ff.

that they are facts of a special sort. More recently, they have identified circumstances in which an issue of foreign law becomes in effect an issue of English law. And in *SACE* they have canvassed another alternative, by suggesting that courts might be permitted to take judicial notice of foreign law. Intriguingly, however, this last approach re-affirms the traditional view that foreign laws are facts—facts of which judicial notice may be taken. And it sharpens the question we should ask. The issue is not whether foreign laws are facts or laws, but whether they are facts subject to the rules of evidence.

As this suggests, resort to the doctrine of judicial notice might introduce the necessary flexibility. And the Court of Appeal may have seen in the doctrine a familiar, effective means to that end. But there is no need to invoke judicial notice to achieve the desired effect, as the solution adopted in US federal practice elegantly demonstrates. Rule 44.1 of the Federal Rules of Civil Procedure provides:

> A party who intends to raise an issue concerning the law of a foreign country shall give notice by pleadings or other reasonable written notice. The court, in determining foreign law, may consider any relevant material or source, including testimony, whether or not submitted by a party or admissible under the Federal Rules of Evidence. The court's determination shall be treated as a ruling on a question of law.

Rule 44.1 thus achieves two important objectives.[59] The status of foreign law on appeal is confirmed. Findings on foreign law are findings of law. And, importantly, the strictures of the normal rules of evidence are explicitly removed. But this is achieved without characterizing such issues as simply legal or factual, thereby confirming their hybrid status. True, the court's finding is one of law, thereby ensuring its status on appeal. But the language of the rule's second sentence confirms that the process of establishing foreign law is not necessarily a process of legal determination. It may depend upon expert opinion, like any question of fact. Or it may not. Echoing the Court of Appeal's approach in *Bishopsgate*, its status may change according to the circumstances. But the approach of Rule 44.1, unlike that of the Court of Appeal in *SACE*, is to secure flexibility directly, by allowing recourse to any 'relevant material or source', not indirectly, by interposing the doctrine of judicial notice.

But the purpose of Rule 44.1 is more radical than this suggests. *Bishopsgate* and *SACE* propose in different ways how establishing foreign

[59] The first sentence also relaxes the requirement to plead foreign law, previously a matter of concern in US practice. In English law a matter of which a court has judicial notice need not be pleaded: *Brando v Barnett* (1846) 12 Cl & F 787.

law need not require evidence. But it may, and to that extent foreign law remains a fact, as the concept of judicial notice implies. The theory underlying Rule 44.1 is different. The determination of foreign law is not a matter of evidence at all. And foreign laws should not be seen as facts. Expert testimony might be relied upon. But this does not mean that the rules of evidence apply, merely that this is an effective means of communicating the necessary information about foreign law. The omission of any reference to judicial notice was intended to ensure that the determination of foreign law is outside the law of evidence, and that foreign law should not be seen merely as a fact of which judicial notice might be taken.[60] But what then is the status of foreign law? It is law, as Rule 44.1 provides, yet it may be established by expert opinion. So it does not resemble the law of the forum. It is, perhaps, a question of law of a peculiar kind. Or perhaps, after all, it is just foreign law.

The Presumption of Identity

To ask whether issues of foreign law are merely issues of fact is to ask how far the ascertainment of foreign law is subject to the normal rules of evidence. A related question concerns the status of the evidential presumption that, in the absence of any, or adequate, evidence of foreign law, foreign law is presumed to be the same as English law. This improbable fiction has been put to work in different ways, although its distinct roles are not always properly separated. It is said to justify applying English law, both where the evidence of foreign law is unsatisfactory or conflicting, and where foreign law has been pleaded, but no evidence of the content of foreign law has been introduced. It might also be used to explain why English law applies in a case having foreign elements, which ought in principle to be subject to foreign law, but in which neither party has relied upon foreign law. In each such case it might be said that the necessary evidence of foreign law is absent.

Thus described, the presumption of identity between English and foreign law has always been troublesome. Even if it operates where the proof of foreign law has failed, or has not been attempted, it is uncertain whether it has a role where foreign law has not been pleaded at all. It is unclear what is served by pretending that foreign law is being applied in the guise of English law when nobody has suggested that foreign law applies at all. Doubtless English law will govern in such cases. But, as we

[60] Federal Advisory Committee on Evidence, Note, 56 FRD 207 (1972).

shall see, this is best explained by saying that the parties have in effect chosen English law as the governing law by their failure to rely upon foreign law. Indeed, to explain such cases by reference to the presumption of identity has an unfortunate consequence. It obscures the real issue in cases where foreign law has not been relied upon, which is whether the relevant choice of law regime is mandatory, and whether it permits the parties to choose English law in preference to any foreign law that would otherwise be applicable according to that regime. It makes it look as if the only issue concerns the possibility or plausibility of equating English and foreign law, rather than the mandatory status of the relevant choice of law rule.

But difficulties exist even when foreign law has been relied upon, but evidence of its content is either absent, unsatisfactory, or inconclusive. It has always been casuistry to say that the end result in such cases is that foreign law is applied as if it were English law. As is now widely accepted, the more honest view is that English law becomes the applicable law in such cases, the attempt to apply foreign law having failed for want of evidence.[61]

Again, there may be good reasons to resist deploying the presumption of identity, at least where evidence of foreign law has been introduced. It would be troubling if a court were obliged to apply English law, having heard perhaps extensive (and expensive) evidence which if nothing else establishes that English law and foreign law are different. It would be especially troubling if a court were expected to do so when the evidence of foreign law, though substantial, is conflicting. In such a case the failure to establish foreign law clearly may be attributable more to the process of proof, or to the court's inexperience in foreign law, than to parties or their experts. It is unsurprising, therefore, that English courts have conspicuously refrained from relying upon the presumption of identity in such cases. Typically, they have found a way to arrive at a finding on foreign law, often by discarding the opinion of the parties' experts, and reviewing independently such primary sources as may have been put in evidence.[62]

But the presumption of identity cannot always be circumvented so easily. Sometimes the only solution is to conclude that it does not operate at all. A cluster of important recent cases, in England and Australia, consider the limits to the presumption, and confirm that it is far less secure than might be supposed. Before examining their implications, however, it is important to be clear how limited the presumption has always been.

[61] Fentiman, n 5 above, 146, 184, 290; *Dicey, Morris and Collins*, n 5 above, 269.
[62] *Bumper Development Corpn v Comr of Police* [1991] 1 WLR 1362 (CA).

The Limits to Identity

It has been said that 'to state exhaustively when a court will not assume that the unproved provisions of foreign law are identical with those of the *lex fori* would be a difficult task'.[63] Moreover, although these exceptions are conceptually distinct, they may overlap in practice. There may be more than one reason for jettisoning the presumption in a given case. But there would appear to be four principal situations in which the presumption of identity has been held not to operate: (i) where the application of foreign law is mandatory; (ii) where reliance upon the presumption is unfair; (iii) where the presumption is inoperable; (iv) where identity between foreign law and the law of the forum is implausible.

The Mandatory Application of Foreign Law

To propose that certain rules of English private international law are mandatory in character, requiring the application of the applicable law, is to court controversy.[64] It is uncertain whether in principle any such rules can be mandatory. Even if this is possible in principle, it is unclear which particular rules have mandatory status. It is also unclear whether, or in what circumstances, principle would permit the parties to trump any mandatory rule demanding the application of foreign law by agreeing to the application of English law instead. And it is unclear whether such an agreement may be constituted by a passive omission to plead and prove foreign law. Again, it is unclear whether the parties may subvert the mandatory status of any such rules simply by omitting to introduce evidence of foreign law, and relying upon the presumption of identity.

Prolonged examination of these difficult questions is not for the present discussion. But three points may be made here. First, there are grounds for thinking that certain rules of English private international may have mandatory status. Most obviously, this is so in criminal proceedings whenever liability turns on the content of foreign law. A frequently cited example concerns prosecutions for bigamy, in which it is clear that the validity of any earlier marriage must be established under its governing law.[65] Consider also Articles 3 and 4 of the 1980 Rome Convention on the Law Applicable to Contractual Obligations.[66]

[63] *Damberg v Damberg* [2001] NSWCA 87, para 162.
[64] Contrast, Fentiman, n 5 above, 80–97, with *Dicey, Morris and Collins*, n 5 above, 259.
[65] *R v Naguib* [1917] 1 KB 359 (CA).
[66] Contracts (Applicable Law) Act 1990, Sch I.

Expressed in imperative language, these provide rules for identifying the law applicable to contractual obligations.[67] A further example might be the statutory choice of law regime in tort supplied by the Private International Law (Miscellaneous Provisions) Act 1995.[68] Again, it may be that certain English choice of law rules concerning personal status have mandatory effect. In such cases, policy may demand that such questions are determined strictly in accordance with the correct law. Thus, in *Male v Roberts*,[69] Lord Eldon famously declined to treat the Scots law concerning the capacity of infants to contract as the same as English law. And in *Guepratte v Young*[70] Knight Bruce VC refused to equate English with French law in the matter of matrimonial property.

Secondly, the suggestion that foreign law must be positively pleaded and proved when the relevant choice of law is mandatory is open to an objection.[71] Arguably, the reason why the application of foreign law can never be mandatory is precisely that a party who is required to rely upon that law may rely also upon the presumption of identity. This is, however, unconvincing. In so far as the application of foreign law is sometimes mandatory, it is surely unlikely that any such rule could be subverted by reliance on the presumption of identity. It would be anomalous if an evidential presumption were permitted to defeat a rule of substantive law. Certainly, one might expect that the purpose of rules of procedure is to further, not frustrate, substantive rules of law.

No doubt, as traditionally stated, the presumption tempts us to think that this may be possible, by implying that foreign law is being applied, albeit in the guise of English law. But, if the effect of the presumption is that English law becomes the applicable law in the absence of evidence of foreign law, as is now accepted,[72] it would be contradictory to hold that any given choice of law rule is mandatory, and at the same time to deploy the presumption of identity.

Thirdly, we may or may not accept that the parties may invariably escape the operation of the choice of law, simply by omitting to plead foreign law. But it cannot be denied that the collision between the choice of law process and the rules of pleading and proof creates a serious problem of principle. It certainly cannot be assumed that it is self-evident that the latter qualify the former. The difficulty was alluded to in the leading Canadian case. In *Amosin v The Mercury Bell*[73] Marceau J was concerned

[67] Fentiman, n 5 above, 80–97.
[68] ibid 97–106.
[69] (1800) 3 Esp 163.
[70] (1851) 4 De G & Sim 217.
[71] *Dicey, Morris and Collins*, n 5 above, 259.
[72] *Shaker v Al-Bedrawi* [2002] 4 All ER 835 (CA).
[73] (1986), 66 NR 361 (FCA).

that the presumption of identity might subvert the choice of law process. As he said:

> This English jurisprudential rule that, in the absence of proof of the foreign law governing the case, the judge will apply the law of the forum should not and cannot be seen, it seems to me, as a pure abandonment of the rule of conflict, as if the rule of conflict was so unimportant that its application could be left to the whim of the parties.[74]

Again, as was said, in *Damberg v Damberg*,[75] a leading Australian case:

> The problem of when a civil court can or must refuse to be bound by a failure of the parties to prove relevant foreign law and a consensus between them that the *lex fori* applies is but one part of a wider problem. The wider problem is the extent to which the parties, by their conduct of proceedings, can prevent the court from deciding a case in accordance with the law or the facts.[76]

It is, therefore, controversial whether rules for choice of law—and thus the application of foreign law—may be mandatory in English law. More precisely, it is uncertain whether the mandatory effect of such rules may be extinguished because the proof of foreign law is a voluntary matter for the parties. But in so far as the application of foreign law is indeed required, it is surely unlikely that litigants (and the courts) could satisfy their obligation to apply foreign law by relying upon the presumption that English and foreign law are the same.

The Presumption is Unfair

There are cases in which the courts have been reluctant to employ the presumption of identity where it has the potential to cause injustice. Its role has been doubted where principle requires that a party relying upon foreign law should establish its case positively, as where fraud is alleged against the other party.[77] Nor has it been applied where the evidence before the court is necessarily incomplete, as in applications for summary judgment,[78] or applications for a stay of proceedings on *forum non conveniens* grounds.[79] The presumption may only operate, it seems, at a full trial where comprehensive evidence is available.

There may also be support in the cases for a broader proposition. There are suggestions that a party who relies upon foreign law cannot, by

[74] At 365. [75] [2001] NSWCA 87. [76] para 148.
[77] *Österreichische Länderbank v S'Elite Ltd* [1981] 1 QB 565, 569.
[78] *Western National Bank of New York v Perez, Triana & Co* (1860) 6 TLR 366; *National Shipping Corp v Arab* [1971] 2 Lloyd's Rep. 363.
[79] *The Polessk* [1996] 2 Lloyd's Rep 40, 43.

declining to introduce evidence of that law, impose on the other party the burden of proving that English law is different. The proposition that the presumption of identity is not available to such a party is consistent with some prominent decisions,[80] and was articulated clearly in an important Australian case:[81]

> The application of the presumption is intended to operate against, not in favour of, the party whose obligation it is to prove the foreign law, so that he is deprived of the benefit of a right or exemption given by that foreign law.[82]

Fairness has also led the courts to avoid the presumption of identity by other means. In one case the effect of the presumption was neutralized because the court considered that an attempt to rely upon the laws of several foreign countries, without pleading or proving their content, amounted to an abuse of process.[83] There the claimants could not seriously have believed that the laws of several countries were all the same as English law.

The Presumption is Inoperable

Sometimes the presumption of identity is ousted because English law cannot be applied by default. In such cases, the application of foreign law is not mandatory in choice of law terms, nor is it unfair to deploy the presumption. The presumption is simply inoperable. Most obviously, there may be no rule of English law equivalent to the applicable rule of foreign law. In one case, for example, the problem in French maritime law to which an answer was sought could not have arisen in English law, which adopted an entirely different approach to such matters.[84] Unable to deploy the presumption of identity, the court was forced (somewhat unconvincingly) to assume that a French court would do the just thing, and determined French law accordingly.

Different but related problems arise in cases concerning the construction of documents (typically, contracts or wills), when English courts encounter foreign expressions or terms of art, which can only meaningfully be understood by reference to foreign law. In such cases courts are sometimes asked to construe such language without evidence. The courts

[80] *McElroy v McAllister* 1949 SC 100; *Dynamit AG v Rio Tinto Co* [1918] AC 260 (HL).

[81] *BP Exploration Ltd v Hunt* [1980] 1 NSWLR 496. [82] At 503.

[83] *Mother Bertha Music Ltd v Bourne Music Ltd* (unreported), 31 July 1997.

[84] *The Spirit of Independence* [1999] 1 Lloyd's Rep 43; R Fentiman, 'Foreign Law in National Courts' in G Canivet, M Andenas, and D Fairgrieve (eds), *Comparative Law before the Courts* (London: BIICL, 2004), 17 ff.

have sometimes avoided the difficulty of doing so by determining what the parties must have meant by the term in question.[85] But in others it may be 'absolutely necessary' to hear evidence as to the correct meaning of the term, regardless of the presumption of identity.[86]

Identity is Implausible

In some cases it is counter-intuitive to suppose that English and foreign law are the same. This may be the case where a party relies upon several foreign laws, each of which is alleged to be the same as English law. It may be unlikely that English law is the same as each of them.[87] It may also be implausible to apply the presumption when it is apparent that the relevant foreign law is different, notwithstanding the lack of evidence to that effect. In the unusual case of *Saxby v Fulton*,[88] Bray J declined to conclude in the absence of evidence that gaming was illegal in Monte Carlo, as under English law, because the opposite was notoriously true. Conversely, it may be apparent that English law is unique, and differs from other legal systems, even if it is not clear that it differs from the relevant foreign law. The distinctiveness of English law's former approach to matrimonial property has been said to explain Knight Bruce VC's refusal to equate English with French law in *Gueprattc v Young*.[89] More recently, in *Fourie v Allan le Roux*, [90] the Court of Appeal concluded that it was unlikely that South African law contained provisions identical to English law's insolvency rules, given that the leading work on comparative insolvency law indicated otherwise.[91]

The most important reason for concluding that identity between the *lex causae* and *lex fori* is implausible is that the relevant rules of the forum are distinctively local in character, rather than universal. If those rules serve purely local interests, and regulate matters of purely local concern, it may be implausible to suppose that they exist also in other legal systems. This is not, as might be supposed, a matter of whether the law of forum is capable of applying by default. It does not concern whether the case is comprehended by that law. It is a matter of testing the likelihood that a foreign law has the same content as the law of the forum.

[85] *Stafford Allen & Sons Ltd v Pacific Steam Navigation Co* [1956] 1 Lloyd's Rep 105.

[86] *Di Sora v Phillipps* (1863) 33 LJ Ch 129, 130; *Eglington v Lamb* (1867) 15 LT 657; *Stafford Allen & Sons Ltd v Pacific Steam Navigation Co* [1956] 1 Lloyd's Rep 105.

[87] ibid. [88] [1909] 2 KB 208, 211.

[89] (1851) 4 De G & Sim 217, 224; see *Damberg v Damberg* [2001] NSWCA 87, para 129. [90] [2005] EWCA Civ 204.

[91] P Wood, *International Insolvency* (London: Sweet & Maxwell, 1995), para 1–25. But this may have merely reinforced their view that the presumption was inapplicable because the relevant English rules were strictly local in scope.

The leading analysis of the universality test is to be found in an important Canadian decision. In *Amosin v The Ship 'Mercury Bell'*,[92] questions arose concerning a labour dispute between a vessel's crew and its owners. It was accepted that Liberian law governed, but no evidence was introduced as to its content. Instead it was alleged that a Canadian statute, the Canada Labour Code, should apply on the basis that Canadian and Liberian law were presumptively identical. This prompted an extensive review of the scope of the presumption. Marceau J appears to have adopted a sophisticated view of the mechanics of the presumption. He never doubted that identity between the *lex fori* and *lex causae* might sometimes be presumed. But he did not apparently conclude that foreign law then applies as if it is the same as the *lex fori*. Instead, he seems to have assumed that the presumed identity between the two laws entitles the forum to apply its own law.[93] He also considered, but rejected as unsupported by Canadian authority, the simplistic proposition that the presumption was inapplicable where the relevant rules of the forum were statutory. Instead, he drew on suggestions in the Canadian case law that it was inapplicable only if 'special statutory provisions' were involved.[94] He distinguished between 'substantive provisions of a general character and others of a localized or regulatory character'.[95] The former might be subject to the presumption of identity, but not the latter. As he remarked, the presumption 'can be rationally acceptable only when limited to provisions of the law potentially having some degree of universality'.[96]

This sensitive approach is compelling, but it is incomplete. The distinction between local and universal laws may be conceptually robust, but its content is uncertain. When precisely is a law 'regulatory'? Arguably all law, certainly all statute law, has this character. Again, if a law is not so designated, how is universality to be judged? Is a rule universal if it reflects a principle which it may be assumed is common to all legal systems? Alternatively, is a rule local when it can be meaningfully applied only in a local context?

Marceau J's application of this principle to the facts of *The Mercury Bell* suggests some answers. Analysing the Canada Labour Code, he concluded that the presumption could embrace those of its rules concerning 'recognising the role of labour unions, giving effect to collective agreements, and, as interpreted by the courts, recognising the right of each individual employee to sue for his wages under the agreement'.[97] Such rules were universal in character. They were 'fundamental'. By contrast,

[92] (1986) 27 DLR (4th) 641. [93] At 645.
[94] *Gray v Kerslake* [1958] SCR 3; *Hellens v Densmore* [1957] SCR 768.
[95] At 650. [96] ibid. [97] At 650.

the rules of the code concerning the role of the Canada Labour Relations Board, and the settlement of disputes by arbitration in Canada, were local, because 'linked to Canadian circumstances and purposes'. Such rules were connected with Canadian institutions, and could only sensibly be applied in a Canadian context, within the structure of Canadian law.

In English law, this approach was anticipated by Westlake, who wrote in an important passage: 'Foreign law is presumed to be the same as English, of course excluding those parts of the latter which only exist as special institutions with special machinery, such as bankruptcy . . . '.[98]

Explicit treatment of such issues is rare in English proceedings. However, in *Österreichische Länderbank v S'Elite Ltd*[99] it was doubted that English and Austrian law could be deemed to be identical in a case concerning the effect of fraud on a bill of exchange, as regulated by the Bills of Exchange Act 1882. It is likely that the Court of Appeal's reluctance owed much to the fact that fraud had been alleged, thus making it unfair for the claimant to allege fraud without proof positive. But another possible explanation is that it may be unlikely that one country's view of what constitutes improper is shared elsewhere. As Roskill LJ said:

> In proper cases, of course, the presumption may be applied but I question whether it has any place in a matter of this kind where an assertion is made of fraud, based upon a provision of an English statute which does not have any direct application, at any rate at first sight, to the law of the country of the incorporation of the company whose conduct is complained of—or indeed, of the bank, whose conduct is complained of.[100]

It is uncertain what principle underlies Roskill LJ's remarks, which were extempore. Perhaps the best explanation, consistent with the analysis in *The Mercury Bell*, is that the provisions of the Act concerning fraud are regulatory in nature. They are in a sense punitive, and express English law's interest in the conduct of financial transactions. As such, they should be treated as local in operation, and thus exempt from the presumption of identity.

The Presumption Reviewed

In a cluster of recent cases the courts in England and Australia have considered the status of the presumption of identity, with important and potentially radical consequences.

[98] J Westlake, *A Treatise on Private International Law* (6th edn) (London: Sweet and Maxwell, 1922), para 353.

[99] [1981] 1 QB 565.

[100] At 569.

Damberg and *Neilson*—Plus Ça Change?

In two important cases in recent years, the foreign law problem has been closely scrutinized in Australia, with ambiguous results. In one the presumption of identity was criticized, and confined; in the other its position was apparently restored.

The Presumption Criticized

Damberg v Damberg[101] concerned the effect of German tax law on certain property transactions in Australia. In a dispute between a father and his children, the question was whether he was prevented from relying on a resulting trust of the proceeds of those transactions, on the ground that he had avoided German capital gains tax. Relying on the presumption of identity, the children had argued that under Australian law, and thus under German law, taxpayers were required to declare all their income, which their father had not done. Speaking for the Court, Heydon JA accepted that the presumption might apply in other cases. But it could not apply in *Damberg*, for two reasons. First, the presumption was implausible. Although no expert opinion was offered as to German law, the father's German accountant had outlined the position under German law in his evidence relating to the transactions. That was enough to suggest that German and Australian law were not the same. Secondly, in one respect, it was impossible to operate the presumption. At the time when most of the transactions were effected, there was no provision in Australian law for taxing any but short-term capital gains, as there appeared to be in German law.

The decision in *Damberg* is unobjectionable, even obvious. But it has significance beyond its facts. Importantly, Heydon JA (Spiegelman CJ and Shellar JA concurring never doubted the existence of the presumption of identity. They focused on the applicability of the presumption, on whether it was both plausible and possible to apply it. In doing so, they accepted that foreign law can sometimes be equated with the *lex fori*, and thus that foreign law continues to apply when the presumption operates.[102] At no time was it suggested that, if foreign law is not proved, the *lex fori* applies as the applicable law. But in reaching this conclusion, Heydon JA undertook a particularly thorough comparative survey of the position in several common law jurisdictions, including England. Conspicuously, Heydon JA resisted deriving any principles from the case law, and declined to specify when the presumption might be inapplicable.[103] But the numerous authorities cited in the judgment correspond

[101] [2001] NSWCA 87. [102] para 119. [103] para 162.

with the exceptions we have already identified. And they confirm beyond doubt that the presumption of identity is significantly qualified in its operation.

The Presumption Restored?

Such is the breadth and detail of the *tour d'horizon* offered in *Damberg*, and the persuasiveness of the argument that the presumption is qualified, that it is hard to see how any future case involving the presumption of identity could fail to engage with the decision. Yet the presumption of identity was considered again, this time by the High Court of Australia, in *Neilson v Overseas Projects Corporation of Victoria Ltd.*[104] And *Damberg*, and its implications, seem largely to have been ignored.

Neilson concerned an action by the claimant for injuries sustained while living in China in a flat provided by the defendant, an Australian company. The action was time-barred under that law, but not in Australian law. Which law governed? Application of the Australian choice of law rule in tort led to the law of China, the *lex loci delicti*.[105] But Chinese courts have discretion to apply the law of the parties' common nationality or domicile to a claim in tort.[106] The relevant provision of Chinese law was Article 146 of the General Principles of Civil Law of the People's Republic of China: 'If both parties are nationals of the same country or domiciled in the same country, the law of their own country or of their place of domicile may also be applied'.

The High Court began by confirming (controversially), that the *lex loci delicti* rule is absolute in Australian law.[107] Unlike Chinese law—and, indeed, English law[108]—there is no discretion to apply any other law with which the tort might have a stronger connection. But the question was whether an Australian court should apply Chinese domestic law, or the choice of law embodied in Article 146. Did *renvoi* operate or not? The High Court accepted that it did. But was there sufficient evidence concerning Article 146 to enable the court to exercise the discretion to disapply the *lex loci delicti*? If not, could the court presume that Chinese and Australian law were the same, supplying a basis for exercising the discretion provided by Chinese law?

It must have seemed unlikely from the outset that the court would find that the evidence of Chinese law was sufficient. As Chief Justice Gleeson

[104] [2005] HCA 54.
[105] Applying *Regie Nationale des Usines Renault SA v Zhang* (2002) 210 CLR 491.
[106] Article 146, General Principles of Law of the People's Republic of China.
[107] Endorsing *Regie Nationale des Usines Renault SA v Zhang* (2002) 210 CLR 491.
[108] Private International Law (Miscellaneous Provisions) Act 1995, s 12.

candidly admitted: 'Not much was said in evidence about Article 146'.[109] Only the respondent had led expert evidence, and the respondent's expert did not consider that Article 146 applied at all, apparently because he thought it was irrelevant as a matter of Australian law.[110] But in cross-examination he 'assented rather hesitantly to the proposition that, if it appeared just and reasonable, a court in Wuhan might treat Australian (presumably meaning Western Australian) law as applicable'.[111] Unsurprisingly, therefore, a majority concluded that there was insufficient evidence of Chinese law,[112] although, strikingly, a minority thought the evidence adequate.[113]

The effect of the majority view was to raise squarely the question whether the presumption of identity applied. At first sight, it is hard to see how it could. Although Chinese law confers upon courts a discretion to apply a law other than the *lex loci delicti*, Australian law does not. The absence of such flexibility is a distinctive feature of Australian law, confirmed by the High Court in *Neilson* itself. There was thus no equivalent Australian rule which could have been applied. Unsurprisingly, therefore, a minority of three justices held that the presumption of identity was inapplicable.[114] But a majority of the High Court concluded that the presumption might operate. In the absence of proof of how the Article 146 discretion should be exercised, reference to Australian law was justified.[115]

None of the four justices who were prepared to apply the presumption apparently regarded it as suspect in principle. Only one, Heydon J, referred to doubts about its status.[116] But he did so without elaboration. This is in striking contrast with the same judge's extensive survey of possible exceptions to the presumption in *Damberg*, and sits uneasily with the conclusion in *Damberg* that it should not apply. Nor did the majority engage with the compelling objections which had persuaded other members of the Court not to apply the presumption on the facts. That a majority took this view is striking. At first sight, if there is any case in which the presumption should not operate, it is *Neilson*.

On inspection, however, *Neilson* does not endorse unqualified resort to the presumption of identity. As Heydon J observed, the 'general correctness' of the presumption had not been put in issue by the parties.[117]

[109] para 8. [110] para 117. [111] para 10.

[112] McHugh, Kirby, Callinan, and Heydon JJ.

[113] Gleeson CJ, Gummow, and Hayne JJ.

[114] Gleeson CJ, McHugh and Kirby JJ, who for these reasons regarded the presumption as inapplicable. See especially, the discussion by Kirby J at para 193 ff.

[115] Gummow, Hayne, Callinan, and Heydon JJ, a view rejected by Gleeson CJ, McHugh and Kirby JJ.

[116] para 267, citing Fentiman, n 5 above, 149–156.

[117] para 267.

The question was only whether it applied to the facts of *Neilson*. Again, although Gummow and Hayne JJ, in their joint opinion, would have been content to apply the presumption, they did not in fact do so. Certainly, they expressed no concerns about the presumption in principle.[118] And they would have been prepared to apply it if necessary. But they concluded that the evidence of Chinese law, though scant, was sufficient to allow an Australian court to decide that Australian law was the applicable law.[119] Strictly *obiter*, their remarks did not involve the consideration of the matter that would have been necessary had everything turned upon the presumption of identity.

Moreover, although Callinan and Heydon JJ did apply the presumption, this is understandable, given their perception of the issue before them. Both considered at some length the application of the presumption to the facts. Importantly, both concluded that the question of Chinese law before them was a matter of construction, not choice of law. It concerned the principles governing the statutory interpretation of Article 146, not the substantive principles whereby a Chinese court might displace the *lex loci delicti*. The question therefore was whether Australian principles of statutory construction could be applied by default, rather than Australian choice of law principles. Indeed, Callinan J expressly followed those English cases in which English courts have readily applied the *lex fori* in the construction of foreign statutes, where there is no evidence that the relevant foreign principles are different.[120]

To regard the issues surrounding Article 146 merely as issues of statutory construction is perhaps surprising. Arguably, they concerned the substantive legal principles upon which Chinese law might be dis-applied in favour of another law. But the assumption that only the construction of Article 146 was involved explains how the presumption could apply to the unpromising facts of *Neilson*. It answers the argument that Australian law does not recognize the existence of a flexible exception to application of the *lex loci delicti*, which means there was no Australian law which could apply in place of Chinese law. That argument would be well taken if we assume that an Australian court would be required to employ substantive principles relevant to the operation of such an exception. But not if the relevant Australian law concerns merely the principles of statutory interpretation.

As this suggests, *Damberg* and *Neilson* may not be at odds, and *Neilson* may stand for less than it seems. The difference of opinion in *Neilson*

118 para 125. 119 para 127.
120 Notably *F & K Jabbour v Custodian of Israeli Absentee Property* [1954] 1 WLR 139.

concerning the applicability of the presumption of identity may say more about how different members of the court understood the question before them, than about the presumption's status.

Shaker—The Presumption Ousted

The status of the presumption of identity in English law was comprehensively reviewed by the Court of Appeal in *Shaker v Al-Bedrawi*.[121] *Shaker* involved complex questions relating to the reflective loss rule in company law—the *Prudential* principle—which prevents shareholders from suing company directors for loss suffered as shareholders, if the company itself has a cause of action against the director. [122] In proceedings brought by Mr Shaker, a shareholder, against Mr Al-Bedrawi, a director, the question was whether ANA Inc, the company, itself had an action against Mr Bedrawi. Difficulty arose because the company was incorporated in Pennsylvania, so that Pennsylvania law governed its rights against Mr Al-Bedrawi. But no evidence had been offered as to whether the company could sue Mr Bedrawi under that law. Applying the presumption of identity, Collins J concluded that Pennsylvania law was the same as English law, whereby Mr Bedrawi was liable to the company for an unlawful distribution of company funds. But an appeal from the judge's decision was allowed , *inter alia* because it was wrong to presume that English and Pennsylvania law were the same.

The relevant English law, concerning unlawful distributions from company funds, is contained in Part VIII of the Companies Act 1985, which implements the provisions of the Second EC Company Law Directive.[123] Part VIII restricts the circumstances in which distributions can be made, and subjects such distributions to strict accounting requirements. Collins J held in particular that Mr Bedrawi had failed to keep 'relevant accounts', in the form required by Part VII. He accepted, as did the parties, that whether the presumption of identity applied turned upon whether this rule was local or universal in nature, as suggested in *The Mercury Bell*. He concluded that the rule was universal, being a generally applicable rule of law, and applied the presumption.

The appeal was allowed for two reasons. The proceedings did not involve a trial on the merits, but only the preliminary issue whether the

121 [2002] 4 All ER 835 (CA), applied *Fourie v Allan le Roux* [2005] EWCA Civ 204.
122 *Prudential Assurance Co Ltd v Newman Industries Ltd (No 2)* [1982] Ch 204.
123 (EEC) 77/91.

Prudential principle applied, such that Mr Shaker's claim failed *in limine*. The Court of Appeal seems to have accepted the position taken in several previous cases involving abbreviated proceedings that it might thus be unfair to apply English law by default.[124]

More significantly, the Court of Appeal concluded that English law was not applicable by default.[125] Part VIII of the Companies Act could not be applied according to its terms. It was applicable only to companies incorporated under the Act itself. In particular, it would have been impossible to extend the accounting requirements of Part VIII to a foreign company, because such a company was under no obligation to submit accounts in the form required by the Act.

The approach of the Court of Appeal is significant for two particular reasons.

A Broad Approach to Foreign Law

The determination of the appeal in *Shaker* aside, the Court of Appeal adopted a broad and flexible view of the treatment of foreign law. They rejected the view, long taken by the editors of *Dicey and Morris on the Conflict of Laws*, that the only true qualification to the presumption of identity is in cases of bigamy, when the existence of a previous marriage must be positively established.[126] They identified several other possible exceptions. The default rule does not operate where the equivalent English rule represents a special institution of English law, or in cases involving the legality of acts abroad, or in proceedings for summary judgment, or in cases involving foreign terms of art. But these were merely examples of English law's flexible approach, and the court referred to academic writing suggesting the existence of other exceptions.[127]

In doing so, the Court of Appeal implicitly rejected the assumption, underlying the account in *Dicey and Morris*, that only the formulation of the default rule was problematic, rather than its scope. The editors of *Dicey and Morris* had proposed that the machinery of a presumption should be jettisoned, and with it the fiction that foreign law remains applicable, in favour of recognizing that English law applies when the proof of foreign law fails. But, at the time *Shaker* was decided, they would not apparently have accepted that the cases in which English law applies by default might be limited (other than in cases of bigamy). And it is presently uncertain how far they would do so now.[128]

[124] para 65. [125] para 66. [126] N 5 above, para 9.025.
[127] Fentiman, n 5 above, Chs 3 and 4; Hartley, n 5 above.
[128] See *Dicey, Morris and Collins*, n 5 above, 269, describing *Damberg* and *Shaker*.

English Law as the Lex Causae

Strikingly, the Court of Appeal concluded that there is, after all, no presumption of identity between English and foreign law.[129] Departing from the view endorsed in *The Mercury Bell, Damberg*, and *Neilson*, they denied that foreign law applies on the fictive basis that it has the content of English law. Instead, English law is the *lex causae* in such cases. In practice, therefore, the application of English law when foreign law is not proved is not an aspect of the process of proof, an evidential rule. Rather, the default rule is a choice of law rule, determining which law governs. This important development reflects concern in the courts and the literature about the desirability of the presumption.[130] And it affected the court's approach in *Shaker* in significant ways.

First, the Court of Appeal denied that the plausibility of equating English and foreign law is a relevant issue.[131] Whether it is realistic to expect a foreign law to contain a provision found in English law is an irrelevant consideration 'in deciding whether to apply English as the *lex causae* in default of proof of foreign law'.[132] It thus becomes irrelevant to ask—as Collins J had asked—whether the relevant rule of English law is universal or local in character. To enquire whether the applicable English rule is universal or local goes to whether it is plausible to suppose that it might also be a rule of the foreign *lex causae*. If local in kind, it is not. But if universal, it may be assumed that it might.

Secondly, once it is recognized that English law is the *lex causae*, the only question is whether the case is within the scope of the relevant English rule. It depends on the familiar process of legal—usually, statutory—interpretation. Unsurprisingly, therefore, the Court of Appeal insisted that the Companies Act had to be applicable according to its terms. They rejected the suggestion that the accounting requirements of Part VIII might be made to apply to a Pennsylvania company, if it were required only to supply accounts in the form recognized by Pennsylvania law, rather than as required by the Companies Act. Because English law is the *lex causae*, it cannot be adapted just because a case has foreign elements, for then the court would not be applying English law at all: 'Either it applies to a Pennsylvanian company or it does not'.[133]

On the facts, the court concluded that the Companies Act could not be applied 'literally' to the facts of *Shaker*, because it governed only UK companies.[134] But, even had the statute been more ambiguous, the

[129] para 66.
[130] Fentiman, n 5 above, 146, 184, 290; *Dicey, Morris and Collins*, n 5 above, 269.
[131] para 68. [132] ibid. [133] para 66. [134] para 66.

answer would it seems have been the same. Part VIII originated in an EC directive, aimed at harmonization in the Community. Arguably, it reflects a distinctive Community policy, and should not therefore be extended to a corporation incorporated in a third state.

A Radical Departure

Shaker marks a radical departure in English law. There is no longer a presumption of identity between English and foreign law. Instead, if foreign law is not proved, English law is the applicable law. This approach differs from that of the Australian courts in *Damberg* and *Neilson*. There it was accepted that the presumption exists, even if there may be circumstances in which it is inapplicable. But, as *Shaker* confirms, the difference is not merely one of idiom. It turns the default rule from a rule of evidence into a choice of law rule. And it means that the relevant English law, to be applied by default, must be strictly applicable in its terms. For, if English law is the applicable law, it must be applicable. This approach also differs from the hybrid principle suggested in *The Mercury Bell.* There, as we have seen, Marceau J apparently thought that the effect of the presumption was that the law of the forum applied. But he accepted that this was because foreign law and the law of the forum could be taken to be the same, and thus that the plausibility of such an assumption in any given case was the decisive issue.

But this important development begs two questions.

First, what is the status of the now-familiar exceptions to the application of English law by default? It is no longer necessary (or possible) to enquire whether it is plausible to equate foreign law and English law, because identity is no longer to be presumed, and is no longer in issue. It is now redundant to ask (as was asked in *The Mercury Bell*), whether the relevant English law is universal or local, for the purposes of testing whether foreign law could be the same. But presumably it remains true that English law will not apply by default if there is no relevant English rule, or if it would be unfair, or if the application of foreign law is mandatory. In such cases, however, the idiom of presumption is now inapt.

Secondly, if the presumption of identity is abolished, what bearing does this have on the principle that reliance upon foreign law is generally optional? Presumably, it has none. As we have seen, whether foreign law or English law is relied upon is in principle a choice of law matter. It concerns whether the relevant choice of law rule is mandatory or, as is more usual, voluntary. It is not affected by the demise of the presumption of identity, which was of relevance only when the applicable law was clearly foreign. Only if we make the mistake of assuming that the presumption operated when foreign law was not pleaded, might we be tempted to conclude that *Shaker* makes reliance upon foreign law mandatory.

Conclusions—And a Question

The treatment of foreign law in Australia is still cast in a recognizably traditional mould. Although (importantly), *Damberg* exposes the numerous possible exceptions to the presumption, it adheres to the presumption of identity, while the facts of *Neilson* (or the way the issue was perceived by the High Court) offered little scope for creativity. But the English decisions in *Bishopsgate*, *Sace*, and *Shaker* promote a more radical agenda. They suggest a trend towards treating issues of foreign law as issues more of law than fact. Whether they are treated for some purposes overtly as issues of law, or as facts of which judicial notice may be taken, the effect is to recognize the legal quality of foreign law. *Bishopsgate* and *Sace* mark the apotheosis of the legal tendency in the cases. Adherence to the rules of evidence should not obscure the reality that the determination of foreign law depends in part upon an English court's skill and experience in English law. And *Sace* goes further, by suggesting that English courts should take judicial notice of foreign law. *Shaker* reflects a different but parallel development. When proof of foreign law is absent (or deficient), the remedy is not to deploy the presumption of identity, an evidential device, but to recognize that English law applies by default. This transforms what was an aspect of the law of evidence into a feature of the choice of law process: if proof fails, the applicable law is English. There need be no pretence that foreign law is something it is not.

Both developments reflect the assumption that English courts should aspire to apply the foreign law correctly (or not at all). It is not sufficient to apply foreign law only as well as the law of evidence allows, and certainly not by making spurious assumptions about its content. But this seemingly laudable position begs the question with which we began, a question at the heart of the conflicts process: how far must we accept that the application of one country's laws in another country's courts is inevitably compromised? Those who favour an evidential approach to foreign law insist that both practicality and principle require that the ascertainment of foreign law is inescapably (and properly) subject to local practice and procedure.[135] Others, who favour a more normative approach, see the process as going to the legal basis of the decision.

This tension is evident in the different approaches to the foreign law problem apparent in *Neilson*. There a minority of the High Court considered (surprisingly) that there was sufficient evidence of Chinese law. As we have seen, such evidence was scant indeed. All that was known was that Article 146 of the Civil Code applied, and that the respondent's expert was prepared to accept counsel's surmise as to how it might be applied. How then could three members of the court consider that Chinese law was proved?

Of the three justices in the minority, Gummow and Hayne JJ considered that there was sufficient evidence of at least one consideration relevant to exercising the Article 146 discretion. Both parties had to be foreign. As both were Australian, this pointed to applying Australian law. Conversely, there was no evidence concerning what other considerations might favour the application of Chinese law. So, on the evidence, the application of Western Australia 'was inevitable'.[136] Any uncontradicted evidence is evidence enough.

But the minority approach may rest on deeper assumptions. For Gleeson CJ, it was a judge's duty to decide on the evidence, and the parties' responsibility to supply it:

> It is possible, perhaps even likely, that the evidence of foreign law was incomplete. Nevertheless, it was necessary for the trial judge to decide the issues raised by the parties on the evidence which they presented. This is adversarial litigation, and the outcome of such litigation is commonly influenced by the way in which the parties have chosen to conduct their respective cases.[137]

Again, for Hayne and Gummow JJ, the risk of inaccuracy in establishing foreign law was consistent with the status of foreign law as fact: 'The trial is not an inquisition into the content of relevant foreign law any more than it is an inquisition into other factual issues that the parties tender for decision by the court'.[138]

But, even if the proof of foreign law is inevitably compromised, there may be minimal constraints on doing merely as the evidence dictates. Gleeson CJ suggests two. He was prepared to act on the available evidence of Chinese law because it was not 'inherently implausible' that Article 146 requires a consideration of what is 'just and reasonable in the circumstances' (as the respondent's expert had suggested).[139] Again, he was

[135] A Briggs, 'The Meaning and Proof of Foreign Law' [2006] *LMCLQ* 1.
[136] para 127. [137] para 1. [138] para 118. [139] para 17.

satisfied that the outcome would cause no offence in China: 'The Chinese authorities are totally unaffected by the outcome of the litigation, no Chinese interests are involved, are there appears to be no reason of policy for a Chinese court to resist the proposition'.[140] For Gleeson CJ, the proof of foreign law is not a search for truth about foreign law, but a question of evidence. Any finding on foreign law may be acceptable, provided that it has support (however slight) in the evidence, that it is plausible (or not 'inherently implausible'), and that the interests of the relevant foreign state are not implicated.

A strikingly different view informs the decision of Kirby J, who was concerned throughout that Chinese law should have been clearly and accurately determined, and who concluded not only that there was insufficient evidence of foreign law, but also that the presumption of identity was inapplicable. For Kirby J, absent evidence as to how the flexible exception in Article 146 would be applied, and given that the presumption was inapplicable, the contention that Australian law displaced Chinese law simply failed. The reason is articulated in a revealing passage:

> If, then the purpose of ascertaining, and applying, the law of the place of the wrong (*lex loci delicti*) is to ensure consistency of outcomes, to deny advantages of forum shopping and to fulfil ordinary human expectations, the only way this can be done, in a case such as the present, is according to evidence... there is a commensurate need for expert testimony to bridge the gulf that exists between the substantive law known to an Australian court and the law that would be observed in China, were proceedings brought there.[141]

This implies two distinct reasons for treating the proof of foreign law as more than a matter of evidence. First, to do so promotes the objectives of the choice of law process—consistency, uniformity, and the satisfaction of expectations. Indeed, Kirby J apparently considered that respect for these objectives was compulsory. He took the relevant Australian choice of law rule, whereby the *lex loci delicti* governs claims in tort, to be a mandatory rule.[142] Secondly, he assumed that applying foreign law means applying it as the foreign court would. It is desirable in principle for a court to replicate the behaviour of foreign courts when applying foreign law. Unsatisfactory evidence of foreign law could not be excused by adverting to the factual nature of foreign law, and holding the evidence to be sufficient. Nor could it be circumvented by relying upon the evidential fiction that foreign law is the same as local law.

This difference of opinion exposes clearly a tension which arises the moment we allow one country's courts to apply another country's laws.

[140] para 17. [141] para 199. [142] paras 215, 220.

To what extent should an English court aspire to apply foreign law as a foreign court would? To what extent is it acceptable that the treatment of foreign law is domesticated, trimmed to suit local policies and conditions? Is justice served merely if an English court approaches the evidence fairly and transparently, or only if foreign law is applied as a foreign court would apply it?

Commonsense and practicality demand that some compromise in the treatment of foreign law is inevitable. And the most any court can aspire to is authenticity in its approach to foreign law, not the simulation of foreign proceedings.[143] But recent developments—at least in English law—teach an important lesson. Compromise in the treatment of foreign law may be required on practical grounds. But that is no reason to tolerate the misapplication of foreign law where it can be avoided. There is certainly no reason to do so by forcing issues of foreign law into the category of evidence not law, and by adhering slavishly to the old shibboleth that foreign laws are facts not laws.

143 Fentiman, n 5 above, 292 ff.

The World Trade Organization after Ten Years: The Role of the WTO in a Globalized World

John Jackson

While the topic undertaken here seems to be vast, its goal is simple: to look at the World Trade Organization (WTO) at the end of its tenth year in existence, with particular focus on the jurisprudence resulting from the WTO Dispute Settlement System.[1] By most accounts, it has been quite an exceptional decade, and my examination may be fairly detailed and technical. This examination is, as academics love to say, a 'work in progress'. However, all of my work is a work in progress, as events move and change, and so one has to continuously cope with those changes.

The last decade and a half have been particularly challenging for international law generally, but also for international economic law more specifically. The period between the 'bookends' of the fall of the Berlin Wall in 1989, through the destruction of the twin towers in New York in 2001, has had profound significance. At the early part of that period there was almost a euphoria that came with the end of the Cold War along with the ensuing belief that there was going to be a peace dividend. Things indeed looked very solid for international law, with the first Gulf War going quite satisfactorily. But then things began to turn sour in various ways, including protests against the WTO, International Monetary Fund (IMF), and World Bank, and finally came the tragedy of 11 September 2001. It is interesting to reflect on the impact that these events have had on international law generally, and on international economic law, some of which I dealt with in the Lauterpacht Lecture series that I delivered at Cambridge two years ago, and which is now becoming part of a book that will be going to press shortly.[2] But here I am taking a somewhat different focus than that taken in those works in progress.

[1] Hereafter 'the DSS'.

[2] Hersch Lauterpacht Memorial Lectures, delivered at Cambridge University on 5–7 November 2002.

The primary focus here is to look through the lens of particular WTO DS cases, thus taking a 'bottom up' approach. But I will also fit that into the broader context of both international law and international economic law, to recognize some emerging patterns. It is not always obvious, but there are some interesting relationships emerging in the WTO jurisprudence, relationships which can have a considerable impact, not only on the specifics of international economic law, trade policy, and economic policy, but also on general international law itself. Some of the cases I will mention are extremely complex, some involve mathematical formulas, but I am aiming for an overall survey to lay the groundwork for the emerging patterns or relationships. The landscape behind these trends, which cannot be ignored, of course, is the impact of globalization. Globalization is a word that is both overused and misused, and thus I will define the elements of that concept that are most relevant for my purposes. Another background theme, in addition to the impact of globalization, is the role of a juridical institution at the international level in today's world. Thus, I will examine how the WTO jurisprudence shapes that role.

The rest of this comment will be divided into four parts. First will be a general look at the policy and legal landscape. This landscape is broad, but it is important to establish this context before getting into the detail. Secondly, I will take up the architecture of the World Trade Organization. Next, the biggest section will be a look at a series of WTO DS cases and a series of jurisprudential issues. I have chosen five jurisprudential issues, out of the dozens that could be taken up. Finally, after a look at the cases and these jurisprudential issues one by one, I will step back and reprise with some generalizations that can be drawn and end with some perceptions and conclusions about the future.

The Policy and Legal Landscape

As legal professionals, we have to look at the facts in the context of the real world—the so-called exogenous circumstances—and cannot examine these subjects in isolation. In other words, we have to look at the 'facts on the ground'. Globalization is the reality of that world. The literature on globalization is vast, including an excellent book by Martin Wolf,[3] but amidst all of the rhetoric, it is hard to know what the word 'globalization' really means. There are three elements that are extremely important for

[3] M Wolf, *Why Globalization Works* (New Haven: Yale University Press, 2004).

the purposes of this essay, and those three elements are communication, transport, and weapons. These three have changed dramatically in the last half century, although there are those who claim that globalization is not new to this world, that we had an even more globalized world at the turn of the previous century, at the beginning of the 1900s. At that time, there was perhaps, as some claim, freer movement of people, fewer governmental restraints on certain kinds of trade and transactions, and so forth. But the big difference arriving in the last three or four decades is the technological innovation that affects communication, transport, and weaponry.

The cost and time of communication have dramatically dropped, as we can see instant shifts of billions of dollars with a computer key. We can see instant talk and messaging of all kinds. We can see groups—non-governmental organizations, business groups, and other organizations—depending heavily on communication, and its relative inexpensiveness and speed. Furthermore, the methods of production are changing as a product moves from one country to another, coordinated by the communication revolution that has been brought about by technology.

The same dramatic change has occurred in terms of efficiency of transportation. A hundred years ago, transport was a natural barrier to certain kinds of globalization facets. For instance, people employed in one country had less to fear, at least in the short run, from foreign products that might invade their territory, or from foreign labor that might be competitive. But today, because of the decline in the cost of transport, of humans, products, and services, as well as the reduced time required, transport is no longer much of a barrier at all. There remain some barriers, of course, including various kinds of governmental interventions, which is the subject of an entirely separate set of warnings. Finally, the technology of weapons has changed dramatically in the last few decades. The technology for all kinds of weapons, not just weapons of mass destruction, has become extraordinarily refined, resulting in very precise weaponry. Delivery of these weapons is also cheaper now because of the cheaper transportation costs, and all of this is coordinated by the speed and reduced cost of communication.

Thus, those are the three main elements, or 'facts on the ground', of globalization that are changing the fundamentals of international economic law, and international law generally, elements that we must grapple with as we examine the specific context of the WTO. But first, it is worth examining how these elements shape the general international law landscape. In considering this landscape, I have written a variety of works over the past decade concerning the question of sovereignty.[4] In doing so, I have surveyed some of the vast literature that has been critical of the concept of sovereignty. There is an enormous disrespect for the concept of sovereignty, but at the same time, the concept of sovereignty is clung to by advocates, who are usually politicians. The concept is repeated almost like a mantra, without really looking at its implications, leading one very prominent author in the US, Professor Steven Krasner, at Stanford University, to title his book on sovereignty *Organized Hypocrisy*.[5]

So there is an enormous challenge to the concept of sovereignty, particularly as the concept is sometimes viewed in its traditional shape—sometimes called the Westphalian sense of sovereignty—which is an absolute idea of sovereignty, an idea which no one sensible believes still pertains in the world in which we are now operating. Thus, old concepts of sovereignty have proven inconsistent with reality, contrary to values that we trust, that is, we no longer believe that a potentate who is a sovereign in a particular nation-state has the right to do anything he wants to his citizens—chop off heads, violate virgins, etc. This shift in attitude about sovereignty has current relevance in the debate about what is sometimes called 'regime change' and also for the problem of 'rogue states'. But there may yet be something worth salvaging and examining more carefully within the concept of sovereignty. Although Professor Louis Henkin, perhaps the most renowned American professor of international law, has written that we should get rid of the ' "s" word', he also says that we need to disaggregate the sovereignty concept and to look at it in more precise detail.[6]

When we examine the concept more closely, we see that there are many elements of sovereignty. I write about 'sovereignty in slices', and one of those slices that it is valuable to look at is the idea of allocating power. After all, does not sovereignty really mean that some people think that a particular decision should be made at a certain level of governance, for example in Geneva, instead of in Washington, DC, or proceeding further

[4] See eg J H Jackson, 'Sovereignty Modern: A New Approach to an Outdated Concept' (2003) 97 *American Journal of International Law* 782; J H Jackson, 'Sovereignty, Subsidiarity, and Separation of Powers: The High-Wire Balancing Act of Globalization' in D L M Kennedy and J D Southwick (eds), *The Political Economy of International Trade Law: Essays in Honour of Robert E. Hudec*, (Cambridge: Cambridge University Press, 2002), 13; J H Jackson, 'The Great 1994 Sovereignty Debate: United States Acceptance and Implementation of the Uruguay Round Results' (1997) 36 *Columbia Journal of Transnational Law* 157.

[5] S D Krasner, *Sovereignty: Organized Hypocrisy* (Princeton: Princeton University Press, 1999).

[6] See L Henkin, *International Law: Politics and Values* (Dordrecht: Kluwer, 1995), discussed in Jackson, 'The Great 1994 Sovereignty Debate', n 4 above, 149.

down the list, in Sacramento, California or Berkeley, California, or even a neighborhood in Berkeley? Thus, the question becomes: how do you allocate power to make decisions that operate in the world today, given the challenges presented by globalization? Globalization's most controversial implications are that the sovereign nation-state can no longer regulate in a way that can deliver to its constituents without a coordinated effort in a broader world.

Further challenging the general underpinnings of sovereignty, we begin to recognize the implications for other concepts that are derivative of sovereignty, at least historically derivative. Two of these concepts are consent theory and the equality of nations. There may exist independent policy grounds for these concepts, but they are inextricably linked to sovereignty in current discussions, particularly to the mantra-like use of the word. Taking first the concept of consent in international law, the theory is that the nation-state must consent before it is bound by an international norm. If you remove traditional concepts of sovereignty as its basis, consent theory has to be re-evaluated in order to find the credibility, or the legitimacy, of international norms.

Secondly, the idea of equality of nations, that each nation is equal, is an idea that takes the form of a 'one nation, one vote' rule in many international organizations. Clearly, the international organizations and many of the key players in the world do not really believe in the validity of a one nation, one vote system. Therefore, various other devices—a veto power, a super-majority, a consensus rule, etc.—are employed to prevent that impact. Powerful players like China, India, the United States, and Europe, refuse to be out-voted by a series of 'mini-states'. Calculations indicate that when ranking the entire list of countries in the world that are called sovereign, from the most populous to least populous, you can move up from the least populous to a majority, and still only have 5 percent of the population represented. There is also the sovereignty slice of non-interference, particularly non-interference from the outside. Internal trade policy and economic actions by nation-states can have an impact well beyond their borders and that is an aspect of sovereignty that must be rethought.

The final part of the landscape worth mentioning, although it is pretty clear to most people in the world, is that the view of international law on either side of the Atlantic varies a bit. That can be understood partly from the experience of Europe compared to that of the United States. An illustration is the different answers to the following question that might be heard on either side of the 'pond': what is it that an individual who has a family and a lifestyle, and goals in life can depend upon to maintain the lifestyle she enjoys? In the United States, it is felt that the individual must rely on his or her nation-state. But in Europe, it is doubtful that an individual would always feel likewise reliant on the nation-state, particularly after the first half of the last century, given the double civil war problem, plus the nature of some oppressive governments.

The Architecture of the WTO and its Dispute Settlement System

It is with the facts on the ground outlined above that we begin to lay the framework of the WTO jurisprudence, but not without first examining the origin and structure of the organization. The WTO is probably not the most important institution that has come on the international scene since 1950—that title now probably goes to the European Union, because of its power to promote peace and prosperity in Europe and consequently, to contribute similarly to the world—but the WTO is potentially the second most important. A rash of innovation followed the end of World War II, with the Bretton Woods system, and the United Nations topping the list. But after that, we limped along without an international trade organization. The General Agreement on Tariffs and Trade (GATT) was serving as a rather poor substitute, and was obviously subject to what I call 'birth defects', because of the way it came about.[7] But 1995 brought into being the third 'leg' contemplated by the Bretton Woods conference—the component for trade in the name of the WTO.

The two original goals embodied in the failed attempt at an International Trade Organization (the so-called 'Havana Charter of 1948'[8]) were also goals of the GATT. Those goals are: to keep the peace and increase world welfare. Today we do not often think of peace as a goal of trade and international economics institutions and policies, but the speeches and the dialogue of the 1940s emphasized the importance of international institutions in the economic area in order to keep the peace and avoid another world conflagration. The second goal was to increase world welfare, or to make the whole world richer, although the question of distribution was

[7] See J H Jackson, 'The Role and Effectiveness of the WTO Dispute Settlement Mechanism' in *Brookings Trade Forum 2000* (Washington: Brookings Institution Press, 2001), 179; and J H Jackson, *The World Trading System* (2nd edn) (Cambridge, Mass: Massachusetts Institute of Technology Press, 1997), 31.

[8] Havana Charter for an International Trade Organization 1948 (never in force); Final Act and Related Documents, United Nations Conference on Trade and Employment, Havana, Cuba (21 November 1947–24 March 1948) UN Doc ICITO/1/4 (1948).

not much addressed. That is a key and important question: how is that increasing wealth in the world distributed? The idea is that using the appropriate economic principles of trade would make the world richer and would allow families everywhere to have better and more satisfying lives.

We have added, over the decades, two more goals to this list. One is the reduction of world poverty, which has become a basic goal of the WTO—the new Doha Trade Negotiating Round is sometimes called the 'development round'.[9] The final goal is risk management—management of the new risks that have been spawned by globalization. The speed of communication, the speed and cost of transport, and weaponry make nation-states increasingly interdependent, which sometimes prevents governments acting alone from being able to achieve what is really necessary for the benefit of their domestic institutions in response to these newly created dangers.

Underlying the world trading system and its goals is the concept of the market. The last fifteen years have witnessed a swing away from socialist planning concepts and favoring the idea of the market. There is broader recognition of the value of markets in increasing world welfare and improving the lives of the constituents. But several Nobel Prize winning economists—Joseph Stiglitz (2001), Douglass North (1993), and Ronald Coase (1991)—have emphasized that the market will not work unless there is an institutional framework supporting it.[10] I agree with this widely held view and disagree with the so-called 'pure marketeers'—for example, on the right wing of American politics—who believe that a market can function without government intervention. Furthermore, an institutional structure implies there are rules that must be complied with, and that implies, in turn, a dispute settlement system of some kind. A rule-oriented dispute settlement system brings a modicum of predictability and stability essential to proper market function. Those two words—predictability and stability—incidentally, are used in the WTO Dispute Settlement Understanding (DSU) treaty text, because it is recognized that entrepreneurs are often willing to accept a lower rate of return on

[9] The so-called 'Doha Development Round' of trade negotiations, launched in late 2001, and in the aftermath of the 11 September 2001 terrorist attacks, aimed at leveling the global playing field, by eg reducing unfair advantages enjoyed by farmers in rich nations. See eg G de Jonquieres, 'Fresh Road Map to Help Find the Exit Trade' *The Financial Times* (London, 1 October 2004), 4.

[10] See R H Coase, *The Firm, the Market and the Law* (Chicago: University of Chicago Press, 1988), ch 5; D C North, *Institutions, Institutional Change and Economic Performance* (Cambridge: Cambridge University Press, 1990); J E Stiglitz, *Globalization and its Discontents* (New York: W W Norton & Company, 2002), 219.

their investments in exchange for a lowered risk. A lowered risk premium means greater efficiency. But there are opposing views of the market organization and structure, or at least opposing policies that value goals other than reducing the risk premium, including the environment, human rights, reduction of poverty abroad, etc. Thus, inevitably, some balancing of these different goals is necessary. At the nation-state level, this balancing occurs constantly. Those in the legal profession recognize this need for balancing, which, especially in Europe, is often called 'proportionality'.

Thus, we have seen the WTO develop as an organization, with the backdrop of the goals mentioned above, particularly through the last trade round of the GATT, 1986–94. An indication of its success in achieving some of those goals is that there are already 148 members. The most important member accession recently was China in 2001, and Russia is currently negotiating for entry, as are several dozen other countries.[11] Therefore, it is obvious that governments see the advantages to be gained from this institution, although there clearly are some problems associated with it. But when looking explicitly at the dispute settlement system, there is broad agreement—including the WTO Consultative Board, in which I participated recently for the WTO, and which issued a report in January 2005[12]—that the WTO DSS is probably the most powerful and most significant international tribunal system today. With compulsory jurisdiction, and an automatic obligation to perform or comply with the result of the system, this is indeed a powerful institution. Further, the scope of the DSS is vast: every dispute involving the WTO covered agreements is supposed to be brought, in accordance with international law treaty obligation, to this system.

Besides the goals of predictability and stability mentioned above, the DSS also aims for prompt and satisfactory settlement. A tension among its goals is quickly apparent and requires a process of balancing because prompt settlement does not always mean quality with respect to predictability and stability. The story is further complicated by the fact that there exist at least twelve different goals for international dispute

[11] See list of members and observer countries (including those that have begun the accession process): <http://www.wto.org/english/thewto_e/whatis_e/tif_e/org6_e.htm>.

[12] P Sutherland, 'The Future of the WTO: Addressing Institutional Challenges in the New Millennium', Report by the Consultative Board to the Director-General Supachai Panitchpakdi (Geneva: WTO, 2005): <http://www.wto.org/english/thewto_e/10anniv_e/10anniv_e.htm#future>. The Consultative Board is comprised of: Mr Peter Sutherland (Chairman of the Consultative Board), Professor Jagdish Bhagwati, Dr Kwesi Botchwey, Mr Niall W A Fitzgerald, Professor Koichi Hamada, Professor John Jackson, Professor Celso Lafer, and Professor Thierry de Montbrial.

settlement systems and the very idea of what goals such a system should promote is very complex.

The architecture of the DS system is worth examining before getting further into the details of the cases. There are ad hoc panels, usually three persons, at the first level, which was also the practice under the GATT. The First Level Panel Report is automatically adopted under a procedure called 'reverse consensus'. But unique and new under the WTO is the appeals process. There is an Appellate Body (AB) of seven persons who sit in divisions of three at a time, designed and selected so that no potential appellant will know which three AB members will hear their appeal. It is a secret process, partly random, and partly according to a distribution of the workload, with a very quick turnaround time. The DSS statistics thus far are impressive. In the ten years, up until October 2006, 350 complaints have been filed. Fewer than half of the complaints actually go on to a panel, so in other words, there is a lot of settlement going on, which can be viewed as a strength of the system. There have been 120 adopted First Level Panel Reports and 78 adopted Appellate Body Reports. The number of panel reports appealed has been declining, as a percentage of cases, and is currently at about 65 percent. Of the 'big' players, the US and EU are involved in nearly half of the cases, as complainant or respondent. But we are also finding that the developing countries are major participants in this process, and that they are involved in almost 80 percent of the cases, either as complainants or respondents, and they are very assertive complainants—133 complaints, which is about 38 percent of the total.[13]

Jurisprudential Issues

Hopefully having adequately laid the groundwork and context for our subject, I turn now to the complex jurisprudential issues that arise in the WTO DSS. I will briefly take up five issues. Unfortunately, we can only explore the 'tip of the iceberg' of each issue, as some are so complex that entire books have been written about them. The five I have chosen, out of the many that could be selected, are as follows: first, the international law relationship to the WTO system, or the international law context; secondly, the concept of deference, sometimes called standard of review; thirdly, the reference to, or use of, precedent; fourthly, I will take up the

[13] See Update of WTO Dispute Settlement Cases (11 October 2006) WTO Doc WT/DS/OV/24. More recent statistics are available at <www.worldtradelaw.net> see also K Leitner and S Lester, 'WTO Dispute Settlement 1995–2004: A Statistical Analysis' (2005) 8 *Journal of International Economic Law* 231.

different techniques of interpretation; and finally, the fifth issue is compliance. All of the cases discussed below are Appellate Body cases, with the exception of the US—301 case.[14] The prevalent attitude about that jurisprudence, which now is over 25,000 pages, is that it is quite extraordinary. It is very detailed, complex, and many would argue it is very high quality, even when compared with national legal systems, as well as other international systems. This good reputation and high quality does not mean that mistakes have not been made.

International Law Context

First, I will look at the international law context of the jurisprudence. The very first case in the DSS, serendipitously, but interestingly, was brought against the United States by Venezuela and Brazil, in which it was argued that US regulations on the importation of gasoline were discriminatory when compared with regulation of its own gasoline.[15] The regulation in question was an environmental regulation, designed to improve the environment through the chemical composition of gasoline. The case held against the US, the US appealed, and the appeal held against the US. But on appeal, the US was granted a point it wanted, which was a different form of the logic, and thus a different ruling, and so the US claimed victory. But the other side also claimed victory—the US was required to change its regulation, and it did so—making it, essentially, the perfect diplomatic outcome. A critical point in this case was that the Appellate Body began by saying that the WTO is clearly part of international law, and not a separate, independent regime, as some political scientists had said a decade or two earlier of the GATT. Although by the later years of GATT, it was clear that it was not an independent regime: this WTO ruling clinched that issue. The Appellate Body, deciding that the WTO is not an independent legal regime, but is part and parcel of international law, logically turned to customary international law of interpreting treaties, a phrase that is actually mentioned in the Dispute Settlement Understanding.[16] It was agreed that even though the Vienna Convention

[14] US Trade Act of 1974, ss 301–10 (adopted 27 January 2000) WTO Doc WT/DS152/R.

[15] US—Standards for Reformulated and Conventional Gasoline WTO Doc WT/DS2/AB/R.

[16] Understanding on Rules and Procedures Governing the Settlement of Disputes, Art 3.2; Marrakesh Agreement Establishing the World Trade Organization, Annex 2 (15 April 1994) in WTO, *The Legal Texts: The Results of the Uruguay Round of Multilateral Trade Negotiations* (Cambridge: Cambridge University Press, 1999), 354. Hereafter 'the DSU'.

on the Law of Treaties[17] is not specifically named in the treaty text, the VCLT best answers this question of how to interpret treaties under customary international law. The Appellate Body went so far as extensively quoting Articles 31 and 32 of the VCLT, on treaty interpretation. The Appellate Body's view of the VCLT is challengeable, and this author has some hesitations as to whether that treaty is actually the best guide for treaty interpretation, particularly in the context of the WTO DSS, but the *US—Gasoline* case was clearly a pivotal point for situating the DSS in customary international law.

Another case, very soon after *US—Gasoline*, was *Japan—Alcoholic Beverages*,[18] another discrimination case. In the case brought by the US and EU, Japan was alleged to be discriminating against imported alcoholic beverages. In reality, at base this was a case of imported vodka versus domestic shochu, shochu being a Japanese clear liquid alcohol beverage. The holding was that Japan was discriminating, and that these two products were 'like products'. Thus, the phrase being interpreted was 'like products'. That simple little phrase is enormously complex. A doctoral graduate of Georgetown University Law Center, a Mr Won Mog Choi, of Korea, has written an entire book on how to interpret 'like products'.[19] He describes dozens of ways to interpret the phrase, based on different kinds of assumptions, some economic assumptions, others assumptions dependant on your particular bias—whether it be a tilt toward the producer or one toward the consumer—giving rise to the question of who are the actual intended beneficiaries of this system that is part of international law. Are they the sovereign nation members of the WTO? They clearly are some of the intended beneficiaries, but they are not the only ones.

This line of questioning leads us to the *US—301* case, brought by the EU and eight other countries, to challenge the US on its so-called Section 301 statute, allowing it to take retaliatory measures against other countries in some circumstances. The First Level Panel ruled that the US statute was inconsistent with the requirements of the WTO. In other words, even if there had been no measure taken under it, because the statute allowed a measure which, if taken, could have constituted a violation, the statute itself is in violation of WTO law. The Panel went on to say that the US had assured panel members, and had given them written

[17] Hereafter 'the VCLT'.

[18] Japan—Customs Duties, Taxes and Labeling Practices on Imported Wines and Alcoholic Beverages (adopted 10 November 1987) GATT L/6216, 34S/83.

[19] W-M Choi, *'Like Products' in International Trade Law: Towards a Consistent GATT/WTO Jurisprudence* (Oxford: Oxford University Press, 2003).

representations to the effect that the US executive branch has the authority to interpret the 301 Statute, and will never interpret it to violate the WTO rule. The Panel declared that because the US's interpretation, as represented to the Panel, in effect trumps what the statute actually says, the US is not inconsistent with its WTO obligations. But the US was warned that it would be 'watched' on this matter. The 301 case has sometimes been called a 'diplomatic masterpiece and a jurisprudential disaster'. Regardless of which way you choose to view the outcome of the case, the point here is that the market participants are also beneficiaries of the WTO DSS, not just governments. The language of the Section 301 case stresses that when decisions are made, account must be taken of a whole group of people who are not at the table, who are, in a sense, third party beneficiaries.

There are some other international law concerns imbedded in this broader analysis that are worth mentioning. One of these is the concept of good faith. Good faith is problematic because it is such an open and general international law concept that there is a fair amount of fear about using and relying on it. The fear is that, without a strict guideline on its meaning, judges can 'pour into that bottle' a lot of personal predilections. Another problem is the very elaborate remedy system set up in the DSU, involving what some people loosely call 'retaliation'. The more precise word is 'compensation', although this does not imply a 'check in the mail' concept, but rather, compensatory measures. There are people who, unhappy with the concept of compensation under the DSU, argue for a shift to customary international law, and the use of some of the principles of remedies thereunder. But that kind of shift is technically wrong under law, because one could argue *lex specialis*, for instance, or that the treaty trumps customary international law, as long as it is not a matter of *jus cogens*.

Deference and Standard of Review

The second jurisprudential issue I will take up is deference, or standard of review. A crucial question throughout the operation of an international organization is the amount of deference that should be given to the nation-state sovereign. The *EC—Hormones* case,[20] brought by the US and Canada, against the EC, was one of the first WTO cases to dig into the standard of review issue. But the outcome of the case did not provide

[20] EC Measures Concerning Meat and Meat Products (Hormones) (adopted 13 February 1998) WTO Docs WT/DS26 & 48/AB/R.

very much guidance going forward. It held that the EU had not done an adequate risk assessment—had not adequately assessed the risks of the use of artificial hormones for the production of beef—and therefore, was not consistent with the Sanitary and Phyto-Sanitary Texts[21] of the WTO. The hormones in question make it less costly to produce beef. The US tended to use hormones in beef production, while Europe had not and had taken the step of banning all hormones. The First Level Panel and Appellate Body grappled with the standard of review question, of how much deference should be given to the nation-state, because, of course, there is a certain amount of ambiguity in the treaty language. This kind of ambiguity is unavoidable, incidentally, as it is nearly impossible to negotiate with a hundred nations a treaty text without leaving some gaps and ambiguity. The Appellate Body said that complete deference is not owed, but neither is the standard *de novo*. There is a lot of grey area between complete deference and *de novo* review, and it remains unsettled as to where on the spectrum analysis should begin.

Precedent

The third issue is how much precedent should weigh in the WTO DS system. Some have argued that the system approaches one of *stare decisis*, similar to the very strong precedent system known in 'common law' countries. It is quite clear that the WTO DSS does not operate by *stare decisis*, but instead by the principle that there is no binding force as a result of an opinion, except between the parties to that litigation in that particular case. This is the more common international law approach found, for instance, in the World Court statute.

Although there is some ambiguity, the DSU itself, with its explicit goals of stability and predictability, suggests that some continuity is required. In addition, the WTO Charter[22] contains a clause stating that GATT decisions should serve as guidance to WTO decisions, but are not to be automatically implemented as a matter of treaty law. The word 'guidance' is very important in that context. Likewise, in the WTO Charter, there is a measure, Article IX, that allows the members, by a three-quarters majority of the entire membership, to make a definitive interpretation and that that interpretation would be binding. But because it rarely happens that three-quarters of the WTO membership is together

[21] Agreement on Sanitary and Phytosanitary Measures in WTO, *The Legal Texts*, n 16 above, 59.

[22] 'Charter' is an informal term. See Marrakesh Agreement, n 16 above.

in a room, and even rarer that they could get their respective governments to agree on such a thing, a binding interpretation is not likely.

Another way to tackle this question of precedent is to examine the VCLT language of 'subsequent practice in the application of the treaty'.[23] It could be argued that these WTO decisions are practice under the WTO agreement. But in the *Japan—Alcoholic Beverages* case, the Appellate Body said that one case does not constitute *practice*—that there must be something more than one case, although they did not elaborate on what that 'something more' must be.[24]

Also instructive in this context is the *US—Steel Safeguards* case.[25] This case involved an escape clause safeguards question about the steel industry and was enormously complex. Approximately 80 law firms were involved in this case brought by the EC, Brazil, China, Japan, and five more countries, and it hit on a lot of 'hot button issues'. The First Level Panel Report was almost 1,000 pages long because there were thirteen different practices that had to be evaluated against five different standards. Almost all of the 5,800 footnotes were references to prior cases of the WTO Appellate Body. Thus, it is simply not credible to argue that there is no precedent effect in the WTO DSS. The critical question actually becomes: how much precedent is there? The Appellate Body ruled against the US in the *Steel Safeguards* case, and the President of the United States withdrew the measures, but said that the withdrawal had nothing to do with the WTO decision, and was done solely for US domestic constituents. David Sanger, of the New York Times, however, wrote this case was the *Marbury v Madison* of the WTO.[26] Those who know something about US Constitutional law know that *Marbury* is the fundamental case establishing the power of the judiciary over the other branches of government through 'judicial review'.

One could imagine a ladder of precedent effects, with *stare decisis* at the top. There are a lot of weaker precedent effects, further down the ladder, with some that are so far down the list that, in some administrative decision-making, such as is prevalent in some regulatory agencies in the US

[23] The Vienna Convention on the Law of Treaties, Art 31.3(b) (opened for signature 23 May 1969, entered into force 27 January 1970) 1155 UNTS 331, reprinted in (1969) 8 *International Legal Materials* 679.

[24] Japan—Taxes on Alcoholic Beverages (adopted 1 November 1996) WTO Doc WT/DS8, 10 & 11/AB/R, 7, 13–16.

[25] US—Definitive Safeguard Measures on Imports of Certain Steel Products (adopted 10 December 2003) WTO Docs WT/DS248/R and WT/DS248/AB/R.

[26] D E Sanger, 'A Blink From the Bush Administration' *The New York Times* (New York, 5 December 2003), 28.

government, there exists no sense of precedent whatsoever. But in my view the WTO is not very far below the *stare decisis* top rung of the precedent ladder.

Interpretation

Although interpretation is related to the precedent issue, it is a vast topic, and thus, I will address it as the fourth jurisprudential issue. There are literally dozens of different kinds of interpretive techniques. The VCLT goes through a series of about ten or twelve techniques in Articles 31 and 32, but there are a myriad of other possible techniques not mentioned therein. This raises the question of whether the VCLT is really appropriate in the WTO context.

The Appellate Body began with a very strong textual bias, a very stark textualism, relying on the dictionary. But a problem exists because textualism itself is not a 'settled science'. There are several dictionaries, and when the same word is looked up in three different dictionaries, you will sometimes find three different definitions. One could question what textualism is, after all. Nevertheless, the DSS strives very hard to follow the text, which has led to some decisions that have surprised the negotiators of the WTO treaty text. The negotiators have claimed that the interpretation handed down was not the result they had intended. The answer the negotiators invariably receive is 'but that's what the treaty language says'. Thus, the question is raised whether more attention should be given to the negotiators' intent. The VCLT seems to downplay the importance of preparatory work, and there are good reasons to downplay such work—for instance, the lack of a satisfactory record.

In the *Japan—Alcoholic Beverages* case, the Appellate Body said they were going to follow the VCLT, and implied that they were not looking at preparatory work. But then they came to a point in the opinion where they said, 'we have to look at the text, but it also is in the context, and in the light of object and purpose'.[27] A footnote to 'object and purpose' cites a preparatory work document.[28] The further question raised was, can not preparatory work be brought in under the VCLT, through its 'object and purpose' language? That question has been debated at length, and is not yet settled.

Another issue that comes with textualism is what happens when you have a measure that just does not quite fit the text. One of those ill-fitting

27 Japan—Taxes on Alcoholic Beverages, n 24 above, 12.

28 ibid, n 39.

measures is now a very lively issue in the United States, under the so-called *Byrd Amendment* case.[29] This is a set of facts that is truly scandalous, involving a very complex anti-dumping situation, whereby, if an American company or industry brings a case through the United States administrative processes, and is able to demonstrate a practice of dumping by a foreign entity, that entity is selling goods into the US market at less than their normal value, or at a lower price than is charged in its home country, and then an anti-dumping duty equivalent to that difference in price—the margin of dumping—is applied. But the duty is paid into the US Treasury and held to be paid out to the complainants. That practice constitutes a 'double dip'. The complainant, the American industry, reaps the benefit of the monopoly rent by raising their prices as the competition has had to raise their prices because of the added duty, and in addition, is paid the subsidy from the amount that has been collected on the anti-dumping duty. Because of this subsidy, parties are actually induced to bring complaints. The background 'static' on this policy is that the complaints process often manipulates the numbers to the benefit of American complainants.

There is a provision in the anti-dumping text that, it can be argued, fairly strongly prohibits this practice. The text uses the very curious wording: 'no specific action against dumping shall be done, except in accordance with the rules'. Proceeding to analyze the text, the first question is whether there is a 'specific action'. The First Level Panel and Appellate Body struggled with that, but determined that indeed this was a specific action, because it was related to the dumping practice, and only occurred in dumping cases with certain criteria. Next, the First Level Panel and Appellate Body played for pages with the meaning of the single word 'against'. After this textual analysis, they finally held the *Byrd Amendment* to be inconsistent with the US's WTO obligations. There are critics who admit that although the US policy was terrible, the language of the text simply does not support what the dispute settlement system did. I am not one of those critics.

Finally, I want to mention one very important case, and that is the *Shrimp-Turtle* case.[30] The *Shrimp-Turtle* case brings to bear a lot of interesting concepts, and I assert that even given the many new cases that are quite interesting, the *Shrimp-Turtle* case is the single most significant and

[29] US—Continued Dumping and Subsidy Offset Act of 2000 (adopted 16 January 2003) WTO Docs WT/DS217 & 234/AB/R.

[30] US—Import Prohibition of Certain Shrimp and Shrimp Products (adopted 6 November 1998) WTO Doc WT/DS58/AB/R.

important case of the jurisprudence of the WTO. More specifically, I also assert that paragraph 121 of that case is the single most important paragraph of that case, and I go even further to say that the word may, in that paragraph, is the most important word. The Appellate Body says that it may be the case that unilateral measures are inherently those that must be permitted under the exceptions of Article XX of the GATT. Article XX has a series of exceptions, including moral reasons, which has not been used except recently, in a services case, and conservation of natural exhaustible resources, which was the basis of the *US—Gasoline* case, and is the basis of the *Shrimp-Turtle* case. The *Shrimp-Turtle* case involved a United States law that prohibited the importation of shrimp that had been gathered in a process that killed an endangered species of turtle. The United States domestic environmentalists pushed for this law and got it through. The problem was that it did not accord with the normal rules of trade, and so prima facie that law was a violation by the US of its WTO obligations, and was so held by the Appellate Body. But there is an exception in Article XX for the conservation of natural resources, and the US claimed that exception applied in this case. The Appellate Body agreed, and since an exception was cited, there was a next series of criteria to be fulfilled, against discriminatory measures and unjustifiable measures, in the so-called 'Chapeau', or Preface to Article XX.

In evaluating whether those chapeau criteria were fulfilled, the Appellate Body looked to a variety of different sources, including documents and practices outside the trade discipline. The Appellate Body said, with respect to evaluating the words 'natural resources', that their interpretation had to be evolutionary, because they believed that the phrase could now apply to living species, not just to water, minerals, and the like. They went on to say that they were looking at such things as the 'Convention on International Trade in Endangered Species' and other environmental measures, and at the Preamble of the WTO, which is certainly appropriate, and which calls for a sustainable development policy. In looking at these various sources, the Appellate Body said that they were interpreting the Preamble or Chapeau to Article XX, which has the language about arbitrary or unjustifiable discrimination, and were bringing to bear this language from outside sources. This constituted the first instance of jurisprudence in all of GATT and WTO history thus far which had dealt with policies other than trade policies. The First Level Panel had looked only within the trade discipline, and the Appellate Body said that was wrong, instead calling for a balancing of different policies. That decision created a firestorm of criticism. Critics claimed that it is not up to an international organization to do this balancing, but that the sovereign nation must do it. I do not believe that conception is sustainable in light of the globalization landscape described above.

Compliance

Compliance with WTO decisions has generally been quite good. The remedies are outlined in the DSU, and discussed above. Some observers question whether remedies such as compensatory measures, if freely chosen, do away with the obligation to perform by the losing party in the long run. In my view there persists an international law obligation to perform the result of a case in which a country is held not to be consistent with its obligations under the WTO, even though, for an interim period, it may be willing to tolerate retaliatory measures or compensatory measures.[31]

There are many domestic law implications of this system because at least in some systems such as that in the US, and maybe still in the UK (although it may depend on what the EU legal system is going to do), the result of a case in the dispute settlement system is not *ipso facto* part of the domestic law. There is a lag time, so to speak, between the decision, and the creation of the required act of transformation of the decision into domestic law. There is the potential difficulty involved in getting compliance from a nation-state like the US, because, in the US, it is often up to the Congress.

Furthermore, some cynical countries, including the US, have decided to often go ahead with whatever action they intended, and 'take their lumps' in the dispute settlement process. This attitude is largely due to the fact that it takes three years to get through the dispute settlement process, and countries have a three year 'free pass'. If the results of a three year free pass are higher duties during that period of time, and there are monopoly rents, it adds up to millions, if not billions, of dollars.[32] There is no provision for retrospective remedies, or even provisional remedies. This creates a compliance incentive problem. In addition, asking the winning country to impose so-called 'retaliatory measures' means asking it to shoot itself in the foot, because the measures pose an economic harm to the imposing country, and often affect third parties that have nothing to do with the case and who are usually innocent bystanders.

[31] See J H Jackson, 'Editorial Comment: International Law Status of WTO DS Reports: Obligation to Comply or Option to "Buy-Out"?' (2004) 98 *American Journal of International Law* 109.

[32] eg in the steel industry, it would amount to billions of dollars.

Conclusions

To reprise, first of all, it is clear that the international juridical system has increasing importance. The loose term 'juridical', incidentally, is much preferred by the WTO system, which is loathe to use words like 'court', 'tribunal', and even 'arbitration panel'. It could be argued that that shift toward juridical systems is happening all over the world in many different types of international institutions.

There is general approval of the WTO dispute settlement system, coming from many sources, including ambassador reactions to the WTO Consultative Board Report,[33] and also evident from the high frequency of use. This approval is a testament to the quality of the jurisprudence and appreciation of the depth of analysis carried out. But there also remains a constant tension concerning the 'slice of sovereignty' dealing with the allocation of power. Here, the devil really is in the detail of how the nation-state is going to be compared to the international institution. That tension has presented many difficulties, and will continue to do so, and that is part of the landscape going forward.

Another aspect to keep in mind going forward is the disaggregation of treaties. It is important to regard different treaties individually, particularly in terms of interpretation. Some treaties, particularly those that are broad and multilateral, are designed to establish an institution with certain goals, hopes, and objectives over a long period of time, and ought to be appreciated as such. Treating them as constitutions, however, is quite controversial in the international context. I have been rebuked for using the word 'constitution' in various works on this general subject matter.[34] But it is an apt word, in some cases. If it is deemed to be apt, then we ought to be thinking more broadly of what are some of the interpretive methodologies needed for an organization to be sustainably relevant to its subject matter, given the fact of treaty rigidity. Quite often, a treaty, especially large membership treaties, cannot effectively be amended. Some kind of flexibility is essential. That flexibility of interpretation again evokes

[33] P Sutherland, 'The Future of the WTO: Addressing Institutional Challenges in the New Millennium', Report by the Consultative Board to the Director-General Supachai Panitchpakdi (WTO, 2005). See also W J Davey, 'Introduction to Mini-Symposium on the Consultative Board's Report on the Future of the WTO' (2005) 8 *Journal of International Economic Law* 287.

[34] See eg *The World Trade Organization: Constitution and Jurisprudence* (London: Chatham House Papers, 1998); J H Jackson, 'The WTO "Constitution" and Proposed Reforms: Seven "Mantras" Revisited' (2001) 4 *Journal of International Economic Law* 67.

the question of the effective allocation of power, and that allocation of power involves attention to this kind of detail, and needs a juridical institution to hammer out the detail. And yet, we must also keep in mind that the detail of a juridical institution can undermine completely or dangerously the ability of an international institution to perform assigned tasks and achieve goals. An interesting balancing act continues to play out and will be the subject of scholarly attention for years to come.

Better Regulation in Europe

*Jonathan B Wiener**

Introduction

'Better Regulation' is sweeping Europe. Based on a White Paper on Governance[1] and an expert group report,[2] both issued in 2001, the European Commission under President Prodi adopted a suite of regulatory reform measures in 2002, including guidelines on impact assessment.[3] Following a Communication from the new Barroso Commission in March 2005,[4] these guidelines were revised in 2005[5] and updated again in 2006.[6] Impact Assessment (IA) is now required for all regulatory proposals on the Commission's Work Programme. In addition, the Commission is pressing for simplification of existing laws (through

* Perkins Professor of Law, and Professor of Enviromental Policy and Public Policy, Duke University; University Fellow, Resources for the Future (RFF); Visiting Professor, Paris, 2005–6. For support of this research, the author thanks the Eugene T. Bost, Jr Research Professorship of the Charles A. Cannon Charitable Trust No 3 at Duke University. For helpful comments and discussion, the author thanks Joanne Caddy, Luigi Carbone, Cary Coglianese, Heidi Dawidoff, Marie-Anne Frison-Roche, John Graham, Olivier Godard, Robert Hahn, James Hammitt, Jane Holder, Stephane Jacobzone, Josef Konvitz, Gert-Jan Koopmans, Andreas Kraemer, Ragnar Lofstedt, Giandomenico Majone, Richard Macrory, Nikolai Malyshev, Patrick Messerlin, Lars Mitek Pederson, Charles-Henri Montin, Shainila Pradhan, Ray Purdy, Cornelia Quennet-Thielen, Manuel Santiago, Robert Scharrenbourg, Michel Setbon, Bernard Sinclair-Désgagné, Richard Stewart, Cass Sunstein, Tim Swanson, Nicolas Treich, Matti Vainio, and participants in meetings held at University College London, the OECD, the US-EU High-Level Regulatory Cooperation Forum, and the French Ministry of Finance Economy & Industry.

[1] European Commission, 'European Governance: A White Paper', COM(2001) 428.

[2] Mandelkern Group on Better Regulation, Final Report, November 2001.

[3] European Commission, Communication from the Commission on Impact Assessment, COM(2002) 276, 5 June 2002 (hereafter 'IA Guidelines 2002').

[4] European Commission, Communication from the Commission to the Council and the European Parliament, 'Better Regulation for Growth and Jobs in the European Union', COM(2005) 97, SEC(2005) 175, 16 March 2005.

[5] European Commission, Impact Assessment Guidelines, SEC(2005) 791, 15 June 2005 (hereafter 'IA Guidelines 2005').

[6] European Commission, Impact Assessment Guidelines, SEC(2005) 791, 15 June 2005, with 15 March 2006 update (hereafter 'IA Guidelines 2006').

consolidation, codification, and repeal), reduction of administrative costs ('cutting red tape'), and consultation with those affected by regulatory policies.

The member states of the European Union (EU) are likewise adopting programs of Better Regulation, some predating and spurring the Commission's efforts, and others in turn spurred by the Commission.[7] In 2004, a coalition of four of the rotating six-month Presidencies of the European Union (Ireland, Netherlands, Luxembourg, and Britain) issued a joint statement of their intention to pursue Better Regulation efforts during their upcoming Presidencies; this letter played an important role in spurring the European Commission to update and strengthen its IA Guidelines.[8] To note one prominent example of action by a member state, the UK has launched a Better Regulation Executive[9] and an external advisory Better Regulation Commission. In May 2005, UK Prime Minister Tony Blair delivered a speech on 'Risk and the State', emphasizing that risk regulation is absolutely necessary, but criticizing overregulation of small risks in the futile effort to reduce risks to zero (often as an overreaction to a recent crisis), thus impeding innovation and inducing perverse effects that 'do more damage than was done by the problem itself'. As a remedy, he advocated the program of 'Better Regulation' based on a 'rigorous risk-based approach' that will employ impact assessments and 'regulate only after reflection'.[10]

Will Better Regulation make a difference? Will it make things better? This study begins by examining the Better Regulation initiative as an exercise of legal borrowing, and by framing the question whether Better Regulation will really yield better results. After several transatlantic conflicts over regulatory topics such as the precautionary principle, genetically modified foods, and climate change, Europe and America now appear to be converging on the analytic basis for regulation. In a process of hybridization, European institutions are borrowing 'Better Regulation' reforms from both the US approach to regulatory review using benefit-cost analysis and from European member states' initiatives on administrative

[7] The Communication of 16 March 2005, COM(2005) 97, above, included a colourful chart of relative progress on Better Regulation among the member states. Highest marks went to Denmark, the UK, and Poland; lowest marks went to France, Portugal, and Cyprus. See below in the section on European Experience at n 88.

[8] See Joint Initiative on Regulatory Reform, a Letter from the EU Presidencies of Ireland, Netherlands, Luxembourg, and the UK, 26 January 2004, at <http://www.finance.gov.ie/documents/pressreleases/2004/janmcc12462. pdf>.

[9] See <http://www.betterregulation.gov.uk/> and < http://www.cabinetoffice.gov.uk/regulation/>.

[10] Prime Minister Tony Blair, 'Speech on Risk and the State', 26 May 2005, available at < http://www.number-10.gov.uk/output/Page7562.asp>.

costs and simplification; in turn the European Commission is helping to spread these reforms among the member states.

In the following sections, this study addresses in more detail the main components of Better Regulation—impact assessments and administrative simplification—and advocates the adoption of several institutional improvements. (Other aspects of regulatory reform in Europe, such as transparency, consultation, and subsidiarity, are mentioned here but are not the focus.) In many respects, the Better Regulation initiative promises salutary reforms, such as wider use of regulatory impact assessments and a reduction in unnecessary bureaucracy. In other respects, the European initiative speaks more of Procrustean deregulation than of better regulation. Meanwhile the European Commission still needs to establish the institutional infrastructure needed to succeed. I argue that the European program of Better Regulation is well-founded but could be even better if it adopted several strategies: enlarging the scope of impact assessment and benefit-cost analysis toward a broader, 'warmer', and more evenhanded application of these tools, with greater attention to multiple risks; moving beyond a narrow focus on cutting administrative costs or simplification for their own sake, toward criteria that address benefits as well as costs; centralizing expert oversight so that impact assessments actually influence decisions, both to say 'no' to bad ideas and 'yes' to good ideas; and undertaking *ex post* evaluation of policies for adaptive policy revision and for improvement of *ex ante* assessment methods. These reforms would help Better Regulation achieve its true objective: better, not just less or more. In turn, the US could study these European innovations and borrow from them where they prove successful.

Legal Borrowing

The Better Regulation initiative is a conscious exercise of legal borrowing. This borrowing has been both horizontal and vertical. Horizontal legal borrowing occurs when one co-equal legal system borrows from another, such as Europe borrowing from the US, or one European member state from another EU member state.[11] Vertical legal borrowing occurs when a supra-governmental regime borrows from its own constituent members, such as the EU-level institutions borrowing from EU member states.[12]

[11] The literature on horizontal legal borrowing (across states) is extensive; the classic is Alan Watson, *Legal Transplants: An Approach to Comparative Law* (2nd edn) (Athens, Ga: University of Georgia Press, 1993).

[12] A framework of legal borrowing that adds the vertical dimension (between states and federal and international bodies) is developed in Jonathan B Wiener, 'Something

The Better Regulation initiative in Europe borrows along both of these dimensions. It is an outgrowth of ideas percolating up from (vertically) and spreading across (horizontally) the EU member states; of the integration of EU institutions and the current EU platform of competitiveness, good governance, and sustainable development;[13] and also of deliberate (horizontal) borrowing from American law. It is thus a perfect example of legal 'hybridization', an evolutionary process involving the exchange and recombination of traits (here, legal ideas) from different species (here, legal systems) into new hybrid versions in response to changing needs.[14] As in biological evolution, legal hybrids do not always succeed. Mixing together legal concepts can be ineffective or incoherent.[15] As in biology, legal hybrids succeed when they possess novel combinations of traits that enable them to occupy new niches opened up by changing external demands. Better Regulation in Europe is a hybrid package of reforms attempting to respond to changing needs for regulatory management.

In its Impact Assessment Guidelines, the Commission tellingly quotes US President Woodrow Wilson: 'I not only use all the brains that I have, but all that I can borrow'.[16] The Commission's immediate point here is to espouse borrowing ideas from public input and interservice consultation to improve regulation, but the quotation simultaneously invokes the larger project of legal borrowing involved in the European initiative on Better Regulation, which emulates key concepts and tools of regulatory reform developed in the American administrative state over the past four decades.[17]

Borrowed for Something Blue: Legal Transplants in the Evolution of Global Environmental Law' (2001) 27 *Ecology LQ* 1295.

[13] A useful history of the connections of Better Regulation to these three elements of the EU platform is provided in Ragnar Lofstedt, 'The Swing of the Regulatory Pendulum in Europe: From Precautionary Principle to (Regulatory) Impact Analysis' (2004) 28 *J Risk & Uncert* 237–60.

[14] For further discussion on 'hybridization' of legal ideas and the counterpart concepts in evolutionary biology, see Jonathan B Wiener, 'Whose Precaution After All? A Comment on the Comparison and Evolution of Risk Regulatory Systems' (2003) 13 *Duke J Comparative & Int'l Law* 207, 254–61. An overview of evolutionary biology concepts applied to legal evolution is Simon Deakin, 'Evolution for Our Time: A Theory of Legal Memetics' (2002) 55 Current Legal Problems 1–42. See also sources cited in nn 29–31 below on legal borrowing and diffusion.

[15] See Wiener, n 14 above (noting failure of hybrids until new niches open); Willam Reppy, 'Eclecticism in Choice of Law: Hybrid Method or Mishmash?' (1983) 34 Mercer L Rev 645 (criticizing eclecticism as unpredictable and standardless, while endorsing careful construction and transparent selection of new hybrid methods). Moreover, diffusion itself can sometimes undermine incentives to innovate or can invite fads. See David Lazer, 'Regulatory Capitalism as a Networked Order', (March 2005) Annals of the American Academy 52–66.

[16] Quoted in IA Guidelines 2006, at 9.

[17] On the US history, see Richard Pildes and Cass R Sunstein, 'Reinventing the Regulatory State' (1995) 32 *U Chicago L Rev* 1; Elena Kagan, 'Presidential Administration' (2001) 114 *Harv L Rev* 2246.

What is now emerging is a global movement toward regulatory reform and Better Regulation, drawing significantly on American administrative law and oversight mechanisms.[18] The American sources of European Better Regulation are well recognized. For example, the head of Irish government recently observed:

> Better Regulation and EU-US perspectives are foremost in my mind these days. Better Regulation is a core theme of our EU Presidency and featured prominently at the recent Spring Economic Council.... There is a long tradition in American Public Administration of focussing on the quality and impact of regulation. Many of the policies, institutions and tools that support Better Regulation have their origins in the USA. For example, a lot of very significant anti-trust and consumer protection measures were put in place in the USA in the first decades of the 20th century. There is much that we have learned from the United States in relation to regulatory management and, through occasions like this, much that we can continue to learn.... We hope too that there will be shared learning. While we in the European Union are newer to the game, I hope that we have moved beyond our rookie season! The Union is making up ground quickly in respect of Better Regulation. This is as it should be. There is a deeper understanding within the European Institutions and Member States of the need for regulatory reform.[19]

This process is not one-way: American legal ideas are not the only ones being adopted in other countries. At the same time that the Better Regulation initiative is bringing the methods of impact assessment and regulatory review from the US to Europe, other legal concepts are also spreading from Europe and elsewhere to the US and beyond.[20] The precautionary principle is perhaps the best example of a European regulatory law export (adopted, for example, in US statutes and judicial decisions in the 1970s and by the city of San Francisco in 2003);

[18] See Benedict Kingsbury, Nico Krisch, and Richard B Stewart, 'The Emergence of Global Administrative Law', (summer/autumn 2005) 68 L & Contemp Probs 15; Richard B Stewart, 'Accountability and the Discontents of Globalization: US and EU Models for Regulatory Governance' (draft 2006); Robert W Hahn and Robert E Litan, 'Counting Regulatory Benefits and Costs: Lessons for the US and Europe' (2005) 8 J Int'l Econ Law 473–508; Robert W Hahn, *Reviving Regulatory Reform: A Global Perspective* (Washington, DC: AEI Press, 2001).

[19] Speech by the Taoiseach (head of government of Ireland), Mr Bertie Ahern, TD, at the IBEC Conference on EU-US Perspectives on Regulation, Dublin, 19 April 2004, available at <http://www.betterregulation.ie/index.asp?docID=57>.

[20] This mixed and multi-directional pattern stands in contrast to the claim that the globalization of law is a one-way process of imperious Americanization, eg Ugo Mattei, 'A Theory of Imperial Law: A Study on US Hegemony and the Latin Resistance' (2003) 10 Indiana J Global Legal Studies 383. Contrary to Mattei, European legal ideas are also being borrowed, including by America. And (as Mattei also recognizes) America is frequently a borrower of other countries' immigrants and ideas, so even the export of nominally 'American' legal ideas is often the reception, recombination, and re-export of others' ideas.

environmental contracts or covenants are another. The larger picture of globalization is one of shared hybridization across legal systems, that is, the mutual borrowing of many legal ideas across many countries and the creation of new hybrid legal concepts.[21] The Better Regulation initiative is itself a hybrid, combining the American tool of regulatory impact assessment (RIA) with European strands such as simplification and a standardized approach to measuring administrative costs.

Moreover, Better Regulation is not just an American idea. Considered as a form of structured reasoning to inform sound public policy and bureaucratic governance, as I describe below (recalling Benjamin Franklin's 'prudential algebra'), it is also a European idea: one need only think of Bentham, Hume, Smith, and Mill, and of Montaigne, Descartes, Rousseau, Voltaire, and Max Weber, to name a few. America did not invent the ideas of forecasting future risks, reasoned decision-making, and rigorously assessing public policy options, even if the US government has by now constructed a highly developed system for implementing these concepts. In recent years, British, Australian, and Italian scholars have made important contributions to Better Regulation.[22] And French scholars, across the political spectrum, have championed evidence-based reasoning for government policy; they include figures as diverse as Bertrand de Jouvenel[23] and Pierre Bourdieu.[24]

[21] On the spread of the precautionary principle and hybridization across legal systems, see Wiener, n 14 above.

[22] Eg N Gunningham and P Grabosky, *Smarter Regulation: Designing Environmental Policy* (Oxford: Oxford University Press, 1998); Christopher Hood, Henry Rothstein, and Robert Baldwin, *The Government of Risk: Understanding Risk Regulation Regimes* (Oxford: Oxford University Press, 2001); Richard Macrory, 'Regulatory Justice: Sanctioning in a Post-Hampton World' (The Macrory Review of Penalties) (consultation document, March 2006); Claudio Radaelli, *What Does Regulatory Impact Assessment Mean in Europe?* AEI-Brookings Joint Center for Regulatory Studies, Related Publication 05–02, January 2005; Andrea Renda, *Impact Assessment in the EU* (Brussels: CEPS, 2006); Giandomenico Majone, *Regulating Europe* (London: Routledge, 1996).

[23] Bertrand de Jouvenel, *L'Art de la Conjecture* (Monaco: Editions du Rocher, 1964). This call for rigorous thinking about the future influenced Herman Kahn and Anthony J Wiener, *The Year 2000: A Framework for Speculation* (New York: Macmillan, 1967), which helped bring scenario-based forecasting and decision-making to the US government.

[24] Bourdieu is cited by Joseph Stiglitz, *Globalization and its Discontents* (London: Penguin, 2002), p x for the point that politicians need to engage in scientific debate based on facts and evidence before adopting public policies. Bourdieu was a leading French sociologist, 1930–2002, at L' Ecole des Hautes Etudes en sciences sociales (EHESS) and then at the Collège de France, a theorist of social fields and social capital, a leftist activist, and an opponent of liberal markets and globalization; he was the author of *Acts of Resistance: Against the Tyranny of the Market* (New York: New Press, 1999) and 'Utopia of Endless Exploitation: The Essence of Neoliberalism' *Le Monde Diplomatique*, December 1998, at <http://mondediplo.com/1998/12/08bourdieu> (denouncing market liberalism promoted by economists, and favoring public interest based on collective institutions and empirical verification of theory); he was also the subject of the documentary film *La*

It is worth noting that US Supreme Court Justice Stephen Breyer, in his book on what is now called Better Regulation, held up the French Conseil d'Etat as a model to transplant to the US.[25] And it was a French expert, Dieudonné Mandelkern, who led the multinational group whose report proposed the EU Better Regulation initiative in 2001.[26]

Legal borrowing of the concepts and nomenclature of 'better regulation' and 'regulatory impact assessment' does not necessarily mean convergence in the content of policies and procedures adopted to implement those ideas. As Claudio Radaelli has emphasized, the 'diffusion of a common RIA "bottle"' does not necessarily produce the same 'wine'.[27]

Nonetheless, it is striking that European regulatory policy is now expressly borrowing ideas from American law, even when transatlantic relations are relatively strained. It is even more striking that chief among these borrowed ideas is impact assessment as a check on regulation, or more precisely as a way to shape regulation. The contrast to the debate over the precautionary principle in the 1990s is stark: there Europe sought to export its aggressive platform over the objections of a reluctant US government, and to position Europe (at least rhetorically) as a distinct pro-environment alternative to American pro-market regulatory policy in the post-Cold War era.[28]

Sociologie est un Sport de Combat (2003). Said Bourdieu: 'Observation of reality puts us on our guard against the temptation to construct over-simple models' (from Bourdieu's work on the peasantry in Béarn; quoted in Douglas Johnson, ' Obituary: Pierre Bourdieu' the *Guardian* 28 January 2002, at <http://www.guardian.co.uk/obituaries/story/0,,640396,00.html>).

[25] Stephen G Breyer, *Breaking the Vicious Circle: Toward Effective Risk Regulation* (Cambridge, Mass: Harvard University Press, 1993), part III.

[26] Mandelkern Group Report, n 2 above.

[27] Claudio M Radaelli, 'Diffusion without Convergence: How Political Context Shapes the Adoption of Regulatory Impact Assessment', (October 2005) 12 *Journal of European Public Policy* 924–43.

[28] See Wiener, n 14 above (reporting the evolution of precaution in EU and US legal systems, and the claim that the EU had become more precautionary than the US by the 1990s). Studies in the 1980s typically found that the US used scientific and economic analysis more than did Europe, although the ultimate standards set were similar. Eg Sheila Jasanoff, *Risk Management and Political Culture* (New York: Russell Sage, 1986); David Vogel, *National Styles of Regulatin: Environmental Policy in Great Britain and the United States* (Ithaca, NY: Cornell University Press, 1986). Whether Europe *actually* adopted a more precautionary regulatory system than the US in the 1990s is, however, open to question. Several cases support that claim, including greater European precaution on hormones in beef, genetically modified foods, climate change, and toxic chemicals. On the other hand, several cases point the other way, including greater US precaution on mad cow disease (BSE) and vCJD in blood, particulate matter emissions from power plants and diesel vehicles, youth violence, and terrorism, see Wiener, n 14 above. But these cases are not a representative sample from which reliable generalizations can be drawn about trends in all risk regulation. We therefore studied a data set of all of the 2,878 risks identified in the US

What explains this rapprochement? First, it illustrates the view that legal borrowing is ubiquitous, occurring all the time in multiple directions.[29] Legal borrowing has played a strong role in the evolution and diffusion of environmental regulation in the past.[30] Borrowing has helped spread such legal concepts as environmental impact assessment, pollution discharge information disclosure registries, economic incentive instruments including emissions trading, and precaution. Scholars often write about these patterns of diffusion after they have occurred. Sometimes scholars also play a role in the process of transplantation as it occurs;[31] Better Regulation is one of those cases, as experts share ideas across the Atlantic through papers, conferences, and sabbaticals. A central point here is that the current borrowing of Better Regulation tools has not been much constrained by abstract ideological or rhetorical commitments, nor by supposed national styles or mentalities of law.[32]

and Europe over 1970–2004; we found no significant trend toward greater European precaution over the period. James K Hammitt, Jonathan B. Wiener, Brendon Swedlow, Denise Hall, and Zheng Zhou, 'Precautionary Regulation in Europe and the United States: A Quantitative Comparison' (October 2005) 25 *Risk Analysis* 1215–28.

[29] See Watson, n 11 above, 22; cf Jack L Walker. 'The Diffusion of Innovation Among the American States' (1969) 63 Am Poli Sci Rev 880–9 (within the US); Anne-Marie Slaughter, *A New World Order* (Princeton: Princeton University Press, 2004) (across international networks). There are parallel literatures on the diffusion of business and technological innovations, see Everett M Rogers, *Diffusion of Innovations* (5th edn) (New York: Free Press, 2003) (first pub 1963); on the diffusion of social innovations, see eg Torsten Hägerstrand, 'The Diffusion of Innovations' (1968) 4 *International Encyclopedia of Social Sciences* 194; A J Toynbee, (1961) 12 'A Study of History: Reconsiderations' 343 (describing as 'mimesis' the process of cross-cultural diffusion); and on the diffusion of political systems, see eg Kurt Weyland, 'Theories of Policy Diffusion', (2005) 57 *World Politics* 262–95; Zachary Elkins and Beth Simmons, 'On Waves, Clusters and Diffusion: A Conceptual Framework' (2004) *Annals of the American Academy* (AAPSS); Beth Simmons, Frank Dobbin, and Geoffrey Garrett, 'The International Diffusion of Liberalism', (Fall 2006) *International Organization.*

[30] See Peter H, Sand, *Transnational Environmental Law: Lessons in Global Change* (The Hague and Boston: Kluwer Law International, 1999) 241; Wiener, n 12 above; Per-olof Busch and Helge Jörgens, 'The International Sources of Policy Convergence: Explaining the Spread of Environmental Policy Innovations' (October 2005) 12 *Journal of European Public Policy* 860–84.

[31] Watson argues that much borrowing is carried out by elite jurists who borrow what they happen to know or come across in their travels, communications, and research (n 14 above, at 112–13). In a similar way, Peter Galison writes about the exchange of ideas across scientific disciplines occurring when experts participate in a 'trading zone' such as by collaborating on a common research tool. Peter Galison, *Image & Logic: A Material Culture of Microphysics* (Chicago: The University of Chicago Press, 1997).

[32] For the view that national styles or mentalities of law are highly influential, see Vogel, n 28 above; K Zweigert and H Kotz, *An Introduction to Comparative Law* (3rd edn, T Weir trans) (Oxford: Oxford University Press, 1998) (styles of legal systems are seen in their history, their 'predominant and characteristic mode of thought', their institutions, and their ideology, ibid 68); Pierre Legrand, 'European Legal Systems are Not Converging' (1996)

Contrasts between allegedly US and European approaches to law and regulation are overstated,[33] as intergroup contrasts often are.[34] Instead, the ongoing Better Regulation experience suggests that legal borrowing can readily occur across ostensibly different legal systems, as change agents of legal evolution (such as scholars or policy entrepreneurs within government) import legal concepts and as those legal concepts offer net benefits to the receiving society or its institutions.[35]

Second, economic and political globalization are increasing the opportunities for exchange of legal ideas. Trade, transnational and transgovernmental networks, epistemic communities of experts, and telecommunications (especially the internet) have made it more likely, even in just the last fifteen years, that legal concepts used in one country can be researched and cross-fertilized in another country. Even if national legal styles or mentalities governed in the past, increasing exchange across legal systems is leading those old ways to evolve toward more open, cosmopolitan attitudes, and a process of 'hybridization' in which mixtures of legal ideas create new hybrid modes that populate both sources.[36]

Third, 'it's the economy'. A major objective of Better Regulation is economic competitiveness.[37] The US adopted regulatory reform efforts in the 1970s and 1980s in part to combat inflation and recession. Europe turned to Better Regulation in the last five years to remedy its sluggish economy, which has been growing at about 2 percent per year of late, in contrast to roughly 3 to 4 percent per year in the US and nearly 10 percent per year in China. The Lisbon Strategy adopted in 2000 aims to make

45 ICLQ 52 (emphasizing distinctive national legal mentalities); Robert A Kagan, *Adversarial Legalism: The American Way of Law* (Cambridge, Mass: Harvard University Press, 2001). But see John Bell, *French Legal Cultures* (London: Cambridge University Press/Butterworths, 2001) (finding different legal cultures in the different institutions within France).

[33] Some have argued that Europe now follows the Precautionary Principle whereas the US does not, eg David Vogel, 'The Hare and the Tortoise Revisited: The New Politics of Consumer and Environmental Regulation in Europe', (2003) 33 British J Poli Sci 557–80, but our research finds little evidence of such a divergence. See Wiener, n 14 above (reviewing the debate); Hammitt *et al*, n 28 above (surveying a large array of risks and finding little or no trend toward greater European precaution).

[34] Cf Henri Tajfel, 'Experiments in Intergroup Discrimination' (1970) 223 *Scientific American* 96–102 (showing that people tend to exaggerate intergroup differences); Amartya Sen, *Identity and Violence: The Illusion of Destiny* (New York: WW Norton, 2006) (showing that group characterizations are misleading because they ignore enormous variation among individuals).

[35] For a model of legal borrowing supplied by change agents and potentially subject to benefit-cost analyses in the receiving jurisdiction (depending on the voting rules for adoption of law in the receiving institutions), see Wiener, n 12 above, at 1344–62.

[36] On hybridization of regulatory law, see Wiener, n 14 above, at 254–61.

[37] Better Regulation builds on the continuing program of regulatory reform of *economic* regulation—reform or deregulation of price controls, subsidies, and limits on

Europe the most productive economy in the world by 2010, while maintaining the European social model and fostering environmentally sustainable growth. The Better Regulation initiative is explicitly tied to the Lisbon Strategy. The Prodi Commission stressed good governance; the Barroso Commission stresses competitiveness.[38] Slow economic growth and high unemployment in Europe prompted the Lisbon Strategy to boost growth and jobs; the World Bank's 'Doing Business' reports added pressure on European governments to attract business via legal reform.[39] The four Presidencies' letter of January 2004 began with this opening paragraph:

> The European Commission's recent review of the European economy pointed out that regulatory reform is a key element in seeking to achieve the goals of the Lisbon strategy. The IMF has made it clear that improvements in the EU regulatory framework could deliver as much as a 7 per cent increase in GDP and a 3 per cent increase in productivity in the longer term.[40]

It almost goes without saying that one key purpose of regulatory reform is to reduce costs.[41] In the 1980s the US had a Task Force on Regulatory Relief, later called the Competitiveness Council; the EU now has a Competitiveness Council of Commissioners. The UK Better Regulation Executive was earlier called the Regulatory Impact Unit, and before that the Deregulation Unit in the 1990s. Reducing the costs of regulation is driven by both internal and external pressures. Because regulation

market access in regulated industries such as aviation, trucking, and banking. Despite the predictions of public choice theory that reform of economic regulation was unlikely to occur (because such regulation benefits concentrated industry interests who would lobby to maintain it), much reform and deregulation have in fact occurred. On the US experience focusing on telecommunications, see Robert Horwitz, *The Irony of Regulatory Reform* (Oxford: Oxford University Press, 1991); on the experience in the UK and Japan, see Steven Kent Vogel, *Freer Markets, More Rules: Regulatory Reform in Advanced Industrial Countries* (Ithaca, NY: Cornell University Press, 1998).

[38] In the Communication of 16 March 2005, COM(2005) 97, SEC(2005) 175, 'Better Regulation for Growth and Jobs in the European Union', the first objective identified is 'competitiveness', ibid 3.

[39] See n 176 below.

[40] See Joint Initiative on Regulatory Reform, n 8 above, at 1, citing European Commission, 'The EU Economy: 2003 Review', COM(2003) 729, and IMF, 'When Leaner isn't Meaner: Measuring Benefits and Spillovers of Greater Competition in Europe' 2003.

[41] Much of the debate addresses its efficacy in reducing costs. See Robert Baldwin, 'Is Better Regulation Better for Business?' (2004), at <http://www.lse.ac.uk/collections/pressAndInformationOffice/newsAndEvents/archives/2004/Is_BetterRegulation_betterForBusiness.htm> (criticizing inadequate regulatory relief meant to help industry); Corporate Environment Observer, 'Better Regulation: For Whom ?' (2004), at <http://www.corporateeurope.org/observer9/regulation.html> (criticizing regulatory relief undertaken at industry's behest).

imposes costs on the domestic economy, there is internal pressure for reform. Because some regulation favors domestic producers over foreign producers, yielding international trade disputes, there is external pressure for reform. (Meanwhile, of course, regulations also may have benefits, such as health and environmental protection, which could be lost if regulations were rescinded or diluted.)

Corroborating this point is the remarkable fact that Europe has also borrowed the regulatory tool of emissions trading from the US in order to implement the Kyoto Protocol. During the 1990s, European negotiators resisted and criticized US proposals for greenhouse gas emissions trading. Now, even while criticizing the US for its reluctance to join the Kyoto Protocol, Europe has adopted the very policy proposal that the US had been urging as the flagship instrument to achieve greenhouse gas emissions reductions.[42] The basic reason is no mystery: cost-effectiveness. When Europe ratified Kyoto and finally got down to implementing its targets, it became clear that emissions trading would be a cost-saving, highly effective method of reducing emissions.[43] Cost drove legal borrowing of emissions trading, despite a previously strong rhetorical opposition to this very legal tool and to its source—a rhetoric that one no longer hears in Europe.

Fourth, a related but somewhat different motivation for regulatory reform is to enable the Executive (the President, Prime Minister, or other head of government) to respond to the growth of the regulatory state. The Executive is held accountable by the public for both the costs of regulation (hence pressure to reduce regulation or its costliness), and for the harms of risks not prevented (hence pressure to regulate effectively). In the US, the Administrative Procedure Act of 1946 followed the New Deal expansion of administrative regulation, and Presidential Executive Orders on regulatory review in the 1970s, 1980s, and 1990s followed the

[42] See Wiener, n 12 above; Joseph Kruger and William Pizer, 'Greenhouse Gas Trading in Europe' (October 2004) *Environment* magazine, 8–23.

[43] One current concern is that states may distort the operation of the CO_2 allowance market, partly by allocating excess allowances to shield their industries, arguably leading to price volatility in the EU Emissions Trading System (ETS) in the spring of 2006 when this allocation pattern became apparent (and the market price dropped from 30 to 9 euros in one week). On the general problem, see Jonathan B Wiener, 'Global Environmental Regulation: Instrument Choice in Legal Context' (1999) 108 *Yale LJ* 677–800 , at Part V (warning that nation-states may interfere or 'meddle' with the operation of international allowance trading markets). Carol Rose observed that such 'meddling' is not always 'frivolous', because states may be protecting against local hotspots, see Carol Rose, 'Expanding The Choices for the Global Commons: Comparing Newfangled Tradable Allowance Schemes to Old-Fashioned Common Property Regimes', 10 *Duke Envtl L & Pol'y F* 45, 61 and n 69 (2000). But in CO_2 markets there are no serious hotspot concerns to justify state interference.

Great Society adoption of major health and environmental legislation. The President was compelled to deal with Congressional enactment of regulatory statutes (often delegating substantial power and discretion to regulatory agencies, and foisting on agencies the hard choices of reconciling competing objectives such as health versus cost); and to respond to judicial review of agency action (which is non-expert and not politically accountable, and may distort or ossify regulatory policy). Likewise in Europe, the Better Regulation initiative follows the increasing integration of EU institutions and the greater competency of the EU to regulate health and the environment after the Single European Act and the Maastricht, Amsterdam, and Nice treaties. Better Regulation is in part a move to find a common basis for regulation among the EU institutions (in particular the Commission, the Parliament, and the Council) and the member states, facilitating trade in the Single European Market and ensuring political accountability of government policy.[44] And Better Regulation responds to the need to re-establish the credibility and legitimacy of effective regulation in Europe after a series of public health crises such as mad cow disease (BSE), foot and mouth disease, and scares over dioxin in animal feed, benzene in Perrier, and genetically modified foods. In short, Better Regulation recognizes the need for sound management of the regulatory state, on both sides of the Atlantic.

Is Better Regulation Better?

Given that the EU is borrowing regulatory reform from the US, a normative evaluation of this exercise is in order. It would perhaps be typical for an American legal expert to espouse this flattering imitation, saying, yes, do as we have done, copy our system. But here I write to say: do as we have learned, not simply as we have done. Europe should not simply borrow directly from the US. Europe should innovate, not imitate. Moreover, regulatory reform in Europe must be adapted to suit European institutions. Through this process, Europe should experiment with institutional innovations that can make Better Regulation even better. Europe has an opportunity to do a better job at Better Regulation than the US has

[44] This is true even though the EU does not have the same type of executive branch as the US, headed by a President popularly elected for a term of four years. The EU has a college of Commissioners, appointed as a slate for a term of five years; the President of the Commission is its leader but is also a somewhat equal colleague and is not popularly elected. And the EU as a whole has a Presidency held in rotation by each member state for six months at a time. In these respects, the EU Executive function is weaker or more decentralized than the US Presidency. At the same time, the European Commission has a monopoly on the initiation of legislation, a power that the US President lacks.

done, or, at least, to try out new approaches that can be compared to the US system. If Europe demonstrates improvements in regulatory policy, those advances can and should be borrowed back by the US. Further, the adoption of Better Regulation in Europe can itself create a common language and platform for greater transatlantic communication and collaboration about regulatory policy.[45]

A key theme of this article is that where there are problems in regulatory reform and Better Regulation, such as the debate over benefit-cost analysis (BCA), there are valuable institutional remedies. Where there are controversies regarding the limitations or biases in analytic methods, the underlying sources of these problems are often institutional, not analytic, and can often be ameliorated by institutional reorientations. Thus Europe, and in turn the US, can make Better Regulation even better by investing in intelligent institutional structures and approaches.

'Better regulation' clearly expresses a more sympathetic view of regulation than does 'deregulation', or cost-cutting for greater competitiveness, or even than 'regulatory reform'. 'Reform' could imply improvement, but also pruning and paring, whereas 'better' casts a brighter light on creative approaches.[46] Critics of regulatory reform fear that it really means less regulation, that is, less protection, not better. Of course, cost reduction is desirable, as long as benefits are not reduced even more. European legal systems may need cost reduction and increased flexibility, for example in labor law. But 'better' regulation puts the focus on better results,

[45] One example is the series of US–High-Level Regulatory Cooperation Forum meetings now being held (the latest in January and May 2006).

[46] The Irish government defines 'Regulatory reform' as ' "changes that improve regulatory quality i.e. enhance the performance, cost-effectiveness or legal quality of regulations and related government formalities" [quoting OECD, *Regulatory Reform in Ireland* (2001), at 17]. . . . Examples of changes to the process of regulation include: impact analysis/assessment techniques; the use of alternatives to traditional regulation such as market mechanisms and economic incentives and "sunsetting" arrangements whereby regulations are formally reviewed at a future date to establish whether or not they are still valid or if they could be improved, reduced or even revoked'. By contrast, ' " Regulatory management, Better Regulation and Smarter Regulation" are the terms which are increasingly being used to convey the concept of an ongoing commitment to improving the processes of policy formulation, legislative drafting and enhancing the overall effectiveness and coherence of regulation. The idea of "Better Regulation" also helps to draw an important distinction between the wide reform agenda and deregulation. It is accepted that in some cases consumer, investor and the broader public interest may be better served by introducing new regulation and that in other cases it may be better served by removing regulation. No initial assumption is being made about either the existing quality or quantity of regulation or the need to deregulate. Instead, it is suggested that the goal of Better Regulation will not be achieved by simply seeking to minimise the volume of regulation but rather by using as simple and straightforward measures as possible to achieve policy objectives'. See <http://www.betterregulation.ie/index.asp?locID=20&docID=-1>.

outcomes, performance—not just on less regulation *per se* (nor more). The European initiative on Better Regulation has not gone into detail about what it means by 'better' results, apart from emphasizing accountability and competitiveness. At a first approximation, better results should mean improving societal well-being, that is, increasing societal net benefits, via less cost or more protection or, ideally, both.[47] 'Better' could in some cases imply 'less', but that depends on the calculus of better outcomes, not on a pre-analytic commitment to less regulation for its own sake. And sometimes 'less is more',[48] in the sense that better results can be achieved by more streamlined and lower-cost approaches, but again this is 'less' as a route to 'better' rather than less for its own sake. (Meanwhile, one can also question whether a much-touted program of Better Regulation is really making a difference, or whether it is just rhetoric and symbolic politics. Answering this question requires assessing the quality of impact assessments, the staff and resources being brought to bear, the structures and rules being adopted, and the actual influence on regulatory decisions. I discuss these issues further in the sections on Impact Assessment and Oversight below.)

The Better Regulation initiative could indeed yield better results. The use of impact assessment has the potential to improve regulatory policies and outcomes, increasing net benefits. Administrative cost reduction and simplification can reduce regulatory burdens and untangle needless bureaucratic rigidity. And the Better Regulation initiative, especially the use of IA, is moderating the earlier fervor for the precautionary principle;[49] indeed the European Commission has redefined the precautionary principle as requiring benefit-cost analysis.[50] Precaution can be worth-while to prevent uncertain and potentially irreversible risks, but it can also be excessive, incurring the costs of false positives, innovation foregone, and new countervailing risks (themselves uncertain and potentially

[47] This is plainly a first approximation. There is not space here to compare alternative conceptions of welfare, efficiency, Bentham, Kaldor-Hicks, Pareto, fairness, and other formulations. Suffice to say here that competitiveness is only one element of the overall social well-being that 'better' should entail; and that the European stewards of Better Regulation should develop a more thorough explanation of what they mean by 'better'. See below on 'warm analysis'.

[48] See UK Better Regulation Task Force report, *Regulation: Less is More* (March 2005).

[49] See Wiener, n 14 above, at 220–25; Lofstedt, n 13 above.

[50] See European Commission, Communication from the Commission on the Precautionary Principle, COM(2000) 1, Brussels, 2 February 2000 (available at <http://europa.eu.int/comm/dgs/health_consumer/library/pub/pub07_en.pdf>) (providing that precautionary regulation must satisfy proportionality and must be based on an analysis of benefits and costs).

irreversible).[51] Yet if the Better Regulation initiative focuses exclusively on competitiveness, that is, on reducing costs to industry, without considering social and environmental benefits, it risks yielding less regulation instead of better results. Moreover, increasing net benefits expands the social surplus that can be distributed to engage allies. To succeed and endure, the Better Regulation initiative needs to increase the net benefits of regulation.

In my experience, both in government and in academia, there is a huge swath of interests who favor less regulation regardless of its benefits, and a huge swath who favor more regulation regardless of its costs. In both cases, the alternative to analysis is sanctimony—supposing one knows the right answer without analyzing the consequences. In between these two potent and vocal campaigns is a narrow slice of those who genuinely want to compare the consequences (benefits and costs) of regulatory choices. It is very difficult for governments to maintain a steady commitment to comparing benefits and costs when great political pressure is brought to bear from one swath or the other.

In that light, I assess the Better Regulation initiative in terms of the major reform strategies it invokes, and their counterparts in US law. I address Impact Assessment (including both benefit-cost analysis (BCA) and risk assessment as an input to BCA), the problem of addressing multiple risks in concert, administrative costs, simplification, oversight, and *ex post* evaluation. For each of these issues, I offer suggestions on how to make Better Regulation even better, focusing on institutional innovations.

Impact Assessment

US Experience

In the United States, every President since the 1970s has formally required some form of regulatory impact assessment. President Nixon ordered a Quality of Life review, and President Ford ordered an inflationary impact review. President Carter issued Executive Order (EO) 12044 (23 March 1978), requiring economic analysis of regulations, and creating the Regulatory Analysis Review Group to provide interagency

[51] See Jonathan B Wiener, 'Precaution in a Multirisk World' Dennis J. Paustenbach (ed), in *Human and Ecological Risk Assessment: Theory and Practice* (New York: John Wiley, 2002) 1509–31.

oversight. In 1980, through the Paperwork Reduction Act,[52] the US Congress created the Office of Information and Regulatory Affairs within the Office of Management and Budget (OMB/OIRA). On 17 February 1981, less than a month after taking office, President Reagan signed EO 12291,[53] requiring regulations to yield benefits that 'outweigh' their costs, with a goal of maximizing net benefits, and directed OMB/OIRA to serve as the White House office with the authority to oversee regulatory impact analyses (RIAs).

On 30 September 1993, President Clinton issued EO 12866,[54] which confirmed the bipartisan commitment to RIA using benefit-cost analysis (BCA). EO 12866 replaced the word 'outweigh' with 'justify' (a less quantitative term, embracing a broader public judgment about the policy's merits). Section 1 of EO 12866 maintained the requirement to 'maximize net benefits', and in section 6 it expressly required full analysis of the range of types of costs and benefits, including economic, social, and environmental. EO 12866 also added emphasis on qualitative and distributional impacts, added an instruction to evaluate the countervailing health and environmental risks induced by regulation of a target risk (risk-risk tradeoffs), and added new procedures for transparency (including reporting by OIRA of outside contacts, inclusion of agency representatives at OIRA meetings held to discuss the agency's policies, and oversight of OIRA by a committee chaired by the Vice President).

Since the year 2001, the administration of current President Bush has retained the Clinton EO, reconfirming the bipartisan character of regulatory review. The Bush administration OIRA has issued more 'return' letters (saying 'no' to deficient regulations) than did the Clinton administration OIRA, but at the same time the Bush OIRA has also innovated the new device of 'prompt letters' (using BCA to say 'yes' to desirable regulations and urging agencies to adopt them; examples include requiring trans-fat content labels on food to reduce heart disease, and installing automatic electronic defibrillators in the workplace). OIRA has also issued new RIA Guidelines in Circular A-4,[55] calling for more use of

[52] Codified at 44 USC 3501 ff. Despite the name of this law, the US approach (mandated by the series of Presidential EOs) focuses on BCA—full assessment of both benefits and costs—rather than on trying to reduce paperwork costs (administrative costs) alone.

[53] 46 Fed Reg 13193 (published 19 February 1981).

[54] Executive Order 12866, 'Regulatory Planning and Review', 58 Fed Reg 51735 (4 October 1993), available at <http://www.whitehouse.gov/omb/inforeg/eo12866. pdf>. As a senior staff person in the President's Council of Economic Advisers (CEA) at the time, I assisted in the drafting of EO 12866.

[55] OMB/OIRA, Circular A-4, 'Regulatory Analysis', 17 September 2003, available at < http://www.whitehouse.gov/omb/circulars/a004/a-4.pdf>.

cost-effectiveness analysis (C-EA), lower discount rates (3% as well as 7%, and potentially even lower than 3% for long-term intergenerational effects), risk-risk tradeoff analysis, and probabilistic scenarios of impacts exceeding $1 billion. Further, OIRA has issued guidelines as required by the Information Quality Act, a bulletin on peer review, and a proposed Bulletin on Risk Assessment. President Bush transferred oversight of OIRA from the office of the Vice President to the office of the White House Chief of Staff.[56] And OIRA now posts all significant documents on its website, <http://www.whitehouse.gov/omb/inforeg/regpol.html>.

In short, there is a bipartisan consensus among US Presidents of both political parties over the last four decades to require agencies to produce RIAs and to use BCA for risk management. One prominent author has heralded the era of the 'cost-benefit state'.[57] Another says that monetized BCA has become 'the norm for government policy'.[58] It should also be noted that BCA in the US addresses all types of costs and benefits—including economic, social, and environmental—and thus is comparable to the 'Integrated Impact Assessment' conducted in the EU.[59]

But BCA is still not applied to all regulatory policies in the US. Federal agencies in the US appear to quantify some benefits or costs of regulatory proposals most of the time, but to quantify and monetize both benefits and costs only about half the time.[60] One reason for this incomplete use of BCA may be that federal statutes vary in whether they require, permit, or prohibit reliance on BCA in agency regulatory decision-making. Congress often requires agencies to use BCA, as in the Consumer Product Safety Act (CPSA 1972) (consumer products), Federal Insecticide, Fungicide and Rodenticide Act (FIFRA, 1975) (pesticides), Toxics Substances Control Act (TSCA, section 6 (1977) (toxic substances), and Unfunded Mandates Reform Act (UMRA, 1995) ('unfunded mandates'

[56] EO 13258 (2002), at <http://www.whitehouse.gov/omb/inforeg/eo13258.pdf>. This shift in roles was apparently requested by Vice President Cheney, who preferred to focus on other issues. In some administrations, there can be a difference of perspectives and even competition between the President and Vice President, so the transfer of oversight from the Vice President to the White House Chief of Staff may bring regulatory review more closely in line with the President's policy agenda. This would continue a trend toward Presidential direction of regulatory matters that was already under way in the earlier Carter, Reagan, Bush, and Clinton administrations, see Elena Kagan, 'Presidential Administration', (2001) 114 Harv L Rev 2246.

[57] Cass R Sunstein, *The Cost-Benefit State: The Future of Regulatory Protection* (Chicago: American Bar Association, 2002).

[58] W Kip Viscusi, 'Monetizing the Benefits of Risk and Environmental Regulation' (2006) 33 *Fordham Urban Law Journal* 1033–44.

[59] IA Guidelines 2006, Annex 13, make clear that BCA in the EU also includes economic, environmental, and social impacts.

[60] Hahn and Muething, (2003) 55 *Admin L Rev* 608–42.

on states, businesses). Sometimes Congress permits BCA without requiring its use in decision-making, for example, in the Occupational Safety and Health Act (OSHAct 3(8), 1972) (as to workplace hazards other than toxics), Clean Water Act (CWA, section 304, 1972) (water pollution technology standards), and Safe Drinking Water Act (SDWA, 1996 amendments) (drinking water contaminants). But some Congressional statutes prohibit agencies' use of BCA in regulation, such as the Clean Air Act (CAA, section 109, 1970) (national ambient air quality standards), OSHAct section 6(b)(5) (1972) (workplace toxics), Endangered Species Act (ESA, section 7, 1973) (endangered species), Resource Conservation and Recovery Act (RCRA, section 3004m, 1984) (hazardous waste treatment standards), and Comprehensive Environmental Response, Compensation and Liability Act (CERCLA, section 121, 1986) (hazardous waste cleanup standards). The Presidential EOs requiring BCA do not countermand a Congressional prohibition on using BCA to set standards, but they can require the agency to conduct a BCA as an informative analytic matter even if the agency is prohibited by the statute from relying on the BCA in setting a standard. Thus, the incomplete application of BCA suggests that OMB/OIRA has limited resources to supervise agency conduct, that some impacts are difficult to quantify or monetize, and that spreading the culture of impact assessment across the agencies is still a work in progress.

Moreover, BCA is not required for several other aspects of US regulation. It is not required for Congressional legislation, although the Unfunded Mandates Reform Act (UMRA, 1995) encourages it. Nor is it required for international treaties involving regulatory commitments.[61] Nor is BCA adequately employed in evaluating federal spending decisions, including both new spending and cutbacks,[62] nor in evaluating public works such as water resource projects (despite the history of BCA being developed to evaluate dams since the 1930s),[63] nor in evaluating

[61] Agency regulations adopted pursuant to an international treaty would presumably be subject to EO 12866, but by the time such a regulation reaches OIRA the international treaty has already been negotiated and ratified and the regulation is therefore difficult to revise. To address this problem, the US State Department has recently proposed requiring agencies to consult with OMB/OIRA earlier, on the regulatory impacts of pending new international agreements. 71 Fed Reg 28831 (18 May 2006). The State Department already requires agencies to consult with OMB before making new budgetary commitments in international agreements. See 22 CFR § 181.4(e).

[62] See Robert W Hahn, 'The Cost-Benefit of Budget Cutting', AEI-Brookings Policy Matters 06–12 (May 2006).

[63] The federal Reclamation Act of 1902 required economic analysis of projects, and the federal Flood Control Act of 1936 required projects to demonstrate that 'the benefits to

national forest logging (despite section 6(k) of the 1976 National Forest Management Act (NFMA), requiring economic suitability for timber cutting). Nor is BCA required for major federal actions (such as projects or policy decisions) under the environmental impact statement (EIS) provision of the National Environmental Policy Act (NEPA), despite an early effort to incorporate BCA into the EIS as a way to strengthen environmental protection.[64] Nor is BCA adequately employed in evaluating trade measures, despite the requirement in Section 201 of the Trade Act of 1974 that trade safeguards must 'provide greater economic and social benefits than costs'.[65] Nor is BCA yet employed to evaluate counterterrorism operations (despite the early history of BCA and systems analysis being brought to the US military by Defense Secretary

whomsoever they may accrue are in excess of the estimated costs', 33 USC § 701a. Although federal water agencies such as the Bureau of Reclamation, US Department of the Interior, evaluate some project benefits and costs, they typically have not conducted a full BCA including environmental impacts. See Alan V Kneese, 'Whatever Happened to Benefit-Cost Analysis?' (2000) 116 Water Resources Updates 58–61, at <http://www.ucowr.siu.edu/updates/116/index.html>. Economists have long argued for correcting this omission and thereby protecting the environment by making *greater* use of BCA, including environmental impacts. See Maynard M Hufschmidt, 'Benefit-Cost Analysis: 1933–85' (2000) 116 Water Resources Update 42–9, at <http://www.ucowr.siu.edu/updates/116/index. html> (noting studies in 1950, 1958, and 1962 espousing this view, and changes proposed by the Carter administration to expand BCA to ensure environmental protection in water projects). Economist and BCA advocate Kip Viscusi wrote an early paper for the pro-environment Ralph Nader group making this point: federal water agencies' BCA was unduly narrow and should be expanded to account for environmental impacts. See Richard L Berkman and W Kip Viscusi, *Damming The West: Ralph Nader's Study Group Report on the Bureau of Reclamation* (New York: Grossman Publishers, 1973). Viscusi continues to advocate BCA for both public works projects and regulations, see W Kip Viscusi, 'Monetizing the Benefits of Risk and Environmental Regulation', AEI-Brookings Joint Center Working Paper 06–09 (April 2006).

64 See Judge Skelley Wright's opinion in *Calvert Cliffs Coordinating Committee v AEC*, 449 F 2d 1109 (DC Cir 1971) (finding that the EIS provision in NEPA section 102(2)(C) requires BCA of federal projects, in order to take into account their previously neglected environmental costs), *cert denied*, 404 US 942 (1972). The US Supreme Court subsequently held that NEPA requires only a 'purely procedural' exercise of informed decision-making—a so-called 'stop and think' exercise—with no substantive criteria for such decisions. See *Stryker's Bay Neighborhood Council Inc v Karlen*, 444 US 223 (1980). NEPA has been held by the courts not to apply to international trade agreements like NAFTA, see *Public Citizen v United States Trade Representative*, 5 F 3d 549 (DC Cir 1993), nor to federal spending laws, *Andrus v Sierra Club*, 442 US 347 (1979). In addition, various exemptions to NEPA have been adopted, including statutory exemptions for EPA actions under the Clean Air Act, 15 USC § 793(c)(1), and many actions under the Clean Water Act, 33 USC § 1371(c)(1); and judicial exemptions for EPA actions under environmental laws deemed to require the 'functional equivalent' of the EIS process. See Jonathan M Cosco, 'NEPA for the Gander: NEPA's Application to Critical Habitat Designations and Other "Benevolent" Federal Action' (1998) 8 *Duke Envtl L & Pol'y F* 345.

65 19 USC 2251(a).

Robert McNamara's 'Whiz Kids' in the 1960s), and it is only beginning to be applied (with difficulty) to the new wave of homeland security regulations.[66]

European Experience

In the European Union, Impact Assessment of new regulations is now required in almost all countries and at the EU level, and BCA is increasingly employed. There is a long history of the use of environmental impact assessment used to inform decision-makers (as under NEPA in the US), with some versions requiring actual financial compensation for the environmental harms of projects,[67] and thus a kind of BCA imposed on projects through tort law or the law of expropriation (takings) of neighbors' property.

BCA applied to modern regulatory decisions is also increasingly required in Europe. Most generally, the Proportionality Principle, a general principle of European law,[68] has been held to imply some version of BCA. In the *Pfizer* case, the court observed (paras 410–11):

> The Court considers that a cost/benefit analysis is a particular expression of the principle of proportionality in cases involving risk management . . . . the

[66] See Jessica Stern and Jonathan B Wiener, 'Precaution Against Terrorism' (2006) 9 *J Risk Research* 393–447 and also in Paul Bracken, Ian Bremmer, and David Gordon (eds), *Managing Strategic Surprise* (Cambridge: Cambridge University Press, forthcoming 2007). Analysis of counterterrorism policies (both domestic homeland security and external intelligence and military operations) is particularly urgent, because effective counterterrorism is essential, but counterproductive policies can do serious damage to national security as well as to human life. See ibid (arguing that little serious *ex ante* analysis was done of the Iraq invasion, with the result that serious countervailing risks were neglected, including collateral civilian deaths, blowback, bog-down, distraction, and theft; and advocating subjecting counterterrorism policies to a joint OIRA-NSC oversight process using analytic tools of BCA and risk-risk tradeoff analysis); Linda Bilmes and Joseph E Stiglitz, 'The Economic Costs of the Iraq War' (2006) National Bureau of Economic Research (NBER) Working Paper 12054, available at <www.z.gsb.columbia.edu/faculty/jstiglitz/newworks.cfm> (arguing that the costs of the Iraq War were greatly underestimated *ex ante*, and calling for BCA of future such interventions). See generally Barbara Tuchman, *The March of Folly* (New York: Knopf, 1984) (on the counterproductive results of military campaigns undertaken without adequate analysis of likely outcomes). Yet these policies are difficult to analyze because information may be classified, because terrorists are strategic agents who respond to preventive measures hence requiring dynamic game theory models, and because some consequences may be hard to quantify (eg loss of privacy and freedom).

[67] See Jane Holder, *Environmental Assessment: The Regulation of Decision Making* (Oxford: Oxford University Press, 2005) (focusing on the history in the UK), including her discussion of the compensation requirement under the writ *ad quod damnum* in the thirteenth century.

[68] Nicholas Emiliou, *The Principle of Proportionality in European Law: A Comparative Study* (London: Kluwer Law International, 1996).

principle of proportionality, which is one of the general principles of Community law, requires that measures adopted by Community institutions should not exceed the limits of what is appropriate and necessary in order to attain the legitimate objectives pursued by the legislation in question, and where there is a choice between several appropriate measures, recourse must be had to the least onerous, and the disadvantages caused must not be disproportionate to the aims pursued . . . .[69]

The Communication on the Precautionary Principle of February 2000 requires precautionary regulations to be *proportional* to the chosen level of protection, *non-discriminatory* in their application, *consistent* with similar measures already taken, *based on an examination of the potential benefits and costs* of action or lack of action (including, where appropriate and feasible, an economic cost/benefit analysis), *subject to review* in the light of new scientific data, and *capable of assigning responsibility for producing the scientific evidence* necessary for a more comprehensive risk assessment. In effect, the Communication reclaims the PP as part of decision analysis.[70]

Adopted late in 2000, the Nice Treaty of the EU (building on the Amsterdam and Maastricht treaties) provides in Article 174(3) that European environmental policy must be based on an assessment of 'the potential benefits and costs of action or lack of action'. Unlike in the US, it does not appear that any European Union laws prohibit the use of BCA, although such prohibitions may exist in member states' laws.

[69] Case T-13/99, *Pfizer Animal Health SA v Council*, 2002 WL 31337 (European Court of First Instance, 11 September 2002). But the court remarked in para. 456: 'The Court observes that the importance of the objective pursued by the contested regulation, i.e. the protection of human health, may justify adverse consequences, and even substantial adverse consequences, for certain traders . . . The protection of public health, which the contested regulation is intended to guarantee, must take precedence over economic considerations.'

[70] Several scholars have developed approaches to melding the PP with consequentialist decision analysis. See eg Ralph L Keeney and Detlof von Winterfeldt, 'Appraising the Precautionary Principle—A Decision Analysis Perspective' (2001) 4 *J Risk Research* 191; John D Graham, 'Decision-Analytic Refinements of the Precautionary Principle' (2001) 4 *J Risk Research* 127; Olivier Godard, Claude Henry, Patrick Lagadec, and Erwann Michel-Kerian, *Traité des Nouveaux Risques* (Paris: Gallimard, 2002); Richard B Stewart, 'Environmental Regulatory Decisionmaking under Uncertainty' (2002) 20 *Research in Law and Economics* 71–152; Michael Dekay, Mitchell Small, Paul Fischbeck, Scott Farrow, Alison Cullen, J B Kadane, Lester Lave, Granger Morgan, and K Takemura, 'Risk-Based Decision Analysis in Support of Precautionary Policies' (2002) 5 *J Risk Research* 391; Scott Farrow, 'Using Risk-Assessment, Benefit-Cost Analysis, and Real Options to Implement a Precautionary Principle' (2004) 24 *Risk Analysis* 727; Christian Gollier and Nicolas Treich, 'Decision Making under Uncertainty: The Economics of the Precautionary Principle' (2003) 27 *J Risk & Uncertainty* 77; Pauline Barrieu and Bernard Sinclair-Dégagné, 'On Precautionary Policies' (forthcoming 2006) Management Science.

The new EU 'Better Regulation' initiative has launched Impact Assessment Guidelines (2002, revised 2005, updated 2006) requiring a form of BCA.[71] The IA Guidelines require identification of the problem, consideration of alternative policy options (including no action), and assessment of the 'positive and negative' economic, social, and environmental impacts (including direct and indirect impacts) of each policy option.[72] The Guidelines use the terminology of 'positive and negative impacts' to include both a fully quantified and monetized BCA, and a partially quantified/partially qualitative 'multi-criteria analysis', as well as a cost-effectiveness analysis where relevant.[73] This is similar to the provisions of US EO 12866 and of OMB Circular A-4, calling for an RIA including both quantitative and qualitative evaluation of all benefits and costs and giving guidance on BCA and C-EA. (The US uses the term BCA to refer to both the fully quantified and monetized BCA, and the partially quantified/partially qualitative analysis of benefits and costs, described in the EU Guidelines.) Further, like EO 12866, the EU Guidelines provide that 'A measure is considered justified where net benefits can be expected from the intervention'.[74]

Of the 70 Extended IAs conducted by the European Commission so far (2003–5), fewer than 40 percent quantify and monetize either benefits or costs, and only 17 percent compared net benefits.[75] These figures are lower than the comparable statistics for the US (cited above), but the EU system has been in operation for a much shorter period of time. Also, in principle, the EU RIA system applies to all legislation, at least to directives and regulations initiated by the European Commission, and to amendments adopted by the European Parliament. The Commission's monopoly on initiating legislation means that requiring IA of European Commission proposals is in a sense more akin to requiring IA of Congressional bills in the US—a power that US Presidents and OMB/OIRA do not have.

[71] See IA Guidelines 2005 and 2006, nn. 5–6 above. For discussion, see Andrea Renda, *Impact Assessment in the EU* (Brussels: Center for European Policy Studies, 2006); Lucas Bergkamp, *European Community Law for the New Economy* (Antwerp: Intersentia, 2004), 169. By 'a form of BCA', I mean some analysis of benefits and costs, ie of positive and negative impacts, and not a particular version that eg requires or eschews quantified monetized values.

[72] IA Guidelines 2006, Part III, at 16–46.

[73] See IA Guidelines 2006 at 13 and at 39 and n 45, and Annex 13, 'Methods on Comparing Impacts'.

[74] See IA Guidelines 2006, Annex 13.1.

[75] Andrea Renda, *Impact Assessment in the EU*, n. 71 above, at 63.

Several EU member states have adopted strong Better Regulation programs with RIA procedures.[76] For example:

- The UK has conducted several reviews of its risk regulation system,[77] created the Better Regulation Executive[78] in the Cabinet Office, and the external advisory Better Regulation Commission. The government announced a Better Regulation Action Plan,[79] and developed comprehensive guidelines on risk management which instruct government bodies to seek transparency and proportionality through the use of risk assessment, analysis of market failures, valuation (of monetary and non-monetary impacts, including attention to public concerns), impact assessment including benefit-cost analysis of alternative policy options, and monitoring of policy implementation.[80]
- Ireland has created a regulatory reform office in the Department of the Taoiseach, and a Statutory Law Revision and Consolidation Unit in the Office of the Attorney General.[81] Ireland began these efforts through a Coordinating Group of Secretaries in 1995, which issued a report on Delivering Better Government in 1996.[82] These efforts were organized under the Strategic Management Initiative and its Working Group on Regulatory Reform. The government issued a report on Reducing Red Tape in 1999,[83] and a report on Regulating Better in 2004,[84] committing to rigorous use of Regulatory Impact Analysis.

[76] For more on RIAs in a variety of countries, see OECD, *RIA Inventory* (Paris: OECD, 2003).

[77] These include the Hampton review on Reducing Administrative Burdens (2005) at <http://www.hm-treasury.gov.uk/budget/budget_05/press_notices/bud_bud05_presshampton.cfm>, the Macrory review on Regulatory Penalties (interim consultation document, May 2006) at <http://www.cabinetoffice.gov.uk/regulation/reviewing_regulation/penalties/index.asp>, and the Davidson review on implementation of EU legislation (forthcoming 2006), as well as the Better Regulation Task Force (now Commission) report on *Regulation—Less is More* (March 2005) at <http://www.brc.gov.uk/publications/lessismoreentry.asp>. For further details and links to each document see <http://www.cabinetoffice.gov.uk/regulation/>.

[78] See <http://www.cabinetoffice.gov.uk/regulation/>.

[79] See <http://www.hm-treasury.gov.uk./newsroom_and_speeches/press/2005/press_50_05.cfm>.

[80] See HM Treasury, *The Green Book* (2003); HM Treasury, 'Managing Risks to the Public: Appraisal Guidance' (June 2005). For an overview of these efforts, see UK House of Lords, Economic Affairs Committee, *Government Policy on the Management of Risk* (June 2006), at <http://www.publications.parliament.uk/pa/ld200506/ldselect/ldeconaf/183/183i.pdf>.

[81] See <http://www.betterregulation.ie/>.

[82] Available at <http://www.betterregulation.ie/attached_files/upload/static/1151.pdf>.

[83] Available at <http://www.betterregulation.ie/index.asp?docID=37>.

[84] Department of the Taoiseach, *Regulating Better: A Government White Paper Setting out Six Principles of Better Regulation* (January 2004), available at <http://www.betterregulation.ie/upload/Regulating_Better_html/index.html>.

In June 2005 it decided to require RIA across all departments, and in October 2005 the government issued RIA Guidelines.[85]

- The Netherlands has adopted a strong program of Administrative Cost reduction, including pioneering the Standard Cost Model which is now being borrowed by many other countries,[86] and setting a goal of 25 percent reduction of administrative burden.[87] But it remains to be seen whether the Netherlands will undertake a broader program of Better Regulation using Impact Assessment and BCA.
- France, although it did not begin to adopt Better Regulation measures until more recently, has now created a Better Regulation office at the Ministry of Finance, Economy and Industry (transferring functions there from the Réforme de l'Etat previously in the Prime Minister's office, in order to combine regulatory oversight with budgetary oversight). France has also launched a Better Regulation program in the Conseil d'Etat. And France has proposed a new law requiring impact assessment of all new legislation.
- Germany, under its new coalition government headed by Chancellor Angela Merkel, has made better regulation a high priority. Under the rubric 'Scaling Back Bureaucracy', the Merkel government has appointed a minister to lead the program, adopted the Standard Cost Model as well as RIA Guidelines, and begun an assessment of administrative burdens with a view to adopting a political goal to reduce such burdens in the near future.

In its 16 March 2005 Communication on Better Regulation, the European Commission attached a chart summarizing progress on Better Regulation and Impact Assessment (see below, pp. 472–3).[88] Events are moving quickly in this field, so this chart may already be out of date. Still, the chart is noteworthy for its very clear effort to shame laggard countries into adopting Impact Assessment procedures. Denmark, Poland, and the

[85] See RIA Guidelines: 'How to Conduct a Regulatory Impact Analysis', and 'Regulatory Impact Analysis: Lessons from the Pilot Exercise', both available at <http://www.betterregulation.ie/eng/index.asp?docID=80>.

[86] The Standard Cost Model Network, a consortium of countries using this approach, is at <www.administrative-burdens.com>.

[87] See Bert Doorn and Christiaan Prins, 'A Dutch Treat: The Netherlands Presidency and Regulatory Reform', *Challenge Europe*, Issue 13—What Future for Europe's Economic and Social Model? (30 January 2005), at <http://www.theepc.be/en/ce.asp?TYP=CE&LV=177&see=y&t=42&PG=CE/EN/detail&l=2&AI=417>.

[88] Adapted from European Commission, Communication from the Commission to the Council and the European Parliament, 'Better Regulation for Growth and Jobs in the

UK scored the highest (10 points out of a possible 11); France, Portugal, and Cyprus scored zero. But as noted above, already France has taken important actions since this chart was published.

Of course, even where countries have adopted IA systems, they may be implementing such reviews in different ways. For example, Radaelli finds that IA is aimed at improving substantive policy consequences in the US, at managing the bureaucracy in the UK, at transparency in the Netherlands, and at formal adherence to rules in countries like France and Germany.[89] But IA arguably serves all of these objectives in each of these countries; certainly it does in the US. And IA is also an evolving program, so that the substantive consequentialism of US regulatory review and the transparency of Dutch administrative cost measurement may well be adopted in other countries over time.

A Brief Evaluation

It is by now fairly clear that the choice to use IA and BCA is not a partisan matter. IA is a tool for better decision-making employed on both the center-left and the center-right, and it is a mechanism of interbranch relations—to enable Presidential management of the regulatory state (both in the US and in the European Union). It has become the mainstream consensus approach, albeit with critics on each flank. In the United States, IA using economic analysis such as BCA has been espoused by a wide array of actors across the political spectrum, including not only Republican Presidents Nixon, Ford, Reagan, and both Bushes, but also Democratic Presidents Carter and Clinton, Judge Skelley Wright (in the *Calvert Cliffs* case cited above), US Supreme Court Justice Stephen Breyer[90] (appointed to the Court by President Clinton), and law professors Cass Sunstein[91] and Buzz Thompson,[92] among many others, as well

European Union', COM(2005) 97, SEC(2005) 175, 16 March 2005, n 4 above, at 17 (footnote omitted). The footnote in the table (omitted here) references the chart to 'Commission Staff Working Paper: Report on the Implementation of the European Charter for Small Enterprises in the Member States of the European Union—SEC(2005) 167, 8.2.2005, p. 36', but the chart addresses Impact Assessment procedures in general and only the last two columns address impacts on small businesses.

89 See Radaelli, n 27 above.

90 Breyer, n 25 above.

91 Cass R Sunstein, *Risk and Reason* (New York: Cambridge University Press, 2002); Sunstein, n 57 above. Sunstein is also the author of *Radicals in Robes: Why Extreme Right-Wing Courts are Wrong for America* (New York: Basic Books, 2005).

92 Barton Thompson, Jr, 'People or Prairie Chickens: The Uncertain Search for Optimal Biodiversity', (1999) 51 *Stanford Law Review* 1127.

Overview of measures in the area of Better Regulation and impact assessment*

	Better regulation programme	Specific RIA policy	Obligatory RIA	Alternative instruments considered	Guidelines on RIA	Coordinating body for RIA	Consultation part of RIA	Formal consultation procedures	Direct stakeholder consultation	Tests of impact on small enterprises	Exemptions for SMEs	*Total Y+(Y)*
Belgium	(Y)	N.A.	(Y)	N.A.	(Y)	(Y)	N	(Y)	(Y)	(Y)	N	*7*
Czech Republic	Y	N.A.	N	Y	N.A.	N.A.	N.A.	N.A.	N.A.	(Y)	N	*3*
Denmark	Y	Y	Y	Y	Y	Y	Y	Y	Y	Y	N	*10*
Germany	Y	N.A.	N.A.	N.A.	Y	Y	Y	Y	N.A.	N.A.	N.A.	*5*
Estonia	N	N	Y	Y	Y	N.A.	N.A.	N	N	N.A.	Y	*4*
Greece	(Y)	(Y)	N	N	N	N	Y	N	N	N	N.A.	*3*
Spain	Y	(Y)	Y	Y	(Y)	(Y)	N	N	N	N	N.A.	*6*
France	N.A.	N.A.	N.A.	N.A.	N.A.	N.A.	N.A.	N.A.	N.A.	N.A.	N.A.	*0*
Ireland	Y	N	N	(Y)	(Y)	N	(Y)	(Y)	N	N	N	*5*
Italy	(Y)	Y	N	(Y)	Y	(Y)	(Y)	N	Y	(Y)	N	*8*
Cyprus	N	N	N	N	N	N	N	N	N	N	N.A.	*0*
Latvia	Y	Y	Y	Y	Y	Y	Y	Y	N	Y	N	*9*
Lithuania	N.A.	Y	Y	Y	Y	N.A.	N.A.	N.A.	N	N.A.	N.A.	*4*
Luxembourg	Y	N.A.	Y	Y	N.A.	Y	Y	Y	N	N	Y	*7*

Hungary	Y	(Y)	Y	N	N	Y	(Y)	(Y)	N	N	N	*6*
Malta	Y	N.A.	N.A.	N	N.A.	(Y)	N	N	Y	N	Y	*4*
Netherlands	Y	Y	N.A.	Y	Y	Y	N	N	Y	(Y)	Y	*8*
Austria	Y	Y	Y	Y	Y	N	Y	Y	Y	N.A.	N	*8*
Poland	Y	Y	Y	Y	Y	Y	Y	Y	(Y)	N	Y	*10*
Portugal	N	N	N	N	N	N	N	N	N	N	N	*0*
Slovenia	Y	N.A.	N.A.	N.A.	N.A.	N.A.	N.A.	N.A.	N.A.	N.A.	N.A.	*1*
Slovakia	N.A.	N.A.	N.A.	N.A.	N.A.	N.A.	N.A.	N.A.	(Y)	N.A.	N	*1*
Finland	Y	Y	Y	Y	Y	(Y)	Y	Y	Y	N.A.	N.A.	*9*
Sweden	Y	Y	Y	Y	Y	Y	Y	Y	Y	N	N	*9*
United Kingdom	Y	Y	Y	Y	Y	Y	Y	Y	Y	Y	N	*10*
Total Y+(Y)	*19*	*13*	*12*	*15*	*15*	*14*	*12*	*12*	*11*	*7*	*5*	

Legend:

Y Measures exist	*(Y) Measures planned/Available partially*	*N No measures exist*	*N.A. Information not available*

* See above, p. 470, n. 88.

as many economists of diverse political persuasions,[93] including Alan Blinder[94] and Joseph Stiglitz.[95] In Europe, Better Regulation via IA is espoused by a chorus of political leaders across the political spectrum, including Tony Blair, Gordon Brown, Bertie Ahern, Romano Prodi, Jose Manuel Barroso, Gunther Verheugen, and others; and it has been adopted by both the European Commission and the EU member states.

At the same time, IA of regulations, especially IA using BCA, has been criticized as anti-environmental, chiefly on the grounds that it tends to delay regulations and to overstate costs and understate health and environmental benefits (such as human life, ecological vitality, and aesthetics) which are difficult to measure.[96] Similarly, environmental IA under NEPA has been criticized—notably by industry and the military—for delaying new projects. (As I point out below, another distinct problem with BCA occurs when it focuses narrowly on a target risk and on industry compliance costs, to the neglect of countervailing risks and ancillary benefits.)

Advocates of BCA answer that if BCA is done well, it will measure all important impacts. They are optimistic about the ability of economic methods to develop quantified and monetized measures even of amenities

[93] Eg Kenneth Arrow, Maureen Cropper, George Eads, Robert Hahn, Lester Lave, Roger Noll, Paul Portney, Milt Russell, Richard Schmalensee, Kerry Smith, and Robert Stavins, 'Is There a Role for Benefit-Cost Analysis in Environmental, Health, and Safety Regulation?', (1996) 272 *Science* 221–2 (advocating the use of BCA as a tool to help inform regulatory policy decisions).

[94] See Alan Blinder, *Hard Heads, Soft Hearts: Tough-Minded Economics for a Just Society* (Reading, Mass: Addison-Wesley, 1988). Prof Blinder was a member of the Council of Economic Advisers (CEA) appointed by President Clinton.

[95] Joseph Stiglitz was first a member and later Chair of CEA under President Clinton, and winner of the Nobel Prize. While a critic of *laissez-faire* globalization (see Stiglitz, n 24 above), Prof Stiglitz has espoused BCA with improvements to reflect advances in economic understanding, as reflected in his support and role in the drafting of President Clinton's EO 12866, and in his scholarship such as Joseph E Stiglitz, *Economics of the Public Sector* (3rd edn) (New York: WW Norton, 2000); Joseph E Stiglitz, 'The Rate of Discount for Cost-Benefit Analysis and the Theory of the Second Best', in R Lind (ed), *Discounting for Time and Risk in Energy Policy* (Washington, DC: RFF Press, 1982) 151–204. And he has recently written: 'The most important things in life—like life itself—are priceless. But that does not mean that issues involving the preservation of life (or a way of life), like defense, should not be subjected to cool, hard economic analysis'. Joseph E Stiglitz, 'Analysis on True Cost-Benefit of Iraq "Project" Virtually Absent', Daily Yomiuri Online, 4 March 2006, at <http://www.yomiuri.co.jp/dy/columns/syndicate/20060313dy02.htm>. See also Bilmes and Stiglitz, n 66 above (advocating BCA).

[96] See David Driesen, 'Is Cost-Benefit Analysis Neutral?' (2006) 77 *U Colo L Rev* 335; Frank Ackerman, Lisa Heinzerling, and Rachel Massey, 'Applying Cost-Benefit to Past Decisions: Was Environmental Protection ever a Good Idea?' (2005) 57 *Admin L Rev* 155. Other critiques attack the ethics of monetizing health and environmental benefits, see Frank Ackerman and Lisa Heinzerling, *Priceless: Knowing the Price of Everything and the Value of Nothing* (New York: The New Press 2004). Rebuttals to these critiques include Viscusi, n 58 above; and Robert W Hahn, *In Defense of the Economic Analysis of Regulation* (Washington, DC: American Enterprise Institute Press, 2005).

not traded in markets.[97] And they point to the transparency gains of forcing decisions to be based on a rigorous analysis made available to the public.

An additional point is that, if costs to industry will inevitably be pressed by industry lobbyists (with or without BCA), then failing to quantify health and environmental benefits (by eschewing BCA) will actually lead to underprotection of those social values. If interest group politics favors concentrated industry groups over diffuse environmental beneficiaries, then BCA is more important to clarify the benefits than the costs. If risk reduction or other benefits are not quantified and compared via BCA, those benefits will be neglected in a political calculus that inevitably focuses on cost. To be sure, much costly environmental legislation has been enacted without quantification of benefits (or costs), but those laws may represent interest group deals more than a maximization of public net benefits.

And, fundamentally, advocates respond: if government does not use some version of comparing benefits and costs, then on what alternative basis will it make decisions? Critics of BCA often fail to explain an alternative method for making decisions.[98] Not comparing benefits and costs may simply lead to decisions which are less transparent, less subject to debate and correction, and more arbitrary and biased than is BCA, that is, to decisions which are driven by overreaction to crisis events,[99] underreaction to routine, systemic, or unseen concerns,[100] and raw political

[97] Eg Viscusi says: 'any regulatory benefit from a risk regulation or environmental regulation that should be legitimately recognized in the policy analysis process potentially can be quantified in monetary terms'. Viscusi, n 58 above.

[98] Some advocate setting standards 'as low as feasible', but a feasibility test would be insensitive to benefits, would regulate more profitable industries more tightly than less profitable industries (sending perverse signals and potentially conflicting with environmental justice concerns by protecting poorer communities less than richer communities), and would be less protective than BCA where BCA would warrant shutting down a noxious industry but the 'feasible' constraint would keep the industry in business.

[99] See Robert V Percival, 'Environmental Legislation and the Problem of Collective Action', (1998) 9 *Duke Envtl L & Pol'y F* 9; Thomas Birkland, *After Disaster: Agenda Setting, Public Policy, and Focusing Events* (Washington, DC: Georgetown University Press, 1997); Thomas Birkland, *Lessons of Disaster: Policy Change after Catastrophic Events* (Washington, DC: Georgetown University Press, 2006).

[100] See Cass R Sunstein, 'Cognition and Cost-Benefit Analysis' (2000)29 *Journal of Legal Studies*, reprinted in Mathew Adler and Eric Posner (eds), *Cost-Benefit Analysis* (Chicago: University of Chicago Press, 2001); Richard Posner, *Catastrophe: Risk and Response* (New York: Oxford University Press, 2004) (arguing that the public and government give inadequate attention to low-probability high-consequence risks of extreme events, but that on BCA criteria such risks should be addressed more aggressively); Jonathan B Wiener, Book review of Richard Posner, *Catastrophe: Risk and Response* (2004) and Jared Diamond, *Collapse: How Societies Choose to Fail or Succeed* (2005), in (2005) 24 *Journal of Policy Analysis & Management* 885–9; Cass R Sunstein, 'On the Divergent American Reactions to Terrorism and Climate Change', AEI-Brookings Joint Center for Regulatory Studies, Working Paper 06–13 (May 2006).

power (especially of concentrated industry groups) rather than analysis. The alternative to analysis may often be sanctimony—acting without analyzing, on the supposition that we 'know' the right answer—hastily choosing regulation or deregulation, green technologies or counterterror tactics, depending on who is in power.

In advising the European Commission on these questions, the Mandelkern Group Report rejected claims of bias:

> Some see RIAs as an excuse to impose a business-focused, deregulatory agenda on policy makers. For a RIA done well, this is absolutely not the case. Rather, as stated elsewhere, the RIA simply sets out the information in a clear and concise way to inform—not control—the political decision. This point needs to be stressed as appropriate and real efforts need to be made to ensure that both benefits and costs are included in the assessment.
>
> Another possible problem is the political pressure to do something—anything—now, irrespective of a proper assessment (sometimes known in its most extreme form as a 'knee-jerk reaction') .... development of a good RIA system is likely to reduce the incidence of this reaction as the need for good assessment becomes commonly understood and supported....
>
> A further situation can be where the main political decision has already been taken (perhaps in a government programme or party manifesto). In these cases there can be a reluctance to undertake assessment of the implementation options available. However, almost always details remain to be resolved where an assessment can play an important role in informing, in a very explicit manner, those taking the decisions on the details about the trade-offs that they are making. Finally, there is often the perception that doing RIA takes too much time and delays the policy development process to an unacceptable degree. However, when RIA is an integrated part of the process, any delays in the earlier stages are minimised and often outweighed by time and cost savings later in the process where the greater defensibility of the policy solutions and the increased buy-in by stakeholders are important.[101]

There is not the space here to sort out this entire debate. After briefly assessing the pros and cons of IA in this subsection, I suggest in the next subsection that Europe, committed as it already is to using IA in Better Regulation, should experiment with a set of institutional innovations which will test whether the criticisms can be overcome and whether IA can thus be made to perform even better than it has so far.

The criticisms of IA (especially using BCA) seem to me to be worth taking seriously, but not fatal to a sensible application of weighing the pros and cons of important decisions. There is no better alternative way of

[101] Mandelkern Group Report (2001) at 25.

making policy, and it has become the mainstream consensus approach. The criticisms should therefore motivate better policy analysis, not its rejection. The concerns about omission of important impacts, including countervailing risks and ancillary benefits, are crucial; as I suggest below, they warrant a broader more embracing form of BCA. The concern about delay is quite important, but delay is amenable to a weighing of its own pros and cons. The benefit of delay is that additional analysis can improve decisions (and defer policy burdens); the cost is that delay can forfeit the value of earlier policy adoption (eg earlier protection of victims, or earlier authorization of a useful invention). Weighing these conflicting effects is the task of Value of Information/Cost of Information (VOI/COI) techniques, one component of BCA. This idea is reflected in the European IA Guidelines' doctrine of 'proportionate analysis', and roughly in the difference between initial IA and Extended IA in Europe, as well as initial Environmental Assessments versus full Environmental Impact Statements under US NEPA law, and insignificant versus significant regulatory actions under OMB review. Note that the cost of delay cuts both ways: who bears its costs depends on the default rule in force while the analysis is pending. Regulatory impact assessment (RIA) may delay regulation of private actors, while environmental impact assessment (EIA) may delay projects sought by private actors. The delays posed by RIA themselves can cut both ways, depending on who bears the cost of the delay: if the law requires IA before adopting a regulation that would restrict a risky product or facility (as for many pollution controls), then delay favors industry and the cost is borne by victims; but if the law requires IA before licensing of a new product or site (as for new drugs or pesticides or energy facilities), then delay favors victims and the cost is borne by industry and consumers. The question is institutional rather than analytic. Moreover, as the Mandelkern group points out, a careful IA can resolve and avoid problems that would yield delay later on, so it can achieve less delay overall. In short, delay turns out to be a problem that calls for better BCA, not avoiding BCA.

Meanwhile, retrospective analyses of a variety of policies do not bear out the concern that BCA is biased toward overstating costs and understating benefits. *Ex post* evaluations of a growing set of cases (though not yet a representative sample) have found that *both* benefits and costs appear to have been overstated in *ex ante* RIAs.[102] Certainly specific cases

[102] See OMB, *Validating Regulatory Analysis: 2005 Report to Congress on the Costs and Benefits of Federal Regulations and Unfunded Mandates on State, Local, and Tribal Entities* (Washington, DC: US Office of Management and Budget, 2005), ch III, 41–9; Winston Harrington, Richard D. Morgenstern, and Peter Nelson, 'On the Accuracy of Regulatory Cost Estimates' (2000) 19 *Journal of Policy Analysis and Management* 297–332.

can be cited of BCA recommending less stringent regulation, but perhaps those recommendations were warranted. In several other key cases, RIA and BCA have been used to identify and promulgate some of the most important advances in more stringent environmental and health protection. These include the phaseout of CFCs, the phasedown of lead (Pb) in gasoline (petrol), and the restrictions on particulate matter emissions from power plants and diesel engines.[103] Indeed these are three policies on which the US, using BCA, adopted policies that were substantially more precautionary (earlier and more stringent) than Europe.[104] Critics contend that in the past BCA has more often been used to reduce than to increase the stringency of new regulations.[105] As I argue below, even if this is true, it is as much or more a result of the institutional posture of BCA as of the analytic methodology of BCA, and both of these can be ameliorated in the European program of Better Regulation.

Why might costs and benefits be over- or understated in *ex ante* BCA? Costs may be overstated *ex ante* if industry opposes regulation citing high cost estimates, and then once a rule is imposed, industry finds less costly means of complying than it thought or said it could (though at some expense of managerial time); and if the extent of implementation of the policy is predicted *ex ante* to be greater than it actually turns out to be. On the other hand, costs could be understated *ex ante* if they focus on a subset of costs such as industry compliance costs and neglect wider or longer-term effects such as foregone innovation.

Benefits may be understated *ex ante* if risk assessments focus on one risk at a time and omit multiple simultaneous exposures; if they neglect low-probability extreme events; if they neglect sensitive subpopulations; or if they omit ancillary benefits from unintended reductions in other risks.

[103] Ackerman *et al*, n 96 above , review the Lead Phasedown and argue that it does not show the success of BCA in supporting a more stringent policy on lead (Pb) in gasoline because the BCA came late in the story (in the 1980s), after several decades of the use of lead in gasoline (since the 1920s) and after a prior regulation to reduce lead in gasoline had been adopted in the 1970s without reliance on BCA. By contrast, Driesen, n 96 above, at 364, states that 'this case does seem to offer reasonably good evidence of CBA motivating an increase in stringency'. In addition, the conclusion to be drawn from the Ackerman *et al* critique is not that BCA did not support a more aggressive phaseout of lead in gasoline (it did), but that BCA should have been undertaken decades earlier. Ackerman *et al* say that BCA could not have been conducted earlier because the data on health effects of lead were lacking, yet they cite evidence of the longstanding scientific appreciation of the adverse health effects of lead exposure; and they neglect the endogenous character of benefits data: if BCA had been required or undertaken, evidence to quantify the benefits would have been sought and collected. The reduction in lead emissions due to the first regulation in the 1970s was not the only way to generate exposure and dose-response data, as Ackerman *et al* assert; variations across locations, and changes in exposure over prior decades, could also have been studied.

[104] See Wiener, n 14 above.

[105] See Driesen, n 96 above.

And benefits may be understated *ex ante* if monetized BCA omits or underestimates impacts that are difficult to measure in monetary terms. On the other hand, benefits may be overstated *ex ante* if the implementation of the policy is predicted to be greater than actually turns out to occur; if countervailing risks created by the policy are omitted; if the methods of valuation used to monetize environmental benefits (such as contingent valuation surveys regarding non-market assets such as ecosystems) tend to overstate benefits or if the risk assessments which underlie the calculation of policy benefits use conservative default assumptions and methods that tend to overstate risks and hence benefits (due to such factors as overstated linear no-threshold dose-response extrapolations, use of most sensitive test species, identifying any observed effect as adverse, making animal-to-human extrapolations without accounting for mechanistic differences ('modes of action'), using 'maximum exposed individual' exposure assumptions, and using large safety factors for extrapolation to human subpopulations).

The result is that risk assessment exhibits simultaneous excessive attention to some (small) risks, and inattention to other (larger) risks. To address many of these problems, US EPA has adopted new cancer risk assessment guidelines,[106] which require greater use of evidence before resorting to conservative default assumptions, greater attention to modes of action, and more attention to children and other susceptible sub-groups. And US OMB/OIRA has issued a proposed Bulletin on Risk Assessment in January 2006,[107] seeking to ensure greater transparency and realism, use of central estimates, and consistent criteria for identifying adverse effects. In addition, although few statutes specify the criteria for scientific risk assessment,[108] courts have begun to apply general statutory edicts to use the 'best available science' to require agencies to conduct high-quality risk assessments.[109]

[106] US Environmental Protection Agency (2005), Guidelines for Carcinogen Risk Assessment, EP/630/P-03/0001F <www.epa.gov/cancerguidelines>.

[107] US OMB, Proposed Bulletin on Risk Assessment, 9 January 2006, available at <www.whitehouse.gov/omb/inforeg/infopoltech.html#iq>. This initiative is endorsed in concept by Nicholas Bagley and Richard L Revesz, 'Centralized Oversight of the Regulatory State', AEI-Brookings Joint Center for Regulatory Studies, Related publication 06–12 (April 2006), at 44–53 (forthcoming in (2006) 106 *Columbia L Rev*, Section IV.A).

[108] See Kelsey Stansell, Mark Marvelli, and Jonathan B Wiener, ' "Adverse Effects" And Similar Terms In U.S. Law', Report for the Dose Response Specialty Group of the Society for Risk Analysis (SRA) (July 2005), available at <www.sra.org/drsg/docs/Adverse_Effects_Report.pdf>.

[109] Eg *Chlorine Chemistry Council v EPA*, 206 F 3d 1286 (DC Cir 2000) (vacating goal for maximum level of chloroform because agency set goal based on linear low-dose extrapolation when it had just found that a threshold model was superior). See also Leather Industries v EPA, 40 F 3d 392 (DC Cir 1994) (remanding standard for selenium content in sewage sludge because the exposure assumption—children eating sludge on highway median strips—was not credible).

To make Better Regulation effective, European institutions need to address these questions of risk assessment as well. So far, the approach of European institutions to risk assessment has been ad hoc or ill-defined. In the EU, the move toward quantitative risk assessment has been more recent than in the US (where it accelerated in the 1980s following the US Supreme Court's *Benzene* decision[110] and the 1983 publication of the National Academy of Sciences 'Redbook'.[111]) EU use of risk assessment has been driven in part by WTO decisions under the Agreement on Sanitary and Phytosanitary Standards (SPS), which requires a scientific risk assessment to support international trade restrictions.[112] The European Commission has espoused scientific risk assessment as a predicate to any invocation of the precautionary principle,[113] and the European Court of Justice held, in a case on mad cow disease (BSE) quite reminiscent of *Benzene*, that member state governments may not invoke precaution to regulate risks that the Commission has deemed insignificant.[114] Still, major risk regulations within the EU sometimes proceed without risk assessments, as in the recent *Pfizer* and *Alpharma* cases regarding antibiotics in animal feed,[115] in which the Court of First Instance held that a ban could be adopted without a risk assessment and even when the relevant scientific advisory committee had recommended against a ban or had not been consulted at all (despite a requirement for such consultation). The court ruled in the *Pfizer* case, paras 139 and 142–44:

> . . . a risk assessment cannot be required to provide the Community institutions with conclusive scientific evidence of the reality of the risk and the seriousness of the potential adverse effects were that risk to become a reality . . . . [But] a preventive measure cannot properly be based on a purely hypothetical approach to the risk, founded on mere conjecture which has not been scientifically verified . . . a

110 *Industrial Union Dept, AFL-CIO v American Petroleum Institute*, 448 US 607 (1980).

111 NAS/NRC, *Risk Assessment in the Federal Government: Managing the Process* (Washington, DC: National Academies Press, 1983).

112 See Steve Charnovitz, 'The Supervision of Health and Biosafety Regulation by World Trade Rules' (2000) 13 *Tulane Envtl LJ* 271.

113 Commission of the European Communities, Communication from the Commission on the Precautionary Principle, COM(2000) 1, Brussels, 2 February, 2000, available at <http://europa.eu.int/comm/dgs/health_consumer/library/pub/pub07_en.pdf>.

114 Case 1/00, *Commission of the European Communities v French Republic* (Failure of a Member State to fulfill its obligations—Refusal to end the ban on British beef and veal), 2001 ECR I-09989 (European Court of Justice, 2001).

115 Case T-13/99, *Pfizer Animal Health SA v Council*, 2002 WL 31337 (European Court of First Instance, 11 September 2002); Case T-70/99, *Alpharma Inc v Council*, 2002 WL 31338 (European Court of First Instance, 11 September 2002).

preventive measure may be taken only if the risk, although the reality and extent thereof have not been 'fully demonstrated by conclusive scientific evidence,' appears nevertheless to be adequately backed up by the scientific data available at the time when the measure was taken.

This statement is confusing. The court appears to misunderstand the purpose of a risk assessment, which is never to provide 'conclusive scientific evidence' (which does not exist) but rather to provide a forecast of (inevitably uncertain) future risks. The court holds that a 'purely hypothetical' risk or 'mere conjecture' is inadequate, but that a risk assessment is not required, and it remains unclear what the court means by its alternative of 'adequately backed up by the scientific data'—an invitation to further litigation. The Better Regulation initiative should resolve these confusions by requiring risk assessment (as called for in the European Commission's February 2000 Communication on the Precautionary Principle), setting criteria for risk assessments, and explaining that risk assessment is a method to forecast uncertain future scenarios.

Nor is incomplete information a reason to reject BCA. Information about future events is never complete or certain. Given uncertainty, some form of BCA seems superior to the alternative methods of decision-making. A raw political (non-analytic) choice of goals would be arbitrary or distorted by rent-seeking politics; even if well-intentioned, it may simply neglect important costs and benefits (especially to those who lack effective political voice) and thereby yield policy errors.[116] The Mandelkern Group advised that it is certainly sometimes the case that there is a

paucity of good quality data on benefits and costs, including the difficulty of estimating the value of non-marketed goods (e.g. environmental degradation or damage to human health). Whilst this will indeed affect the overall quality of the assessment—which can only be as good as the inputted data—it is not a sufficient argument for not carrying out any assessment at all. Use of error estimation and ranges (rather than single figures) for benefits and costs can help, as can the input from consultation with stakeholders and intelligent use of available data, consultants and academic expertise. Seeking input from a wide range of stakeholders can help avoid the kind of bias otherwise possible from vested interests.[117]

Likewise, the US Council on Environmental Quality (CEQ) guidelines for environmental IA under NEPA address uncertainty by requiring the

[116] See John D Graham and Jonathan B Wiener, *Risk vs. Risk: Tradeoffs in Protecting Health and the Environment* (Cambridge, Mass: Harvard University Press, 1995) (arguing that failure to analyze full impacts of policy choices often results in selective neglect of impacts on constituencies lacking effective political voice; thus, good impact assessment can advance both efficiency and equity).

[117] Mandelkern Group Report (2001), at 24.

agency to obtain additional information at reasonable cost, to describe the remaining uncertainties, and to make an express judgment about the importance of such questions for the impacts being assessed.[118] As noted above, in its IA Guidelines in 2005, the European Commission addressed this issue through the doctrine of 'proportionate analysis', requiring services of the Commission to invest in additional information where the benefits of doing so (in improved decisions) justify the costs.[119]

Institutional Innovations

Given its commitment to IA as the key tool for Better Regulation, Europe now faces the debate over the pros and cons of BCA, and, at the same time, an opportunity to make progress through institutional innovations. Many of the real problems with IA and BCA are institutional, not analytic. Economics is not fundamentally opposed to ecology: both words derive from the Greek *oikos* for household, and they should be able to cohabit graciously. The concern that the tools of IA and BCA are biased against environmental protection arises largely because of the institutional postures in which the tools are applied: too coldly, to 'just say no', and too narrowly. Making progress on these institutional biases by using BCA more 'warmly', using it to say 'yes' as well as no, and using it more widely, would make Better Regulation even better.

IA and BCA are tools, not rules. They are mechanisms to inform decision-making, not the decision itself. The decision itself is and must be an exercise of judgment by a public official. Policy must be based on and express that judgment, rather than be dictated by a cold numerical

[118] 40 CFR 1502.22 (promulgated at 51 Fed Reg 15625, 25 April 1986) ('(a) If the incomplete information relevant to reasonably foreseeable significant adverse impacts is essential to a reasoned choice among alternatives and the overall costs of obtaining it are not exorbitant, the agency shall include the information in the environmental impact statement. (b) If the information relevant to reasonably foreseeable significant adverse impacts cannot be obtained because the overall costs of obtaining it are exorbitant or the means to obtain it are not known, the agency shall include within the environmental impact statement: (1) A statement that such information is incomplete or unavailable; (2) a statement of the relevance of the incomplete or unavailable information to evaluating reasonably foreseeable significant adverse impacts on the human environment; (3) a summary of existing credible scientific evidence which is relevant to evaluating the reasonably foreseeable significant adverse impacts on the human environment, and (4) the agency's evaluation of such impacts based upon theoretical approaches or research methods generally accepted in the scientific community. For the purposes of this section, "reasonably foreseeable" includes impacts which have catastrophic consequences, even if their probability of occurrence is low, provided that the analysis of the impacts is supported by credible scientific evidence, is not based on pure conjecture, and is within the rule of reason.').

[119] IA Guidelines 2006, Part II, s 5, at 8.

calculus. At the same time, that public policy judgment will often be better made when it is informed by a careful structured comparison of consequences, whether that is termed an analysis of 'benefits and costs' or 'positive and negative impacts'. Simply choosing policy goals on unstated or raw political criteria would be arbitrary, invite partisan volatility, and lack transparency. At least some version of BCA offers a transparent opportunity to evaluate and debate the reasons given. The key should be this function of considering alternatives and consequences and giving reasons for decisions, rather than quantification *per se*.

Here I suggest several institutional innovations that Europe could pursue to make Better Regulation even better.

'Warm Analysis'

Given its determination to use IA and BCA, Europe should employ what I will call 'Warm Analysis'. Along a spectrum from 'hot' to 'cold', one can locate policy based on moral outrage at the hot end (imagine the crowd or the politician who reacts intensely, often to a recent crisis or scandal, expressing moralistic norms of sin, blame, and punishment, and giving little or no attention to, or even opposing, analysis of wider consequences), and one can locate policy based on strict monetized BCA at the end of cool or cold analysis (imagine the accountant wearing a green eye shade who counts statistics, manages only what is measured, and maximizes wealth dispassionately).[120] 'Warm analysis' would occupy the center of this spectrum, embodying serious analysis of the full variety of impacts and tradeoffs, some quantitative and some qualitative, with compassion for both those who incur risks and those who incur abatement costs. As I will argue here, warm analysis can be understood as the application of BCA to BCA—or optimal optimization—recognizing

[120] See Christopher H Schroeder, 'Cool Analysis Versus Moral Outrage in the Development of Federal Environmental Criminal Law', (1993) 35 *William and Mary Law Review* 251, 253–8. Schroeder limits 'cool analysis' to self-interested utility maximization in which risks are calculated as the 'thin' expected value of probability and harm. Two aspects that Schroeder puts under the heading of 'moral outrage'—the inclusion in an individual's utility function of effects on others and on society as a whole, and the recognition of 'thick' qualitative attributes of risk—do not seem to me to fit the notion of moral outrage, and would fit better under what I am calling 'warm analysis'. By contrast, moral outrage at the hot end of the spectrum is characterized by an intense and moralist or absolutist response focused on sin, blame, and prohibition, lacking (or even opposed to) analysis of consequences, tradeoffs, and proportionality. Schroeder describes the moral outrage felt by environmentalists who see pollution as a sin and compliance as an obligation; consider also the moral outrage felt after a terrorist attack and the call for a 'crusade' of 'shock and awe' to strike back. See Stern and Wiener, n 66 above.

that information and analysis are themselves costly (chiefly in delay) and that omitting important effects is itself a costly error of analysis. Sensible application of BCA requires applying it not only to regulatory policies but also to the analytic review process itself. Hot moral outrage neglects important impacts and tradeoffs, and is vulnerable to heuristic errors; cold analysis applies monetized BCA to policies but neglects the costs of delay and of omitting important but unquantified impacts. Warm analysis is thus more embracing than either hot or cold approaches, while remaining truer to the core principle of BCA.

The crucial task for good public policy is to think through decisions. It is therefore to engage in a structured consideration of the major alternatives and consequences, in order to inform sound judgment through reason. The crucial task is not just an accounting exercise, nor strict economic optimization, though economic tools can be helpful. That is the key reason that in EO 12866 we chose to use the term 'justify' in place of 'outweigh', and to expressly allow consideration of non-quantified impacts (while encouraging quantification). 'Warm analysis' compares pros and cons in a structured decision framework but without limiting the comparison to strictly quantified and monetized impacts.

This approach is the 'prudential algebra' recommended by Benjamin Franklin in 1772:

> In the Affair of so much Importance to you, wherein you ask my Advice, I cannot for want of sufficient Premises, advise you *what* to determine, but if you please I will tell you *how*. When those difficult Cases occur, they are difficult, chiefly because while we have them under Consideration, all the Reasons *pro* and *con* are not present to the Mind at the same time; but sometimes one Set present themselves, and at other times another, the first being out of Sight . . . . To get over this, my Way is, to divide half a Sheet of Paper by a Line into two Columns; writing over the one Pro, and over the other Con. Then during three or four Days Consideration, I put down under the different heads short Hints of the different Motives, that at different Times occur to me, *for* or *against* the Measure. When I have thus got them all together in one View, I endeavour to estimate their respective Weights . . . and thus proceeding I find at length where the Ballance lies . . . And, tho' the Weight of Reasons cannot be taken with the Precision of Algebraic Quantities, yet, when each is thus considered, separately and comparatively, and the whole lies before me, I think I can judge better, and am less liable to make a rash Step; and in fact I have found great Advantage from this kind of Equation, in what may be called *Moral or Prudential Algebra*.[121]

[121] Benjamin Franklin, 'Letter to Joseph Priestley', London, 19 September 1772, in *Benjamin Franklin: Representative Selections, with Introduction, Bibliography and Notes*, Frank Luther Mott and Chester E. Jorgenson (eds) (New York: American Book Company, 1936), 348–9.

Franklin describes a careful structured approach to ensuring that all the important consequences are 'on screen',[122] quantifying their weights as much as possible but not insisting on algebraic precision, and coming to a considered judgment about the best course of action. He emphasizes that errors—'rash Steps'—are principally due to omitting important reasons and not to quantifying each reason too little or too much. Similarly, John Maynard Keynes remarked that 'it is better to be roughly right than precisely wrong'.[123] Cass Sunstein has advocated BCA as a cognitive approach to informed decision-making rather than as a strictly numerical calculus of optimization,[124] and Amartya Sen has advocated broadening the types of impacts and valuations incorporated into BCA.[125] As quoted above, the Mandelkern Group urged the use of ranges rather than point estimates, to account for uncertainties in the forecasts of benefits and costs—an insight borne out in the *ex post* studies of BCAs.

Warm Analysis is not a rejection of BCA using quantified, monetized values. Indeed, BCA itself justifies the Warm Analysis approach. With limited resources to analyze decisions, there is some tradeoff between accuracy (getting the decision right) and precision (calculating exact numbers), which suggests that on standard BCA criteria, it would often do more to improve policy decisions to get the full set of consequences before the decision-maker (so that 'the whole lies before me', in Franklin's words) than it would to invest in precisely quantifying only a few of those consequences while neglecting others or unduly delaying the decision. This is akin to the question of how much analysis is optimal: more analysis yields fewer policy errors, but also incurs costs in money and time (delay), so one must compare the Value of Information (VOI) versus the Cost of Information (COI). Such a BCA of BCA, or meta-BCA, shows that it is better to assess the full consequences than to quantify precisely just a few. A Cold Analysis that quantifies some impacts but omits other recognized important impacts (or takes too long) is in effect assigning a weight of zero to those omitted impacts, which is a greater error than including them in a qualitative or partly quantified way.[126] If the cost

[122] See Howard Margolis, *Dealing with Risk* (Chicago: University of Chicago, Press 1996).

[123] Quoted in Alan Greenspan, Chairman of the Federal Reserve Board, 'Bias in the Consumer Price Index', Testimony before the Committee on the Budget, US House of Representatives, 4 March 1997, at <http://www.federalreserve.gov/Boarddocs/testimony/1997/19970304.htm>.

[124] See Sunstein, n 100 above.

[125] See Amartya Sen, 'The Discipline of Cost-Benefit Analysis', (2000) 29 *J Legal Stud* 931–52 (favoring BCA if it uses a broader set of values instead of only market valuations).

[126] Thus either inadequate comparison of benefits and costs (as espoused by critics of BCA) or excessive quantification of a few benefits and costs (as undertaken in some BCAs)

(including delay) of precisely quantifying all the impacts is lower than its benefits, then full quantification is warranted. And this meta-BCA suggests that, over time, as we find ways to quantify and monetize more impacts—to reduce the COI or increase the VOI—more exacting analysis would be warranted. Our methods of quantification and valuation are endogenous and should respond to the use of BCA, as qualified by meta-BCA, to become 'Warm Analysis' by improving our ability to make diverse impacts more understandable.[127]

While the academic debate over BCA often pits advocates of Cool Analysis against sharp critics who reject statistics and monetization without clearly identifying a preferred alternative decision-making method (implying a preference for populist moral outrage), the practical reality is that the approach to Warm Analysis that I am describing is already available, even required, under the major legal requirements for BCA. In the US, EO 12866 expressly requires analysis of both qualitative and quantitative factors, and calls on agencies to show that benefits 'justify' (not 'outweigh') the costs. OMB/OIRA Circular A-4 requires attention to unquantified as well as quantified impacts. CEQ guidelines on environmental IA require assessment of impacts despite incomplete information. In the EU, the IA Guidelines require analysis of 'all positive and negative impacts', with the

would threaten what Franklin called a 'rash step'. In a similar vein, the late Allen Kneese—an economist and advocate of using BCA in environmental policy—worried that overly precise BCAs may 'let method outrun content'. Kneese, n 63 above, at 60. Likewise, the joint statement by eleven noted economists advocating BCA was careful to say that BCA has an important role to play in helping inform regulatory decision-making, although it should not be the sole basis for such decision-making, that agencies 'should not be bound by strict benefit-cost tests', and that agencies should take into account uncertainties, ranges of estimates, unquantified impacts, and distributional impacts. See Arrow *et al*, n 93 above.

[127] I do not propose to leave everything 'blurry', as one critic of BCA has urged, see Lisa Heinzerling, 'Regulatory Costs of Mythic Proportions', (1999) 107 *Yale LJ* 1981, 2069. My point is that a comprehensive Warm Analysis offers greater clarity than either a Cold Analysis that omits important factors, or a non-BCA approach that omits important factors. Nor do I agree that a careful structured analysis of pros and cons lacking full quantification would be 'vacuous' (see Sunstein, n 100 above) or 'vapid' (see Driesen, n 96 above). The key point is to get the decision-maker to consider the full portfolio of important choices and consequences, see Margolis, n 122 above, Graham and Wiener, n 116 above. This approach avoids the 'false promise of determinacy' that critics fear in strictly quantified BCA, see Amy Sinden, 'Cass Sunstein's Cost-Benefit Lite: Economics for Liberals', (2004) 29 *Colum J Envtl L* 191, 194. At the same time, I am optimistic about the ability to improve methods of analysis over time to quantify more kinds of impacts (especially through investment in research and staff capacity, through greater demand for such analysis via initiatives such as Better Regulation, and through *ex post* evaluations to improve *ex ante* methods, as discussed below). For another effort to find a 'middle way between all or nothing analytically' that bears similarities to my version of 'warm analysis'—yet authored by a critic of quantitative analysis—see Richard Parker, 'The Empirical Roots of the Regulatory Reform Movement: A Critical Appraisal', (2006) 58 *Admin L Rev* 359, 394–5.

possibility of using formal BCA or C-EA where warranted.[128] (They do not, however, set a goal of 'maximizing net benefits', as the US orders do; the EU should consider adding this objective in its next updated IA Guidelines.) And the EU IA Guidelines call for 'Proportionate Analysis', to choose the degree of analysis warranted by the problem.[129]

A particular question, to which little space can be devoted here, is—given a decision to monetize valuations of impacts—what monetary estimates should be used for the values of health, life, and environmental impacts? Willingness-to-pay (or to accept) is a useful but imperfect proxy for utility, limited by ability to pay and variations in marginal utility of income, by market imperfections in mobility and information, and by heuristic misperceptions of risk.[130] There is a lively controversy over whether and how to adjust monetized values of the value of a life to account for the expected years of life lost when risks occur at different ages, or to account for different levels of income and associated demand for risk protection. Using a single value of a statistical life (VSL) for all premature deaths seems insensitive to the timing of the death occurring early or late in life, as well as insensitive to other attributes of the risk that people find more or less undesirable.[131] But devising schedules of

128 IA Guidelines 2005, updated 2006, at 39, Part III s 5.1 and n 45 and Annexes 12 and 13. As the EU moves from the hotter (less or non-)analytic side toward greater use of IA and BCA, it may need to do more to quantify impacts and compare options rigorously. One of the leaders of the Better Regulation effort recently remarked: 'I will also be following with great interest the external evaluation of our Impact Assessment system which will report next year and which should provide further input for improvements. Without prejudging the results of the assessment, I personally believe that a more rigorous quantification of the costs and benefits—economic, social and environmental—will be very important. Only if we can demonstrate through hard data that the benefits of what we propose outweigh the costs will we be fully convincing.' Günter Verheugen, Vice-President of the European Commission responsible for Enterprise and Industry, Better Regulation for Jobs and Growth, Former Members Dinner, European Parliament Former Members Association, Brussels, 10 May 2006, SPEECH/06/287, available at <http://ec.europa.eu/commission_barroso/verheugen/speeches/speeches_en.htm>.

129 IA Guidelines 2006, Part II, s 5, at 8. Similarly, 'The depth and scope of the assessment respects the principle of proportionate analysis, i.e. more Impact Assessment resources will be allocated to those proposals that can be expected to have the most significant impacts'. Communication of 16 March 2005, n 4 above, at 13. See also Renda, n 75 above, 92 (discussing the meanings of proportionality in regulatory standards and proportionate analysis in the IA process).

130 See Ezra J Mishan, *Cost-Benefit Analysis: An Informal Introduction* (London: Allen & Unwin, 1971; 4th edn, Routledge, 1994); Sunstein, n 100 above; Jonathan B Wiener, 'Risk in the Republic', (1997) 8 Duke Envtl Law & Policy F 1–21; Matthew D Adler and Eric A. Posner, 'Implementing Cost-Benefit Analysis when Preferences are Distorted', (2000) 29 J Legal Stud 1105, 1146.

131 See Cass R Sunstein, 'Valuing Life: A Plea for Disaggregation', (2004) 54 Duke LJ 385; George Tolley, Donald Kenkel, and Robert Fabian (eds), *Valuing Health for Policy: An Economic Approach* (Chicago: University of Chicago Press, 1994).

different VSL or value of a statistical life-year (VSLY) for different risks, populations, and ages is criticized as unfair and even as inconsistent with willingness to pay.[132] Here, I simply point out that the US and Europe are already using monetized VSL figures in regulatory IAs, but not the same figures: the US uses a range of figures clustered around $3 to $6 million per VSL saved,[133] whereas Europe is using numbers closer to $1.5 million.[134] This implies that the US puts greater value than does Europe on preventing health risks—an observation contrary to the conventional wisdom of greater European concern about such risks. Whether that difference is due to the income elasticity of demand for risk prevention, or to other factors,[135] it deserves greater attention—as does the fact that the US now

[132] Using the same VSL for all deaths appears to treat all victims alike, but it also values younger victims' remaining years of life at less per year than older victims' remaining years of life. On the other hand, using a simple VSLY (ie the VSL divided by years of average life expectancy at birth), which values each year the same regardless of age (and hence values younger victims more than older victims), is inconsistent with WTP if people put different values on different times of life, and in particular if they value the last few years of life (scarce time) more highly than earlier years. See W Kip Viscusi, 'Regulation of Health, Safety and Environmental Risks', NBER Working Paper 11934 (January 2006), at 46–49, available at <http://www.nber.org/papers/w11934> Laura J Lowenstein and Richard L Revesz, 'Anti-Regulation under the Guise of Rational Regulation: The Bush Administration's Approaches to Valuing Human Lives in Environmental Cost-Benefit Analyses', (2004) 34 *Environmental Law Reporter* 109–54. The Lowenstein and Revesz article criticizes OIRA for undervaluing older people, but in fact it was EPA during the Clinton administration that began doing so (based on studies in the UK and Canada) and it was OIRA in 2003 that instructed EPA and other agencies not to use a crude 'senior discount' nor a simple VSLY approach, see John D Graham, 'Memorandum on Benefit-Cost Analysis and Lifesaving Rules', 30 May 2003, available at <http://www.whitehouse.gov/omb/inforeg/pmc_benefit_cost_memo.pdf> (noting that saving ten years of life is more valuable than saving one year of life, but not ten times more valuable). Studies to date suggest that total VSL decreases in older age, but less than proportionately, so that VSLY is increasing in older age, although with little overall impact on benefits valuation, see Viscusi, n 58 above, at 14–17, 30–1.

[133] See Sunstein, n 131 above, table 1, at 396–8 ($1.5 to $6.5 million); Lisa Robinson, background paper for National Academy of Sciences/Institute of Medicine, Current Federal Agency Practices for Valuing the Impact of Regulations on Health and Safety (2004) ($1 m–$8 m).

[134] Presentation by Matti Vainio, DG Environment, European Commission, 'Impact Assessment of Thematic Strategy on Air Pollution', at the US–EU High Level Regulatory Cooperation Forum (25 January 2006), powerpoint slide 27. In November 2000 the European Commission had issued 'Recommended Interim Values for the Value of Preventing a Fatality in DG Environment Cost Benefit Analysis', at <http://europa.eu.int/comm/environment/enveco/others/recommended_interim_values.pdf> (from a workshop at <http://ec.europa.eu/environment/enveco/others/value_of_life.htm>), recommending that the VSL be 1 to 1.5 million euros, with a range from 0.65 to 2.5 million euros.

[135] On variation in the VSL across countries, see Sunstein, n 131 above, at 415; W Kip Viscusi and Joe Aldy, 'The Value of a Statistical Life: A Critical Review of Market Estimates throughout the World', (2003) 27 *J Risk & Uncertainty* 5.

uses discount rates of 7 and 3 percent (or even lower for long-term intergenerational effects), while the EU Guidelines require a discount rate of 4 percent.[136] These and other differences could serve as the point of departure for a wider comparative review of US and EU approaches to monetizing in BCA and to Cool versus Warm Analysis in general.

Using BCA to say 'Yes' as well as 'No'

The second institutional innovation Europe should pursue is to use RIA and BCA evenhandedly, not only to say 'No' to the Bad (ie reject or 'return' regulation proposed by agencies), but also to say 'Yes' to the Good (ie 'prompt' new regulation). This is especially apt in the EU, where the European Commission initiates legislation, so it could use BCA to identify the best new policies to pursue—even more directly than can the White House in the US system, because the US Presidency is so often reacting to Congressional legislation and to agencies' implementing regulations. But it is also highly important in the US, where RIA and BCA have traditionally been positioned as a one-way 'No' check by the Presidency on the tide of lawmaking by the Congress and concomitant regulating by the agencies. It is this institutional posture, more than any analytic bias, that puts BCA in the position cited by critics[137] of being used more often to restrain regulation than to promote it. That posture erodes the credibility of BCA; a more evenhanded posture is needed that uses BCA to maximize net benefits by *both* adding and subtracting regulations as warranted. There are good reasons to think that, even as some proposed regulations would yield benefits that do not justify their costs and should be revised or rejected, there are other regulations that agencies are not proposing that would increase net benefits—such as health and environmental regulations that would yield broadly diffuse benefits but concentrated costs.[138] To fill this institutional gap, in the last five years, OMB/OIRA has adopted the pathbreaking innovation of 'prompt letters' to urge agencies to consider adopting new regulations that look attractive on BCA criteria. Such evenhanded application of BCA would increase net benefits, while incidentally shoring up the credibility of BCA. The US should develop a more routine approach to identifying

[136] IA Guidelines 2006, Annex 12 (adding in footnote 45 that 'This rate broadly corresponds to the average real yield on longer-term government debt in the EU over a period since the early 1980s'.).

[137] Eg Driesen, n 96 above; Bagley and Revesz, n 107 above.

[138] This is indeed a standard prediction of public choice theory. See William N Eskridge, Jr, 'Politics without Romance: Implications of Public Choice Theory for Statutory Interpretation' (1988) 74 *Va L Rev* 275.

promising subjects for prompt letters, such as by issuing an annual request for proposed prompt letters (as a counterpart to OIRA's annual request for burden-reducing proposals), by assigning one or more OIRA staff to identify and develop prompt letters, and by including prompt letters more explicitly in the next revision of the Executive Order.[139] Europe, too, should also develop this kind of an evenhanded approach to IA and BCA.

Wider Application

Third, IA and BCA should be applied more widely, not just to health and environmental rules but also to other important policies, such as trade measures, forest management, projects such as dams and highways, and homeland security and counterterrorism. As discussed in detail above, BCA was initially applied to many of these topics, but no longer is, or is not adequately conducted. Broadening its application would, in many of these domains, position BCA institutionally on the side of health and environmental protection—and as a more powerful tool than environmental groups have often had in these arenas to date. Combined with the continued application of BCA to regulations, this broadened role for BCA would help achieve the more neutral posture to which it aspires, while also bringing more sensible policy results in each domain.[140]

BCA should be used not only to limit costs, but also to increase net benefits. That is the explicit instruction of EO 12866. Thus, if BCA indicates that a regulation should be made more stringent than proposed, that finding should be on the same footing as a BCA in another case indicating that less stringent regulation would be preferable. BCA should correct both over- and under-regulation. And BCA should be applied to deregulation as well as to new regulation.[141] There is no reason to assume in the abstract that every deregulatory move will reduce costs more than benefits; that question should be subject to BCA.

Applying BCA to legislation would be more straightforward in the EU (where the European Commission initiates legislation and is also committed to IA), than in the US (where Congress initiates legislation but is not committed to IA—unless the Congress itself would take seriously the proposals to establish a BCA process and review office, such as

[139] See Bagley and Revesz, n 107 above.

[140] See Robert W Hahn and Cass R Sunstein, 'A New Executive Order for Improving Federal Regulation? Deeper and Wider Cost-Benefit Analysis', (2002) 150 *U Pa L Rev* 1489, 1499 (advocating broader use of BCA to render it a more neutral tool).

[141] See OMB Circular A-4, n 55 above, at 1 (covering both regulation and deregulation).

in the General Accountability Office or the Congressional Budget Office, and listen to the analyses produced by that office).

Optimal Analysis

Fourth, the meta-BCA idea should be incorporated in an institutional mechanism. Where BCA remains highly contested, its application should be based on its own pros and cons (judged by the implementing agency, subject to executive branch review), rather than mandated or prohibited by law. In US law, EO 12866 and Circular A-4 already give some discretion to agencies to tailor the type of BCA or C-EA to the regulatory matter in question. Going further, Congress could enact a 'superauthorization' to authorize (but not mandate) agencies to use BCA or C-EA or other analytic techniques where optimal, notwithstanding prohibitions (or requirements) in existing individual laws.[142] In EU law, the European Commission should develop a regular system to animate its 'proportionate analysis' criterion through routine, considered selection of the optimal type and degree of analysis for each major policy initiative.

Multiple Risks

As it constructs its program of Impact Assessment, the EU can tackle a difficult but inescapable problem that risk regulators have not yet fully addressed: the phenomenon of multiple risks. Government agencies and scientists typically assess the risk of one chemical or technology at a time.[143] For the most part, agencies regulate one risk at a time.[144] Many individual risks have thereby been reduced. But increasing recognition of the interconnectedness among multiple risks poses new demands, including the need to forecast the joint effects of simultaneous exposure to multiple risks, and to analyze the full portfolio effects, including ancillary benefits (AB) and countervailing risks (CR), of any effort to reduce a target risk.

One reason for the single-risk approach is that the cost of information (COI) increases as the problem becomes more complex. Another is institutional fragmentation—dividing up problems into smaller pieces to be addressed by different government bodies—which is the logical result

[142] See Jonathan B Wiener, Testimony on Regulatory Reform Legislation before the Committee on Governmental Affairs, US Senate, 1995.

[143] International Life Sciences Institute (ILSI), *A Framework for Cumulative Risk Assessment*, ILSI Risk Science Institute Workshop Report 5 (1999), available at <http://rsi.ilsi.org/file/rsiframrpt.pdf> (visited 10 September 2003) ('Traditionally, these risk assessments have been conducted on individual chemicals medium by medium; however, humans are exposed to multiple chemicals by multiple routes concurrently in daily life').

[144] See J Clarence Davies and Jan Mazurek, Pollution Control in the United States: Evaluating the System (Washington, DC: RFF Press, 1999).

of special interest politics, legislators' credit-claiming, and specialization in governance. Such specialization can be desirable, and some degree of specialization is inevitable because a monolithic government entity could not handle all issues at once (and would raise other concerns about concentration of power). But fragmentation can also yield problems when issues are interconnected. Fragmentation into specialized agencies with narrow missions exacerbates the inattention to risk-risk tradeoffs, by causing spillover effects into the domains of other agencies (eg the EPA asbestos ban yielding weaker brake linings and hence increased highway accidents, or EPA limits on air toxics emissions yielding increased exposures to workers inside factories). Even within an agency's own domain, these tradeoffs can occur (eg NHTSA requiring higher fuel efficiency levels without assessing vehicle safety, or requiring airbags without assessing injuries to children; or the Iraq war plans addressing cost—albeit underestimated—but omitting the countervailing risks of collateral damage, blowback, theft, degraded combat readiness, and distraction from other threats). Actions by one government entity can impose spillover effects on others—'regulatory externalities'. Some version of coordination or integration is therefore needed.

The real world is one of interconnection and complexity, in which people and ecosystems are exposed to multiple risks at the same time. Naturalist John Muir famously remarked in 1869 that 'when we try to pick out anything by itself, we find it hitched to everything else in the universe'.[145] The modern science of ecotoxicology is moving to formalize that insight in models of simultaneous 'multiple stressors'.[146] Modern legal scholars see the same thing: 'It only takes a moment's reflection to see that multiple-risk situations are quite common'.[147] 'Most of today's environmental law violates basic principles of ecology. Nature teaches the connectedness of all activities, but most current-generation law regulates separate pollutants with little consideration of ecosystems as a whole.'[148]

[145] John Muir, *My First Summer in the Sierra* (San Francisco: Sierra Club Books, 1988), 110 (journal entry for 27 July 1869).

[146] See Nico M Van Straalen, 'Ecotoxicology Becomes Stress Ecology' (1 September 2003) *Envtl Sci & Tech* 325A; JA Foran and SA Ferenc (eds), *Multiple Stressors in Ecological Risk and Impact Assessment* (Pensacola, Fla: Society of Environmental Toxicology and Chemistry (SETAC) Press, 1999); SA Ferenc and JA Foran (eds), *Multiple Stressors in Ecological Risk and Impact Assessment: Approach to Risk Estimation* (Pensacola, Fla: SETAC Press, 2000).

[147] Mark Grady, Book Review, 'Discontinuities and Information Burdens', reviewing William Landes and Richard Posner, *The Economic Structure of Tort Law* (1987), 56 *Geo Wash L Rev* 658, 664 (1988).

[148] E Donald Elliot, 'Toward Ecological Law and Policy', in Marion R Chertow and Daniel C Esty, (eds)., *Thinking Ecologically* (New Haven: Yale University Press, 1997).

The multirisk world poses challenges for risk assessment. First, risk assessors should develop the means to forecast the joint effects of simultaneous exposure to multiple risks. The joint effect may be synergistic (supralinear), linear (additive), or offsetting (subtractive), but the key point is that it is the joint effect rather than the sum of the individual effects that must be forecast. Second, increasing interconnections may accelerate the transmission of risks (such as disease or terrorism) across countries and continents, through increasingly dense networks among ecological, trade, travel, and telecommunications systems (including the internet). Risk assessment needs to account for these propagation vectors. Third, rather than simply forecasting single variables (such as exposure to a chemical), risk assessors need to develop multiple scenarios incorporating the mix of multiple variables affecting risk, weighted by probability judgments and sensitivity analyses.[149] US OMB Circular A-4 (September 2003) now requires a formal probabilistic portfolio of scenarios for policies with impacts exceeding $1 billion.

The multirisk world also challenges risk management. In theory, BCA embraces all effects. But in practice, BCA is often limited to looking only at the reduction in the target risk (TR) versus the increase in industry compliance cost. The problem is that risk-risk tradeoffs—the phenomenon that efforts to reduce a target risk may induce new countervailing risks[150]—are thereby ignored. The focus on TR omits countervailing and ancillary effects. And the focus on industry compliance cost favors options in which the cost of shifting from a restricted product or activity to a new substitute is low; but these substitutes can pose their own countervailing risks.

The solution is a full portfolio analysis (to 'treat the whole patient' rather than focusing on one risk or symptom at a time) that applies BCA more broadly, to maximize overall risk reduction (including countervailing risks (CR) and ancillary benefits (AB), as well as target risk (TR) reductions) less overall social costs (c, including administrative costs, compliance costs, and foregone innovation).[151] Thus risk-risk tradeoff

[149] Kahn and Wiener, n 23 above; de Jouvenel, n 23 above; Stephen Schneider, 'Can We Estimate the likelihood of Climatic Changes at 2100? An Editorial Comment', (2002) 52 *Climatic Change* 441–51 (criticizing single-scenario forecasts and calling for probability-weighted portfolios of scenarios).

[150] See Graham and Wiener, n 116 above.

[151] A short version is: $\max(\Delta TR - \Delta CR + \Delta AB - C)$. See Jonathan B Wiener, 'Managing the Iatrogenic Risks of Risk Management', (1998) 9 *Risk: Health Safety Environment* 39–82. Equal attention to ancillary benefits (as well as countervailing risks) is urged by Samuel J Rascoff and Richard L Revesz, 'The Biases of Risk Tradeoff Analysis: Towards Parity in Regulatory Policy' (2002) 69 *U Chi L Rev* 1763. I agree, as we stated expressly in Grahan and Wiener above n 116, at 2, 37, 232. Indeed several of the examples of ABs offered by Rascoff and Revesz are the same examples we cited in ibid. No normative bias was intended; the goal should be an evaluation of the full portfolio of consequences.

analysis needs to be made an explicit part of BCA (or conducted on its own where BCA is prohibited or otherwise not used). Even opponents of BCA agree that these risk-risk tradeoffs deserve analysis.[152]

EO 12866 expressly requires consideration of adverse health and environmental impacts in section 6. OMB/OIRA's Circular A-4 (2003) contains narrative instructions to perform risk-risk tradeoff analysis, although the table it attaches as a scorecard to guide agency calculations does not contain a line on which risk-risk impacts (countervailing or ancillary effects) are to be entered.[153]

The EU IA Guidelines simply say: 'Identify (direct and indirect) environmental, economic and social impacts and how they occur'.[154] They should pay closer attention to countervailing risks and ancillary benefits, because these factors are so often neglected in the IA process.

The phenomenon of multiple risks underscores the need for Integrated Impacts Assessment—not different IA requirements segmented into particular topics. In the US the RIA is an integrated IA, but there are also specialized IAs on environment, federalism, takings, small business, children, and others. OMB Circular A-4 encourages agencies to combine these into one document. In the EU there is one Integrated IA on economic, social, and environmental impacts (but there is also talk of creating a special IA on

[152] Thomas O McGarity, 'A Cost-Benefit State' (1998) 50 *Admin L Rev* 7, 40–2 ('There is a grain of truth in the proposition that single-minded regulation of some health and safety risks can increase others. For example, when the Consumer Product Safety Commission promulgated a flammability standard for children's sleepwear, some manufacturers responded by treating the sleepwear with the chemical TRIS, which was later found to be carcinogenic. Health and safety agencies should take care not to create more risks than they eliminate. To the extent feasible, agencies should address ancillary risks that flow in a direct causal sequence from the conduct required or induced by their regulations. [Internal footnote: All of the risk-risk tradeoffs described in the case studies of the recent book, *Risk Versus Risk: Tradeoffs in Protecting Health and the Environment*, are of this variety]. Agencies should also coordinate regulatory initiatives with other agencies to ensure that one agency's regulation does not unduly increase risks within another agency's domain.')

[153] Other approaches do not achieve this full portfolio analysis. For example, 'income-risk' ('health-health') analysis translates costs into risk units by estimating the amount of household income reduction (due to regulatory cost) associated with a death (due to reduced household expenditures on health). This in effect 'riskizes' costs, instead of the standard practice of 'monetizing' health risks, to achieve a common numeraire; but it does not address the risk-risk phenomena of CR or AB, which are additional effects apart from regulatory costs. 'Precaution' typically looks only at ΔTR and ignores CR and C (although the European Commission's Communication calls for attention to C). A focus on 'Administrative Costs' ('red tape') is only a subset of C, and reducing Administrative Costs could increase social costs, for example if a good BCA would necessitate some administrative costs, or if requiring industry to do more paperwork for information disclosure would save lives.

[154] IA Guidelines 2006, at 26.

competitiveness). The Commission's Communication of 16 March 2005 (at 13) remarks:

> Impact Assessment system was introduced to integrate and replace all previous single-sector assessments, as un-integrated analyses had been found to have little effect on the quality of policy-making. It requires the Commission to systematically assess, on an equal basis, the likely economic (including competitiveness), environmental and social implications of its proposals and to highlight the potential trade-offs. This new impact assessment system aims at helping the Commission to improve the quality and transparency of its proposals and to identify balanced solutions consistent with Community policy objectives.

Beyond risk-risk analysis in policy development, there should be networks of notification across agencies of cross-domain side effects. In the US, EPA now notifies OSHA when air toxics regulations may induce employers to stop exterior emissions by sealing the factory, thereby trapping toxics inside the workplace. But this was agreed only after OSHA complained, and there is still no government-wide process for such notifications across all agencies. The EU has a process of 'Interservice Consultation',[155] but it is not yet clear whether it will address the problem of cross-domain regulatory externality, or act as a more general invitation to comment on others' proposals.

At the legislative level, a key move is toward methods of Integrated Pollution Control.[156] In the 1990s, the United Kingdom made significant efforts to adopt IPC, in its 1990 and 1995 Environmental Protection Acts and its creation of an integrated pollution control agency.[157] The EU and other countries have considered borrowing the IPC.[158] In the US, this

[155] IA Guidelines, updated 15 March 2006, Part II, s 7, at 9–12.

[156] Lakshman Guruswamy, 'The Case for Integrated Pollution Control' (Autumn 1991) 54 *Law & Contemp Probs* 41; Nigel Haigh and Irene Erwin (eds), *Integrated Pollution Control* (Washington, DC: The Conservation Foundation and the Institute for European Environmental Policy, 1990).

[157] Richard Macrory, 'Integrated Prevention and Pollution Control: The UK Experience' in C Backes and G Betlem (eds), *Integrated Pollution Prevention and Control* (The Hague: Kluwer International, 1991) 53–64; Albert Weale, 'Environmental Regulation and Administrative Reform in Britain' in Giandomenico Majone (ed). *Regulating Europe* (London: Rountledge, 1996) 106; Michael Purdue, 'Integrated Pollution Control in the Environmental Protection Act 1990: A Coming of Age of Environmental Law?' (1991) 54 *Mod L Rev* 534; Neil Carter and Philip Lowe, 'The Establishment of a Cross-Sector Environment Agency' in T Gray (ed), *UK Environmental Policy in the 1990s* (New York: St Martin's Press,1995) 38.

[158] See Chris Backes and Gerrit Betlem (eds), *Integrated Pollution Prevention and Control: The EC Directive from a Comparative Legal and Economic Perspective* (The Hague: Kluwer Law International, 1999); Johannes Zöttl, 'Towards Integrated Protection of the Environment in Germany?' (2000) 12 *J Envtl L* 281.

may require statutory changes to enable, for example, EPA's program offices for air, water, and waste to develop joint multimedia regulations, or several agencies to collaborate. Ultimately, the numerous narrowly targeted statutes could be combined into a Comprehensive Environment (or Risk) Act that integrates regulatory standards and instruments while ensuring attention to multiple risks.

The EU concept of 'Interservice Steering Groups' is also promising.[159] Similarly, the US White House often fosters interagency collaboration. Interagency teams assembled to deal with shared or spillover problems connect the matrix by linking horizontally across the set of vertically isolated government silos.

More aggressively, one could pursue structural integration. This could include merger of related agencies, to internalize cross-domain regulatory externalities. For example, in the United States, EPA (Environmental Protection Agency) and OSHA (Occupational Safety and Health Administration) might be merged, or those two might be combined into a new Risk Department along with others such as the CPSC (Consumer Product Safety Commission), NHTSA (National Highway Traffic Safety Administration), the aviation safety branch of FAA (Federal Aviation Authority) (now partly of TSA, the Transportation Security Administration), and the food safety branch of the FDA. Land and resource management agencies such as the Forest Service, National Park Service, BLM (Bureau of Land Management), FWS (Fish and Wildlife Service), and NMFS (National Marine Fisheries Service) could also be merged into an integrated resource conservation agency. In the EU, one can imagine combining DG (Directorates General) such as DG Environment and DG SANCO (Health and Consumer Affairs). But all these mergers would only be worthwhile if they improved decision-making on complex multirisk problems. They would yield little if the statutory authority to regulate were not also revised, or if the cultures of the pre-existing units remained so balkanized that they continued to regulate without regard for their effects on each other. Merged agencies may continue to operate with fragmented internal structures (as EPA's different program offices are fragmented despite the integrationist agenda for

[159] IA Guidelines, updated 15 March 2006, Part II, s 6, at 9 ('An Inter-Service Steering Group is compulsory for all items of a cross-cutting nature. The Roadmap asks DGs to provide valid justification in those instances when no Inter-Service Steering Group is envisaged. These groups are there to provide specialised inputs and to bring a wider perspective to the process. Involving other DGs from the early stages will also make it easier to reach agreement during the Inter-Service Consultation').

founding EPA). The recent merger of several US agencies into the new Department of Homeland Security offers an opportunity to study and learn from a mega-merger of risk regulatory agencies. In addition to the concern that mergers may mean greater centralization of power, there is also the concern that more centralized management could be more rigid even as a multirisk world demands more agile and creative policymaking. All things considered, merger of agencies seems not as urgent as inculcating a multirisk approach in each agency.

Finally, the White House and the European Commission could each create a Primary Risk Manager to help coordinate risk regulation across the government.[160] Like a primary care physician who monitors the whole patient but refers more serious ailments to specialists, the primary risk manager would dispatch specific problems to expert agencies while supervising and monitoring the whole. The primary risk manager could help coordinate responses to multiple simultaneous risks, and ensure attention to ancillary effects that cross agency jurisdictions. It could also ensure within-agency consideration of ancillary effects.

One point here is that Better Regulation of multiple interconnected risks can imply the need for more, not less regulation—for more comprehensive regulation to avoid perverse shifts (induced regulatory externalities). That is, when narrow regulation creates countervailing risks, rather than regulate the target risk less, the optimal strategy may be to adopt more embracing regulation that internalizes both the market externality (target risk) and the regulatory externality (countervailing risk). Such comprehensive approaches can also be less costly than the sum of separate regulations for each risk. For example, if regulating CO_2 alone induces perverse shifts to emissions of methane (CH_4) that increase net global warming, the optimal solution might be to regulate both in a comprehensive multigas approach—both more protective and less costly.[161]

Administrative Simplification

The leading phalanx of Better Regulation in European member states is currently the campaign to reduce administrative costs and adopt simplification measures. For example, the Netherlands developed the standard

[160] Graham and Wiener, n 116 above ch 11.

[161] See Jonathan B Wiener, 'Protecting the Global Environment' in ibid, ch 10; Richard B Stewart and Jonathan B Wiener, *Reconstructing Climate Policy* (Washington, DC: AEI Press, 2003).

cost model to measure administrative costs, the UK is cutting red tape, the Merkel government in Germany is scaling back bureaucracy, and France hosted a June 2006 conference on administrative simplification. The EU has programs on administrative cost reduction and simplification. The OECD has developed a red tape scoreboard and is conducting a pilot exercise in the road freight transport sector.

Administrative costs are the costs of furnishing information and of processing government functions. Reducing administrative costs can be pursued both *ex ante* (in review of proposed new regulations and information requirements) and *ex post* (to reduce the costs of existing programs). 'Simplification' entails combining, codifying, or repealing old laws, in order to make them easier to understand, to reduce the complexity of bureaucratic steps the public must navigate, and to remove obsolete provisions.

Administrative cost reduction and simplification can be highly desirable, especially in legal systems encumbered with outdated and uncodified rules and a labyrinth of bureaucracy. But administrative cost reduction and simplification pursued narrowly could be counterproductive. They need to be evaluated in terms of their full social costs and benefits.

Administrative Costs

Reducing administrative costs can be one important way to remove barriers to business activities, facilitate new business startups, and diminish the hassles and intrusions faced by individuals. In Europe, the standard cost model (SCM) is being applied to measure and reduce paperwork burdens and time consumption due to information demands imposed on businesses and individuals by regulation. The Netherlands pioneered the SCM in 2002, and there is now an SCM Network involving at least nine EU member states.[162] Further, European governments are setting political targets, such as a 20 or 25 percent reduction in administrative costs from a base level estimated by the SCM inventory.[163] European member states face both national (member state) and EU administrative

[162] See the SCM Network website at <http://www.administrative-burdens.com/>. A brief discussion of progress to date is in European Commission, Communication from the Commission on an EU common methodology for assessing administrative costs imposed by legislation, SEC(2005)1329, COM(2005) 518 final (Brussels, 21 October 2005), at 4.

[163] See examples at the SCM Network website, n 162 above. For example, on 27 April 2006, Austria set a target of reducing administrative costs by 25 percent by 2010 using the SCM, see <http://www.administrative-burdens.com/default.asp?page=1&article=69>.

requirements, but reducing the latter may increase the former.[164] The European Commission has developed a common methodology for measuring administrative burden[165] and is undertaking a pilot project to measure administrative costs in industry sectors (initially construction, with others to be added next year) across Europe. In May 2006, European Commission Vice President Günter Verheugen announced the EU's own 25 percent target to reduce administrative costs, to be achieved in partnership with the member states' own cost reduction programs.[166]

In the US, the Paperwork Reduction Acts of 1980 and 1995, and OMB Circular A-130,[167] established the objective and methods of cutting administrative costs. OMB measures the time spent by businesses

[164] The Commission pointed out: 'Administrative obligations should therefore not be presented as mere "red tape", a term normally reserved for needlessly time-consuming, excessively complicated or useless procedures. Nor should EU administrative obligations be presented as a mere cost factor, as it often replaces 25 different national legislations and thus decreases operating costs at EU level'. European Commission, Communication from the Commission on an EU common methodology for assessing administrative costs imposed by legislation, SEC(2005)1329, COM(2005) 518 final (Brussels, 21 October 2005), at 2 (footnote omitted).

[165] See IA Guidelines 2006, Annex 10 (on administrative cost measurement); European Commission, Communication from the Commission on an EU common methodology for assessing administrative costs imposed by legislation, SEC(2005)1329, COM(2005) 518 final (Brussels, 21 October 2005).

[166] He said: 'I believe that we should give particular attention to the administrative costs of regulation since these costs can be cut without affecting the objectives of the legislation itself. They are the proverbial "low hanging fruit" of our Better Regulation agenda. And they are the major irritants European citizens and businesses are confronted with in their daily lives. Crucially, work done by several Member States, notably the Netherlands, suggests that both these costs and the potential for reducing them are very significant. If these estimates are correct, Europe is spending more than 2.5% of its GDP—or some 275 billion euros every year—on reporting requirements and other administrative obligations linked to our regulatory system. Moreover, these costs fall disproportionally on small and medium sized enterprises—the job engine of the European economy. This is patently absurd at a time that we are putting competitiveness at the heart of our policy agenda. I am, therefore, of the opinion that we should look at cutting these costs by 25% and I will take a proposal to the Commission suggesting how this objective can be achieved. To lay the foundations for this proposal, I have instructed my services to launch the necessary studies, which will provide a baseline against which we can measure administrative costs, as soon as possible. . . . There will . . . have to be a shared responsibility for reaching the 25% objective. I am optimistic that we can achieve this partnership since 17 Member States have already announced administrative cost reduction measures in their Lisbon National Reform Programmes. Through the newly created High Level Group on Better Regulation we are working closely with experts from all the Member States to prepare this ambitious project'. Günter Verheugen, Vice President of the European Commission responsible for Enterprise and Industry, Better Regulation for Jobs and Growth, Former Members Dinner, European Parliament Former Members Association, Brussels, 10 May 2006, SPEECH/06/287, available at <http://ec.europa.eu/commission_barroso/verheugen/speeches/speeches_en.htm>.

[167] 44 USC s 35; OMB Circular A-130, Management of Federal Information Resources, at <http://www.whitehouse.gov/omb/circulars/a130/a130trans4.html>.

and individuals in filling out each form, works to reduce that time, and requires new surveys and other information-gathering projects to receive OIRA approval. But OIRA has gone beyond that task—as directed by EOs 12291 and 12866—to assess the full social costs and benefits of policies.

Better Regulation should address administrative costs, but should not focus solely or predominantly on administrative costs. 'Cutting red tape' is popular, but does not assess the full costs or benefits of a policy. The political targets of 20 or 25 percent reductions in administrative costs are like Procrustes' insistence that guests be cropped to fit his bed: these targets arbitrarily crop information-based programs without considering the benefits of such information collection or the other costs that might increase if information collection is curtailed. Even granting that administrative costs are too high in many countries, the 20 or 25 percent reduction targets have not been based on an analysis of the optimal reduction in such costs. In some countries or sectors the optimal reduction in administrative costs might be greater than 25 percent; in others it might be less than a 20 percent reduction, or even an increase in administrative costs if gathering new information would yield net benefits.

Focusing exclusively on cutting administrative costs could be perverse. It could forfeit the large social benefits of some information disclosure programs, such as the US Toxics Release Inventory[168] and similar European pollutant discharge registries.[169] Cutting administrative costs could be accomplished by swiftly adopting highly precautionary regulations, based on little information or analysis, that impose high social costs in foregone innovation. Administrative costs could also be cut by eschewing the information demands of BCA and proceeding to adopt regulations that impose lower administrative costs but greater social costs.[170]

[168] See James T Hamilton, *Regulation through Revelation: The Origin, Politics and Impacts of the Toxics Release Inventory Program* (Cambridge: Cambridge University Press, 2005).

[169] See Peter H Sand, 'Information Disclosure' (2003) 63 *Heidelberg Journal of International Law* (*Zeitschrift für ausländisches öffentliches Recht und Völkerrecht*) 487–502 (revised as Peter H Sand, 'Information Disclosure and the Atlantic Divide' in Jonathan B Wiener *et al* (eds), *The Reality of Precaution: Comparing Risk Regulation in the United States and Europe* (forthcoming 2006)).

[170] Consider these four hypothetical policies and their associated costs and benefits:

> Policy A: Admin cost 10, Full cost 13, Benefit 20. Net Benefit = 7.
> Policy B: Admin cost 7, Full cost 10, Benefit 19. Net Benefit = 9.
> Policy C: Admin cost 4, Full cost 7, Benefit 12. Net Benefit = 5.
> Policy D: Admin cost 2, Full cost 16, Benefit 10. Net Benefit = −6.

To reduce administrative costs alone, one would prefer option D. To reduce full costs alone: prefer C. To maximize benefits alone: prefer A. To maximize net benefits: prefer B.

Vice President Verheugen's remarks (just quoted) express optimism that administrative costs 'can be cut without affecting the objectives of the legislation itself', but in many cases administrative costs support valuable information collection efforts that are necessary for policies to yield benefits or reduce other costs. The 20 or 25 percent targets to reduce administrative costs do not appear to take these benefits and other savings into account.

To reduce administrative costs while avoiding these potentially counterproductive results, rather than simply setting targets to cut administrative costs alone, European Union institutions and member states should use IA and BCA to assess the full social costs and benefits of policy changes to reduce administrative costs. This point was recently recognized by the European Commission: On 15 March 2006 the Commission inserted a warning to this effect, as a new 'Box 11' in the updated version of the IA Guidelines. Box 11 now reads:

> The fact that one option would impose lower administrative costs is *not* in itself a sufficient reason to prefer it. For example, a measure . . . likely to impose relatively fewer administrative costs [by mandating specific technical standards, instead of requiring labels that disclose product data] . . . could give manufacturers less flexibility and could reduce consumer choice, [so that] its overall costs may be higher than the 'administrative' requirement to display data . . . [171]

This Box 11 was not present in the June 2005 IA Guidelines. Its addition in the updated 2006 Guidelines indicates that the Commission is responding to the zeal for cutting red tape and tempering that zeal with attention to full costs.[172] The Commission should now go further to add explicit consideration of benefits as well as costs, and should address this issue in the member states as well.

Simplification

The EU and several member states have also embarked on ambitious programs of simplification. In October 2005 the European Commission announced 'a three year programme to simplify the existing thousands of pages of EU legislation ("acquis") adopted since 1957', including a

[171] See EU IA Guidelines 2006, Part III, s 5.1, at 39, Box 11.

[172] As the Commission remarked, 'Regulatory costs, of which administrative obligations are just one element, must be analysed in a broad context, encompassing the economic, social and environmental costs and benefits of regulation'. European Commission, Communication from the Commission on an EU common methodology for assessing administrative costs imposed by legislation, SEC(2005)1329, COM(2005) 518 final (Brussels, 21 October 2005), at 3.

proposal 'to repeal, codify, recast or modify 222 basic legislations and over 1,400 related legal acts in the next three years' and 'to tackle administrative burden, especially for small business, by simplifying cumbersome statistics form-filling or by modernizing the customs code to facilitate electronic exchange of information'.[173] The Communication issued to launch this policy outlined each of these strategies (repeal, codify, recast, modify), as well as efforts to make greater use of information technology, to use performance standards instead of technical design standards, and to replace some EU 'directives' (which call on member states to transpose their instructions into national law—akin to 'cooperative federalism' in the US) with EU 'regulations' (which are effective throughout the EU without such transposition—akin to federal pre-emption in the US), in order to achieve more uniform and hence simpler rules across the European single market.[174]

The best understanding of simplification is that it attempts to modernize a body of law by editing, pruning, organizing, and streamlining the laws so that they are more clear, understandable, and effective as well as less burdensome to navigate. It may well be that legal rules in some countries in Europe (and in the US) are so labyrinthine that businesses and individuals must incur high costs just to figure out what the law means. Simplification in the EU is thus reminiscent of the codification movement in the US led by David Dudley Field in the mid-1800s, and the effort in the last several decades in some US states and the federal government to write laws in plain understandable language. This was one of the goals of the Clinton–Gore 'National Performance Review' and the Presidential Memorandum of 1 June 1998. As simplification moves beyond consolidation and codification to undertake the repeal of obsolete or superfluous laws, it is also expressing the view that venerable vintage is not a sufficient reason to preserve a law—perhaps best crystallized by US Supreme Court Justice Oliver Wendell Holmes, Jr:

'It is revolting to have no better reason for a rule of law than that so it was laid down in the time of Henry IV. It is still more revolting if the grounds upon which

[173] See DG Enterprise and Industry, 'Better Regulation—Simplification', 25 October 2005, posted at <http://ec.europa.eu/enterprise/regulation/better_regulation/simplification.htm>.

[174] European Commission, Communication of the Commission to the European Parliament, the Council, the European Economic and Social Committee and the Committee of the Regions, 'Implementing the Community Lisbon Programme: A Strategy for the Simplification of the Regulatory Environment', COM(2005) 535 final (Brussels, 25 October 2005), available at <http://ec.europa.eu/enterprise/regulation/better_regulation/simplification.htm>.

it was laid down have vanished long since, and the rule simply persists from blind imitation of the past'.[175]

But in the EU simplification effort there is also an unmistakable bent of, if not deregulation, then selective excision of obsolete laws. The French example is telling: after laws enacted in 2003 and 2004 to reduce costs to businesses and individuals, France is now considering enactment in 2006 of the 'loi anti-loi'—the so-called 'anti-law law' or 'killer law', which can be used to abrogate outdated or meaningless laws. Belgium has a 'Kafka test' to identify maddening bureaucratic puzzles. These may be a good idea—casual observation and a series of World Bank studies[176] both hint at the possibility that some European law could use some tidying up, flexibility, and codification (rather than the opaque system of citation by date of enactment)—but success depends on the *criteria* for determining which laws to rescind or revise or reorganize, and who has the power to make these decisions. At a meeting on Administrative Simplification in Paris on 9 June 2006, I asked what these criteria might be, and the response was that laws that 'have been in disuse for a long time' ('*en désuétude*') would be deemed obsolete and slated for repeal. This standard is too vague, inviting biased selective enforcement. And it neglects the possibility that while some old laws are indeed obsolete, others may be dormant because they are widely accepted and rarely violated, but the act of repealing them signals open season to transgress the old norm in undesirable ways.

The Mandelkern Group emphasized that simplification does not mean simplistic deregulation:

> The Group's concept of simplification is not to be mistaken with deregulation. The two concepts cannot be regarded as synonyms. Deregulation simply refers to the abolition of rules in a certain sector, whereas simplification—a more

[175] Oliver Wendell Holmes, Jr, 'The Path of the Law' (1897) 10 *Harv L Rev* 457, 469. Holmes was referring to common law rules, which judges can change. Statutes enacted by the legislature may be more difficult for judges to reform and may deserve reform programs or phaseout schedules to enable periodic review and revision or repeal. See Guido Calabresi, *A Common Law for the Age of Statutes* (Cambridge, Mass: Harvard University Press, 1983).

[176] World Bank, 'Doing Business in 2006: Creating Jobs' (2006), 'Doing Business in 2005: Removing Obstacles to Growth' (2005), and 'Doing Business in 2004: Understanding Regulation' (2004), all available at <http://www.doingbusiness.org/>. In the 2006 report, in the summary ranking on 'Ease of Doing Business', France ranked 44th and Italy 70th, while Denmark, the UK, and Ireland were eighth, ninth, and eleventh. The top three spots in both 2006 and 2005 were held by New Zealand, Singapore, and the USA. These reports focus on economic (price and entry) regulation, not on risk (health, safety and environmental) regulation. There can also be debates about the methodologies used to compile the rankings.

> advanced stage in governing regulation—is aimed at preserving the existence of rules in a certain sector, while making them more effective, less burdensome, and easier to understand and to comply with.... Therefore, by simplification we refer to the process of reform of existing regulation, which seeks to streamline administrative procedures and to reduce the burden of compliance on citizens, businesses and the public sector itself, while preserving the intended (political) goals of the regulation.[177]

But sometimes the original intended goals of the legislation also become obsolete. Changes in economics, technology, and social values may well call for repeal or replacement of old laws. The key, again, is the criteria for such choices. Standing alone, the simplification initiative lacks clear criteria for identifying and modifying laws.

Instead, I suggest applying IA and BCA to decide on the rescission or revision of existing laws. IA and BCA should be used to evaluate existing regulations as well as new regulations, and to evaluate deregulation and simplification as well as new regulatory proposals. Such evenhandedness would reduce the current new/old bias in regulatory review. It would also correct the bias toward cutting regulatory costs or repealing old laws without considering benefits. Some existing laws and regulations should be phased out, and others strengthened, depending on new information and learning, but this process should be guided by sensible analysis rather than only by political impulses. More blunt approaches—such as predetermined 'sunset' dates at which regulations automatically expire, or political targets to cut administrative costs by a certain percentage, or deregulation without BCA, or simplification programs to rescind laws on the ground that they have not been used recently—are crudely effective but arbitrary; they neglect the benefits of existing policies and administrative requirements (including costly policies that generate worthwhile benefits, and laws that have not been used recently because compliance is universal as long as the law is in effect). Applying BCA criteria to the review of existing policies would be better: it would put the focus on benefits as well as costs, and it would enable net benefits to be maximized by strengthening, revising, weakening, or eliminating these policies, as the merits warrant.[178]

[177] Mandelkern Group Report (2001), n 2 above, at 33.

[178] The Commission appears to be heading in this direction: 'Simplification is not merely an exercise in improving accessibility and readability. It is intended to operate within the Competitiveness policy and for this reason a reinvigorated simplification programme, to be launched in 2006/7, will reinforce the mechanisms for identifying legislation that requires simplification; namely legislation which careful assessment shows to be disproportionately burdensome for EU citizens and businesses in relation to the public

One promising tack for simplification programs would be to rescind perverse subsidies.[179] Governments spend billions of taxpayer dollars (and euros) on subsidizing agriculture, energy, mining, water use, logging, and many other industries. Such policies often endure long after their initial usefulness has ebbed, yet continue to support activities that are both environmentally harmful and economically wasteful. They are resilient in part because they are supported by concentrated beneficiary constituencies, and impose diffuse costs on the general tax-paying public who face free-rider incentives not to complain. To surmount these rent-seeking pressures in favor of subsidies, the EU and the US could consider setting up non-political commissions to identify subsidies for rescission (based on BCA), with the recommendations to take effect unless the relevant legislature acts to preserve them. Transitions to systems of support payments that are not tied to output could be added to assist dependent communities to wean themselves off subsidies. This approach would be similar to the US military base closure commission. And it would use the power of simplification under Better Regulation to address a problem of enormous domestic and international concern. Such a 'subsidy-closing commission' could not only save costs and the environment in the US and EU, but also benefit farmers in poor countries, and make progress in the stalemate over international trade liberalization.

Oversight

All of this analysis and reform will not make Better Regulation succeed if it does not influence policy decisions. Impact assessment can change minds, but it can also become merely cosmetic—a 'relookage' as they say in France—if there is no oversight mechanism to ensure that the analysis is taken into account in decisions. Some mechanism to check, review, and shape legislation is needed in the EU institutions.

In the US, environmental impact assessment under NEPA has persistently faced the criticism that agencies do the EIA, but merely attach it to

interests that the legislation aims to safeguard. . . . It is only when the assessment of proportionality clearly confirms that public interests might be equally well served by simpler means that the repeal or modification of the legislation should be considered'. DG Enterprise and Industry, 'Better Regulation—Simplification', 25 October 2005, posted at <http://ec.europa.eu/enterprise/regulation/better_regulation/simplification.htm>.

[179] See Norman Myers and Jennifer Kent, *Perverse Subsidies* (Washington, DC: Island Press, 2001); Barton Thompson, n 92 above (suggesting rescission of perverse subsidies in order to protect biodiversity).

the decision they would have made anyway. This is despite the availability of judicial review of NEPA law, including the courts' power to issue injunctions halting projects. One reason is that judicial review is infrequent enough to be a weak deterrent. Another is that NEPA has been held by the US Supreme Court to be 'purely procedural', a 'stop and think' law, requiring agencies to assess environmental impacts but not imposing substantive criteria or constraints on the ultimate decision.[180]

By contrast, RIA is sometimes criticized as overly influential, binding agencies too much as they seek to satisfy OIRA's criteria for BCA; and yet sometimes criticized as inadequately influential, because only about half of agency RIAs monetize the benefits and costs. Still, OIRA's own data show that net benefits have increased over time in response to the RIA and BCA requirements.[181] Yet there is no judicial review of RIAs (although courts can and do take note of RIAs in their decisions under other laws, such as the 'arbitrary and capricious' standard of the Administrative Procedure Act). The reason for even the partial success of the RIA process is undoubtedly the role of OIRA in reviewing the RIAs and returning proposed rules when the criteria are not met. OIRA is more successful at supervising RIA than the courts are at supervising EIA because judicial review is decentralized and non-expert, whereas centralized executive branch oversight is expert and potent while helping to obviate judicial oversight.[182]

In the EU, at least at the European Commission, the Better Regulation initiative is still in search of an oversight mechanism. The Mandelkern Group Report suggested several options, including central, lateral, interinstitutional, and external models.[183] The crucial criterion

[180] See *Strycker's Bay Neighborhood Council v Karlen*, n 64 above. Others have, to be sure, criticized NEPA and judicial review of the EIS for delaying federal projects. See Holder, n 67 above. One study found that NEPA impact analyses usually imposed low costs of delay and did influence agencies to consider and avoid environmental impacts. Serge Taylor, *Making Bureaucvacies Think: The EIS Strategy of Administrative Reform* (Stanford, Calif: Stanford University Press, 1984).

[181] See OMBOIRA Annual Report, 2005 n 102 above.

[182] Justice Breyer's suggestion in *Breaking the Vicious Circle* (1993), n 25 above, was an elite expert group that could manage the risk regulation system to avoid the distortions of interest group politics and heuristic errors. He cited the French Conseil d'Etat as a potential model. Some criticized this proposal as unduly technocratic and insulated from democratic input. That same year, President Clinton issued EO 12866, maintaining OIRA authority over regulation while expanding its transparency and public accountability.

[183] The Mandelkern Group Report (2001), at 50, considered several options: 'There are five main best practice options for effective structures, of which the first is recommended by OECD guidelines:

— A primary unit based at or near the centre of the administration, with or without a network of satellite units across the main Ministries or Directorates-General;

is an effective ability to influence decisions. As the Mandelkern Group wrote:

'[T]he issue of appropriate **structures** is an absolutely **crucial topic**. The success of efforts on better regulation will ultimately depend on this very issue .... Based on the experience in various administrations there are four main elements that seem to be essential for the chosen structure to be effective:

— **Strong political support**. Better regulation programmes need very strong political support to produce the desired outcome;
— **Support from the centre**. The best results are often achieved with the Head of Government personally and/or at least institutionally interested and involved;
— **A horizontal approach**. Very clearly, an all-government approach is necessary; sectoral approaches limited to individual Ministries or Directorates-General will not achieve optimum results and a coherent, horizontal approach is needed; and
— **A strategic approach**. Close connection to the strategic planning of the government/administration is of real benefit.'[184]

This body/structure must, by virtue of its qualified staff with a range of expertise, its specific position in the administration, its recognised authority and its expertise in managing regulatory quality tools, be able to ensure adherence to the process that contributes towards improving regulatory quality. At the same time this body/structure must have an appropriate level of autonomy, as well as objectiveness with regard to the policy officials who prepare regulations .... the body/structure might also be given a gate-keeping function.'[185]

Yet despite this advice from 2001, and the US model in place since at least 1981, the European Commission appears still to be searching in 2006 for the best way to handle the oversight question. Constructing an oversight mechanism is a work in progress. Vice President Verheugen recently declared:

I will be campaigning for three major new initiatives: First, President Barroso and I will significantly strengthen central oversight in the Commission to police the

— A primary unit based in a part of the administration other than the centre (e.g. Public Administration or Economic Affairs Ministry), probably with a network of satellite units;
— An inter-ministerial co-ordination committee;
— A network of units/responsibilities across the main Ministries or Directorates-General, with or without support from a primary unit; and
— A body external to the administration (a body of such type may especially be apt to be integrated into the evaluation of the consequences of already existing regulation)'.

[184] Mandelkern Group Report (2001), at 47–8 (emphasis in original).
[185] Ibid at 49.

quality of our Impact Assessment. While the Impact Assessments must be carried out by the services responsible for the development of the proposals, we must also ensure that they are rigorously scrutinised by an 'independent party' within the Commission but with no involvement in the preparation of the file. This is why as a first step, we are creating a standing committee of senior officials who will be tasked with ensuring that the Impact Assessments are in full conformity with the exacting requirements we have set ourselves. These officials should report directly to the President and myself. In this way we can strengthen the system of checks and balances in the Commission.[186]

Where this independent review will be located is still an open question. Within the European Commission, the office of the Secretariat General has the authority to perform this function, but does not yet have the expert staff to review IAs, and has not yet issued an 'avis negatif' based on an IA. Perhaps it will soon bolster its capacity. Other options for a central oversight body include the Bureau of European Policy Advisors attached to the Presidency; a new Presidential office; or a shared group of DGs or an interinstitutional body linking several units such as DG Enterprise, DG EcoFin, DG Environment, DG SANCO, the Legal Service, and others with expert staff.

But none of these has yet been adopted at the EU level.[187] The structure of power in the Commission to some extent inhibits a strong central role, because the President of the Commission is not popularly elected and remains one member of the College of Commissioners, all of whom are appointed at the same time and are expected to work together. Moreover, the objective of the European Union is in substantial part to prevent conflicts among the countries of Europe, and as a result the collegial and courteous style of work within the Commission seems, at least to an outsider accustomed to the tough debates within the White House 'family', to be unreceptive to the sharp and hierarchical confrontations over policies that central regulatory oversight might entail. The question is whether a Commission could decide collegially to establish an oversight office with real power, an office that would sometimes oppose the position of one or another individual Commissioner, or whether instead such a reform must await more radical governance reform such as the advent of a popularly elected European President who could install such an office.

[186] Günter Verheugen, Vice-President of the European Commission responsible for Enterprise and Industry, Better Regulation for Jobs and Growth, Former Members Dinner, European Parliament Former Members Association, Brussels, 10 May 2006, SPEECH/06/287, available at <http://ec.europa.eu/commission_barroso/verheugen/speeches/speeches_en.htm>.

[187] Several have been tried at the member state level. See Hahn and Litan, n 18 above. The UK has a central expert body in its Better Regulation Executive. Finland assigns the

Meanwhile, filling the open niche, DG Enterprise has developed substantial staff expertise and appears to be acting, in effect, as the 'lateral' oversight arm. If so, this is progress, but it is not yet the ideal. Lateral oversight offers staff capacity, but typically lacks the power to enforce supervisory decisions on other co-equal units. And lateral oversight lacks the perspective and legitimacy of central oversight. Even if DG Enterprise does a very fine job, its lateral posture will yield the appearance (if not the reality) of factionalized or parochial review, if it appears to represent the interests of business rather than of full social impacts, in turn raising questions about its credibility and hence its sustainability.[188] The review function (including staff with expertise) should thus be relocated to the center, that is, to the Presidency of the Commission. DG Enterprise could continue its review activities in support of this central office, or the current review team at DG Enterprise could (along with others) be promoted to become the staff of the central office.[189]

This central oversight office should not be just a referee, nor simply a check on regulation percolating up from the DGs. That is too reactive a posture. The central oversight office should be closely attached to the Presidency of the Commission and should carry out the President's strategy for regulatory policy (such as Better Regulation using IA).[190] Of course the Commission President could lead this initiative along with one of the Vice Presidents (just as the US Executive Orders originally designated the Vice President to oversee OMB/OIRA, a role now transferred to the White House Chief of Staff by EO 13258). In addition to waiting

oversight role to its Trade Ministry, and Hungary to its Justice Ministry. Recently, France shifted its Better Regulation office from the office of Réforme de l'Etat, attached to the Prime Minister, to the Ministry of Finance, Economy and Industry. Although this creates a lateral review rather than a central office, its objective was to combine regulatory review with fiscal budgetary review in the Finance Ministry and thereby to add effective teeth to the review function.

188 Radaelli, n 27 above, at 940, argues that 'credibility is the Achilles heel of impact assessment. [If] RIA is tilted towards one actor's preferences to the detriment of others, there is no economic analysis that can compensate for the credibility deficit'.

189 I emphasize that I am not criticizing the individuals at DG Enterprise, nor the quality of their work; they are filling a niche left open and a role that the Better Regulation initiative demands be filled, and by all accounts are doing so quite ably. The point here is about institutional structure.

190 See Kagan, n 17 above, ('We live today in an era of Presidential administration . . . presidential control of administration, in critical respects, expanded dramatically during the Clinton years, making the regulatory activity of the executive branch agencies more and more an extension of the President's own policy and political agenda'); James F Blumstein, 'Regulatory Review by the Executive Office of the President' (2001) 51 *Duke LJ* 851. For doubts whether the Presidential agenda and expert BCA can fully coexist in regulatory review, see Stuart Shapiro, 'Politics and Regulatory Policy Analysis', (summer 2006) *Regulation* magazine 40–5.

for regulatory proposals to arrive from the DGs for review, the central oversight office should play an early role in shaping the regulatory priorities of the Commission, working with DGs to identify subjects warranting regulation, to improve their policy proposals, to reconcile tradeoffs, and to ensure best practices across DGs. It should issue 'prompt' letters to stimulate new regulation that its expert analysis deems desirable, and 'return' letters (or *avis negatifs*) to reject regulations where the analysis is inadequate.

In the EU system the Commission initiates new legislation, so IA within the Commission is important, especially at a central oversight office that can reconcile competing interests across the DGs. Otherwise the lead DG may simply carry the day, or there may be horse trading among DGs (among Commissioners) in which each gets its priority initiatives adopted but none is truly assessed for overall net benefit to the EU.

> 'Complicated regulation arises in large part from current practice of the Commission, by which regulation is drafted primarily by more than 20 Directorates-General, with an imperfect degree of co-ordination among them. This does not optimise collegiate action and often forsakes the benefits that could be gained by a more deliberative form of decision-making. On this crucial topic, it has been widely observed that different DGs draw up draft directives in themselves perfectly compatible with the objectives and administrative culture of a particular DG, but compatibility with general EU interests is weakly ensured.'[191]

Central oversight of the IA process in the Commission would thus be important to ensure that EU-wide net benefits are considered in important regulatory policies.

Even if the Commission does establish centralized review, there may also be a need for an external check on the Commission because of the Commission's monopoly on initiating legislation. This external check could be situated in the Council, the Parliament, or an Interinstitutional body.

The Council is currently ill-suited to this task because the Council members who meet on a particular matter, although ostensibly representing each member state's prime minister or government, in fact tend to be the ministers from the single ministry concerned with the specific issue of the legislation (eg all the Environment ministers), and therefore tend to support the legislation. 'At the European level, even if the proposals have to come from the Commission, which, operating in collegiate fashion, seeks to weigh the various demands and interests, the competent

[191] Mandelkern Group Report (2001), at 64.

Council is composed of just the sectoral ministers, who are in charge of the final decision. This asymmetry leads to a systematic tendency towards the growth of regulation.'[192] The Council's role in IA could be strengthened if the member states insisted on a full consideration of impacts before deciding on instructions for their delegates to the Council, and, furthermore, if the member states conducted their own IAs. There is now talk of member state parliaments doing so in order to assess EU directives before they are adopted and must be transposed into member state law. The Council's role in EU-level Better Regulation could be best supported if the member states created a network or pool of member state experts (drawn from each member state's own central regulatory oversight office)—the Council's own 'regulatory analysis review group', to borrow the title of President Carter's interagency body—available to conduct IAs for the Council and to deliberate together on regulatory proposals. The Commission's Communication of 16 March 2005, at 10, announces a 'group of high-level national regulatory experts', although this group may or may not be in a position to advise the Council.

Apart from the Council, external oversight would be left to the European Courts or the European Parliament. The Courts are not equipped with the staff or expertise to perform IA, and they tend to defer to the Commission and the Council (as in the *Pfizer* case discussed above). But if the other EU institutions do not effectively oversee regulatory policy, the courts may step in. The European Parliament, meanwhile, has the motivation to check legislative initiatives coming from the Commission, but so far does not have the political clout. In the US, the adoption of the Congressional Review Act in 1996 authorized a special procedure for Congress to reject an agency regulation (a power Congress always had via legislation, so long as the President did not veto the law or Congress could override the veto), but Congress did not create an expert body to conduct IA, so exercise of the CRA remains an essentially political act. And it remains rare—of almost 42,000 rules including 610 major rules promulgated in the last ten years, the Congressional Review Act has only been used to reject one: the ergonomics rule rescinded in March 2001.[193] Adding an expert body equipped to perform IA in the US Congress and in the European Parliament (as a counterpart to IA by the

[192] Mandelkern Group Report (2001), at 64.

[193] Statement of Morton Rosenberg, Congressional Research Service, before the House Subcommittee on Commercial and Administrative Law, Committee on the Judiciary, Concerning Oversight of the Congressional Review Act on the Tenth Anniversary of its Enactment, 30 March 2006, <http://judiciary.house.gov/media/pdfs/rosenberg033006.pdf>, at 3.

White House and the Commission) could raise the Parliament's stature and enable it to engage actively in reasoned debate over regulatory policy (to reject, revise, or prompt policies, as the net benefits warrant). In the US, such a body could also, perhaps even more importantly, enable IA of legislative proposals in Congress, which currently are not subject to IA. But if no such expert IA body is created, then Congressional or Parliamentary review of regulatory policy could be seriously dysfunctional: driven by the vicissitudes of political winds and caprice, unrelated to societal net benefits, it could mark a return to horse trading among parties and parochialisms that would harm rather than help yield Better Regulation.

In sum, a central oversight office is needed in the EU regulatory system, but the unique features of EU governance imply that 'centralized' could be within the Commission (overseeing the DGs), at the Council (with support from the member states), at the Parliament, or in a new interinstitutional body. This oversight office needs the capacity to conduct excellent analysis, embracing the broad set of topics outlined above, with skills not only in economics but in other fields as well, including the science underlying benefits estimates and risk assessments. It needs the power to influence decisions: to say no (return), yes (prompt), or revise. It needs to follow clear procedures of transparency, posting its meetings and decisions for public view, to avoid the appearance of backroom deals.[194] And it needs the expertise not only to evaluate regulatory proposals and IAs, but also to assist the DGs with their policy development and analyses:

> Education as to the usefulness of the tool in assisting the policy process is vital—policy officials need to see what is 'in it for them' in using the system. But there must also be a credible deterrent element—if the process is not completed properly (timing and quality), the progress of the policy can be delayed, halted completely or challenged subsequently.[195]

At present, the most likely candidate for such a central oversight office is within the Commission, either in the Secretariat General or in a new body attached to the Presidency (and a Vice President). The Commission's Competitiveness Council might play this role, if it were equipped with an expert staff and if it took a full-portfolio view of overall impacts rather than focusing only on competitiveness. But over time the creation of oversight mechanisms in the Council and the Parliament could supplement and check the Commission's oversight role. A new interinstitutional body

[194] This was a key improvement made in EO 12866 in 1993, and redoubled by OIRA after 2000 when it posted all its activities on a public website at <www.omb.gov>.

[195] Mandelkern Group Report (2001), at 24.

remains the least well-defined option; it would be the most 'central' but perhaps the least potent. Failing all these options, the courts may begin to take a tougher role in reviewing EU regulatory policies.

Ex Post Evaluation and Adaptive Management

Do policies actually work? With what results? This question is often neglected, perhaps because agencies have scarce resources which they prefer to devote to new initiatives. Most wealthy countries currently conduct some kind of *ex ante* assessment through IA, but few conduct *ex post* review. In the US, EO 12866 requires *ex ante* review of major rules but does not require *ex post* evaluation.

One reason to conduct *ex post* evaluation is to improve policies over time based on the updated information about effectiveness, benefits, costs, and unintended countervailing or ancillary effects.[196] The use of performance monitoring data to revise policies is often called 'adaptive management'. A second reason to conduct *ex post* evaluations is to determine how accurate the *ex ante* RIA estimates were, and to validate and improve the *ex ante* methodologies for subsequent decision-making. As noted above, initial retrospective studies by OMB and by Harrington *et al*,[197] while not representative samples, find both over- and underestimates in the *ex ante* analyses.[198]

[196] Charles Herrick and Daniel Sarewitz, 'Ex Post Evaluation: A More Effective Role for Scientific Assessments in Environmental Policy', (2000) 25 *Science, Technology, and Human Values* 309–31.

[197] See OMB, n 102 above; Harrington *et al*, n 102 above. An early call for such evaluations was W Kip Viscusi, *Risk by Choice: Regulating Health and Safety in the Workplace* (Cambridge, Mass: Harvard University Press 1983), 162–3 (criticizing the absence of *ex post* evaluation of cost estimates, and urging creation of a staff group to conduct these analyses).

[198] *Ex post* evaluations face methodological challenges. See James K Hammitt, 'Risk Assessment and Economic Evaluation', ch 112 in William N. Rom (ed), *Environmental and Occupational Medicine* (4th edn) (Philadelphia: Lippincott-Raven, 2006), 33–6 (noting that 'retrospective values are also estimates because, although one can observe some of the consequences once the rule is implemented, one cannot observe what the consequences would be if the rule had not been adopted and so the counterfactual situation must be estimated. In addition, the health benefits of a regulation may remain quite uncertain in cases where the individuals suffering the health effects due to the agent that is regulated may not be identifiable'). One should not draw the conclusion from *ex post* evaluations that *ex ante* predictions can always be easily improved. *Ex post* evaluations may yield 'hindsight bias'—the misimpression that outcomes were more easily predicted *ex ante* when in fact they were difficult to predict *ex ante*. Terrorist attacks and corporate fraud may look predictable in hindsight when *ex ante* clues are turned up, but those *ex ante* clues may have been buried among many other clues pointing in other directions. See Scott A. Hawkins and Reid

As it implements Better Regulation, the EU and its member states should take the opportunity to build in regular *ex post* evaluations of policies and of *ex ante* IAs. In the future, *ex post* evaluation exercises should address a representative sample of past IAs rather than a convenience sample. They should quantify the degree of error rather than just whether the *ex ante* IA over- or underestimated. They should address countervailing risks and ancillary benefits (both those forecast *ex ante* and those observed *ex post*). Eventually, *ex post* evaluations should be undertaken as a routine matter for every major rulemaking, both to improve *ex ante* methods and to revise policies through adaptive management.

Some observers urge more *ex post* evaluation and adaptive revision, and less reliance on *ex ante* evaluation via BCA.[199] But why not do both? One cannot just do *ex post* analysis alone—because one needs some way to choose which policies to adopt at first, and then review later. One still needs some sensible criteria for initial choices.[200]

The adaptive management aspect of *ex post* review corresponds to the 'provisional' character of precautionary regulation, meant to be updated as science evolves. But this still leaves open the question of who will conduct the additional research and who will apply that research to *ex post* policy evaluation and revision. JB Ruhl worries that 'decisionmakers need to be in a position to adjust decisions based on reliable monitoring feedback [and] in a manner that is transparent and accountable [and] subject to some objective boundaries', but in practice this gets bogged down by interest groups and judicial review; it 'cannot flourish . . . in the conventional [US] administrative law context', so we need 'new institutions . . . that allow agencies to use adaptive management while ensuring adequate agency accountability'.[201] *Ex post* review using BCA could serve this role.

Hastie, 'Hindsight: Biased Judgments of Past Events after the Outcomes are Known', (1990) 107 *Psychol Bull* 311, 312; Mitu Gulati, Jeffrey J Rachlinski, and Donald C Langevoort, 'Fraud by Hindsight', (2004) 98 *Northwestern University Law Review* 773.

[199] Sidney A Shapiro and Robert L Glicksman, *Risk Regulation at Risk: Restoring a Pragmatic Approach* (Stanford, Calif: Stanford University Press, 2003).

[200] Cf Ackerman *et al*, n 96 above (arguing that BCA mistakenly skews decisions against environmental protection, as illustrated by the authors' *ex post* reconstructions of *ex ante* BCA rejecting selected past decisions that they contend were good). But on what criteria do they determine that the initial decisions were good? If *ex post* BCA shows that the decisions were good but *ex ante* BCA would not have done so, this is the kind of *ex post* review that can be used to improve the methods of *ex ante* BCA. A more complete sample would also include cases where BCA did favor adoption of the policy *ex ante* but would not *ex post*, and cases where BCA would have favored adoption of the policy *ex ante* but was not used and hence the policy was not adopted.

[201] See J B Ruhl, 'Regulation by Adaptive Management—Is it Possible?' (2005) 7 *Minn J Law, Sci & Tech* 21, 53–5.

And perhaps Europe, with a less ossified system of judicial review, could do better at this task than the US.

Such *ex post* evaluation should also apply to the choice among regulatory instruments. There is ample theory on the different costs and effectiveness of technology standards, emissions trading, taxes, information disclosure instruments, environmental contracts, and other instrument options. But there is insufficient empirical evidence on how these tools operate in practice. *Ex post* evaluation of these interventions could go a long way to improving future policy choices.[202]

The move toward regular *ex post* evaluations of regulations has been slow, but recent activity is promising. US EPA only began to conduct *ex post* evaluations in the late 1990s,[203] including a major retrospective study of the Clean Air Act required by Congress.[204] US OMB/OIRA is now beginning to conduct *ex post* evaluations of agency RIAs, as noted above.[205] The OECD held a meeting on *ex post* evaluations in

[202] One recent effort is Winston Harrington, Richard Morgenstern, and Thomas Sterner (eds), *Choosing Environmental Policy* (Washington, DC: RFF Press, 2004), collecting *ex post* studies of the impacts of technology-based and incentive-based environmental policies in the US and Europe.

[203] According to a GAO report, of the more than 100 major rules issued by EPA from 1981 to 1998, only five were subject to *ex post* evaluations, with all of those five reviews occurring after 1997. GAO, 'Environmental Protection: Assessing the Impacts of EPA's Regulations through Retrospective Studies', GAO/RCED-99–250 (September 1999). GAO concluded: 'While EPA devotes substantial resources to cost-benefit analyses when developing new regulations, the agency seldom looks back at the actual costs and benefits after those regulations have been implemented'. Ibid at 13. GAO recommended that EPA develop a plan for systematic *ex post* evaluations, ibid at 14. See also Thomas O McGarity and Ruth Ruttenberg, 'Counting the Cost of Health, Safety, and Environmental Regulation' (2002) 80 *Tex L Rev* 1997 (criticizing *ex ante* cost estimates and the lack of *ex post* evaluation).

[204] US EPA, 'The Benefits and Costs of the Clean Air Act, 1970–1990, Section 812 Retrospective Study' (October 1997).

[205] OMB, n 102 above. Scholars' *ex post* evaluations of BCA include Harrington *et al*, n 102 above; James K Hammitt, 'Are the Costs of Proposed Environmental Regulations Overestimated? Evidence from the CFC Phaseout' (2000) 16 *Envtl & Resource Econ* 281–301; P W Kolp and W Kip Viscusi, 'Uncertainty in Risk Analysis: A Retrospective Assessment of the OSHA Cotton Dust Standard' (1986) 4 *Advances in Applied Microeconomics* 105–30. For more general reviews of OIRA's influence on regulatory policy (as opposed to *ex post* validation of BCAs), see eg OMB/OIRA Annual Report 2005, n 102 above (finding that OIRA *ex ante* reviews have yielded rules promising substantial net benefits); Steven Croley, 'White House Review of Agency Rulemaking: An Empirical Investigation' (2003) 70 *U Chicago Law Review* 821 (finding that OIRA has had a discernible and beneficial influence on rules, with little evidence of bias); Hahn and Muething, n 60 above (finding fully monetized BCA in about half of US agencies' RIAs); Scott Farrow, 'Improving Regulatory Performance: Does Executive Oversight Matter?' (draft July 2000, available at <http://www.aei-brookings.org/admin/authorpdfs/page.php?id=123>) (finding little impact on rejections of rules); Stuart Shapiro, 'Unequal Partners: Cost-Benefit Analysis and Executive Review of Regulations' (2005) 35 *Envtl L Rep* 10433 (arguing that

2003.[206] The European Environment Agency has attempted to conduct *ex post* analyses (of effectiveness and cost-effectiveness, though not necessarily of BCA), but has been hampered by lack of comparable information across member states.[207] To address that need, the EU IA Guidelines now direct attention to planning for *ex post* review in the initial policy design and *ex ante* IA.[208]

The lesson for Better Regulation is to learn from medicine: Treat the whole patient, not just one ailment at a time, and measure success by 'evidence-based' *ex post* review or 'outcomes studies' of patients after treatment.[209] Better Regulation should develop large-scale outcomes studies to track the effects of regulatory policy choices over time, and across jurisdictions (where policies vary spatially). These *ex post* outcomes studies could be conducted by regulatory agencies and oversight offices, but could also be delegated to an independent body to ensure greater objectivity. In this effort, the US and EU could collaborate on a transatlantic policy laboratory—a joint effort in the *ex post* epidemiology of regulatory interventions and their empirical impacts.

Conclusions

In many respects, the Better Regulation initiative promises salutary reforms, such as wider use of regulatory impact assessments (IAs) to evaluate regulatory decisions *ex ante*. In other respects, including some of its

BCA has had little effect on rulemaking because OIRA has put more emphasis on coordinating Presidential priorities); Bagley and Revesz, n 107 above (arguing that BCA has had a significant impact on rulemaking, but that OIRA should instead put more emphasis on coordinating Presidential priorities); Richard D Morgenstern (ed), *Economic Analysis at EPA: Assessing Regulatory Impact* (Washington, DC: RFF Press, 1997) (finding beneficial impact). A challenge in these studies is to identify the counterfactual baseline of what would have happened absent regulatory review. See Cary Coglianese, 'Empirical Analysis and Administrative Law', (2002) *Univ Illinois L Rev* 1111.

[206] OECD, *Regulatory Performance: Ex Post Evaluation of Regulatory Policies* (Paris, 22 September 2003) (noting at p 5 the increasing interest in evidence-based empirical evaluation of policy impacts).

[207] European Environment Agency (EEA), 'Reporting on Environmental Measures: Are We Being Effective?' Environmental Issues Report no. 25 (November 2001) (calling for greater attention to data collection and comparability to enable *ex post* evaluations); EEA, 'Effectiveness of Packaging Waste Management Systems in Selected Countries: An EEA Pilot Study', Report 3/2005 (2005) (noting at p 8 that 'The sixth environment action programme of the European Community (6EAP) highlights the need to undertake "*ex-post* evaluation of the effectiveness of existing measures in meeting their environmental objectives",' but finding such analysis inhibited by non-comparable data across member states).

[208] IA Guidelines 2006, at 44–6.

[209] See Wiener, n 151 above (advocating evidence-based outcomes studies for risk regulation, as in medical care). See also Cary Coglianese and Lori Snyder Bennear, 'Measuring

rhetoric, its focus on administrative costs and simplification, and its institutional structure, the EU initiative speaks more of deregulation than of better regulation. Questions also remain whether particular regulatory programs, such as those regarding genetically modified foods and chemicals (REACH), can be reconciled with the tenets of Better Regulation.

Truly better regulation—maximizing societal well-being—would involve reducing or eliminating some regulations, but strengthening or expanding others, depending on the full social consequences of each choice. Better Regulation will often mean cutting costs. But it will also sometimes mean more regulation, or more comprehensive regulation: of issues that BCA shows warrant more regulation; of risks understated by risk assessment; of multiple simultaneous risks; of countervailing risks induced by intervention to reduce a target risk; and of risks addressed through more cost-effective instruments that reduce costs and hence make the optimal degree of regulation more protective. The 'less versus more' dichotomy is fairly unhelpful in making regulatory policy choices. 'Better' can be neither less nor more.

The EU is borrowing the concepts of Better Regulation from US regulatory reform and from initiatives in the EU member states, but Europe can make Better Regulation even better. Regulatory tools and institutions can be improved based on learning from past approaches, and tailored to suit European governance. The problems with impact assessment and benefit-cost analysis to date appear to be institutional: not that they are used too much, but rather too little and too narrowly or one-sidedly. IA and BCA in Europe would be more successful and credible if they were expanded to become self-reflective proportionate Warm Analysis of full portfolio impacts, to say yes to the good as well as no to the bad, to apply to a wider array of public policies (such as trade and counterterrorism) beyond the current focus on risk regulation, to embrace multiple countervailing risks and ancillary benefits, and to guide administrative simplification to consider benefits as well as costs. In addition, Europe should establish a centralized expert oversight body with the authority to use IA to influence decisions, and a system of *ex post* policy evaluations for adaptive revision and for improvement of *ex ante* assessment methods. These reforms would help Better Regulation become even better and achieve its true objective: better, not less or more.

Progress: Program Evaluation of Environmental Policies' (2005) 47(2) *Environment* magazine 22–40 (lamenting lack of *ex post* evaluation and advocating establishment of systematic program evaluation to measure policies' actual impacts); Cary Coglianese and Lori Snyder Bennear, 'Program Evaluation of Environmental Policies: Toward Evidence-Based Decision Making', in *Social and Behavioral Science Research Priorities For Environmental Decision Making* (Washington, DC: National Research Council, National Academies Press, 2005) 246–73.

Europe should experiment with these institutional innovations under its Better Regulation strategies, and evaluate their performance over time. Europe has an opportunity to develop new and improved approaches to regulation, not only borrowing but also adapting and creating anew. The innovations suggested here can help Europe manage its regulatory system, facilitate trade in the Single European Market, and advance European competitiveness, while ensuring that Better Regulation really means better. In turn, the US could improve its own regulatory regime by monitoring and borrowing from Europe's successes.

The exercise of legal borrowing involved in Better Regulation, and the normative evaluation of that borrowing that I have offered, show that—at least in this case—the focus is, and should be, on the particular merits of legal ideas, not on abstract ideology or supposedly fixed national legal mentalities. Blake overstated the case: 'To generalize is to be an idiot. To particularize is alone the distinction of merit.'[210] That itself is a hasty generalization, perhaps unintentionally proving its point, because some generalizations are useful.[211] But the point remains that particularization adds insight; the details matter, even when they are difficult to grasp. Observed La Rochefoucauld: 'Pour bien savoir les choses, il en faut savoir le détail, et comme il est presque infini, nos connaissances sont toujours superficielles et imparfaites.'[212] Better Regulation itself consists in large measure of knowing the important details, without seeking perfection in every last detail, and in using those details to offer and to test different reasons for alternative regulatory choices, toward a considered judgment about the better course of action. Mr Franklin's advice to avoid 'rash steps' by a prudential evaluation of the consequences now finds fruition in what Mr Blair has called 'regulation after reflection'.

[210] William Blake, Annotations to Sir Joshua Reynolds' *Discourses* (1814).

[211] For a provocative discussion, see Frederick Schauer and Richard Zeckhauser, 'Regulation by Generalization', AEI-Brookings Joint Center, Working Paper 05–16, August 2005.

[212] La Rochefoucauld, *Maximes* (Montreal: Les Editions Variétés, 1946), no 106 (p 61) (translated into English, 'To know things well, one must know the details, but as these are almost infinite, our understanding is always superficial and imperfect.').

Index

Accountability 53, 460
  popular 53
Adjudication 91, 94–8, 102, 108–9, 112–13, 115, 119–20, 123, 125–6
  constitutional 91, 94–8, 102, 108–9, 112, 115, 119–20, 123, 125–6
  process of 113
  regional 96
Affirmative action 289
Anti-Social Behaviour Order 135–6, 146–7, 292
Appeal, right to 30
Association, right of 30
Authority 53, 61, 80, 82, 101, 112, 150
  constitutional 82, 112
  executive, of 53
  public 61, 82
  sovereign 53
Autonomy 59–60, 62, 72, 74–5, 80, 150, 179, 239–43, 244, 249, 251–4, 264–5, 507
  comprehensiveness 59, 72
  interpretative 60, 74
  procedural 74
  self-definition 59, 72, 74
  self-enforcement 59–60, 72, 74
Austin, John 267–70, 272, 276
Australia 102–3, 106–7, 111, 116–17, 319, 388, 414–17, 422–3, 425
  aboriginal land rights 319
  courts 422
  equality 103
  foreign law 423
  representative democracy 102–3
  tax 388

Bentham, Jeremy 268, 452
Blackstone, William 268–9, 272, 276
Brazil 440
British Columbia, Supreme Court of 103
Broadcasts 32–4
  broadcasters' obligations 32
  censorship 34
  good taste and decency 32–4
  offensive material 33
  party political 32, 34

Canada 102–3, 105–6, 112, 118, 122–4, 210, 216, 285, 388, 413, 438
  Labour Code 413
  Supreme Court of 122, 124, 210, 216, 279, 285
  tax 388
  World Trade Organisation 438
China 416–18, 424–5, 431, 434, 440, 455
  law of *lex loci delicti* 416
Citizenship 51, 369, 387
  tax, and 369, 387
Civil 133, 145–6, 288, 394
  liberties 133, 145–6
  procedure 288; international 394
Commission for Equality and Human Rights 290
Commons 278–9, 287–8, 319–57
  adverse possession 344
  commonhold associations 350, 352–5
  communal land rights 319–57
  companies 350–2; directors, accountability of 351, 354; guarantee 351, 353; limited liability 350–1, 353
    winding up 352
  co-ownership 349
  councils 345–7, 350
  covenants 349
  de facto 327, 347–56
  defence of 324–6
  easements 339–40, 349
  Jennings Report 320, 331–8, 345, 347
  land registration 336–45
  private property 319–57
  profits à prendre 339–40
  property rights, theory of 320
  public interest/access 328–9, 331–8, 340, 346–7
  town/village greens 341–5, 347–8
  tragedy of the commons 320–7, 331–3

Commons (*cont.*)
trusts 278–9, 287–8, 355–6
universal rights 323
Common law 27–50, 97, 110–11, 113
Company law, reflective loss rule 419–20
Comparative law 91–127
functionalism 121–3
private 120–2, 124
Compatibility, European Convention on Human Rights, and 27–9, 31, 33, 37
Comprehensiveness 59
Conscience 30
Conseil d'Etat 506
Conservative Party 133, 143, 145, 154, 163–4
Consequentialism 81
Conspiracy 185–230
Constitution 30–1, 33, 35–6, 39–41, 44, 46, 48, 51–89, 97, 108–9, 112–14, 445
authority of 109
common law 30, 39–40
conception/meaning of 113–14
European Union 51–89
Reason, of 31, 33, 35, 46
unwritten 31, 41, 44
Will, of 31, 36, 48
written 54, 97
Constitutional 11, 27, 38, 65, 67–8, 71, 82, 91–2, 94–8, 102, 105, 108–10, 112–13, 115, 119–20, 123, 125–7, 177
adjudication 91, 94–8, 102, 108–9, 112, 115, 119–20, 123, 125–6
authority 11, 82
Court of South Africa 105
efficacy 68
evolution 113
history 65, 127
interpretation 92, 95, 109–10, 113
justice 38
law 27, 98, 110, 113, 177
norms 67–8
universal standards 71
Constitutionalism 30, 44, 51–89
constitutionality 30
documentary 83–9
European 51–89
liberal 44
modern 68
post-state 89
state 51–89
Consumerism 152
Contract 268, 270, 272, 275, 277–9, 312, 376–7, 389, 391, 409
breach of 275, 278
damages 277
freedom of 312
non-contractual obligations 391
obligations 409
specific performance 272, 277, 279
tax, and 376–7, 389
third parties, and 277
Co-ownership 349
Court 96, 100–1, 105, 108
constitutional, of South Africa 105
deliberative process 100
domestic 101
Crime 30, 39, 48, 130, 135, 140–3, 148, 151–5, 175, 185, 189–227, 230, 293
actus reus 189, 192–3, 197
British Survey 140–3, 148, 151–4
burden of proof 39
bystander, reasonable 195
capital punishment 130
conduct 193–4, 199, 201, 209, 218, 221–5
criminal proceedings 30
damage 189, 194–7, 199–200, 202
detection of 175
disability, and 293
knowledge/intention 194, 197–226; actual 192–3, 212–13; belief 215–16; conditional 221–2, 224–6; constructive 212, 214; meaning 206–9, 218; oblique/direct 218–21, 224; proof of 193–4, 196, 199, 204, 210, 217–18; second degree 212; third degree 212; unconditional 224; wilful blindness 206, 211–16, 220–1
law enforcement 175
liability 185, 190–1, 201, 204, 220, 222–23
secondary 210
strict offence 193–5, 201, 229
meaning 130, 133–40
mens rea 185–230
money laundering 197–9, 202, 204–5, 208, 214–15, 222, 224, 227, 230

negligence, proof of 196
presumption of innocence 30, 39
proceeds of 190, 194, 198, 200–3, 205, 210
property 205
proportionality 213
punishment 48, 135, 155
rape 207
recklessness 186, 192, 194–5, 202, 206–7, 209, 212, 216–18, 225–226; *Caldwell* 195–6; proof of 217; subjective 197
trends in 130
Criminology 137–8, 140

Data protection 161–83
Decision-making 49, 61, 63, 77–8, 83, 86
collective 61, 86
judicial 49
legislative 49
non-unanimous 83
participation, and 77
Delegation theory 79
Democracy 30–2, 34, 41, 43, 48–51, 54, 62–3, 69, 77–8, 80–1, 84–5, 102–3, 105, 108, 118, 123, 150
framework of 32
holistic 78
liberal 30, 41, 43, 50
no demos 69
postnational 78, 84–5
process of 48
representative 102–3
social 150
substantive 105
Defamation, malice 104, 122–4
Deference 150, 435
Descartes, René 452
Detention 43–4, 49–50
detainees 50
indefinite 49–50
Parol Board 44
without trial 49–50
Deterrence 44, 152
Devlin, Patrick 137
Dicey, Albert Venn 394
theory of national sovereignty 394
vested rights theory 394
Dignity 31, 41, 46–7, 104, 178
Disability 289–318
affirmative action 289
crime, and 293
economics of 309–14
employment, and 310, 316–17
Disability Rights Commission 290, 316
discrimination 303
history of 295
law 289–318
medical model of 296, 305
public 307–8, 310, 315–17; authorities, duty on 315–17; transport, and 307–8, 310
social 296–7, 300, 305, 311–12; justice 311–12; model of 296–7, 300, 305
Studies 293–7
welfarism 302–3, 315
Discretion 104, 113–15, 167
administrative 167
executive 104
judicial 113–15
Discrimination 28, 38, 40, 289–90, 292–3, 298–9, 303–4, 307, 310, 312–18, 437, 443
Access to Work 313
anti-discrimination 289, 292, 303, 307, 310, 312, 318
Commission for Equality and HumanRights 290
comparator 303–4
disability 303
equality 293, 298–9, 303, 309–10, 314–17
foreign nations, against 50
gender 290, 293, 298–9, 303, 318
institutional 315
race 290, 303, 318
sexual orientation 298–9, 303
unfair 38
unjustified 40, 443
Dispute resolution 63, 444–5
World Trade Organisation 445

Easements 339–40, 349
Employment 175, 310, 316–17
disability, and 310, 316–17
Environmental law 447–518
administrative costs/simplification 449, 460–1, 470, 497–505, 517
benefit–cost analysis 448, 459–60, 462–3, 466, 468, 470–1, 474–5, 477–8, 481–6, 489–91, 493–94, 500–1, 504–6, 514, 516–17
default rule 477

Environmental law (*cont.*)
deregulation 459, 503–4
European 448, 451, 453, 455, 457–9, 466–71, 474, 478, 480, 482–3, 486, 488–9, 491, 494–6, 498–503, 505–6, 508, 510, 514, 516–18; social model 456
externalities 492, 497
impact assessment 447, 449, 451, 454, 460–97, 505, 508, 516–17; integrated 494; statements 477
integrated pollution control 495–6
legal borrowing 449–58
precautionary principle 448, 450–1, 453–4, 460, 480
public choice theory 456
risk 478–81, 493, 512; assessment 478–81, 493, 512; management 493; risk tradeoff 494–5
standard cost model 470, 498
sustainable development 450, 456
Equality 103, 293, 298–9, 303, 309–10, 313–17
Equity 267–88
Europe 431–2, 439–40, 502, 518
Single Market 502, 518
European Institutions 66–9, 74, 76, 105, 389, 447–50, 456, 458, 460, 468, 474, 476, 480, 482, 489–91, 497, 499, 501, 506–8, 510–12
Commission 76, 447–50, 456, 458, 460, 468, 474, 476, 480, 482, 489–91, 497, 499, 501, 506–8, 510, 512;
Competitiveness Council 512
Council 76, 458, 510–11
Court of Human Rights 105
Court of Justice 74, 480; implied powers, doctrine of 74; self-authorship 66–9, 74, 76; tax law 389
democratic deficit, and 76
Parliament 76, 458, 468, 510–11
European Union 27, 46, 51–89, 101, 107, 112, 124, 150, 162, 303, 432, 435, 437, 444, 448, 451, 453, 455, 457–9, 466–71, 474, 478, 480, 482–3, 486, 488–9, 491, 494–6, 498–503, 505–6, 508, 510, 514, 516–18
Action Plan 303
authority 53, 61, 67, 80, 82, 101,112, 150
autonomy, *see* Autonomy
citizens 499
collective self 66
competence 59, 70, 74, 81
constitution 51–89; constitutionalism 51–89; adaptation 53, 55–8; constructivism 50, 84–8; continuity 52, 56; history 65; holism 68–9; legal order 58–60, 67–9, 71–6, 79, 87; miscategorization perspective 52, 57; modern 68; nominalist 53–4; postnational 56, 84–5; projection 68; reflexivity 58, 66–9, 71, 76, 81, 83–4, 88–9; self-authorization 58, 61–3, 76; social integration 58, 63–8, 76, 81, 86; specialised political system 58, 60–1, 75–83, 87; state 52; tradition 57; traditional-framed novelty 55–6; truncated 69–89; vindication approach 88
decision-making 61, 63, 69, 78, 81, 83, 86
delegation theory 79
democracy, *see* Democracy
direct effect 72–3
directives 468, 502
dispute resolution 63
environmental law 448, 451, 453, 455, 457–9, 466–71, 474, 478, 480, 482–3, 486, 488–9, 491, 494–6, 498–503, 505–6, 508, 510, 514, 516–18
free trade 77
Hans Ipsen special purpose 76–7
infraction 61
interdependence 89
internal market 80
international 27, 46, 73–4, 79; law 27, 46, 73–4, 79; relations 79
judicial review 53
justice 54
law 403, 503
law-making 53
norms, *see* Norms
ordoliberal tradition 76–7
political 70, 72; identity 70; morality 76, 81; rule 72
political-ethical debate 65

popular accountability 53
regulations 468, 502
risk regulation 77
rule of law 54, 60
security 74; external 74; internal 74; policy 80, 162
self-: amendment 60, 74–5; containment 59, 60, 73, 75; government 66, 82; institution 67
separation of powers 53
social constituency 65
sovereignty, *see* Sovereignty
strict liability 74
supranationalism 51–89
supremacy 72–3
veto power 74, 81
Westphalian order 70–1
Evidence 136, 300, 392, 394, 396–8, 402, 404–8, 411, 421–3, 425–6
excited utterance rule 300
rules of 136, 392, 396–8, 402, 404–8, 411, 421–3, 425
Executive 53, 104
authority 53
discretion 104

Fair trial, 41, 134
Fairness 31, 50, 103
electoral 103
procedural 50
Feminism 300
France, national security 161
Franklin, Benjamin 484–5, 518
prudential algebra 484, 518
Fraud 414, 513
corporate 513
Free speech 30, 32–3
Freedom 18–19, 31, 41, 47, 161–83, 312
contract, of 312
individual 41, 161–83
liberty 47
Fuller 10–1, 18–24
governance, and 18–24, 76–7, 79; desiderata 18, 22–3; European Union 76–7, 79
official sanctions 11

Germany 105, 118, 123–4, 166–7, 169–80, 415
constitutional law 177
Federal Constitutional Court 170–2, 179
National Identity Register 169–72
national security 166, 169–80
tax law 415
Globalisation 96, 126–7, 159–60, 428, 452, 455
economic 455
political 455
Good faith 42, 438
concept of 438
deference 42
Governance 18–22, 76–7, 79, 517
European Union 76–7, 79, 517
law, by 19
Raz, and 19
Government, according to law 50

Harm 137, 247, 249, 261–5
Mill, John Stuart, and 249
prevention of 249
Hart, HLA, *see* Theory of law, Hart, HLA
Hobbes, Thomas 5–6
Homosexual 28, 38, 40, 93
partnerships 28
relations 38, 93; criminalisation of 93
same-sex partner, rights of 38, 40
unmarried heterosexual survivors 38
Human rights 31, 33, 123, 136, 178–81
data protection 178–81
protection of 123

Identity cards 161–183, 302
Immigration 175
Impartiality 25, 113
Incompatibility, Declaration of 41, 49–50
Independence 25, 50
value of 25
Independent Police Complaints Commission 148
Individualism 146, 150
Infraction 61
Insolvency rules 412
International 27, 46, 73–4, 79, 94–7, 127, 427–31, 435–9, 445
law 27, 46, 73–4, 79, 94–7, 127, 391, 408, 416, 427–31, 434, 435–9, 445; consent 431; economic 427–9; judicial system 445; *jus cogens* 438; *lex specialis* 438

International (*cont.*)
Monetary Fund 427
private law 391, 408, 416
relations 79
tribunal 434
Internationalization 96
Interpretation 27–9, 31–47, 50, 84–8, 92, 95, 109–10, 113, 400–1, 404, 418, 441–45
constitutional 92, 95, 109–10, 113
creative 37
flexibility of 445
foreign law, of 401
interpretative obligation 28, 40
judicial 29, 37, 42, 113
legitimate 39; boundaries of 40–6
nature of 28
restrictive 41
retrospective 38
statutory 27, 32, 46, 400, 418; ambiguity 27; amendment 34, 38, 45–6; construction 36–7, 404, 418; constitutional 45; purposive 42; constructivism 50, 84–8; Convention-compatible 27–9, 31, 33, 37; Convention-incompatible 40, 47; express words 28; language 29; legislative intent 29, 34, 36, 38, 40, 43–4; literal 36, 39, 41–2, 44; ordinary meaning 27–9, 37–40, 42; revision 37–8
World Trade Organisation, and 441–44
Israel 98, 102, 104–5, 115, 118, 123
basic rule 104–5
executive discretion 104
legislative/executive power 118
Supreme Court of 115, 123

Japan 437, 440
Judgment 1–26
justification 5, 13–17, 33; moral 5; technical 5
Judges 7–16, 15–17, 24–5, 33–5, 46, 49–50, 93, 111, 115, 395
duty of 24–5, 50; administer justice 50; fidelity to law 24–5
Hart, HLA, and 7–16
personal preference 115
Raz, Joseph, and 16
sentencing 49
Judicial 25, 29, 35, 37, 42, 44–5, 53, 108, 111, 113–19, 108, 126, 396, 402–5, 423, 440, 458, 506
activism 126
appointment 108
decision-making 114
discretion 113–15
disobedience 35
impartiality 25, 113
independence 111
interpretation 29, 37, 42, 113
method 113–18
notice of foreign law 396, 402–5, 423
reasoning 115, 118–19
review 44–5, 53, 108, 113, 440, 458, 506
role 108
vandalism 42, 44
Justice 24–50, 54, 113, 116, 130, 138–41, 146–47, 149, 153, 161, 178, 309, 311–12, 397, 426
access to 397
according to law 50, 113
administration of 116, 178
concept of 24
constitutional 38
criminal 48, 130, 138–41, 146, 149, 153, 161
equality, and 25
European Union 54
judicial concern for 25
miscarriage of 42
natural 49
Plato, *The Republic* 25–6
process of 147
requirements of 38
social 309, 311–12
value of 25
youth 146

Kant 5, 23
law's nature 23
natural law 5
universal law of freedom 5
Kelsen, basic norm, theory of 9
Keynes, John Maynard 145–6, 153, 485

Labour Party 130, 143–8, 154, 156–7, 163
New 143, 145–8, 154, 156–7
Law 1, 3–7, 9–10, 15–23, 27–50, 59, 76–7, 79, 81, 91–127, 129–60, 289–318, 391–431, 435–39, 445, 503, 517

common 27–50, 97, 110–11, 113
company, reflective loss rule 419–20
comparative 91–127
concept of 17–9, 35
constitutional 27, 98, 110, 113
disability 289–318
European Union 403, 503
foreign 91–127, 391–426; facts 391–426; identity 406–26; legitimacy of 94; notice of 396, 402–4
governance, and 18–22; European Union 76–7, 79, 517
international 27, 46, 73–4, 79, 94–7, 127, 427–31, 435–39, 445
lex causae 421–22
morality, and 7, 15, 50; political 76, 81
natural 5, 28, 59
nature of 1, 3–7, 9–10, 15, 18–23; *ius* 5; Grotius 6; *lex* 5–6; self-preservation 6; univocal 4–5
obedience, idea of, and 21
order, and 129–160
positivism 5, 15–6, 21, 23, 28, 59, 134, 137–38
public 34; judicial review, *see* Judicial review
status 49
tax 415
theory of, *see* Theory of law
Legality 1–27, 29, 34, 43–4, 48
justificatory force of 19
legal validity 6, 9–10, 21; Hart, HLA, and 10
rule of recognition, of 10
Legislation 53, 129, 177
primary 177
public order 129
Legitimacy 94–5, 97, 102, 107–18, 126
illegitimacy 107–8
ius gentium 110
per se 108–10
Liability 74, 185, 190–1, 284–5
solicitors' 284–5
state 74
strict 185, 190–1
Liberal 129, 327
Classic 327
Liberties, *see* Civil liberties
Locke, John 82

MacCormick, Neil 14–7
Market, concept of 433
Mass media 139–40
Mill, John Stuart 137, 452
Morality 31, 36, 76, 81, 153, 383–4
constitutional 36
political 31, 76, 81
tax, and 383–4

Nationalism 126
Negligence, reasonableness, and 300
Neo- 145–6, 150, 153, 158–60
conservative 145
liberal 145–6, 150, 153, 158–60
New Deal 145
New Zealand 98, 112, 116
Norms 67–8, 96–7, 99
constitutional 67–8, 96–7, 99
institutional 68
international 96
legal 96–7, 99
substantive 68

Offence 41, 47
serious 47
sexual 41
Orwell, George 129

Plato, *The Republic*, 25–6
Pluralism 82, 84
Political–ethical debate 65
Political party 32–3
Positivism 5, 15–6, 21, 23, 28, 59, 134, 137–8
Hart, HLA, and 15–16
law, and 5,15, 28
positivists 23, 59; criminal law and 134, 137–8; inclusive legal 23
rule of recognition, positivist account of 21
Posner, Richard 301
Precautionary principle 448, 450–1, 453–4, 460, 480
Precedent, doctrine of 110–11, 395, 435, 439–41
Press, freedom of 122
Proportionality 136, 174, 176, 213, 434, 466–7, 469, 482–3, 487, 491
Property law 205, 319–57
Public 31, 34, 41, 61, 82, 122, 133, 315–17
authority 61, 82, 315–17
good 41, 82

Public (*cont.*)
  interest 31
  law 34, 122; judicial review, *see* Judicial review
  private divide 122
  protection 133
Punishment 44, 48, 130, 135, 152, 155
  capital 130
  deterrence 44, 152

Rawls, John 240, 309–10
  original position 240
  undue influence 240
  veil of ignorance 240, 309–10
Raz, Joseph 16–17, 19–22, 76–7, 79, 517
  concept of law, and 19
  governance 19, 76–7, 79, 517; European Union 76–7, 79, 517
  judges, and 16
  rule of law, and 19–20
  rule of recognition 20
Realists 59, 144
Reflexivity 66–7
Registration of land 336–45
Republicanism 51
Restitution 270–71, 280
Right of way 301
Rights 27–8, 31, 33, 97, 136, 303, 313, 323
  constitutional 27–8
  human 31, 33, 136
  individual 303
  universal 303, 313, 323
Roman, jurists/law 269
Rousseau, Jean-Jacques 452
Rule of law 19–24, 29–32, 35, 39, 41–6, 48–50, 54, 60, 105, 108, 118, 123, 132, 409, 419
  doctrinal legal scholarship 23–4
  elements of 30
  European Union 54, 60
  independence 19, 22
  necessity 19, 22
  protection of 46
  requirements of 32
  universality 19, 22, 419
  violation of 132
Rule of recognition 2–3, 7–18, 20, 22–5
  legality, *see* Legality
  MacCormick, acceptance of 14; justifications 15; underpinning reasons for 14–6
  penumbral cases 7, 24–5
  positivist, account of 21
Rules 7–12, 409
  procedure of 409
  system of 7–12
Russia 434

Security 161–83, 284–86
  loans 284–6
  national 161, 166, 169–80
  public 161–83
Sentence, life 47
Separation of powers 29, 37, 43, 49, 53, 97, 105, 118
Sieyès, Emmanuel Joseph 82
Social 131, 133, 144–5, 150, 158–60, 179, 309–12
  democratic 133, 144–5, 150, 158,160; deficit 160
  exclusion 158–9
  inequality 133
  justice 145, 309–12
  security benefits 179
  theory, classical 131
Socialism 156
South Africa 101–2, 105–7, 112, 117, 124
  apartheid 105
  Bill of Rights 112
  Constitutional Court of 101–2, 105
  new constitutional order 105
Sovereign, authority 53
Sovereignty 28–9, 31, 34, 36, 40, 44–5, 47, 59, 62, 73, 79, 82, 109, 124, 394, 430–1, 445
  conception of 124, 430–1
  legal 59
  national 79
  parliamentary 28–9, 31, 34, 36, 40, 44–5, 47
  popular 62, 82, 109
  theory of national 394
  ultimate 73
  Westphalian sense of 430
Soviet Union 145
Speech 30, 32–3, 52, 293
  European 52
  free 30, 32–3
  hate 293
  political, censorship of 32
State 51–52

Standing, doctrine of 112, 439–41
Statutes 29
Supranationalism 51–89, 96, 127, 160
Supremacy, legislative 35
Sustainable development 450, 456
Switzerland 124

Tax 359–90, 415
 anti-avoidance 359, 371–2, 388
 avoidance 359–90; culture 372; meaning 361–5
 citizenship, and 369, 387
 companies, directors' duties 381–2
 concept of 369
 contract, and 376–7
 corporate 360–1; governance 361, 380; social responsibility 360–1, 366–8, 379–85
 corporation 369–70
 credit/benefit 374, 376
 direct 390
 Honoré 380
 law 415
 liability 378, 384
 national insurance 371, 376, 378
 planning 366–7, 378
 reduction 368
 salary sacrifice 372–9
 statutory relief 374
Terrorism 126, 129, 145, 148, 161–2, 166, 513
Theory of law 1–26, 33, 137
 basic norm 9
 detached observer 2–5
 Hart, HLA 7–16; legal reasons, partial autonomy 7, 13; positivism 15–16; internal point of view 15; judges 16
 justification 5, 13–17, 33
 Nietzsche Friedrich 4
 non-reflexive 2
 object 2
 participant 4
 reflexive 2
 rule of recognition, *see* Rule of recognition
Tort law 270, 277, 293, 391, 416, 425, 466
 damages 270, 277
Trade Unions 129, 133, 145
Trust 278–9, 287–8, 355–6
 commercial 288
 exclusion clause 287
 funds 278–9
 mixing 355
 perpetuity rule 355–6
Trustee 271–88, 356
 beneficiaries 274–80, 282–3, 286; rights of 276–84; vulnerability of 287
 deterrence 287
 disbursements, and 279–82
 duty 271–7; account to 280, 282; breach of 271, 274, 276–80, 282–6, 356; care of 283; fiduciary 286–8
 liability 280, 285; solicitors' 284–5
 mitigation of loss 281
 negligence 283–4
 remedies 271–3
 remoteness 281

Ultra vires 45
Undue influence 137, 231–66
 actual/class 1, 233, 265
 attachment theory 241
 autonomy 239–43, 244, 249, 251–4, 264–5; detached 240–41; individual 251; negative 265; personal 247, 249; positive 247, 249, 265; relational 241–3, 252; self-authorship 239; value of 251, 254
 burden of proof 236, 239, 255
 civil 231, 251; law 231; liability 251
 conduct 237
 consent 231, 233–4, 239–40, 253, 265; defective 237–9, 243–4; impaired 239, 262; transactional 244–6
 contract 231
 criminal law 231
 faith 237
 Finnis, John 242
 freedom 231, 240; individual 231; transaction, of 231, 233
 Freud, Sigmund 241
 gifts/guarantees 254, 258, 260–1
 harm 137, 247, 249, 261–5
 Hart, HLA 233, 244–6
 liability 244, 250; transactional 244, 246
 Nietzsche, Friedrich 241

Undue influnence (*cont.*)
  perfectionism 247–8
  plurality, moral 247
  positive autonomy 233
  presumed/Class 2, 234, 265
  Raz, Joseph 233, 246–52
  relational theory 233, 250, 265
  restitution 231, 237
  substantive unfairness 236–7
  unjust enrichment 231
  welfare 253–61
  wills 254, 257, 263
United Nations 109, 432
  General Assembly 109
United States 91–3, 103–6, 108–11, 118, 122–4, 126, 130, 155–6, 161–2, 228, 301, 354, 394, 421, 431–2, 435–40, 442, 443–4, 449, 451, 453, 455–9, 461–91, 494–5, 497, 499–500, 502, 505–7, 511–18
  administrative/constitutional law 440, 514
  Bill of Rights 91
  commons 354
  Congress 92, 444, 462–4, 489–91, 511–12, 515
  cooperative federalism 502
  dispute settlement 444
  environmental law 449, 451, 453, 455–9, 461–8, 471, 478–81, 486, 488–90, 494–5, 497, 499–500, 502, 505–7, 511–18
  fact doctrine 394
  Federal Court of Appeals 301
  national security 161–2
  Pennsylvania law 421
  Right-wing policies and 130
  Supreme Court of 91, 104, 109, 228, 465, 480, 506
Universalism 71, 93, 101, 323, 413, 421–2
Unjust enrichment 270

Weber, Max 452
Welfarism 302, 432
World Trade Organisation 427–46
  Canada 438
  compliance 444
  dispute settlement 432–5, 445
  interpretation 441–4